London

BARS
PUBS & CLUBS

timeout.com

Time Out Guides Ltd
Universal House
251 Tottenham Court Road
London W1T 7AB
Tel + 44(0)20 7813 3000
Fax + 44(0)20 7813 6001
guides@timeout.com
www.timeout.com

Editorial
Editor Tom Lamont
Deputy Editor Cath Phillips
Copy Editors Elizabeth Winding, Yolanda Zappaterra
Researchers Cathy Limb, Fiona Shield
Proofreader Anna Norman
Subject Indexer Lesley McCave

Managing Director Peter Fiennes
Financial Director Gareth Garner
Editorial Director Sarah Guy
Series Editor Cath Phillips
Editorial Manager Holly Pick
Accountant Ija Krasnikova

Design
Art Director Scott Moore
Art Editor Pinelope Kourmouzoglou
Senior Designer Henry Elphick
Junior Graphic Designer Kei Ishimaru
Digital Imaging Simon Foster
Ad Make-up Jodi Sher

Picture Desk
Picture Editor Jael Marschner
Deputy Picture Editor Tracey Kerrigan
Picture Researcher Helen McFarland

Advertising
Sales Director & Sponsorship Mark Phillips
Sales Manager Alison Wallen
Advertising Sales Ben Holt, Jason Trotman
Advertising Assistant Kate Staddon
Copy Controller Declan Symington

Marketing
Group Marketing Director John Luck
Marketing Manager Yvonne Poon
Sales & Marketing Director, North America Lisa Levinson

Production
Group Production Director Mark Lamond
Production Manager Brendan McKeown
Production Coordinator Caroline Bradford

Time Out Group
Chairman Tony Elliott
Financial Director Richard Waterlow
TO Magazine Ltd MD David Pepper
Group General Manager/Director Nichola Coulthard
Managing Director, Time Out International Cathy Runciman
TO Communications Ltd MD David Pepper
Group Art Director John Oakey
Group IT Director Simon Chappell

Contributors

Claire Ainsley, Simone Baird, Joseph Bindloss, Hal Brown, Addie Chinn, Richard Clarke, Simon Coppock, Peterjon Cresswell, Rob Crossan, Guy Dimond, Alexi Duggins, Will Fulford-Jones, Jan Fuscoe, Francis Gooding, Sarah Guy, Gwynnie, Martin Hemming, David Jenkins, Emma Howarth, Tom Lamont, Susan Low, Rhodri Marsden, Jenny McIvor, Norman Miller, Jenni Muir, Anna Norman, Cath Phillips, Hugh Reilly, Cyrus Shahrad, Fiona Shield, Andrew Shields, Mark Smith, Andrew Staffell, Sejal Sukhadwala, Charlotte Thomas, Elizabeth Winding. Features in this guide were written and researched by: When London pours, it reigns Richard Ehrlich; Sign of drinks to come, Old haunts, Darting about Peter Watts; Getting saké Guy Dimond; Booze talking Fiona Shield.

The Editor would like to thank Hal Brown, Guy Dimond, Francis Gooding, Julien Sauvalle, Christina Theisen and all the landlords and bar owners who agreed to be interviewed.

Maps john@jsgraphics.co.uk

Cover Artwork Simon Foster
Wall Background Photography © Craig Aurness/CORBIS

Photography pages 3, 5, 7, 8, 12, 25, 34, 50, 51, 56, 57, 68, 69, 74, 75, 76, 77, 80, 81, 194, 195 Ming Tang Evans; pages 5, 12, 59, 88, 228, 231 Heloise Bergman; pages 5, 12, 96, 97, 100, 102, 103, 114, 116, 117, 122, 126, 127, 130, 131, 134, 138, 139, 140, 141, 148, 149, 154, 155, 234, 235 Gemma Day; pages 5, 32, 33, 62, 84, 85, 87, 92, 133, 135, 168, 172, 179, 184, 185, 198, 199, 237, 238 Britta Jaschinski; page 5 Laurent Garnier; page 12, 191 Michael Grieve; page 18 Ross Fortune; pages 20, 21 Haris Artemis; pages 45, 247 Rogan McDonald; pages 53, 99, 120, 125 Marzena Zoladz; pages 89, 144 Rob Greig; pages 108, 109 Nigel Tradewell; pages 113, 171, 230 Christina Theisen; page 119 Heikki Aho; page 157 Michael Franke; page 165 Martin Daly; page 175 Oliver Knight; page 196 Jonas Rodin.

Printer Cooper Clegg, Shannon Way, Tewkesbury Industrial Centre, Tewkesbury, Gloucestershire GL20 8HB.

Time Out Group uses paper products that are environmentally friendly, from well managed forests and mills that use certified (PEFC) Chain of Custody pulp in their production.

ISBN 978-1-905042-15-9
ISBN 1-905042-15-9
ISSN 1753-7924
Distribution by Seymour Ltd (020 7429 4000)
For details of distribution in the Americas, see www.timeout.com

About the guide

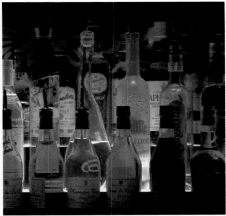

Opening times
We list only the opening times of the bar or pub at the time of going to press. We do not list those of any attached shop, restaurant or brasserie (though these may be the same).

Food served
We list the times when food is served in the bar or pub or, where relevant, in any attached restaurant or brasserie. 'Food served' can mean anything from cheese rolls to a three-course meal. When the opening times and food serving times are run together (Open/food served), it means food is served until shortly before closing time.

Admission
In some cases, particularly in central London, pubs and bars charge admission after a certain time. Where there is a regular pattern to this, we list the details. Note that more and more venues are becoming members-only after a fixed time (usually when pubs close), although the rules are often blurred. We've chosen not to include in this guide places that are strictly members-only.

Credit cards
The following abbreviations are used: **AmEx** American Express; **DC** Diners Club; **MC** MasterCard; **V** Visa.

Babies and children admitted
Under-14s are only allowed into gardens, separate family rooms and restaurant areas of pubs and wine bars, unless the premises has a special 'children's certificate'. If the establishment has such a certificate, children are allowed in as long as they're accompanied by an adult. Those aged 14-17 can go into a bar, but only for soft drinks. It's an offence for a licensee to serve alcohol in a bar to anyone under 18. Unless drinkers can prove they're at least 18, the licensee can refuse to serve them and may ask them to leave the premises.

Disabled: toilet
If a pub claims to have a toilet for the disabled, we have said so; this also implies that it's possible for a disabled person to gain access to the venue. However, we cannot guarantee this, so it's best to phone in advance to check.

Smoking ban
The ban comes into force in London on 1 July 2007, shortly after this guide is published. As a result, we no longer include smoking information in our listings. The fine for smoking in an indoor public place is £50; expect to see die-hard puffers huddled in pub doorways.

Star ratings/new entries
Those venues that we particularly like are marked with a ★ in this guide. Those added since the last edition are marked **NEW**. These aren't necessarily brand-new businesses, but they are new inclusions to the guide.

Themed index
This guide is arranged by area because we reckon that's how most people drink. But if you're after something other than just the closest or most convenient pub or bar, turn to **Where to go for...** (starting on p249), an index of establishments arranged by theme.

During the year-long lifetime of this guide, bars and pubs will inevitably change name, change hands or close. We strongly recommend giving the venue a ring before you set out – especially if your visit involves a long trip.

Reviews featured in this guide are based on the experiences and opinions of Time Out's reviewers. All pubs and bars listed are visited – anonymously – and Time Out pays the bill. No payment or incentive of any kind has secured or influenced a review.

SPONSORS & ADVERTISERS
We would like to thank our sponsor, Peroni, for its involvement in this guide. However, we would like to stress that sponsors have no control over editorial content. The same applies to advertisers. No venue has been included because its owner has advertised in the guide. An advertiser may receive a bad review or no review at all.

Contents

The finest bars in and around Soho...

When London pours, *it reigns*

A decade ago, our first guide listed just 11 good cocktail bars. Now, thanks to some innovative training schemes, London boasts the finest cocktails in the world. **Richard Ehrlich** celebrates.

Ten years ago, when the first edition of this guide was published, serious cocktail lovers ordering a martini or a manhattan in London would be taking a major gamble. Outside a small collection of bars, all of them clustered in the West End, cocktail bartending was virtually a write-off. You could get great margaritas at Café Pacifico, and great anything at the grand hotel bars or a few of the newer cocktail havens that were just starting to open up, but outside those places… well, let's just say the odds were against you. Looking again at the first edition, I found just 11 bars where I'd have felt confident ordering a cocktail.

How far have we come since then? Well, in the 2006/7 edition I found 44 places where I'd happily order a cocktail, across a much wider geographical spread. And there are a few more that hadn't made it into the guide, or have opened in the past year. That's what I call progress.

It's easy to be smug when you're living in the capital, but you don't have to take the word of proud Londoners boasting about the level of liquid artistry we enjoy here. Listen instead to Audrey Saunders, one of the best cocktail bartenders in New York. In a *New York Times* article by Kate Sekules published in February 2007, Saunders said: ►

'London is the best cocktail city in the world right now. I hate to admit it, but it's true.' And Sekules herself added: 'The explosion of sheer quality and variety in the city now strikes connoisseurs of mixed drinks as so fortunate and so welcome.'

Audrey Saunders is a protégée of Dale DeGroff, often regarded as the premier bartender in the US, and she has gone from overseeing the fabled Bemelmans Bar in Manhattan's Carlyle Hotel to running her own place, the Pegu Club in Lower Manhattan. I can testify from personal experience of a marathon tasting of her cocktail creations (spitting, not swallowing) that she is as good a cocktail bartender as you'll find anywhere on the planet. So when she says London is the best cocktail city in the world, you should sit up and take notice.

This has all happened in the last ten years or so, but its roots go deeper. To understand the genesis of London's cocktail greatness, you have to look back to the 1970s and '80s. For much of those two decades, you could count on one hand the places where good cocktails were made. Almost all were in swanky hotels catering for an international – and especially American – clientele. For British customers, roughly speaking, the culture of alcohol split along class lines: wine and good whisky for the middle classes and above (plus the obligatory G&Ts of well-heeled suburbia); beer and cheaper spirits for the working classes. People with money knew plenty about claret and champagne, but they knew zilch about cocktails.

In the US, by contrast, cocktails have always been taken seriously, even by people who could afford to drink Dom Pérignon as an aperitif. And there was no split between the concept of the standalone cocktail bar and fine dining, as there often is in London.

Every halfway decent restaurant in Manhattan, Chicago and San Francisco – and many smaller cities as well – employed a skilled bartender working with a full stock of spirits. These bartenders knew that their customers would expect their martinis, manhattans and whisky sours to be made well – and more often than not, with a particular brand in a particular way.

The breadth and depth of American cocktail culture hasn't reached Britain yet, and perhaps it never will. But something else of value has happened here, and partly because of the American influence. As a new generation of newly affluent drinkers arose in the 1990s, well-travelled and aspiring to the sophistication of a US drinking culture, they began to see that there was more to fine alcohol than wine and single malts. And as their tastes became more sophisticated, a new generation of bar owners and bartenders grew to meet it. Supply and demand have grown together: as customers asked for more, the bartenders taught the customers to expand their horizons.

The magnificent three

The inspiration came originally from the great bartenders working in the fancy hotels, almost all of them Italian. A triumvirate of seminal figures is always mentioned in this regard, and with good reason. Peter Dorelli at the American Bar of the Savoy, Gilberto Preti at Dukes Hotel and Salvatore Calabrese (originally at Dukes, then at the Lanesborough, and now with his own members' club, Salvatore at 50) set standards of professionalism and craftsmanship that are still regarded as hugely influential. All of them had an encyclopedic knowledge not just of cocktails but of the spirits from which they are made,

Peroni con amici.

Great nights out with friends, that's what Peroni was made for. Imported from Italy, this unmistakably stylish beer is brewed for an equally unmistakable crisp, refreshing taste. Need a guide to the best places in town? Just ask if they serve Peroni.

peroniitaly.com

▶ and that knowledge is a cornerstone of good bartending. They also knew the business inside and out, and they struck the right balance between correctness and adaptability.

Part of their professionalism lay in their understanding that it isn't enough for a bartender to know how to make good drinks or turn a profit for the owner. He or she must also know how to train junior bartenders, who are essential not just for the bar where they're working, but for all the places they'll go on to afterwards. Prior to his retirement from the Savoy, Peter Dorelli said: 'I try to prepare them in their approach to life as well as work.' When his bartenders left for other jobs, they knew about the whole business – budgets, costs, management, training. Sitting in the American Bar, bartender Dick Bradsell said of Dorelli: 'We're in the presence of a god here. His standards and dedication are incredible. For me, cocktail bartending is more about fun. This is different. It's a religious experience. The American Bar is a temple, and Peter Dorelli is the priest.'

If Dorelli and his two colleagues were the seminal figures of their era, then Bradsell is their equivalent for this current cocktail explosion. After the long dominance of the hotel bars, his creation of Dick's Bar at the Atlantic Bar & Grill in 1994 signalled the birth of a new idea – that great cocktails could be served in places where you didn't have to wear a suit or run a merchant bank to fit in, and that cocktails could, as Bradsell put it, be 'about fun.' And the idea didn't take long to catch on.

To begin with, however, there was too much emphasis on fun and not enough on professionalism. The showmanship of flair-bartending, and a premature leap into 'creative' cocktail-making, valuing novelty and appearance over substance, dominated the offerings of lesser bars that didn't have someone like Bradsell running the show. Bradsell described this as the tendency to 'put seven or eight ingredients in every cocktail and making artificial concoctions that are clever but clashing.' Cocktails were cool, but there just weren't enough good,

well-trained people making them – and drinkers lacked the sophistication to know that they were getting an inferior product. Which is only to be expected: it takes time to create a true cocktail culture. It doesn't just appear overnight.

What changed things – and brought us to our current happy state – was that Dick Bradsell and a few others had the same training ethos that made those hotel bars so good. Bradsell trained bartenders who now work all over the world. The London Academy of Bartenders (founded in 1996) and IP Bartenders (1999) provided a more formal setting for training, and the people who learned there in turn went on to train others. Jonathan Downey's Match group (whose first bar opened in 1999) began with Bradsell at the helm and is now, with its three Match bars and members' bars Milk & Honey and the Player, a veritable university of cocktail training.

The effect is akin to a pyramid scheme, but a benign one: one bartender trains four, those four train another four apiece, and so on. The result: a large and growing base of skilled practitioners who spread out all over the capital. They know their spirits. They know how to please and educate their customers. And increasingly they are leading cocktail-making in the right direction: favouring brown spirits over well-marketed but often insipid vodkas (the favoured spirit of the first generation of cocktail bars), and valuing enlightened classicism over inventiveness for the sake of inventiveness.

There's been progress in various areas of London's drinking scene over the period covered by the ten editions of this guide. Dingy boozers serving keg beer are fewer in number, the gastropub phenomenon has exploded, wine bars have kept pace with the growing diversity of wine-making styles and origins. But it's in the capital's cocktail bars that the greatest leaps have taken place. If you'd asked me a decade ago, I'd never have predicted such fantastic improvements both in quality and quantity. And in this instance, I am only too happy to have been proved wrong. ●

Hello!

Notable arrivals in the last year.

Big Chill House

Mahiki

Fat Badger

Pigalle Club

Central

Artesian
Langham Hotel,
1C Portland Place,
W1B 1JA (7636 1000/
www.artesian-bar.co.uk).
Extravagantly
refurbished bar in the
Langham Hotel. Grand
or OTT? You decide.
See p48.
Bedford & Strand
1A Bedford Street,
WC2E 9HH
(7836 3033/
www.bedford-
strand.com).
Stylish, convivial wine
bar tucked just off the
Strand. A real don't
miss. *See p35.*
Big Chill House
257-259 Pentonville
Road, N1 9NL (7427
2540/www.bigchill.net).
Take a knackered old
venue, put it in the care
of the famously friendly
Big Chill folk and you
get this: a cracking bar.
See p45.
5th View
5th floor, Waterstone's,
203-206 Piccadilly,
W1J 9HA (7851 2468/
www.5thview.co.uk).
Ace cocktail bar
atop Waterstone's
bookshop. *See p58.*
Hat & Feathers
2 Clerkenwell Road,
EC1M 5PQ
(7490 2244).
Restoration and
refurbishment of a long-

derelict Victorian boozer,
now a fine pub and
restaurant. *See p29.*
Mahiki
1 Dover Street, W1S
4LD (7493 9529/
www.mahiki.com).
Absurdly popular
Hawaiian-themed bar,
beloved of monied
youngsters. *See p55.*
Moose
31 Duke Street,
W1U 1LG (7224 3452/
www.vpmg.net).
Likeable, cosy cocktail
bar from the Vince
Powers Music Group.
See p50.

City

Hawksmoor
157 Commercial Street,
E1 6BJ (7247 7392/
www.thehawksmoor.com).
American-inspired
cocktail bar and
restaurant. *See p87.*

West

Fat Badger
310 Portobello Road,
W10 5TA (8969 4500/
www.thefatbadger.com).
Cosy pub serving
adventurous bar snacks
– smoked sprats
anyone? *See p108.*
Montgomery Place
31 Kensington Park
Road, W11 2EU (7792
3921/www.montgomery
place.co.uk).
Self-described 'lounge
bar kitchen' that's

above all else a cocktail
bar – and a very good
one. *See p111.*

South West

Amuse Bouche
51 Parsons Green Lane,
SW6 4JA (7371 8517/
www.abcb.co.uk).
Busy modern bar – and
one of the best places
in town dedicated to
quality champagne.
See p129.

South

Vinifera
20-26 Bedford Road,
SW4 7HJ (7498 9648).
Miniature wine bar
hidden behind Clapham
North tube. *See p152.*

South East

Hide Bar
39-45 Bermondsey
Street, SE1 3XF
(7403 6655).
Bermondsey cocktail
bar with a drinks list
made in bar heaven –
all the premium spirits
you've ever heard of,
plus quite a few you
haven't. *See p162.*

East

Narrow Street
Pub & Dining Room
44 Narrow Street,
E14 8DQ (7265 8931).
The first Gordon Ramsay
gastropub – and it's a
good 'un. *See p182.*

Favela Chic
91-93 Great Eastern
Street, EC2A 3HZ
(7613 4228/www.
favelachic.com/london).
Wild party bar and
sister to the über-cool
Parisian venue of the
same name. *See p188.*

North East

Empress of India
130 Lauriston Road,
E9 7LH (8533 5123/
www.theempress
ofindia.com).
Old boozer transformed
into an impressive
gastropub, run by
the same group as
Dockland's the Gun.
See 195.

North

Gilgamesh
Stables Market,
Chalk Farm Road, NW1
8AH (7482 5757/www.
gilgameshbar.com).
Opulent, theatrical bar
and restaurant with a
splendid mosaic bar.
See p206.

Clubs

Pigalle Club
215 Piccadilly,
W1J 9HN (0845
345 053/www.the
pigalleclub.com).
Sleek, chic basement
supper club, harking
back to the glamour of
the 1940s. *See p247.*

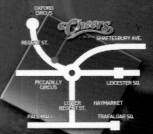

The Triangle

1 Ferme park road, N4 4DS (8292 0516)
Finsbury park tube. Open 6pm-12am Mon-Fri; 11am-12am Sat-Sun.
www.thetrianglerestaurant.co.uk

Prepare to be transported to another world. Inside this palace of curiosities between Crouch End and Finsbury Park, with its rich fabrics, beaten metalwork, glowing candles and enchanting alcoves is a food-lover's heaven. Moroccan-inspired but with elements of Asian, European and even Australasian cuisine, the menu is as eclectic as the decor. We ate sardine salad with couscous - the fish moist with a perfectly crispy exterior, the couscous tender and spicy - then Thai green chicken curry, once again the ideal heat, texture and taste. My companion's sirloin steak had a garnish of ginger which had her squeaking with pleasure.

Owner Aziz Begdouri devised both the exotic interior (including a surreal bed with furniture stuck to the ceiling) and the funky fusion menu, having been a chef in both his native Morocco and in London. Triangle won Archant's Best Moroccan restaurant in London award in 2006.

Combined with the chilled music, the gracious and happy service, the small but idyllic garden, the low-level den where you sit cross-legged on cushions, the inventive wine list (try the Moroccan sauvignon blanc - it's knockout) and the plethora of intricate, lovingly worked details everywhere you look, this is a stunning triumph of a restaurant.

By David Nicholson

Don't be  go ●
to the ▲

Central

Provincials, tourists, gay hedonists, after-work gluggers, early-hours groovers – Soho is diverse enough to accommodate the lot. If you're after famous old boozers, squeeze into the **French House** or the lovely little **Dog & Duck**. Further into the night, hit the cocktails – few places mix them as well as the **Player** or serve them as stylishly as **Milk & Honey** (book before you arrive). The gay scene is focused on the west end of Old Compton Street, around the **Admiral Duncan** and **Comptons of Soho**; lesbians have the **Candy Bar**.

Holborn is somewhat more restrained, but does have a few pubs to be proud of – **Edgar Wallace** for one. Slicker is neighbouring Aldwych, which has dramatic venues the **Lobby Bar** and **Bank Aldwych**. Snug pubs and glitzy bars are Mayfair's forte. **Claridge's**, **Donovan Bar**, **American Bar** and **Galvin at Windows** add to the glamour of their respective hotels; **Mô Tea Room** is funky and welcoming, **Mahiki** less so but undeniably popular. And those snug pubs? The **Red Lion** is our pick. Marylebone has a wealth of its own fine boozers, many with the feel of a local – Crawford Place's **Windsor Castle** (one of two in the area) is a cracker, as is vintage tap the **Golden Eagle**. The bar scene has improved of late, with the addition of hotel cocktail bar **Artesian** and the music-driven **Moose**.

Teetering on the edge of the West End, Bloomsbury has a clutch of grand traditional pubs that draw tourists from the British Museum; ignore these and head for the homely **Lamb** instead. Rival bowling alleys **All Star Lanes** and **Bloomsbury Bowling Lanes** do a fine rolling trade; **Vats Wine Bar** is a more discrete place for a chat and a sip. Though (legend says) named after a pub, Fitzrovia is better served by its bars than its unimaginative boozers. Cocktails are a must at **Match Bar** and **Crazy Bear**; Japanese spirit shochu should be supped at the attractive **Shochu Lounge**. Pub-goers do have something to cheer: the pies at the **Newman Arms** are delicious.

You'll find the side-streets of Covent Garden more promising than its tourist-heavy Piazza, yielding traditional old boozers like the **Lamb & Flag** (packed to its bare beams most days) and the cosy **Cross Keys**. South to the Strand and Trafalgar Square, tucked-away wine bar **Gordon's** is hard to beat for a shared bottle; whisky is the speciality at **Albannach**, standing-looking-cool the same at the **ICA Bar**. Piccadilly, meanwhile, has been bolstered by excellent wine bar **1707** within Fortnum & Mason (shame it isn't open later); Leicester Square is as drab as ever, Dutch bar **De Hems** the pick of a poor bunch.

In Westminster, politicians cram into the **Red Lion**, complete with division bell and BBC Parliament on the telly. St James's has more (albeit pricier) choices, with classic cocktails at **Rivoli at the Ritz** and a new bar atop Waterstone's bookshop, **5th View**. For an old school pub, head for one of the three **Lions** – two **Red** (on Crown Passage and Duke of York Street) and one

Golden. For a stronger tipple, choose from the 18-page whisky menu at **Boisdale.**

Pimlico pubs are quiet affairs frequented by affluent locals and office workers: typical is the **Morpeth Arms.** Round the corner, cocktails at **Millbank Lounge** should not be missed. In Belgravia, the Lanesborough Hotel's stylish **Library** bar is expensive but worth a splash – perhaps before you head off for a pint at the cheerful little **Nag's Head.** In South Kensington, look past the curious mingle of Sloanes, rootless cosmopolitans and crims to find some of London's most pristine cocktail bars. Typical of the genre is **Collection:** clever, expensive and a little soulless unless you're part of a monied clique. Better is **190 Queensgate:** a miracle of swankiness on an otherwise desolate stretch between the Albert Hall and the Bulgarian Embassy.

With regeneration in full swing, new venues are popping up all over King's Cross and Euston – **Big Chill House,** a new venue from the Big Chill group, is the most exciting. Clerkenwell, however, still dominates the nightlife scene in these parts. No wonder, considering its collection of ace, niche bars (**St John, Café Kick, Vinoteca**), top gastropubs (the **Eagle** and the **Coach & Horses**) and one-of-a-kind boozers (**Jerusalem Tavern, Old China Hand**). Why go anywhere else?

Aldwych

Bank Aldwych
1 Kingsway, WC2B 6XF (7379 9797/www.bank restaurants.com). Holborn or Temple tube. **Open** 11.30am-11.30pm Mon-Thur, Sat; 11.30am-1am Fri; noon-3.30pm Sun. **Credit** AmEx, MC, V. Bar/restaurant
Bank Aldwych uses its high-ceilinged space and prime location to good effect. A bronze duck and an urban seafront mural add a funky touch to this blue-chip bar and adjoining Modern Euro restaurant. The extensive cocktail menu (£7-£11) features a list of Off Shore cocktails, including a Dark & Stormy with Gosling Black Seal rum, and a Singapore Sling with Hendrick's gin. Reyka vodka and Lapponia cranberry liqueur in the Glacier Martini, and Monkey Shoulder triple malt and fresh kumquats in the Asian Monkey display a similarly well-sourced, classy touch on the Signature list. Bitburger and Innis & Gunn are among the bottled beers; 16 wines come by the glass.
Babies and children admitted. Disabled: toilet. Dress: smart casual. Function room. **Map p275 M6.**

Edgar Wallace
40 Essex Street, WC2R 3JE (7353 3120). Temple tube. **Open** 11am-11pm Mon-Fri. **Food served** noon-9.30pm Mon-Fri. **Credit** MC, V. Pub

Tucked beside Middle Temple, between the Strand and the Embankment, the pleasantly historic Edgar is a great corner pub, well stocked and well run. Anywhere more prominent and it would clean up. As it stands, custom ticks along as steadily as any crime novel by the writer this pub was named after. Pumps of Edgar's Pale Ale (brewed specially for the pub by the Nethergate brewery), Adnams, Suffolk County, Wood's Parish and Moor Withy Cutter, along with a host of other regular ales, illustrate the place's dedication to bringing in the better obscure brews. Staropramen should suit lager drinkers. The wines, 18 by the bottle, eight by the glass, are also well sourced, and include a Philippe Zinck pinot blanc (£15) and a Castillo Rioja Bodegas Palacio (£15.50). Food is standard pub grub (burgers, fish and chips, salads, garlic bread).
Function room. Games (darts, golf machine). Restaurant. TVs. **Map p275 M6.**

George IV
28 Portugal Street, WC2A 2HE (7955 7743). Holborn or Temple tube. **Open** noon-11pm Mon-Fri. **Food served** noon-10pm Mon-Fri. **Credit** MC, V. Pub
A quality pub this, located next to the pleasant, pedestrianised hub of the LSE. But don't expect drinks promo nights and plastic glasses; instead, a sturdy bar counter dispenses guest ales (Hancock HB was a recent example), Adnams Explorer, Bombardier, Abbot, Beck's Vier and Hoegaarden, even two draught wines. A board of other bottles – Casa La Joya merlot (£2.85/£10.30), Château Labory Fronsac (£13.65) – stands in the roomy main bar, resplendent with varnished wood. The relaxing upstairs darts room has been decorated with equally simple aplomb. Superior all-day food caters well for vegetarians, with the likes of wild mushroom or asparagus risotto.
Function room. Games (darts). TVs. **Map p275 M6.**

La Grande Marque NEW
Middle Temple Lane, EC4Y 9BT (7583 5946/ www.lagrandemarque.co.uk). Temple tube. **Open/ food served** 11am-11pm Mon-Fri. **Credit** (over £10) AmEx, MC, V. Bar
Opened in 2006, this branch of the classy La Grande Marque in Ludgate Hill makes best use of its erudite surroundings. Set halfway down Middle Temple Lane, it comprises two smart rooms, the larger one to the rear a library illustrated with imperial pastimes and portraits of stern bewigged lords. Both rooms overlook a well-manicured courtyard garden. The drinks menu is the same as at its sister branch. Of the 40 champagne choices are bottles for birthdays (Joseph Perrier 1998, £55) and engagements (Bollinger Grande Année 1997, £80), and half-bottles for personal treats (Veuve Clicquot, £25). There are also 40 red and white wines, starting at £14.50 a bottle, with a Les Crillotis Pouilly-Fumé 2004 and a Domaine Pabiot Sancerre Rouge 2002 both in the £30 range.
Babies and children admitted. Disabled: toilet. Function room. Restaurant. Tables outdoors (garden). **Map p275 N6.**

★ Lobby Bar
One Aldwych, WC2B 4RH (7300 1070/www.one aldwych.com). Covent Garden or Temple tube. **Open** 8am-11.30pm Mon-Sat; 8am-10.30pm Sun. **Food served** noon-5pm, 5.30-11.30pm Mon-Sat; noon-5pm, 5.30-10.30pm Sun. **Credit** AmEx, DC, MC, V. Hotel bar
The lobby bar of the One Aldwych hotel innovates as much as it sparkles. It offers an improbable 30 kinds of

THE RESTAURANT
Paper

With a modern British themed menu and a capacity of 100 for a seated meal or 150 for canapés the Restaurant is an ideal place to start your evening at Paper Club London.

Our delicious 3 course menu also includes complimentary entrance into the Club after your meal.

Opening times: Thursday, Friday, Saturday 7:30pm until late

Paper Club, 68 Regent Street, London W1B 5EL
For reservations please call the following number
T +44 (0)207 439 7770   F +44 (0)207 434 0077
E info@paperclublondon.com
www.paperclublondon.com

Nag's Head

martini (£9.40-£20), based on original mixes (Snow Cat with Snow Leopard vodka, strawberry purée and Limoncello) or brand (Junipero, Ciroc, Kauffman Vintage 2003). The six-strong house selection allows the use of crushed fresh chilli (with Agavero tequila liqueur) in a Chilli del Toro, and fresh tamarillo (with Wyborowa) in a tamarillo martini. De Venoge is the base for the champagne cocktails, Prosecco for the bellinis. Fresh cantaloupe melons flavour the cantaloupe daiquiri, fresh passion fruit pulp the Mexican Passion. Evening bar snacks (organic gravadlax, mini wagyu steak burgers, £8.95) maintain quality control. The whole proceedings are overseen by an impeccable staff. Pure class.
Babies and children admitted. Disabled: toilet. Separate rooms for parties. **Map p275 M7.**

Also in the area...
Cellar Door *Zero Aldwych, WC2E 7DA (7240 8848).* Subterranean bar converted from an ex-public lavatory. Drinks are one-third off before 8pm; later in the evening, there's always some form of entertainment, from cabaret to jazz. Admission is free. **Map p275 M7.**
Devereux *20 Devereux Court, Essex Street, WC2R 3JJ (7583 4562).* Ancient hideaway pub with four cask ales at the bar and an upstairs restaurant. **Map p275 N6.**
Queen Mary *Waterloo Pier, Victoria Embankment, WC2R 2PP (7240 9404/www.queenmary.co.uk).* Boat bar anchored in a killer spot near Temple tube station, overlooking the South Bank. Shame about the scuffed furniture, flatscreen TVs and poor cocktails. **Map p275 N7.**

Belgravia

Blue Bar
The Berkeley, Wilton Place, SW1X 7RL (7235 6000/ www.the-berkeley.co.uk). Hyde Park Corner tube.
Open/food served 4pm-1am Mon-Sat; 4-11pm Sun. **Credit** AmEx, DC, MC, V. Hotel bar
With its glass walls and watery blue interior, walking into the David Collins-designed Blue Bar feels akin to being immersed in an aquarium teeming with some of the most exotic and expensive fish on earth. Seating is limited to just 50, so each new entry halts conversations as heads crane to rate celebrity status on a sliding scale. Displays of wealth regularly border on vulgar (rappers with supermodels draped over their arms like size-zero fur pieces), but the glamour tones are pitched to such a surreal sheen that it all feels strangely normal. Cocktails are seriously well crafted – the Spicy Queen blends 12-year-old Chivas whisky, fresh figs and lime juice with own-made caramel and chilli – but there's only one reason people come here, and it ain't the drinks. In terms of social statements, the Blue Bar is a great, glittering exclamation mark.
Disabled: toilet (in hotel). Dress: no shorts or caps.

Horse & Groom
7 Groom Place, SW1X 7BA (7235 6980/www.horse andgroom.net). Hyde Park Corner tube/Victoria tube/ rail. **Open** 11am-12.30pm Mon-Fri. **Food served** noon-3pm Mon-Fri. **Credit** AmEx, MC, V. Pub
Due for a revamp at the time of writing, the Horse & Groom offers a relaxing pint down a cobbled mews. Informal and unpretentious – the kind of place whose upstairs function

room would suit any office department – this Shepherd Neame pub features the strong and splendid Swiss Hürlimann on draught, along with the stable Spitfire, Master Brew and Oranjeboom. Todd's provide the wines, so you can find a Domaine du Petit Soumard Pouilly-Fumé (£16.50) and a Timara cabernet sauvignon merlot (£14.50) from New Zealand, as well as the tenner-a-bottle stuff (Berticot sauvignon blanc). All but one variety comes by the glass. The revamp will pair off the right-angle of tables, matching intimacy with comfort.
Bar available for hire Sat, Sun (free). Function room. Games (darts). Tables outdoors (10, pavement). TVs.

★ Library
Lanesborough Hotel, 1 Lanesborough Place, Hyde Park Corner, SW1X 7TA (7259 5599/www.lanesborough. com). Hyde Park Corner tube. **Open** 11am-1am Mon-Sat; noon-10.30pm Sun. **Food served** 11am-midnight Mon-Sat; noon-10.30pm Sun. **Credit** AmEx, DC, MC, V. Hotel bar
Walk through the lobby of the Lanesborough Hotel to the Library and you are handed a book by staff in *Casablanca* attire. Within it you'll find, as you survey the towering fresh flowers and roaring fire of the elegant surroundings, spells. In the house champagne cocktail (£13.50), Aperol works with the orange juice and Limoncello. Fresh garlic, cognac and ginger beer combine in a Garlic Affair (£12.50). Wokka saké, fresh mint and strawberry purée mingle in the house martini (£12.50). The collection of vintage armagnacs and cognacs is legendary. Of the dozen wines, all, including a Puligny-Montrachet La Garenne Larue (£19/£76), come by the glass. It's magic at a price – £19 for spicy lobster nachos – but magic none the same.
Disabled: toilet. Function rooms. Music (pianist 6.30pm daily; free). Restaurant.

★ Nag's Head
53 Kinnerton Street, SW1X 8ED (7235 1135). Hyde Park Corner or Knightsbridge tube. **Open** 11am-11pm Mon-Sat; noon-10.30pm Sun. **Food served** noon-9pm daily. **No credit cards.** Pub
No mobiles and no credit cards at this charming time warp of a pub – it's a wonder they accept decimal coinage. The Nag's Head echoes a time when National Service was a given (note the cravats and regimental heraldry), James Mason was a sex bomb (note the line drawings) and glamorous destinations (Paris, New York) could only be glimpsed in crank-up machines, such as the one stood here beside a wireless-era Spangles sweets dispenser. The beer, served by what appear to be dwarfs behind the sunken counter in the main bar (and sold with sandwiches in the basement), is draught Adnams and Bitburger. Handle the steps in between with care.
Games (antique what-the-butler-saw machine). No mobile phones. Tables outdoors (1, pavement).

Star Tavern
6 Belgrave Mews West, SW1X 8HT (7235 3019). Hyde Park Corner or Knightsbridge tube/Victoria tube/ rail. **Open** 11am-11pm Mon-Sat; noon-10.30pm Sun. **Food served** noon-2.30pm, 6-9.30pm Mon-Fri. **Credit** AmEx, MC, V. Pub
Despite the slight refurb in early 2007, this two-room pub tucked in a quiet mews behind a phalanx of embassies still smacks of the 1960s. Back then, it was a star tavern indeed – crims, models and actors fraternising around the fireplace in the spacious side room or around the small horseshoe bar area. It was said that the Great Train

Robbery was planned here. Not over a pint of Bitburger it wasn't, but the ST still offers traditional British ales from the Fuller's stable. There are whiskies too – Laphroaig, Glenmorangie, and so on. Sundry continental clerks will go to their next posting with pleasant memories of peaceful, sozzled lunchtimes here. The Star Tavern is on the straight and narrow these days.
Babies and children admitted. Function room. Games (board games, darts). No piped music or jukebox.

Also in the area...
Ebury *11 Pimlico Road, SW1W 8NA (7730 6784/ www.theebury.co.uk).* Trendy gastrobar that gets packed with young families at weekends.
Ebury Wine Bar & Restaurant *139 Ebury Street, SW1W 9QU (7730 5447/www.eburywinebars. co.uk).* Old-fashioned in looks, but sparky in style, with an admirable 38 choices by the glass.
Prince Edward *73 Princes Square, W2 4NY (7727 2221).* Unpretentious oldies' boozer with a choice of Badger ales on draught.

Bloomsbury

AKA
18 West Central Street, WC1A 1JJ (7836 0110/ www.akalondon.com). Holborn or Tottenham Court Road tube. **Open** 10pm-5am Tue (6pm-5am 1st Tue of mth); 6pm-3am Wed; 8pm-3am Thur; 6pm-4am Fri; 7pm-5am Sat; 10pm-5am Sun. **Food served** 6-11.30pm Tue-Fri; 7-11.30pm Sat. **Admission** £5 after 11pm Tue; £5 after 10pm Thur; £7 after 11pm Fri; £10 after 9pm Sat; varies Sun. **Credit** AmEx, DC, MC, V. Bar
Dropping in for a post-work snifter, we found AKA's two-storey warehouse space pleasantly empty. The new Friday night, Blind Tiger, has taken on the vogueish speakeasy mantle to predictably brilliant effect – witness the Sazerac using 18-year-old Sazerac Rye (£8.50). For the fools not sampling the cocktails there are nine well-chosen reds and whites, plus a couple of rosés and 18 champers, and premium spirits mostly listed by country to facilitate choice for those bewildered by pages of options. The beers don't fare brilliantly; half a dozen, with only Kronenbourg on draught, but bottles include Theakston's Old Peculier and Bulmers cider as well as lagers. Food comes courtesy of the nearby Pizza Express. The punters? Chilled, but picking up momentum. Soundtrack? The same. Bar staff? Friendly, enthusiastic, well informed.
Bar available for hire. Comedy (7.30pm 2nd Thur of mth; £8). Disabled: toilet. Music (DJs 10pm daily; free). Quiz (8pm 1st Tue of mth; free). Screening facilities (call for details). **Map p272 L6.**

★ All Star Lanes
Victoria House, Bloomsbury Place, WC1B 4DA (7025 2676/www.allstarlanes.co.uk). Holborn tube. **Open/ food served** 5-11.30pm Mon-Wed; 5pm-midnight Thur; noon-2am Fri, Sat; noon-11pm Sun. **Bowling** (per person per game) £7.50 before 5pm; £8.50 after 5pm. **Credit** AmEx, MC, V. Bar/Bowling alley
Doing for ten-pin bowling what the Elbow Room did for pool and Café Kick did for table football, All Star Lanes is a well-realised, high-end endeavour. It's the gold-card brigade's foil to grungier Bloomsbury Bowling nearby, sporting four bowling lanes (plus two private ones) and a red leather bar serving up good cocktails. It's not a cheap

night out – the kitchen serves lobster, for gawd's sake – but All Star goes about its business with confidence and panache. Celebrities, they say, flock here, and the venue was recently featured as a 'treat' for Alan Sugar's winners on *The Apprentice*. Praise indeed. Look out for new branches in Bayswater and Shoreditch by 2008. *Babies and children admitted (until 6pm). Booking essential. Disabled: toilet. Separate room for parties.* **Map p272 L5.**

★ Bloomsbury Bowling Lanes

Basement, Tavistock Hotel, Bedford Way, WC1H 9EU (7691 2610/www.bloomsburylive.com). Russell Square tube. **Open/food served** noon-2am Mon-Wed; noon-3am Thur-Sat; noon-midnight Sun. **Bowling** from £36/hr 1 lane. **Credit** AmEx, MC, V. Bar/Bowling alley
Do you like sleek cocktails, flashy bartending, celebrity-spotting? Get thee to nearby bowling rival All Star Lanes. But if you prefer a pint while you bowl, the freedom to spill it on worn carpeting, and a joystick-jiggle on retro arcade games such as Galactica, this is your venue. With low-key decor, booths in the restaurant (burgers for £6.75) and swivel stools dotted around, this is a more authentic representation of Americana. Cocktails adhere to the theme; the list includes a white russian (£3.50), linked to bowling forever more thanks to *The Big Lebowski*. The beer selection features Bitburger, Bernard and the Meantime Brewery's Kölsch on tap, plus a further 15 by the bottle. Two karaoke rooms have been added in the last year, and films are occasionally screened in the sloping entrance hall. *Booking essential. Disabled: toilet.Games. No under-18s after 4pm.*

Duke

7 Roger Street, WC1N 2PB (7242 7230/www.duke pub.co.uk). Chancery Lane, Holborn or Russell Square tube. **Open** noon-11pm Mon-Sat; noon-10.30pm Sun.

Food served noon-10pm Mon-Sat; noon-9.30pm Sun. **Credit** MC, V. Gastropub
Even on a quiet weekday, the Duke contrives a hospitable feel with lustrous jazz crooning and Edith Piaf on the stereo, and newpapers at the handsome curved bar. Fixed-seat dark wood booths and red, black and white tile-effect lino give the place the feel of a café, while the inter-war decadence of a pink piano and Bakelite phone is enhanced by monochrome paintings of screen legends: among them a Louise Brooks styled rather like the diffident barmaid. Expect well-kept Greene King IPA and Adnams Broadside, food from sea bass to own-made tiramisu, and bar snacks of the chips-with-dips order. There's a second room with nicely laid tables and a deco-ish etched mirror; a couple of tables sit outside for banned smokers. *Babies and children admitted. Restaurant. Tables outdoors (3, pavement).* **Map p274 M4.**

King's Bar

Russell Hotel, Russell Square, WC1B 5BE (7837 6470/ www.principal-hotels.com). Russell Square tube. **Open** 7am-midnight Mon-Sat; 8am-11pm Sun. **Food served** 7am-9pm Mon-Sat; 8am-9pm Sun. **Credit** AmEx, DC, MC, V. Hotel bar
Visually, the King's Bar has plenty going for it, not least its prime location in a Gothic hotel recently party to a £20 million refurbishment. Then there's the unapologetically imperial aesthetic of the bar itself, where big mirrors and stern-looking portraits jostle for space on the wood-panelled walls, carriage clocks tick away slower-than-usual hours over the ornamental fireplace, and seating comes in the form of leather upholstered couches and chairs. It provides the sort of unreconstructed gentlemen's club atmosphere beloved of the fusty old brokers from *Trading Places*. Not that you'll find a Mortimer or Randolph Duke unwinding here: instead, the menu of premium spirit cocktails (from £9) and wines (from £5.25 a glass, £20.95 a bottle)

is pored over by a mute mix of hotel guests and bewildered tourists, making for a strangely funereal atmosphere that somewhat skewers the architectural sense of occasion. *Babies and children admitted. Disabled: toilet. Function room. No piped music or jukebox. Restaurant.* **Map p272 L4**.

★ Lamb

94 Lamb's Conduit Street, WC1N 3LZ (7405 0713). Holborn or Russell Square tube. **Open** 11am-midnight Mon-Sat; noon-10.30pm Sun. **Food served** noon-9pm daily. **Credit** AmEx, MC, V. Pub
Founded in 1729, this beautifully restored etched glass and mahogany masterpiece is class itself. Today the snob screens have a decorative role above the horseshoe island bar, but, back in the days when music hall stars were regulars here, they were used to deflect unwanted attention. The stage stars are remembered with two rows of small, gilt-framed portraits running around the walls, and other vintage theatrical touches are provided by a polyphon (the old mechanical musical instrument in the corner), dinky brass balustrades around the bar tables and the Pit, a sunken back area that gives access to a summer patio. The beer is Young's (and always served with correctly branded pint and beer mat), the wines a well-chosen half-dozen of each colour from Cockburn and Campbell, and the menu seasonal, with most main plates costing under a tenner – try the own-made steak and mushroom pie (£8.75). Pub excellence. *No piped music or jukebox. Separate room for parties. Tables outdoors (3, patio; 3, pavement).* **Map p274 M4**.

Museum Tavern

49 Great Russell Street, WC1B 3BA (7242 8987). Holborn or Tottenham Court Road tube. **Open** 11am-11.30pm Mon-Thur; 11am-midnight Fri, Sat; noon-10.30pm Sun. **Food served** 11am-8.30pm Mon-Sat; noon-8pm Sun. **Credit** AmEx, DC, MC, V. Pub

All Star Lanes. *See p19.*

A rare example of a pub as popular with locals as tourists, rejoicing in both a noble history (the current, splendid interior dates to a mid 19th-century refurb) and an ideal location (opposite the front gates of the British Museum). Ignore the logoed T-shirts for the six real ales (Greene King IPA, Pride, Theakston's Old Peculier, Timothy Taylor Landlord and guests Harviestoun Bitter & Twisted and, disappointingly, Bombardier) that decorate an expansive bar backed by mirrors advertising liquor manufacturers. Wines run to half a dozen of each by glass and bottle (reasonably priced at around a tenner), plus a couple of champagnes and rosés, and food is pub staples prodded a little upmarket. A row of flimsy tables cling to the pavement along Museum Street. *Children admitted (until 5pm, over-14s only). Games (board games, darts). Tables outdoors (5-8, pavement).* **Map p272 L5**.

mybar

11-13 Bayley Street, WC1B 3HD (7667 6050/ www.myhotels.com). Goodge Street or Tottenham Court Road tube. **Open** 11am-12.30am daily. **Food served** 7am-10.30pm daily. **Credit** AmEx, DC, MC, V. Bar
That myhotel sells its 'award-winning hospitality brand' with the line 'you're unique, you're an individual' invites cynicism, but, among the globular silver lightshades and arty light boxes, this sleek and comfortable two-room bar has made distinct improvements. There are now half a dozen beers by the bottle (including St Peter's Organic), the cocktail list has some intriguing inventions (perhaps an £8 Basilistic of basil and strawberry with Centenario Plata Tequila, passion fruit, lime juice and ginger ale) and a 'Wellbeing' selection of mocktails. There are premium liquors (£6-£15), decent wines (nine of each, seven fizz, two rosé) and appropriate booze fodder (chips and dips, £3.50). Surprisingly raucous on a recent Friday evening, mybar was nonetheless able to accommodate two individuals quietly attending to a pot of tea. Not bad. *Bar available for hire. Disabled: toilet. Function rooms. Tables outdoors (7, pavement).* **Map p272 K5**.

Oporto

168 High Holborn, WC1V 7AA (7240 1548/www.bar oporto.com). Holborn or Tottenham Court Road tube. **Open/food served** noon-midnight Mon-Wed; noon-1am Thur, Fri; 1pm-1am Sat. **Credit** MC, V. Bar
Sombre paintwork – the steely grey side of black – is enlivened at this skinny bar by the people-watching opportunities from bar stools set along the large windows on Endell Street. There are tables at either end of the bar, but floorspace is mainly left clear to facilitate crowds of post-work punters. The drinks options are mostly good – half a dozen of each colour of wine, half by the glass, plus half a dozen sparklers (up to an optimistic £165 vintage Dom Perignon); three dozen cocktails (£6-£7), divided into Rocks, Long, Straight Up, Cocktails, Mocktails and £3.50 Shots – but the taps are a disappointing flurry of San Miguel, Staropramen, Hoegaarden and Stella. The reassuringly dive-like downstairs combines squashy black leather armchairs and a dancefloor. *Function room. Games (pool). Tables outdoors (4, pavement). TV.* **Map p272 L6**.

Perseverance

63 Lamb's Conduit Street, WC1N 3ND (7405 8278). Russell Square tube. **Open** noon-11pm Mon-Thur, Sat; noon-midnight Fri. **Food served** noon-4pm, 5-9pm Mon-Sat; noon-6pm Sun. **Credit** MC, V. Gastrobar

Relaunched under new management with a slick maroon paint-job, the Perseverance attracts much the same crowd it always did: cool youngsters enjoying the loud, chatty, pub-cum-bar vibe inside, spilling out into the traffic-free street in good weather. The more quiet-minded head upstairs to a peaceful, armchair-filled lounge. Peroni has been added to an otherwise standard draught lager line-up; we were disappointed to find only one real ale available (London Pride) on our last visit. Service, though, has improved. It used to be a real problem – sporadic, surly and rushed – but the new regime has beefed-up the numbers behind the bar to good effect. Undemanding food of the burger and fish cake variety is available. *Function room. Tables outdoors (3, pavement).* **Map p274 M4.**

Point 101
101 New Oxford Street, WC1A 1DB (7379 3112/ www.vpmg.net). Tottenham Court Road tube. **Open/ food served** 5pm-3am Mon-Thur; 4pm-4am Fri, Sat; 4pm-2.30am Sun. **Admission** £3 after midnight Fri, Sat. **Credit** AmEx, MC, V. Bar
Arrive around closing time to make the most of the late licence and you might just wish you were on the nightbus instead. Just beyond the profusion of bouncers, the young, drunken punters have mostly already danced themselves down to a lascivious jiggle. Those still having fun would be as happy in an airport, given some booze and music played a little too loud. But during happy hour (5-9pm) the music's mellower, the drinkers more mixed, and the retro-futurist furniture that gets corralled behind the bar later on spreads over the whole space. One side of laminated A4 does the drinks – lacklustre beer, wine at £8.50 and cocktails easily bettered for £6.50. Outside seats appeal to exhaust-fume addicts.
Function room. Music (DJs 10pm daily). Tables outdoors (4, pavement). **Map p272 K6.**

Rugby Tavern
19 Great James Street, WC1N 3ES (7405 1384). Holborn tube. **Open** 11am-11pm Mon-Fri. **Food served** noon-2.30pm, 5.30-9pm Mon-Fri. **Credit** AmEx, MC, V. Pub
The sporting connection may be a mere quirk of geographical fate (Rugby Street is nearby) but nevertheless there are two dartboards, and a flatscreen TV showing all the major rugby and football matches. The rest of the interior is pub-standard – wooden stools at the bar, comfortable booths, a blackboard listing burgers and sandwiches – leaving the outdoor seating as the Rugby Tavern's USP. Benches line up along one front wall (look out for the pre-served harlequin tiling); in front of the other, a pleasant courtyard is filled with tree-sheltered tables and chairs. As soon as the weather even hints at clemency, office workers swarm here for an alfresco pint of Asahi or Oranjeboom lagers, Early Bird, Spitfire or Master's Brew real ales.
Function room. Games (darts). Tables outdoors (10, pavement). TV. **Map p274 M4.**

Truckles of Pied Bull Yard
Off Bury Place, WC1A 2JR (7404 5338/www.davy. co.uk). Holborn or Tottenham Court Road tube. **Open/food served** 11am-10pm Mon-Fri; (summer only) 11am-3pm Sat. **Credit** AmEx, DC, MC, V. Pub
Hidden in an enclosed square next to the London Review Bookshop, this branch of wine chain Davy's is a two-decked affair. Upstairs, spotlights and light pine furniture give unwelcome reminders of All Bar One. Downstairs is

better: a partitioned cellar bar, darker and more intimate, stretches far underground. Local office workers drink pints of Old Wallop served in pewter tankards. Otherwise, a dozen of Davy's own wines – fine French claret (£4.75/ £17.75), Australian chardonnnay (£4.85/£18.25), Rioja of Marqués de Vitoria, Alavesa (£4.75/£17.95) – come by the glass or bottle. But Truckles' key USP is its outdoor space: the pub's tables colonise most of Pied Bull Yard, creating a pleasant boozy piazza when weather allows.
Babies and children admitted (restaurant). Bar available for hire. Tables outdoors (20, courtyard). **Map p272 L5.**

Vats Wine Bar
51 Lamb's Conduit Street, WC1N 3NB (7242 8963). Holborn or Russell Square tube. **Open** noon-11pm Mon-Fri. **Food served** noon-2.30pm, 6-9.30pm Mon-Fri. **Credit** AmEx, DC, MC, V. Wine bar
This is the kind of old-fashioned place that attracts regulars: men in pinstriped suits served by long-standing staff amid etchings and wood panels. Although the front area has been lightened up considerably, the wine list is rather in the dark ages, relying on the competent if not wildly exciting Louis Latour for basic Burgundy – his logo appears on the wine list to confirm he won't be shifting for a while. A 2003 Rioja from Cune by the glass had decent acidity, with redcurrant and buttery notes, but the fruit wasn't bright enough, suggesting the bottle had been open a while. Trimbach, with its 2003 Gewürztraminer from Alsace, and South African winery Vergelegen stood out, the latter's 2003 blend of cabernet sauvignon and merlot made popular in Bordeaux being an excellent choice. Food starts in the 1970s with salmon and filo tapenade, plus green beans, and dips into the late 1990s with a Jamie-style duck leg, borlotti bean and thyme ragoût. As a venue for a lunchtime business meeting, it's perfect.
Babies and children admitted. Function room. Restaurant. Tables outdoors (4, pavement). **Map p274 M4.**

Also in the area...
Angel *61 St Giles High Street, WC2H 8LE (7240 2876).* Ancient pub, with Young's ales at the bar and a well-used dartboard. **Map p272 K6.**
Grape Street Wine Bar *222-224A Shaftesbury Avenue, WC2H 8EB (7240 0686).* Well-priced, two-roomed wine bar that attracts an office crowd. There's a café-like space at street level and, next door, a more conspiratorial wine-bar basement. **Map p272 L6.**
King's Arms *11A Northington Street, WC1N 2JF (7405 9107).* Regally themed expansive pub, popular with the lunchtime crowd; three ales on tap. **Map p274 M4.**
Lord John Russell *91 Marchmont Street, WC1N 1AL (7388 0500).* Rustic-looking pub serving pies, pasties and pints of ale (three on tap). **Map p272 L4.**
Marquis of Cornwallis *31 Marchmont Street, WC1N 1AP (7923 5960).* Refurbed pub (opposite the new-and-improved Brunswick Centre) with an attractive open-plan interior. **Map p272 L4.**
Plough *27 Museum Street, WC1A 1LH (7636 7964).* Corner pub in sight of the British Museum; expect lots of tourists. **Map p272 L5.**
Yorkshire Grey *29-33 Grays Inn Road, WC1X 8HR (7405 2519/www.alphabetbar.com).* Bustling pub with attractive dark wood interior. Under the same ownership as Alphabet, Amber and Cantaloupe. **Map p274 M5.**

Clerkenwell & Farringdon

Al's Café Bar
11-13 Exmouth Market, EC1R 4QD (7837 4821).
Angel tube/Farringdon tube/rail. **Open** 8am-2am
daily. **Food served** 8am-10pm Mon-Fri; 9am-10pm
Sat, Sun. **Credit** AmEx, MC, V. Café/Bar
With its huge windows overlooking Exmouth Market, Al's
is at its best in summertime when chatty punters spill out
on to the pavement by the pair of cheery classic red phone
boxes. Inside, a blue ceiling bedecked with faux art
nouveau chandeliers contrasts with bright red walls and
exposed metal ducting. Seating is an eclectic mix of red
chesterfields, black leather sofas and utilitarian chairs,
reflecting a similarly eclectic clientele: gaggles of women,
media blokes and arty types sporting thick-rim specs. The
bar (an imposing slab of concrete) is a shrine to continental booze, particularly wheat beers such as the caramel-
tinged König Ludwig – though the friendly bar staff are
as happy to serve you a cocktail or a coffee. On busy
nights there's a downstairs bar that some find bunkerish,
but we think is a cool concrete den brightened by illuminated 1960s images.
Babies and children welcome: high chairs. Function
room. Music (DJ 10pm Thur-Sat; free). Tables outdoors
(12, pavement). TVs. **Map p274 N4.**

Apple Tree
45 Mount Pleasant, WC1X 0AE (7837 2365).
Farringdon tube/rail. **Open** noon-11.30pm Mon-Fri;
6pm-1am Sat; 5-10.30pm Sun. **Food served** noon-3pm,
6-9pm Mon-Fri. **Credit** AmEx, DC, MC, V. Pub
Given the area's long association with the giant Mount
Pleasant postal sorting office, it's fitting that this old brick
corner hangout should be a first-class spot. It's hidden in
the shadow of an old bridge beneath Rosebery Avenue. A
high ceiling brings a roomy atmosphere to the front part
of a cosy L-shaped bar, which is decorated with vintage
green wallpaper, chandeliers and antique mirrors above
worn floorboards and an old rug. The long, thin section of
the bar to the rear is more intimate; oil paintings provide
the only distraction from punters' appreciation of excellent
beer like Abbot and Batemans. Expect media types from
the nearby ITN and *Guardian* offices.
Bar available for hire (Sat, Sun). Entertainment
(Poker 6pm Wed; £2). Function room. Music
(Americana/bluegrass; phone for details). Tables
outdoors (3, pavement). **Map p274 N4.**

Bishops Finger
9-10 West Smithfield, EC1A 9JR (7248 2341/www.
shepherdneame.co.uk). Farringdon tube/rail. **Open**
11am-11pm Mon-Thur; noon-3pm Fri. **Credit** AmEx, MC, V. Pub
A fine boozer on Smithfield's lesser-patronised southern
edge, with more character than better-known places on the
other side of the meat market. Beer choice is better too,
thanks to the pub's Shepherd Neame ownership: excellent
Porter is served alongside Master Brew, Spitfire and, of
course, the eponymous (and equally good) Bishops Finger.
Bar staff are a friendly bunch, cheerfully serving younger
suits and older locals sat at a mix of low and high polished
wood tables. Brass lights cast a sepia glow; period prints
and old advertising signs complete the decor. For diners,
a gold-framed blackboard offers honest British ballast like
broccoli and stilton soup – though the Finger is most
famous for the dozen or so juicy sausages it offers.

Babies and children admitted. Bar available for hire
(Sat, Sun). Disabled: toilet. Function room. Tables
outdoors (3, pavement). TV. **Map p274 O5.**

Bleeding Heart Tavern
Bleeding Heart Yard, 19 Greville Street, EC1N 8SJ
(7404 0333/www.bleedingheart.co.uk). Farringdon
tube/rail. **Open** 11am-11pm Mon-Fri. **Food served**
Bar 7-10.30am, 12.45-10.30pm Mon-Fri. *Bistro/tavern*
noon-3pm, 6-10.30pm Mon-Fri. **Credit** AmEx, DC,
MC, V. Wine bar
With its blood red walls and ruddy wooden floorboards,
drinking in the Bleeding Heart can often feel like exactly
that. The upstairs bar is too small to support the place's
enduring after-work popularity with local lawmakers, but
it's a top spot once things quieten down later in the evening.
Charming French staff serve goodies from a formidable
cellar of 450 bottles, listed in a comprehensive menu
(there's also an abridged version for beginners). Most wines
are from a New Zealand vineyard in which the owners have
a share; prices start low, but quickly skyrocket on more
exclusive vintages. Food in the downstairs dining room is
traditional British, with an emphasis on organic meats siz-
zling on an open rotisserie and grill.
Function room. No piped music or jukebox. Restaurant.
Tables outdoors (10, terrace). **Map p274 N5.**

Bowler NEW
28-32 Bowling Green Lane, EC1R 0BJ (7837 4141/
www.thebowler-ec1.co.uk). Farringdon tube/rail.
Open noon-midnight Mon-Fri. **Food served** noon-
9pm Mon-Fri. **Credit** MC, V. Bar/Restaurant
Reactions to the Bowler's shamelessly psychedelic
makeover will no doubt be split between those viewing it
as a triumph of the imagination and grumbling locals wondering exactly what the new owners have been smoking.
Either way, it certainly makes for a striking entrance; walls
are festooned with kaleidoscopically swirling Finnish
prints, the fireplace filled with candles. Step further inside,
however, and it becomes clear that this is little more than
cultural camouflage; the Bowler is still very much a bog-
standard boozer, from the silver branded pumps dispensing big-name lagers to the typo-riddled menu of swanky
burgers and bangers. Only eleven days reborn on our visit,
it remains to be seen whether the Bowler's new look gives
it a shot in the arm or a slap in the face.
Babies and children welcome: high chairs. Bar available
for hire (Sat, Sun). Function room. Quiz (phone for
details). Restaurant. **Map p274 N4.**

★ Café Kick
43 Exmouth Market, EC1R 4QL (7837 8077/www.cafe
kick.co.uk). Angel tube/Farringdon tube/rail. **Open**
noon-11pm Mon-Thur; noon-midnight Fri, Sat; 4-10.30pm
Sun (Mar-Dec). **Food served** noon-3pm, 6-10pm Mon-
Fri; noon-10pm Sat; 4-9.30pm Sun. **Credit** MC, V. Bar
This worn and weathered scout hut of a bar – long, thin
and dotted with footie memorabilia – is the setting for competitive high jinks of the highest order, courtesy of three
well-oiled René Pierre table football tables. Tokens are purchased from jovial bar staff, rules are clearly posted and
there are regular monthly tournaments. An area at the back
with Formica-topped café tables offers sparse seating and
menus listing a Champions' League of Euro beers: 14 by
the bottle, including Kronenbourg (France), Peroni (Italy),
Duvel (Belgium), San Miguel (Spain), Sagres (Portugal),
Krombacher Pils (Germany) and Brahma (a ringer from
Brazil). Cocktails come in the form of 'long kicks' and 'short

kicks', food is tapas, platters and sandwiches, and the cigarettes sold behind the bar are, appropriately enough, Lucky Strikes. Premier league stuff.
Babies and children admitted (until 5pm). Games (table football). Tables outdoors (2, pavement). TVs. **Map p274 N4.**

Castle

34-35 Cowcross Street, EC1M 6DB (7553 7621). Farringdon tube/rail. **Open** noon-11pm Mon; noon-midnight Tue-Thur; noon-1am Fri, Sat; noon-10.30pm Sun. **Food served** noon-10pm daily. **Credit** AmEx, MC, V. Pub

Don't be put off by the rather nondescript exterior, with its pub chain-style promise of food and booze (yes, we know that's a likely combination). Though perfectly situated (by Farringdon station) to suck in passing commuters, the boho vibe of this engaging corner pub attracts local creatives – Clerkenwell designers and arty hacks – rather than suits. Dark polished wood and old wallpaper provide a backdrop for a changing art display – big pop art paintings on our last visit, but there's a welcome edge of shabbiness that makes it feel more thrown together than carefully designed. Red banquettes beckon once you've grabbed a pint of Bombardier or something continental, while the peckish can choose the likes of cassoulet and mash from the Comfort Food menu. A decent mix of non-chart sounds helps delay any plans for departure home.
Disabled: toilet. Function room. Games (arcade machine, fruit machine). Music (DJs 7.30pm Fri, Sat; free). TV. **Map p274 N5.**

★ Cellar Gascon

59 West Smithfield, EC1A 9DS (7600 7561/7796 0600/ www.cellargascon.com). Barbican tube/Farringdon tube/ rail. **Open** noon-midnight Mon-Fri; 6pm-midnight Sat. **Tapas served** noon-11.30pm Mon-Fri; 6pm-midnight Sat. **Credit** AmEx, MC, V. Wine bar

Attached to the much-fêted Club Gascon, this bar opened to take advantage of the clamour for the restaurant's foie gras done a number of ways. Owner Vincent Labeyrie has built a room with City workers in mind: leather-style banquettes line a cool blue wall for a clubby vibe – an odd look, perhaps, for a region that's known for stuffing corn down goose necks. There's a large selection of expertly chosen bottles from south-west France, such as Pacherenc du Vic-Bilh, Château Montus 2002, a barrel-fermented petit corbu with full, honeyed flavours, and a delicious range of nibbles including slices of fatty, rich Gascon black ham. Most unusually, the tasting notes are as good as the wines themselves: 'mountain fresh, bristling with pithy, lemon-edged fruit' being a great description of the 2004 Xuri d'Ansa Cave de Saint-Etienne de Baïgorry.
Bar available for hire. **Map p274 O5.**

Charterhouse

38 Charterhouse Street, EC1M 6JH (7608 0858/www. charterhousebar.co.uk). Farringdon tube/rail. **Open** noon-11pm Mon, Tue; noon-midnight Wed, Sun; noon-2am Thur; noon-4am Fri; 5pm-4am Sat; noon-5pm Sun. **Food served** noon-9.30pm Mon-Fri; 5-9.30pm Sat; noon-5pm Sun. **Admission** £5 after 10pm Fri, Sat. **Credit** AmEx, MC, V. Bar

Central

Hat & Feathers. See p29.

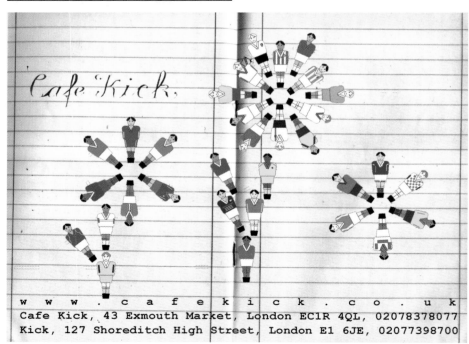

Where better to get pie-eyed than a pie-shaped bar? This wedge-shaped glass enclosure opposite Smithfield Market is an alternative to Fluid along the road. In place of the latter's retro Asian theme, however, Charterhouse opts for a more straight-up approach, relying on stylishly wrapped music and booze. A concise cocktail list tweaks classics with panache: a Big Bison martini makes use of Zubrówka bison grass vodka, Krupnik honey vodka and apple juice. As a warm-up (or cheaper alternative) to neighbouring Fabric, weekend music nights range from soulful house to pumped-up funk. It's handy too for a quick lunch from a nifty menu; the likes of chickpea cakes with tomato chutney cost around a fiver, and there's a Sunday brunch too. *Bar available for hire. Function room. Music (DJs 8pm Fri, Sat). Tables outdoors (3, pavement). TVs (big screen).* **Map p274 O5.**

Cicada

132-136 St John Street, EC1V 4JT (7608 1550/ www.cicada.nu). Farringdon tube/rail. **Open/food served** noon-11pm Mon-Sat. **Credit** AmEx, DC, MC, V. Cocktail bar

Looking for a date venue that's vaguely sophisticated but not too trendy or expensive? Cicada seems to fit the bill if the thirty-plus coupley clientele on our visit was typical. Lighting up a corner site, its huge glass windows wrap around a bright, clean-lined interior split into two-thirds restaurant, one-third bar. Dark stone flags contrast with bare white walls pierced by the glowing slit of a modern fake fire, and big geometric lampshades continue the theme of pale modernity. Cocktails show more understanding of mixology than Zetter down the road, as well as costing less (especially without the 'optional service charge'); try a Mekong Mule, which adds fresh coriander and ginger to the traditional mix. A decent wine list offers large glasses from £4, while bar food has an Asian theme if you don't want to move across to the bustling restaurant. *Babies and children admitted (until 7pm). Booking advisable. Separate room for parties. Tables outdoors (5, pavement).* **Map p274 O4.**

★ Coach & Horses

26-28 Ray Street, EC1R 3DJ (7278 8990/www.the coachandhorses.com). Farringdon tube/rail. **Open** 11am-11pm Mon-Fri; 6-11pm Sat; noon-4pm Sun. **Food served** noon-3pm, 6-10pm Mon-Fri; 6-10pm Sat; noon-3pm Sun. **Credit** AmEx, MC, V. Gastropub
Tucked away down a side street near Farringdon station, it's easy to see why this is a popular haunt of hacks from the nearby *Guardian* and *Observer* HQ. Art adorns panelled walls beneath a beautifully moulded ceiling, and a classy menu of changing specials (such as cockles with pancetta) rivals anything on offer at the nearby Eagle. The beer's fine too, with the likes of Adnams, London Pride and Timothy Taylor, while the wine list is as good as you'd expect in an area mixing journos and lawyers. Food is excellent – we were impressed by an unexpectedly delicious cauliflower pie, £10 – and the garlicky, rock-salted chips should not be missed. A patio garden makes an ideal place to enjoy a bowl during the summer. *Babies and children welcome: high chairs. Restaurant available for hire. Tables outdoors (16, garden).* **Map p274 N4.**

Crown Tavern

43 Clerkenwell Green, EC1R 0EG (7253 4973). Farringdon tube/rail. **Open** noon-midnight daily. **Food served** noon-10pm daily. **Credit** AmEx, MC, V. Pub

Tastefully refurbished a couple of years back, the Crown has retained much of its period charm while adding an overlay of modern touches. But whether you prefer to gaze at Clerkenwell Green through etched Victorian glass or big modern fishbowl glazing, you're likely to find something here to appeal. The space is nicely divided into sections, each offering a slightly different ambience – a rear room nods to past times with its old paint-job and vintage fireplace, while sofas and red banquettes give a more contemporary feel to the brighter front sections. Beers include Adnams alongside Hoegaarden and Kirin, backed by a good bottled selection and decent wine list. From an extensive menu, the likes of duck breast on roasted veg sits happily alongside pub grub favourites. Music, like the clientele, tends to the perky and contemporary. *Babies and children admitted (until 7pm). Function room. Music (April-Sept jazz 7pm Tue; free). Tables outdoors (10, pavement).* **Map p274 N4.**

Dollar

2 Exmouth Market, EC1R 4PX (7278 0077/ www.dollargrills.com). Farringdon tube/rail. **Open** 6pm-1am daily. **Food served** noon-4pm, 6-11pm Mon-Thur; noon-4pm, 6-11.30pm Fri, Sat; noon-5pm, 6-10pm Sun. **Credit** AmEx, MC, V. Cocktail bar
Occupying a corner site on Exmouth Market, this is a fine cocktail-focused complement to the neighbouring Al's Café Bar and the Eagle across the road. Skip the food operation at street level and sidle down a little staircase into the slick, glamorous subterranean bar. Dim red lights and candles reveal silvery columns rising from old boards, plus dark brick walls punctuated by seductive little alcoves for those seeking privacy. The more showy disport themselves on ornate gilded vintage chairs near a huge screen, which, thankfully, offers vintage film classics rather than sport. The drinks are classy too, with both invention and quality among the array of well-priced martinis and other classics from £6.50 – a Lemongrass Collins hits the right notes, while drinkers are offered a choice of premium spirits such as Tanqueray 10. *Babies and children admitted. Bar available for hire. Music (DJs 8pm Fri, Sat; free). Restaurant. Tables outdoors (5, pavement). TV (plasma screen).* **Map p274 N4.**

★ Eagle

159 Farringdon Road, EC1R 3AL (7837 1353). Farringdon tube/rail. **Open** noon-11pm Mon-Sat; noon-5pm Sun. **Food served** 12.30-3pm, 6.30-10.30pm Mon-Fri; 12.30-3.30pm, 6.30-10.30pm Sat; 12.30-3.30pm Sun. **Credit** MC, V. Gastropub
If there's a person left in London who doesn't know of this pioneering venue – 'the grandfather of gastropubs', set up by Michael Belben and David Eyre in 1991 – we'll eat Philip Treacy's entire winter collection, never mind a single hat. Of course, it would be much more pleasant to lounge at one of the Eagle's big wooden tables, watch the grey-faced *Guardian* journos make their way to and from work down the road, and tuck into some of the food that made the pub's name (steak sandwiches, tapas and heartier Med-influenced meat and fish dishes). Drinkers are well taken care of, with Kirin and Red Stripe, plus Bombardier and Eagle IPA for ale-heads; there's also a good wine list. The only complaint we have about this stalwart is that, 15 years in, it's still near impossible to get a seat. To have a hope, come early – once people get settled, they shift for no one. *Babies and children welcome: children's portions. Tables outdoors (4, pavement).* **Map p274 N4.**

Easton

22 Easton Street, WC1X 0DS (7278 7608/www.the easton.co.uk). Farringdon tube/rail. **Open** noon-11pm Mon-Thur; noon-1am Fri; 5.30pm-1am Sat; noon-10.30pm Sun. **Food served** 12.30-3pm, 6.30-10pm Mon-Fri; 6.30-10pm Sat; 1-4pm Sun. **Credit** MC, V. Gastropub

It's been four years since strip joint the Queen's Head was transformed into the Easton, and in that time it has become a very assured boozer. Airy and spacious, it has plenty of large tables that are just the thing for drunken birthday gatherings and lazy Sunday sessions. A changeable menu is short but interesting – think big, unfussy portions of pork belly or risotto – and the Sunday roasts (or excellent veggie pie) are justifiably popular. Drinks-wise, things have improved in the last year; at last there's a real ale (Timothy Taylor Landlord) among the roster of lagers and continental beers. Later openings at weekends (plus DJs on Fridays) mean that the good times can now roll on for a little longer.

Babies and children admitted (until 9pm). Music (DJs 9pm Fri; free). Restaurant available for hire. Tables outdoors (4, pavement). **Map p274 N4**.

Fluid

40 Charterhouse Street, EC1M 6JN (7253 3444/ www.fluidbar.com). Barbican tube/Farringdon tube/rail. **Open** noon-midnight Mon-Wed; noon-2am Thur; noon-4am Fri; 7pm-4am Sat. **Food served** noon-10pm Mon-Fri. **Admission** £3 after 9pm, £5 after 10pm Fri, Sat. **Credit** AmEx, DC, MC, V. Bar

Epitomising Clerkenwell retro-chic, Fluid draws a discerning flow of laid-back urbanites to its low-level leather seating. The Far East provides motifs galore, from giant koi carp strikingly engraved on the huge windows to an excellent snacking menu of around 30 Asian nibbles (£3-£6). There's Japanese beer to wash it all down, with quirky offerings like a bottled ginseng beer alongside more familiar names like Asahi. A fair cocktail list rounds things off. For entertainment, get misty-eyed with a few rounds of the retro computer games – go Galaxians! – while music spins pleasantly through the lower tempos during the week before speeding up at the weekend.

Babies and children admitted (until 9pm). Function room. Games (retro video games). Music (DJs 7pm Tue-Sat). Tables outdoors (3, pavement). TV (big screen, satellite). **Map p274 O5**.

Green

29 Clerkenwell Green, EC1R 0DU (7490 8010). Farringdon tube/rail. **Open** noon-11pm Mon-Wed, Sun; noon-midnight Thur-Sat. **Food served** noon-3pm, 6-10pm Mon-Wed; noon-3pm, 6-11pm Thur, Fri; noon-4pm, 6-10pm Sat; noon-8pm Sun. **Credit** AmEx, MC, V. Gastropub

Twinkly lights pick out this corner bar perched above the Farringdon station tracks. The interior is pretty too, with gilded mirrors setting off black walls. Blackboards offer a selection of Tasty Tapas for under £4 as well as more substantial bar grub such as seared tuna loin on the specials board. The clientele are as scrubbed as the tables, with enough Hoorays for you to wonder if you've been transported to SW1 from EC1. Adnams offers a solitary ale amid continental lagers at the bar, alongside a decent enough wine list. Though the Green scores on proximity to the Clerkenwell Green boutiques, it can't really compete in the gastropub stakes with either the nearby Coach & Horses or the venerable Eagle.

Babies and children admitted. Bar available for hire. Disabled: toilet. Function room. Music (DJ 7pm Sat, Sun; free). Tables outdoors (6, pavement). **Map p274 N4**.

Gunmakers

13 Eyre Street Hill, EC1R 5ET (7278 1022/www.the gunmakers.co.uk). Farringdon tube/rail. **Open** noon-11pm Mon-Fri; noon-5pm Sun. **Food served** noon-3pm, 6-10pm Mon-Fri; noon-5pm Sun. **Credit** MC, V. Pub

The sign says gastropub but we'd describe this hidey-hole, tucked down a lane off the Clerkenwell Road, as a fine little boozer. The gastro bit of the equation, y'see, is a long list of pub standards like sausage and mash, stuffed mushrooms and tempura prawns. Sound enough for lunch or a post-work snack, washed down with Bombardier, Greene King IPA or Hoegaarden, but nothing too special. Decor is traditional but offers the odd surprise; lots of well-worn wood, engraved bar mirrors and vintage firearms augmented by a modern landscape mural. A yellow-walled back room offers the loudest buzz; in the front bar, punters seem more reflective, enjoying the beer and banter with the barmaids before ambling off contentedly into the night.

Babies and children admitted (until 6pm). Bar available for hire (Sat). Tables outdoors (10, conservatory). **Map p274 N4**.

Hand & Shears

1 Middle Street, EC1A 7JA (7600 0257). Barbican tube. **Open** 11am-11pm Mon-Fri. **Food served** noon-3pm Mon-Fri. **Credit** AmEx, MC, V. Pub

There's old and there's old. A pub has stood here since the 12th century, though the present building is a mere 1840s stripling. There's still something of a medieval air about the place though, with its division into a series of sparse worn wooden spaces concealed from the street by opaque period windows. Decor restricts itself to antique prints in black and white or muted colours. A predominantly legal clientele dress in similar vein as they sup decent beer – Courage Best, Directors and changing guest ales – and house wine while cogitating on tricky cases or the cosmos. While it lacks a little in atmosphere, the Hand & Shears compensates with a rare sense of privacy – especially if you nab the solitary table in the Private Bar.

Function room. Games (darts). No piped music or jukebox. Quiz (weekly; call for details). Restaurant. **Map p274 O5**.

Hat & Feathers NEW

2 Clerkenwell Road, EC1M 5PQ (7490 2244). Barbican tube/Farringdon tube/rail. **Open** noon-1am Mon-Sat. **Food served** noon-2.30pm, 6-10.30pm Mon-Fri; 6-10.30pm Sat. **Credit** AmEx, MC, V. Pub

Long derelict, this Victorian corner boozer has reopened its doors. Happily, the lovely acid-etched windows and wood panelling have been retained, and restorers have replaced the gold leaf on the cornicing and reinstalled the atmospheric gas lighting. The resulting look is distinctly contemporary – neutral colours, black leather chairs and faux ostrich-skin banquettes – and this sense of style is further reflected in the fine Modern European cuisine served on the first floor. On our Saturday night visit the ground-floor bar was less than half full and had a slightly sterile look. However, the customers seemed happy enough, perhaps because they can partake of some of the fanciest pub grub around; Gressingham duck risotto or fat chips sure beats a packet of peanuts. The wine list has an admirably wide range of bottles and prices, with 12

under £20 and five by the glass (including Chablis 1er Cru Montmains, £8.95). There's also an impressive list of whiskies and bourbons.
Babies and children admitted. Bar available for hire. Disabled: toilet. **Map p274 O4.**

★ Jerusalem Tavern

55 Britton Street, EC1M 5UQ (7490 4281/www.stpeters brewery.co.uk). Farringdon tube/rail. **Open** 11am-11pm Mon-Fri. **Food served** noon-3pm Mon, Tue, Fri; noon-3pm, 6-10pm Wed, Thur. **Credit** AmEx, MC, V. Pubs
So faithful are the devotees regularly massing for the Jerusalem's yeasty concoctions that some of them seem to think this may well be the promised land itself, an opinion given slight credence by the fact that St Peter's (the brewery, not the bloke) runs the place. Inside you'll find a range of interesting beers chalked up behind the small bar, from the always-popular Honey Porter and Golden Ale to seasonal favourites and fruit brews. But it's not just a beer bores' establishment: with its wooden interior painted green and its clutter of tucked-away tables in countless nooks and crannies, the Jerusalem is like something straight out of Tolkien's Shire, and justly popular with punters of all ages and occupations. Certainly worth a trip.
Babies and children admitted. Bar available for hire (weekends only). No piped music or jukebox. Tables outdoors (2, pavement). **Map p274 O4.**

Match EC1

45-47 Clerkenwell Road, EC1M 5RS (7250 4002/ www.matchbar.com). Farringdon tube/rail. **Open** 11am-midnight Mon-Fri; 6pm-1am Sat. **Food served** noon-11pm Mon-Fri; 6-11pm Sat. **Credit** AmEx, DC, MC, V. Bars
It may be a shade less lusty and a touch longer in the tooth, but there's still plenty of spark in the bar that in 1997 set London alight with its aggressively chic *Bladerunner* aesthetics and endlessly innovative cocktail laboratory. The latter is still firing on all cylinders, with a miniature bible of imaginative concoctions featuring several bespoke numbers by renowned New York mixologist Dale DeGroff, including his patented Vodka Espresso and a mighty champagne fruit punch. Whether the decor has aged as well is open to debate, but with the box lights turned low and the first fingers of a mojito creeping up the spine, it still offers a uniquely luminescent experience – somewhat akin to drinking inside an elaborate Japanese lantern. Regularly tested staff really know their (cocktail) onions.
Babies and children admitted (before 5pm). Bar available for hire. Disabled: toilet. Tables outdoors (4, pavement). **Map p274 O4.**

Medcalf

38-40 Exmouth Market, EC1R 4QE (7833 3533/ www.medcalfbar.co.uk). Farringdon tube/rail. **Open** noon-11pm Mon-Thur, Sat; noon-12.30am Fri; noon-5pm Sun. **Food served** noon-3pm, 6-10pm Mon-Thur; noon-3pm Fri; noon-4pm Sat, Sun. **Credit** MC, V. Bar
In an area that prides itself on flamboyance, Medcalf is a picture of stylish understatement. Little touches make a big difference: there are trendy light fixtures aplenty, but the former butcher's storefront remains largely unaltered and bread is sliced on Albert Medcalf's original chopping block. Artfully distressed metal tables and ramshackle wooden school chairs are staggered over a narrow dining area running alongside the bar to a well-lit sofa space in the rear. A new room has appeared behind the bar in the last year, an extension into the building next door: it hosts

eclectic contemporary art shows and weekend DJs. A good range of French and Spanish wines complements a bold British menu, but it's also as fine a place to blow the froth off one of two real ales after work, especially if you're quick enough to grab a couch.
Babies and children welcome (until 7pm): high chairs. Disabled: toilet. Games (darts). Music (DJs 7pm Fri; free). Tables outdoors (5, garden; 6, pavement). **Map p274 N4.**

Old China Hand

8 Tysoe Street, EC1R 4RQ (7278 7678/www.oldchina hand.co.uk). Angel tube. **Open** noon-2am Mon-Sat; noon-10pm Sun. **Food served** 6-10pm Tue, Sat; noon-3pm, 6-10pm Wed-Fri; noon-6pm Sun. **Credit** MC, V. Pub
Equal parts Cockney 'my old China' and authentic oriental eatery, this diminutive bar is a glorious cultural muddle. Delicate dim sum from the kitchen is fused with a fiery affection for rugby and football (major games are beamed over two big screens) and a good range of beers, including international bottles (Brahma, Chimay, Liefmans Kriek) and cask ales courtesy of O'Hanlon's, erstwhile owner of the premises. The drab grey walls and heavy-set wooden furniture won't tickle everyone's fancy, but we like it – and few will be inclined to complain after a mouthful of dim sum courtesy of head chef Ngan Tung Cheung, formerly of the Michelin-starred Dorchester Oriental.
Babies and children admitted (until 6pm). Bar available for hire. Separate room for parties. Tables outdoors (4, pavement). Takeaway service. **Map p274 N3.**

Pakenham Arms

1 Pakenham Street, WC1X 0LA (7837 6933). King's Cross tube/rail. **Open** 9am-1am Mon-Thur, Sat; 9am-1.30am Fri; 9am-10.30pm Sun. **Food served** noon-2pm, 6-9pm Mon-Fri; noon-6pm Sat, Sun. **Credit** MC, V. Pub
The Pakenham's bright painted exterior offers a welcoming face towards the Mount Pleasant sorting office across the road, especially as the accompanying shrubbery is about the biggest patch of greenery in the area. Inside, it's a cornucopia of wood – worn benches, polished boards, aged bar – overseen by vintage mirrors, Jack Vettriano prints and illuminated beer advertising signs. Game machines and a dartboard provide distraction for idle hands on one side. This is a geezers' pub, popular with postal workers who think the (excellent) Apple Tree nearby is too poncey, as well as solitary types reading the paper over a pint: London Pride, Adnams, Greene King IPA or Bombardier. The chef's specials are just what you'd expect: chilli, curry and black forest gateau for pud.
Babies and children admitted. Games (darts). Quiz (7pm Mon; £2). Tables outdoors (7, pavement). TVs (satellite). **Map p274 M4.**

★ Peasant

240 St John Street, EC1V 4PH (7336 7726/www.the peasant.co.uk). Angel tube/Farringdon tube/rail. **Open** noon-11pm Mon-Sat; noon-10.30pm Sun. **Food served** noon-10.45pm Mon-Sat; noon-10pm Sun. **Credit** AmEx, MC, V. Gastropub
Soaring since its refurbishment by the aptly named Wright brothers in 2001, the Peasant is a model gastropub: classy without being condescending, adventurous without being ridiculous and, above all, blessed with a richness of personality absent at more aloof establishments. An array of original fixtures – from the mosaic tiled floor to the grand horseshoe bar – hark back to its days as a Victorian gin

• cocktails • beers • wine • shooters • jugs • bar food •
• spirits • champagne • spirits by the bottle • dj's •

**40 Hoxton Square, Shoreditch
London N1 6PB**
alternative entrance at 331 Old Street EC1V 9LE

• Happy hours daily from 5.30pm • Open til 2am (sunday midnight) •
• Basement bar available for private hire • No hire fee •
• Deposit and minimum spend required • Table reservation available •
• Runner up best late night bar in Shoreditch - *myshoreditch.com* •
• Pole dancing lessons hosted by www.polestars.net (women only) •

• pr@trafikinfo.co.uk • 020 7613 0234 • www.trafikinfo.co.uk •

palace, while its velvety red walls are replete with antique fairground art and framed period posters of Iggy Pop, the Sex Pistols and friends. The Peasant's culinary storm is largely localised in the upstairs restaurant, although there's an excellent bar menu (mains like steak sandwich for under a tenner), and a range of draught delights including Cruzcampo, Bombardier and 'house ale' Wat Tyler. Bottled beers like Grimbergen and Chimay wink in the cooler. *Babies and children welcome (until 9pm): high chairs. Games (board games). Tables outdoors (4, garden terrace; 5, pavement).* **Map p274 O4.**

Queen Boadicea

Potemkin
144 Clerkenwell Road, EC1R 5DP (7278 6661/ www.potemkin.co.uk). Farringdon tube/rail. **Open/food served** noon-11pm Mon-Fri; 6-11pm Sat. **Credit** AmEx, DC, MC, V. Bar
Anyone whose appreciation of vodka begins and ends with a quick shot before staggering on to the dancefloor might want to think about a voyage on the good ship Potemkin. More than 40 varieties of colourless chaos propel eager pupils into a cultural education all too easily forgotten the next day. Largely free of Russian trinkets and disarmingly nondescript in terms of decor (excluding some tasteful bottle-based wall art), Potemkin more than makes up for its aesthetic shortcomings with effusive enthusiasm for the strong stuff; a cheerful Russian barmaid was more than happy to explain the extensive menu on our visit. A swanky downstairs restaurant dispenses Russian cuisine for those seeking a more complete cultural immersion. *Babies and children admitted (dining only). Bar available for hire. Booking advisable. Restaurant. Takeaway service.* **Map p274 N4.**

Queen Boadicea **NEW**
292-294 St John Street, EC1V 4PA (7278 9990/ www.thequeenboadicea.com). Angel tube. **Open** 11.30am-midnight Mon-Thur; noon-2am Fri, Sat; noon-11pm Sun. **Food served** noon-10pm Mon-Sat; noon-7pm Sun. **Credit** AmEx, MC, V. Pub
Formerly the Bull, this corner pub's recent renovation and renaming as the Queen Boadicea marks a return to form following mixed fortunes over the years. The new management's biggest success has been its work on the pub's exterior, stripping away all the ugly black paint to reveal regal Georgian tiling. Inside, there's more original tilework, offset by a funky trim of bright, patterned wallpaper. A dining room to the rear is gussied up with a grand chandelier and a hanging made from what looks like deer antlers. Journalism students from the nearby City University make up much of the clientele (perhaps explaining the rather unimaginative beer choice), so watch what you say: these hacks-in-waiting would sell their sister for a breakthrough scoop. Simple bar food like sandwiches and roasts are prepared in a kitchen upstairs. *Babies and children admitted (until 8pm). Bar available for hire. Music (DJs 8pm Fri, Sat; free). Quiz (7pm Wed; £2). Tables outdoors (3, pavement). TV.* **Map p274 O3.**

★ St John
26 St John Street, EC1M 4AY (7251 0848/4998/ www.stjohnrestaurant.com). Barbican tube/Farringdon tube/rail. **Open/food served** 11am-11pm Mon-Fri; 6-11pm Sat. **Credit** AmEx, DC, MC, V. Bar-Restaurant
For the discerning drinker, there are few better options than this roomy ground-floor bar, attached to the world-renowned British restaurant. The welcoming, competent bar staff, low-key whitewashed decor and conversation-friendly acoustics greatly enhance the pleasure of a pint of Timothy Taylor Landlord or Black Sheep. The range of drinks goes well beyond beer, though: you might try one of the sherries, single malts or even an absinthe; the French wine list starts at £15, with a third of the options available by the glass. And the bar food is a draw in itself. The likes of welsh rarebit, doorstep cheese or beef sandwiches or a changing selection of heartwarming fillers (lentils with goat's curd, say) are rarely less than excellent. *Babies and children welcome: high chairs. Disabled: toilet (bar). Restaurant. Separate room for parties, seats 18.* **Map p274 O5.**

Smiths of Smithfield
67-77 Charterhouse Street, EC1M 6HJ (7251 7950/ www.smithsofsmithfield.co.uk). Farringdon tube/rail. **Open** *Ground floor bar* 11am-11pm Mon-Sat; noon-10.30pm Sun. *Wine room* noon-3pm Mon-Fri; noon-5pm Sat. **Food served** 11am-4.15pm Mon-Sat; noon-4.15pm Sun. **Credit** AmEx, DC, MC, V. Bar
TV chef John Torode's four-floor operation is as big and muscular as you'd expect in a place opposite a meat market, particularly in the ground-floor bar, which, as the website boasts manfully, is moulded from 'raw concrete, industrial steel, cast iron and sand-blasted brickwork'. Savvy, bruv? The effort of turning out the quality nosh on offer on the three upper floors seems, however, to have diverted energy away from the bar. Sure, it's got sofas, but it's also got a dismal drinks selection based on lager and plonk, while the overloud funk blaring out on our visit didn't win points either. The clientele seem to be office workers impressed by Torode's name, but as bars go this is as characterless as white bread.

Central

the same bottles available with food to sit down. And sure enough the compact main room has the feel of a packed tapas bar in Spain rather than an old-fashioned English pub, a young crowd sitting down to enjoy the wine plus Simon Hopkinson-inspired food. The choice of wine is outstanding, ranging from one of the world's best whites in 1981 Viña Tondonia Rioja to a new entry 2004 cabernet sauvignon from Miolo in Brazil that is top of no one's list, but which has a pleasant chocolatey and ripe tannin edge nonetheless. It worked well with a melting rump of lamb (from next-door Smithfield market), which was served on a plate with pommes dauphinoise. There's a new private room in the basement for larger parties, but this busy bar is worth savouring among the general public.
Babies and children admitted. Bookings not accepted for dinner. Function room. Off-licence. Tables outdoors (4, pavement). **Map p274 O5.**

Vivat Bacchus
47 Farringdon Street, EC4A 4LL (7353 2648/www. vivatbacchus.co.uk). Chancery Lane tube/Farringdon tube/rail. **Open/food served** noon-10.30pm Mon-Fri. **Credit** AmEx, DC, MC, V. Wine bar
Runner-up in 2006 for Time Out's Best Wine Bar award, this is one serious outfit, comprising restaurant and wine bar. The firm originated in South Africa, so that country is well represented on the impressive list (which runs to around 250 bins); a filleted version is also available. In the bar, suits and ties are to the fore (this is the edge of the City, after all), and there are plenty of waiters to see to their every need. But it's not a stuffy place – the decor is all polished wooden furnishings and fashionable metal pipes running along the ceiling. There are five wine cellars; ask nicely and you can have a look around. Accompany your choice of wine with an equally special selection of cheeses.
Bar available for hire. Disabled: toilet. Off-licence. Restaurant (booking advisable). Wine club (7pm Mon; £15). TV (satellite). **Map p275 N5.**

Babies and children welcome (restaurant): high chairs. Disabled: toilet. Entertainment (DJs 7pm Thur-Sat (ground floor); free). Separate room for parties. Tables outdoors (4, pavement; 6, terrace). **Map p274 O5.**

★ Three Kings of Clerkenwell
7 Clerkenwell Close, EC1R 0DY (7253 0483). Farringdon tube/rail. **Open** noon-11pm Mon-Sat. **Food served** noon-3pm Mon-Fri. **No credit cards.** Pub
In a town where characterful pubs succumb all too often to closure or, arguably worse, big chain buyouts, it's a relief to find a boozer with such brazen personality. From the frankly bonkers figurines standing guard over the entrance to the triumphant collection of tat cluttering every available surface inside (Egyptian cat statues, snowglobes, a fake rhino's head above the fireplace), the Three Kings is a true original. For all that, the pub takes one thing seriously: its music. Framed jazz prints hint at the interest, a superb jukebox in the upstairs room bears it out, and DJ nights and spoken word events emphasise it. The crowd, unsurprisingly, is big on bohos reading Bukowski through a haze of rollie smoke – but it's nonetheless lively for that. Three real ales on tap complete the picture.
Babies and children admitted (until 5.30pm). Function rooms. Games (board games). Quiz (9pm Mon; £5 per team). TV. **Map p274 N4.**

★ Vinoteca
7 St John Street, EC1M 4AA (7253 8786/www.vinoteca. co.uk). Farringdon tube/rail. **Open** 11am-11pm Mon-Sat. **Food served** noon-2.45pm, 6.30-10pm Mon-Sat. **Credit** MC, V. Wine bar
The owners of this successful new bar were inspired by the overseas trend of having wine in an attached shop, with

Well
180 St John Street, EC1V 4JY (7251 9363/www. downthewell.com). Farringdon tube/rail. **Open** 11am-midnight Mon-Thur; 11am-1am Fri; 10.30am-1am Sat; 10.30am-11pm Sun. **Food served** noon-3pm, 6-10.30pm Mon-Fri; 10.30am-4pm, 6-10.30pm Sat; 10.30am-4pm, 6-10pm Sun. **Credit** AmEx, MC, V. Gastropub
The Well draws deep on the tenets of gastro interior design, its striking blue façade giving way to a mix of bare brick walls, scrubbed wooden floors and painted metal beams – although its diminutive size means that diners get dibs on the tables and drinkers are often left to hover at the bar when the place is heaving. Food is the main event here, but there's also a downstairs room for those seeking purely liquid kicks, complete with red lights, banquette seating and fish tanks set into the leather-panelled walls. DJs provide the noise on weekends – to the consternation of more conservative diners – while a decent wine list is complemented by a range of colourful cocktails (most £6).
Babies and children welcome: high chairs. Separate room for parties. Tables outdoors (6, pavement). **Map p274 O4.**

Zetter
86-88 Clerkenwell Road, EC1M 5RJ (7324 4455/ www.thezetter.com). Farringdon tube/rail. **Open/ food served** 7am-midnight Mon-Sat; 7am-11pm Sun. **Credit** AmEx, MC, V. Cocktail bar

Bedford & Strand

Lists are fickle things, creatures of the moment. While *Conde Nast Traveller* voted the Zetter hotel into the top 50 in Europe within nanoseconds of opening, its bar doesn't even make it into the top 50 in central London. We can't vouch for the hotel rooms, but the boozing bit seems very much an afterthought. Crammed into a little semi-circular space between foyer and restaurant, the decor – stylish wooden slats mixed with pale stonework – is pleasing enough, but drinks are lacklustre, from the martinis and other classics (£7-£8) to the 20 or so unimaginative alternatives for a quid or two more. The 'optional' 12.5% service charge adds insult to injury given the desultory service on our visit. Fellow drinkers are likely to be hotel guests, oblivious to the better drinking opportunities all around. *Babies and children welcome. Bar available for hire. Disabled: toilet. Restaurant. Separate rooms for parties. Tables outdoors (14, pavement). TV (big screen, satellite).* **Map p274 N4.**

Also in the area...

Calthorpe Arms *252 Gray's Inn Road, WC1X 8JR (7278 4732).* Quiet, roomy Young's pub. **Map p274 M4.**
City Pride *28 Farringdon Lane, EC1R 3AU (7608 0615).* Fuller's pub serving ESB, London Pride and Adnams; 3am licence on Fridays and Saturdays. **Map p274 N4.**
Cock Tavern *East Poultry Avenue, Central Markets, EC1A 9LH (7248 2918).* Early opening pub that's popular with market traders. Pop in for a pint of Courage Best at 6am. **Map p274 O4.**
Dovetail *9 Jerusalem Passage, EC1V 4JP (7490 7321/www.belgianbars.com).* Branch of Dove; stocks exclusively Belgian beers – 101 varieties of the stuff. **Map p274 O4.**
Heads & Tails *64-66 West Smithfield, EC1A 9HE (7600 0700).* Branch of Jamies. **Map p274 O5.**
Leonards EC1 *42 Northampton Road, EC1R 0HU (7278 9983/www.leonards-ec1.co.uk).* Spacious three-roomed bar with a centrepiece tropical fish tank. Table football, pool and weekend bands make up for an uninspiring choice of beers on tap. **Map p274 N4.**
Parker McMillan *47 Chiswell Street, EC1Y 4SB (7256 5883/www.parkermcmillan.co.uk).* Impressive New York-style cocktail bar with music nights (7pm Wed and Fri) and a pool table. **Map p276 P5.**
Puncheon *Unit 5, Cowcross Place, Cowcross Street, EC1M 6DQ (7250 3336).* Branch of Davy's. **Map p274 O5.**
Slaughtered Lamb *34-35 Great Sutton Street, EC1V 0DX (7253 1516).* Aptly named pub catering to a young crowd that seek to get slaughtered; two real ales on tap help them. **Map p274 O4.**
Trading House Bar *12-13 Greville Street, EC1N 8SB (7831 0697/www.thetradinghouse.net).* Jazzy bar with a monied target audience: glittery enough, but offputtingly smug at times. **Map p274 N5.**

Covent Garden

★ Bedford & Strand `NEW`
1A Bedford Street, WC2E 9HH (7836 3033/ www.bedford-strand.com). Charing Cross tube/rail. **Open/food served** noon-midnight Mon-Fri; 5pm-midnight Sat. **Credit** AmEx, MC, V. Wine bar

From the rows of Perrier-Jouët lining the dark-wood bar to the carefully selected wine menu, we like everything about this place. The convivial atmosphere the owners have aspired to create is in full swing, enhanced by professional yet informal staff and stylish lighting that contrasts the dark height of the impressive bar with the intimacy of brighter candlelit tables. The red and white wine list is extensive in scope and price, with wine served by the glass (starting at £4.60), by the carafe (from £12.95) and by the bottle (from £18). Bedford & Strand more than meets its brief as a classic wine bar with style. Tucked downstairs just off the Strand, you could almost miss it. Don't. *Babies and children admitted. Bar available for hire. Wine club (5.30pm 1st Mon of mth; £10-£15).* **Map p273 L7.**

Box
32-34 Monmouth Street, WC2H 9HA (7240 5828/ www.boxbar.com). Covent Garden or Leicester Square tube. **Open** 11am-11pm Mon-Sat; noon-10.30pm Sun. **Food served** 11am-5pm daily. **Credit** MC, V. Bar
A relaxed gay bar-café that's welcoming to straights, Box has an easy-going vibe that attracts a (mainly male) laid-back crowd. It has an enviable location just south of Seven Dials, displayed to advantage through a fold-back glass frontage or even better, weather permitting, from pavement tables on Upper St Martin's Lane. The drinks selection is more sophisticated than usual – quality lagers such as Staropramen backed with boutique beers (Hoegaarden, Leffe Blonde), cocktails, a fair wine selection and coffees. There's a decent food menu during the day. The original paintings exhibited across the back wall give Box an arty feel, even if the rest of the furnishings are a touch on the pedestrian side. *Babies and children admitted. Tables outdoors (3, pavement).* **Map p273 L6.**

Brasserie Max
Covent Garden Hotel, 10 Monmouth Street, WC2H 9LF (7806 1000/www.coventgardenhotel.co.uk). Covent Garden tube. **Open/food served** 7am-11pm Mon-Fri; 8am-11pm Sat; 8am-10.30pm Sun. **Credit** AmEx, MC, V. Hotel bar
Beyond the lobby of the exclusive Covent Garden Hotel lies Brasserie Max, a very elegant hotel bar offering impeccable service for those who like to sup with style. Customers powwow at polished dark wood tables over flutes of pink fizz or retire around the corner to banquettes that provide alcove-intimacy; all the while a lively buzz centres on the long, continental-styled zinc bar counter. For those who care, the table count is as high as at most Soho members' clubs. Cocktails are supremely well made, with top-quality brands and fresh fruit, while some 20 wines are categorised into light, medium and full bodies. Light snacks and bottled beers are also on the menu. Expect to pay the price for exclusivity – £10.50 for a martini, and wines averaging £30 a bottle. *Babies and children welcome: high chairs. Function rooms. Restaurant. Screening facilities (8pm Sat; dinner plus film £35). Tables outdoors (10, pavement).* **Map p272 L6.**

Café des Amis
11-14 Hanover Place, WC2E 9JP (7379 3444/ www.cafedesamis.co.uk). Covent Garden tube. **Open** 11.30am-1am Mon-Sat. **Food served** 11.30am-11.30pm Mon-Sat. **Credit** AmEx, DC, MC, V. Wine bar

atmosphere. Beers aren't bad either; there's an excellent line-up of mainly Young's ales, supplemented by guests that typically include the likes of Bombardier, Courage Best and Ridley's IPA. Pub grub and doorstep sandwiches are also served.

Babies and children admitted (lunch only). Games (darts). Music (jazz 7.30 Sun; free). No piped music or jukebox. TV. **Map p273 L7.**

Langley

5 Langley Street, WC2H 9JA (7836 5005/www.the langley.co.uk). Covent Garden tube. **Open/food served** 4.30pm-1am Mon-Sat; 4.30-12.30pm Sun. **Admission** £3 after 10pm Thur; £7 after 10pm Fri, Sat. **Credit** AmEx, MC, V. Bar

An inauspicious entrance just off Acre Lane brings you into one of the area's most deservedly popular bars. On the site of a former tube station and flower market, the Langley has two large underground bars, a restaurant and two smaller booth areas. The bare bricks of the Hudson Bar are offset by the swirly decor of the Geneva Bar, and all in all create a sense of spaciousness favoured by a regular crowd of twenty- and thirtysomethings. A decent selection of cocktails, including some delicious fruity capirinhas, is averagely priced, as is the reasonable bar food menu. It's particularly worth heading down for the 5-7pm happy hour, when £4 is knocked off a bottle of wine usually starting at £12.75 (red and white).

Bar available for hire. Disabled: toilet. Music (DJs 8pm Thur-Sat). Restaurant. TVs (plasma). **Map p273 L6.**

★ Lowlander

36 Drury Lane, WC2B 5RR (7379 7446/www.lowlander. com). Covent Garden or Holborn tube. **Open** noon-11pm Mon-Sat; noon-10.30pm Sun. **Food served** noon-10.30pm Mon-Sat; noon-9.30pm Sun. **Credit** AmEx, MC, V. Café/Bar

Choose from the finest Dutch and Belgian beers at Lowlander, a treat for hop lovers. No fewer than 15 tall, gleaming chrome beer taps are lined up on the bar, offering pilsners, blondes, wheat beers, red and dark ales, fruit beers and miscellaneous speciality beers; there are also more than 40 bottled options. For the undecided, three third-of-a-pint tasters start at £5; for the enthusiast, tutored tastings start at £14. The high ceilings and light-wood communal tables all add to the buzz, overlooked by a mezzanine that can be hired out for private bashes. The good food menu reflects the Dutch and Belgian influence, with meat and cheese platters for around a fiver. Always popular, it's a shame there are so few staff, so expect a leisurely pace – which is probably how you want to enjoy these beers anyway.

Babies and children admitted. Function room. Tables outdoors (4, pavement). TV (big screen, satellite). **Map p272 L6.**

Maple Leaf

41 Maiden Lane, WC2E 7LJ (7240 2843). Covent Garden tube. **Open** 11am-11pm Mon-Sat; noon-10.30pm Sun. **Food served** noon-9.30pm daily. **Credit** (over £10) AmEx, MC, V. Pub

London's only Canadian pub (so we're told) pulls out all the stops to stamp its national identity on this regular-looking pub. There's a stuffed bear, framed ice hockey paraphernalia and mounted Mounties set within the log-walled bar. As you would expect, Canadian beers are served on draught (Molson and Sleeman Silver) and by the bottle (Moosehead). It's a sizeable slice of Canada: a large all-in-one bar area and logged lounge, with plenty of snug corners. There are no less than nine TV screens set around the room showing Premiership games, along with American football (NFL) and basketball (NBA). Food is the kind of pub grub you'd get anywhere. What makes the place unmistakably Canadian, though, is the hockey scoreline engraved on the wall: Canada 5, USA 2, Olympics 2002.

Babies and children admitted (before 5pm). Bar available for hire. Games (fruit machine, quiz machine). TV (satellite). **Map p273 L7.**

Nell of Old Drury

29 Catherine Street, WC2B 5JS (7836 5328/www.nellof olddrury.com). Covent Garden tube. **Open** noon-3pm, 5-11.30pm Mon-Fri; noon-midnight Sat. **Credit** MC, V. Pub

This fine traditional pub in the heart of Theatreland is so close to the Theatre Royal opposite it offers a handy pre-ordered interval drinks service. The connection between the two is literal: there is an underground tunnel that connects them, which allegedly was used by Charles II to visit his mistress Nell Gwynne, after whom the pub is named. While geared towards the pre- and post-theatre crowds, it's worth visiting when shows are underway so you can enjoy the friendly welcome and perhaps grab prime position in the lovely red velvet-cushioned window seats. The upstairs bar makes it more accommodating than many of the tiny boozers in the neighbouring streets, and in summer tables are set up outside for alfresco drinking.

Function room. **Map p273 L6.**

Porterhouse

21-22 Maiden Lane, WC2E 7NA (7836 9931/ www.porterhousebrewco.com). Covent Garden tube/ Charing Cross tube/rail. **Open** 11am-11pm Mon-Wed; 11am-11.30pm Thur-Sat; noon-10.30pm Sun. **Food served** noon-9pm Mon-Sat; noon-7pm Sun. **Credit** AmEx, MC, V. Bar

Irish favourite it may be, but the Porterhouse has a truly international beer menu that runs to 28 pages, listing beers from Argentina to Vietnam. The multi-levelled maze of mezzanines, galleries and walkways lined with copper piping railings means half your fun will be in finding your mates. The other half, of course, will be working your way through the beers, and the fair-minded selection balances Israel's Macabee with the Palestinian Taybeh. Instruction is also provided on choosing a good beer: 'Avoid "lite". Avoid "ice". Avoid "smooth". Avoid beer advertised with words ending in "flow". Avoid beer with a sports tournament named after it.' We almost forgive them for their £10 souvenir baseball caps and £25 rugby shirts. One great play pen for would-be inebriates.

Disabled: toilet. Function room. Music (bands 9pm Wed-Sat; Irish band 5.30pm Sun; free). Tables outdoors (3, pavement). TV (big screen, satellite). **Map p273 L7.**

Roundhouse

1 Garrick Street, WC2E 9BF (7836 9838/www. spiritgroup.com). Covent Garden or Leicester Square tube. **Open** 11am-11.30pm Mon-Thur; 11am-midnight Fri, Sat; noon-10.30pm Sun. **Food served** noon-9pm daily. **Credit** AmEx, MC, V. Pub

Occupying pole position on the busy corner between Garrick Street and King Street, the Roundhouse provides a 180° view of Covent Garden life. Its pedestrian-friendly location makes it a favourite for outdoor drinking as soon as the weather shakes off the cold, and service is friendly with a local touch. The one-time clientele of luvvies and traders has now been replaced by tourists and transients, with a corresponding vacuum where the atmosphere should be. However, the selection of beers is strong: Adnams Broadside, Fuller's London Pride, Spitfire, Bombardier and Old Peculiar as well as foreign draught beers. Wine is well priced, starting at £2.95 a glass. Plasma screens fixed up high make for easy match viewing. *Games (fruit machine). Tables outdoors (3, pavement). TVs.* **Map p273 L7.**

Also in the area...

Bünker *41 Earlham Street, WC2H 9LD (7240 0606/www.bunkerbar.com).* One of London's last surviving microbreweries, offering three unique house draughts. Under the same ownership as Alphabet, Amber and Cantaloupe, and similar in ambience. **Map p273 L6.**
Cove *1 The Piazza, WC2E 8HB (7836 7880).* Touristy pub above a pasty shop that *would* be one to avoid – were it not for the sizeable terrace overlooking Covent Garden Piazza and St Paul's church. **Map p273 L7.**
Crusting Pipe *27 The Market, WC2E 8RD (7836 1415).* Branch of Davy's. **Map p273 L7.**
Opera Tavern *23 Catherine Street, WC2B 5JS (7379 9832).* Attractive Victorian pub, popular with stagehands from nearby theatres; offers five real ales. **Map p273 L6.**
La Perla *28 Maiden Lane, WC2E 7JS (7240 7400).* Branch. **Map p273 L7.**
Segar & Snuff Parlour *27A The Market, WC2E 8RD (7836 8345).* Branch of Davy's. **Map p273 L6.**

Euston

Norfolk Arms NEW

28 Leigh Street, WC1H 9EP (7388 3937/www.norfolk arms.co.uk). Russell Square tube/King's Cross tube/ rail. **Open** 11am-11pm Mon-Sat; noon-10.30pm Sun. **Food served** 12.30-3.30pm, 6.30-10.15pm daily. **Credit** AmEx, MC, V. Gastropub
A promising new joint – with definite glitches. The bad things first. We can just about understand an overworked barman handing over a shoddy pint (in our case, a watery, end-of-the-barrel Greene King IPA, the glass only two-thirds full) but his reluctance to pour a new one was plain bad service. And we couldn't help feeling sorry for the woman next to us, unceremoniously turfed from her table to make way for new customers; the reason ('It's reserved but we forgot to put the sign out') wasn't convincing. Still, the new Norfolk has much going for it. We love the design – English boozer meets European charcuterie – and food is top-notch. Set menu entries like duck confit and seafood broth (a tenner with starter or dessert) impressed on one of our lunchtime visits. At night, the place buzzes. In an area devoid of good beer options, its two real ales are very welcome – as long as they're poured right. With tweaks, this place could really shine.
Babies and children admitted. Separate room for parties. Tables outdoors (10, pavement).

Positively 4th Street

119 Hampstead Road, NW1 3EE (7388 5380/www. positively4thstreet.co.uk). Euston tube/rail. **Open** 5-11pm Mon-Thur; 5pm-1am Fri; 7pm-1am Sat. **Food served** 5-9.30pm Mon-Fri. **Credit** MC, V. Cocktail bar

Although it's not known exactly which 4th Street Dylan was referring to in the song that lends its name to this bar, we can be pretty confident it's nowhere in the vicinity of the 1960s town-planning hell that is the Hampstead Road. Thankfully, this dark little bar is pure escapism. The decorative theme is somewhere between New York mob speakeasy and Indiana Jones and the Temple of Booze, the food hails from Japan, and the cocktails (£5.95 for a Singapore Sling) and hypnotic ceiling fans (they paddle rather than spin) put one in mind of Raffles – albeit a budget version you can reach on the N29 bus. What's more, the barman was very gracious when we sent chilli sauce flying the length of the bar.
Bar available for hire. Function room. Music (DJs 8pm Fri; free).

Prince Arthur NEW

80-82 Eversholt Street, NW1 1BX (7387 2165). Euston tube/rail. **Open** noon-midnight Mon-Fri. **Food served** noon-3pm, 5.15-10pm Mon-Fri. **Credit** AmEx, MC, V. Pub
Surrounded as it is by three mucky vid shops, the Euston Massage Parlour and the back-end of one of London's ugliest stations, the Prince Arthur ain't the most appealing prospect. But over the last few years, under landlord Tom Helliwell, it's had a major face-lift. Out have gone the mouldy furniture, the clogged pumps and the drug dealers. In have come leather chairs, colourful artwork and a Thai menu. Fresh flowers on every table, a shelf stacked with literary oddities and a jumpy soundtrack complete the new look, though the original Arthur's essentials remain: gorgeous wood-panelled walls and a stained glass skylight to the rear. Greene King IPA, Timothy Taylor Landlord and Deuchars are pumped by chummy, mainly Gallic staff. There's also table service for those who like their pint with a splash of servitude. Recommended.
Bar available for hire (Sat, Sun). Games (darts). Tables outdoors (10, pavement). TV (plasma).

Somerstown Coffee House

60 Chalton Street, NW1 1HS (7691 9136). Euston tube/rail. **Open/food served** noon-11pm Mon-Sat; noon-6pm Sun. **Credit** AmEx, MC, V. Gastropub
This grade II-listed building is best described as half pub, half bistro, with a smaller, smarter 'restaurant' section screened off from the main bar. This latter is a successful variation on the usual gastropub template; rich wood panelling, crystal lampshades and a hotchpotch of sofas and wooden chairs accompany rustic tables. There's a small garden area out the back and a spacious forecourt too. In terms of drinks, particularly notable is the long list of bottled beers (including Hoegaarden, Cobra, Grolsch, San Miguel) and the international wine list with all bottles under £20; commendably, around half are available by the glass. The draught ales include Bombardier and Young's Special. Food is French, like the owners, and is taken seriously.
Babies and children admitted (until 5pm). Bar available for hire (Mon-Wed). Function room. Tables outdoors (5, terrace; 10, garden).

Also in the area...

Davy's of Regent's Place *Unit 2, Euston Tower, Regent's Place, NW1 3DP (7387 6622).* Branch. **Doric Arch** *1 Eversholt Street, NW1 1DN (7388 2221).* Formerly the Head of Steam, this pub by Euston station is now owned by Fuller's. Four real ales make it fine enough for a pitstop pint.

Fitzrovia

Annex 3
*6 Little Portland Street, W1W 7JE (7631 0700/
www.annex3.co.uk). Oxford Circus tube.* **Open** 5pm-
midnight Mon-Fri; 6pm-midnight Sat. **Food served**
6.30-11pm Mon-Sat. **Credit** AmEx, MC, V. Bar
You would expect nothing less from the people behind Les
Trois Garçons and Loungelover. A few blocks north of
Oxford Street, Annex 3 is an explosion of camp, like the
interior of a spaceship from *Barbarella*. A dozen different
1960s chandeliers dangle from the roof. Wall surfaces
shimmer with DayGlo and glitter, and columns are wrapped
in sparkling foil and brocade. The front half of Annex 3 is
a restaurant – and a posh one at that – while the back room
is full of couples sipping cocktails in psychedelic pools of
coloured light. Racks of spirits are used for the house cocktails – the dreamy Chocolate Mistress (£8) has shots of
Frangelico, Tuaca, Baileys and gingerbread liqueur, shaken
with cocoa. Every table is different, so listen to your inner
interior designer before choosing where to sit.
Bar available for hire. Music (DJs Sat; free).
Map p272 J5.

Bradley's Spanish Bar
*42-44 Hanway Street, W1T 1UT (7636 0359).
Goodge Street or Tottenham Court Road tube.*
Open noon-11pm Mon-Sat; noon-10.30pm Sun.
Credit MC, V. Bar
This much-loved off-Oxford Street institution remains a
fine place in which to spend a gloomy winter afternoon
(tucked into a dark corner of the scruffy downstairs bar)
or summery evening (when everyone spills out on to the
street, much to the dismay of chauffeurs and cabbies driving their charges to nearby Hakkasan). Though some
lament a slight smartening up that has seen kitsch tunes
removed from the jukebox and tacky bullfighting posters
taken off the walls, Bradley's has found a new generation
of drinkers drawn to its (rather pricey) pumps of Amstel,
San Miguel, Cruzcampo, Bitburger and Guinness. It's still
a fabulously louche place to drink, as long as you don't
mind a bit of grime: the men's toilets, for example, remain
a bit of a challenge.
Map p272 K5.

Champion NEW
*12-13 Wells Street, W1T 3PA (7323 1228).
Oxford Circus, Tottenham Court Road or Goodge
Street tube .* **Open** 11.30am-11pm Mon-Fri; noon-
11pm Sat; noon-10.30pm Sun. **Food served** noon-
2.30pm, 6.30-8.30pm Mon-Thur; noon-2.30pm Fri,
Sat. **No credit cards.** Pub
A standard corner pub exterior does little to prepare you
for the decorative Victorian opulence within. Sporting
greats of the era are depicted window-frame by window-
frame in glorious stained glass. Cricket's WG Grace, golf's
Young Tom Morris and Channel swimmer Captain
Matthew Webb look over a church-like interior of dark
wood and frosted glass. Plump leather banquettes and
curved alcoves allow a generational mix of customers to
relax over standard Samuel Smith brews and a menu of
wild boar sausages, liver and bacon, and jacket potatoes.
It's a place for easy chatter around the island bar, a round
of darts, a post-work pint or nonchalant pre-match analysis. You might knit it in any Yorkshire market town. Here
in West One, it's unique.
Games (darts). **Map p272 J5.**

Cock Tavern
*27 Great Portland Street, W1W 8QE (7631 5002).
Oxford Circus tube.* **Open** 11.30am-11pm Mon-
Sat; noon-10.30pm Sun. **Food served** noon-
3pm, 5.30-8.30pm Mon-Thur; noon-3pm Fri.
Credit MC, V. Pub
On the junction of Great Portland Street and Great
Titchfield Street, the Cock stands proud as a traditional
corner boozer amid a sea of trendy bar-eateries and post-
work drinking troughs. A century old or more, the place
is a masterpiece of pub interior woodcraft, evident as soon
as you set foot on its sturdy floor tiles. A grand doorframe
topped with a clock divides the entrance area from the
main part of the bar. A fireplace at the back attracts winter drinkers, large lamps augmenting the sense of comfort. It's a Samuel Smith pub, the standard brews
providing an ideal accompaniment for a steak-and-mush-
room pie or fish and chips. There are tables upstairs for
busy lunchtimes.
*Games (fruit machines). No piped music or jukebox.
Tables outdoors (3, pavement).* **Map p272 J5.**

★ Crazy Bear
*26-28 Whitfield Street, W1T 2RG (7631 0088/
www.crazybeargroup.co.uk). Goodge Street tube.*
Open/food served noon-10.45pm Mon-Fri;
6-10.45pm Sat. **Credit** AmEx, DC, MC, V.
Bar/Restaurant
Stylish, decadent yet supremely comfortable, the London
outpost of the Oxfordshire-based hotel and pub chain comprises restaurant upstairs and opulent bar below. You may
have trouble finding it – the building is almost entirely
unmarked. As are the toilets within; they're hidden behind
a fake wall and signposted only by a spotlight. You'll have
no problem finding the swivel cowhide bar stools, red
padded alcoves or low leather armchairs in the downstairs
bar – a charming hostess will escort you down the ornate
staircase. Once settled, choose from classic bellinis (£9.50)
or house creations such as Thai Sunset (a twist on the
tequila sunrise, £8.50) – all are mixed with high-end
brands, exotic fruits and inventive purées. Fine dim sum
keeps hunger pangs at bay.
*Babies and children admitted (lunch).
Booking advisable.* **Map p272 K5.**

Crown & Sceptre
*26-27 Foley Street, W1W 6DS (7307 9971).
Goodge Street, Oxford Circus or Tottenham
Court Road tube.* **Open** noon-11pm Mon-Sat;
noon-10.30pm Sun. **Food served** noon-9.30pm
daily. **Credit** AmEx, MC, V. Pub
The finest in Fitzrovia? The lively, high-ceilinged C&S is
certainly well run. Picture windows let sunlight warm the
bare-wood furniture while your food is cooked to order.
Taps of Kirin Ichiban, Sleeman, Schneider Weisse,
Maredsous, Greene King, Bombardier, Früli, Liefmans
Frambozen, dark Budvar, and Addlestones cider line an
island bar counter, each with a descriptive tag. Bottled vari-
eties include Mexican Pacifico Claro and Liverpool's Cains.
Nearly all of the 20 wines also come by the glass, cate-
gorised by taste, so you can choose from a 'voluptuous'
Alamos Malbec (£3.65/£14.50) or a 'fruity' Persimmon
Viognier (£3.30/£12.90) – or just order a Chablis (Domaine
Laroche, £17.50) to share. Saturdays mean board games,
Sundays a bloody mary before a roast and Mondays iPod
DJs. Commendable.
*Disabled: toilet. Music (DJ 6.30pm Sat; free).
Tables outdoors (4, pavement).* **Map p272 J5.**

Eagle Bar Diner

3-5 Rathbone Place, W1T 1HJ (7637 1418/
www.eaglebardiner.com). Tottenham Court Road tube.
Open/food served noon-11pm Mon-Wed; noon-1am
Thur, Fri; 10am-1am Sat; 10am-6pm Sun. **Credit** MC,
V. Bar/Restaurant
Despite a fine selection of hamburgers (£5.95-£8.50), this
funky diner is a rather disconcerting place to eat in the
evening, due to the loud jammin' tunes played throughout the dark-hued, boothed, one-room space. As a bar,
though, it's very good: who needs conversation when
you've got such an imaginative cocktail list to peruse? Try,
perhaps, a peanut butter martini (made with Finlandia
vodka, £6.95) or an Eagle Mary (jalapeno Sky vodka, dry
sherry and tomato juice, £6.95). In honour of diner-fan
Quentin Tarantino, shooters are listed under the heading
Kill Bill Vol. 3. On our most recent vist, a new line of champagne cocktails (£8.50) had just been added in anticipation of summer. Dixie, Liberty, Brooklyn and Anchor
feature among the bottled beers, or you could go for a
sumptuous milkshake (£3.75).
Babies and children admitted (until 9pm if dining).
Booking advisable. Disabled: toilet. Music (DJs
7.30pm Wed-Sat). Takeaway service. **Map p272 K5.**

★ Hakkasan

8 Hanway Place, W1T 1HD (7907 1888).
Tottenham Court Road tube. **Open** noon-12.30am
Mon-Wed; noon-1.30am Thur-Sat; noon-midnight Sun.
Food served noon-3pm, 6-11.30pm Mon-Wed; noon-
3pm, 6pm-12.30am Thur, Fri; noon-4pm, 6pm-12.30am
Sat, Sun. **Credit** AmEx, MC, V. Bar/Restaurant
Clearly aware of the importance of making an entrance,
upmarket Chinese restaurant Hakkasan whisks customers
off an arterial alley and plunges them into a hidden Narnia
of Oriental other-worldliness. A cavernous descent opens
into a stone-cut cloakroom peppered with purple blossoms
and flickering candles, which in turns leads to the dining
room itself; a three-dimensional Chinese woodcut of interlocking, intimate little booths. Along one side runs the bar,
where aquamarine backlighting and flickering water patterns projected on to grey slate walls lend a dreamy liq-
uidity. Cocktails (£8.50) are the stuff of Asian-influenced
fantasy: the Purple Emperor is sharp with a mix of
Matusalem ten-year-old rum, saké and jasmine tea, and
comes topped with a clipped purple pansy, while the Long
Dragon is a blend of lime saké, Noilly Prat and ginger ale.
A fully immersive experience for the discerning drinker.
Babies and children admitted (not recommended after
7.30pm). Disabled: toilet. Music (DJs 9pm daily).
Restaurant available for hire. Separate room
for parties, seats 65. **Map p272 K5.**

Hope

15 Tottenham Street, W1T 2AJ (7637 0896).
Goodge Street tube. **Open** 11am-11pm Mon-Sat.
Food served noon-3pm daily. **Credit** MC, V. Pub
Quality sausages and ale await the work crowd at this
homely, two-floor pub on a corner of Noho away from the
media hubbub. The clientele here all do proper jobs – fil-
ing, faxing, fitting – and look forward to a warming plate
of venison and wild mushroom or wild boar and apple
sausages accompanied by a pint of Adnams, Fuller's
London Pride, John Smith's, Timothy Taylor Landlord,
Hoegaarden or Guinness. There are standard wines too.
Puddings (citrus sponge, sticky toffee) and hot custard fill
any remaining gaps. Upstairs is for cosy, conversational
dining; downstairs offers the distraction of a large screen
in the corner and board games. Historic prints and framed
copies of the *Illustrated London News* adorn the walls
throughout, and there are a few outdoor tables.
Babies and children admitted (until 7pm).
Function room. Games (board games, fruit machine).
Tables outdoors (3, pavement). TV (big screen).
Map p272 J5.

Jerusalem

33-34 Rathbone Place, W1T 1JN (7255 1120/
www.fabbars.com). Tottenham Court Road tube.
Open noon-11pm Mon; noon-midnight Tue, Wed;
noon-1am Thur, Fri; 7pm-1am Sat. **Food served**
noon-3pm, 6-10.30pm Mon-Fri; 7-10.30pm Sat.
Credit AmEx, MC, V. Bar/Restaurant
This gloomy, Gothic basement chugs along, once the flagship operation of the Breakfast Group, now just another
cheap lunch option in Mediadonia. The meal deal early in
the week is a tenner-for-two; colleagues scoff in dark
alcoves ill-lit by fat candles. Jerusalem has upped the ante
after dark, with DJs and late closing, which helps the spacious bar area look less bare. The half-dozen white wines,
three by the glass, run from a standard Pleno Blanco or
Tinto (£4.20/£13.50) from Navarre to a Petit Chablis
(Château du Val de Mercy, £20) on a Bourgogne rouge pinot
noir (£19.50). Look out for bin-end bargains. Bottled
Michelob, Sol, Brahma and Tiger complement the draught
Leffe, Hoegaarden and Grolsch on offer.
Music (DJs Thur-Sat; £5 after 10pm Fri, Sat).
Restaurant. **Map p272 K5.**

Long Bar

The Sanderson, 50 Berners Street, W1T 3NG
(7300 1400). Oxford Circus or Tottenham Court Road
tube. **Open** noon-2.30am Mon-Sat; noon-10.30pm Sun.
Food served noon-2.30pm, 6-11pm Mon-Sat; noon-
2.30pm, 6-10pm Sun. **Credit** AmEx, DC, MC, V.
Hotel bar
There's an Italian touch these days to the Long Bar at the
high-design Sanderson. It's not only the neat, able staff
working the long bar in question, a thin onyx affair lined
with eyeball-backed bar stools. Limoncello has crept in to
the mix, slowly stirred with Ketel One and elderflower
water in the Citroen martini (£12), one of 12 on offer.
Quality spirits monopolise the menu; the Wyborowa
Lemon and Polstar Cucumber in the Sanderson martini,
the Kurrant Absolut in the Long Bar Hi Ball (£11), the
Sauza Gold tequila in the Apassionata martini. Fresh fruit
– grapes, Scottish raspberries, passionfruit – are used for
flavourings throughout. Four pricey wines of each colour
come by the bottle and glass, a Rizzardi pinot grigio weigh-
ing in at £7.50/£27.
Babies and children admitted (terrace). Disabled: toilet
(in hotel). Tables outdoors (20, terrace). **Map p272 J5.**

Market Place

11-13 Market Place, W1W 8AH (7079 2020/
www.marketplace-london.com). Oxford Circus tube.
Open/food served 11am-midnight Mon-Wed; 11am-
1am Thur, Fri; noon-1am Sat; 1-11pm Sun. **Admission**
£7 after 11pm Fri, Sat. **Credit** AmEx, MC, V. Bar
The Market Place on this busy pedestrianised square of
terrace eateries tries to give its young(ish) urban clientele
global variety. Draught Erdinger Weissbier, Budvar and
Amstel and bottled Sagres, Moretti and Duvel represent
six EU members, not to mention the fat litre bottles of
Cruzcampo (£6.50), and the South American streetfood
slant to the menu. Upstairs, decked out in rough planks of

wood, is for brunching, lunching and munching post-work; downstairs, DJs get to work every evening. There's wine too, a Rioja Livor Viña Ijalba (£17.50) or a Chablis Antique Jean-Marc Brocard (£24.50). The ten cocktails (£6-£7) include a bellini with Moët Imperial and a Mango Royale with Russian Dovgan vodka, both flavoured with the appropriate Funkin fruit purée.
Disabled: toilet. Music (DJs 8pm daily). Tables outdoors (8, terrace). **Map p272 J6.**

Mash
19-21 Great Portland Street, W1W 8QB (7637 5555/ www.mash-bar.co.uk). Oxford Circus tube. **Open** 10am-2am Mon-Fri; noon-2am Sat. **Food served** noon-3pm, 6-10.30pm Mon-Sat. **Admission** £5 after 9pm Fri; £5 after 9pm, £10 after 10pm Sat. *Both* **Credit** AmEx, MC, V. Bar
Mash has gone off the boil somewhat of late, but is still concocting its microbrewed ales, the big orange retro vats with equally retro Apollo-age numbers occupying the back wall. Mash Blonde, Belgian Wheat and Vienna-style Lager are pumped at the bar for around £3 a pint, half this during happy hour from 5pm. Much like the curves of every corner – bar counter hatch, business cards, menus – the look here seems dated. The mural in the sunken chat area (1970s scenes with a tragic twist) is still brilliant, though. For its cocktails (£7), Mash has gone overboard on fruit, churning watermelon, passionfruit and strawberries by the chunkload with Havana 3 rum, Luksusowa and Ketel One vodkas. Lassis come by the pitcher (£15.50).
Babies and children admitted. Bar available for hire. Disabled: toilet. Dress: smart casual. Music (DJs 9pm Wed-Sat). Separate room for hire, seats 28. Tables outdoors (4-8, pavement). **Map p272 J6.**

★ Match Bar
37-38 Margaret Street, W1G 0JF (7499 3443/ www.matchbar.com). Oxford Circus tube. **Open/food served** 11am-midnight Mon-Fri; noon-midnight Sat; noon-10.30pm Sun. **Credit** AmEx, DC, MC, V. Cocktail bar
As original as ever, even though they're now into a second decade, London's Match bars celebrate the craft of the bartender. Dale DeGroff oversees the annual drinks menu, a selection ranging from his authentic concoctions (£6.50-£7), such as a grapefruit julep (Wyborowa, grapefruit, lime, pomegranate, drizzled with honey), to those conceived by his contemporary counterparts here in recent years (Tom Ward's Kamomilla Fizz, perhaps, made from Wyborowa and camomile syrup with fresh lemon and cucumber). Opening in Geneva for the skiing season, the Match group still runs the three London branches, this West End one being a narrow but not squeezed space. Two rows of seating, one raised, connect a convivial front area to the bar, suiting the sharing of bowls of punch (£12), noodles and curries that Match encourages.
Disabled: toilet. Music (DJs 7.30pm Thur-Sat). Tables outdoors (2, pavement). **Map p272 J6.**

Newman Arms
23 Rathbone Street, W1T 1NG (7636 1127/ www.newmanarms.co.uk). Goodge Street or Tottenham Court Road tube. **Open** noon-midnight Mon-Fri. **Food served** noon-3pm, 6-9pm Mon-Fri. **Credit** MC, V. Pub
Though a former haunt of George Orwell, and the exterior setting for scenes in Michael Powell's 1960 classic *Peeping Tom*, the Newman Arms' main draw now is its Famous Pie Room on the first floor. Duvet-sized puffs of pastry

cover fillings such as venison in red wine, steak and kidney and chicken and broccoli; there's always a veggie option too. You'll need to book, but it's worth it. Downstairs, the interior is poky, but not without its charms – look out for the framed Orwell pic and a daffy poem by Ken Hilton bemoaning the life of a rep. The bar dispenses London Pride and Adnams, as well as standard draught lagers, Guinness and a 15-strong wine list.
Restaurant. **Map p272 J5.**

Nordic
25 Newman Street, W1T 1PN (7631 3174/ www.nordicbar.com). Tottenham Court Road tube. **Open** noon-11pm Mon-Fri; 6-11pm Sat. **Food served** noon-3pm, 5.30-10pm Mon-Fri; 6-10pm Sat. **Credit** AmEx, MC, V. Bar
London's Scandinavian bar has had some minor decorative readjustment, but Max von Sydow's triptych mural remains, as does the meticulously sourced selection of regional beers and spirits. Where else would you find small-batch Reyka vodka, filtered through the lava rock of Iceland, Sweden's Blossa glögg (fortified mulled wine) or Spendrups Old Gold Pils? Akvavits and vodkas feature highly, some flavoured with every berry known to Nordic man, many used in the 30-strong cocktail list. Lingonberry juice is one of nine elements in the Longberry cocktail (£6.95), along with Finlandia Lime, Lapponia Blueberry and more muddled berries. It's an intimate basement, so it can get lively. Lunch is a little formal, accompanied by ambient images of winter sports on the flat-screen TV.
TV (big screen, plasma). **Map p272 J5.**

Nueva Costa Dorada
47-55 Hanway Street, W1T 1UX (7631 5117/ www.costadoradarestaurant.co.uk). Tottenham Court Road tube. **Open** noon-3am Tue-Fri; 5pm-3am Sat. **Food served** noon-3pm, 5pm-3am Tue-Fri; 5pm-3am Sat. **Credit** AmEx, DC, MC, V. Bar
The revamped Costa Dorada is no longer a tiled flophouse for post-midnight fun. A smart lounge area by the bar makes for a pleasant start to the evening or a preamble to a dinner and flamenco show in the adjoining main space. No more crass bullfighting posters; tasteful black and white photographs include an iconic shot of Carmen Sevilla. Staying with the theme, the drinks menu offers Montesquis cava (£4.50/£24), Riojas (£4/£15) red and white, plus bottled San Miguel and Estrella. Of the 13 cocktails (£7), an El Matador of Havana 3 and port seems the most appropriate. No more gloopy *albóndigas* soup to overheat in the microwave – proper *comida* (grub to you and me) till the early hours.
Entertainment (flamenco shows 9.30pm Tue-Sat). Music (DJ 11pm Thur-Sat). **Map p272 K5.**

Oscar
Charlotte Street Hotel, 15 Charlotte Street, W1T 1RJ (7806 2000/www.charlottestreethotel.com). Goodge Street or Tottenham Court Road tube. **Open** 7am-11pm Mon-Sat; 8am-9pm Sun. **Food served** 7-11am, noon-10.30pm Mon-Sat; 8am-8pm Sun. **Credit** AmEx, MC, V. Hotel bar
The bar half of the restaurant adjoining the lobby at the media-mobbed Charlotte Street Hotel is now more open-plan and accomodating, with a splash of primary colour. The drinks menu is still encyclopedic, a memory test for the slightly snooty but swift bar staff. Cocktails (£9.50-£10) come in the contemporary, classic, martini, bellini or after-dinner variety, stand-outs including an Oscar Passion

of Grey Goose L'Orange, Chambord and passionfruit liqueur (note the chilled glass) and a kiwi-themed NZ-politan of 42 Below Honey, lychee liqueur and pomegranate juice. All 40 wines are served by the glass – it's not often you can sip a Châteauneuf-du-Pape, Château Mont-Redon label (£11.75/£45) and not shell out for the whole bottle. What the hell. It's all on expenses.

Babies and children admitted. Film screenings (8pm Sun; £35 incl meal, book in advance). Separate rooms for parties, seating 10, 14 and 32. Tables outdoors (10, pavement). **Map p272 K5.**

La Perla

11 Charlotte Street, W1T 1RQ (7436 1744/ www.cafepacifico-laperla.com). Goodge Street or Tottenham Court Road tube. **Open** 5-11pm Mon-Sat. **Food served** 5-10pm Mon-Sat. **Credit** AmEx, MC, V. Bar/Restaurant

Plentiful seating and an alluring happy hour (5-7pm daily) make this low-ceilinged Mexican-theme bar a contender in an area of superficially superior bars. It's loud, shouty and entirely without reserve (pictures of Latino models are there for the ogling in the men's loos), but staff are friendly and bar snacks such as quesadillas and nachos at around a fiver per plate do a fine job of soaking up the booze. This comes in the form of frosted margaritas (£5.75 for a glass, £14.75 for a half-pitcher), bottled cervesas (Sol, Pacifico, Dos Equis, Bohemia, Negra Modelo) and an incredible array of 100% agave tequilas. Impeccably sourced, this is arguably the best selection of the spirit in London. Shot prices start at £3.75 and rise to £100 (order this and your name goes on a plaque behind the bar).

Babies and children admitted (restaurant). Booking advisable. **Map p272 J5.**

Roxy

3 Rathbone Place, W1T 1HJ (7255 1098/ www.theroxy.co.uk). Tottenham Court Road tube. **Open/food served** 5pm-3am Mon-Fri; 9.30pm-3.30am Sat. **Happy hour** 5-7.30pm Mon-Fri; 9.30-10.30pm Sat. **Admission** £3 after 10pm Mon, Tue; £5 after 10pm Wed, Thur; £4 after 8.30pm, £9 after 10.30pm Fri; £7 after 9.30pm, £9 after 10.30pm Sat. **Credit** (bar) AmEx, MC, V. Bar

A more palatable kind of happy-hour haunt, the retro Roxy is pleasingly unpretentious, its basement ample enough for groups of laptop-lugging wage slaves any night of the week. The Roxy pitches its seven £7.95 half-price post-work pitchers to pre-clubbers for a swift late hour on Saturdays. Glug a Kung Fu (tequila, vodka, Midori and white rum) before cutting one in Soho. Single glasses (£6) include a vanilla margarita, a lemongrass mojito or a Bramble Rox of gin and blackberry liqueur. Beers are bottled and include Red Stripe, Budvar or San Miguel; wines include a house Condessa de Leganza (£3.80/£11.95), a J Moreau Chablis (£22.50) and a Faustino Rioja (£16.75). Toasted ciabattas (£4.95) or feta-stuffed olives (£2) provide sustenance. Soundtrack is *Smash Hits* era.

Games (backgammon, chess). Music (DJs 6pm nightly; admission varies). **Map p272 K5.**

Ship

134 New Cavendish Street, W1W 6YB (7636 6301). Oxford Circus tube. **Open** 11am-11pm Mon-Fri. **Food served** 11.30am-3pm Mon-Fri. **Credit** MC, V. Pub

It's been here for generations, this masculine corner boozer, harking back to the days of National Service and the intoxicating smell of firelighters on winter mornings.

Its exterior has been smartened up, but the interior is still a visual assault of gleaming nautical brass, neon beer signs and regimental insignia. Bass, Grolsch, Caffrey's and Guinness line the bar counter, despite a board above it advertising defunct brewery Wenlock. Ambience is matey, but be warned, if you're looking for something a bit more friendly – there's a 'No Soliciting' sign over the gents' – passing sailors do pop in, but they're here to talk tides and tillers. Breakfasts, burgers and jackets are brought in from the caff next door. The pub closes at weekends.

Function room. Games (fruit machine). Tables outdoors (2, pavement). TV. **Map p272 J5.**

★ Shochu Lounge

Basement, Roka, 37 Charlotte Street, W1T 1RR (7580 9666/www.shochulounge.com). Goodge Street or Tottenham Court Road tube. **Open/meals served** noon-midnight Mon-Fri; 5pm-midnight Sat; 6pm-midnight Sun. **Credit** AmEx, DC, MC, V. Bar/Restaurant

The wooden vats and rustic bar counter, low tables and plush, boxy red seats in enclaves make for a setting that's half 21st-century style bar, half feudal Japan. The dim lighting and low ceiling confer a louche yet sociable mood. And as befits a bar in the basement of trend-setting Japanese restaurant Roka, there's a pioneering focus on shochu. Here, this vodka-like spirit is tinctured with things such as cinnamon (for joy of life) or lemon (for virility) and served neat or in cocktails by Tony Conigliaro. Try a Hallo Kitty (shochu, raspberries, rose, lemon and sparkling water, £8.60) or a Plum Plum (shochu and plum vodka, £8.30). And to really push the boat out, note that anything on Roka's tempting menu can be ordered in the bar.

Music (DJs 8pm Thur-Sat). **Map p272 J5.**

★ Social

5 Little Portland Street, W1W 7JD (7636 4992/ www.thesocial.com). Oxford Circus tube. **Open/ food served** noon-midnight Mon-Wed; noon-1am Thur, Fri; 1pm-1am Sat; 6pm-midnight Sun. **Credit** AmEx, MC, V. Bar

Fine beers, wines and cocktails, Dad food (even Twiglets!), great music including quality weekend DJs in an evening-only downstairs bar, intimate ambience, sparky bar staff and just the right crowd. Business as usual at Social. Daytime unfolds in the street-level diner, walls decked out in rotating exhibitions of black and white photography with punky themes, while five rounded tables bearing ketchup and HP await a fishfinger sarnie (£3.70) or Square Pie (£7). A long bar bookended by a Heavenly Jukebox begs your backside for company. Beers include San Miguel and Grolsch on tap, plus bottled A. Le Coq from Estonia, Tsingtao from China, Red Stripe and Pilsner Urquell. The eponymous house cocktail features Teichenné, a butter-scotch variety mixed with Frangelico Hazelnut.

Babies and children admitted (until 5pm). Music (DJs/bands 7pm Mon-Sun; £3-£5 entry for bands Sun-Wed; free Thur-Sat). **Map p272 J5.**

Wax

4 Winsley Street, W1W 8HF (7436 4650/www.wax-bar.co.uk). Oxford Circus tube. **Open/food served** noon-3am Mon-Sat. **Happy Hour** 5-7pm Mon-Sat. **Admission** £7 after 10pm Fri; £10 after 9pm Sat. **Credit** AmEx, MC, V. Bar

Unashamed and unsophisticated but certainly not unnecessary, Wax is a post-work trough for caning it and copping off. There are sporadic speed dating nights, but if

Leicester Square

★ Cork & Bottle
44-46 Cranbourn Street, WC2H 7AN (7734 7807/
www.donhewitson.com). Leicester Square tube.
Open/food served 11am-11.30pm Mon-Sat; noon-
10.30pm Sun. **Credit** AmEx, DC, MC, V. Wine bar
Don Hewitson's intimate, atmospheric Cork & Bottle
matures with age. Accessed from parallel streets leading
to Leicester Square, this permanently popular operation is
approaching 40. In that time the passionate New Zealander
has curated a collection of world wines he shares at reasonable prices with a grown-up clientele of colleagues and
couples not afraid of a bit of fun. Wine, accompanied by
appropriate cold plates and hot dishes, is an unpretentious
pleasure. A thick, quarterly pamphlet in parish newsletter-
style lists the selection, from Don's Specials (Chablis 2004,
Domaine de Vauroux £23.50; Chinon Rouge, Domaine du
Grand Bouqueteau, £25), through France (seven
Beaujolais, £17.95-£26), 'the new Spain', southern Europe,
the southern hemisphere and 'the Glories of Oz'. The champers (£31.50) is his own vintage.
Babies and children admitted. **Map p273 K7.**

De Hems
11 Macclesfield Street, W1D 5BW (7437 2494).
Leicester Square tube. **Open/food served** noon-
midnight Mon-Sat; noon-10.30pm Sun. **Credit** AmEx,
DC, MC, V. Pub
Dutch down to its clogs, De Hems originated as a refuge
for homesick sailors, became a base for the Resistance and
is now a pleasant, two-floor pub, its gold-lettered frontage
attracting punters wandering through Chinatown.
Upstairs is conviviality itself, a relaxing space decorated
with old beer ads. A downstairs of dark wood quickly
packs out, the best seats at the back invariably taken. A
sturdy bar counter is thus lined with customers on one side,
colourful taps of Benelux beers on top, and a fridge of bottled varieties behind. Belle-Vue Kriek and Oranjeboom
stand out among the standard Amstels and Heinekens,
with Westmalle, Orval, Kwak and Chimay of both colours
among the bottles. Dutch snacks (bitterballen, vitsmitter,
frikadellen) are also available.
*Disabled: toilet. Function room. Games (fruit machine).
Music (DJ 8pm Fri, Sat; free). Tables outdoors
(2, pavement). TVs.* **Map p273 K6.**

Harp
47 Chandos Place, WC2N 4HS (7836 0291).
Charing Cross tube/rail. **Open** 11am-11pm Mon-Sat;
noon-10.30pm Sun. **Food served** noon-3pm daily.
Credit MC, V. Pub
Fine ales, award-winning sausages and a genuine Irish
atmosphere bring punters to this lovely little pub near
Charing Cross. No need for shillelaghs or signposts to
Kilkenny, just titular harps in the glazed-window frontage,
and a buzz of conversation around the centrepiece bar
counter. Talk centres on the day's racing form; decor is provided by portraits lining the walls of the narrow saloon.
And the ales? Harveys Sussex Best, Timothy Taylor
Landlord, St Peter's Suffolk Gold and the wonderfully
named Home Wrecker from the Milestone brewery.
O'Hagan's finest sausages, proudly announced on the
board outside, sizzle in a pot on the hob atop the bar
counter. Moroccan lamb and Lincolnshire pork and ale
were the standouts on our most recent visit.
Function room. **Map p273 L7.**

International
116 St Martin's Lane, WC2N 4BF (7655 9810/
www.theinternational.co.uk). Leicester Square
tube/Charing Cross tube/rail. **Open/food served**
noon-2am Mon-Sat; noon-10.30pm Sun. **Credit**
AmEx, MC, V. Bar
Very swish this, but not too swish that it can't offer cheap
lunchtime deals on food and wine. Park yourself on a low
black seat or comfy divan amid a modern interior overlooking St Martin's, order an £8 bottle of plonk and you're
away. The 20 vintages are in the £13-£15 range, nearly all
available by the glass. Classier choices include a Bodegas
Mureza, Rioja Vega Blanco (£5.25/£22) and South African
Groote Post merlot (£6.50/£32). It's a cocktail bar too, very
much so, with a large selection (£6.95-£7.95) categorised
by spirit base. You'll be mixed 42 Below and passionfruit
in the caipiroska 42, Cariel Vanilla and Frangelico Hazelnut
in the chocolate martini and Wokka saké, Amaretto and
ginger beer in the Weekend Away.
*Babies and children admitted (restaurant). Bar available
for hire. Disabled: toilet. Function room. Restaurant
(available for hire). Tables outdoors (3, pavement).
TV (plasma screen).* **Map p273 L7.**

Salisbury
90 St Martin's Lane, WC2N 4AP (7836 5863).
Leicester Square tube. **Open** 11am-11pm Mon-Thur;
11am-midnight Fri; noon-midnight Sat; noon-10.30pm
Sun. **Food served** noon-9pm daily. **Credit** AmEx,
DC, MC, V. Pub
Pubs don't get more palatial than the Salisbury, nor more
Victorian. The place was transformed by its namesake
leaseholder and turn-of-the-century prime minister, who
had an interior created of beautifully carved mahogany,
etched glass and art nouveau lamps. The current management treats this legacy with respect, offering the the-
atre and tourist crowd a superb range of ales, a choice of
20 superior pub meals, well-priced wines and, as it boasts,
no TV sports. St Austell Tribute, John Holt, Young's,
Bombardier and Hook Norton Old Hooky stand out among
the beers. Lager drinkers are offered Peetermans Artois,
Leffe and Budvar, with the American version by the bottle.
Most wines come by the glass and bottle, including a
Chablis Ropiteau (£3.85/£5.30/£14.90).
*Function rooms. Games (board games, chess).
Tables outdoors (8, pavement).* **Map p273 L7.**

Also in the area…
Oxygen 17-18 Irving Street, WC2H 7AZ (7930
0907/www.oxygenbar.co.uk). Party bar with a
decent choice of wines, beers and cocktails to
prepare punters and tourists for a long night in
the DJ basement. **Map p273 K7.**

Marylebone

★ Artesian NEW
Langham Hotel, 1C Portland Place, W1B 1JA
(7636 1000/www.artesian-bar.co.uk). Oxford Circus
tube. **Open/food served** 7.30am-2am Mon-Fri; 8am-
2am Sat; 8am-midnight Sun. **Credit** AmEx, DC, MC, V.
Hotel bar
Some of the design features at the Langham Hotel's
Artesian bar – reopened after a hugely expensive
makeover by top designer David Collins – sail nervously
close to OTT, especially the vast back bar with its

Chinese-Chippendale references and the massive chandeliers combining glass and wood. But a subdued colour scheme makes the total effect soothing rather than imposing, and it's a most suitable setting for an evening of grand cocktails, expertly made and served in remarkably beautiful glassware. Rum takes centre stage, with a 50-strong list growing steadily as the staff are trained in each new variety (the sign of a classy bar). Cocktailhounds can choose from four lists, the top billing going to signature and luxury rum cocktails. Prices are serious (£11-£14.50), but if you want an extremely good cocktail with all the trappings, Artesian is a well you might want to dive into.
Babies and children admitted (until 6pm). Disabled: toilet (in hotel). Games (dominoes). **Map p270 H5.**

Chapel
48 Chapel Street, NW1 5DP (7402 9220). Edgware Road tube. **Open** noon-11pm Mon-Sat; noon-10.30pm Sun. **Food served** noon-2.30pm, 7-10pm daily. **Credit** AmEx, DC, MC, V. Gastropub
Plenty of places try to please both foodies and drinkers, but end up pleasing nobody – the Chapel crosses the divide perfectly. Half the bar feels like a pub, the other half is like a rustic restaurant, a feeling reinforced by the chalkboard menu and chunky wooden furniture. After-work drinkers come here for the accessible gastropub fare: exotic soups and salads and plenty of steaks and grilled seafood. At the bar, mainstream lagers are joined by Adnams, Greene King IPA, Hoegaarden, Pilsner Urquell and Addlestones' scrumptious (or should that be scrumpylicious?) cloudy cider. It's always loud and on Thursday and Friday nights it can be positively heaving – but you can always pull back to the beer garden, screened from Old Marylebone Road by a baffle of hedges.
Babies and children admitted. Function room. Tables outdoors (12, garden; 4, pavement). TV (big screen). **Map p270 F5.**

Cocomomo NEW
79 Marylebone High Street, W1U 5JZ (7486 5746). Baker Street or Bond Street tube. **Open** 10am-11pm Mon-Thur; 10am-midnight Fri; 9am-midnight Sat; 9am-10.30pm Sun. **Food served** noon-5pm Mon-Fri; 9am-5pm Sat, Sun. **Credit** AmEx, MC, V. Bar
Cocomomo knows its clientele: young professionals who enjoy a few glasses of pinot on the way home from the office. Accordingly, the drinks menu focuses on mid-range wines and cocktails as much as beer, though Guinness, Leffe, Amstel and San Miguel are all available on tap. This is the second reinvention of this pub in the last few years – it used to be Dusk, and before that, the Rising Sun – and the minimalist decor of the current incarnation can come across as rather soulless. Food and fuel is the concept, so there's a decent choice of gastropub-style food at breakfast and lunch. In the evenings, tables are crammed with drinkers inside and out, but it feels like a place in which to start an evening rather than finish it.
Babies and children admitted (before 5pm). Disabled: toilet. Tables outdoors (7, pavement). **Map p270 G5.**

deVigne NEW
Mandeville Hotel, 8-14 Mandeville Place, W1U 2BE (7935 5599). Bond Street tube. **Open** 11am-midnight Mon-Sat; noon-11pm Sun. **Food served** noon-10pm Mon-Sat; noon-9pm Sun. **Credit** AmEx, MC, V. Hotel bar

Don't be put off by the *101 Dalmations* pun in the name: deVigne is a classy dame. Everything inside is designer, from the kitsch 1960s chandeliers and neon candelabras etched in glass to the DayGlo Regency trim – collected together by *Wallpaper** darling Stephen Ryan. Sure, it's over the top and pricey, but this is what designer hotel bars should feel like. There are no taps here – everything fizzy comes in bottles – but the wine, champagne and cocktail lists are exemplary and the spirits lining the mirrored shelves behind the bar are impressively varied. Take the whiskies – a broad sweep of prestige Scots brands, plus exotics like Japanese Suntory. It's often quiet, but bar staff know their drinks, and the slick decor provides a welcome break from gastropub sofaland.
Disabled: toilet (hotel). Function room (in hotel). Restaurant. **Map p270 G6.**

Dover Castle
43 Weymouth Mews, W1G 7EQ (7580 4412). Oxford Circus or Regent's Park tube. **Open** 11.30am-11pm Mon-Fri; noon-11pm Sat. **Food served** noon-2.30pm, 6-8.30pm Mon-Fri. **Credit** MC, V. Pub
Young people love Samuel Smith's pubs: the small independent brewery serves a full range of own-brand ales, lagers, stouts, ciders, wines and spirits at penny-saving prices. The cosy Dover Castle is no exception. Tucked away in a quiet mews off Weymouth Street, this refreshingly ungentrified pub attracts younger drinkers who appreciate being able to sit down for the evening. There are no leather sofas, just flowery curtains, chintzy carpets and the laid-back atmosphere of a small-town local. Tables and chairs are spread out over several rooms and there's a small outdoor area at the back for balmy evenings. The unpretentious pub grub is as cheap and satisfying as the beer, but the kitchen closes at 8.30pm.
Games (board games). No piped music or jukebox. Tables outdoors (6, patio). **Map p270 H5.**

Duke of Wellington
94A Crawford Street, W1H 2HQ (7224 9435). Baker Street tube/Marylebone tube/rail. **Open** 11am-11pm Mon-Fri; 4.30-11pm Sat; noon-10.30pm Sun. **Food served** noon-2pm Mon-Fri. **Credit** AmEx, MC, V. Pub
Pubs like the Duke of Wellington are few and far between, particularly in this part of Marylebone. This unashamedly old-fashioned public house is practically a museum. The front windows have been converted into display cases housing a glorious collection of Duke of Wellington memorabilia and tat – busts, money boxes, toy soldiers, mugs, military prints. Scan the walls inside and you'll find a genuine lock of Napoleon's hair. It's an old man's pub, but in a good way: the publican is as likely to be chatting to regulars as manning the bar. Taps include a few standard lagers and Blackthorn cider, plus Adnams and Bombardier, and there's a small but adequate choice of spirits lined up in the optics. A real piece of local history.
Tables outdoors (4, pavement). TV. **Map p270 F5.**

Golden Eagle
59 Marylebone Lane, W1U 2NY (7935 3228). Bond Street tube. **Open** 11am-11pm Mon-Sat; noon-7pm Sun. **Food served** 11.30am-9pm Mon-Sat. **No credit cards.** Pub
The Eagle wears its heart on its sleeve. This is a vintage London boozer, down to the rickety bar stools and beer-soaked upright piano in the corner. The ivories are covered by a dust sheet except on Tuesday, Thursday and Friday evenings – when everyone joins in an old-fashioned pub

singalong. The public bar is tiny – just a small back room and a handful of bar stools along the window – but you can swig Tetley's, London Pride, Guinness and a rotating selection of ales from the Cornish St Austell Brewery while you belt out a few choruses of 'Moon River'. Come here for a reminder of what pubs were like before gastropub fever swept through town.
Music (pianist 8.30pm Tue, Thur, Fri; free). TV.
Map p270 G5.

Inn 1888
21A Devonshire Street, W1G 6PG (7486 7420).
*Baker Street or Regent's Park tube . * **Open** 11am-11.30pm Mon-Wed; 11am-midnight Thur-Sat; 11am-10.30pm Sun. **Food served** noon-4pm, 5-10pm Mon-Sat; noon-8pm Sun. **Credit** MC, V. Pub
Amazing what you can do to a fading Victorian pub with a few licks of paint. The original interior of Inn 1888 was covered over during a misjudged refit a few years back, but the pub has been bought back to life with a shiny new coat of red gloss. The etched glass and tilework are gorgeous, but the lipstick colour scheme won't appeal to everyone. There are no gastropub pretensions here, just a small corner bar with a decent stock of wines and Greene King IPA, Abbot and Hoegaarden joining the usual lager and cider options on tap. Bar staff can knock up a convincing mojito and there are six different rums on the spirit shelf. Our conclusion? Cute and refreshingly uncrowded compared to most of the Marylebone competition.
Bar available for hire. Tables outdoors (3, pavement).
Map p270 G5.

Low Life
34A Paddington Street, W1U 4HG (7935 1272/
www.lowlifelounge.com). Baker Street tube.
Open/food served 5-11pm Mon-Sat; noon-10.30pm Sun. **Credit** AmEx, MC, V. Bar
A subterranean cavern of a bar, hidden behind a Marylebone shopfront. With its Mars-red interior, bubbling aquarium, superhero murals and upbeat DJ soundtrack, Low Life feels like it should be open later. Even constrained by standard licensing hours, the curtained vaults beneath Paddington Street are great places to order cocktails and settle in for the night. There are only bottles behind the bar, but the fridge is commendably stocked with international beers – Sierra Nevada wheat beer, Coopers Brewery ale and Brooklyn Lager among them – and the bar carries an impressive array of spirits and mixers. After a change of management, the cocktail menu has gone back to basics: martinis, mules, daiquiris and sours. Weekends are party nights; stick to weekdays for deep conversations.
Bar available for hire. Games (board games).
Music (DJs 7pm Thur-Sat; free). Tables outdoors (2, pavement). **Map p270 G5**.

Mason's Arms
51 Upper Berkeley Street, W1H 7QW (7723 2131).
Marble Arch tube. **Open** noon-11.30pm Mon-Sat; noon-10.30pm Sun. **Food served** noon-2.30pm, 6-9pm Mon-Thur; noon-3pm, 6-9pm Fri-Sun. **Credit** MC, V. Pub
Not one but two open fires warm the cockles at this old-fashioned London alehouse. Not much has changed around here in decades: flower baskets hang along the front window, the wood-panelled walls are dotted with framed prints of Queen Victoria, and the stereo in the corner plays whole albums of whatever takes the barman's fancy. Wines and spirits are fairly limited, but the pumps feature full-flavoured ales from the Dorset-based Badger

Brewery – Best Bitter, Golden Ale and Hofbräu lager in 'export', 'premium' and 'cold' – plus Guinness and Blackthorn cider. Everything is arranged around a square central bar, but wooden partitions create space for private conversations; come early if you want to bag the one tiny cubicle for a particularly intimate chat.
Babies and children admitted (separate area).
Function room. Games (fruit machine). Tables outdoors (5, pavement). TV. **Map p270 F6**.

★ Moose NEW
31 Duke Street, W1U 1LG (7224 3452/www.vpmg.net).
Bond Street tube. **Open** 4pm-2am Mon-Thur; 4pm-3am Fri, Sat. **Food served** 4-10pm Mon-Sat. **Credit** AmEx, MC, V. Cocktail bar
We can't imagine anyone not liking this place. The latest venture from the Vince Power Music Group is a rarity in the West End: cosy, reasonably priced and with decor that's simultaneously eccentric and inviting. There are two spaces: a small ground-floor bar and a much larger downstairs bar with DJs six nights a week. The decorative motif is that of a ski lodge in the Canadian Rockies, big pictures of which grace the walls. Antlers adorning the ceiling lights and cowhide on the seating downstairs complete the rugged, rustic look. At 7.30pm on a Monday, both rooms

were pleasantly quiet, perfect for a pre-dinner drink. A daiquiri made with three-year-old Havana Club was excellent; a Beefeater martini excessively vermouthy but quickly replaced by a charming bartender when told of the fault. We had no complaints about pricing: the extensive cocktail list is £6.50, or £8.50 for champagne cocktails, and an impressively long happy hour (6-9pm) offers ordinary cocktails at a delightfully cheap £3.75.
Booking advisable on weekends. Music (DJs 9pm Mon-Wed, Sat; 6pm Thur, Fri). **Map p270 G6.**

Occo Bar & Kitchen
58 Crawford Street, W1H 4NA (7724 4991/ www.occo.co.uk). Edgware Road tube. **Open** noon-midnight Mon-Fri; 10am-11.30pm Sat, Sun. **Food served** noon-3pm, 6.30-10pm Mon-Fri; 6.30-10pm Sat. **Credit** AmEx, MC, V. Bar
A Moroccan-themed bar in Marylebone could have gone either way. Fortunately the owners of Occo thought the concept through before filling the place with beanbags and waiters in kaftans. Instead, you'll find subtle mood lighting, flickering Moroccan lanterns and a menu of Moroccan-fusion cooking with just enough spice to keep things interesting. The drinks menu features 22 red and 22 white wines, some novel takes on familiar

Burlington Club. *See p53.*

cocktails – rose petal martinis anyone? – plus Amstel on tap for drinkers who insist on beer. There are actually four different rooms here: a ground-floor lounge full of patinated copper, a beat-filled basement bar, a pale-blue conservatory and a tiny 'boudoir' full of red divans. If you're feeling flush, you can puff on a fruit-flavoured shisha for £15.
Babies and children admitted (daytime only). Disabled: toilet. Separate rooms for parties. Tables outdoors (6, pavement). **Map p270 F4.**

Prince Regent
71 Marylebone High Street, W1U 5JN (7467 3811). Baker Street tube. **Open** noon-11pm Mon-Sat; noon-10.30pm Sun. **Food served** noon-10pm Mon-Sat; noon-9pm Sun. **Credit** AmEx, MC, V. Pub
The Prince Regent is partner pub to the Volunteer on Baker Street, but the Marylebone High Street location lends it a more sophisticated air. The old Victorian interior has been gentrified with the usual whistles and bells: glass chandeliers, baroque mirrors and, of course, those inescapable leather sofas. Some drinkers feel the styling is a little contrived, but it's a good place to start an evening and people are always moving on, so tables become free quite often. Draught ales include Adnams and Timothy Taylor, and we were pleased to see Deuchars as a guest beer, but it's the Belgian imports that stand out – Leffe, fruity Frûli and Liefman's Frambozenbier with its unmistakable raspberry tang. The accompanying bar food is good but not quite up to gourmet standards.
Disabled: toilet. Function room. Music (DJs, Sun afternoons). Tables outdoors (6, pavement). **Map p270 G4.**

Queen's Head & Artichoke
30-32 Albany Street, NW1 4EA (7916 6206/ www.theartichoke.net). Great Portland Street or Regent's Park tube. **Open** 11am-11pm Mon-Sat; noon-10.30pm Sun. **Food served** 12.30-10pm daily. **Credit** AmEx, MC, V. Gastropub
After going 'gastro' a few years back, the Queen's Head & Artichoke has never looked back. It's a welcome retreat in a rather quiet corner of Marylebone. The smart upstairs dining room has brass chandeliers, freshly cut flowers and a Modern European menu with a noticeable bias towards hearty roasts. There's a huge list of tapas, with plenty of plates for under £5. Downstairs, the main lounge recalls the inside of a Wren church, dark wood at the bar and an orderly spread of wooden tables and chairs beneath soaring windows. Drinkers may be slightly disappointed by the choice of spirits, but the wine list trots the globe and Pedigree and Adnams are tap bitters. It gets busy after work, but a pleasant Parisian café mood creeps in later.
Babies and children admitted. Disabled: toilet. Function room. Tables outdoors (4, garden; 8, pavement). **Map p270 H4.**

Temperance NEW
74-76 York Street, W1H 1QN (7262 1513). Baker Street or Marble Arch tube. **Open** noon-11pm Mon-Sat; noon-10.30pm Sun. **Food served** noon-3pm, 6-10pm Mon-Sat; noon-5pm Sun. **Credit** AmEx, MC, V. Gastropub
This gastropub's name may be suggestive of Prohibition and women's tea parties, and it does feel a bit like a boozer that's only recently come out of rehab. It's gone distinctly 'healthy' – there's even a basket of fruit on the bar. The decor is as fresh as spring rain and the smell of recently

ment squeezed into a dark and narrow Mayfair building make it feel like somewhere you wouldn't want to linger when it's quiet. But cocktails are top-dollar, with long drinks such as the house cocktail (Bison Grass vodka, apple juice, lime, mint, sugar) costing £9.50; not unusual for Mayfair. The wine list is long, with excellent bottles at predictably steep mark-ups.
Bar available for hire. Disabled: toilet. Music (DJ 10pm daily). **Map p273 J7.**

Cecconi's
5A Burlington Gardens, W1S 3EP (7434 1500/ www.cecconis.co.uk). Green Park or Piccadilly Circus tube. **Open/food served** 7am-11pm Mon-Sat; 8am-11pm Sun. **Credit** AmEx, MC, V. Cocktail bar
Brave the cold, rather uninviting glass exterior and the forest of post-work posh folk dining within and head straight for the gloriously classic, Italian-NY cocktail centrepiece. Then take a perch at this elegant, white marble island-bar as the old-school bartenders, immaculately clad in white DJs, greet you with bar snacks and a leather-bound menu. While the cocktails are hardly innovative, they are entirely adequately mixed. The Cecconi martini (£8), with a blend of vodka, strawberry and black pepper, was rather delightful; if that doesn't entice, there's Prosecco on tap at £4.50. Though hardly a venue to settle into for the night, it's certainly worth a passing dram if you're in the area and don't mind the incessant chatter of Mayfair dahlings.
Babies and children welcome: high chairs. Disabled: toilet. Tables outdoors (10, pavement). **Map p273 J7.**

Claridge's Bar
Claridge's Hotel, 49 Brook Street, W1K 4HR (7629 8860/www.claridges.co.uk). Bond Street tube. **Open** noon-1am Mon-Sat; 4pm-midnight Sun. **Food served** noon-11pm daily. **Credit** AmEx, DC, MC, V. Hotel bar
Claridge's bar has become a mainstream byword for urban sophistication. Catch its immaculate blend of Old World grandeur and 21st-century chic on a quiet night and you can see why. However, on an average busy evening, the atmosphere is inappropriately boisterous – Fenella and Tania from marketing shrieking it up over their third bottle of pinot grigio while a couple of suited swells skip the appetising (if expensive) cocktail menu in favour of bottled beer. Instead, sneak over to the Fumoir, a tiny art deco room just off the main lobby that might be the most beautiful bar in London. Post-smoking ban, the humidor has gone (though at the time of writing the name was still the same), but we're assured the timeless elegance of decor, service and cocktail list will remain.
Disabled: toilet (hotel). Restaurant. **Map p271 H6.**

★ Donovan Bar
Brown's Hotel, 33-34 Albemarle Street, W1S 4BP (7493 6020/www.roccofortehotels.com). Green Park tube. **Open/food served** 11am-midnight Mon-Sat; noon-midnight Sun. **Credit** AmEx, MC, V. Hotel bar
The polarised black and whiteness of the diminutive Donovan bar is a fitting testament to its muse, Stepney-born photographer Terence Donovan, whose monochrome prints of the international celebrities and semi-clad women that characterised swinging '60s London are liberally peppered over the walls. Black leather upholsters both chairs and bar, while music on our last visit came courtesy of a laconic jazz guitarist bearing a passing resemblance to Johnny Depp. It's the epitome of nostalgia-chic, but the cocktail list is surprisingly forward-thinking, with an eclectic range of manhattans, mojitos and martinis (the latter

including saffron, pomegranate and apple variations) alongside the award-winning Space Race, a patented mix of Sputnik rose vodka, lychee liquor and Cointreau. All in all, the perfect spot to raise a glass to a more glamorous and reckless generation.
Disabled: toilet (hotel). Music (jazz 7.30pm Mon-Sat; free). **Map p273 J7.**

43
43 South Molton Street, W1K 5RS (7647 4343/ www.43southmolton.com). Bond Street tube. **Open** *Club* 10.30pm-3am Thur-Sat. *Members' bar* 5.30pm-3am Mon-Sat. **Food served** *Restaurant* 11.30am-7.30pm daily. *Members' bar* 5.30pm-3am Mon-Sat. **Credit** AmEx, MC, V. Cocktail bar
Is it a bar? Is it a club? Is it someone's living room? 43 appeared to be suffering from an identity crisis on a latest visit: the red carpet and bouncer hint at a private members' club; but the front door could easily be mistaken for a residential entrance… and you have to climb a narrow flight of stairs to reach it. In fact, this is a very beautiful, cool yet homely, cocktail bar – despite, on our visit, the complete absence of a cocktail list. To be fair, there was a note on the limited menu (eight reds, nine whites – three of each by the glass at £7.50; one bottled beer or cider) explaining that the list was currently under construction, and inviting drinkers to order whatever they desired – adding that the bartenders like a bit more of a challenge than just a sea breeze or a Long Island iced tea. The candlelit tables, kooky wall painting, cosy atmosphere and friendly service are a rarity this side of Soho.
Babies and children admitted (restaurant). Music (bands/DJs 10.30pm Fri, Sat; admission varies). Restaurant. Tables outdoors (5, pavement). **Map p271 H6.**

Galvin at Windows
28th floor, London Hilton, 22 Park Lane, W1K 1BE (7208 4021/www.galvinatwindows.com). Hyde Park Corner tube. **Open** 10am-1am Mon-Wed; 10am-3am Thur, Fri; 5.30pm-3am Sat; 10am-10.30pm Sun. **Food served** noon-2.30pm, 6-10.30pm Mon-Fri; 6-10.30pm Sat; noon-3pm Sun. **Credit** AmEx, DC, MC, V. Hotel bar
Windows is at the top of the Park Lane Hilton – the 28th floor, to be precise – and the views are naturally sumptuous, but the cost of drinking here is pretty staggering too. The starting price for a bottle of wine is £22, and the cheapest glass of red is £11.25 (for 175ml), just 25p less than a glass of champagne. At least the wines are well selected; a La Poda Corta Carmenere, a red from Chile's Rapel Valley, was fabulous. There was nothing technically wrong with the small martinis served either, but £10.50 each plus service (and no nibbles provided) is, well, a bit rich. The bar is stylish and not too trendy; on our visit a singer-guitarist in Jack Johnson mode hit the right note of late-evening entertainment.
Babies and children admitted (restaurant). Disabled: toilet (in hotel). Restaurant. **Map p271 G8.**

Living Room
3-9 Heddon Street, W1B 4BE (08701 662225/ www.thelivingroomw1.co.uk). Piccadilly Circus tube. **Open** 10am-1am Mon-Sat; 11am-11pm Sun. **Food served** noon-11pm Mon-Sat; noon-10.30pm Sun. **Credit** AmEx, MC, V. Bar/Restaurant
This popular Mayfair hangout certainly looks the part. Grey slate flooring, dark wooden furniture and smokeless fireplaces reek of expensive Swedish chalets, while

eccentrically framed paintings and some of the most peculiar loos we've ever seen (Radio 4 is piped individually into each cubicle and the walls are lined with garish pub carpets) set it apart from the All Bar One formula. But there's an unfortunate overlap with the aforementioned's clientele, on weekend evenings at least. The braying of post-work drinkers trying to pull high-heeled office girls drowned out the establishment's classy entertainment: a pianist on the full-size grand piano. It must be a tad depressing for the management, who have clearly laboured over an impressive drinks menu featuring over 100 cocktails, many developed exclusively for the Living Room. The subtle Waldorf martini (eight-year-old Bacardi, Frangelico, apple juice, cinnamon; £6.95) deserves to be enjoyed in the laid-back lounge atmosphere that this place is clearly aiming for.

Babies and children admitted (restaurant). Bar available for hire. Music (pianist 8pm Tue-Sat; 2.30pm Sun; free). Restaurant (available for hire). **Map p273 J7.**

Mahiki NEW
1 Dover Street, W1S 4LD (7493 9529/www.mahiki. com). Green Park tube. **Open** 5.30pm-3am Mon-Sat. **Food served** 5.30-10.30pm Mon-Sat. **Admission** £10 after 9.30pm Wed-Fri; £15 after 9.30pm Sat. **Credit** MC, V. Cocktail bar

Informed by style mags and gossip pages that this is The Place To Be, yodelling trustafarians form a semi-circle around the door and fight to get into Mahiki every night of the week. We find the underground venue cramped and rather tacky – a Hawaiian theme means wall-to-wall bamboo – but the cocktails are truly first-rate. Some of the best mixologists in London have been lured in, despite an obligation to wear open Hawaiian shirt and garland of flowers; they stir up 31 mixes from the standard menu alone, leisurely and at their own pace, but with undoubted aplomb. Our Zombie (£12) was sublime: four types of premium rum, maraschino, lime and grapefruit juices, finished with a slug of flaming absinthe. Unless armed with daddy's credit card, you might feel out of place among the children of rock stars and minor royals, but cocktail devotees should certainly take a look.

Bar available for hire. **Map p273 J7.**

Met Bar
Metropolitan Hotel, 18-19 Old Park Lane, W1K 1LB (7447 1000/www.metropolitan.co.uk). Hyde Park Corner tube. **Open/food served** 10am-3am Mon-Sat; 10am-1.30am Sun. **Credit** AmEx, DC, MC, V. Hotel bar

These days the Met's members- or hotel guests-only exclusivity can seem a little tired, but if you can get past the chic concierge and don't mind the hiked-up prices necessitated by its Park Lane postcode, then you could do much worse. Service is remarkably attentive, and while our Fig & Honey whisky cocktail (£10.50) missed the mark, the passionfruit and champagne Passion Blush (£13.50) was spot-on – as you'd expect at that price. The bar is smaller than you might presume, and its curved architecture can leave it feeling a tad hollow when empty, but stick around because when it packs out the vibe gets a lot better.

Disabled: toilet (hotel). Music (DJs 10pm Mon-Sat; free). Restaurant. **Map p271 G8.**

Mews of Mayfair NEW
10-11 Lancashire Court, W1S 1EY (7518 9388/ www.mewsofmayfair.com). Oxford Circus tube. **Open** Cocktail bar 11am-11pm Mon-Sat; 11.30am-10pm Sun. *Lounge bar* 6pm-1am Tue-Sat. **Food served** noon-11pm Mon-Sat; noon-6pm Sun. **Credit** AmEx, MC, V. Cocktail bar

Lancashire Court was rammed on our Friday evening visit to Mews of Mayfair. It was hard to tell who was at the new venue and who was at Rocket bar and pizzeria opposite, such was the crush of post-work drinkers thronging outside. Indoors, the ground-floor bar is decked with chandeliers and gilt-framed mirrors. The soothing first-floor restaurant (serving the likes of sea bass soused in a Japanesey bonito-flavoured dressing) is all creamy white with glittering coloured butterflies adorning the walls, plump fabric-covered chairs and pretty white floral porcelain. There's also a lounge bar in the basement, and private dining facilities at the top.

Babies and children admitted (until 8pm). Disabled: toilet. Function room. Tables outdoors (10, pavement). TV. **Map p271 H6.**

Mô Tea Room
23 Heddon Street, W1B 4BH (7434 4040/www.momo resto.com). Oxford Circus tube. **Open** noon-midnight Mon-Sat; noon-10.30pm Sun. **Food served** noon-11.30pm Mon-Sat; noon-11pm Sun. **Credit** AmEx, DC, MC, V.

If you're lucky enough to bag one of the beautiful Moroccan tables at Mô (easier said than done after 6pm; expect to queue after 7pm), you could almost believe you're in a sub-Saharan souk. The interior is impressive: whitewashed walls, moulded enclaves any Berber house would be proud of, scented shisha smoke, unobtrusive Arabic music, genuine North African furniture – and, like a real bazaar, some of the lanterns and slippers are for sale. But the staff (efficient to the point of neurotic) and the suited-and-booted clientele rather spoil what should be a relaxing ambience. There's wine (15 whites, 28 reds), 15-plus champagnes, alcoholic and non-alcoholic cocktails, mint tea and delicious meze-style plates (which cost half what they would at sister restaurant Momo next door). Prices are Mayfair, but not unfair; our Black Banshee (Bombay Sapphire, crushed blackberries, elderflower cordial, sloe gin, crème mûre and apple juice) cost £8.50.

Babies and children admitted (terrace only). Bar available for hire. Table outdoors (15, terrace). **Map p273 J7.**

★ Polo Bar
Westbury Hotel, New Bond Street, W1S 2YF (7629 7755/www.westburymayfair.com). Bond Street or Oxford Circus tube. **Open** 11am-1am Mon-Sat; noon-midnight Sun. **Food served** 11am-11pm daily. **Credit** AmEx, DC, MC, V. Hotel bar

Despite being part of a hotel, Polo succeeds where so many others fail; it's an exceptionally good bar in its own right. Maybe it's because the entrance is independent of the hotel, or maybe it's down to the mature sophistication and impeccable quality, but Polo manages to tick every box as the perfect post-work wind-down venue. The understated luxurious interiors and some of the most polite, attentive staff in London still manage to allow the drinks to speak for themselves. Signature cocktails clock in at a pricey £18, but you get what you pay for; the beguiling black cherry and lavender martini (Ultimat cherry vodka, fresh lavender syrup) was pure sensuality; intense and fragrant rather than overwhelmingly perfumed. Standard martinis, such as the Chili Raspberry (chilli vodka, framboise liqueur, raspberry syrup, £11) are anything but, and there's a wine list to match (in price as well as quality).

The crowd is refreshingly unpretentious for a venue of this calibre – definitely one for the grown-ups. *Babies and children admitted (until 6pm). Bar available for hire. Disabled: toilet (hotel).* **Map p273 J7**.

Red Lion

1 Waverton Street, W1J 5QN (7499 1307). Green Park tube. **Open** noon-11pm Mon-Fri; 6-11pm Sat. **Food served** noon-2.30pm, 6-9.30pm Mon-Fri; 6-9.30pm Sat. **Credit** AmEx, MC, V. Pub

A slice of the English countryside in the bowels of Mayfair, the Red Lion exudes rural bonhomie. Age-old pub ephemera hangs from hooks and sits on shelves, while an affable bunch of drinkers sup a well-kept range of ales (Greene King IPA, London Pride) and chow down on familiar pub grub. Only the foreign accents on the bar staff and the suits on a fair proportion of the clientele give away the pub's urban location. It's notoriously difficult to run a local in central London that appeals equally to regulars and outsiders, but the people behind this likeable spot have pulled it off. When we last visited, philandering controversialist Rod Liddle was lurching rowdily around the room. Such was the warm feeling engendered by the room that we felt absolutely no desire to commit violence. *Babies and children admitted. Bar available for hire. Restaurant (available for hire).* **Map p271 H7**.

Shepherd's Tavern

50 Hertford Street, W1J 7SS (7499 3017). Green Park or Hyde Park Corner tube. **Open** 11am-11pm Mon-Sat; noon-10.30pm Sun. **Food served** 11am-10.30pm Mon-Sat; noon-9.30pm Sun. **Credit** AmEx, MC, V. Pub

A boisterous but inviting place, this. The downstairs room is loud and often very busy, with attention keenly focused on the mounted TV when the footie's showing. Indeed, the raucousness can be a bit of a shock if you arrive from gentrified Shepherd's Market. There's a quiet lounge upstairs, though, with plenty of seating; it's a real looker, with acres of wood cladding and a great view over one of Mayfair's prettiest corners. Fine puff-topped pies are served (there are usually three or four own-made options on the menu), often accompanied by a glass or two from the varied wine list (ten of each colour). Downstairs, back in the bar, London Pride and Bombardier bolster the usual lagers. *Babies and children admitted (under-10s dining area only). Games (fruit machines). Restaurant (available for hire). TV.* **Map p271 H8**.

Trader Vic's

London Hilton, 22 Park Lane, W1K 4BE (7208 4113/ www.tradervics.com). Hyde Park Corner tube. **Open/ food served** noon-1am Mon-Thur; noon-3am Fri; 5pm-3am Sat; 5pm-1am Sun. **Admission** £7 after 11pm Mon-Sat. **Credit** AmEx, DC, MC, V. Hotel bar

On his visit to this Polynesian-themed cellar, Warren Zevon famously spotted a werewolf drinking a pina colada. We didn't, but the other sights on show provided plenty of entertainment. The resident musician, for example, mooching through jauntily familiar melodies as though providing a soundtrack for the elevator to hell. The waitresses, clad in loud dresses and expressions of deep misery. The decor, roughly 35,000ft over the top. And, of course, the illustrated cocktail menu, offering such concoctions as Doctor Funk of Tahiti, the Suffering Bastard and, most preposterously, the Munich Sour ('Asbach Uralt, German brandy at its best'). *Babies and children welcome: high chairs. Booking advisable (restaurant). Disabled: toilet (hotel). Music (musicians 10.30pm daily). Separate room for parties, seats 50.* **Map p271 G8**.

Mahiki. *See p55.*

Windmill

6-8 Mill Street, W1S 2AZ (7491 8050/www.windmill mayfair.co.uk). Oxford Circus tube. **Open** 11am-midnight Mon-Fri; noon-4pm Sat. **Food served** noon-9.30pm Mon-Fri; noon-3.30pm Sat. **Credit** AmEx, DC, MC, V. Pub
This warm, welcoming pub is in stark contrast to its location – scant metres from the shopping maelstrom of Oxford Circus – and its sanctuary status is well valued by its customers. The Windmill comes into its own after work, when Young's ales are the drink of choice. Decor is sub-Victoriana, heavy on the red, with portraits of immensely sideburned men, and golden cherubs high on the walls. Basic food is also up to standard: steak and kidney pies, fish and chips and veggie shepherd's pie go down a treat. Finding a chair (never mind a table) can prove a challenge at peak times, but the congenial atmosphere is enough to make you not resent drinking while standing.
Function room. No piped music or jukebox. Restaurant (available for hire). TV. **Map p273 J6.**

Zeta Bar

35 Hertford Street, W1J 7TG (7208 4067/ www.zeta-bar.com). Green Park or Hyde Park Corner tube. **Open** 5pm-1am Mon, Tue; 5pm-3am Wed-Fri; 8pm-3am Sat. **Food served** 6-10pm Mon-Sat. **Admission** £10-£15 after 10pm Wed-Sat. **Credit** AmEx, MC, V. Cocktail bar.
In the last edition of this guide we described Zeta as 'an excellent cocktail bar in search of clientele'; judging from our most recent visit, not a lot has changed. At 9.30pm on a Thursday night, staff easily outnumbered the customers. A shame, as it's still a very pleasant venue; no doubt business picks up on Fridays and Saturdays when there are DJs. Design-wise, a good decision lay in moving the grim

entrance on Hertford Street, easily missed; it's now accessed via the hotel lobby, from which you cross a delightful bamboo-dressed footbridge into the bar. This expansive space is subtly decorated in neutral colours, scattered with crafted night-shades and oriental-style trellising; unobtrusive music hums in the background. The cocktail menu is extensive and imaginative: our Mother's Milk (Wyborowa pear vodka, passoa liqueur, honey and guava juice, £7.50) was delicious – and at least there was no risk of having to drink it standing up.
Bar available for hire. Dress: smart casual. Music (DJs 9pm Wed-Sat). **Map p271 H8.**

Also in the area...

Balls Brothers *34 Brook Street, W1Y 1YA (7499 4567).* Branch. **Map p271 H6.**
Chopper Lump *10C Hanover Square, W1R 9HD (7499 7569).* Branch of Davy's. **Map p271 H6.**
Guinea *30 Bruton Place, W1J 6NL (7499 1210/www.theguinea.co.uk).* Unpretentious, rough-and-ready boozer with a rather incongruous (but decent) grill restaurant in its rear. **Map p271 H7.**
Mulligan's of Mayfair *14 Cork Street, W1S 3NS (7409 1370).* Branch of Balls Brothers. **Map p271 J7.**
Red Bar *111 Park Lane, W1K 7AW (7499 6363).* Posh hotel bar that's so red it's almost like returning to the womb – except for the big-screen sport. **Map p271 G7.**
Running Horse *50 Davies Street, W1K 5JE (7493 1275).* Pub-cum-bar with a fine selection of (pricey) wine and three real ales on tap. **Map p271 H6.**

Piccadilly

Cocoon

65 Regent Street, W1B 4EA (7494 7609/www.cocoon-restaurants.com). Piccadilly Circus tube. **Open** 5.30pm-midnight Mon-Wed; 5.30pm-3am Thur-Sat. **Food served** noon-3pm, 5.30pm-midnight Mon-Fri; 5.30pm-midnight Sat. **Credit** AmEx, MC, V.
Cocktail bar
Professional and imaginative, Cocoon is underused as the holding bar for the somewhat space-age first-floor restaurant of the same name. Dinky bar stools revolve around a circular bar counter at the far end. The restaurant being oriental, there are plenty of Japanese drinks on the sumptuous menu: eight types of shochu and a dozen sakés. Beer is bottled Asahi and Kirin Ichiban. The four-dozen cocktails (£8-£9) are either contemporary or classic, or have an oriental twist, such as the Akari of fresh Jonagold apple and fragrant lychee shaken with saké and grapes, or the Japanese Mule of fresh ginger, coriander and Imo-shochu. Fresh ingredients (berries, rhubarb, watermelon) and high-end spirit bases are used throughout. *Babies and children admitted (restaurant). Disabled: toilet. Music (DJs 11pm Thur-Sat; free). Function room.* **Map p273 J7.**

5th View NEW

5th floor, Waterstone's, 203-206 Piccadilly, W1J 9HA (7851 2468/www.5thview.co.uk). Piccadilly Circus tube. **Open** 10am-10pm Mon-Sat; noon-5pm Sun. **Food served** noon-3pm, 5-9pm Mon-Fri; noon-4pm, 5-9pm Sat; noon-4pm Sun. **Credit** MC, V. Bar
Bookshops ain't what they used to be. These days you'll find not only author signings and talks, but jazz sessions, quizzes, wine-tasting evenings, singles events… and in the case of Waterstone's in Piccadilly, a damn fine cocktail bar perched on the fifth floor. We were impressed by a jazzy kir royale, served with a cube of berry jelly and little spoons to scoop up the cassis foam on top; the Bloody Mary, meanwhile, was as spicy as a Jackie Collins novel. Tarts with toppings like crab, chilli and lime were served to the peckish. The view is worth a mention too – though not as glamorous as, say, Vertigo 42, you do get a fine skyline vista that takes in Big Ben. *Babies and children admitted (until 5pm). Disabled: toilet. Function rooms.* **Map p273 J7.**

Glass

9 Glasshouse Street, W1R 5RL (7439 7770/www.paperclublondon.com). Piccadilly Circus tube. **Open** 5-11pm Mon-Thur; 5pm-1am Fri; 7pm-1am Sat. **Food served** 5-11pm Mon-Fri; 7-11pm Sat. **Credit** AmEx, MC, V. Bar
Glass starts with plenty of it: floor-to-ceiling reflections bounce around the lobby before a curtain beckons to a main room of soothing cream and black. With towers of irises, and tea lights shimmering in the shiny tabletops, it's an oasis of taste behind the gaudy bustle of Piccadilly Circus. Private functions occupy the back room, and often the main bar too. Cocktails (around £8) feature serious use of BNJ scotch, Sputnik and Belvedere vodkas, with own-made caramelised peaches, fresh passion fruit and melon – most notably in a Phone Number of Sputnik, Midori and lime, or an Orient Express of Belvedere and melon. It's knowingly chic, and the service could be quicker – much quicker – but it's a classy start to any evening. *Disabled: toilet.* **Map p273 J7.**

Jewel

4-6 Glasshouse Street, W1B 5DQ (7439 4990/www.jewelbarlondon.co.uk). Piccadilly Circus tube. **Open/food served** 5pm-1am Mon-Wed; 4pm-1am Thur-Sat; 6pm-12.30am Sun. **Credit** AmEx, MC, V. Bar
Less ostentatious than when it opened, or than the adjoining Blanca bar, Jewel still attracts a mix of well-dressed grown-ups on the pull and random traffic from Piccadilly Circus, just visible from the front window. Views of prey and Piccadilly have been improved by an uncluttering of the main space around the bar, while the back area is table service only. A mildly upscale cocktail menu stands out for its odd pricing (£8.10 martinis, £7.60 contemporary varieties) and themed drinks. Try a Jewel bellini of peach or strawberry liqueur and Devaux champagne; a Jewel in the Crown of Finlandia, melon and passion fruit liqueurs; or a Soho Grand (£7.90) of Grand Marnier blended cognac liqueur, Cherry Marnier and Devaux champagne. *Disabled: toilet. Function rooms. Music (DJs 8.30pm Wed-Sun; £5 after 9pm Fri, Sat).* **Map p273 J7.**

Rivoli at the Ritz

Ritz Hotel, 150 Piccadilly, W1J 9BR (7493 8181). Green Park tube. **Open** 11.30am-1am Mon-Sat; noon-midnight Sun. **Food served** noon-10pm daily. **Credit** AmEx, DC, MC, V. Hotel bar
Jacket and tie only at the Ritz – what else are you going to wear in Piccadilly's smartest hotel, after all? The Barclay Brothers invested eight years and a small fortune into renovating this landmark hotel and its classic art deco cocktail bar, accessed through a quite modest doorway then a hard right once you get past the flunky in the lobby. Gold, glass and leopardskin suitably dazzle. Prices are silly, even for a spot so opulent: £16 for a standard bellini of peach juice and Ritz Selection Champagne, £15 for an old fashioned of 'bourbon whiskey' and Angostura bitters. When your drink arrives, impeccably served, it's fine, it's dandy – but not £15 worth of fine and dandy. And let's not even mention the £18.50 club sandwiches… *Babies and children admitted (lounge area). Disabled: toilet (hotel). Dress: jacket, no jeans or trainers.* **Map p273 J8.**

★ 1707 NEW

Fortnum & Mason, 181 Piccadilly, W1A 1ER (7734 8040/www.fortnumandmason.com). Piccadilly Circus tube. **Open** 11am-8.30pm Mon-Sat; 11am-6pm Sun. **Food served** noon-8.30pm Mon-Sat; noon-5.30pm Sun. **Credit** MC, V. Wine bar
At the heart of the new basement in the famous old store, this place is a stylish take on the traditional wine bar. Unpolished wooden slats line the walls, propping up cream-painted arches, all from the hand of restaurant designer-to-the-celebrity-chef David Collins. But the wine list outdoes even this, taking in choice selections from Clare Valley in Australia and fortifieds from Jerez, plus a pre-selected range of wines either from a particular region or made from the same grape, known as a 'flight'. 'Red Austrian', for example, is good value at under a tenner for three wines from that country. You can bring in bottles from the shop if nothing on the list appeals, with corkage at £10. Decent food is a bonus: Fortnum pork pie with scotch egg, deliciously crumbly montgomery cheddar and a pot of chutney definitely complemented an unctuous Alsace pinot gris from Bruno Sorg, 2004. 1707 shows off F&M's outstanding wine collection in fine style. *Babies and children welcome. Disabled: toilet. Restaurant.* **Map p273 J7.**

Mews of Mayfair. *See p55.*

Sports Café
80 Haymarket, SW1Y 4TE (7839 8300/www.thesports cafe.com). Piccadilly Circus tube/Charing Cross tube/rail. **Open** 11.30am-3am Mon, Tue, Fri, Sat; 11.30am-2am Wed, Thur; 11.30am-midnight Sun. **Food served** noon-11pm daily. **Admission** £5 after 10pm Mon, Tue, Fri, Sat. **Credit** AmEx, DC, MC, V. Sports bar Rammed on Champions League nights, the West End branch of this global chain originating from Toronto offers the usual common denominators of sports memorabilia (racing cars, signed shirts), themed food (knockout fillet £14.95, main event ribs £11.95) and standard drinks. An Antipodean touch is added by the draught Foster's and bottled Victoria beers. Downstairs contains two dining areas, with little TV screens for each of its eight tables; the slightly smarter upstairs bar boasts pool tables at one end. Essentially, though, it's a trough of £3.30 lager, banks of TV screens and boisterous, partisan viewing, the authentic icing on the cake coming at half-time when half the bar queues for the upstairs toilets.
Children admitted (until 9pm, dining only). Disabled: toilet. Music (DJs 10pm Mon, Tue, Fri, Sat). Restaurant available for hire. **Map p273 K7.**

Pimlico

Chimes
26 Churton Street, SW1V 2LP (7821 7456/www.chimes-of-pimlico.co.uk). Pimlico tube. **Open/food served** noon-2.30pm, 5.30-10.15pm Mon-Sat; noon-3pm, 5.30-10pm Sun. **Credit** AmEx, DC, MC, V. Cider bar Three taps of draught cider – Biddenden, Weston's and Weston's Old Rosie's cloudy scrumpy – await as you enter

this quaint, wooden establishment. Hand-pumped from the cellar, these are sold by the half-pint glass (£1.60) or two-pint jug (£6-£7), along with bottles of Biddenden Sweet and Weston's Special Vintage. The wines too have a rustic touch to them, with silver birch, gooseberry and damson varieties (£2.30/£2.85/£11.50). There are a dozen more conventional ones of the grape genre, including a Mâcon-Lugny Louis Latour (£16.95) and a Sancerre Dominique Baud (£18.95). Amid timeless Kentish scenes of traditional cider-pressing displayed around the two-area interior, Spitfire and Fuller's London Pride are the bottled beers on offer, Kronenbourg 1664 the French contribution.
Function room. Tables outdoors (3, pavement). **Map p281 J11.**

Jugged Hare
172 Vauxhall Bridge Road, SW1V 1DX (7828 1543). Victoria tube/rail. **Open** 11.30am-11pm Mon; 11.30am-11.30pm Tue-Sat; noon-10.30pm Sun. **Food served** noon-9.30pm daily. **Credit** AmEx, DC, MC, V. Pub
A flagship of the Fuller's fleet, the Jugged Hare makes the most of its premises: a bank built in the 1800s. An impression of life as it looked then is spread over one wall of the tidy main bar, adjoining a mezzanine and back room. The space is carefully thought out, and equal care is taken with the food, the jugged hare in question being slow-cooked in a pie with ESB and the roasts (pork, beef, nut cutlet) making a pleasant Sunday distraction along this otherwise moribund stretch of the Vauxhall Bridge Road. Most meals cost under a tenner. Along with draught offerings from the house brewery – Chiswick, Discovery, Honey Dew – there are 15 mainly mid-priced wines. Gunshearer riesling (£21) and cabernet sauvignon (£22) stand out.
Games (fruit machine). TV. **Map p281 J10.**

★ Millbank Lounge

City Inn Hotel, 30 John Islip Street, SW1P 4DD (7932 4700). Pimlico or Westminster tube. **Open** 11am-11pm Mon-Sat; noon-10.30pm Sun. **Food served** 11am-10pm Mon-Sat; noon-9.30pm Sun. **Credit** AmEx, DC, MC, V. Hotel bar

This quality hotel bar is criminally underused, hidden away down a Pimlico backstreet on the first floor of a city hotel. You'll have no trouble finding a relaxing low chair in the expansive bar area – but you'll need to take your time over the impressive drinks menu. Lounge Selective is the core choice: mojitos, daiquiris and other classics made with standard (Mount Gay Eclipse, £8.25), superior (Havana 7 or Matusalem, £10.50) or deluxe (Mount Gay XO, Appleton 21, £15-£19) brands. Lounging Nostalgia offers a more eclectic mix: Plymouth gin mixed with elder-flower in the Elderflower collins or Absolut Vanilla smashed with raspberries and strawberries in the Cascade. Wines run from a house Lézard chardonnay or merlot (£3.75-£14.50) to a Napa Valley zinfandel (£48). *Babies and children admitted (until 6pm). Disabled: toilet (hotel). Function room (hotel). Restaurant.* **Map p281 K10.**

Morpeth Arms

58 Millbank, SW1P 4RW (7834 6442). Pimlico tube. **Open** 10am-11pm Mon-Sat; 11am-10.30pm Sun. **Food served** 10am-10pm Mon-Sat; 11am-9.30pm Sun. **Credit** AmEx, DC, MC, V. Pub

The railinged terrace overlooking the Thames and the MI6 building beyond is not typical of your average Young's pub. The Morpeth's comfortable main bar may have the standard Young's beers, equally standard wines (Hawke's Bay sauvignon £3.80/£15.95, El Coto Rioja Crianza £3.65/£15.25) and plates of liver and onions or grilled cumberland sausages (£8-£9), but down below, something stirs. Built on the site of the former Millbank penitentiary, the pub hides a network of tunnels said to be haunted by the ghosts of prisoners who never escaped. Equally, the man sitting next to you tucking into his tra-ditional roast might be an off-duty spy from over the river. If you're starting to feel paranoid, find a table in the upstairs lounge. *Games (fruit machine, quiz machine). No piped music or jukebox. Quiz (8.30pm alternate Mon; £1). Tables outside (25, riverside terrace). TV.* **Map p281 K11.**

White Swan

14 Vauxhall Bridge Road, SW1V 2SA (7821 8568). Pimlico tube. **Open** 11am-11pm Mon-Thur, Sat; 11am-midnight Fri; noon-10.30pm Sun. **Food served** noon-9pm daily. **Credit** AmEx, DC, MC, V. Pub

Down by the Thames, this well-run, renovated pub exudes a rare touch of character amid the blandness of Pimlico. Done out in a traditional style, with old light fittings and flagstone tiles set around the central bar area, the White Swan provides honest ales – Bombardier, Adnams, Greene King IPA, Morland Old Speckled Hen, London Pride – to clientele drawn from the locality. The wines are on the cheaper end of the price scale, of the New Zealand Montana (sauvignon blanc and pinot noir) variety, but that's not what brings people in. It's a place for a quiet pint and a home-baked pie, a ketchup-on-the-table kind of establish-ment – and none the worse for it. *Babies and children welcome (dining only). Games (fruit machine). Tables outdoors (2, pavement). TV (widescreen).* **Map p281 K11.**

Also in the area...

Gallery *1 Lupus Street, SW1V 3AS (7821 7573).* Oddly named neighbourhood pub with little in the way of art; instead, try three real ales on tap. **Map p281 K11.**
Page *11 Warwick Way, SW1V 1QT (7834 3313/ www.frontpagepubs.com).* Front Page pub with a decent choice of draught ales and a Thai menu. **Map p281 J10.**

St James's

Aura

48-49 St James's Street, SW1A 1JT (7499 6655/ www.the-aura.com). Green Park tube. **Open** 8.30pm-3.30am Tue-Sat; 9pm-1.30am Sun. **Food served** 8.30-9.30pm Tue-Sat. **Credit** AmEx, MC, V. Cocktail bar

Is there an aura about Aura? Definitely, particularly when they dim the lights and there's a faint glow around the edges of the smart but intimate interior, backdropped by a proper bar counter fronting a proper cocktail bar. The drinks menu, presented like a schoolboy's exercise book (soon to be toned down), offers an imaginative range of sassy concoctions, most with a £9 price tag. A Berry Smash of Stoli, berries, grapes, myrtle and apple juice should do the trick, or a Reggae Superstar of Appleton 151, watermelon liqueur and Coco Lopez. There's Grey Goose Citron in the cosmopolitan and Maker's Mark in the man-hattan. The loyal, discerning urban clientele shimmy from bar to adjoining club most nights of the week. *Bar available for hire. Music (DJ 10.30pm Tue; DJs 11pm Wed-Sun; £20). TV.* **Map p273 J7.**

★ Dukes Hotel

35 St James's Place, SW1A 1NY (7491 4840/www. dukeshotel.co.uk). Green Park tube. **Open** noon-11pm Mon-Sat; noon-10.30pm Sun. **Food served** noon-3.30pm daily. **Credit** AmEx, DC, MC, V. Hotel bar

Tucked away by the lobby of the Duke's Hotel, itself hid-den away in a courtyard of St James's Place, this discreet cocktail bar comprises four seating areas of striped walls and stately portraits. Settle into your leather chair with your complimentary nuts and nibbles and peruse the famed martini (£14.50) menu. House versions are based with Plymouth gin or Potocki vodka, frozen for 24 hours; eight Modern Classics also involve U'Luvka and Królewska vodkas, with Iranian saffron, fresh passion fruit juice or 'copious' olive juice. These quality brands are used in the 25 Classics (£13-£16). Vintage malts (McPhail's 1948, £50) and cognacs are another speciality. Some 20 wines include a Châteauneuf-du-Pape Domaine du Grand Tinel (£9.50/ £40) and a merlot Faucon Bleu (£6.50/£23). *Dress: smart casual. Tables outdoors (3, garden).* **Map p281 J8.**

Golden Lion

25 King Street, SW1Y 6QY (7925 0007). Green Park or Piccadilly Circus tube. **Open** 11am-11pm Mon-Fri; noon-6pm Sat. **Food served** noon-3.30pm Mon-Fri; noon-3pm Sat. **Credit** AmEx, MC, V. Pub

As cosy a hostelry as it was when frequented by Oscar Wilde and Lillie Langtry in between performances at the long-gone St James' Theatre opposite, the dark wood Golden Lion hides a range of quality ales behind the heraldic crests of its glazed windows. Adnams, Greene King IPA, Hogs Back and London Pride all feature, with enough high-end spirits (Grey Goose L'Orange, Ketel One Citron, Sagatiba cachaça, Hendrick's gin) and carefully sourced flavours (Amazonian superfruits acerola and acaí berry, fresh berries, rose syrup) to satisfy the most jaded Soho-ite. Beers, bottled only, include Warsteiner, Budvar and Tiger. Wines, 16 by the bottle, eight by the glass, feature a Barolo Ravello (£25) and a Chablis La Colombe (£23). The decor is interesting: a rotating exhibition space in the airy, street-level bar; signature A-Z floor map in the lived-in basement where DJs spin. Finally, the food – snacks and mains from the kitchen hatch upstairs – hits the spot. *Babies and children admitted (until 5pm). Music (DJs 7.30pm Thur-Sat; free).* **Map p273 J6.**

Amber
6 Poland Street, W1F 8PS (7734 3094/www.amber bar.com). Oxford Circus or Piccadilly Circus tube. **Open** noon-1am Mon-Sat. **Food served** noon-11pm Mon-Sat. **Credit** AmEx, MC, V. Bar
The Latin lilt here differs from the more adult tastes of Amber's nearby sister, Alphabet, although the pair share the same wine selection. Amber is for a younger, partying crowd, more at ease tucking into a sharing platter of tapas (£10) than approaching a well-composed lunch. Cocktails (£6.30) are based on Agavero tequila, Bombay Sapphire gin, Frangelico… the ideal start for a couple of hours of fun before heading out into Soho. Tequilas are a speciality: Sauza Blanco, Herradura Reposado, Sotol Reposado, plus the premier Anejo varities. Bottled beers include Estrella Damm and San Miguel – there'd be no room in the narrow, main bar for taps on the counter anyway. The bar downstairs, similarly narrow and bright, hosts DJs. *Function room. Music (DJs 8pm Fri, Sat; free). Restaurant.* **Map p273 J6.**

Argyll Arms
18 Argyll Street, W1F 7TP (7734 6117). Oxford Circus tube. **Open** 8am-11pm Mon-Thur; 8am-midnight Fri, Sat; 8am-10.30pm Sun. **Food served** 8am-10pm daily. **Credit** AmEx, MC, V. Pub
Set between the London Palladium and Oxford Circus, the mahogany-and-etched-glass Victoriana of the Argyll maintains singular elements of British tradition while the world tramps through its partitioned interior. Taps of Marston's Pedigree, London Pride, Timothy Taylor Landlord, Black Sheep, Shepherd Neame Spitfire, Bombardier, Hook Norton Old Hooky and Abbot ale are one thing. But how do you explain portraits of Ken Dodd and Frankie Howerd, gaga or gurning, to the curious Japanese tourist? More school milk-era celebs haunt the Palladium Bar upstairs. It's a Nicholson's pub, so it's the usual pies and sausages for tea. Given that you're drinking on the green bit of the Monopoly board, wine is cheap, most of the dozen choices costing £12 a bottle and Chablis Laroche at £16.95. *Babies and children admitted (restaurant). Games (fruit machines). Restaurant. Tables outdoors (6, pavement).* **Map p272 J6.**

Bar Chocolate
27 D'Arblay Street, W1F 8EN (7287 2823/www.bar choc.co.uk). Oxford Circus or Tottenham Court Road tube. **Open/food served** 10am-11pm Mon-Sat; noon-10.30pm Sun. **Credit** MC, V. Bar
A regular on the circuit, Bar Chocolate is as smooth an operation as its name suggests, having shed its pleasantly bohemian wrapping. The decor is now a plain maroon and white on black and white tiling. The lack of brown is compensated for by chocolate in the desserts (£4-£4.80) of

cake and mousse, the hot drink itself (£2.40) and the crème de cacao in some of the 16 cocktails (£8). Absolut in the Bar Chocolate martini and Ketel One in the Smartini both undergo these unusual mixes. Lunches are a whopping £9, although Baltika, Budvar and Corona by the bottle are welcome accompaniments. There's draught San Miguel too. Wines, ten by the bottle and glass, include a white Rioja Vega (£4.55/£18). *Babies and children admitted (until 6pm). Tables outdoors (3, pavement).* **Map p272 J6.**

Bar Soho
23-25 Old Compton Street, W1D 5JQ (7439 0439/ www.sohoclubsandbars.com). Leicester Square or Piccadilly Circus tube. **Open/food served** noon-1am Mon-Thur; noon-3am Fri, Sat; 2pm-12.30am Sun. **Admission** £3 after 10pm Mon-Thur; £5 after 9.30pm Fri, Sat. **Credit** AmEx, DC, MC, V. Bar
Dinky menus in new signature red, dining tables across half the main bar space at lunchtime (portobello mushroom burger, £6) and 'I Heart Soho' merchandise suggest this party bar and pick-up joint is now punting for daytime trade. Come nightfall, most customers are mainly intent on reaching first base before moving on à deux. They're aided in this task by an improved wine selection – ten on offer, four by the glass (Les Bateaux merlot £4/£14.50, Silterra pinot grigio £4.10/£14.90) – and standard cocktails at £6.20. No surprises among the draught beer options, but you can find bottled Peroni, Michelob and Sol, as well as Bulmers cider and fruit Quinn's. Despite the upgrade, Bar Soho's sturdy wrought-iron and flagstone interior can still tell a few tales of nights gone by. *Babies and children admitted (until 6pm). Function room. Music (DJs 9pm nightly). Tables outdoors (4, pavement). TV (big screen, satellite).* **Map p273 K6.**

Blue Posts
28 Rupert Street, W1D 6DJ (7437 1415). Leicester Square or Piccadilly Circus tube. **Open** 11am-11.30pm Mon-Thur; 11am-midnight Fri, Sat; noon-10.30pm Sun. **Food served** noon-9pm daily. **Credit** MC, V. Pub
Someone's been round with the duster at this cosy little corner pub, put a few houseplants in the window and tidied the place up a bit. It attracts a chatty gay/straight mix, the conversation fuelled by pints of Timothy Taylor Landlord, Fuller's London Pride, Hoegaarden, Leffe and Peeterman. The half dozen wines include a Painter Bridge chardonnay and a La Garenne syrah. Drinks are served over a busy bar counter, brightened by dinky long-wired lights and manned by that genial barman that some punters may remember from when the Dive Bar was going strong. They've improved the food menu too: broccoli and stilton was the soup of the day. *Babies and children admitted (until 6pm). Function room. Music (jazz 4-7pm Sun; free). Tables outdoors (2, pavement).* **Map p273 K7.**

Boulevard Bar & Dining Room
57-59 Old Compton Street, W1D 6HP (7287 0770/ www.boulevardsoho.com). Leicester Square tube. **Open** 11am-1am Mon-Sat; noon-midnight Sun. **Food served** 11am-11pm Mon-Tue, Sun; 11am-midnight Wed-Sat. **Credit** AmEx, MC, V. Bar/Restaurant
As the only quality contemporary cocktail bar and eaterie on the street, the simple, modern Boulevard appeals to a gay/straight mix deep in alcopop territory. Bar and diner intertwine, so you can order a proper martini (£6.50) with Ketel One or Bombay Sapphire at the same table as an

asparagus risotto with truffle oil (£6/£9) – although there are separate dining areas in the partitioned interior. Fresh fruit (strawberries, pomegranate, berries) and superior brands (Stoli Razberi, Sauza Hornito tequila) are just some of the ingredients of an impressive cocktail selection, many invented by the Boulevard bar team. Brooklyn and Sierra Nevada number among the bottled beers, and there are ten well-chosen wines (Marquis de Lissac chardonnay, Bodegas Navajas Rioja) from £4.50/£13.
Babies and children admitted (dining only). Music (DJs 8pm Fri, Sat; free). Restaurant. Tables outdoors (3, pavement). **Map p273 K6.**

Café Bohème
13 Old Compton Street, W1D 5JQ (7734 0623/ www.cafeboheme.co.uk). Leicester Square tube. **Open** 8am-3am Mon-Sat; 8am-midnight Sun. **Food served** 8am-2.30am Mon-Sat; 8am-11pm Sun. **Admission** £5 after 11pm Fri, Sat. **Credit** AmEx, DC, MC, V. Café/Bar
Daytime café, white-tableclothed restaurant and after-hours bar, the corner Bohème is French in most aspects. Croissants sit on the zinc counter of the bar area; aproned staff waiting on dining tables. The 40-strong wine list, including a handful by the glass or half bottle, is predominately French, as is the champagne (Mumm £6.50/£32.50, Veuve Clicquot £45) and the small plates, salads and sandwiches. There also a choice of 30 cocktails (£6-£7), featuring La Fée absinthe in the Bohemian Mule and Mumm in the Bohème bellini. Draught Stella comes by the half pint (£1.85) or two-pint pitcher (£7.40) .
Babies and children admitted (before 7pm). Music (jazz 5pm Thur, Sun). Tables outdoors (9, pavement). **Map p273 K6.**

Candy Bar
4 Carlisle Street, W1D 3BJ (7494 4041/www.the candybar.co.uk). Tottenham Court Road tube. **Open** 5-11.30pm Mon-Thur; 3pm-2am Fri, Sat; 3-11pm Sun. **Admission** £5 after 9pm Fri, Sat. **Credit** MC, V. Bar
A kitsch, glowing pink squiggle of neon just off Charing Cross Road signifies the longest-established lesbian bar in London, still going strong after more than a decade. Entry policy is strictly regulated: lesbian and bisexual women, and men only if gay and accompanied. An intimate interior consists of three floors containing an upstairs lounge bar, a long main bar at street level and a sweaty basement space. Drinks involve strong shots and cocktails and halves of Red Stripe, complemented by snacks of ciabatta toasties, fuel before the fiery interaction downstairs. There's a full entertainment programme of nightly DJs and weekly karaoke, with regular pole-dancing and striptease shows to raise temperatures.
Entertainment (karaoke 9pm Wed, free; strip shows hourly from 9pm Thur, Sat, £3). Music (DJs 9pm nightly; £5 Fri, Sat after 9pm). **Map p272 K6.**

Clachan
34 Kingly Street, W1B 5QH (7494 0834). Oxford Circus tube. **Open** 11am-11pm Mon-Thur; 11am-11.30pm Fri, Sat; noon-10.30pm Sun. **Food served** noon-10pm daily. **Credit** (over £10) AmEx, MC, V. Pub
Tucked away behind Liberty, beside its goods entrance in fact, the Clachan was once an outer part of London's most characterful department store. The style still shows in the dark wood, glass and chandeliers, and equal care is taken over the ales served. There is little pretension, just proper

beers, well kept, served to satisfied tourists and locals on their lunch hour. Taps for Old Speckled Hen, Marston's Pedigree, Timothy Taylor Landlord, Fuller's Chiswick and London Pride line the island bar counter that serves the main saloon. There are more intimate seats in a raised alcove at the back, and a Liberty bar upstairs. Lagers include Staropramen and Erdinger, and there's pub grub of the traditional variety.
Function room. Games (fruit machine). Restaurant. **Map p273 J6.**

Club Bar & Dining NEW
21-22 Warwick Street, W1B 5NE (7734 1002/ www.theclubbaranddining.co.uk). Piccadilly Circus tube. **Open** 10am-midnight Mon-Fri; 2pm-midnight Sat. **Food served** 10am-3pm, 6-11pm Mon-Fri; 2-11pm Sat. **Credit** AmEx, MC, V. Bar/Restaurant
This pricy new option at the Piccadilly end of Soho caters for the brunch (soft-boiled eggs with brioche soldiers, £4.50), lunch, dinner and post-work drinking crowd. At the back of the expansive, sturdy main room, an open kitchen adjoins the bar counter. Of the 40-strong wine list, a dozen come by the glass. Options begin with a standard Cuvée d'Etoiles or Le Havre L'Hérault (£3.30/£12.50) and move through a Malbec Finca Beltrán (£20) or a Château du Val de Mercy Chablis (£30). Eight champagnes start from a Perrier-Jouët (£9/£39.50), the rosé variety mixed with Wyborowa pear and poached pear in the house Clubtini, a standout among the standard cocktails. Touches of pink neon announce a brighter bar downstairs.
Bar available for hire. **Map p273 J6.**

Coach & Horses
29 Greek Street, W1D 5DH (7437 5920). Leicester Square or Piccadilly Circus tube. **Open** 11am-11pm Mon-Sat; noon-10.30pm Sun. **Credit** AmEx, MC, V. Pub
A user-friendly Coach? Whatever next! Famous for its rude landlord Norman Balon and his pricing policy (London Pride at £3.20 a pint – the cheek!), the Coach has turned a corner. The replacement of the Matthau-esque Balon by Alistair Choat has changed the climate at the Coach from chilly to warm. Food (Norman's Rude Pies, including steak and London Pride) forms part of a pie-and-pint daytime deal before the regular rootless cosmopolitans convene in the familiar wood-panelled saloon. The caricatures, the louche Sohoites, the retro back bar of illuminated Ind Coope and Double Diamond signage… what is sacrosanct, stays. Draught Löwenbräu, Beck's Vier and Leffe still appeal – as does, these days, a decent muscadet (£3.50/£13) or Viura Rioja (£4.20/£16.50).
No piped music or jukebox. **Map p273 K6.**

Couch
97-99 Dean Street, W1D 3TE (7287 0150/ www.massivepub.com). Tottenham Court Road tube. **Open** 11am-11pm Mon-Fri; noon-10.30pm Sun. **Food served** 11am-9pm Mon-Fri; noon-9pm Sat, Sun. **Credit** AmEx, MC, V. Bar
The kind of bar that does nothing wrong, but nothing spectacularly right – except, perhaps, for its location, at the Oxford Street end of Dean Street. The usual after-work crowd range around an expansive single main interior, all institutional wooden chairs and the odd black sofa. There's a choice of 20 wines, with 15 by two sizes of glass, from a house Zingano (£3.60/£4.60/£13) to an Australian Penny's Hill Red Dot shiraz (£25.50) and Petit Chablis Domaine Jean Goulley (£24.50). Draught beers are San Miguel and

with Ayala Brut champagne. Portraits of famed regulars line the saloon and its cherished back alcove.
Babies and children admitted (restaurant). Restaurant. **Map p273 K6.**

Kettners
29 Romilly Street, W1D 5HP (7734 6112/www.kettners. com). Leicester Square tube. **Open** 11am-midnight Mon-Wed; 11am-1am Thur-Sat; 11am-10.30pm Sun. **Food served** noon-midnight Mon-Wed; noon-1am Thur-Sat. **Credit** AmEx, DC, MC, V. Champagne bar
Kettners boasts as opulent an interior as you'd expect from somewhere founded by the former chef to Emperor Napoleon III. Seating comes in the form of leather sofas spread across three rooms, the walls of which are hung with a mix of po-faced portraits and eccentric architectural sketches in heavy gilt frames. Black-shirted staff reverently scoop ice into silver buckets behind the bar, which is home to as comprehensive a selection of champagnes as you could hope to find: the menu lists them alphabetically over three pages, from £21 to £1,250 per bottle. Mark-ups are commendably low. A glass of house champagne is £8.25, and there are also a few wines, whiskies, brandies and champagne cocktails. Kettners is part of the Pizza Express chain, so pizzas, pasta, burgers and salads are available to soak up the bubbly.
Babies and children admitted. Music (pianist 1-3.30pm, 7-10pm daily). Restaurant. **Map p273 K6.**

Lab
12 Old Compton Street, W1D 4TQ (7437 7820/ www.lab-townhouse.com). Leicester Square or Tottenham Court Road tube. **Open** 4pm-midnight

Mon-Sat; 4-10.30pm Sun. **Food served** 6-11pm Mon-Sat; 6-10.30pm Sun. **Credit** AmEx, MC, V. Cocktail bar
Founded by Douglas Ankrah, Lab has long been at the forefront of London's cocktail scene. Some see it as the most innovative and exciting bar in the capital, others find it distinctly unenjoyable. We've been forced to side with the latter on occasion – affronted by overzealous doormen, drowned in a crush of intoxicated trendies and dying of thirst by the time we've been tended to at the bar – but then you'd be a fool to come here for a quiet drink, especially at weekends. What Lab does is exuberance with panache, its intimate two-floor interior decked out with colourful retro aesthetics, its music euphoric and its (fairly priced) cocktail list among the finest in town – and handled by some of the best mixologists in the world. From the Streets Ahead section, you could try an Unbeetable (Miller's gin, fresh beetroot and thyme, with a dash of passionfruit syrup, £6.90), or, from the Hall of Fame, a Kool Hand Luke (Myer's rum, fresh limes muddled with dark brown sugar and Angostura bitters).
Bar available for hire. Dress: no ties. Music (DJs 8pm Mon-Sat). **Map p273 K6.**

Lucky Voice
52 Poland Street, W1F 7NH (7439 3660/www.lucky voice.co.uk). Oxford Circus tube. **Open/food served** 6pm-1am Mon-Thur; 3pm-1am Fri, Sat; 3-10.30pm Sun. **Credit** AmEx, MC, V. Karaoke bar
Karaoke has become inexplicably fashionable, and this upscale karaoke bar was dreamed up by its owner, internet entrepreneur Martha Lane Fox, while she was recuperating in hospital. The small, stylish bar, decorated in contemporary red and black Japanese design motifs, offers reasonably priced oriental cocktails like Sen Chai bellini

Club Bar & Dining. *See p65.*

Toucan

*19 Carlisle Street, W1D 3BY (7437 4123/www.the
toucan.co.uk). Leicester Square or Tottenham Court
Road tube.* **Open** 11am-11pm Mon-Fri; noon-11pm Sat.
Food served 11am-3.30pm Mon-Sat. **Credit** MC, V.
Pub

Just off Soho Square, the black-fronted, two-floor Toucan
is a shrine to Guinness and its iconic advertising over the
decades. Toucans are prominent, of course, although the
pub could conceivably have also been called the Seal or
the Ostrich when it was converted from a sandwich store
ten years ago. Along with the black stuff, and Grolsch,
Irish whiskeys are offered in number. These are either
hard-to-find single malts – Locke's, Tyrconnell, peated
Connemara – or some very rare varieties, such as the
Tullamores of 42-year, 41-year and 38-year vintage.
There's poitin too, at £4 a shot. Thai curries and standard
lunchtime fare can be ordered separately or in a £10 two-
pint meal deal.
TV (satellite). **Map p272 K6.**

22 Below

*22 Great Marlborough Street, W1F 7HU (7437 4106/
www.22below.co.uk). Oxford Circus tube.* **Open** 5pm-
midnight Mon-Fri; 7.30pm-midnight Sat. **Food served**
5-9pm Mon-Wed; 5-10pm Thur-Sat. **Credit** AmEx, DC,
MC, V. Cocktail bar

Under discerning mixologist Tim Schofield, 22 Below, hidden underneath the Café Libre, once offered a balanced,
imaginative range of cocktails. The more the merrier seems
to be today's motto. A pastiche pulp fiction menu cover
('The Case of the Backward Mule') contains four-person
glug-jug Massives for Four (XL margarita with Olmeca
tequila and Grand Marnier, £25). The mixes are odd, such
as a champagne cocktail with Earl Grey tea (the Earl Grey
Fizz), or a Merlot Magic with red wine, Stoli Razberi and
Chambord. However, there's nothing wrong with the 14
wines (Ropiteau L'Emage Sauvignon or merlot, £4.30/
£12.50) or the three bottled beers (Kastel Cru, Pacifico, Klug).
Bar available for hire. Music (DJ 8pm Thur, Fri; free).
TV. **Map p273 J6.**

Babies and children admitted (daytime only). Bar available for hire. Tables outdoors (2, courtyard). **Map p273 J6.**

Yard

57 Rupert Street, W1D 7PL (7437 2652). Piccadilly Circus tube. **Open** 4-11pm Mon-Sat; 4-10.30pm Sun. **Credit** AmEx, MC, V. Bar

Its gateway tucked amid the porn stores, obscure shopfronts and gaudy neon of the more cruisy gay bars of Soho, the rather respectable Yard can still throw a good party. Comprising the titular small square of courtyard (offering sought-after shaded bar tables on sunny afternoons), a main street-level bar and upstairs Loft Bar, Yard attracts a relaxed, friendly crowd, more mixed and grown-up than other gay bars in the immediate vicinity. Beers on tap include Coors and Grolsch, complemented by Guinness and Strongbow, and a fridge full of Budvar and Breezers. The amiably busy bar staff could sort you out a shooter or cocktail too – there just seems no need to advertise 'Cocksucking Cowboys' over the bar.
Function room. Music (DJs 8pm Fri, Sat; free). Tables outdoors (4, courtyard). **Map p273 K6.**

Zebrano

14-16 Ganton Street, W1F 7BT (7287 5267/ www.zebrano-bar.com). Oxford Circus tube. **Open** Bar 5pm-12.30am Mon-Sat; 7pm-12.30am Sun. **Food served** 11am-midnight Mon-Sat; noon-10.30pm Sun. **Credit** AmEx, MC, V. Bar

After a quick refurb, the two-storey Zebrano is back as a party hub. Punters – whether upstairs, perched on pedestrianised Ganton Street or in the busy bar – glug pints of San Miguel. Each dimly lit alcove contains an illuminated table bearing a tall red drinks menu. Encouraged by the pumping party music at just the right volume, you might consider a Zebrano (£7) of vodka, Passoa, cucumber, passionfruit and ginger ale; or a flavoured caipirinha (£7), kiwi, melon or mango. Frozen cocktails (margarita, pina colada or daiquiri) are another speciality. The bottled beers include Baltika, and a dozen wines start with a house Lerane Terret Viognier (£3.25/£12).
Bar available for hire. Music (DJs 7pm Tue-Sat; free). Tables outdoors (6, pavement). **Map p273 J6.**

Also in the area...

Barcode *3-4 Archer Street, W1D 7AP (7734 3342/ www.bar-code.co.uk).* Cruisy gay bar with a nightly programme of entertainment and dangerously discounted drinks for the boys. **Map p273 K7.**
Black Gardenia *93 Dean Street, W1D 3SZ (7494 4955).* An atmospheric, intimate 1940s throwback, with swing, jazz and blues musicians nightly and a basic choice of drinks. **Map p272 K6.**
Romilly Room *Teatro Club, 93-107 Shaftesbury Avenue, W1D 5DY (7494 3040/www.teatrosoho. co.uk).* A bar troubled by pretension: the dark wood interior is impressive, as is the drinks menu, but smirking staff are a real turn-off. **Map p273 K6.**
Shaston Arms *4 Ganton Street, W1F 7QL (7287 2631).* Countrified Hall & Woodhouse pub, serving Dorset's Badger ales amid mirrored booths and low-ceilinged, dark wood alcoves. **Map p273 J6.**
Village Soho *81 Wardour Street, W1D 6QD (7434 2124).* Landmark bar and mainstay of Soho's gay scene. Fun is fuelled by four dozen cocktails by the glass or jug. **Map p273 K6.**

Two Floors

3 Kingly Street, W1B 5PD (7439 1007/www.barworks. co.uk). Oxford Circus or Piccadilly Circus tube. **Open** noon-11.30pm Mon-Thur; noon-midnight Fri, Sat. **Food served** noon-4pm Mon-Sat. **Credit** AmEx, DC, MC, V. Bar

A fine, fine bar this, reasonably priced, modest, understated. There's no sign – look out for an old No.3 along a Kingly Street rapidly becoming bar central. Inside, furniture institutional and loungey fills an informal, long bar space, each table bearing a drinks menu with a black two of diamonds on the cover. Cocktails (£6) feature mules, sours and caipirinhas, many with Reyka vodka. Bottled beers include Red Stripe, Modelo Especial, Brooklyn and St Peter's Ale. Four taps of Kirin stand atop a seen-it-all bar counter, behind which friendly staff prepare £4 ciabattas and salads. Also on offer are eight, mainly Med, wines, such as Monte Clavijo Rioja Joven (£4/£15) and Palena sauvignon blanc (£4.50/£16). Downstairs, Handy Joe's intimate Tiki Bar is open most evenings.

Babies and children welcome: children's room.
Games (fruit machines). Restaurant. Map p281 J9.

bbar
43 Buckingham Palace Road, SW1W 0PP (7958
7000/www.bbarlondon.com). Victoria tube/rail.
Open 11.30am-11pm Mon-Fri. **Food served**
noon-10.30pm Mon-Fri. **Credit** AmEx, DC, MC,
V. Bar/Restaurant
Some 65 cocktails and 90 wines are on offer at this smart,
contemporary bar-restaurant near the Rubens Hotel. Like
the decor – black and white safari scenes, a running chee-
tah statuette, leopard-spotted lampshades over the bar –
the drinks selection has a South African flavour. Bouchard
Finlayson varieties (a Sans Barrique chardonnay or a
Walker Bay sauvignon blanc) feature heavily and cost
about £6 a glass, £20 a bottle; the BF full-bodied reds
(Galpin Peak pinot noir, £10/£38) are a little pricier. The
bottled beers – Castle, Savanna, Windhoek from Namibia
– are of similar provenance. Mention must be made of the
martinis (£6-£7), apricot-infused Plymouth gin used in the
apricot one, fresh passionfruit and vanilla mixed with
Finlandia in the Passionate Vanilla Kiss.
Babies and children admitted (daytime). Bar available
for hire (weekends). Disabled: toilet. Function room.
Restaurant. Tables outdoors (8, pavement).
Map p281 H9.

Boisdale
13 Eccleston Street, SW1W 9LX (7730 6922/
www.boisdale.co.uk). Victoria tube/rail. **Open/food**
served noon-1am Mon-Fri; 7pm-1am Sat. **Admission**
£10 (£3.95 if already on premises) after 10pm Mon-Sat.
Credit AmEx, DC, MC, V. Bar
Boisdale has cornered the market in whiskies, Cuban cigars and quality Scottish fare. This main branch, 'of
Belgravia' but actually round the corner from Victoria
coach station, also specialises in jazz, with regular live
shows. The USP, though, is the whisky menu of rare dis-
tinction – 18 pages thick – spanning distilleries large and
small across the Scottish Lowlands, Highlands and
Islands. Most are sold by the 50ml glass, for £6-£8, but
there are a number of historic exceptions. Macallan is
given special consideration, such as the 1946 vintage
(£625.50); potent Speyside varieties include an Aberlour
(£9.10) and a Benromach 1982 (£14.20), both around 60
per cent ABV. Irish whiskeys are given the thumb-nose
treatment – Jameson is notably 10p cheaper than all the
other brands.
Babies and children admitted (restaurant). Function
room. Music (jazz 10pm Mon-Sat). Restaurant.
Map p281 H10.

Cardinal
23 Francis Street, SW1P 1DN (7834 7260).
Victoria tube/rail. **Open** 11.30am-11pm Mon-Fri;
noon-11pm Sat; noon-10.30pm Sun. **Food served**
noon-3pm, 5.30-9pm Mon-Fri; noon-3pm Sat.
Credit AmEx, MC, V. Pub
Quite an obscure place this, although often busy with
lunchtime and post-work crowds. It's a Samuel Smith pub,
the standard brewery range served from an imposing
island bar counter dominating an interior lined with portraits of cardinals past and ancient. Patterned wallpaper
adds to the somewhat stern appearance. Equally concentrated gazes are given to the dartboard, allotted its own
area to one side, while a gloomy back room is given over
to the devouring of standard mains (£5.95), lite bites and

baguettes. Perhaps it's the slightly lower-than-average
food prices that have kept this place popular – tucked away
in a quiet street behind Westminster Cathedral, you have
to know it to find it.
Games (darts, fruit machine). No piped music
or jukebox. Map p281 J10.

Cask & Glass
39-41 Palace Street, SW1E 5HN (7834 7630). Victoria
tube/rail. **Open** 11am-11pm Mon-Fri; noon-9pm Sat;
noon-4.30pm Sun. **Food served** noon-2.30pm Mon-Fri.
Credit AmEx, DC, MC, V. Pub
The recent opening of the steel-and-glass Cardinal Walk
development, practically on top of this petite Shepherd
Neame pub, only underlines its obscurity. It's almost as if
developers didn't notice it was here. Overflowing hanging
baskets of flowers and a cottage-like façade lend a village-
like appearance to the exterior. Once inside – if you can get
inside, it's so compact – you're set for the usual SN on-tap
treats like Master Brew, Spitfire, Kent's Best, Bishops
Finger, Oranjeboom and Holsten. There's Asahi by the bottle too. The management has taken down the retro collection of model aeroplanes that lined the top skirting –
hopefully for a careful dusting – but apart from that, the
place remains pretty much unchanged from when the
Beatles were strumming.
No piped music or jukebox. Tables outdoors
(4, pavement). TV. Map p281 J9.

Plumbers Arms
14 Lower Belgrave Street, SW1W 0LN (7730 4067).
Victoria tube/rail. **Open** 11am-11pm Mon-Fri.
Food served 11am-9.30pm Mon-Thur; 11am-
2.30pm Fri. **Credit** AmEx, DC, MC, V. Pub
'A Great British Tradition' announces this cosy little
boozer. Sure enough, the PA offers good ales and proper
(recently improved) pub grub. But, if only by historical

Babies and children admitted (daytime only). Bar available for hire. Tables outdoors (2, courtyard). **Map p273 J6.**

Yard

57 Rupert Street, W1D 7PL (7437 2652). Piccadilly Circus tube. **Open** 4-11pm Mon-Sat; 4-10.30pm Sun. **Credit** AmEx, MC, V. Bar

Its gateway tucked amid the porn stores, obscure shopfronts and gaudy neon of the more cruisy gay bars of Soho, the rather respectable Yard can still throw a good party. Comprising the titular small square of courtyard (offering sought-after shaded bar tables on sunny afternoons), a main street-level bar and upstairs Loft Bar, Yard attracts a relaxed, friendly crowd, more mixed and grown-up than other gay bars in the immediate vicinity. Beers on tap include Coors and Grolsch, complemented by Guinness and Strongbow, and a fridge full of Budvar and Breezers. The amiably busy bar staff could sort you out a shooter or cocktail too – there just seems no need to advertise 'Cocksucking Cowboys' over the bar.

Function room. Music (DJs 8pm Fri, Sat; free). Tables outdoors (4, courtyard). **Map p273 K6.**

Zebrano

14-16 Ganton Street, W1F 7BT (7287 5267/ www.zebrano-bar.com). Oxford Circus tube. **Open** Bar 5pm-12.30am Mon-Sat; 7pm-12.30am Sun. **Food served** 11am-midnight Mon-Sat; noon-10.30pm Sun. **Credit** AmEx, MC, V. Bar

After a quick refurb, the two-storey Zebrano is back as a party hub. Punters – whether upstairs, perched on pedestrianised Ganton Street or in the busy bar – glug pints of San Miguel. Each dimly lit alcove contains an illuminated table bearing a tall red drinks menu. Encouraged by the pumping party music at just the right volume, you might consider a Zebrano (£7) of vodka, Passoa, cucumber, passionfruit and ginger ale; or a flavoured caipirinha (£7), kiwi, melon or mango. Frozen cocktails (margarita, pina colada or daiquiri) are another speciality. The bottled beers include Baltika, and a dozen wines start with a house Lerane Terret Viognier (£3.25/£12).

Bar available for hire. Music (DJs 7pm Tue-Sat; free). Tables outdoors (6, pavement). **Map p273 J6.**

Also in the area...

Barcode 3-4 Archer Street, W1D 7AP (7734 3342/ www.bar-code.co.uk). Cruisy gay bar with a nightly programme of entertainment and dangerously discounted drinks for the boys. **Map p273 K7.**
Black Gardenia 93 Dean Street, W1D 3SZ (7494 4955). An atmospheric, intimate 1940s throwback, with swing, jazz and blues musicians nightly and a basic choice of drinks. **Map p272 K6.**
Romilly Room Teatro Club, 93-107 Shaftesbury Avenue, W1D 5DY (7494 3040/www.teatrosoho. co.uk). A bar troubled by pretension: the dark wood interior is impressive, as is the drinks menu, but smirking staff are a real turn-off. **Map p273 K6.**
Shaston Arms 4 Ganton Street, W1F 7QL (7287 2631). Countrified Hall & Woodhouse pub, serving Dorset's Badger ales amid mirrored booths and low-ceilinged, dark wood alcoves. **Map p273 J6.**
Village Soho 81 Wardour Street, W1D 6QD (7434 2124). Landmark bar and mainstay of Soho's gay scene. Fun is fuelled by four dozen cocktails by the glass or jug. **Map p273 K6.**

Two Floors

3 Kingly Street, W1B 5PD (7439 1007/www.barworks. co.uk). Oxford Circus or Piccadilly Circus tube. **Open** noon-11.30pm Mon-Thur; noon-midnight Fri, Sat. **Food served** noon-4pm Mon-Sat. **Credit** AmEx, DC, MC, V. Bar

A fine, fine bar this, reasonably priced, modest, understated. There's no sign – look out for an old No.3 along a Kingly Street rapidly becoming bar central. Inside, furniture institutional and loungey fills an informal, long bar space, each table bearing a drinks menu with a black two of diamonds on the cover. Cocktails (£6) feature mules, sours and caipirinhas, many with Reyka vodka. Bottled beers include Red Stripe, Modelo Especial, Brooklyn and St Peter's Ale. Four taps of Kirin stand atop a seen-it-all bar counter, behind which friendly staff prepare £4 ciabattas and salads. Also on offer are eight, mainly Med, wines, such as Monte Clavijo Rioja Joven (£4/£15) and Palena sauvignon blanc (£4.50/£16). Downstairs, Handy Joe's intimate Tiki Bar is open most evenings.

South Kensington

Admiral Codrington

17 Mossop Street, SW3 2LY (7581 0005/www.
admiralcodrington.com). South Kensington tube.
Open 11.30am-midnight Mon-Thur; 11.30am-1am Fri,
Sat; noon-10.30pm Sun. **Food served** noon-2.30pm
Mon-Fri; noon-3.30pm Sat; noon-4pm Sun. **Credit**
AmEx, MC, V. Pub
So neatly revamped it's almost a bar – the stripped-back
furniture, the dark browns and greens, the yin-and-yang
fish logo – the Cod still behaves like a pub, and one with
a good restaurant attached. Pints of Bombardier, Greene
King IPA, Guinness and Heineken are dispensed from the
island bar counter. The 30-strong wine list also serves diners, so those in the bar can order a decent tipple by the
glass – an Avila pinot noir San Luis Obispo (£6.50/£26.50)
for example, or a Chablis Domaine du Colombier (£7/£28).
Pub food is of the superior traditional variety: pints of
prawns, own-made cumberland sausage rolls and so on.
An enclosed courtyard allows for outdoor drinking in
warmer weather.
Babies and children welcome: high chairs. Function
room. Games (backgammon, bridge, perudo).
Restaurant (available for hire). Tables outdoors
(3, garden). TV (big screen). **Map p279 D3.**

Anglesea Arms

15 Selwood Terrace, SW7 3QG (7373 7960/www.
capitalpubcompany.com). South Kensington tube.
Open 11am-11pm Mon-Sat; noon-10.30pm Sun.
Food served noon-3pm, 6.30-10pm Mon-Fri; noon-
5pm, 6-10pm Sat; noon-5pm, 6-9.30pm Sun. **Credit**
AmEx, MC, V. Pub
Dickens and DH Lawrence both frequented this splendid
free house, and both would probably still enjoy it today.
There's a sympathetically dated feel to the sturdy wood
interior – the large erotic painting, the sign saying 'To the
loos' – but the drinks selection is bang up to date. With
Kirin Ichiban and San Miguel on draught and Erdinger
Weissbier, Tiger, Budvar and Peroni by the bottle, global
lager drinkers are well catered for. Ales, though, are the
Anglesea's speciality: Hardys & Hansons Olde Trip, Hogs
Back, Brakspear Special, Adnams Broadside and London
Pride all currently feature. The 18 wines, ten by the glass,
include a Bouchard Père et Fils pinot noir (£8.40/£24.50)
and a Montmains Chablis 2005 (£10.10/£29.90). The front
terrace overlooks the quiet residential corner.
No piped music or jukebox. Restaurant (available
for hire). Tables outdoors (12, terrace). TVs.
Map p279 B4.

Cactus Blue

86 Fulham Road, SW3 6HR (7823 7858/www.cactus
blue.co.uk). South Kensington tube. **Open/food**
served 5pm-midnight Mon-Sat; noon-11.30pm Sun.
Credit AmEx, DC, MC, V. Bar/Restaurant
Part Navajo, part Mexico, this fun bar and diner on the
Fulham Road attracts a lively crowd tucking into quality
'South West Tapas' (burgers and chicken wings) at tables
surrounding an illuminated island bar counter. Punters on
surprisingly springy stools prop up the bar, which is
tended by efficient and attentive staff dispensing drinks
with a North American flavour. Many involve tequila –
including the Aztec Gem (with orange and strawberry,
topped with champagne). The nine Cactus Favourites
(£7.50), the ten martinis (£7.50) and ten classics (£7) might

mix Plymouth gin with a Bramble or Zubrówka Bison,
crowned with Goldschlager. Four Latin beers (Modelo
Negra and Modelo Especial among them) and 20 wines
(Rioja, Chilean) continue the theme. The toilets being way
upstairs is our only complaint.
Babies and children admitted (daytime, restaurant
only). Function room. Music (DJs 7pm Thur-Sat;
noon Sun; free). Restaurant. **Map p279 B4.**

Collection

264 Brompton Road, SW3 2AS (7225 1212/
www.the-collection.co.uk). South Kensington tube.
Open 5-11pm Mon-Fri; noon-11pm Sat; 6-10.30pm
Sun. **Food served** 5-10.30pm Tue-Sun. **Credit**
AmEx, MC, V. Bar/Restaurant
This is a party bar for Kensington types, grown-ups and
impressionable, attractive 20-year-olds looking to shape
a lifestyle in London. The overblown entrance, flaming
torches, red ropes and stern Balkan bouncers add to the
illusion of class – you almost expect valet parking. You
enter a sturdy two-level interior, one side lined with a long,
copper-topped bar manned by staff who, on the night we
were there, had an annoying sense of self-importance.
Screens above show Fashion TV. No complaints about the
cocktails, though: four £10 champagne varieties based on
Taittinger (plus Stoli and fresh raspberry in the Russian
Punch) and seven Collection Specials (£9), including a
Lychee Tang of Absolut Citron, Midori and lychee purée.
Absolutely delicious.
Babies and children admitted (restaurant). Bar available
for hire. Booking advisable. Disabled: toilet. Music
(DJs 8pm daily; £10 after 10pm Sat, Sun.). TVs
(big screen, satellite). **Map p279 C3.**

Drayton Arms
*153 Old Brompton Road, SW5 0LJ (7835 2301).
Earl's Court or Gloucester Road tube.* **Open** noon-
midnight daily. **Food served** noon-4pm, 6-10pm
Mon-Fri; noon-10pm Sat; noon-9pm Sun. **Credit**
AmEx, DC, MC, V. Bar
The slightly trendy Drayton Arms lends a youthful, urban
touch to the South Ken bar scene. Sunlight floods the large
main bar through the picture windows and falls on the
scuffed wooden tables and loungey, mismatching sofas.
The selection of beer taps on the bar counter is impressive
– Sleeman, Erdinger, Budvar, Amstel, Hoegaarden, Früli,
Bass, Addlestones cider – as is the wine list. Bin-end spe-
cials complement a two-dozen strong main selection, from
a £2.55/£10 Silverland malbec to a £19 Pouilly-Fumé
Domaine Pabiot or a £25 St-Émilion Grand Cru Château
Teyssier. The Drayton is big on snacks and sharing plates
(potato wedges, breaded calamari) and Sunday roasts; it's
also packed out on rugby weekends.
*Babies and children admitted. Disabled: toilet. Music
(DJs 8pm Fri; free). Quiz (8.30pm Mon; £2). Tables
outdoors (6, pavement). TVs.* **Map p279 A4.**

Enterprise
*35 Walton Street, SW3 2HU (0871 332 4601/
www.theenterprise.co.uk). Knightsbridge or South
Kensington tube.* **Open** noon-11pm Mon-Sat; noon-
10.30pm Sun. **Food served** noon-3pm, 6-10.30pm
Mon-Fri; noon-3.30pm, 6-10.30pm Sat, Sun. **Credit**
AmEx, MC, V. Bar/Restaurant
Equally divided between intimate restaurant and bar, the
Enterprise gives the illusion of space by having a floor-to-
ceiling mirror at one end of the bar counter. The feel is

190 Queensgate

continental – indeed, the wine list (six sauvignon blancs,
five Burgundys, a dozen Bordeaux) relies heavily on
France and, to a lesser extent, Spain and Italy. Four choices of the month – such as an unusual chardonnay
(£4.25/£16) from the Stimson Estate Cellars, Washington
State – preface any decision. Among the French chardonnays are a Chablis Laroche (£27) and a Domaine Vincent
Girardin Puligny-Montrachet La Truffière (£57); elsewhere
there's a Châteauneuf-du-Pape Haute Pierre Delas Frères
(£44). Taps of Beck's, Grolsch, Guinness and Budvar stand
between warrior figurines on the bar.
*Babies and children welcome: high chairs. Restaurant.
Tables outdoors (4, pavement). TV (big screen,
satellite).* **Map p279 C3.**

★ 190 Queensgate
*The Gore Hotel, 190 Queensgate, SW7 5EX
(7584 6601/www.gorehotel.co.uk). Gloucester Road
or South Kensington tube.* **Open/food served**
noon-1am Mon-Wed, Sun; noon-2am Thur-Sat.
Credit AmEx, DC, MC, V. Hotel bar
The perfect pub, cocktail bar and destination lounge, this
annexe of the Gore Hotel hides between the Albert Hall and
the Bulgarian Embassy. Upholstered seating and carved
dark wood surround a sturdy bar, and table service frees
you of the transactional bullshit of the metal change tray.
Bar food of the charcuterie plate variety and an ambient
soundtrack also feature. Underpinning it all is a 20-strong
list of cocktails (£8.50), mules and martinis made with
Ketel One, Belvedere and Absolut, mixed with fresh raspberries, lychees and so on. The high-end brands can be
ordered singly too, a shot of Matusalem Clasico is £6. Four
quality champagnes (£9.95-£17) also come by the glass,
including Veuve Clicquot.
*Music (DJs 10pm Sat; free). Separate room for parties,
seats 60.*

Oratory
*234 Brompton Road, SW3 2BB (7584 3493/
www.brinkleys.com). South Kensington tube.* **Open**
11am-11pm Mon-Sat; 11am-10.30pm Sun. **Food
served** noon-4pm; 6-11pm Mon-Sat; noon-4pm,
6-10.30pm Sun. **Credit** AmEx, MC, V. Bar/Brasserie
Just over the road from the V&A, this bright, chic brasserie
(part of the Brinkley's chain) offers a taste of France in your
glass and on your plate. Of the 40 wines, most come from
just across the Channel, although you can also find a
Fontanafredda Barolo Nebbiolo (£26.50). You might splash
out on a Chassagne-Montrachet Jean-Marc Pillot (£35) or
opt for one of ten half bottles – a Châteauneuf-du-Pape
Domaine des Sénéchaux (£12.50), perhaps. Not everything
requires a heavy outlay: a simple Macon Blanc is £4 a
glass. The ordered layout of the sparkling interior lends
itself to dining, so try to snag one of half a dozen continental tables outside. If you're celebrating, Brinkley's
house champagne is £20 a bottle.
*Babies and children admitted (restaurant).
Booking advisable. Tables outdoors (6, pavement).*
Map p280 C3.

Also in the area...
Duke of Clarence 148 Old Brompton Road,
SW5 0BE (7373 1285/www.geronimo-inns.co.uk).
Triangular, Geronimo-owned corner pub that
resembles a ship; fine selection of home-grown
and international beers on tap. **Map p279 A4.**
Eclipse 158 Old Brompton Road, SW5 0BA
(7259 2577). Branch. **Map p279 A4.**

Queen's Arms *30 Queens Gate Mews, SW7 5QL (7581 7741).* Tidy gastropub with a picturesque mews location; a fine selection of bottled beers includes Innis & Gunn.

Strand

★ American Bar
The Savoy, Strand, WC2R 0EU (7836 4343/www. fairmont.com/savoy). Covent Garden or Embankment tube/Charing Cross tube/rail. **Open** noon-1am Mon-Sat; noon-10.30pm Sun. **Food served** noon-10.30pm Mon-Sat; noon-10pm Sun. **Admission** £5.50 after 8pm. **Credit** AmEx, DC, MC, V. Hotel bar
Entrance to the Savoy Hotel may be a veritable fanfare of otherworldly opulence, but there's something strangely cosy about the art deco American Bar, which has been shaking and stirring high society's 'mixed drinks' for more than a century. Atmospherically, the emphasis remains firmly on the kind of jazz that dresses for dinner: well-mannered waiters in white ties bustle between the tables and an elegant curved bar with a space-age Kubrick aesthetic; music comes courtesy of a besuited crooner at the central grand piano; and the walls are replete with black and white prints of the Newmans, Streisands and Rossellinis of this world. Cocktails are first-class: the Espresso Martini kicks like a mule, thanks to the mix of Absolut Vanilla, Kahlua and a coffee shot, while long drinks like the potent Monkey Trouble (Monkey Shoulder whisky, with peach and apricot brandy) come served in glasses more usually seen holding knickerbocker glories. A real treat. *Music (pianist/singer 7pm Mon-Sat).* **Map p273 L7.**

Coal Hole
91 Strand, WC2R 0DW (7379 9883). Embankment tube/Charing Cross tube/rail. **Open** 11am-midnight Mon-Sat; 11am-10.30pm Sun. **Food served** noon-10pm daily. **Credit** MC, V. Pub
Once part of the Savoy Hotel complex, the historic Coal Hole still exudes dark, decorative class: baronial wood beams, Greco-Roman friezes and fancy stained glasswork. Bacchanalian actor Edmund Kean and his louche Wolf Club fraternity were also fixtures here, honoured in name by an equally grand gallery. It's a Nicholson's pub, so the food is of the hearty pies-sausages-puddings variety. Draught ales of similar character – Adnams, Timothy Taylor Landlord, Fuller's London Pride, Greene King IPA and Abbot – are occasionally complemented by less commonly found brews, such as (at the time of our visit) Hook Norton Old Hooky, Black Sheep and Brains. The fairly priced pub wines branch out to include a Châteauneuf-du-Pape grenache (£18). *Babies and children admitted (until 4pm). Games (fruit machines). Tables outdoors (2, pavement). TV.* **Map p273 L7.**

★ Gordon's
47 Villiers Street, WC2N 6NE (7930 1408/ www.gordonswinebar.com). Embankment tube/ Charing Cross tube/rail. **Open** 11am-11pm Mon-Sat; noon-10pm Sun. **Food served** noon-10pm Mon-Sat; noon-9pm Sun. **Credit** AmEx, MC, V. Wine bar
The history of this candlelit warren of a wine bar (the oldest in London, established in 1890) isn't confined to the Coronation-era newspaper clippings or schooners of sherry dispensed from the ageing barrels behind the bar. There's the name itself. When vintner Arthur Gordon

founded the place, it already had a history – Samuel Pepys lived here in the 1600s. Rudyard Kipling had a room upstairs. Having established the kind of hideaway where Laurence Olivier would woo Vivien Leigh – it still feels like a cellar of naughty Londoners getting intimately frisky away from the stern torch of the ARP warden – Arthur was then followed by Luis Gordon, no relation. The family of bon vivant, newly departed Luis are still the owners, but little else has changed: fine wines from £3.40 a glass, £11.95 a bottle, detailed in a huge menu, barrels of fino, amontillado and oloroso, port and Madeira, ploughman's lunches and Sunday roasts. *Babies and children admitted. Bookings not accepted dinner. Tables outdoors (20, terrace).* **Map p273 L7.**

Nell Gwynne
1-2 Bull Inn Court, WC2R 0NP (7240 5579). Covent Garden tube/Charing Cross tube/rail. **Open** 11am-11pm Mon-Sat. **Food served** noon-3pm Mon-Fri. **No credit cards.** Pub
'The Friendliest Free House in the West End' could also be its most hidden hostelry. A blanked-out sign at a narrow opening on the Strand beckons those in the know to this welcoming cubby hole of a pub. Perhaps this is what attracted its namesake and her royal lover Charles II here, NG nipping out for a quick one before treading the boards of the nearby theatres. Fellow royal-rocker Lillie Langtry is still honoured in picture form. Today's regulars are drawn to the Old Speckled Hen, John Smith's, Bombardier and Holsten Pils on draught, filling the dark interior with the friendly cheer promised on the sign behind the bar. Mind the steps to the toilet – Charlie boy must have tripped and flipped his wig. *Babies and children admitted. Games (darts, fruit machines). Jukebox. Tables outdoors (12 chairs, pavement). TVs (satellite).* **Map p273 L7.**

Also in the area...
Savoy Tup *2 Savoy Street, off Strand, WC2R 0BA (7836 9738).* Branch of Tup.
Tappit Hen *5 William IV Street, WC2N 4DW (7836 9839).* Branch of Davy's. **Map p273 L7.**

Trafalgar Square

Albannach
66 Trafalgar Square, WC2N 5DS (7930 0066/ www.albannach.co.uk). Charing Cross tube/rail. **Open/food served** noon-1am Mon-Sat. **Credit** AmEx, DC, MC, V. Bar/Restaurant
If you thought it was just wine buffs who got to rattle on about the underlying hints of teak in their tipple, think again: the menu at this upmarket Scottish bar and restaurant is a slim bible of regional whiskies, each one glowingly described in terms of composite flavours (seaweed, TCP, chocolate-coated cherries). There are also plenty of whisky-based cocktails: the 1984 is made from a single malt hailing from the island where Orwell spent his last days. But there's less to lure non-whisky lovers: the ground-floor bar is overly bright and aesthetically uninspiring. In avoiding Scottish tokenism (cultural nods are roughly limited to kilted staff, antler-based light fixtures and tasteful black and white Highland prints), the place is strangely bereft of real character. Proof that prime real estate and a novel idea does not a destination make. *Disabled: toilet. Separate room for parties.*

Tables outdoors (3, pavement). TV (projector).
Map p273 K8.

ICA Bar

The Mall, SW1Y 5AH (7930 3647/www.ica.org.uk).
Charing Cross tube/rail. **Open** noon-11pm Mon;
noon-1am Tue-Sat; noon-11pm Sun. **Food served**
noon-2.30pm, 5-10.30pm Mon; noon-2.30pm, 5-11pm
Tue-Fri; noon-4pm, 5-11pm Sat; noon-4pm, 5-10pm
Sun. **Admission** (non-members) £2 Mon-Fri; £2.50
Sat, Sun. **Credit** AmEx, MC, V. Bar
Law dictates that the only establishments permitted to
serve alcohol in the vicinity of Buckingham Palace are
members' clubs – so you have to pay a 'temporary mem-
bership fee' just to get into the bar here. However, this
keeps out the riff-raff, as does the ICA's vaguely intimidating arty credentials. Discerning twenty- and thirtysomethings drink wine (four reds, four whites), beers (five
on tap, including the delicious Früli strawberry brew) and
cocktails (choice of 11 classsics), and dine on the bar's
decent menu, from soups to steaks. The space is airy and
modern, the atmosphere cool but not pretentious; a solo
woman can have a drink without being hassled, and it's an
excellent venue for a first date. Things liven up on weekend nights when there are DJs and one-off club nights.
Babies and children welcome (until 9pm); high chairs.
Disabled: toilet. Function rooms. Internet access (free).
Music (bands/DJs weekly; check website for details).
Map p273 K8.

Old Shades

37 Whitehall, SW1A 2BX (7321 2801). Embankment
tube/Charing Cross tube/rail. **Open** 11am-11pm
Mon-Sat; noon-10.30pm Sun. **Food served** noon-
10pm daily. **Credit** AmEx, MC, V. Pub
A row of faux historic taverns line the Trafalgar Square
end of Whitehall, offering ales, hearty lunches and relief
from weary sightseeing duty. Old Shades is the most sym-
pathetic. It's humble yet spacious, with three bar areas ending in a lovely, panelled dining room. Choosy and careful
about its beers, the Old Shades offered draught Marston's
Pedigree and Fuller's London Pride at the time of review
(Young's wasn't available as the pipes were being cleaned).
Bottled varieties include Budvar, Duvel, Peroni, Beck's,
Leffe, Erdinger and Hoegaarden. Equal discernment has
been shown in the choice of wines, such as in the Laroche
Chablis (£16.95) or the Domaine Pabiot Pouilly-Fumé
(£17.95). Portraits of prime ministers tick a modest box
marked history.
Babies and children admitted (restaurant). Disabled:
toilet. Games (fruit machine). Restaurant (available
for hire). TV. **Map p273 L8.**

Sherlock Holmes

10 Northumberland Street, WC2N 5DB (7930 2644/
www.sherlockholmespub.com). Embankment tube/
Charing Cross tube/rail. **Open** 11am-11pm Mon-Thur;
11am-midnight Fri, Sat; noon-10.30pm Sun. **Food**
served noon-10pm daily. **Credit** AmEx, MC, V. Pub
By Gad, Holmes, I think you've nabbed a few tourists!
Elementary, my dear Watson. I simply lure them in with
a simple trap of souvenirs real and fake, constant black
and white TV re-runs (send for Basil Rathbone!) and a battery of British ales: Old Speckled Hen, Greene King IPA,
Abbot. I include a house variety, Sherlock Holmes, and
themed dishes. Then I set this trap in the perfect location
of the former Northumberland Hotel, exactly where Sir
Henry Baskerville stayed when he came up to town to meet

us. Finally, Watson, I suggest a few souvenirs, a £24.95
deerstalker hat, say, or a £12.95 tankard for the thrifty,
throwing in a £2.50 Sherlock Holmes walking tour for good
measure. Case solved, Holmes!
Babies and children admitted (until 6pm). Games
(fruit machine). Restaurant (available for hire).
Tables outdoors (6, terrace; 3, pavement). TVs.
Map p273 L7.

Ship & Shovell

1-3 Craven Passage, WC2N 5PH (7839 1311).
Charing Cross tube/rail. **Open** 11am-11pm Mon-Sat.
Food served noon-3.30pm Mon-Fri; noon-4pm Sat.
Credit AmEx, MC, V. Pub
Prow to prow at the Thames end of the Arches, these facing taverns of the same name and ale selection honour the
corpulent captain who fought Barbary pirates in the 1700s,
only to be run aground and done for on the Scilly Isles. Sir
Clowdisley Shovell stares out amid the wood panelling and
historic nautical prints in the smaller venue. The larger one
is similarly decorated. Beers include Badger, Tangle Foot
and Sussex, with a big, blue Bavarian tap of HB from
Munich for lager drinkers. Baguettes and pub lunches are
scoffed at appropriate times, a little privacy accorded by
booths at the S&S junior or a snug at the back just big
enough for the cabin boy.
Babies and children admitted (Sat only). Function room.
Games (darts, fruit machine). TV. **Map p273 L7.**

Also in the area...

Champagne Charlies *17 The Arches, off Villiers*
Street, WC2N 4NN (7930 7737). Branch of Davy's.
Map p273 L7.
Rockwell *Trafalgar Hitlon Hotel, 2 Spring Gardens,*
SW1A 2TS (7870 2959/www.thetrafalgar.hilton.
com). London's first bourbon bar (over 100
varieties); its appeal has faded somewhat in
recent years in the face of competition from
superior Albannach. **Map p273 K7.**
Tattershall Castle *Kings Reach, Victoria*
Embankment, SW1A 2HR (7839 6548). Boat pub
that's been smartened up of late; five bars serve
John Smith's plus standard lagers. **Map p273 L8.**

Victoria

Albert

52 Victoria Street, SW1H 0NP (7222 5577). St James's
Park tube/Victoria tube/rail. **Open** 11am-11pm Mon-
Thur; 11am-midnight Fri, Sat; 11am-10.30pm Sun.
Food served 11am-10pm Mon-Sat; noon-9.30pm Sun.
Credit AmEx, DC, MC, V. Pub
The minor refurb slated for 2007 shouldn't alter the Albert.
You can't tamper with tradition, not in a place like this.
Steeped in parliamentary lore, with a grand wooden stair-
case lined with portraits of past prime ministers that leads
to a carvery containing a division bell, the Albert is the per-
fect example of pub design from the days of empire. Carved
wood and frosted glass abound, embellishing a spacious
interior always busy with tourists, able to pay in dollars
or euros. Draught Fuller's London Pride, Greene King IPA,
Courage Directors and Bombardier provide a suitably
British pint to accompany the pies and similar food also
on offer. Kids will be pleased with the sticky puddings –
and a room to get messy in.

Babies and children welcome: children's room.
Games (fruit machines). Restaurant. **Map p281 J9**.

bbar
43 Buckingham Palace Road, SW1W 0PP (7958
7000/www.bbarlondon.com). Victoria tube/rail.
Open 11.30am-11pm Mon-Fri. **Food served**
noon-10.30pm Mon-Fri. **Credit** AmEx, DC, MC,
V. Bar/Restaurant
Some 65 cocktails and 90 wines are on offer at this smart,
contemporary bar-restaurant near the Rubens Hotel. Like
the decor – black and white safari scenes, a running chee-
tah statuette, leopard-spotted lampshades over the bar –
the drinks selection has a South African flavour. Bouchard
Finlayson varieties (a Sans Barrique chardonnay or a
Walker Bay sauvignon blanc) feature heavily and cost
about £6 a glass, £20 a bottle; the BF full-bodied reds
(Galpin Peak pinot noir, £10/£38) are a little pricier. The
bottled beers – Castle, Savanna, Windhoek from Namibia
– are of similar provenance. Mention must be made of the
martinis (£6-£7), apricot-infused Plymouth gin used in the
apricot one, fresh passionfruit and vanilla mixed with
Finlandia in the Passionate Vanilla Kiss.
Babies and children admitted (daytime). Bar available
for hire (weekends). Disabled: toilet. Function room.
Restaurant. Tables outdoors (8, pavement).
Map p281 H9.

Boisdale
13 Eccleston Street, SW1W 9LX (7730 6922/
www.boisdale.co.uk). Victoria tube/rail. **Open/food**
served noon-1am Mon-Fri; 7pm-1am Sat. **Admission**
£10 (£3.95 if already on premises) after 10pm Mon-Sat.
Credit AmEx, DC, MC, V. Bar
Boisdale has cornered the market in whiskies, Cuban cigars and quality Scottish fare. This main branch, 'of
Belgravia' but actually round the corner from Victoria
coach station, also specialises in jazz, with regular live
shows. The USP, though, is the whisky menu of rare dis-
tinction – 18 pages thick – spanning distilleries large and
small across the Scottish Lowlands, Highlands and
Islands. Most are sold by the 50ml glass, for £6-£8, but
there are a number of historic exceptions. Macallan is
given special consideration, such as the 1946 vintage
(£625.50); potent Speyside varieties include an Aberlour
(£9.10) and a Benromach 1982 (£14.20), both around 60
per cent ABV. Irish whiskeys are given the thumb-nose
treatment – Jameson is notably 10p cheaper than all the
other brands.
Babies and children admitted (restaurant). Function
room. Music (jazz 10pm Mon-Sat). Restaurant.
Map p281 H10.

Cardinal
23 Francis Street, SW1P 1DN (7834 7260).
Victoria tube/rail. **Open** 11.30am-11pm Mon-Fri;
noon-11pm Sat; noon-10.30pm Sun. **Food served**
noon-3pm, 5.30-9pm Mon-Fri; noon-3pm Sat.
Credit AmEx, MC, V. Pub
Quite an obscure place this, although often busy with
lunchtime and post-work crowds. It's a Samuel Smith pub,
the standard brewery range served from an imposing
island bar counter dominating an interior lined with portraits of cardinals past and ancient. Patterned wallpaper
adds to the somewhat stern appearance. Equally concentrated gazes are given to the dartboard, allotted its own
area to one side, while a gloomy back room is given over
to the devouring of standard mains (£5.95), lite bites and

baguettes. Perhaps it's the slightly lower-than-average
food prices that have kept this place popular – tucked away
in a quiet street behind Westminster Cathedral, you have
to know it to find it.
Games (darts, fruit machine). No piped music
or jukebox. **Map p281 J10**.

Cask & Glass
39-41 Palace Street, SW1E 5HN (7834 7630). Victoria
tube/rail. **Open** 11am-11pm Mon-Fri; noon-9pm Sat;
noon-4.30pm Sun. **Food served** noon-2.30pm Mon-Fri.
Credit AmEx, DC, MC, V. Pub
The recent opening of the steel-and-glass Cardinal Walk
development, practically on top of this petite Shepherd
Neame pub, only underlines its obscurity. It's almost as if
developers didn't notice it was here. Overflowing hanging
baskets of flowers and a cottage-like façade lend a village-
like appearance to the exterior. Once inside – if you can get
inside, it's so compact – you're set for the usual SN on-tap
treats like Master Brew, Spitfire, Kent's Best, Bishops
Finger, Oranjeboom and Holsten. There's Asahi by the bottle too. The management has taken down the retro collection of model aeroplanes that lined the top skirting –
hopefully for a careful dusting – but apart from that, the
place remains pretty much unchanged from when the
Beatles were strumming.
No piped music or jukebox. Tables outdoors
(4, pavement). TV. **Map p281 J9**.

Plumbers Arms
14 Lower Belgrave Street, SW1W 0LN (7730 4067).
Victoria tube/rail. **Open** 11am-11pm Mon-Fri.
Food served 11am-9.30pm Mon-Thur; 11am-
2.30pm Fri. **Credit** AmEx, DC, MC, V. Pub
'A Great British Tradition' announces this cosy little
boozer. Sure enough, the PA offers good ales and proper
(recently improved) pub grub. But, if only by historical

5th View. *See p58.*

coincidence, a drop of doolally aristocracy and murder most foul are thrown into the mix. One night in 1974, the bonhomie was broken by Lady Lucan bursting in to blurt of her family nanny's fate. News of this most famous crime is displayed on a pillar beside the long, wooden bar counter. Of more interest to today's chatty clientele are the taps of Adnams, Young's, London Pride, John Smith's and Guinness, discussion perhaps concerning the next guest ale, in this case Hook Norton Old Hooky. Wines include a Ropiteau Chablis and a Wolff Blass chardonnay.
Bar available for hire. Function room. Games (board games, darts, quiz machine). Tables outdoors (3, pavement). TV. Map p281 H10.

Thomas Cubitt

44 Elizabeth Street, SW1W 9PA (7730 6060/ www.thethomascubitt.co.uk). Victoria tube/rail. **Open** noon-11pm daily. **Food served** noon-10pm daily. **Credit** AmEx, MC, V. Bar/Brasserie
The former Joiner's Arms is now a busy, upscale brasserie, serving superior roasts and seriously good British fare. The street-level bar area and terrace fill at peak Sunday lunchtimes; weekday evenings attract casual drinkers. From the island bar, draught Bitburger, Brakspear and Adnams are dispensed by a flustered staff, who may take a while with the wine list. No gripes with the two-dozen strong selection, ten by the glass. Denis Pommier Chablis (£6/£25) and Château Lacroix Bordeaux (£5.50/£22) are the solid mid-range choices of a list running from a £3.50 glass of house sauvignon blanc or merlot to a £54 bottle of Puligny-Montrachet Les Charmes. A list of ten cocktails (£7-£8) includes Absolut martinis and Havana Club pear daiquiris.
Babies and children welcome: high chairs. Bar available for hire. Disabled: toilet. Function rooms. Games (board games). Tables outdoors (8, pavement). Map p281 H10.

Tiles

36 Buckingham Palace Road, SW1W 0RE (7834 7761/ www.tilesrestaurant.co.uk). Victoria tube/rail. **Open** noon-11pm Mon-Fri. **Food served** noon-2.30pm, 5.30-10pm Mon-Fri. **Credit** AmEx, MC, V. Wine bar
Discerning about its wine without being pretentious, the informal Tiles offers racks of well-priced labels to be enjoyed with a full meal or simple snack. Both fare and tiled decor of this two-floor venue are Mediterranean in character. The main wine list – there's a cellar collection and vineyard selection too – is comprehensive but easy to negotiate: ten whites by the glass, ten reds, and another ten each in the £20-£25 range by the bottle. Prices are reasonable: a Baron Philippe de Rothschild viognier 2001 costs £4.25 by the glass, £15.50 by the bottle; a 2000 Château les Morleaux Bordeaux likewise. Delving into the cellar collection reveals a Château Cissac Cru Bourgeois, Haut-Medoc 1975 (£48.50) or Château Leoville-Poyferre St-Julien (£55) from the same year.
Babies and children admitted. Bar available for hire (Sat, Sun). Booking advisable. Separate room for parties, seats 50. Tables outdoors (5, pavement). Map p281 H10.

Zander Bar

45 Buckingham Gate, SW1E 6BS (7379 9797/ www.bankrestaurants.com). St James's Park tube/ Victoria tube/rail. **Open** 11am-11pm Mon, Tue; 11am-1am Wed-Fri; 5pm-1am Sat. **Food served** noon-2.45pm, 5.30-11pm Mon-Fri; 5.30-11pm Sat. **Credit** AmEx, DC, MC, V. Cocktail bar
Such places are almost standard now, but in the 1990s, this upscale cocktail bar was the bee's knees. Sister to Bank Aldwych, it shares the same classic and contemporary selection of superior mixes, but appeals more to the discerning barfly. The counter goes on forever. On it, you can have your expert barman plonk something quite unusual

– a new-age gin such as a Blue Saffron (£7) with fresh blueberries, say – or something traditional with a twist. A ginger margarita (Gran Centenario Plata tequila, Cointreau and fresh ginger, £7) would fall into that category. The Hedonist (U'Luvka vodka and a dash of Noilly Prat, £12) is the stand-out martini.

Babies and children admitted (restaurant only). Disabled: toilet. Function rooms. Restaurant. Tables outdoors (60, terrace). **Map p281 J9.**

Also in the area...

Balls Brothers *50 Buckingham Palace Road, SW1W 0RN (7828 4111).* Branch. **Map p281 H10.**

Colonies *25 Wilfred Street, SW1E 6PR (7834 1407).* Cosy watering hole with an outdoor yard and three ales on tap. **Map p281 J9.**

Grouse & Claret *14-15 Little Chester Street, SW1X 7AP (7235 3438).* Refined Hall & Woodhouse pub fitted out with secluded booths, serving King & Barnes Sussex Bitter alongside Badger ales. **Map p281 H9.**

Phoenix *14 Palace Street, SW1E 5JA (7834 3547).* Refurbished Geronimo Inns gastropub with Doom Bar, Adnams bitter, a weekly guest ale and Aspall Suffolk Cyder on tap. **Map p281 J9.**

Tapster *3 Brewers Green, Buckingham Gate, SW1H 0RH (7222 0561).* Branch of Davy's. **Map p281 J9.**

Westminster

Cinnamon Club

The Old Westminster Library, 30-32 Great Smith Street, SW1P 3BU (7222 2555/www.cinnamonclub.com). St James's Park or Westminster tube. **Open** *Library bar* 11am-11.45pm Mon-Sat. *Club bar* 6-11.45pm Mon-Sat. **Food served** 6-10.45pm Mon-Sat. **Credit** AmEx, DC, MC, V. Cocktail bar

Set in the old Westminster Library, this upscale Indian establishment comprises a restaurant and two bars. One lends itself to the quiet sipping of a fine whisky; the other is sleek and contemporary. Bollywood movies play across a wall while black-shirted staff mix serious cocktails. The signature selection (£9-£10) continues the theme: a Rupee Rush involves Manor Farm sloe gin and microbrewed ginger beer; a Cricket Club mixes Canadian bourbon, Drambuie and Vermouth with a green tea and kola nut infusion sold separately as a Cricket. Martinis (£8-£9) come in pomegranate, cardamom and lychee varieties. Bottled beers include a rice one from Laos (£4) and double fermented King Cobra (£15). Platters (£8-£12) of seafood, meat and vegetarian delicacies are predictably classy.

Babies and children welcome: high chairs. Bars available for hire. Booking advisable. Disabled: toilet. Separate room for parties. **Map p281 K10.**

Red Lion

48 Parliament Street, SW1A 2NH (7930 5826). Westminster tube. **Open** 10am-11pm Mon-Fri; 10am-9.30pm Sat; noon-9pm Sun. **Food served** noon-8.30pm Mon-Fri; noon-8pm Sat, Sun. **Credit** AmEx, MC, V. Pub

Stern, sideburned politicians from the days of empire gaze down from the walls of this traditional, dark wood pub. The draught ales available at the crowded bar counter towards the back of the main saloon keep the place in character: Timothy Taylor Landlord, Tetley's,

Bombardier, Greene King IPA, Adnams Broadside, Deuchars IPA and Fuller's London Pride. These are supped in wooden alcoves in the busy back of the bar. A whisky such as a Laphroaig or a Glenlivet would seem a suitable chaser. A new selection of something to sip, wine-wise, is promised soon. Upstairs there is an underused restaurant with its own separate entrance; tables are spread outside the sturdy, corner building in the warmer months.

Babies and children admitted (dining only). Bar available for hire. Comedy (7.30pm Mon). Tables outdoors (5, pavement). **TV. Map p281 K9.**

St Stephen's Tavern

10 Bridge Street, SW1A 2JR (7925 2286). Westminster tube. **Open** 10am-11.30pm Mon-Thur, Sat; 10am-midnight Fri; 10.30am-10.30pm Sun. **Food served** 10.30am-9.30pm daily. **Credit** MC, V. Pub

Most brewery bosses would give their drinking arm for a venue such as this one, diagonally opposite Big Ben. Somehow it seems apt that it should be traditional old Hall & Woodhouse running such a time-honoured establishment, and a thoroughly good job they've done of it too. The decor of this restored gem is all carved wood and etched glass, with towering displays of fresh flowers reaching up to the high, high ceilings. Three bar areas – two at street level overlooked by a mezzanine – are served by the same, well-staffed counter, where pints of Tangle Foot, Sussex and Badger and authentic Munich lager HB are dispensed. Tea and muffins (£4.25) and English breakfasts (£6.25) keep with the general air of decorum.

Disabled: toilet. Function room. No piped music or jukebox. **Map p281 K9.**

Westminster Arms

9 Storey's Gate, SW1P 3AT (7222 8520). St James's Park or Westminster tube. **Open** 11am-11pm Mon-Fri; 11am-8pm Sat; noon-6pm Sun. **Food served** 11am-8pm Mon-Fri; noon-5pm Sat, Sun. **Credit** MC, V. Pub

Attached to Storey's Wine Bar downstairs, the traditional Westminster Arms squeezes tourists and sundry parliamentary staff into an intimate space of dark wood and busy chatter. Ales on the prominent bar counter include Thwaites Lancaster Bomber, Fuller's London Pride, Abbot, Young's and Adnams Bitter and Broadside. Beck's by the bottle is probably the best option for lager drinkers. There are wines too, starting from the house Marquis de Lassine. Sustenance comes in the form of belly-filling mains of beef lasagne and traditional fish and chips. It's not all staid – for some bizarre reason there's a framed display of violins and sheet music for Viennese waltzes, a decorative touch that the long-established French barman is delighted to keep a mystery.

Babies and children admitted. Tables outdoors (4, pavement). TV (big screen). **Map p281 K9.**

Also in the area...

Speaker *46 Great Peter Street, SW1P 2HA (7222 1749).* 'No big screen, no music, no fruit machines' at this Waverley TBS pub with three ales on tap and caricatures on the walls. **Map p281 K10.**

Two Chairmen *39 Dartmouth Street, SW1H 9BP (7222 8694).* This little gem has bucketloads of historic character with its mahogany panelling and open fire in an upstairs sedan room; Adnams Broadside, Young's and Deuchars are on tap. **Map p281 K9.**

City

Over the course of an average day, the City suffers a Jekyll and Hyde-like transformation. By day, it's mobbed by nearly half a million office workers, plus a small army of tourists. By night (and at weekends) the streets are eerily quiet. The effect this has on nightlife is twofold. First, there tends to be little in the way of boozy frolics before Thursday and Friday. Second, chains have a *very* strong presence, particularly Balls Brothers, Corney & Barrow, Davy's, and Jamies. Still, the Square Mile holds some wonderfully historic drinking dens: Fleet Street's **Viaduct Tavern** and Blackfriar's appropriately named **Black Friar**, to list two. It has more modern one-offs too: try the near-flawless **Bar Bourse** or new cocktail venture **Hawksmoor**.

Chancery Lane

Cittie of Yorke

22 High Holborn, WC1V 6BN (7242 7670). Chancery Lane tube. **Open** 11.30am-11pm Mon-Sat. **Food served** noon-3pm, 5-9pm Mon-Sat. **Credit** (over £10) AmEx, MC, V. Pub

One of many historic taverns hereabouts, the Cittie of Yorke comprises a quite remarkable market-sized back room fit for a Hogarth scene, and an unremarkable front bar lined with some of the worst likenesses of historic figures in portrait form you'll ever laugh at. Ignore them and walk right through to the back. Opposite a row of soon-snagged snugs, upturned beer-barrel tables and powerful stand-up heaters arranged around the crowded floor space, a long, long bar counter dispenses the usual brews from the Samuel Smith stable. This is only half the story as there are other (mainly function) rooms below.

Babies and children admitted (downstairs, until 5pm). Games (darts, fruit machine). **Map p274 M5.**

Seven Stars

53 Carey Street, WC2A 2JB (7242 8521). Chancery Lane or Holborn tube. **Open** 11am-11pm Mon-Fri; noon-11pm Sat; noon-10.30pm Sun. **Food served** noon-3pm, 5-10pm Mon-Fri; 1-9pm Sat, Sun. **Credit** AmEx, MC, V. Pub/Restaurant

By the Royal Courts of Justice, Roxy Beaujolais' magic little pub-cum-bar-cum-eaterie fulfils its (admittedly complex) brief to near perfection while keeping a healthy tongue in cheek. Posters for courtroom dramas – *Action for Slander*, *Trial and Error*, Spence and Kate Hepburn on opposing toilet doors upstairs – overlook the legal fraternity tucking into well-chosen (and well-priced) merlots, malbecs and house Dulucs. Craftily conceived daily dishes chalked up by the bar (Napoli sausages and mash, dill-cured herring) are devoured on green and white checked tablecloths in one side room; the other, purple in hue, copes with the inevitable bar overflow. A bar counter offers draught Bitburger, Adnams Bitter and Broadside, Licher Weizen, London Pride and Crouch Vale's Brewers Gold. *No piped music or jukebox.* **Map p275 M6.**

White Swan Pub & Dining Room

108 Fetter Lane, EC4A 1ES (7242 9696/www.the whiteswanlondon.com). Chancery Lane or Holborn tube. **Open** 11am-11pm Mon; 11am-midnight Tue-Thur; 11am-1am Fri. **Food served** noon-3pm, 6-10pm Mon-Fri. **Credit** AmEx, MC, V. Gastropub

As slick as its sister venues (the Gun, the Well and newcomer the Empress of India), the White Swan is a cheerful alternative to the olde pubs and chain wineries that dominate in this area. In detail, it actually borrows from both: decorative touches like a stuffed swan and a ship's bell nod to tradition; an exhaustive wine list (more than a hundred strong) should appeal to the modern connoisseur. Just three tables in the downstairs pub make stand-up pints of Adnams Broadside and London Pride a likely order – if you do nab a seat, try superior pub grub like pheasant pie and braised pig's cheek for under a tenner. In the mirrored and panelled dining room upstairs, a sit-down menu is offered at £28 for three courses, £23 for two.

Babies and children admitted (restaurant). Restaurant. Tables outdoors (4, pavement). **Map p275 N6.**

★ Ye Old Mitre
*1 Ely Court, Ely Place, at the side of 8 Hatton Gardens,
EC1N 6SJ (7405 4751). Chancery Lane tube/Farringdon
tube/rail.* **Open** 11am-11pm Mon-Fri. **Food served**
11am-9.30pm Mon-Fri. **Credit** AmEx, MC, V. Pub
This oldie (established 1546) is only accessible through a
narrow passage – incongruously described as 25m long.
Still, the Mitre needs no yard conversion or 'ye olde' embell-
ishment to prove its worth. Walk into its venerable,
cramped three-room space, see what's on as the guest ale
(Orkney Dark Island on our visit) then settle down amid
the portraits of Henry VIII and sundry beruffed luminaries. The taps of Adnams Bitter and Broadside, Deuchars
and Guinness will be easier to pick out than the extended
history in small type lining the hatch of the bar counter.
The handful of wines – Chilean San Rafael merlot, La Serre
cabernet sauvignon – are well priced at under £15. There
are stand-up tables in the courtyard too.
*No piped music or jukebox. Tables outdoors
(10 barrels, pavement).* **Map p274 N5.**

Also in the area...
Bottlescrue *Bath House, 53-60 Holborn Viaduct,
EC1A 2FD (7248 2157).* Branch of Davy's.
Map p275 O5.
Bung Hole Cellars *Hand Court, 57 High Holborn,
WC1V 6DX (7831 8365).* Branch of Davy's.
Map p274 M5.

Fleet Street & Blackfriars

Black Friar
*174 Queen Victoria Street, EC4V 4EG (7236 5474).
Blackfriars tube/rail.* **Open** 11am-11pm Mon-Wed,
Sat; 11am-11.30pm Thur, Fri; noon-10.30pm Sun. **Food
served** noon-10pm daily. **Credit** AmEx, MC, V. Pub
Sir John Betjeman justifiably and successfully led the campaign to save this remarkable venue, now a Nicholson's
pub. Built in the 1880s on the site of a medieval Dominican
friary, the Black Friar had its interior completely remod-
elled by H Fuller Clark and Henry Poole of the Arts and
Crafts movement, a forerunner of art nouveau. Bright
panes, intricate friezes and carved slogans ('Industry is
Ale', 'Haste is Slow') make a work of art out of the main
saloon. This is adjoined by a prosaic second space, linked
by a doorway and marble-topped bar. Upon it stand taps
of Timothy Taylor Landlord, Adnams, London Pride and,
on our visit, guest beer Robinsons Unicorn. Standard
Nicholson's wines (none costing over £12) may also
accompany the range of pies.
Tables outdoors (10, pavement). TV. **Map p275 O6.**

Cockpit
*7 St Andrew's Hill, EC4V 5BY (7248 7315).
Blackfriars tube/rail.* **Open** 11am-11pm Mon-Sat;
noon-2.30pm, 7-10.30pm Sun. **Food served**
11am-2.30pm Mon-Fri. **Credit** MC, V. Pub
A cock-fighting pit back in the day, this unreconstituted
Courage pub – the shape of a Trivial Pursuit wedge – adds
an unpretentious touch to drinking in Blackfriars. Courage
Best and Directors are accompanied on the tightly packed
bar counter by Adnams, John Smith's and Marston's
Pedigree. Beneath a mock balcony of additional seating,
the ales attract a blokey clientele who sup and scoff
between working hours, comfortable with *The Sweeney*-
era decor (house plants, cockerel iconery) and menu

La Grand Marque. *See p86.*

(chicken kiev). Bottled Peroni provides a gratuitous nod to
Europe while a large TV screen relays the latest on groin
strains and transfer rumours. Given the chance, one half
of the population would happily spend a lifetime here – not
unlike the 1600s, in fact.
Games (fruit machine, shove-halfpenny). **Map p275 O6.**

El Vino
*47 Fleet Street, EC4Y 1BJ (7353 6786/www.elvino.co.uk).
Chancery Lane tube/Blackfriars tube/rail.* **Open** 8.30am-
9pm Mon; 8.30am-10pm Tue-Fri. **Food served** 8am-
11.30pm. **Credit** AmEx, DC, MC, V. Wine bar
One of four branches, El Vino was established in 1879 by
the great-grandfather of the current owner. So steeped in
tradition you could almost believe guineas or promissory
notes were accepted, each outlet is a sturdy wooden
Rumpolesque affair, thick with legal banter or silently
heavy with solitary crossword compilation. Two drinks
menus serve all: green for glasses, half-bottles and bottles
to drink on the premises, white for premium and mail order.
The former offers six chardonnays (Petit Chablis £22.50),
14 sauvignons (St Bris £19.50), four merlots (Barossa
Valley Black Label £18.15), as well as gamays, grenaches,
pinots noirs and German rieslings. House Velvin or Choisi
de Boyier are under £4 a glass. Snacks include the house
sandwich of Norfolk turkey and best back bacon (£8.95).
*Booking advisable. Separate room for parties, seats 50.
Tables outdoors (4, courtyard).* **Map p275 N6.**

Evangelist
*33 Blackfriars Lane, EC4V 6EP (7213 0740).
Blackfriars tube/rail.* **Open** noon-11pm Mon-Fri. **Food
served** noon-9pm Mon-Fri. **Credit** AmEx, MC, V. Bar
A popular destination in the modern scrubbed-pine style,
Evangelist, with its quality open kitchen in the sunken bar,
has a loyal lunchtime and post-work following; a table of

Old Bank of England

194 Fleet Street, EC4A 2LT (7430 2255). Chancery Lane or Temple tube. **Open** 11am-11pm Mon-Fri. **Food served** noon-9pm Mon-Thur; noon-8pm Fri. **Credit** AmEx, MC, V. Pub
As the giveaway postcards relate, this stately building was once two taverns, the Cock and the Haunch of Venison, which were demolished to accommodate a branch of the Bank of England. Fuller's refurbished it ten years ago. As a historical aside, Sweeney Todd worked nearby, allegedly burying the bodies somewhere downstairs. Accountants' quills, old notes and scenes of London deck the walls, which rise and rise to ceilings so high they must have their own climate. An equally vast island bar dispenses Fuller's London Pride and Discovery, and is also used to serve the sausages, pies, fish and other superior pub grub on offer. An excellent wine choice includes Domaine de Vauroux Chablis (£22) and Château de Trignon Sablet (£19.50).
Tables outdoors (11, courtyard). **Map p275 N6**.

Old Bell Tavern

95 Fleet Street, EC4Y 1DH (7583 0216). Blackfriars tube/rail. **Open** 11.30am-11pm Mon-Fri. **Food served** noon-9pm Mon-Fri. **Credit** (over £10) AmEx, MC, V. Pub
This slopey-floored pub on the Nicholson's roster was built by Sir Christopher Wren for his workers during the construction of nearby St Bride's Church. Red buses and black taxis blur past the glazed front panels; behind them, men nurse pints of London Pride, Adnams Broadside or Timothy Taylor Landlord in armchairs by the fireplace. This is London, guv. To cater for more modern (and female) tastes, there's a decent wine list, offering ten reds and whites by the bottle, four by the glass. Aside from a bargain house Argentine chardonnay (£2.55/£7.95), you'll find a Laroche Chablis, Spy Valley riesling or Domaine Clavel Côtes du Rhône for under £17.
Babies and children admitted. Games (golf machine). TV. **Map p275 N6**.

Punch Tavern

99 Fleet Street, EC4Y 1DE (7353 6658). Blackfriars tube/rail. **Open** 7am-11pm Mon-Wed; 7am-midnight Thur, Fri. **Food served** 7am-10.30pm Mon-Fri. **Credit** AmEx, MC, V. Pub/Wine bar
A sense of gravitas comes over visitors to this venerable establishment, its narrow tiled corridor opening into an indulgent main bar of velour banquettes, candles and a fireplace. The back room, used mainly for dining, shows decorative evidence of the venue's role in publishing history: it was here that *Punch* was founded in the 1840s. The back conservatory is a welcome later addition. Wine is the drink of choice, with some 30 varieties, including ten by the glass. Try a low-cost Obikwa chenin blanc (£3.40/£13), a Château de Galoupet rosé (£4.25/£17.75) or the pricier Chapitre Sancerre and Lost Valley merlot. Monthly wine tastings (£20) are also held. Timothy Taylor Landlord and San Miguel feature on draught.
Babies and children admitted. Games (board games). Quiz (6.30pm 1st Mon of mth; £10 per team). Wine tasting (monthly; call for details). **Map p275 N6**.

Shaw's Booksellers

31-34 St Andrew's Hill, EC4V 5DE (7489 7999). St Paul's tube/Blackfriars tube/rail. **Open** noon-11pm Mon-Fri. **Food served** noon-3.30pm, 5-9pm Mon-Fri. **Credit** AmEx, DC, MC, V. Bar/Gastropub

regulars were celebrating a lottery win (how much money do these people need?) as we arrived. The pretty European staff are savvy enough to refuse drinks, amicably dispensing pints of Bombardier, San Miguel and Kronenbourg Blanc, bottles of Red Stripe and wine by the bucketload. Twenty wines come by the glass or bottle (Foundstone unoaked chardonnay £3.90/£15, Berton Vineyard Black shiraz £4.50/£17.95), and a select ten by the bottle (Fortia Châteauneuf-du-Pape £35, Domaine de la Rossignole Sancerre £24.95). Cocktails (Honey Royale with Krupnik, Jealous Lover with Woodford Reserve bourbon; both £7) are also available.
Disabled: toilet. Function room. Restaurant. TV (big screen). **Map p275 O6**.

Ochre

2-3 Creed Lane, EC4V 5BR (0871 223 5106). St Paul's tube/Blackfriars tube/rail. **Open** 11am-11pm Mon-Fri. **Food served** noon-3pm, 6-10pm Mon-Fri. **Credit** AmEx, MC, V. Bar
Falling between the stools of cool lounge destination and gastrobar, Ochre appeals to the kind of City workers who like to think of themselves as tuned in. It does nothing wrong, but there must have been a checklist of requirements when it was put together (loungey seats, institutional wooden furniture, picture windows, standard cocktails and shooters, bar food of the fish cake variety). Reasonable house wines, Trebbiano d'Abruzzo or Pasquiers shiraz, start at an equally reasonable £2.90/£12, but an Artesa Rioja (£3.70/£15) or a Taltami Estate sauvignon-semillon (£16.50) won't break the bank either. Southern European beers (draught San Miguel and Perretti, bottled Cruzcampo and Sol) are complemented by 20 standard cocktails and shooters.
Bar available for hire (weekends). Disabled: toilet. Function room. TV (big screen). **Map p275 O6**.

Shaw's is hard to categorise, being a great mix of pub, bar and eaterie. It's set in two adjoining areas: a sunken one for dining, and a drinking space with picture windows overlooking the incline of St Andrew's Hill. Here, a bar counter embellished with icons of baby-boom boyhood (Colin Bell, comics annuals) presents taps of Kirin Ichiban, Hoegaarden and Fuller's London Pride, Discovery and Honey Dew. Bottled Cruzcampo, Budvar, Singha and Asahi also feature. A big board of wines – Louis Latour chardonnay, Vita di Storie pinot grigio, Marqués de Griñón Rioja, Argentine Trivento pinot noir – stands beside a similar one keeping tabs on the Shaw's Premiership sweepstake. It's a place for regulars. Good whiskies (Ardbeg, Laphroaig) too.
Disabled: toilet. TV. **Map p275 O6.**

Tipperary
66 Fleet Street, EC4Y 1HT (7583 6470/www.tipperary pub.co.uk). Blackfriars tube/rail. **Open** 11am-11pm Mon-Fri; noon-6pm Sat, Sun. **Food served** 11am-10pm Mon-Fri; noon-5.30pm Sat, Sun. **Credit** AmEx, MC, V. Pub
London's first Irish pub is still pleasingly authentic. Built of brick in 1605, the then Boar's Head survived the Great Fire. It was given Gaelic touches by an Irish brewery chain in the early 1700s and renamed two centuries later by local print workers returning from the trenches. Dark and panelled, with shamrock motifs in the tiled floor and framed black and white images of Gaelic life on the wall, the Tip offers Irish stew, chicken boxty (both under £7) and portions of soda bread to complement the Caffrey's, Guinness, Abbot and Greene King IPA on draught. Hot drinks include Irish coffee with Jameson whiskey and a Baileys chocolate cup. A small room above the narrow main bar does its best to cope with the overflow.
Babies and children admitted. Function room. Games (fruit machine). TV. **Map p275 N6.**

Viaduct Tavern
126 Newgate Street, EC1A 7AA (7600 1863). St Paul's tube. **Open** 11am-11pm Mon-Fri. **Food served** noon-3pm Mon-Fri. **Credit** AmEx, MC, V. Pub
Built as a Victorian gin palace, this Fuller's pub has kept its classy interior hidden behind a dark, circular façade that tends to be ignored by passing traffic. Inside, the 16 stone heads around the ceiling represent the hanging judges of Newgate Prison, opposite. Friezes of virginal women in light, off-the-shoulder numbers cover one wall; mirrors are etched in 24-carat gold and silver. There's also an original till area, used for dispensing tokens when the gin-sozzled could only focus on the serving girl's cleavage. Suitably, a decent range of gins (Hendrick's, Plymouth, Quintessential Warrington) today complements the usual Fuller's draught options (London Pride, Discovery, Honey Dew) plus Grolsch and Hoegaarden. Fourteen wines include Gun Shearer shiraz (£21.50) and Domaine de Vauroux Chablis (£22).
Games (quiz machine). TV (widescreen). **Map p275 O6.**

Ye Olde Cheshire Cheese
145 Fleet Street, EC4A 2BU (7353 6170/www.yeolde cheshirecheese.com). Blackfriars tube/rail. **Open** 11am-11pm Mon-Sat; noon-6pm Sun. **Food served** noon-9.30pm Mon-Fri; noon-8.30pm Sat; noon-5pm Sun. **Credit** AmEx, DC, MC, V. Pub
This dark, historic warren of a pub does a roaring trade with tourists, but less lunchtime business than the many other pubs on this busy stretch of Fleet Street. Why is it less popular with locals now than when Dickens came

here? It could be the limits of the beer range (it's a Samuel Smith's pub), the guidebook-wielding Americans in attendance or a sprawling layout that incorporates a long descent to the Cellar Bar and a cramped entryway to the Chop Room. The YOCC is so sprawling, in fact, that staff need to use pagers to alert diners of their impending rustic platter (£3.95), chef's salad (£6.25-£6.75) or daily specials of cumberland sausage or scampi.
Babies and children admitted (restaurant). No piped music or jukebox. Restaurant. **Map p275 N6.**

Also in the area...
Corney & Barrow *3 Fleet Place, EC4M 7RD (7329 3141)* **Map p275 O6; 10 Paternoster Square, EC4M 7DX (7618 9520)** **Map p275 O6.** Branches.
Davy's *10 Creed Lane, EC4M 8SH (7236 5317).* Branch. **Map p275 O6.**
El Vino *30 New Bridge Street, EC4V 6BJ (7236 4534).* Branch. **Map p275 O6.**
Hodgsons *115 Chancery Lane, WC2A 1PP (7242 2836).* Branch of Jamies. **Map p275 N6.**
Jamies *34 Ludgate Hill, EC4M 7DE (7489 1938).* Branch. **Map p275 O6.**
La Grande Marque *47 Ludgate Hill, EC4M 7JU (7329 6709/www.lagrandemarque.co.uk).* Fine bar conversion in an old bank; under the same management as Temple. **Map p275 O6.**
Saint *Rose Street, Paternoster Square, EC4M 7DQ (7600 5500).* Branch of Jamies. **Map p275 O6.**
St Brides Tavern *Bridewell Place, EC4V 6AP (7353 1614).* Greene King pub boasting an elegant wood-panelled interior. **Map p275 O6.**

Liverpool Street & Moorgate

George
Great Eastern Hotel, 40 Liverpool Street, EC2M 7QN (7618 7400). Liverpool Street tube/rail. **Open** 7am-11pm Mon-Fri; 7.30am-10.30pm Sat, Sun. **Food served** 7-10am, noon-2.30pm, 6-9.30pm Mon-Fri; noon-5pm, 6-9pm Sat, Sun. **Credit** AmEx, DC, MC, V. Hotel bar
A two-room, high-ceilinged wood-panelled bar and adjoining restaurant, this is the public face of the Great Eastern Hotel beside Liverpool Street station. The cross of the saint in question features gratuitously: on the pub sign, the matchboxes, the staff uniforms (poor Antipodeans!), the ashtrays. But what's draught Beck's doing between the proud pumps of London Pride and Bombardier? A predictable selection of wines accompany meals – upscale dishes brought out on sturdy white plates, tucked into by smartly dressed members of middle management, making a good fist of being uncomfortably balanced on high stools and tables. A surprisingly upbeat soundtrack plays throughout, guitar-driven rock bouncing off the gilt-framed faux historic prints and Bishopsgate 1620 signs.
Babies and children admitted. **Map p277 R6.**

★ Golden Heart
110 Commercial Street, E1 6LZ (7247 2158). Liverpool Street tube/rail. **Open** 11am-11pm Mon-Sat; 11am-10.30pm Sun. **Credit** AmEx, MC, V. Pub
'Stand still and rot' flashes a sign in this place, a motto for the East End arty types who see it as a home from home. Sandra Esquilant's famed corner boozer has stood still since the 1970s, which is precisely why they like it. The mounted evidence mounts: the moustache worn by one half

Hawksmoor

of 'Mr and Mrs Dennis Esquilant', centrepiecing a Truman Pub of the Year 1983 poster, the Eagle Stout advertising, the neon Americana of the fluoro jukebox. And everyone knows the words to the Carpenters. This is retro at its most indulgent – and it's all marvellous fun. A big tap of Grolsch gets a daily caning, bottled choices include Peroni, Becks and Budvar, and unspecified wine flows like billy-o. *Babies and children welcome. Function room. Jukebox. Tables outdoors (4, pavement). TVs (big screen, satellite).* **Map p276 R5.**

Gramaphone
60-62 Commercial Street, E1 6LT (7377 5332/ www.thegramaphone.co.uk). Aldgate East tube/ Liverpool Street tube/rail. **Open** noon-midnight Mon-Thur; noon-3.30am Fri; 9pm-3.30am Sat. **Food served** noon-10pm Mon-Fri. **Credit** MC, V. Bar/Restaurant
Music powers the rather spiffy Gramaphone, with its DJ decks by the door, its decor and its savvy clientele. Surrounded by archive shots of the Who from the *My Generation* sleeve and the Stones looking commendably mean in a caff, punters gather in an airy space of sturdy furniture and scuffed floorboards. At the back, a large horseshoe bar is crowned by tall taps of Bitburger, Aspall Suffolk Cyder and Guinness; downstairs is a club. There are standard cocktails at £6, while daytime trade is encouraged by Thai curries, chicken satay and the like for around a fiver. Most of all, the Gramaphone – ignore the misspelling – is a trusty spot in which to jaw and jig, just within the Shoreditch orbit. We like it. *Babies and children admitted (until 7pm). Music (DJ 7pm Thur-Sat; bar free; club £5-£7).* **Map p278 S6.**

★ Hawksmoor NEW
157 Commercial Street, E1 6BJ (7247 7392/www.the hawksmoor.com). Liverpool Street tube/rail. **Open** noon-1am Mon-Sat. **Food served** noon-10pm Mon-Sat. **Credit** AmEx, DC, MC, V. Cocktail bar/Restaurant
Yes, there's a worthy selection of wines (six of each colour by the glass, 30 or so by the bottle) and assorted transatlantic bar snacks (macaroni cheese, grilled 'shrimp') but this American-inspired restaurant and bar exists primarily for its meat and its mixology. The former it does well, a selection of hefty cuts offered at around the £20 mark. The latter it does with excellence: the highlights of our last trip, a Tobacco Old Fashioned (£7.50), stirred relentlessly to marry its flavours of sugar, bitter orange and 'tobacco infusion' with a bourbon base, and an own-designed R&R Sour (£6.50), made with redcurrant, Aperol and egg white. As a standalone bar it's limited by space – much of the room is given over to dining tables. But there's a secluded mini-lounge at the back, and barmen are loud and characterful enough to make a plonk on a stool at the counter worthwhile too. Recommended. *Babies and children admitted. Disabled: toilet. Restaurant available for hire. Separate room for parties, seats 30.* **Map p276 R5.**

Poet
9-11 Folgate Street, E1 6BX (7426 0495). Liverpool Street tube/rail. **Open/food served** noon-11pm Mon-Fri; noon-10.30pm Sun. **Credit** MC, V. Pub/Bar
The Water Poet, as it's referred to on advertising boards in Bishopsgate and Folgate Street ('Voted the Best Bar Around!'), is a modern-styled destination for those looking to sink a few drinks and perhaps flirt with a few strangers

City

after a day of drudgery. Helping them in this task are Beck's Vier and Peetermans Artois; the latter's beer tap displays as much shiny metal as the old man-size scales by the bar. Erotic paintings and half a chair mounted on the red walls are an attempt to tick the box marked 'funky'. Still, Poet does the job of providing its punters with a lively opportunity for post-work play, either at the pool tables in a side room or the chat-up zone by the bar.

Babies and children welcome (until 9pm). Bar available for hire (Sat, Sun). Games (fruit machines, pool tables, table football). Restaurant. Tables outdoors (15, garden). TV (big screen, satellite). **Map p276 R5**.

St Paul's Tavern

56 Chiswell Street, EC1Y 4SA (7606 3828). Moorgate tube/rail. **Open** 11am-11pm Mon-Fri. **Food served** noon-9pm Mon-Thur; noon-6pm Fri. **Credit** AmEx, MC, V. Pub

This Greene King boozer – bearing the company's pub sign dated 1799 and boasting a brewing pedigree back to 1750 – is now dwarfed by a huge building site set up for office development in 2008. Nevertheless, a timeless boozer atmosphere reigns within the four-spaced, low-ceilinged cabin of a pub. House ales Morland Old Speckled Hen and Original and Greene King IPA are served over the cramped bar counter. Wines, cheap by the glass (none over £3.50), lend a fine lunchtime accompaniment to the house deli selections of warm camembert, grilled chicken breast and Wiltshire ham. More serious buffs can opt for a Chablis (£17.45) or Ropiteau Frères Fleurie (£17.95), the hungry a steak and ale pie or sausages and mash.

Bar available for hire. Games (golf machines). TVs. **Map p276 Q5**.

Ten Bells

84 Commercial Street, E1 6LY (7366 1721). Liverpool Street tube/rail. **Open** noon-midnight Mon-Wed, Sun; noon-1am Thur-Sat. **Credit** MC, V. Pub

Firmly on the Shoreditch circuit, this prominent stripped-down corner pub is now party central, a century or so after its clientele included Jack the Ripper's last victim enjoying her last drink. Press cuttings line the stairs to the toilets. They've kept the original tiling, but have played the alternative card by chucking in busted sofas, Bogarde-era cinema seats and a glitterball. Market traders from Spitalfields opposite avoid it, despite a fabulous selection of beers: Bombardier, Grolsch, Kronenbourg, John Smith's on draught; Baltika, Leffe, Bishops Finger and San Miguel by the bottle. Ask for a glass of wine and you'll get something equally quaffable. The monthly quiz night is taken as seriously as the need to look interesting.

Quiz (7pm 1st Mon of mth; £1). Tables outdoors (4, pavement).

Throgmorton's

27B Throgmorton Street, EC2N 2AN (7588 5165). Bank tube/DLR/Liverpool Street tube/rail. **Open** noon-9.30pm Mon; noon-11pm Tue-Thur; noon-midnight Fri. **Food served** noon-9pm Mon-Tue; noon-10pm Wed-Fri. **Credit** AmEx, MC, V. Bar

How this place must have looked in its prime… You pass the street-level café, descend a staircase befitting a Grand Tour hotel and enter the main bar. Expansive, tatty, dotted with Throgmorton crests, it now bears dinky modern lights and a contemporary ambient soundtrack. It's like seeing a once-proud public school tie blotted with gravy stains. Adjoining is a long gallery room; downstairs is a

Ballroom. *See p90.*

games room or 'sports bar'. The wide selection of draught beers – Erdinger, Beck's, Küppers Kölsch, Hoegaarden, Franziskaner, Adnams, Timothy Taylor Landlord – attracts ties-off blokes on long liquid lunches. Most of the 30 wines are available by the glass, with only one costing (just) over £4. The superior Domaine Molousson Vaucoupin, £38 a bottle, is probably neglected. *Babies and children admitted.* **Map p277 Q6.**

★ Vertigo 42

Tower 42, 25 Old Broad Street, EC2N 1HQ (7877 7842/www.vertigo42.co.uk). Bank tube/DLR/Liverpool Street tube/rail. **Open** *noon-3pm, 5-11pm Mon-Fri.* **Food served** *noon-2.15pm, 5-9.30pm Mon-Fri.* **Credit** *AmEx, DC, MC, V.* Bar
And you thought the view from Gary Rhodes's restaurant – 18 storeys down – was impressive. Situated on the 42nd floor of the tallest edifice in the City, Vertigo 42 enjoys a truly stunning London panorama. The suits, romantics and view-tourists who come here all react in much the same way – 'Blimey' (or something ruder). Visitors have to earn their vista: the check-in process, including X-ray machines and guest passes, is reminiscent of arrival at an airport. Thankfully, the bar itself no longer looks like the corresponding departure lounge – a thoughtful revamp means a new darker colour scheme to complement the floor-to-ceiling windows and the city-spread beyond. Champers is surely the only appropriate order; bottles start at £44 for Champagne de Castellane and rise to mighty heights of their own. Otherwise, there are cocktails (the likes of a kir royale or bellini, £11.50) and pricey bar snacks. With a bowl of olives at £3.95, this view don't come cheap – but it's a genuine London must-do.
Bar available for hire. Booking advisable. Dress: smart casual. **Map p277 Q6.**

Wall Bar

45 Old Broad Street, EC2N 1HU (7588 4845). Liverpool Street tube/rail. **Open** *noon-midnight Mon-Wed; noon-1am Thur, Fri.* **Food served** *noon-10pm Mon-Fri.* **Credit** *AmEx, DC, MC, V.* Gastropub
Under the same umbrella as the Livery off Cheapside, this terrace bar below Tower 42 makes up for its soulless concrete surroundings with reasonable cheer inside. Once under the red awnings, you're treated to the same extensive drinks menu as at the Livery: 30 wines, 20 cocktails and ten beers. White wines include a Seppelt chardonnay (£4.10/ £15.95) and a Babich sauvignon blanc (£4.70/£18.15); reds a Casillero del Diablo Carmenere (£4.85/£18.45) from Chile and a Côte de Brouilly (£5.85/ £22.45). Half the cocktails are also available by the jug, and include mixes such as a Lynchburg Lemonade with JD and a cosmopolitan with Absolut Citron. You'll find Asahi, Tiger and Leffe among the bottled beers.
Bar available for hire (weekends). Function room. Music (DJs 8pm Thur, Fri; free). Tables outdoors (15, terrace). TV (big screen, satellite). **Map p277 Q6.**

Also in the area...

Balls Brothers *158 Bishopsgate, EC2M 4LN (7426 0567)* **Map p277 R6;** *11 Blomfield Street, EC2M 1PS (7588 4643)* **Map p277 Q6;** *Gow's Restaurant, 81 Old Broad Street, EC2M 1PR (7920 9645)* **Map p277 Q6;** *38 St Mary Axe, EC3A 8EX (7929 6660)* **Map p277 R6.** Branches.
Bangers *Eldon House, 2-12 Wilson Street, EC2H 2TE (7377 6326).* Branch of Davy's. **Map p276 Q5.**

Booze talking
Golden Heart

City

You are?
Sandra Esquilant, landlady of the Golden Heart, Commercial Street.
How did you come to be the landlady here?
My husband and brother were interested and persuaded me to view the place. I remember that first day so well – I fell in love with the pub straight away, and I've never stopped having that feeling, even after 30 years. I eat, sleep and drink in my bar, it's my life. I don't even like leaving it to go on holiday.
You must have seen a lot of changes in the area during those 30 years?
Definitely. At one point everything closed and they pulled down half the market. My husband said we should go, but I said I'm not moving, no matter what. So I worked night and day here on my own for eight years. We're one of only two places around here that has survived.
Do you think you run your pub differently as a woman?
If you've got a licensed premises selling alcohol, you've got to take charge, no matter if you're a man or a woman. I've got eyes in the back of my head. If someone has had a bit too much, I'll politely ask them to leave. If I was tipsy somewhere, I'd want them to send me home to bed too! Though I don't drink myself... only very occasionally. You can't drink and run a pub because you have to be alert. I have tea instead. I drink 25 cups a day.
What does the future hold?
I never want to go anywhere else. I'm hoping my youngest daughter will take over. She used to help me when she was little (though I'd never let her in the pub when we were open). But even when she was ten, I said, 'She's got it, she could do this.'

scarlet
spice bar

the hottest spot
in spitalfields...

for power lunches, canapé platters, brunch,
Indian à la carte haute cuisine dining, fine wine & cocktails.

4 Crispin Sq, Crispin Place (off Lamb St), Spitalfield Market, London E1
Bookings 020 7375 0880 Opening Times Mon - Sun 10am till late
Website www.scarletdot.co.uk Email info@scarletdot.co.uk

THE HOT SPOT IN

Spitalfields
www.spitalfields.co.uk

Bishop of Norwich *91-93 Moorgate, EC2M 6SJ (7920 0857).* Branch of Davy's. **Map p277 Q5**.
Boisdale Bishopsgate *Swedeland Court, 202 Bishopsgate, EC2M 4NR (7283 1763/ www.boisdale.co.uk).* Branch of Boisdale. **Map p277 R5**.
City Boot *7 Moorfields High Walk, EC2Y 9DP (7588 4766).* Branch of Davy's. **Map p277 Q5**.
Corney & Barrow *19 Broadgate Circle, EC2M 2QS (7628 1251)* **Map p276 Q5**; *City Point, 1 Ropemaker Street, EC2Y 9HT (7382 0606)* **Map p276 Q5**; *5 Exchange Square, EC2A 2EH (7628 4367)* **Map p276 R5**; *11 Old Broad Street, EC2N 1AP (7638 9308)* **Map p277 Q6**. Branches.
Cuban *City Point, 1 Ropemaker Street, EC2Y 9AW (7256 2202/www.thecuban.co.uk).* Branch. **Map p276 Q5**.
Davy's *2 Exchange Square, EC2A 2EH (7256 5962).* Branch. **Map p277 R5**.
Jamies *155 Bishopsgate, EC2A 2AA (7256 7279).* Branch. **Map p277 R5**.
Jamies at the Pavilion *Finsbury Circus Gardens, EC2M 7AB (7628 8224).* Branch. **Map p277 Q5**.
King's Head *49 Chiswell Street, EC1Y 4SA (7606 9158).* Smart Greene King pub; three real ales. **Map p276 P5**.
Orangery *Cutlers Gardens, 10 Devonshire Square, EC2M 4TE (7623 1377).* Branch of Jamies. **Map p277 R6**.
Phoenix *26 Throgmorton Street, EC2N 2AN (7588 7289).* Airy, L-shaped pub with four real ales on tap. **Map p277 Q6**.

Mansion House, Monument & Bank

Ballroom NEW
34 Threadneedle Street, EC2R 8AY (7628 0001/ www.ballroom.uk.com). Monument tube/Bank tube/ DLR. **Open** noon-midnight Mon-Wed; noon-2am Thur, Fri. **Food served** noon-3pm, 6-9pm Mon-Fri. **Credit** AmEx, MC, V. Bar
A welcome addition to a dull City drinking scene, Ballroom is a professional cocktail bar that makes an equal fuss over its wines and food. The cocktails (£8.50-£9.50), some 30 in number, are mainly well-made classics (Stoli and Chambord in a french martini, Havana Club Especial in a daiquiri with fruity offshoots (vanilla mango martini with a Stoli Vanil, fresh mango purée and a dash of Galliano; fresh muddled blackberries in a Ballroom Bramble). Three £12.50 'signature' mixtures include a honeycomb margarita with Reserva de la Familia tequila, 100-old-year Grand Marnier and organic honeycomb from New Zealand. The 16 wines begin at a £5-a-glass Côte à Côte house red or white and move onto a Brouilly Mommessin Beaujolais (£28) and a Knappstein riesling (£29).
Music (DJs 8pm; free). **Map p277 Q6**.

★ Bar Bourse
67 Queen Street, EC4R 1EE (7248 2200/2211/ www.barbourse.co.uk). Mansion House tube. **Open** 11.30am-11pm Mon-Fri. **Food served** 11.30am-3pm. **Credit** AmEx, MC, V. Wine bar
The BB logo on the menus, matchboxes and door handles in this stylish basement stands for quality. First, the impeccable decor of striped banquettes and photographs of the Square Mile in all its pomp. Second, the wine list,

which features 20 each of reds and whites, including a Pouilly-Fumé Claude Michot (£6.50/£28) and a Chilean MontGras merlot reserva (£4.75/£18). There are half-bottles too – a Domaine des Valanges Burgundy (£14/£26) for example. Beers (Michelob, Tiger, Peroni, Budvar) are bottled. Light lunches, sandwiches and 'comfort food' such as Neal's Yard cheeses (£10) are well sourced and presented. The staff are sassy and dressed in black. You can even check the share prices on the TV.
Booking advisable. Off-licence. **Map p277 P7**.

Bell
29 Bush Lane, EC4R 0AN (7929 7772). Cannon Street tube/rail. **Open** 11am-10pm Mon-Fri. **Food served** noon-2.30pm Mon-Fri. **Credit** AmEx, MC, V. Pub
A traditional watering hole dating back to the days of the Great Fire, the Bell squeezes fine ales, sport on two TVs and busy lunchtime and post-work buzz into a jigsaw piece-shaped wooden interior. Sharp's Atlantic IPA, Young's, Timothy Taylor Landlord, Courage Best and Deuchars line the modest bar counter, beside which a chalked list of wines includes Pinehurst chenin blanc and El Coto Rioja. At lunch, the smell of onions hints at the pub grub selection, served until 2.30pm. Scenes of London, copper utensils and random heraldic devices compose an unpretentious decor, but the historic tone is set by the beamed ceiling and cramped feel – what shape *were* people in the old days? Fortunately, it's a friendly City crowd, so should shoulders brush or drinks be tipped, apologies are accepted with a smile.
TV (satellite). **Map p277 P7**.

★ Bonds Bar & Restaurant
Threadneedle Hotel, 5 Threadneedle Street, EC4R 8AY (7657 8088). Monument tube/Bank tube/DLR. **Open** 11am-11pm Mon-Fri; 10am-8pm Sat, Sun. **Food served** noon-2.30pm, 6-10pm Mon-Fri; 6-10pm Sat, Sun. **Credit** AmEx, DC, MC, V. Bar/Restaurant
The best bar in the City? All is as it should be: the attentive, black-shirted staff; the padded swivel bar-chairs; the reading lights over the bar; and, above all, the cocktails. Among the six dozen varieties (most costing £8-£10) there's a truffle martini using truffle liqueur, an Indian Touch with Stoli razberi and cardamom, and a Bison Kick with Zubrówka and kiwi syrup – divine. Staff are true pros; many have concocted creations good enough for inclusion on an already impressive menu and are credited accordingly. Meticulously selected wines include 16 by the glass, such as Hélène Perrot Chablis (£8.50) or Hawke's Bay Te Awa syrah (£9). The two bottled beers are Asahi and Lapin Kulta. Superior tapas (£3-£3.50) stretch to £22 land and sea platters. Pricey, but worth every shilling.
Babies and children welcome (restaurant). Disabled: toilet. Function rooms. Restaurant. **Map p277 Q6**.

Bow Wine Vaults
10 Bow Churchyard, EC4M 9DQ (7248 1121). Mansion House tube/Bank tube/DLR. **Open** 11am-11pm Mon-Fri. **Food served** noon-3pm Mon-Fri. **Credit** AmEx, DC, MC, V. Wine bar
This is not a lie: upon walking into this venerable establishment (purveyor of 60 fine wines, from a house red for £13.75 to an Amarone Classico 2000 Guerrieri Rizzardi for £65.50) they were playing 'Anarchy in the UK'. Apparently, even monied fortysomethings need a little attitude with their drinking. Inevitably, the mainly French labels available from the horseshoe bar counter in this cosy,

Gracechurch Street, EC3V 1LY (7283 7712).
Fuller's pub that claims to be the smallest in
the Square Mile. **Map p277 Q7.**
Walrus & Carpenter *45 Monument Street, EC3R
8BU (7621 1647/www.walrusandcarpenter.co.uk).*
Nicholson's pub, heavy with characterful tradition,
that serves London Pride, Young's, Adnams,
Marston's Pedigree, Old Speckled Hen and a guest
beer that regulars can vote for. **Map p277 Q7.**

Tower Hill & Aldgate

Poet
*82 Middlesex Street, E1 7EZ (7422 0000). Liverpool
Street tube/rail.* **Open** 11am-11pm Mon-Fri. **Food
served** noon-3pm Mon; noon-3pm, 5-9pm Tue-Fri.
Credit AmEx, DC, MC, V. Wine bar
This big, smart, slightly bland lounge bar near Petticoat
Lane gets its fair share of market traders and office workers, whose memory of their first job will no doubt be
blurred by too many evening sessions here on the lager or
under-a-tenner house wine. To be fair, the lager is Budvar,
supplemented ale-wise by Morland Original or Greene
King IPA, and the wine list is decent enough. Twenty
labels include a Sherwood Estate pinot noir (£18.50),
Domaine des Fines Caillottes Pouilly-Fumé (£22.95) and
Leredde Sancerre (£25.95). On our visit, all were being
offered, market-like, at a third off. The pool table, big-
screen sports and assorted events – poker, ladies' nights –
keep the punters entertained.
*Babies and children admitted (until 5pm). Bar available
for hire. Disabled: toilet. Games (darts). TVs (big screen,
satellite).* **Map p277 R6.**

Princess of Prussia
*15 Prescot Street, E1 8AZ (7480 5304). Aldgate
East or Tower Hill tube/Tower Gateway DLR.* **Open**
11am-midnight Mon-Fri. **Credit** MC, V. Pub
If it were located nearer the City, and not plopped in its current hinterland of faceless grey buildings, this fine pub
would clean up. Then again, you wouldn't find a spare spot
in its comfortable front bar, spacious back room (decorated with images of London and various battle scenes,
Sebastopol in particular) and back patio garden. But here
you can find your readily-available table and choose your
poison. It's a Shepherd Neame pub, so draught Master
Brew and Spitfire accompany Asahi, Holsten and
Guinness. As in other SN pubs, wines are provided
by Todd's, with Pascal Clement Pouilly-Fuissé (£20)
and Glen Carlos Tortoise Hill cabernet shiraz zinfandel
(£14) among the 15 selections. Some are available by the
glass – ask at the bar.
*Babies and children admitted. Games (quiz machine).
Tables outdoors (8, patio). TV.* **Map p278 S7.**

Still & Star
*1 Little Somerset Street, E1 8AH (7702 2899).
Aldgate tube.* **Open** 11am-11pm Mon-Fri.
Food served noon-4pm Mon-Fri. **Credit**
AmEx, MC, V. Pub
This funny little cabin gives the impression that everyone
is desperately sinking that last drink before the place is
knocked down to make way for the railway. The man with
the title deeds could walk in any minute, so the cluster of
customers clinging to the bar turn their heads as one, mid-
conversation, whenever a stranger walks in. To ward off

undesirables, a bloody big St George's flag fills several
windows upstairs. You won't interrupt the piano player,
only a game of darts (played with such proficiency that
a side area glimmers with silverware). Draught ales
like London Pride, Greene King IPA and Adnams push
the patriotism, as does an offer of pie, mash and – can it
really be true? – licor.
*Bar available for hire. Function room. Games (darts,
tournament 6.30pm Mon, Thur; fruit machines).
Tables outdoors (4, patio). TV.* **Map p278 S6.**

White Swan
*21-23 Alie Street, E1 8DA (7702 0448). Aldgate
tube/Tower Gateway DLR.* **Open** 11am-11pm
Mon-Fri. **Food served** noon-3pm Mon-Fri.
Credit AmEx, MC, V. Pub
Straying from the City into Jack the Ripper territory – note
the newspaper evidence in a pub otherwise mercifully free
of tat – you find this cosy outpost of the Shepherd Neame
stable. They even serve pots of tea. Regulars, who compose the bulk of the clientele, come here for a pint or two
of Master Brew, Spitfire and Porter, or draught Asahi,
Holsten and Oranjeboom. Wines include a Domaine de la
Bouronière Fleurie (£18) and a Château Terre Rouge
Medoc (£17.50); the handful available by the glass
are chalked up behind the bar. In keeping with the
understated surroundings, a simple selection of eats
centres on ciabatta sandwiches and the like; a daily menu
offers more filling grub.
Babies and children admitted. Games (quiz machine).
Map p278 S6.

Also in the area...
Balls Brothers *52 Lime Street, EC3M 7BS
(7283 0841)* **Map p277 R6**; *Mark Lane, EC3R
7BB (7623 2923).* **Map p277 R7.** Branches.
Brown Bear *139 Leman Street, E1 8EY
(7481 3792).* Relaxed pub serving London Pride,
Adnams and Cascade Pale Ale; a dartboard and
a retro Space Invaders machine keep regulars
happy. **Map p278 S7.**
City Flogger *Fen Court, 120 Fenchurch Street,
EC3M 5BA (7623 3251).* Branch of Davy's.
Map p277 R7.
Corney & Barrow *37A Jewry Street, EC3N 2EX
(7680 8550)* **Map p277 R7**; *1 Leadenhall Place,
EC3M 7DX (7621 9201)* **Map p277 R7.** Branches.
Crutched Friar *39-41 Crutched Friars, EC3N 2AE
(7264 0041).* Nicholson's pub with three ales on
tap and a back beer garden. Its modest L-shaped
interior of wood and red-brick alcoves and arches
fills quickly. **Map p277 R7.**
Davy's *Unit 8, Plantation Place, Mincing Lane,
EC3R 5AT (7621 9878).* Branch. **Map p277 R7.**
Fine Line *124-127 The Minories, EC3N 1NT
(7481 8195).* Branch. **Map p277 R7.**
Habit & New Waterloo Room *Friary Court,
65 Crutched Friars, EC3M 2RN (7481 1131).*
Branch of Davy's. **Map p277 R6.**
Jamies *107-112 Leadenhall Street, EC3A
4AA (7626 7226)* **Map p277 R6**; *119-121 The
Minories, EC3N 1DR (7709 9900)* **Map p277 R7.**
Branches.
Vineyard *International House, 1 St Katherine's
Way, E1W 9UN (7480 6680).* Branch of Davy's.
Map p278 S7.
Willy's *107 Fenchurch Street, EC3M 5JF (7480
7289).* Branch of Jamies. **Map p277 R7.**

West

West

No wonder the denizens of W11 often seem smug: Notting Hill has nurtured a spate of quality bars over recent years, including newcomer **Montgomery Place**. Established boho boozers like **Portobello Gold** bring up the rear. In Ladbroke Grove, residents can feel equally smug with two fine new pubs – the gastro-leaning **Fat Badger** and the music-leaning **Pelican**. Holland Park boasts a fine outdoor drinking spot at the **Ladbroke Arms**; Westbourne Grove makes do with its fine gastropubs the **Cow** and **Prince Bonaparte**.

West to Shepherd's Bush, the **Havelock Tavern** is back after closure last year through fire damage; Hammersmith still has the excellent historic boozer the **Dove**. In Acton, the **George & Dragon** has been thoughtfully refurbished in association with English Heritage; Chiswick gastropub the **Swan** needed no such change, and still serves some of the best grub in the area.

Back near central London, Maida Vale's old gin palace **Prince Alfred** continues to impress, though newcomer the **Skiddaw** is certainly worth a stop-in too. But Bayswater has few such decent options – at a push we favour pleasant corner-pub the **Victoria**.

Acton

George & Dragon [NEW]

183 High Street, W3 9DJ (8992 3712/www.thegeorge anddragonacton.com). Acton Central tube/rail. **Open** noon-11.30pm Mon-Wed, Sun; noon-midnight Thur-Sat. **Food served** noon-10pm daily. **Credit** MC, V. Pub
Once a dingy old man's pub at the front and a dingy old

man's club at the back, this historic boozer – dating from 1529 – was refurbished in 2006 in association with English Heritage. The front room still performs its traditional role as pub, with dark mahogany boards and an enormous portrait on one wall facing off against a disarming gold bust of an African colonial on the other ('We're still waiting for someone to come in and tell us who he is,' said a barman). The back room, hidden from view unless you venture through the dining area, is a more spacious bar, its own statues wrapped in twinkly fairy lights. Two bitters – London Pride and Gales HSB – plus draughts of Fuller's Honey Dew, Paulaner and Litovel keep Acton's beer lovers happy. A placard lists all the pub's landlords 'since records began' in 1769: a fine history for all to see.
Babies and children welcome (until 9pm): high chairs. Bar available for hire. Games (board games). Quiz (8pm Mon; £2).

★ Grand Junction Arms

Acton Lane, NW10 7AD (8965 5670). Harlesden tube. **Open** *Front bar* 11am-midnight Mon-Sat; noon-10.30pm Sun. *Back bar* noon-3pm, 6pm-midnight Mon-Fri; noon-midnight Sat; noon-10.30pm Sun. **Food served** noon-3pm, 6-9pm Mon-Fri; noon-9pm Sun. **Credit** MC, V. Pub
Among the insalubrious industrial estates, this is a delicious surprise. The front bar is the most popular, allowing you to gaze over the canal when you tire of shooting pool on one of three tables by the open fireplace. A small lounge area with comfy chesterfields and potted plants leads into a larger room with wooden beams, pictures of barges and gilt-edged mirrors. Best of all is the tripartite beer garden: a decked balcony overlooks a pleasant canalside spot, with a further grassy area at the back overseen by a flat roof from which DJs play in summer. There's jazz on a Sunday afternoon and steak nights on Thursday. Decent Young's ales and Staropramen are the best of the draught choices.
Babies and children admitted (until 7pm). Disabled: toilet. Games (fruit machines, 3 pool tables). Music (3pm Sun; free). Tables outdoors (20, garden). TVs (widescreen).

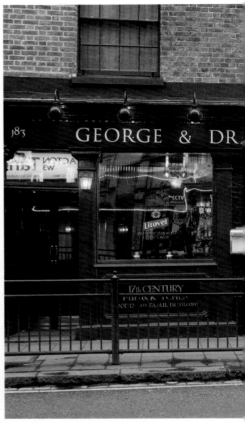

Bayswater

Elbow Room
*103 Westbourne Grove, W2 4UW (7221 5211).
Bayswater or Notting Hill Gate tube.* **Open/food
served** noon-11pm Mon-Sat; noon-10.30pm Sun.
Credit MC, V. Pool bar
Since spawning this simple concept more than a decade
ago, this bar-cum-pool hall has seen the family spread to
Shoreditch and Islington, Bristol and Leeds. This
Westbourne Grove original set the trend, though, the
authentic model being predominately purple and American
in style. Seven full-sized tables ensure a good evening's
entertainment, although it's pretty busy at weekends and
competition nights (7pm Monday). Large drape curtains
separate the baize action from the comfortable booths,
where you can sip a draught Korenwolf or a decent bottle
of La Roche viognier (£12). There's a long list of cocktails
and shooters, including a watermelon martini for £5.90.
Food is of the superior burger and bar snacks variety,
broadening the appeal to both sexes.
*Bar available for hire. Games (7 pool tables; call for
details of competitions). Music (DJs 8pm Sat; free).
TV (big screen).* **Map p279 B6.**

Harlem
*78 Westbourne Grove, W2 5RT (7985 0900/www.
harlemsoulfood.com). Bayswater or Notting Hill Gate
tube.* **Open** noon-1.30am Mon-Fri; 10am-2am Sat;
10am-10.30pm Sun. **Food served** noon-midnight
Mon-Fri; 10am-midnight Sat; 10am-10.30pm Sun.
Credit AmEx, DC, MC, V. Bar/Diner
'Harlem, Here to Serve' says the motto on the shirts of the
sullen staff. Here to Stand Around is more like it. The slow
and inattentive service is frustrating because the menus,
both food and drink, are so enticing. You can hardly wait
for your Harlem Favourite cocktail (£7.50) to arrive, one of
eight elaborately described; there's also a New York Sour
with Kentucky bourbon, a mai tai made according to
Trader Vic's 1944 recipe, Dale DeGroff's cosmopolitan or
Dick Bradsell's Bramble. Food-wise, you're looking at bar-
becued chicken, racks of baby back ribs and bloody big
brunches. Downstairs, in the DJ den, owner Arthur Baker
spins regularly. This intimate joint should be great, a genuine destination. Instead, you just get fed up waiting for
that cocktail to appear.
*Babies and children welcome: children's menu; high
chairs. Music (DJs 10pm Thur-Sat; £10 after 11pm).
Takeaway service.* **Map p279 B6.**

George & Dragon. *See p95.*

Island Restaurant & Bar

Royal Lancaster Hotel, Lancaster Terrace, W2 2TY
(7551 6070/www.islandrestaurant.co.uk). Lancaster
Gate tube. **Open** noon-11pm daily. **Food served**
noon-10.30pm daily. **Credit** AmEx, DC, MC, V.
Hotel bar/Restaurant
With the reopening of Lancaster Gate tube, the Island is
again accessible as a destination bar to all-comers, not just
guests of the Royal Lancaster Hotel. Set on the first floor,
next to the restaurant, the bar is sleek and contemporary
in style, with large windows overlooking the varying
coloured foliage of Hyde Park. The cocktail menu, likewise,
changes with the seasons. A quality selection (£6.50-£7.50)
numbers 50 concoctions. Henriot Souverain champers tops
a French 75 with Plymouth gin and a British 75 with
Hendrick's; Maker's Mark is the bourbon in the whisky
sour, and Ketel One, Zubrówka and Bombay Sapphire are
in the martini mixes. Most of the 20 well-chosen wines
come by the glass – including Hawkes Bay Trinity Hill
pinot gris (£8.50/£34) and Treehouse pinot noir (£8/£33).
In the restaurant proper, diners enjoy poshed-up versions
of burgers and fish and chips (around £12).
Babies and children welcome: high chairs.
Disabled toilet.

Mad Bishop & Bear

Upper Concourse, Paddington Station, Praed Street,
W2 1HB (7402 2441). Paddington tube/rail. **Open**
8am-11pm Mon-Wed, Sat; 8am-11.30pm Thur, Fri;
8am-11pm Sat; 9am-10.30pm Sun. **Food served**
9am-9pm Mon-Sat; 8.30am-9pm Sun. **Credit** AmEx,
DC, MC, V. Pub
One of the better railway station pubs, set amid the bland
shining chrome of Paddington's upper-floor concourse, this
Fuller's hostelry is a functional, high-ceilinged place where
sports fans gather before a train to south Wales or the West
Country. St Austell Tribute, Strongbow and Grolsch complement the usual brewery range (ESB, Discovery, London
Pride, Chiswick) on draught. A short and simple wine selection includes a tenner-a-bottle Chilean Don Segundo merlot as well as a Conway Hills pinot noir (£18) and Domaine
de Vauroux Chablis (£21.35). Breakfasts, ciabattas, home-
made pies (steak and Fuller's ale, chicken and leek) and ribeye steaks are brought out to numbered tables. All is
played out to a soundtrack of drivetime classics. By no
means a bad place to waste time, waiting on a choo-choo.
Babies and children admitted (until 9pm). Disabled: lift.
Games (fruit machines). Tables outdoors (8, terrace).
TV (widescreen).

Mitre

24 Craven Terrace, W2 3QH (7262 5240). Lancaster Gate tube/Paddington tube/rail. **Open** 11am-11pm Mon-Thur; 11am-11.30pm Fri, Sat; noon-10.30pm Sun. **Food served** noon-3pm, 6-10pm Mon-Fri; noon-9pm Sat; noon-8pm Sun. **Credit** AmEx, MC, V. Pub

Decent ales and comfortable, dark wood surroundings are the attractions of this free house on a quiet residential street. Taps of Hardys & Hansons Olde Trip and Hogs Back Hop Garden Gold, plus Bombardier and London Pride, are dispensed from the long, sturdy bar counter, along with San Miguel and Red Stripe lagers. A Henri Bourgeois Sancerre Blanc (£6.20/£24), a Balgownie Estate Yarra Valley pinot noir (£4.45/£17.65) and a Sicilian Nero d'Avola (£4.20/£16.50) are the highlights of a near 20-strong wine selection by the bottle and glass. Chesterfields crown a back area designed for hushed conversation or newspaper perusal. The open fire is an added draw.
Babies and children admitted (separate room). Function room. Tables outdoors (8, pavement). TV.

Royal Exchange

26 Sale Place, W2 1PU (7723 3781). Paddington tube/rail. **Open** 11am-11pm Mon-Sat; noon-10.30pm Sun. **Food served** noon-10pm daily. **Credit** AmEx, MC, V. Pub

This quiet corner pub hides a hive of activity centred on the horse-racing industry. Form is fervently studied beneath a phalanx of flatscreen TVs switching from course to course, thoroughbreds are celebrated in painting and caricature, while a somewhat fanciful image in the con-spiratorial back room depicts a winner cantering past the winning post of the pub itself. To aid concentration and gambling chatter, Timothy Taylor Landlord, Murphy's, Brakspear, Somerset cider and Guinness are served on tap – the slight Irish slant is due to the pub's long-term own-ership. Roast Limerick ham is one of several sandwiches on offer; there's salt beef on Fridays. House wines are cheap (£2.25/£6.95), but if you're celebrating victory on the ponies, you might stretch to a bottle of Moët (£35).
Babies and children admitted (outdoors). Tables outdoors (4, pavement). TV (satellite, digital).

Steam

1 Eastbourne Terrace, W2 1BA (7850 0555). Paddington tube/rail. **Open** noon-midnight Mon-Thur; noon-3am Fri, Sat. **Food served** 11am-11pm Mon-Sat. **Admission** £5 after 11pm Mon-Thur; £10 after 11pm Fri, Sat. **Credit** AmEx, DC, MC, V. Cocktail bar

Attached to both Paddington station and the Hilton hotel, Steam pushes the boat out to offer an extensive selection of imaginative, contemporary cocktails of quality and dis-tinction. Around a smart, spacious interior – equipped with a long, stone bar counter, and decked out with arty black and white photographs of London scenes – well-mixed con-coctions (£7-£9) feature high-end labels and fresh fruits. Muddled green seedless grapes combine with Sauza Hornitos tequila in a Johnny Vaughan; maraschino cher-ries mingle with Finlandia cranberry in a North West 05; and the cachaça in the organic mango caipirinha has been infused with the fruit of the same name. Wines such as a Casa La Joya chardonnay (£5.50/£17.50) and a Raimat Clamor (£6/£21) complement draught Leffe and Stella, and bottled Asahi and Peroni.
Bar available for hire. Disabled: toilet (in hotel). Music (DJs 10pm Fri, Sat). Restaurant. TV (big screen, satellite).

Victoria

10A Strathern Place, W2 2NH (7724 1191). Lancaster Gate tube/Paddington tube/rail. **Open** 11am-11pm Mon-Sat; noon-10.30pm Sun. **Food served** noon-9.30pm Mon-Sat; noon-9pm Sun. **Credit** AmEx, MC, V. Pub

The queen in question looks disdainfully from her sign on to a mini roundabout beside this stately pub, a favourite with Churchill, Dickens, the Dracula Society and sundry debating and speaking clubs. 'Accommodating' would best describe the place, with its fireplaces at each end of a cosy interior lined with historic prints, and tables outside. The Fuller's beer range (Chiswick, Discovery, London Pride) is complemented by a guest ale, usually Gales (now under the Fuller's umbrella). The 14-strong wine list, including eight by the glass, features a Château de Fayolle sauvi-gnon-semillon for around £13 a bottle, as well as a Château Grand Renouil Canon-Fronsac (£22.50) and a Domaine de Durand Sancerre (£18.95). Superior pub food is served well into the evening.
Function rooms. Quiz (9pm Tue; £1). Tables outdoors (7, terrace). TV.

Also in the area...

Gyngleboy *27 Spring Street, W2 1JA (7723 3351).* Branch of Davy's.
Salt Whisky Bar *82 Seymour Street, W2 2JB (7402 1155/www.saltbar.com).* Contemporary spirits bar offering 200 whiskies, bourbons and Japanese labels you didn't know existed. Warning: it gets rowdier than the drinks list would have you expect.

Chiswick

Bollo

13-15 Bollo Lane, W4 5LR (8994 6037). Chiswick Park tube. **Open** noon-11pm Mon-Sat; noon-10.30pm Sun. **Food served** noon-10.30pm daily. **Credit** AmEx, MC, V. Gastropub

Tucked down a residential backstreet, this well-respected pub and dining room seems to have settled for a typical gastro menu rather than the more adventurous cooking that greeted our previous visits; on our Monday visit, tables were full thanks to an offer that sees mains reduced to half-price. The punters – covering a range of ages but uniformly well heeled – get to enjoy candlelight, the ministrations of attentive staff and the scent of the flower arrangements dotted around the L-shaped dining area. There's a popu-lar quiz night on Wednesday, and a roadside terrace for warmer evenings. You can sample Abbot, Greene King IPA, Budvar and Hoegaarden on draught, or choose from an extensive wine list that includes bottles from Portugal and Sardinia for around £20.
Babies and children admitted. Quiz (8pm Wed; £1). Tables outdoors (12, terrace).

George IV `NEW`

185 Chiswick High Road, W4 2DR (8994 4624/www. georgeiv.co.uk). South Acton rail/Turnham Green tube. **Open** 11.30am-11pm Mon-Thur; 11.30am-midnight Fri, Sat; 11.30am-10.30pm Sun. **Food served** noon-3pm, 6-10pm Mon-Sat; noon-3pm Sun. **Credit** AmEx, DC, MC, V. Pub

Voted Fuller's pub of the year twice in a row, this broad-fronted old boozer has its biggest asset in the building that adjoins it to the rear: the Headliners comedy club, which

has hosted the likes of Al Murray, Harry Hill, Bill Bailey and Ed Byrne. The pub can get very busy, especially when there's a big match on, although the dark wood, semi-partitioned areas with comfy leather bench seats that are dotted around offer a degree of seclusion. As you'd expect, there's an impressive range of Fuller's ales, including Pride, ESB, Discovery and Honey Dew, as well as HSB and Swing Low from Gales, Leffe and Hoegaarden. Back in 1838, the pub manager ran an omnibus service to the City; sadly, these days you'll have to make your own way.
Babies and children admitted. Comedy (9pm Fri, Sat; £10). Disabled: toilet. Games (darts). Salsa classes (8pm, 9pm Tue; £6). Tables outdoors (8, garden). TVs.

Mawson Arms
110 Chiswick Lane South, W4 2QA (8994 2936). Turnham Green tube. **Open** 11am-8pm Mon-Fri. **Food served** noon-3pm Mon-Fri. **Credit** MC, V. Pub
The Mawson Arms is a 15-minute hike from Turnham Green tube towards the roar of the A4, and it closes at 8pm. So why would anyone bother coming here? For the ale, quite simply. This Fuller's pub sits right next door to its parent brewery, so its selection of the company's beer is unparalleled: broad and impeccably served. Expect London Pride, Chiswick, ESB, Discovery and Honey Dew on draught, as well as 1845, Swing Low, Golden Pride and London Porter by the bottle. The boozer itself doesn't indulge in many frills, with plain wooden tables and chairs, two open fires and portraits of the brewery's founders: Fuller, Smith and Turner. This is also the starting point for the brewery tour.
Function room. TV.

Old Pack Horse
434 Chiswick High Road, W4 5TF (8994 2872). Chiswick Park tube. **Open** 11am-11pm Mon-Thur; 11am-midnight Fri, Sat; 11am-10.30pm Sun. **Food served** noon-10pm Mon-Sat; noon-9pm Sun. **Credit** AmEx, MC, V. Pub
This imposing four-storey building contains a solid, down-to-earth boozer that's one of the best on Chiswick's main drag. Although it's a spacious place, it has a cosy, old-fashioned feel, with comfortable leather seats, an open fire and old black and white photos of Chiswick High Road alongside posters of the Empire. There are three sectioned-off snugs around the central bar; the rear has been turned into a Thai restaurant, with exotic fauna hanging beneath a large skylight. As you'd expect from a Fuller's pub, there's a great choice of draught ales, including London Pride, ESB and Discovery, and seasonal beer Swing Low from Gales. Leffe is the best lager on offer, although Franziskaner and Belle-Vue Kriek stand out among the bottled options.
Babies and children admitted (restaurant). Games (fruit machines). Tables outdoors (6, pavement; 5, garden).

Pilot
56 Wellesley Road, W4 4BZ (8994 0828). Gunnersbury tube/rail. **Open** noon-11pm Mon-Sat; noon-10.30pm Sun. **Food served** noon-3pm, 6.30-10pm Mon-Fri; noon-10pm Sat; noon-9.30pm Sun. **Credit** AmEx, MC, V. Bar
This upbeat bar is far removed from the usual Fuller's hostelry, edging closer to gastropub territory with its candlelit wooden tables and cream walls adorned with film posters and starlet portraits. The clientele are a mix of well-heeled young locals and professionals, most enjoying a well-balanced menu of Modern British and European

Booze talking
Nag's Head

You are?
Kevin Moran, landlord of the Nag's Head, SW1.
Tell us how you came to be landlord here.
I used to be an actor – not a very secure job – then one day I helped out a friend in his pub and caught the bug. My friends didn't think the Nag's Head was right for me, but I took a chance and I've been here for 25 years.
You don't allow mobiles to be used in the pub.
No. I'm very strict about it. I don't want to listen to someone yabbering away on their phone – it's antisocial. Tell them to meet you here if they want to speak to you.
You're known for your strong opinions...
People should be allowed to smoke in pubs! I'd give up serving food here so that people could carry on smoking. It's part of the place.
And you removed the free house sign outside.
Yes, I did. I replaced it with my name. What is a free house nowadays? There are too many places run by breweries that are pretending to be free houses. Even small chains have to serve certain drinks because they get such big discounts on them. I'm one of the few landlords who chooses the drinks that are served.
Would you say you're a tough landlord?
If you misbehave, you're out. If you behave and enjoy yourself, I'll give you my all. An English pub used to have the character of the landlord or landlady, but they've become so commercialised now...
Who drinks here?
We have about ten real regulars, a couple of whom are homeless. Otherwise, customers are office workers, people from the nearby embassies or tourists. Richard Harris used to come in too; I've got a poem of his on the wall.
Can you imagine yourself doing anything else?
No, I'd be bored. This is my life. For me behind a bar is the same as standing on the boards in the West End.

George IV. *See p98.*

dishes, washed down with a bottle of Conway Hills sauvignon blanc (£18.50) or a Brouilly Château de Nervers Beaujolais (£20). On draught there's London Pride, Honey Dew, Leffe and Kirin, while the bottles include Schneider Weisse, Discovery and Goose Island. At the back is a sheltered courtyard, which gets packed on summer weekends. *Babies and children admitted (until 7pm). Disabled: toilet. Function room. Tables outdoors (12, garden).*

Roebuck NEW
122 Chiswick High Road, W4 1PU (8995 4392). Turnham Green tube. **Open** 11am-11pm Mon-Sat; noon-10.30pm Sun. **Food served** noon-10.30pm Mon-Sat; noon-10pm Sun. **Credit** AmEx, DC, MC, V.
Gastropub
Part of a small but growing gastropub chain that now includes the Queen's in Crouch End and Lots Road in Chelsea, the Roebuck is in many ways just another formula gastropub – albeit executed to a better than usual standard. The dark wood floor, big leather sofas and spacious feel create a comfortable, very English aesthetic. The waiting staff are well-spoken young Englishmen with well-defined cheekbones – you might just as easily expect them to be talking shares, sports cars or sailboarding holidays. To drink, there's Bombardier or Eagle IPA, plus an extensive selection of wines grouped by style, with more than a dozen by the glass. Even if it feels a bit like a blueprint rolled out, the Roebuck is worth a look.
Babies and children welcome: children's menu, high chairs. Disabled: toilet. Tables outdoors (14, garden; 3, pavement).

Sam's Brasserie & Bar
11 Barley Mow Passage, W4 4PH (8987 0555/www. samsbrasserie.co.uk). Chiswick Park or Turnham Green tube. **Open** 9am-midnight Mon-Thur, Sun; 9am-12.30am Fri, Sat. **Food served** 9am-3pm, 6.30-10.30pm Mon-Sat; 9am-3pm, 6.30-10pm Sun. **No credit cards.** Bar/Brasserie
This Time Out award-winning bar and brasserie is on the site of a former paper factory. The warehouse-style space has a smart industrial feel, with visible iron girders and ventilation pipes. To the right of the entrance is the long rectangular bar, opposite rows of tables with leather seating under giant lampshades. There's an extensive list of cocktails (try a strawberry, honey and lavender martini, £6.50) as well as a 60-strong wine list, which includes a New Zealand sauvignon blanc from Seresin, Marlborough (£26) or a Chilean Viña Mar Reserva Casablanca Valley pinot noir (£19). The larger dining area (serving brasserie classics) is separated from the bar by a stack of hollow cubes filled with books and plants, proffering views into a vibrant kitchen through a rectangular slot.
Babies and children welcome: children's menu; high chairs; toys. Booking advisable Thur-Sat. Disabled: toilet. Music (jazz 7pm occasional Sun).

★ Swan
Evershed Walk, 119 Acton Lane, W4 5HH (8994 8262). Chiswick Park tube/94 bus. **Open** 5-11pm Mon-Fri; noon-11pm Sat; noon-10.30pm Sun. **Food served** 7-10.30pm Mon-Fri; 12.30-3pm, 7-10.30pm Sat; 12.30-3pm, 7-10pm Sun. **Credit** MC, V. Gastropub
Tucked away in a residential backstreet, this welcoming gastropub serves some of the best food in Chiswick. The smaller bar area has well-worn leather sofas next to a gas fire, while the larger dining area features quaint rickety furniture and dim lighting. Picture windows means there's

plenty of light during the day, and a good-sized patio garden makes this a top spot in warmer weather. The friendly, attentive bar staff serve a good pint of ale (London Pride, Deuchars IPA and Timothy Taylor Landlord), while lager drinkers get draught Hoegaarden or San Miguel. The 35-strong wine list is chalked on blackboards: try a Franz Haas pinot nero or a La Rocca Soave (both £26). Excellent. *Babies and children admitted (until 7pm). Tables outdoors (30, garden).*

Also in the area...
Raven *375 Goldhawk Road, W6 0SA (8748 6977).* Comfortable, worn-in pub with a lively atmosphere and sheltered garden area. The shelf-length of whiskies should impress fans.

Ealing

Baroque
94 Uxbridge Road, W13 8RA (8567 7346/www. baroque-ealing.co.uk). West Ealing rail. **Open** noon-11pm Mon-Thur; noon-2am Fri, Sat; noon-10.30pm Sun. **Food served** noon-3pm, 6-10pm Mon-Sat; noon-5pm Sun. **Credit** MC, V. Cocktail bar
The Manhattan skyline is emblazoned behind the counter of this trendy little bar, opposite the space-age white cushioning on the walls of the dining area. There's a New Zealand slant to the drinks (try a Kiwi Kiss of vodka, kiwi fruit, schnapps, kiwi syrup, lime cordial and apple juice for £6) and the food (including Maori dishes), and there's usually a smattering of Antipodeans among the clientele of upwardly mobile twentysomethings. The beer selection is unimaginative, but there's an extensive range of cocktails and a good wine list (Whites Bay pinot noir, £23; Amor Bendall pinot gris, £25) and a garden to sip them in. Entertainment includes jazz (Thursday and Friday evenings, Sunday lunch) and funky house DJs (every second Saturday).
Babies and children admitted (Mon-Thur, Sun). Music (DJs/jazz 10pm Thur-Sat, 1pm Sun; free). Tables outdoors (5, garden).

Castlebar
84 Uxbridge Road, W13 8RA (8567 3819/www.castle bar.co.uk). Ealing Broadway or West Ealing tube. **Open** 11am-12.30pm Mon-Wed, Sun; 10am-1am Thur-Fri; 11am-1am Sat; 11am-midnight Sun. **Food served** 10am-10pm Mon-Fri; 11am-10pm Sat, Sun. **Credit** AmEx, DC, MC, V. Gastrobar
This funky gastrobar banned indoor smoking 18 months before the ban came in, so had plenty of time to come up with a ploy to appeal to London's remaining puffers: they've joined together four large outdoor canopies and filled them with heaters. Inside, there's an Irish lilt to the main bar, with Gaelic slogans on mirrors and signs. Adnams Best and Broadside, Leffe and Hoegaarden on draught are backed up by a long list of house and traditional cocktails (£5.50-£6.50); the well-prepared Modern European cuisine can be washed down with the help of an extensive wine list that includes a crisp Rully Chartron et Trébuchet chardonnay (£20.50). Since our last visit, the music has relaxed somewhat, drawing in a slightly older crowd of sophisticated thirtysomethings. Host Abel and his staff offer table service for drinks – a friendly touch. *Babies and children admitted (until 6pm). Disabled: toilet. Tables outdoors (17, garden). TV.*

West

Drayton Court

2 The Avenue, W13 8PH (8997 1019). West Ealing rail. **Open** 11am-11pm Mon-Tue; 11am-midnight Wed-Sat; noon-11pm Sun. **Food served** noon-3pm, 5-9pm Mon-Fri; noon-9pm Sat, Sun. **Credit** MC, V. Pub
This 19th-century hotel is now a massive Fuller's boozer. The main bar alone is about the size of a normal pub, so finding a seat is never a problem. Adjoining it is a quiet, sitting room (with open fire and sink-in sofas); there's also a sports bar, noisier than the other rooms, with big TVs and lively pool matches. At the back a terrace overlooks what might well be the largest beer garden in London – it must be about the size of a football pitch. The well-kept draught ales include the normal Fuller's range (ESB, London Pride, Chiswick, Discovery) plus seasonal brews, while Grolsch and Staropramen are the best of the mostly nitro-keg lagers. There are also quiz nights, salsa and other dance classes, and sporadic comedy evenings.
Babies and children welcome (until 9pm): children's menu. Comedy (8.30pm alternate Fri; £6-£9). Disabled: toilet. Dance classes (lindehop 8pm Mon; salsa 8pm Thur). Function room. Games (pool). Music (jazz 8pm 3rd or last Wed of mth; free). Quiz (9pm Tue; £1). Tables outdoors (40, garden). TVs (big screen, satellite).

Ealing Park Tavern

222 South Ealing Road, W5 4RL (8758 1879). South Ealing tube. **Open** 6-11pm Mon; noon-11pm Tue-Sat; noon-10.30pm Sun. **Food served** 6-10pm Mon; noon-3pm, 6-10pm Tue-Sat; noon-3.45pm, 6-9.30pm Sun. **Credit** AmEx, MC, V. Gastropub
Formerly a student pub called the Penny Flyer, this beautiful old building is probably breathing a sigh of relief since its proprieters decided to go gastro some years back. During the day natural light streams through large windows, illuminating an attractive, understated interior of wood panels, squidgy sofas and roaring open fires. Lamps, rugs and urns containing plants complete the aesthetic. There are three indoor sections – a main bar, smaller standing area and a wood-beamed dining room whose bustling open kitchen turns out Mod European food – plus a spacious garden with concrete tables. A good range of ales and lagers are on offer at the zinc-topped bar, among them Greene King IPA, Tribute, Ruddles County and Wadworth 6X, Leffe, Hoegaarden and Amstel.
Babies and children welcome (until 9pm): high chairs. Music (jazz alternate Wed; free). Restaurant available for hire. Tables outdoors (25, garden).

Red Lion

13 St Mary's Road, W5 5RA (8567 2541). South Ealing tube. **Open** 11am-11pm Mon-Wed; 11am-midnight Thur-Sat; noon-11pm Sun. **Food served** noon-3pm, 7-9.30pm Mon-Sat; 12.30-5pm Sun. **Credit** AmEx, MC, V. Pub
For generations, actors and technicians from the nearby Ealing Studios have considered this cosy little pub their 'Stage Six' (the studios were numbered one to five); there's a modest plaque commemorating this endorsement by the door. The walls are crammed with photographs and posters from the studio's heyday; today's incumbents fill the standing space, joining local eccentrics after work for a restorative tipple. Food is of the comforting, home-cooked variety, to be swilled down with a Fuller's ale from the bar: Chiswick, London Pride, ESB, Discovery, Organic Honey Dew and regular seasonal brews, such as Old Winter Ale. The outdoor area has been thoughtfully landscaped.
Disabled: toilet. Tables outdoors (15, garden).

Fat Badger. *See p108.*

Hammersmith

Blue Anchor
13 Lower Mall, W6 9DJ (8748 5774). Hammersmith tube. **Open** 11am-11pm Mon-Sat; noon-10.30pm Sun. **Food served** noon-3pm, 6-9pm daily. **Credit** AmEx, MC, V. Pub
Despite coming under new ownership last year, this charming little 18th-century pub near Hammersmith Bridge has retained its olde worlde charm. Every nook and cranny is filled with military and boating knick-knacks, including helmets, gas masks and upside-down rowing boats suspended from the ceiling. Gustav Holst, longtime local resident, supposedly wrote his *Hammersmith* here in 1930. The best options on draught are Brakspear Special, London Pride and Peetermans; the bottled choices are limited. The wine list is also basic but the quality is good: Viña Alcorta Rioja at £14.75 or Anapi River sauvignon blanc at £16.50. Champagne is available by the flute at £8. The interior can get a bit cramped, so the outdoor tables next to the river are a bonus – especially in good weather, when its Thames-side location comes into its own.
Babies and children admitted (until 6pm). Function room. Tables outdoors (10, riverside). TV.

Brook Green Hotel
170 Shepherd's Bush Road, W6 7PB (7603 2516). Hammersmith tube. **Open/food served** 11am-11pm Mon; 11am-midnight Tue-Fri; noon-midnight Sat; noon-11pm Sun. **Credit** AmEx, DC, MC, V. Pub
This large Victorian pub, on a prominent corner site opposite Brook Green, is also a 14-room hotel. It's definitely more of a well-preserved pub than a hotel bar, though. The decor is a strange mix of rag-rolled red and mustard ceilings, black and gold architraves and black ceiling roses, with an odd set of orb lights hanging above the bar. The comfiest area is at the back, near a heated patio, while the club downstairs draws in punters with world music, jazz and swing dancing at the weekend. It's a Young's establishment, so there's a fine choice of ale: Special, Bitter, Winter Warmer and Bombardier on tap, plus bottles of Ram Rod, Waggledance and Oatmeal Stout.
Babies and children admitted. Disabled: toilet. Function room. Swing dancing (7pm Sun; £7). Tables outdoors (12, garden). TVs (big screen, satellite).

★ Dove
19 Upper Mall, W6 9TA (8748 5405). Hammersmith or Ravenscourt Park tube. **Open** 11am-11pm Mon-Sat; noon-10.30pm Sun. **Food served** noon-3pm, 5-10pm Mon-Fri; noon-9pm Sat, noon-5pm Sun. **Credit** AmEx, MC, V. Pub
British to its bones, the Dove is a 17th-century riverside inn with all the trimmings: low-beamed ceilings, dark panelled walls and historical gravitas. *Rule Britannia* was penned in an upstairs room, and the manuscript hangs in a display case. Charles II and Nell Gwynne caroused here. The list of former regulars, posted above the roaring fire in the front bar, includes Tommy Cooper and Graham Greene. It's even had an entry in the *Guinness Book of Records* for the tiny front bar – although there are four sections, including a conservatory opening out on to a waterside terrace. It's a Fuller's pub, so ESB, Discovery and London Pride stand alongside standard lagers and there are no surprises on the 25-strong wine list.
No piped music or jukebox. Tables outdoors (15, riverside terrace).

Hope & Anchor
20 Macbeth Street, W6 9JJ (8748 1873). Hammersmith tube/266 bus. **Open** 11am-11pm Mon-Sat; noon-10.30pm Sun. **No credit cards.** Pub
This unpretentious little local remains the only pub in the King Street vicinity to resist a chain takeover or gastro makeover. Perhaps it's the side-street location or, more probably, the fact that it's a pre-war Grade-II listed building. The local preservation society might also like to consider the Bucks Fizz and Shakin' Stevens 45s pinned to the wall of the spartan and slightly frayed interior. The entertainment is equally traditional – darts, pool and a large screen for TV sports – all appealing to a hard core of contented regulars. Everyone seems to be happy with the limited, nitro-keg lager selection, the best choice among the bitters being Theakston Old Peculier.
Babies and children admitted. Games (darts, fruit machines, pool). Jukebox. Music (musicians 8.30pm Sat; free). Tables outdoors (8, garden). TVs (big screen, satellite).

Queen's Arms NEW
171 Greyhound Road, W6 8NL (7386 5078). Barons Court tube. **Open** noon-11pm Mon-Thur, Sun; noon-midnight Fri, Sat. **Food served** noon-3pm, 6.30-10pm Mon-Fri; noon-3.30pm, 6.30-10pm Sat; 12.30-4pm, 6.30-9pm Sun. **Credit** MC, V. Pub
The bar at this tarted-up boozer is a stunning black walnut affair that bends around the ground-floor drinking area. A wide staircase with glass balustrade leads to the first-floor dining room with its open kitchen and retractable roof; wooden venetian blinds help mask the incongruous panorama of the council estate opposite. The aim is to satisfy all-comers: a decent choice of wine and cocktails says 'hello girls', while flatscreen TVs and roomy lounge chairs welcome sports fans. Foodies can have a light meal from the appealing bar menu, or head to the restaurant for a smarter experience. At the taps, Leffe and Beck's Vier complement London Pride and Timothy Taylor Landlord. Look out for Dr Seuss-goes-abstract glass paintings by Zebedee Helm – a quirky, light-hearted touch in keeping with the general vibe.
Babies and children welcome: children's menu, high chairs. Quiz (8pm Mon; £1). Restaurant (retractable roof). TVs (satellite).

Salutation
154 King Street, W6 0QU (8748 3668). Hammersmith tube. **Open** 11am-11pm Mon-Thur, Sat; 11am-midnight Fri; noon-10.30pm Sun. **Food served** noon-2.30pm, 5.30-9.30pm daily. **Credit** MC, V. Pub
The highlight here is the beautifully ornate, claret and blue tiled Victorian frontage of this Grade-II listed building, a colourful feature among the bland shopfronts and constant traffic whirr of Hammersmith. Disappointingly, the interior of this Fuller's pub is more mundane. There's the standard drop-down TV screen, and potted plants and blond wood abound, while a suburban conservatory leads to a good-sized beer garden. The foliage attracted the Queen Mother, whose visit in 1989 as patron of the London Gardens Society is recorded inside. Beers are the expected: Discovery, ESB and London Pride, plus Grolsch on tap, and Golden Pride and Organic Honey Dew among the bottled varieties.
Babies and children admitted (until 6pm). Games (arcade machine, quiz machine). Tables outdoors (24, garden). TV (big screen).

West

Also in the area...

Andover Arms *57 Aldensley Rd, W6 0DL
(8741 9794).* Cosy Fuller's pub tucked down
a sleepy backstreet. Six real ales on the pumps
include a rotating guest.

brb@the hart *383 King Street, W6 9NJ
(8748 6076).* Branch of Bar Room Bar.

Chancellors *25 Crisp Road, W6 9RL (8748 2600).*
A local's local ideally positioned for the pre-show
Riverside Studios crowd.

Rutland *15 Lower Mall, W6 9DJ (8748 5586).*
Not as appealing as its next-door neighbour, the
Blue Anchor, but equally popular on Boat Race day
thanks to its river views.

Holland Park

Julie's Wine Bar

*135 Portland Road, W11 4LW (7727 7985/www.julies
restaurant.com). Holland Park tube.* **Open** 9am-11.30pm
Mon-Sat; 10am-10.30pm Sun. **Food served** 9-11am,
noon-3pm, 7-11pm Mon-Sat; 12.30-3pm, 7-10pm Sun.
Credit AmEx, MC, V. Wine bar
It's as easy to be repulsed as impressed by Julie's Wine
Bar. As if the location wasn't enough – tucked behind a
veritable Rubik's Cube of interlocking BMWs and
Bentleys – there's also a legacy to consider: this is where
Charles and Diana held their engagement party. It also
seems a little too keen on boasting about 'celebrity clients'.
And yet, behind all the nonsense, Julie's is a likeable place
– its warren of wood-clad rooms and arterial corridors are
big on hidey-hole charm. The bar offers an unexpectedly
affordable wine list (bottles start at £16, glasses at £4)
and artful if not exactly adventurous cocktails (£8-£9).
Mod-Euro food, meanwhile, is calibrated to match the
average income of the monied clientele. One for locals and
cultural anthropologists.
*Babies and children welcome (crèche 1-4pm Sun,
free for diners). Function rooms. Restaurant.*
Map p279 Z7.

★ Ladbroke Arms

*54 Ladbroke Road, W11 3NW (7727 6648/www.
capitalpubcompany.com/ladbroke). Holland Park tube.*
Open 11am-11pm Mon-Sat; noon-10.30pm Sun.
Food served noon-2.30pm, 7-9.30pm Mon-Fri;
12.30-3pm, 7-9.30pm Sat, Sun. **Credit** AmEx,
MC, V. Pub
Gorgeous within and without. The tree-shrouded front garden is packed in summer, with drinkers spilling out on to
one of those majestic runs of lofty mini mansions that west
London does so well. A perch here, adjacent to the cobbled
mews and the pub's trailing fronds of ivy, is about as soothing as London boozing gets. Inside, a petite counter serves
a small room beautified by a lovely etched mirror, framed
pictures and some original Victorian stained-glass detailing. To the rear is a small dining room, where diners enjoy
a Gallic-accented menu, and burrowed still further away
is a bunker-like benched area. It's all very snug, and very
popular. The clientele is an equal mix of under- and over-
thirties, prim and poised the way W11 breeds 'em. Real
ales – Abbot, Greene King IPA, Adnams – appease the rugger chaps, a well-chosen wine list the rest.
*Babies and children admitted (dining only).
Bar available for hire. No piped music or jukebox.
Tables outdoors (12, terrace).* **Map p279 A7.**

Prince of Wales

*14 Princedale Road, W11 4NJ (7313 9321). Holland
Park tube.* **Open** noon-11pm Mon-Sat; noon-10.30pm
Sun. **Food served** noon-3pm, 5.30-10pm Mon-Fri;
noon-10pm Sat; noon-9pm Sun. **Credit** AmEx, MC,
V. Pub
Owned by the Michells & Butlers mini-empire, this is an
artfully dishevelled boozer that takes its interior design
seriously. The combination of red-paint and turquoise wallpaper is rather OTT, as are the mismatched chairs (from
retro leather pouffes to a trio of padded seats that look like
they've been ripped from the back of a car). There's also
an undeniable charm to the way everything orbits around
an elliptical wooden bar, right in the centre of the room. It
lends a European feel to the place, complemented by a
range of continental beers on tap (Paulaner, Leffe, Liefmans
Kriek). That said, a stylish facelift goes only skin deep, and
the generally apathetic service and oddly disjointed clientele (from lonesome bookworms to loudmouthed kids
knocking over chairs on their way out) suggests that more
serious surgery may be needed before the Prince feels as
good as it looks.
*Babies and children admitted (before 6pm). Disabled:
toilet. Games (board games). Quiz (7.30pm Sun; £1).
Tables outdoors (15, garden). TV.* **Map p279 Z7.**

Also in the area...

Academy *57 Princedale Road, W11 4NP (7221
0248).* Attractive wine bar with an extensive, well-
chosen selection; rarely busy. **Map p279 Z7.**

Kensington

Abingdon

*54 Abingdon Road, W8 6AP (7937 3339/www.the
abingdonrestaurant.com). Earl's Court or High Street
Kensington tube.* **Open** 12.30-11pm Mon-Sat; 12.30-
10.30pm Sun. **Food served** 12.30-2.30pm, 6.30-
10.30pm Mon; 12.30-2.30pm, 6.30-11pm Tue-Fri;
12.30-3pm, 6.30-11pm Sat; 12.30-3pm, 7-10pm
Sun. **Credit** AmEx, MC, V. Gastrobar
Proof that you can run an attractive, upscale bar and
restaurant in an attractive, upscale part of town – and not
charge the earth. An expansive couch accommodates
lovers or gossiping girlfriends, while checkerboard-motifed
tables suit clusters of grown-ups and nuclear families. The
60-strong wine list is exemplary. Starting with a Sicilian
Borgo Selene Bianco and 2004 Pic St-Pierre Val de
Montferrand, both at £11.95 (£3.95 for a glass), it runs to
a Finca Antigua tempranillo from La Mancha and a
Sangoma chenin blanc, topping off at a 2003 C Perchaud
Chablis and a 2002 St-Emilion Château Haut Gros Caillou,
both £38. A dozen are available by the glass, six by the
half-bottle. The cocktail choice (£6.50-£7) is fairly standard, but ingredients are decent: the martinis, for example,
are made with Absolut or Tanqueray. If you're feeling
peckish, the restaurant serves Modern European food
(chilli and coconut red snapper, roast rump of lamb with
blue cheese sweet potato mash), at around £15 a main.
*Babies and children welcome: high chairs. Tables
outdoors (4, pavement).*

Churchill Arms

*119 Kensington Church Street, W8 7LN (7727 4242).
Notting Hill Gate tube.* **Open** 11am-11pm Mon-Wed;
11am-midnight Thur-Sat; noon-10.30pm Sun. **Food**

West

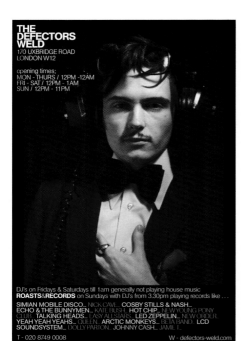

served noon-10pm Mon-Sat; noon-9.30pm Sun. **Credit** AmEx, MC, V. Pub
The clutter of jumble in this landmark pub doesn't relate exclusively to Winston, although his portraits cover one wall of an expansive interior leading to two areas for Thai dining at the back. Other prime ministers, American presidents, Irish sporting line-ups, shiny copper implements… all get a decorative look-in. The imposing main bar counter, invariably two men deep, serves Fuller's brews (Discovery, London Pride, ESB) as well as Hoegaarden, Grolsch and Caffrey's, with Thai beers Chang and Singha available in bottles. The wine list is extensive, focusing on the cheaper brands, including a Gun Shearer riesling (£4.50/£18), a Domaine Durand Loire Sancerre (£4.65/£18.90) and a Marqués de Griñón Crianza Rioja (£3.60/£15). *Babies and children admitted (until 1pm). Games (fruit machine). Restaurant. TV (satellite).*

Elephant & Castle
40 Holland Street, W8 4LT (7368 0901). High Street Kensington tube. **Open** 11am-11pm Mon-Sat; noon-10.30pm Sun. **Food served** noon-8pm Mon-Thur, Sat; noon-3pm Fri, Sun. **Credit** MC, V. Pub
This cosy little corner pub on a quiet residential crossroads prides itself on its real ales. Guest brews on our visit included Skinner's Best, Mordue Geordie Pride, Caledonian Great Scot and JHB from Hansons, whose proposed closure has inspired a CAMRA rescue campaign. Had we arrived a month later, we would have found Wickwar Old Arnold and Robinsons Unicorn. It's not a place for wine drinkers, unless they like the cheap stuff (nothing over £13), but the pub grub is certainly superior. 'Famous for fish & chips', the Elephant also offers swordfish, hake and salmon, plus enormous Sunday roasts (£8.50). A back room of splashes from the *Evening Standard* (John Lennon shot, Edward abdicating) tends to be ignored for the cosy, banquetted front area.
Games (fruit machine, quiz machine). Tables outdoors (4, pavement). TV. Wi-Fi.

Kensington Arms NEW
41 Abingdon Road, W8 6AH (7938 3841/www. kensingtonarms.com). High Street Kensington tube. **Open** 11am-11pm Mon-Sat; noon-10.30pm Sun. **Food served** noon-10pm Mon-Sat; noon-9pm Sun. **Credit** MC, V. Gastrobar
A neighbourhood pub turned gastrobar, the KA is a cousin of the Mariners Rock in Cornwall, hence the Sharp's Doom Bar beer, colourful retro travel posters of Newquay and moody landscapes in black and white. Airy and light, with remnants of its former existence (glazed front windows, picnic table outside), this two-area venue attracts a young, professional clientele, gathered here for the rugger or football on one of three screens. Beck's Vier, Hoegaarden, Peroni and Young's comprise the draught offerings, while 20 wines, eight by the glass, include a Château de Roques sauvignon blanc (£4.25/£15.90) and three champagnes. Gastropub staples and superior Cornish pasties are served via a little hatch in the back room.
Babies and children welcome: high chairs. Disabled: toilet. Tables outdoors (2, pavement).

Scarsdale
23A Edwardes Square, W8 6HE (7937 1811). Earl's Court or High Street Kensington tube. **Open** noon-11pm Mon-Sat; noon-10.30pm Sun. **Food served** noon-10pm Mon-Sat; noon-9.30pm Sun. **Credit** AmEx, MC, V. Pub

Built for Bonaparte's officers before they were set to invade England in the early 1800s (they didn't), the Scarsdale is a traditional pub exuding good taste from the front terrace to the two back dining areas. Quality bitters (London Pride, Bombardier, Young's, guest ale Cumberland) plus Erdinger and Staropramen complement a well-chosen wine selection, monthly highlights at the time of review including bottles of Les Charmes Pouilly-Fumé (£17.95), Ropiteau Fleurie (£15.25) and Rothbury Estate verdelho (£17.80). Typical customers are sturdy rugger types, their well-bred female companions and parents visiting after shopping sprees. Thick steaks and beefburgers complete the picture.
Babies and children admitted (in restaurant). Restaurant. Tables outdoors (8, garden). TV.

Tenth Bar
Royal Garden Hotel, 2-24 Kensington High Street, W8 4PT (7361 1910/www.royalgardenhotel.co.uk). High Street Kensington tube. **Open/food served** noon-2.15pm, 5.30-10.30pm Mon-Fri; 5.30-10.30pm Sat. **Credit** AmEx, DC, MC, V. Hotel bar
Press 'X' in the lift of the Royal Garden Hotel and you are whisked to the same magnificent panoramic view of London that the hotel's guests pay top dollar for. Find a low, brown leather armchair in the unfussy bar area adjoining the larger restaurant. You are soon brought a bowl of spicy nuts while you peruse a drinks menu that includes three dozen cocktails (£8.50-£9.75), 15 champagnes and a host of vintage malts. As a holding bar, the Tenth is big on aperitifs, with apple, lychee or melon martinis mixed with Zubrówka, Stolichnaya or Absolut. A quality Chablis (Domaine de l'Égalité, Jean Durop, £9) stands out of the eight wines available by the glass; Newcastle Brown gives comedy value to the choice of four bottled beers.
Disabled: lift; toilet. Restaurant.

Windsor Castle
114 Campden Hill Road, W8 7AR (7243 9551/www. windsor-castle-pub.co.uk). Notting Hill Gate tube. **Open** noon-11pm Mon-Sat; noon-10.30pm Sun. **Food served** noon-3pm, 5-10pm Mon-Fri; noon-10pm Sat; noon-9pm Sun. **Credit** AmEx, MC, V. Pub
This corner boozer comprises a Cluedo-like warren of bar areas, the main one giving access to smaller ones, each named, accessed by low doorways. Fireplaces, lanterns and historic prints feature throughout. On draught, Timothy Taylor Landlord, Adnams Broadside, Leffe and Grolsch are accompanied by a rare Charlie's Angel from Nottinghamshire's Springhead brewery. Well-priced wines, ten by the glass and bottle, include a Stopbanks sauvignon blanc (£3.80/£16) and a Campden Park shiraz (£3.75/£15). They also run to a superior seasonal selection by the bottle (£11.50-£22), such as a Vitapura organic merlot or a Barolo. An equally superior anglocentric menu offers lamb chops followed by rhubarb crumble and custard. Read the Sundays in the sun outside.
Games (board games). No piped music or jukebox. Tables outdoors (20, garden; 4, pavement).

Also in the area...
Britannia *1 Allen Street, W8 6UX (7937 6905).* Recently refurbished (and now rather swish) Young's pub.
Cumberland Arms *29 North End Road, W14 8SZ (7371 6806/www.thecumberlandarmspub.co.uk).* Gastropub with an Italian-leaning menu and a handsome wine selection.

West

Ladbroke Grove

Fat Badger NEW

*310 Portobello Road, W10 5TA (8969 4500/www.the
fatbadger.com). Ladbroke Grove or Westbourne Park
tube.* **Open** noon-11pm Mon-Thur; 11am-midnight
Fri, Sat; noon-10.30pm Sun. **Food served** noon-3pm,
6-10pm Mon-Sat; noon-10pm Sun. **Credit** AmEx, DC,
MC, V. Pub

A police car waiting outside the Trellick Tower. A bag
lady. Park-bench drinkers. A black man pulling a gun on
a white man. No, not everyday scenes in Ladbroke Grove,
but scenes from the subversive Timorous Beasties wallpaper in the Fat Badger. This is not the Ladbroke Grove
of the very-well-to-do, but the northern end of Portobello
that still retains some edge. The pub is conformist in most
other ways, with its knackered leather sofas, chandeliers
and candles. On our visit, the only real ale was off, leaving
us with a choice of Leffe Blonde, dull lagers or wines by
the glass. But it's cosy enough to attract pre-coital couples,
and casual diners who are adventurous enough to try bar
snacks such as smoked sprats and horseradish.
*Babies and children admitted. Bar available for hire.
Games (board games). Tables outdoors (6, terrace;
2, pavement).* **Map p279 Z5.**

Pelican NEW

*45 All Saints Road, W11 1HE (7792 3073/www.the
pelicanpub.com). Ladbroke Grove or Westbourne Park
tube.* **Open** noon-11pm Mon-Sat; 1-11pm Sun. **Food
served** noon-9pm Mon-Sat; 1-9pm Sun. **Credit** AmEx,
MC, V. Pub

With a prime spot on the corner of Tavistock and All Saints
Roads, it's difficult to understand the succession of closures
on this site. Once a fighter's pub that you wouldn't enter
without a chainmail vest, then an organic restaurant, then
a gastropub, it's now an indie pub. This final incarnation
looks to have some staying power. Plungeable sofas and
tables for snacking are spread around a right-angled bar,
while a pit at the rear accomodates a hideaway booth.
Design kudos is earned by the use of gorgeous Futura lettering all over the place; another highlight is a glassed-off
central staircase, visible behind the drinks shelves, leading to a separate upstairs bar where bands play. On the
taps, Germany (Bitburger and Erdinger), Japan (Kirin) and
good old London town (London Pride) are all represented.
*Games (board games, quiz machines). Jukebox. Quiz
(8pm; free). Music (open mic night 8pm alternate Wed,
8pm Thur; free). Separate room for parties, seats 30.
Tables outdoors (3, pavement).* **Map p279 Z5.**

Ruby & Sequoia

*6-8 All Saints Road, W11 1HH (7243 6363/www.
ruby.uk.com). Ladbroke Grove or Westbourne Park
tube.* **Open** 6pm-12.30am Mon-Thur; 6pm-2am Fri;
11am-2am Sat; 11am-12.30am Sun. **Credit** AmEx,
MC, V. Bar/Restaurant

Despite our experience with an over-zealous bouncer on a
recent visit – turning away hordes of well-mannered
groovers early on a Saturday evening – and a long wait at
the bar, there's a lot to like about Ruby & Sequoia.
Cocktails are ace, for a start: a bloody mary thick and perfectly spiced; an amaretto sour with a real lemon juice kick.
The place looks a treat too, with diner-style seating beneath
a glam gold-flecked ceiling decked out with Perspex lights.

Skiddaw. See p111.

West

Skiddaw. See p111.

Big bay doors let in the bustle of Notting Hill on fair-weather days. At night (assuming you make it past the doorman) sit back and wonder what all those chaps in zoot suits and wraparound sunglasses actually do for a living. *Babies and children admitted (restaurant until 6pm Sat, Sun). Bar available for hire. Disabled: toilet. Music (DJs 9pm Thur-Sat; free). Restaurant. Tables outdoors (2, pavement).* **Map p279 Z5.**

Visible

299 Portobello Road, W10 5TD (8969 0333). Ladbroke Grove or Notting Hill Gate tube. **Open** 3.30-11pm Mon-Thur; 10am-1am Fri, Sat; 10am-10pm Sun. **Food served** 4-11pm Mon-Sat; 4-10pm Sun. **Credit** MC, V. Bar
Visible is exactly that, its bright red exterior and smattering of street-side seating a vivid and inviting sight on a people-saturated Portobello Road. Inside, it's no less colourful, with kaleidoscopically coloured walls surrounding low-slung sofas and flatscreen TVs. On our visit, these were showing muted Bollywood films while the DJ dropped appropriately laid-back funk from a booth beside the bar. A selection of tapas accompanies a range of interesting bottled beers (including the tequila-flavoured Desperado) and cocktails (£5-£7); of these, a Sombrero was thick with real raspberries and packed a genuine punch thanks to a volatile mix of Stolichnaya vodka and passion fruit liquor. A charming hideaway that somehow gets itself noticed on a street with plenty of action. *Babies and children admitted (until 7pm). Music (DJ 8pm Fri; musicians 8pm Sun; both free). Tables outdoors (4, pavement). TVs (big screen, satellite).* **Map p279 Z5.**

Also in the area...

Elgin *96 Ladbroke Grove, W11 1PY (7229 5663).* Mammoth corner boozer with pool tables and sport-showing TV screens. **Map p279 Z5.**

Maida Vale

Bridge House

13 Westbourne Terrace Road, W2 6NG (7432 1361). Warwick Avenue tube/Paddington tube/rail. **Open** noon-11pm Mon-Thur; noon-11.30pm Fri, Sat; noon-10.30pm Sun. **Food served** noon-10pm Mon-Sat; noon-9.30pm Sun. **Credit** (over £5) AmEx, MC, V. Comedy pub
Home to allegedly the world's longest-running comedy show (the satirical News Revue is performed three times a night in the upstairs Canal Café Theatre), Bridge House is an eye-opener. There's an armless mannequin with a feather boa over the door, red lights above the bar that might be earrings stolen from Pat Butcher, and a wicker breakfast bar with high stools. There is nothing frivolous about the beer, though, with draught Greene King IPA, Old Speckled Hen and (the guest on our visit) Six Nations, plus Franziskaner, Sleeman's Honey Brown, Belle-Vue Kriek, Küppers Kölsch, Früli and Leffe. Wine is fairly priced (Domaine de Prion Fleurie, £18; Stonehaven Lime Coast viognier, £19), with plenty of both colours available by the glass.
Babies and children admitted (before 6pm). Comedy (7.30pm & 9.30pm Mon-Sat; 7pm & 9pm Sun; phone to confirm times; £5-£9). Disabled: toilet. Games (board games). Tables outdoors (8, terrace).

E Bar

2 Warrington Crescent, W9 1ER (7432 8455). Warwick Avenue tube. **Open** 5-11pm Tue-Fri; noon-11pm Sat; noon-10.30pm Sun. **Food served** 5-10.30pm Tue-Fri; noon-10.30pm Sat; noon-10pm Sun. **Credit** MC, V. Bar
This subterranean cocktail lounge and tapas bar, owned by the adjacent Colonnade Hotel, is one of a growing number of fine bars in the area. From a small, penned area for alfresco dining, a flight of stairs leads down to the glass-roofed bar. Inside, the decor combines textured off-cream wallpaper with silky beige drapes, black and white shots of Paris and, set into the walls, large spotlit pebbles in rectangular cases. Resident singer Emma-Jane performs every Wednesday evening, DJs spin on Thursdays, and free Wi-Fi attracts the penny wise. At the bar it's unimpressive bottled lager (Lapin Kulta, San Miguel, Corona), a considered wine list (a medium-bodied Château Bel-Air from Bordeaux for £23) or an extensive long, short and martini cocktail list – try a Pink Panther of Malibu, watermelon, maraschino cherry and champagne (£7).
Babies and children admitted (until 6pm Sat, Sun). Function rooms. Games (backgammon, chess). Music (musician Wed; DJs Thur). Tables outdoors (20, terrace). Wi-Fi (free).

Elgin

255 Elgin Avenue, W9 1NJ (7624 2602/www.the-elgin.com). Maida Vale tube. **Open** 9am-11pm Mon-Thur; 9am-midnight Fri; 10am-midnight Sat; 10am-11pm Sun. **Food served** 10.30am-10pm Mon-Sat; 10.30am-9pm Sun. **Credit** AmEx, DC, MC, V. Bar

clement orange and Santa Teresa rums) and Koshiku (lime leaf-infused shochu with passionfruit, honey and fresh ginger), while the Eclipse Cocktail (one of the 20 Eclipse Favourites) features Maker's Mark bourbon, raspberry liqueur, lime and cranberry juice and fresh raspberries. The food – burgers, Asian snacks, weekend brunch – looks sassy enough. The problem is the layout: a long banquette and facing line of chairs, with just enough space for passage to a thin bar. It's fine for couples, provided one can focus on the fireplace should the partner or conversation drift, but confining for groups. Weekdays can be quiet.
Babies and children admitted (lunchtime Sat, Sun). Bar available for hire. Tables outdoors (2, pavement). **Map p279 Z6.**

Electric Brasserie

191 Portobello Road, W11 2ED (7908 9696/www. the-electric.co.uk). Ladbroke Grove tube. **Open** 8am-12.30am Mon-Wed; 8am-1am Thur-Sat; 8am-11.30pm Sun. **Food served** 8am-11pm Mon-Fri; 8am-5pm, 6-11pm Sat; 8am-5pm, 6-10pm Sun. **Credit** AmEx, DC, MC, V. Brasserie
Serving the adjoining cinema of the same name, the stylish Electric buzzes from breakfast to past bedtime as a destination bar and brasserie. There's a long zinc bar counter, square of terrace, efficient uniformed staff and quality wines, cocktails and food (pastries, eggs benedict, oysters, lobster and chips, and much more). The global wine list starts with 'pouring wines' by the glass (from £3.75 for the French house); there are also 50 by the bottle (£13.75-£125) and a selection by the half-litre carafe (£9.50-£16). Fancy something stronger? Try the decent array of rums, tequilas, whiskies and other spirits, or one of the 25 or so cocktails (£7.50-£8). These include a cappuccino martini (with Toussaint, Baileys and a double espresso) and – potentially useful, this – an Electric Hangover Cure (Stoli Gold, lime, mint and a lemonade top).
Babies and children welcome: high chairs. Disabled: toilet. Tables outdoors (8, pavement). **Map p279 Z6.**

★ Lonsdale

44-48 Lonsdale Road, W11 2DE (7727 4080/www.the lonsdale.co.uk). Ladbroke Grove or Notting Hill Gate tube. **Open** 6pm-midnight Mon-Thur, Sun; 6pm-1am Fri, Sat. **Food served** 6-10.30pm daily. **Credit** AmEx, MC, V. Cocktail bar
Dick Bradsell's old establishment is back in contention with the launch of a fabulously original cocktail menu in spring 2007. Simple in concept, it traces the history of the London cocktail, from the mojito conceived in Cuba in 1586, the Sours of the 1700s, the Sangarees of the Antilles, the Flips of the 1860s, the Bucks of the 1920s and contemporary classics. It's a labour of love, a work of art, and it provides meticulously sourced concoctions (£6-£7.50) at fair prices. In truth, Lonsdale was getting as jaded as the Prague Metro-style decor around its bar counter, and the expansive back area was often quiet. A Westbourne Sour (Miller's Westbourne Strength gin, fresh raspberry, gently frothed) should put the whizz back in W11.
Babies and children admitted (8.30pm). Disabled: toilet. Function room. Music (DJs 9pm Fri, Sat; free). Tables outdoors (5, terrace). **Map 10 A6.**

★ Montgomery Place NEW

31 Kensington Park Road, W11 2EU (7792 3921/ www.montgomeryplace.co.uk). Ladbroke Grove tube. **Open** 5pm-midnight Mon-Fri, Sun; 2pm-midnight Sat.

Food served 6-11pm daily. **Credit** AmEx, MC, V. Cocktail Bar
Eclipsing the Eclipse opposite, this recently opened 'lounge bar kitchen' is above all else a cocktail bar – and a very good one. Alex Fitzsimmons and Matt Perovetz from sister bar Dusk (and other London and NYC mixers) have consulted on a cracking cocktail selection. Inspiration for the list comes from great bars of the 20th century and the classic drinks created therein. Concoctions start at £8.50; you might fancy the Montgomery-style martini (Tanqueray, Noilly Prat, named in honour of Field Marshall Montgomery), the Kangaroo vodka martini (with Wyborowa), original manhattans, authentic daiquiris ('¡Viva La Revoluçion!'), long drinks (Vertigo), or whisky (Acqua Vitae) and tequila (Tres Bandidos) mixes. Each category is either meticulously researched (as in the Queen's Park Swizzle of Angostura rum and bitters from Port of Spain, Trinidad) or devised as an homage. The Montgomery is an intimate space and it attracts a grown-up clientele. Recommended.
Babies and children admitted (Sat afternoon). Music (percussion 8pm Sun; free). Tables outdoors (pavement, 2). **Map p279 Z6.**

Negozio Classica

283 Westbourne Grove, W11 2QA (7034 0005/ www.negozioclassica.co.uk). Ladbroke Grove or Notting Hill Gate tube. **Open/food served** noon-midnight Mon-Fri, Sun; 9am-midnight Sat. **Credit** AmEx, MC, V. Wine bar
This bar has airport lounge coffee shop written all over it: red walls, modern lights and tiny dimensions. But the quality of food and wine is top drawer. We enjoyed scouring the shelving of bottles filling one wall; all can be bought to take home, or drunk on site with carpaccio, cheeses and other snacks, alongside the occasional posh local or shaggy-haired Euro student. The usual classic regions plus a smattering of hefty southern Italy dominates – Altecino's 1998 Brunello di Montalcino Montesoli and Liveli 2004 Orion Primitivo from Puglia. There are also some good whites from ever-improving Slovenia, and white port from Churchill's, a commendable inclusion for its rarity. Plenty of other delis offer more change from a £20 note, but none in Notting Hill are as good as this one.
Babies and children admitted. Off-licence. Tables outdoors (2, pavement). **Map p279 Z6.**

Portobello Gold

95-97 Portobello Road, W11 2QB (7460 4900/ www.portobellogold.com). Notting Hill Gate tube. **Open** 10am-midnight Mon-Thur; 10am-12.30am Fri; 9am-12.30am Sat; 10am-11.30pm Sun. **Food served** 11am-11pm Mon-Sat; 1-9pm Sun. **Happy hour** 5.30-7pm daily. **Credit** AmEx, DC, MC, V. Bar/Restaurant
Established enough to say 'Just Gold' outside, PG is the perfect Portobello hangout. With a firm grasp of pop culture – images of Sandie Shaw, the Stones on *Thank Your Lucky Stars*, and a California surfing scene that impressed Bill Clinton – Portobello Gold allows discerning, music-savvy bohos to commune over pints of Thatcher's cider, Fuller's London Pride, Hogs Back IPA or Grolsch. Whiskies line the back bar. The jungle of a rear conservatory serves as a reputable restaurant, so the wine list is decent. Eight labels of each colour, two by the glass, include a McWilliams Harwood Estate chardonnay and a Oak Cask Trapiche pinot noir. The shelving lining the cosy wooden front bar converts into internet work stations, should that be your gig.

West

Sign of drinks to come

With origins dating back to Roman times, pub signs have been a unique feature of British life since the 14th century. They first appeared in the 12th century to help the vast majority of the population who could not read or write identify their local boozer, and in 1393 Richard II passed an act making it compulsory for all pubs and inns to carry a visual sign so they could be clocked by the official 'Ale Taster'. Many were originally heraldic – the Cross Keys, Red Lion – but as pubs took on more interesting names, the signs followed suit.

These days, heraldic imagery still dominates, along with regal portraits, while many opt to just have the name written out in fancy script – but there are some cracking pictorial signs out there. The **Tom Cribb** (36 Panton Street, SW1, 7839 3801) has a beautifully energetic image of two bare-knuckle boxers mid-fight, a tribute to the pub's former landowner, Cribb, a famous pugilist. Some are literal: the **Lamb** on Lamb's Conduit Street depicts a superb fluffy specimen; the **Bull's Head** in Barnes shows just that, while the **Eagle** (2 Shepherdess Walk, NI, 7553 7681) has a swooping beauty. Others are more oblique: the **Three Kings of Clerkenwell** boasts a sign of King Kong, Henry VIII and Elvis, while a pub with almost the same name, the **Famous Three Kings** (171 North End Road, W14, 7603 6071), goes for Elvis, Henry VIII and Charles I. The latter shows that a good pub and good sign do not always go together. While the **Seven Stars** in Holborn has an uninspired sign, its **namesake** on the North End Road (No.253, W14, 7385 3571??) has an atmospheric beauty.

Some pubs take in local London history. The **Doric Arch** (1 Eversholt Street, NW1, 7388 2221) immortalises the long-lost Euston Arch; the **Lea Tavern** (90 White Post Lane, E9, 8985 2179) presents a bucolic image of the Lee Navigation that doesn't quite chime with the present-day reality of dual carriageway and abandoned factories; while the **Widow's Son** (5, Devons Road, E3, 7515 9072) offers a beautiful memorial to the pub's founding folk tale, which sees a new hot cross bun added to an ancient collection every Good Friday in memory of a sailor who went to war and never returned.

Recent years have seen a new trend develop: the three-dimensional sign, as seen outside the **Pillars of Hercules** in Soho and the **Bag O'Nails** in Victoria (6 Buckingham Palace Road, SW1, 7828 7003). But these novelties have nothing on the finest painted pub sign in London – and for this we send you to the **Angel** on St Giles High Street for an absolute masterclass in eye-catching public artwork.

This ambitious bar and restaurant is an ideal spot in which to wind down after the bustle of Goldhawk Road. The bare-brick walls are softened by an open fire, slouchy leather sofas and large orange lampshades that contain ever smaller shades, like matryoshka dolls. The rear dining area has a large open kitchen (dishing out the likes of ribeye, sea bass, burgers and pasta), ornate heraldic mirrors and some intimate enclaves. Curtains section it off from a high-ceilinged chill-out lounge, which has a large golden chandelier, hung beneath ventilation pipes, as its centrepiece. The music is as laid-back as the mixed crowd. Draught options include Adnams Spindrift, Pilsner Urquell, Peetermans and Hoegaarden, and the wine list is compact but eclectic: Domaine Vacheron Sancerre (£18.50), perhaps, or a Griffin Vineyard shiraz (£15.95).
Babies and children admitted. Disabled: toilet. Restaurant. Tables outdoors (3 long tables, garden).

Also in the area...

Davy's White City *Units 4 & 5, Media Centre, White City Media Village, Wood Lane, W12 7ST (8811 2862).* Branch.
Goldhawk *122 Goldhawk Road, W12 8HH (8576 6921).* Spacious modern pub with art displayed on the walls and the likes of Sleeman and Küppers Kölsch on tap.

Westbourne Grove

Cow
89 Westbourne Park Road, W2 5QH (7221 0021/www. thecowlondon.co.uk). Royal Oak or Westbourne Park tube. **Open** noon-11pm Mon-Thur; noon-midnight Fri, Sat; noon-10.30pm Sun. **Food served** noon-3.30pm, 6-10.30pm Mon-Sat; noon-3.30pm, 6-10pm Sun. **Credit** MC, V. Gastropub
Gastrobar guru Tom Conran runs this two-storey operation: an Irish pub downstairs and renowned restaurant upstairs, with another dining area at the back of the pub. The versatile kitchen provides diners on both levels with first-rate seafood and pies. Plates of rock oysters sit atop the bar counter, invariably accompanied by a decent pint of Guinness, and equally invariably devoured by self-important regulars who swarm the modest interior. Other choices on tap include ESB, London Pride, Hoegaarden and delicious amber De Koninck from Antwerp. More Belgian brews feature by the bottle. Not surprisingly, the wine list is discerning – it might take you a while to pick out a La di Motte pinot grigio at £22, but it will be worth it.
Babies and children admitted (lunch). Restaurant available for hire. Tables outdoors (4, pavement).
Map p279 B5.

Crazy Homies
127 Westbourne Park Road, W2 5QL (7727 6771). Royal Oak or Westbourne Park tube. **Open** 6.30pm-midnight Mon-Fri; noon-midnight Sat, Sun. **Food served** 6.30-11pm Mon-Fri; noon-11.30pm Sat, Sun. **Credit** MC, V. Gastrobar
Commendably more downbeat than Tom Conran's other establishments, this vampish, Mexican-themed venue (next to its sister bar-diner, Lucky Seven) is hugely popular, which is why TC is planning to expand it. The odd skull hides amid the cacti and a jukebox full of Tarantino-esque tunes pounds out dark and dirty delights. The food, inspired by the street vendors and neighbourhood *taquerias*

found throughout Mexico, is delectable and reasonably priced. Equally authentic are the margaritas, the main element of the cocktail selection, featuring such delights as a Batanga of tequila, lime and Coke, with a salted rim, for £6. The bottled beers from south of the border include a Dos Equis amber (£3.50) and rarely found Casta Triguera wheat ale (£3.75).
Babies and children admitted. Bar available for hire. Function room. Jukebox. Tables outdoors (1, pavement).
Map p279 A5.

Prince Bonaparte
80 Chepstow Road, W2 5BE (7313 9491/www.the-prince-bonaparte.co.uk). Notting Hill Gate or Royal Oak tube. **Open** noon-11pm Mon-Sat; noon-10.30pm Sun. **Food served** noon-10pm Mon-Thur; noon-9pm Fri-Sun. **Credit** AmEx, MC, V. Gastropub
A large, open-plan Victorian pub-gone-gastro, site for Johnny Vaughan's Strongbow ads, the Bonaparte has a high reputation for its food and variety of drinks. Draught London Pride, Schneider Weiss, Budvar and Hoegaarden are complemented by an eclectic, 37-strong wine list, including a rich Vidal pinot noir from New Zealand and a dry and refreshing Don Pabiot Pouilly-Fumé (both £19). An already healthy crowd expands on Thursday, when the resident female DJ spins an '80s mix, and at weekends, when the loud interaction and background sounds render conversation impossible. On a quiet lunchtime, though, you can recline in a leather armchair by an open fire and browse the paintings in the gallery before taking your place in the dining area for a slap-up meal.
Art exhibitions. Babies and children admitted (until 6pm). Bar available for hire. Disabled: toilet. TV.
Map p279 A5.

Tiroler Hut
27 Westbourne Grove, W2 4UA (7727 3981/ www.tirolerhut.co.uk). Bayswater or Queensway tube. **Open** 6.30pm-1am Tue-Sat; 6.30pm-midnight Sun. **Food served** 6.30pm-midnight Tue-Sat; 6.30-11pm Sun. **Credit** AmEx, DC, MC, V. Bar/Restaurant
Bonkers with bells on, the Tiroler Hut is a kitsch and wonderfully entertaining destination. Run by the same family for four decades, this basement bar gives owner Joseph ample scope to appear in lederhosen, squeezing an accordion. He may yodel. He might tinkle with Tyrolean cowbells. Octagenarian Europeans, ex-Spurs players and people you might have seen on the telly gather at the bar, sipping draught Dortmunder Union or Bergadler, bottled Erdinger Weiss or Dunkel. Unusual but welcome Hungarian wines (Szekszárdi Bull's Blood, £13.90) and spirits, such as the dark and dreadful Unicum, also feature. The food is a central European mix of meats with sauerkraut and dumplings; ravenous vegetarian couples can dive into the cheese fondue (£20.50 for two).
Babies and children admitted. Booking essential (restaurant). Entertainment (cowbell show 9pm Wed-Sun). Restaurant available for hire. Vegan dishes.
Map p279 B6.

Westbourne
101 Westbourne Park Villas, W2 5ED (7221 1332/ www.thewestbourne.com). Royal Oak or Westbourne Park tube. **Open** 5-11pm Mon; 11am-11pm Tue-Fri; noon-11am Sat; noon-10.30pm Sun. **Food served** 7-10pm Mon; 12.30-3pm, 7-10pm Tue-Fri; 12.30-3.30pm, 7.30-10.30pm Sat; 12.30-3.30pm, 6.30-9.30pm Sun. **Credit** MC, V. Gastropub

Sign of drinks to come

With origins dating back to Roman times, pub signs have been a unique feature of British life since the 14th century. They first appeared in the 12th century to help the vast majority of the population who could not read or write identify their local boozer, and in 1393 Richard II passed an act making it compulsory for all pubs and inns to carry a visual sign so they could be clocked by the official 'Ale Taster'. Many were originally heraldic – the Cross Keys, Red Lion – but as pubs took on more interesting names, the signs followed suit.

These days, heraldic imagery still dominates, along with regal portraits, while many opt to just have the name written out in fancy script – but there are some cracking pictorial signs out there. The **Tom Cribb** (36 Panton Street, SW1, 7839 3801) has a beautifully energetic image of two bare-knuckle boxers mid-fight, a tribute to the pub's former landowner, Cribb, a famous pugilist. Some are literal: the **Lamb** on Lamb's Conduit Street depicts a superb fluffy specimen; the **Bull's Head** in Barnes shows just that, while the **Eagle** (2 Shepherdess Walk, NI, 7553 7681) has a swooping beauty. Others are more oblique: the **Three Kings of Clerkenwell** boasts a sign of King Kong, Henry VIII and Elvis, while a pub with almost the same name, the **Famous Three Kings** (171 North End Road, W14, 7603 6071), goes

for Elvis, Henry VIII and Charles I. The latter shows that a good pub and good sign do not always go together. While the **Seven Stars** in Holborn has an uninspired sign, its **namesake** on the North End Road (No.253, W14, 7385 3571??) has an atmospheric beauty.

Some pubs take in local London history. The **Doric Arch** (1 Eversholt Street, NW1, 7388 2221) immortalises the long-lost Euston Arch; the **Lea Tavern** (90 White Post Lane, E9, 8985 2179) presents a bucolic image of the Lee Navigation that doesn't quite chime with the present-day reality of dual carriageway and abandoned factories; while the **Widow's Son** (5, Devons Road, E3, 7515 9072) offers a beautiful memorial to the pub's founding folk tale, which sees a new hot cross bun added to an ancient collection every Good Friday in memory of a sailor who went to war and never returned.

Recent years have seen a new trend develop: the three-dimensional sign, as seen outside the **Pillars of Hercules** in Soho and the **Bag O'Nails** in Victoria (6 Buckingham Palace Road, SW1, 7828 7003). But these novelties have nothing on the finest painted pub sign in London – and for this we send you to the **Angel** on St Giles High Street for an absolute masterclass in eye-catching public artwork.

West

Montgomery Place. *See p112.*

Babies and children admitted (restaurant). Bar available for hire. Internet access. Music (bands 7pm Sun; free). Restaurant. Tables outdoors (3, pavement). TV (satellite, widescreen). **Map p279 A6.**

Prince Albert
11 Pembridge Road, W11 3HQ (7727 7362/www.the-prince-albert.co.uk). Notting Hill Gate tube. **Open** noon-midnight daily. **Food served** noon-11pm Mon-Sat; noon-10pm Sun. **Credit** AmEx, MC, V. Pub
Set at a prominent mini roundabout behind Notting Hill Gate tube, and adjoining the Gate Theatre, the Prince Albert is a popular loungey revamp of a landmark corner boozer. The intimate sunken area at the back, the bare red lightbulbs, the chandelier resembling an upside-down sombrero – all point to a late 20th-century conversion. It also means a decent range of draught beers from Europe (Budvar light and dark, Schneider Weisse, Hoegaarden, Leffe) to complement the traditional ones (Young's, Abbot) from England. There's Weston's organic cider on tap too. Drinks are dispensed from a sturdy, horseshoe island bar, where your choice from the three dozen somewhat pricey wines can also be made. An open kitchen dispatches standard modern bar fare.
Disabled: toilet. Tables outdoors (8, heated garden). **Map p279 A7.**

Sun in Splendour
7 Portobello Road, W11 3DA (7313 9331). Notting Hill Gate tube. **Open** noon-11pm Mon-Thur; noon-midnight Fri; 11am-midnight Sat; noon-10.30pm Sun. **Food served** noon-4pm, 6-10pm Mon-Fri; noon-9.30pm Sat, Sun. **Credit** AmEx, MC, V. Bar
Welcome to Notting Hill in a nutshell, from the black and white photo mural of local women well known because of their fathers, to the 'Snog in Safety!' sign leading to the 'secret garden'. The button stools, the hand-me-down furniture, the flatscreen TV and the *Sopranos* pinball machine for stoners – all is Bohemian in a well-bred kind of way. Trustafarian tipples include Kirin Ichiban, Sleeman, Leffe, Hoegaarden, Früli and Staropramen on draught, Duvel and Liefmans Kriek by the bottle. A blackboard brims with decent mid-priced wine selections, most available by the glass: typical offerings include a Robert Mondavi pinot noir (£3.65/£15) and a Domaine Pabiot Pouilly-Fumé (£19). Another board lists half a dozen mains of the day (perhaps shepherd's pie, or butternut squash and pecorino risotto) and sharing plates.
Games (pinball machine, quiz machine). Music (open mic night 7.30pm Tue; free). Tables outdoors (8, garden). TV. **Map p279 A7.**

★ Trailer Happiness
177 Portobello Road, W11 2DY (7727 2700/www. trailerhappiness.com). Ladbroke Grove or Notting Hill Gate tube. **Open** 5-10pm 1st Mon of mth; 5pm-midnight Tue-Fri; 6pm-midnight Sat; 6-10.30pm Sun. **Food served** 6-10.30pm Tue-Sat. **Credit** AmEx, MC, V. Bar
Ah, a proper bar, no messing. This basement might look trashy – part bordello, part South Pacific – but the drinking is serious. Bloody professional and bags of fun. Along with a homage to great contemporary mixologists – Vincenzo Errico's Red Hook (Peppery Rye whiskey, dry cherry, sweet vermouth) from New York's Milk & Honey circa 2003, for example – Trailer Happiness does its own Grapefruit Julep (with Finlandia, grapefruit and pomegranate juices, and a drizzle of honey) and Hedgerow Sling

(Plymouth and sloe gins, lemon, mure, soda). Sticking with the Pacific theme, 1950s-style Tiki drinks are mixed with reverence to their Californian roots; note that, sensibly, you're limited to two Zombies (five rums, absinthe, 'bitters and trepidation'). Most cocktails cost £6.50, while Tikis go up to £12. Snacks are available, and DJs take to the decks in a corner hatch towards the end of the week.
Music (DJs 8pm Wed-Sat). Tables outdoors (5, pavement). **Map p279 Z6.**

Also in the area...
Beach Blanket Babylon *5 Ledbury Road, W11 2AA (7229 2907/www.beachblanket.co.uk).* Pricey bar with pseudo-French decor, aimed at 'well-heeled socialites'; 70 wines starts at £6.50 a glass. **Map p279 A6.**
Bumpkin *209 Westbourne Park Rd, W11 1EA (7243 9818/www.bumpkinuk.com).* Rurally styled gastropub with friendly service and good beer. **Map p279 A5.**
Corney & Barrow *194 Kensington Park Road, W11 2ES (7221 5122).* Branch. **Map p279 Z6.**
Uxbridge Arms *13 Uxbridge Street, W8 7TQ (7727 7326).* Charming, old-fashioned pub. **Map p279 A7.**

Shepherd's Bush

Albertine
1 Wood Lane, W12 7DP (8743 9593/www.gonumber. com/albertine). Shepherd's Bush tube. **Open** 10am-11pm Mon-Thur; 10am-midnight Fri; 6.30pm-midnight Sat. **Food served** noon-10.30pm Mon-Fri; 6.30-10.30pm Sat. **Credit** MC, V. Wine bar
This long-standing wine bar may look rather old-fashioned – drippy candles, dark church pews, wines chalked on a large board – but it's kept up with trends in the wine world. Australia forms a major part of the list, with the highlight being posh versions of normally rather dull branded wines. Wynns John Riddoch cabernet sauvignon 1996 and Lindemans Pyrus 1998 offer a chance to taste what these companies can really do, and there's an impressively long list of 38 wines by the glass. Don't be afraid to seek advice; the friendly staff wear their considerable knowledge lightly. Albertine is a warm, convivial place, with people chatting loudly and at length rather than kicking off, as tends to happen on the Green outside. A pleasant respite from much of Shepherd's Bush.
Bar available for hire. Bookings not accepted (evenings). Off-licence. Separate room for parties, seats 25.

Anglesea Arms
35 Wingate Road, W6 0UR (8749 1291). Goldhawk Road or Ravenscourt Park tube. **Open** 11am-11pm Mon-Sat; noon-10.30pm Sun. **Food served** 12.30-2.45pm, 7-10.30pm Mon-Sat; 12.30-3.30pm, 7-10pm Sun. **Credit** MC, V. Gastropub
This friendly neighbourhood gastropub is on a quiet suburban street, not far from traffic-clogged Goldhawk Road. A smallish place, it features mahogany panels, old sofas pulled up to the open fire, perimeter bench seats and a few outdoor tables at the front. At the rear is the dining area – lit by a large skylight, with a bare-brick wall enlivened by an African-style mural – where the open kitchen serves excellent gastro fare (we were impressed by a main of roast gilthead bream). The bar has a good selection of ales: Old

West

Havelock Tavern

Speckled Hen, Timothy Taylor Landlord, Deuchars IPA and London Pride among them – indeed, in the 1970s, the Anglesea was one of the first free houses to sell real ale from independent breweries. Lagers include San Miguel, Leffe and Hoegaarden, while fans of the grape get 90 alternatives (Billaud-Simon Chablis, £28.50; Reserva Bodega Ostatu Rioja, £36).

Babies and children welcome: high chairs. Tables outdoors (5, pavement).

Bush Bar & Grill

45A Goldhawk Road, W12 8QP (8746 2111/www. bushbar.co.uk). Goldhawk Road tube. **Open** noon-11pm Mon-Wed, Sun; noon-midnight Thur; noon-1am Fri, Sat. **Food served** noon-11pm Mon-Wed, Sun; noon-midnight Thur-Sat. **Credit** AmEx, MC, V. Bar/Restaurant

A short passageway of spotless white walls and red lights takes you into this former milk-bottling factory, now a swish bar-restaurant. The high ceiling is all ventilation pipes, while huge windows overlook leather bench seats that are large enough to prevent the place from appearing cavernous. The disappointing range of draught lagers is improved by bottles of Vedett, Duvel and Paulaner, and the 40-strong wine list include a Jaffelin, Mâcon Fuisse (£23.75) and a Delta Vineyard pinot noir from New Zealand (£26.50). There's also an extensive range of cocktails (£6.75-£8.50): try a Cabaret of Gordon's gin, Benedictine, Noilly Pratt Blanc vermouth and Angostura bitters. A slit along one wall reveals a kitchen serving Modern European cuisine to the raised dining area; the menu changes monthly, but featured haddock and salmon fishcakes and roast rack of lamb on our most recent visit. New ownership has seen minor alterations to the layout and a major improvement in the staff's demeanour.

a large picture of a greyhound. Entertainment takes the form of a very popular Monday night quiz, bands on Wednesday and a table football table in the corner. It's a Fuller's pub, so selections on tap include London Pride, London Porter, Organic Honey Dew, Hoegaarden and Grolsch. There's also a 30-strong selection of wines, plus a few bottles of bubbly.

Babies and children welcome (until 7pm): high chairs. Disabled: toilet. Games (table football). Music (bands 9pm Wed; free). Quiz (9pm Mon; £2). Tables outdoors (10, garden; 3, pavement). TV.

Defectors Weld

170 Uxbridge Road, W12 8AA (8749 0008/www. defectors-weld.com). Shepherd's Bush tube. **Open** noon-midnight Mon-Thur; noon-1am Fri, Sat; noon-11pm Sun. **Food served** noon-3pm, 5-10pm Mon-Thur; noon-3pm, 5pm-midnight Fri; noon-10pm Sat, Sun. **Credit** MC, V. Pub

This stylish, modern two-storey pub on the corner of Shepherd's Bush Green is part of the Lock Tavern family, and like its forebear it gets packed out with a young, lively and down-to-earth crowd. The best seating is at the rear, in an area sectioned off by patterned drapes, with separate booths beneath large, tassled orange lampshades. Stark, arty photographic portraits hang on the walls, among them a knight and disillusioned bear hanging over the disused fireplace. When things get too busy downstairs, head to the snug candlelit bar upstairs; divided into two by large curtains, it is a thoroughly laid-back affair. On tap you'll find Amstel, Staropramen, Leffe, Franziskaner and Früli; real-ale heads get Greene King IPA and London Pride.

Babies and children admitted (until 5pm). Bar available for hire. Disabled: toilet. Function room. Games (board games). Music (DJs 8pm Fri-Sat, 3pm Sun; free).

Havelock Tavern NEW

57 Masbro Road, W14 0LS (7603 5374/www.the havelocktavern.co.uk). Hammersmith or Shepherd's Bush tube/Kensington (Olympia) tube/rail. **Open** 11am-11pm Mon-Sat; noon-10.30pm Sun. **Food served** 12.30-2.30pm, 7-10pm Mon-Sat; 12.30-3pm, 7-9.30pm Sun. **No credit cards.** Gastropub

This smart, well-established gastropub, located in a quiet residential area near Brook Green, reopened in 2006 after a devastating fire. It's a gastropub in the proper sense: a pub that serves great food, rather than a restaurant in a pub. Hence there's no booking and you have to pay up front by cash or cheque – which, due to the place's undiminished popularity, can be a problem. The atmosphere is lively and informal, attracting a thirtysomething crowd of regulars who enjoy draught Flowers Original, London Pride and Marston's Pedigree, and some rather ordinary lagers. The wine list is well balanced, with a dozen of each colour (Good Hope pinot noir, £22; Four Sisters sauvignon blanc, £19), four of them by the glass. A fine operation – we're glad it's back.

Babies and children welcome: high chairs. Bar available for hire. Bookings not accepted. Tables outdoors (6, garden; 2, pavement).

Seven Stars Bar & Dining Room

243 Goldhawk Road, W12 8EU (8748 0229/www. sevenstarsdining.co.uk). Goldhawk Road tube. **Open** 11am-midnight Mon-Thur, Sun; 11am-2am Fri, Sat. **Food served** noon-3pm, 6-10pm Mon-Sat; noon-10pm Sun. **Credit** MC, V. Bar/Restaurant

Babies and children welcome: high chairs. Booking advisable. Disabled: toilet. Separate room for parties, seats 40. Tables outdoors (16, patio).

Crown & Sceptre

57 Melina Road, W12 9HY (8746 0060). Goldhawk Road or Shepherd's Bush tube. **Open** noon-11pm Mon-Sat; noon-10.30pm Sun. **Food served** noon-3pm, 6-9.45pm Mon-Fri; noon-9.45pm Sat; noon-8.45pm Sun. **Credit** AmEx, MC, V. Gastropub

Despite a gastro conversion and the inevitable open kitchen, this old Victorian pub could be stuck in the late 1950s. Frosted glass doors swing into a bright, open seating area, where tables are pushed into every available space so that getting round them can be difficult during busy times. Red leather benches follow the outer walls, which are rather bare apart from an embossed crown and

This ambitious bar and restaurant is an ideal spot in which to wind down after the bustle of Goldhawk Road. The bare-brick walls are softened by an open fire, slouchy leather sofas and large orange lampshades that contain ever smaller shades, like matryoshka dolls. The rear dining area has a large open kitchen (dishing out the likes of ribeye, sea bass, burgers and pasta), ornate heraldic mirrors and some intimate enclaves. Curtains section it off from a high-ceilinged chill-out lounge, which has a large golden chandelier, hung beneath ventilation pipes, as its centrepiece. The music is as laid-back as the mixed crowd. Draught options include Adnams Spindrift, Pilsner Urquell, Peetermans and Hoegaarden, and the wine list is compact but eclectic: Domaine Vacheron Sancerre (£18.50), perhaps, or a Griffin Vineyard shiraz (£15.95).
Babies and children admitted. Disabled: toilet. Restaurant. Tables outdoors (3 long tables, garden).

Also in the area...
Davy's White City *Units 4 & 5, Media Centre, White City Media Village, Wood Lane, W12 7ST (8811 2862). Branch.*
Goldhawk *122 Goldhawk Road, W12 8HH (8576 6921).* Spacious modern pub with art displayed on the walls and the likes of Sleeman and Küppers Kölsch on tap.

Westbourne Grove

Cow
89 Westbourne Park Road, W2 5QH (7221 0021/www.thecowlondon.co.uk). Royal Oak or Westbourne Park tube. **Open** noon-11pm Mon-Thur; noon-midnight Fri, Sat; noon-10.30pm Sun. **Food served** noon-3.30pm, 6-10.30pm Mon-Sat; noon-3.30pm, 6-10pm Sun. **Credit** MC, V. Gastropub
Gastrobar guru Tom Conran runs this two-storey operation: an Irish pub downstairs and renowned restaurant upstairs, with another dining area at the back of the pub. The versatile kitchen provides diners on both levels with first-rate seafood and pies. Plates of rock oysters sit atop the bar counter, invariably accompanied by a decent pint of Guinness, and equally invariably devoured by self-important regulars who swarm the modest interior. Other choices on tap include ESB, London Pride, Hoegaarden and delicious amber De Koninck from Antwerp. More Belgian brews feature by the bottle. Not surprisingly, the wine list is discerning – it might take you a while to pick out a La di Motte pinot grigio at £22, but it will be worth it.
Babies and children admitted (lunch). Restaurant available for hire. Tables outdoors (4, pavement).
Map p279 B5.

Crazy Homies
127 Westbourne Park Road, W2 5QL (7727 6771). Royal Oak or Westbourne Park tube. **Open** 6.30pm-midnight Mon-Fri; noon-midnight Sat, Sun. **Food served** 6.30-11pm Mon-Fri; noon-11.30pm Sat, Sun. **Credit** MC, V. Gastrobar
Commendably more downbeat than Tom Conran's other establishments, this vampish, Mexican-themed venue (next to its sister bar-diner, Lucky Seven) is hugely popular, which is why TC is planning to expand it. The odd skull hides amid the cacti and a jukebox full of Tarantino-esque tunes pounds out dark and dirty delights. The food, inspired by the street vendors and neighbourhood *taquerias*

found throughout Mexico, is delectable and reasonably priced. Equally authentic are the margaritas, the main element of the cocktail selection, featuring such delights as a Batanga of tequila, lime and Coke, with a salted rim, for £6. The bottled beers from south of the border include a Dos Equis amber (£3.50) and rarely found Casta Triguera wheat ale (£3.75).
Babies and children admitted. Bar available for hire. Function room. Jukebox. Tables outdoors (1, pavement).
Map p279 A5.

Prince Bonaparte
80 Chepstow Road, W2 5BE (7313 9491/www.the-prince-bonaparte.co.uk). Notting Hill Gate or Royal Oak tube. **Open** noon-11pm Mon-Sat; noon-10.30pm Sun. **Food served** noon-10pm Mon-Thur; noon-9pm Fri-Sun. **Credit** AmEx, MC, V. Gastropub
A large, open-plan Victorian pub-gone-gastro, site for Johnny Vaughan's Strongbow ads, the Bonaparte has a high reputation for its food and variety of drinks. Draught London Pride, Schneider Weiss, Budvar and Hoegaarden are complemented by an eclectic, 37-strong wine list, including a rich Vidal pinot noir from New Zealand and a dry and refreshing Don Pabiot Pouilly-Fumé (both £19). An already healthy crowd expands on Thursday, when the resident female DJ spins an '80s mix, and at weekends, when the loud interaction and background sounds render conversation impossible. On a quiet lunchtime, though, you can recline in a leather armchair by an open fire and browse the paintings in the gallery before taking your place in the dining area for a slap-up meal.
Art exhibitions. Babies and children admitted (until 6pm). Bar available for hire. Disabled: toilet. TV.
Map p279 A5.

Tiroler Hut
27 Westbourne Grove, W2 4UA (7727 3981/www.tirolerhut.co.uk). Bayswater or Queensway tube. **Open** 6.30pm-1am Tue-Sat; 6.30pm-midnight Sun. **Food served** 6.30pm-midnight Tue-Sat; 6.30-11pm Sun. **Credit** AmEx, DC, MC, V. Bar/Restaurant
Bonkers with bells on, the Tiroler Hut is a kitsch and wonderfully entertaining destination. Run by the same family for four decades, this basement bar gives owner Joseph ample scope to appear in lederhosen, squeezing an accordion. He may yodel. He might tinkle with Tyrolean cowbells. Octagenarian Europeans, ex-Spurs players and people you might have seen on the telly gather at the bar, sipping draught Dortmunder Union or Bergadler, bottled Erdinger Weiss or Dunkel. Unusual but welcome Hungarian wines (Szekszárdi Bull's Blood, £13.90) and spirits, such as the dark and dreadful Unicum, also feature. The food is a central European mix of meats with sauerkraut and dumplings; ravenous vegetarian couples can dive into the cheese fondue (£20.50 for two).
Babies and children admitted. Booking essential (restaurant). Entertainment (cowbell show 9pm Wed-Sun). Restaurant available for hire. Vegan dishes.
Map p279 B6.

Westbourne
101 Westbourne Park Villas, W2 5ED (7221 1332/www.thewestbourne.com). Royal Oak or Westbourne Park tube. **Open** 5-11pm Mon; 11am-11pm Tue-Fri; 11am-11pm Sat; noon-10.30pm Sun. **Food served** 7-10pm Mon; 12.30-3pm, 7-10pm Tue-Fri; 12.30-3.30pm, 7.30-10.30pm Sat; 12.30-3.30pm, 6.30-9.30pm Sun. **Credit** MC, V. Gastropub

Nectar. *See p124.*

Booze talking

Prince Arthur

You are?
Tom Helliwell, landlord of the Prince Arthur, Eversholt Street, Euston.
Tell us how you came to be landlord here.
The Arthur was in a bad way when I arrived. For years it was a boozer for posties from the nearby sorting office – then the sorting office was moved to Stonebridge Park. In three years the pub lost all of its trade; the only customers were drug dealers and old men talking to themselves. The area itself took a general nosedive too – a strip club, a brothel and three adult video shops were opened on the same road. To cap it all off the manager of the pub was murdered in 1997.
How did you turn around the pub's fortunes?
It was difficult because I had no money to refurbish. Instead I had to change the clientele through good management and good service. To me a pub is like a church – it's based around the service. But I needed a blank canvas before I could make those improvements. In the first three months I barred over 100 people. Then, as the money started coming in, I reinvested. I introduced table service, revived the drinks list to include four real ales and plenty of wines, and changed the ambience by putting on varied background music, dimming the lights and putting candles and fresh flowers on the tables.
When did things begin to look up?
I saw a real change after seven months, when women started to feel comfortable enough to come in. I put a lot of my soul into this place during the first three years and now I have a strong customer core of workers from schools and offices nearby.
What does the future hold?
I've just bought the Woodman over in Highgate – it also has the wrong clientele for its surroundings – and I'm looking forward to fixing things there.

The in-crowd park their flash wheels in front of the large front terrace and join the rest of their Notting Hill ilk here. Inside, the decor is traditional French bistro, including a zinc bar counter, wine racks, mirrors and bare floors. Rough walls are covered in posters depicting film, art and theatre. A decent beer selection includes draught Flowers, Leffe, Warsteiner and Hoegaarden and bottled Belgian brews. Considering the clientele, the wine list is well-priced, with Sicilian Nero d'Avola (£15) and Domaine Champeau Pouilly-Fumé (£19). The tempting menu covers the usual gastro faves (ribeye steak, organic salmon, duck breast), but, unusually, changes twice a day. Given the character of the place and its public, you would expect the service to be aloof. It's not.
Babies and children welcome (until 8pm): high chairs. Bar available for hire. Tables outdoors (14, terrace). Wi-Fi. **Map p279 B5.**

Westbourne Park

Grand Union
45 Woodfield Road, W9 2BA (7286 1886). Westbourne Park tube. **Open** noon-11pm Mon-Thur; noon-midnight Fri, Sat; noon-10.30pm Sun. **Food served** noon-10pm Mon-Sat; noon-9pm Sun. **Credit** AmEx, MC, V. Bar
Once an old boozer used by workers from the nearby bus depot, the Grand Union, in keeping with its upmarket location, is now a gastropub. Pleasingly, the transformation has been kind, with some of its character retained inside a cosy interior – particularly in the dimly lit corner warmed by an open fire. London Pride, Leffe, Hoegaarden and Kirin feature on draught, while an extensive selection of European and New World favourites (Domaine Durand Sancerre, £25) accompany good gastro fare. In summer, the Grand Union's pretty terrace by the famed canal of the same name is handy for barbecues – you just have to ignore the tyre mountain on the opposite bank and the odd floating shopping trolley.
Babies and children admitted (until 6pm). Function room. Tables outdoors (20, canalside terrace). **Map p279 A4.**

Metropolitan
60 Great Western Road, W11 1AB (7229 9254/www. realpubs.co.uk). Westbourne Park tube. **Open** noon-11.30pm Mon-Thur; noon-midnight Fri, Sat; noon-10.30pm Sun. **Food served** noon-3.30pm, 6.30-10.30pm Mon-Fri; noon-10.30pm Sat; 1-8pm Sun. **Credit** AmEx, MC, V. Gastropub
This large gastropub manages – just – to pull back from the brink of out-and-out trendiness. The bar on the ground floor still feels like a local, albeit one filled with the loud and fashionable; the Metropolitan is firmly on the Cow and Grand Union circuit. Property prices can be discussed (and lamented) in the upstairs restaurant, with its alfresco summer terrace. Downstairs, the choice of draught beers includes Adnams Broadside, Hobgoblin and Hoegaarden, and there's no lack of variety on the 30-strong wine list, which features a dark, intense Argentine Cabernet malbec (£15.50). The light and upbeat atmosphere of weekday lunchtimes gives way to the place being politely mobbed on Sunday; quality roasts and DJs are the root cause.
Babies and children welcome (until 7pm): high chairs. Music (DJs 5.30pm Sun; free). Restaurant. Tables outdoors (8, heated garden). TV (big screen). **Map p279 A5.**

West

South West

The King's Road might be the foremost stretch for Chelsea nightlife – maybe flash **Apartment 195**, or mead-specialising cocktail lounge **Nectar** – but its backstreets are where you'll find top-notch gastropubs **Lots Road Pub & Dining Room** and the **Pig's Ear**. To the north-east, Earl's Court boasts eccentric wine bar and music spot the **Troubadour**; to the south-west, Fulham has been bolstered by the arrival of cocktail bar **Mokksh**. Parsons Green's infamous pub the 'Sloaney Pony' (more properly the **White Horse**) might face competition in the form of two new Young's ventures: **Duke on the Green** and the well-located **Waterside**. For live music, there are few London pubs better than Putney's **Half Moon**. In Wandsworth, gastropubs the **Alma** and the **Ship** rule the roost, but we like the quirky boho pub-cum-bar the **Cat's Back**. Both Barnes and Wimbledon boast their own excellent gastropubs (newcomer the **Brown Dog** in the former, the **Leather Bottle** in the latter), but there's something about Barons Court's unreconstructed **Colton Arms** that lures us back time and time again.

Barnes

Brown Dog ![NEW]
28 Cross Street, SW13 0AP (8392 2200/www.the browndog.co.uk). Barnes Bridge rail. **Open** noon-11pm Mon-Sat; noon-10pm Sun. **Food served** noon-3pm, 7-10pm Mon-Fri; noon-5pm, 7-10pm Sat, Sun. **Credit** AmEx, MC, V. Gastropub
Charmingly small, like the cottages around it, the Brown Dog is very much a local gastropub for local gastropeople.

The 150-year-old property is split into a cosy bar and modestly proportioned dining room with just 30 covers; there's also a beer garden. Foodie sensibilities are hinted at via citrus fruit on the bar and mains like lamb shank with braised root veg, while the fleece-lined dog basket on the floor subliminally signals the owner's hope this pub can still be enjoyed as a boozer. The brief, wallet-friendly wine list is mostly French. Beers on tap include Adnams, London Pride, Harveys Sussex Ale and Beck's; there's also bottled Breton cider. A great spot.
Dining room. Disabled: toilet. Games (board games).

Bull's Head
373 Lonsdale Road, SW13 9PY (8876 5241/www. thebullshead.com). Barnes Bridge rail. **Open** noon-midnight daily. **Food served** noon-3.30pm, 6-10.30pm daily. **Credit** AmEx, MC, V. Pub
It wasn't so long ago that this riverside Young's pub had one of the most diverse drinks lists in the area. But the glory days might be over. Its once-lengthy wine list is now pared down to just a handful, plus a white and red of the month, and although there's still an extensive collection of whiskies, the pub does little to promote them – only a few labels were in evidence on our visit. Happily, its reputation as one of London's best jazz venues (since 1959) survives intact, with nightly gigs, and a perch at the large central bar is still a good spot at which to nurse a pint of Young's or chomp through a red curry from the Thai kitchen, housed in the former stables.
Babies and children welcome (family area). Function room. Games (board games). Music (jazz 8.30pm Mon-Sat; 1pm, 8.30pm Sun; £5-£15). TVs (big screen).

Spencer Arms
237 Lower Richmond Road, SW15 1HJ (8788 0640). Putney Bridge tube. **Open** 10am-midnight daily. **Food served** noon-2.30pm, 6.30-10pm Mon-Fri; noon-3pm, 6.30-10pm Sat; noon-4pm, 6.30-9.45pm Sun. **Credit** MC, V. Gastropub
Aged leather sofas on the brink of retirement and a chalky palette of Farrow & Ball paintwork: the interior of the Spencer Arms is a textbook rendition of the gastropub aesthetic, albeit one given the subtle glossy sheen that the

Colton Arms

SW15 postcode demands. The well-made, well-sourced food walks a similar line, with a menu of robust Modern British dishes that's updated twice daily. London Pride, Adnams Broadside and Hogs Back Best Bitter, served in dimpled glass mugs, make for a respectable beer offering, and the predominantly Old World wine list (including 15 by the glass) impresses with its length and range. Sit by the fire in the cosy side area, in the more spartan main room or, come summer, at the pavement tables within sight of the Common. Putney offers few more appealing pubs at which to while away downtime.
Babies and children welcome (until 9pm): children's menu; high chairs. Disabled: toilet. Games (board games). Music (jazz duo 9pm occasional Tue-Thur). Restaurant available for hire. Tables outdoors (8, pavement).

Sun Inn
7 Church Road, SW13 9HE (8876 5256). Barnes Bridge rail. **Open** noon-11pm Mon-Wed, Sun; noon-midnight Thur, Fri; 11am-midnight Sat. **Food served** noon-10pm Mon-Fri; 11am-10pm Sat; noon-9pm Sun. **Credit** AmEx, MC, V. Gastropub
Although the Sun's location, opposite a village duck pond lifted straight out of *The Darling Buds of May*, allows its patrons to live the ersatz bucolic dream for a couple of hours, it's unlikely the average rural boozer could match the diversity of its line-up. A recent makeover has seen the pub expand its already substantial drinks list even further, to include Adnams, guest ales and Weston's Organic Cider on tap, global bottled beers such as Paulaner, Chimay, Kirin and Peroni, plus 28 interesting and keenly priced

wines by the glass. Quality ingredients and a confident kitchen brigade lift the menu of straightforward pub standards above the norm, and the building's layout, a network of low-lit, cosy rooms and snugs, creates an intimate vibe even when the place is mobbed. The outdoor tables in the front yard are packed in fair weather.
Babies and children admitted (until 7pm). Tables outdoors (15, terrace).

Ye White Hart
The Terrace, Riverside, SW13 0NR (8876 5177). Barnes Bridge rail. **Open** 11am-midnight daily. **Food served** 11am-10.30pm Mon-Sat; noon-10.30pm Sun. **Credit** MC, V. Pub
Few pubs in this part of the world don't claim riverside locations, even though there might be the small matter of a car park or an SUV-choked thoroughfare separating them from the actual bank. This, however, is the real deal. Its narrow balcony and pocket-sized terrace hover right above the water, providing the perfect spot for exploring the extensive wine list or working your way to the bottom of a jug of Pimm's. Inside, the shabbily handsome Edwardian decor is kept from being self-consciously 'heritage' by the presence of a few fruit machines, a cashpoint (a useful community service) and volubly happy locals, contentedly necking Young's Ordinary or Special before gingerly tackling the treacherous spiral staircase down to the loos.
Function room. Games (fruit machines). Music (jazz 8pm Sun, winter only; free). Tables outdoors (6, balcony, riverside terrace; 8, garden; 12, tow path). TV (big screen, satellite).

Barons Court

★ **Colton Arms** NEW
*187 Greyhound Road, W14 9SD (7385 6956).
Barons Court tube.* **Open** noon-3pm, 5.30-11pm
Mon-Thur; 12noon-3pm, 5.30pm-midnight Fri; noon-
4pm, 6.30pm-midnight Sat; noon-4pm, 6.30pm-11pm
Sun. **Credit** MC, V. Pub
This wonderful old boozer could be the only reason to
visit the barren 'burbs of Barons Court (unless you're a
devoted *Grange Hill* fan – Fulham Prep, real-life location
of the show for 25 years, is just across the road). Dark oak
throughout gives the Colton's tiny front bar and back-room
seating area a rural feel; completing the picture, toilets are
labelled 'wenches' and 'sires'. A hidey-hole garden is ideal
in summer; time it right and you can hear the thwacks,
plonks and grunts from nearby Queen's Tennis Club, gates
by firm order of landlord Jonathan. He's run the place for
37 years and is on first-name terms with most of the old
war-horses and wellies who gather here.
Tables outdoors (5, garden).

Chelsea

Apartment 195
*195 King's Road, SW3 5ED (7351 5195/www.
apartment195.co.uk). Sloane Square tube then 11, 22
bus.* **Open** 6-11pm Mon-Sat. **Food served** 6-10.30pm
Mon-Sat. **Credit** AmEx, MC, V. Cocktail bar
You need to press a buzzer to gain admittance to this discreet little number (a sure way to impress your mates). But
despite the trappings of highfalutin' exclusivity, a warm
welcome awaits at the top of the stairs. There's a Vivienne
Westwood meets laid-back gentlemen's club feel to the
decor, with sumptuous leathers sofas, a garish pop holo-
gram and royally purple walls adorned with artwork and
an enormous, kitsch Penny Black stamp. The drinking is
all about the cocktails, with legendary mojitos; the delicious and surprisingly potent lulo mojito (containing
Havana Club seven-year-old) costs £8. To celebrate the
bar's fourth anniversary, they've launched a special
London-themed cocktail menu, featuring various fruity
offerings. The star turn is the aptly named Crown Jewels:
a glass of honey-sweetened rare cognac topped with vintage champagne that'll set you back a staggering £350.
Now that really would impress your friends.
Bar available for hire. Function room. **Map p280 C5.**

Beaufort House
*354 King's Road, SW3 5UZ (7352 2828/www.chelsea
venues.com). Sloane Square tube then 11, 19, 22, 211
bus.* **Open** 9.30am-1am Mon-Sat; 9.30am-12.30am Sun.
Food served 9.30am-3.30pm, 7pm-1am Mon-Wed;
9.30am-3.30pm Thur-Sat; 9.30am-11.30pm Sun. **Credit**
AmEx, MC, V. Cocktail bar
Gorgeous twentysomethings abound at this glamorous
Chelsea venue, posing by the bar and oiling the social
wheels with champagne and cocktails before moving on to
the King's Road clubs. And with cocktails packing a sharp
kick and sporting intriguing names like Inga from Sweden
and Cannabis Ice Tea (both £6.50), who wouldn't indulge?
The centrepiece of the room is the gleaming, horseshoe-
shaped bar, where the staff rattle their shakers under the

dim glow of a magnificent art deco-style chandelier; grand
mirrors and leather sofas complete the restrained but opulent decor. Acoustic musicians play early in the week, and
lunch/brunch is served daily, with a full dinner menu some
nights and tapas-style snacks at the weekend. On a Friday
night, the place was comfortably busy without being
packed out. A note of warning to beer drinkers: the bar
only stocks bottled Asahi, Sol and Stella.
*Babies and children admitted (until 6.30pm). Function
room. Music (musicians 10pm Mon-Wed, Sun; free).
Tables outdoors (10, heated patio). Wi-Fi (free).*
Map p280 B5.

Chelsea Potter
*119 King's Road, SW3 4PL (7352 9479). Sloane
Square tube then 11, 22 bus.* **Open** 11am-11pm
Mon-Fri; 11am-midnight Sat; noon-10.30pm Sun.
Food served 11am-9pm Mon-Sat; noon-9pm Sun.
Credit AmEx, DC, MC, V. Pub
Something of an anomaly in this neck of the woods, the
Chelsea Potter is a lively, single-room boozer. It may not
be as flash as the other bars on the King's Road, but it's
a fine place to rest weary feet after a frantic morning traips-
ing the shops, or to drop by for a relaxed pint or two of an
evening. High wooden tables (good for tourists to spread
out their maps on) play host to more down-to-earth Chelsea
folk; the cask ales are London Pride, Spitfire and Greene
King IPA; and the good-value pub grub ('posh bacon &
eggs') doesn't try to overreach itself with unnecessary
frills and furbelows. Stools by the window and tables out
on the pavement provide the perfect vantage point for a
spot of people-watching.
*Babies and children admitted (until 6pm). Games
(fruit machines). Tables outdoors (5, pavement).
TV (satellite).* **Map p280 D5.**

Chelsea Ram
*32 Burnaby Street, SW10 0PL (7351 4008). Fulham
Broadway tube/Sloane Square tube then 11, 22 bus.*
Open 11am-11pm Mon-Sat; noon-10.30pm Sun. **Food
served** noon-3pm, 6.30-10pm Mon-Sat; noon-4pm,
6-9pm Sun. **Credit** MC, V. Pub
Tucked away in a quiet residential area, this Young's pub
affords a civilised retreat from the noisier, glitzier watering holes of the nearby King's Road. Indeed, its sedate
charms are perfectly suited to cosy conversation, or flip-
ping though the Sunday papers over a pint of Special or a
glass of wine from the extensive New World selection. On
a Friday night, we found a delightful mixture of seasoned
regulars, cheery staff and unpretentious young things,
giving the place the feel of a relaxed but decidedly upmarket local. The tasteful matt brown and green colour
scheme, paintings on the walls and artful toilet door
(made up to look like old-fashioned bookshelves) are subtle but unmistakeable signs that you're in the salubrious
surrounds of Chelsea.
*Babies and children admitted. Function room.
Restaurant. Quiz (7.30pm 1st Mon of mth; free).
Tables outdoors (6, pavement). TV (big screen).*

Cooper's Arms
*87 Flood Street, SW3 5TB (7376 3120). Sloane Square
tube then 11, 22 bus.* **Open** 11am-11pm Mon-Sat; noon-
10.30pm Sun. **Food served** 11am-10pm Mon-Sat;
noon-9pm Sun. **Credit** AmEx, MC, V. Gastropub
From the solid red wood bar counter to the barometers and
moose's head on the wall, there's a reassuring air of age
and experience about this place. Young's and Bombardier

South West

are the well-kept ales, and a commendable selection of French wines are sold by the glass. A laid-back thirty-something crowd also seem to appreciate the generous portions of solid, unpretentious fare on offer, ranging from succulent burger staples to beautifully prepared spinach and ricotta ravioli or creamy baked camembert with rosemary and garlic. It's a pleasantly calm, unhurried sort of place, with light streaming through the big windows, a contented hum of chat and, thankfully, no loud background music to disturb the tranquility.
Babies and children admitted (until 6pm). Bar available for hire. Function room. TV. **Map p280 C6.**

Cross Keys
1 Lawrence Street, SW3 5NB (7349 9111/ www.thexkeys.co.uk). Sloane Square tube then 11, 22 bus. **Open** *noon-3pm, 7-11pm Mon-Sat; noon-4pm, 7-10.30pm Sun.* **Food served** *noon-3pm, 6-10.30pm Mon-Sat; noon-4pm, 5-9.30pm Sun.* **Credit** *AmEx, MC, V.* Gastropub
The downstairs bar may seem surprisingly small, given the large and splendidly ornate exterior, but there's more to this historic Chelsea pub than first meets the eye. A spacious conservatory restaurant to the rear is light and leafy, while the gallery area and 'Room at the Top', decked out with purple curtains, curly chandeliers and gilt-framed mirrors, resemble decadent 18th-century French salons. Food in the bar is simple but superior (toulouse sausages and mash with lentil jus, £8.90), while the restaurant's three menus show a promising seasonal focus. At lunchtime, the mix of American tourists and Chelsea ladies (complete with tiny dogs) seemed to be enjoying both the quality wine list and the delicate fussiness of their surroundings.
Babies and children admitted. Function rooms. Private dining rooms. Restaurant.

Fox & Hounds
29 Passmore Street, SW1W 8HR (7730 6367). Sloane Square tube. **Open** *11am-11pm Mon-Sat; noon-10.30pm Sun.* **Food served** *12.30-2.30pm Mon-Fri.* **Credit** *MC, V.* Pub
With its rich red wallpaper, warm dark wood fittings and fox's head mounted on the wall, this tiny, dimly lit Young's pub is the perfect antidote to an overdose of designed-to-the-hilt bars and gastropubs. Expect to see Chelsea pensioners in full regalia whiling away the hours over a Young's Winter Warmer ale at the minuscule bar, while a couple of well-bred sixth-form girls huddle in the corner discussing their A-levels. At the back, two worn red leather chesterfields, fox hunting paintings, old bookshelves and reading lamps give the impression of a small but perfectly formed gentlemen's club. An evening here is a slow, old-fashioned and intimate experience – something we all need every now and then.
Quiz (last Sun of every month 8pm; £1). **Map p280 E4.**

★ Lots Road Pub & Dining Room
114 Lots Road, SW10 0RJ (7352 6645/www.thespirit group.com). Fulham Broadway tube then 11 bus/Sloane Square tube then 11, 19, 22 bus. **Open** *11am-11pm Mon-Thur; 11am-midnight Fri, Sat; noon-10.30pm Sun.* **Food served** *noon-3pm, 5.30-10pm Mon-Fri; noon-10pm Sat, Sun.* **Credit** *AmEx, MC, V.* Gastropub
A stone's throw from posh Chelsea Harbour, Lots is a stylish über-gastropub, complete with huge windows, lofty ceiling and a throng of young Chelsea socialites packed round the L-shaped aluminium bar. Despite the crowd, bar service is quick and polite. The food, prepared in the open-plan kitchen and served in the slick dining area to the side of the bar, has a fearsomely good reputation – particularly the sticky toffee pudding. London Pride and Deuchars IPA compete with continental lagers at the taps, and there's no shortage of excellent wines by the glass. Thursday evenings are 'special' nights (complimentary bar snacks, rum and wine tastings). The only downside is the teeny-weeny toilets, but that's a minor quibble.
Babies and children welcome: high chairs. Disabled: toilet. Restaurant available for hire. Wine tastings (Thur eve).

Nectar
562 King's Road, SW6 2DZ (7326 7450/www. nectarbar.co.uk). Fulham Broadway tube. **Open** *noon-midnight Mon-Thur; noon-2am Fri, Sat.* **Food served** *5-10pm Mon-Sat.* **Credit** *AmEx, MC, V.* Cocktail bar
Coloured lighting, pink chairs and outrageous wallpaper in a spacious, open-plan setting mean that this stylish King's Road bar remains a popular Chelsea venue – and one that lends itself perfectly to private parties. The attractive mixture of cool contemporary design and retro 1970s kitsch is matched by the wild range of cocktails, with the signature Nectopia – Absolut Kurant, Galliano, wild Japanese bee honey and royal jelly are among its ingredients (£8) – being the pick of a honey-infused bunch. Mead is served at £3 a shot, and if you really can't wait to get the weekend fun started, you can pre-order a bottle of spirits with mixers to be ready and waiting on your table when you arrive.
Babies and children admitted (until 9pm). Bar available for hire. Music (DJs 9pm Thur-Sat; £3 after 10pm Fri, Sat). Tables outdoors (6, garden). TV (big screen, satellite).

Orange Brewery
37-39 Pimlico Road, SW1W 8NE (7730 5984). Sloane Square tube. **Open** *noon-11pm Mon-Fri; 11am-11pm Sat; noon-10.30pm Sun.* **Food served** *noon-8.30pm daily.* **Credit** *AmEx, DC, MC, V.* Pub
Ale lovers will find plenty to please at this solid, straight-talking pub, with London Pride, Greene King, Old Speckled Hen and Broadside on draught at the no-frills, L-shaped bar. A separate dining area similarly dispenses with anything too fancy and serves substantial, reasonably priced pub fare, offering sausages or pie of the day to the local office crowd who tend to make up the bulk of the clientele. To clear up the question of the unusual name – they used to brew their own beer on the premises, but sadly ceased operations in 2001, and the orange refers to the Prince of Orange rather than the citrus fruit. So now you know.
Babies and children admitted (until 7.30pm, restaurant only). Function room. Games (fruit machines, quiz machine). Quiz (7.30pm Mon; £1). Restaurant. Tables outdoors (7, pavement).

Phoenix
23 Smith Street, SW3 4EE (7730 9182/www.geronimo-inns.co.uk). Sloane Square tube then 11, 22 bus. **Open** *11am-11pm Mon-Sat; noon-10.30pm Sun.* **Food served** *noon-2.45pm, 7-9.45pm Mon-Fri; noon-4pm, 7-9.45pm Sat; noon-4pm Sun.* **Credit** *MC, V.* Gastropub
Shabby chic is the order of the day in this stylish spot, with its fudge-coloured tiled exterior and welcoming, softly lit saloon. Worn velvet sofas, brown leather pouffes and scuffed wooden flooring exude laid-back elegance, and the narrow bar room is packed with well-to-do Chelsea folk (some even sporting striped scarves swept round their

South West

necks) and the spillover from the King's Road. Ales on tap are Adnams and Doom Bar, and the single malts are ecstatically earthy. The beautiful square dining room at the back aims to soar above run-of-the-mill pub standards and succeeds: crisp plum tomato and parmesan tartlet was surpassed only by a wonderful apple and mixed berry crumble served with crème anglaise.
Babies and children admitted. Dining Room. Games (board games). Tables outdoors (7, patio). Map p280 D4.

★ Pig's Ear
35 Old Church Street, SW3 5BS (7352 2908/www. thepigsear.co.uk). Sloane Square tube then 11, 22 bus. Open noon-11pm Mon-Sat; noon-10.30pm Sun. Food served 12.30-3pm, 7-10pm Mon-Fri; 12.30-4pm, 7-10pm Sat; 12.30-4pm, 7-9.30pm Sun. Credit AmEx, MC, V. Gastropub
Brimming with bohemian London character, this Chelsea treat does indeed serve tasty, deep-fried porcine ears (as well as the excellent Pig's Ear ale from the Uley Brewery in Gloucestershire). Indeed, the food in both the bar and the smart dining room upstairs is decidedly adventurous (chicken livers and sherry vinegar crostini; rock oysters with fennel salsa). The crowd is refreshingly mixed: elderly Chelsea eccentrics, local builders and a group of girlfriends decadently getting drunk on red wine in the middle of the day. Benches set back against the windows provide seating space in front of the attractive metal-topped bar. 'This is very English,' said the barman as he poured a free sample of ale. Very English, very London and very good.
Babies and children welcome: high chairs. Booking advisable (dining room). Games (board games). Restaurant available for hire. Map p280 C5.

Also in the area...
Brinkley's *47 Hollywood Road, SW10 9HX (7351 1683/www.brinkleys.com).* Branch of the Oratory and Putney Station. Map p280 A5.
Eclipse Chelsea *111-113 Walton Street, SW3 2HP (7581 0123).* Branch of Eclipse. Map p280 C3.
mybar *35 Ixworth Place, SW3 3QX (0871 223 7470).* Branch. Map p280 C4.
Tom's Kitchen *27 Cale Street, SW3 3QP (7349 0202/www.tomskitchen.co.uk).* First-floor cocktail bar above Tom Aikens' latest venture, a British-style brasserie. Map p280 D4.

Earl's Court

King's Head
17 Hogarth Place, SW5 0QT (7244 5931). Earl's Court tube. Open noon-11pm Mon-Sat; noon-10.30pm Sun. Food served noon-9.45pm daily. Credit AmEx, MC, V. Pub
The only thing letting down this excellent backstreet local are the cutesy signs written in wobbly lower-case handwriting, telling you that the roasts are 'as good as mum's', and recommending 'rosey rosés' as 'our favourite wine'. If you're serving up excellent food and booze for adult human beings, why the kindergarten-speak? This gripe aside, there's a nicely varied selection of lagers (Amstel, Star, Paulaner, Früli); lip-smacking Fuller's ales with Timothy Taylor Landlord as back-up; and reliable bar food, ranging from wasabi snacks to top-notch sausages and mash (although it's not always quick to arrive). The

Booze talking
Colton Arms

You are?
Jonathan Nunn, landlord of the Colton Arms in Barons Court.
The pub has been run by your family for nearly 80 years now...
That's right. My parents ran the place for 42 years and I took over 37 years ago. How could I not? It's my family heritage. My parents still help out today.
Tell us about the pub.
It's the hub of the community. We've maintained a real community atmosphere. It's hard work, but I make sure I'm here most of the time. Being a landlord is a life choice... and one that's not very conducive to married life, I'm afraid.
Who drinks here?
Everyone, from professionals to retirees, manual workers to royalty. They all blend in together. We're always welcoming and discreet – a sanctuary for people to relax and have a drink in. I pride myself on it being a safe and peaceful environment; a girl can come in and sit on her own and not worry. I take care of my customers and make sure it's always a non-confrontational, happy atmosphere.
So you're quite protective of your regulars?
Absolutely. I always look after them – I have spare house keys, addresses and phone numbers behind the bar. I consider the regulars in all my decisions, because I can't afford to upset them and I don't want to. For example, I rarely close for private parties because they'd have to go elsewhere.
Do you ever drink in other pubs?
Never. I've never been tempted to go anywhere else – this is home for me. It's such a happy place, and most people go home smiling. That includes me.

surroundings are restful and welcoming, with comfortable sofas, framed daubings on the walls, and wooden tables and chairs that are not only higgledy but decidedly piggledy too. Top-rate.

Disabled: toilet. Games (retro arcade machines). Quiz (8pm Mon; £2). TVs (big screen).

One-Eight-One NEW

The Rockwell Hotel, 181 Cromwell Road, SW5 0SF (7244 2000/www.therockwell.com). Earl's Court tube. **Open/food served** 9am-11.30pm daily. **Credit** AmEx, MC, V. Bar

You might not immediately seek out a place on the A4 to kick off your evening and, indeed, the staff of the Rockwell Hotel seemed almost surprised when we asked if we could have a drink in their bar. It's a pristinely decorated little area, divided from the acclaimed restaurant by a small partition. But you don't pay over the odds for the swank; the wines are actually below average pub prices and the well-presented six-quid cocktails come with hefty bowls of high-calibre nuts. The clientele on our visit consisted of a middle-aged couple loudly discussing the ingredients for fish pie over a soundtrack of soporific incidental music – but get a few of your mates in and you could transform the ambience pretty quickly.

Babies and children welcome: high chairs. Disabled: toilet. Tables outdoors (10, garden). Restaurant.

Troubadour

265 Old Brompton Road, SW5 9JA (7370 1434/ www.troubadour.co.uk). Earl's Court tube/West Brompton tube/rail. **Open** *Café* 9am-midnight daily. *Club* 8pm-midnight Mon-Wed, Sun; 8pm-2am Thur-Sat. **Food served** 9am-midnight daily. **Credit** MC, V. Café/Club

Drinking holes don't come much more eccentric than the Troubadour. It's a slice of 1960s bohemia that hasn't yet dragged itself into the 21st century – much to the relief of the regulars, who lounge around sipping coffee or red wine while daydreaming about their unfinished acoustic ballads and surreal novellas. The marble tabletops, wooden stools and ornate mirrors are lifted straight out of a European café, and the music drifting up from the basement venue (where Jimi Hendrix, Bob Dylan, Joni Mitchell and many others have played) is predictably heartfelt and unplugged. Beers are primarily bottled and referred to as 'talking water'; reds, whites and bubbles are around £4.50 a glass; daiquiris and sours are just under £6 and arrive, hilariously, in a Duralex tumbler – but you really wouldn't want it any other way. Idiosyncratically glorious.

Club available for hire. Function room. Games (board games). Music (bands/musicians 8pm Tue, Wed; £5; bands 8pm Thur-Sat; £5-£15). Poetry (8-10pm alternate Mon; £6). Restaurant. Tables outdoors (8, garden; 4, pavement). TV (big screen, satellite). **Map p280 A4.**

Warwick Arms

160 Warwick Road, W14 8PS (7603 3560). Earl's Court or High Street Kensington tube. **Open** noon-midnight Mon-Sat; noon-11.30pm Sun. **Food served** noon-3pm, 5.30-11.30pm Mon-Fri; 5.30-11.30pm Sat; noon-3pm, 5.30-10.30pm Sun. **Credit** MC, V. Pub

Plonked opposite a Homebase in the middle of nowhere, this Fuller's pub has made efforts to outdo its Young's rival a couple of doors down – and it's ahead by several lengths. A large array of Scottish and Irish whiskies are proudly on display, and the range of draught beers includes London Pride, ESB and Adnams. The idiosyncratic junk shop decor (accordions, tubas, jugs, field telephones and other

Arbiter

knick-knacks abound) gives off the unmistakeable ambience of an insane uncle's living room, but in a good way. Rumbling stomachs can be silenced with Indian food brought politely to your table. The flyers advertising forthcoming beer festivals make a visit to the Warwick an even more attractive prospect.
Bar available for hire. Tables outdoors (6, pavement). TV.

Fulham

Arbiter NEW
308-310 North End Road, SW6 1NQ (7385 8001). Fulham Broadway tube. **Open** 5pm-midnight Mon; 12.30pm-midnight Tue, Wed; 12.30pm-1am Thur, Fri; 11.30am-1am Sat; 11.30am-11pm Sun. **Food served** 5-10pm Mon; 12.30-3pm, 5-10pm Tue-Fri; 11.30am-10pm Sat; 11.30am-9pm Sun. **Credit** AmEx, MC, V. Gastrobar
Welcome back to Makeover Corner: another year, another valiant stab at making this venue vaguely attractive to the punters of SW6. This time it's a straightforward gastrobar, but the voluminous armchairs, sofas and standard lamps mean there's only space for about 20 people to sit down. Not that this is a problem; most people strolling up from the Broadway merely look in quizzically, while those that do wander in tend to subsist on bottles of Magners while nodding along to the Kaiser Chiefs on the sound system. It's a shame; there's Timothy Taylor Landlord on tap, the staff are knowledgeable about the wine list and the cocktails are well mixed – but do the locals care? Not really. Will they ever wise up?
Function room. Games (board games). Music (DJ 8pm last Sat of every month; musicians 8pm occasional Wed, Thur; both free).

Fox & Pheasant
1 Billing Road, SW10 9UJ (7352 2943). Fulham Broadway tube. **Open** 11am-midnight Mon-Sat; 11am-11pm Sun. **Food served** noon-2.30pm, 6-9pm Mon-Fri. **Credit** MC, V. Pub
The Fox & Pheasant is one of those backstreet boozers that gives you the feeling that you're having a night out in a grim Lancashire town. Reassuringly English in the details (beer mugs hung on hooks behind the bar, slightly dingy lighting, St George's flag in the corner, a crowd of blokes throwing darts with pinpoint precision despite the effects of several pints), it's a welcome refuge from aspirational Fulham, where an authentic British pub would be viewed with abject horror. You won't find anything exotic to drink – just Greene King IPA, Foster's and a couple of decent wines – but it's cheap, it's cheerful and conversation flows freely, thanks to the sole TV set having a tea towel draped over it.
Babies and children admitted (garden; until 5pm). Games (darts). Tables outdoors (8, heated garden). TV.

Mitre
81 Dawes Road, SW6 7DU (7386 8877/ www.fulhammitre.com). Fulham Broadway tube. **Open** noon-11pm Mon-Sat; noon-10.30pm Sun. **Food served** noon-3pm, 6-9.30pm Mon-Sat; 1-4pm, 6-9.30pm Sun. **Credit** MC, V. Pub
You can't help thinking that there's something of a battle being waged here. One one side is the publican, who has generously laid on some fantastic ales (including the always welcome Deuchars), decorated the bar with fresh flowers, employed a top-notch chef serving excellent gastro fare and assembled an impressive wine selection. On the other side, however, are several hundred twentysomething regulars, who pack the place out night after night,

but are mainly interested in getting lashed on lager and Bacardi Breezers. A garden at the back offers some respite from the shouting and guzzling. The publican may well be happy with his takings, but the Mitre feels like it's become a victim of its own success.
Babies and children admitted (until 7pm). Disabled: toilet. Tables outdoors (30, garden). TV (satellite).

Mokssh NEW
222-224 Fulham Road, SW10 9NB (7352 6548/ www.mokssh.com). Fulham Broadway tube. **Open** noon-midnight Tue-Thur; noon-1am Fri, Sat; noon-10pm Sun. **Food served** noon-3pm, 6-11pm Tue-Thur; noon-3pm, 6pm-midnight Fri, Sat; noon-3pm, 6-9pm Sun. **Credit** AmEx, DC, MC, V. Cocktail bar
This carefully styled Indian bar-cum-restaurant looks like the inside of a gigantic boiled sweet. The cocktails are similarly sugary, with classic recipes given candied, spicy overtones by a couple of serious-looking bartenders. The menu emphasises the staff's dedication to perfection; whisky isn't mixed with mint leaves, it's 'rambunctiously muddled', while cognac is 'reworked' with vanilla liquor. Instead of nuts, you're served exquisite popadoms that hint at the quality of food the kitchen provides; unfortunately, these have the effect of ripping out your taste buds and obscuring the flavour of the drinks. A handful of reds and whites and a couple of Indian lagers (Kingfisher, Cobra) add variety to the drinks list, but it's the Rosebud Martinis and fiery Gingeranis that keep pulling in the punters.
Bar available for hire. Restaurant.

Also in the area...
Cock & Hen Brewpub *360 North End Road, SW6 1LY (7385 6021).* Fulham gastropub with Adnams Oyster Stout and Explorer on tap.
Fulham Tup *1 Harwood Terrace, SW6 2AF (7610 6131).* Branch.
Joe's Brasserie *130 Wandsworth Bridge Road, SW6 2UL (7731 7835/www.brinkleys.com).* Branch of the Oratory and Putney Station (Brinkley's).

Mortlake

Ship
10 Thames Bank, SW14 7QR (8876 1439). Mortlake rail. **Open** 11am-11pm Mon-Fri; 11am-midnight Sat; noon-11pm Sun. **Food served** noon-9pm daily. **Credit** DC, MC, V. Pub
When drinkers are deprived – either by early sunsets or inclement weather – of the distraction of the riverside vista, the Ship is a pretty unremarkable place. The interior is as bland as the Budweiser brewed next door; the beer line-up is conservative, with London Pride the only real ale on offer; and while phrases like 'nuances of brioche' on the wine list and the presence of a few chunky candles represent a spirited stab at making the place more compelling, it's a fairly futile exercise. And the staff seem to know it: it was chairs on tables by 10.30pm on the winter's night we visited. But sit out on the sun-bathed patio on a summer's afternoon, drink in hand, watching rowers sweep their way up this glorious stretch of the Thames, and all that is an irrelevance.
Babies and children admitted (until 8pm). Function room. Games (board games, fruit machines, quiz machine). Music (covers band 9pm alternate Sat; free). Quiz (9pm Sun; £1). Tables outdoors (25, garden). TV (satellite).

Parsons Green

Amuse Bouche NEW
51 Parsons Green Lane, SW6 4JA (7371 8517/ www.abcb.co.uk). Parsons Green tube. **Open** noon-11pm Mon, Sun; noon-midnight Tue-Thur; noon-12.30am Fri, Sat. **Food served** noon-3.30pm, 6-10.30pm Mon, Sun; noon-3.30pm, 6-11pm Tue-Sat. **Credit** AmEx, DC, MC, V. Wine bar
Parsons Green has a busy new place dedicated to good-quality fizz. Wealthy bankers and smart women splash out at will in this calmly modern venue. And Amuse Bouche has an advantage over those central London hotel bars forced to list wines from one sponsoring champagne house alone. It has 30 different kinds, from the crisply dry Laurent-Perrier Ultra Brut to the sweet Louis Roederer Rich. Some smaller growers could be included along with Larmandier-Bernier, and it's a shame that a medium-sized house, Ruinart, has been dropped. But the fizz comes at the right temperature (cold but not freezing), with plenty of bubbles and acidity plus elegance in the case of Pol Roger White Label. Some will be put off by the braying customers, but you can't ignore one of the best places in town dedicated to champagne.
Babies and children admitted. Booking advisable. Off-licence. Separate room for parties, seats 40. Tables outdoors (6, courtyard).

Aragon House
247 New King's Road, SW6 4XG (7731 7313/www. aragonhouse.net). Parsons Green tube. **Open** 11am-11pm Mon-Sat; noon-10.30pm Sun. **Food served** noon-3pm, 6-10pm Mon-Fri; noon-9pm Sat, Sun. **Credit** AmEx, DC, MC, V. Pub
At Aragon (named after Catherine of Aragon, who lived in a manor house on this site in the 16th century), it's forever Sunday afternoon in the sumptuous inherited residence of a privately educated Oxbridge graduate. Chandeliers dangle, upholstery beckons, cigars lie patiently in humidors and a pair of antlers stick out of the wall. All this lies, somewhat inconspicuously, behind a black door on the New King's Road, making you feel like an opportunistic burglar when you walk in – particularly if you're wearing a parka. But it's worth plucking up courage; the real ales (Hogs Back TEA and two guest ales), delicate Sancerres and glasses of Pimm's are predictably delicious, and are insouciantly sipped by the immaculately manicured clientele. It's not that pricey, either, with food coming in at under a tenner for a main course. But then the true upper classes never did need to flash their cash.
Function rooms. Tables outdoors (5, garden; 12, patio).

Duke on the Green NEW
235 New King's Road, SW6 4XG (7736 2777/www. dukeonthegreen.co.uk). Parsons Green tube. **Open** 11am-midnight Mon-Fri; 10.30am-midnight Sat; 10.30am-11.30pm Sun. **Food served** noon-3pm, 6-10.30pm Mon-Fri; 10.30am-1pm, 6-10.30pm Sat; 10.30am-4pm, 6-9.30pm Sun. **Credit** AmEx, MC, V. Pub
This huge Young's pub on the south side of Parsons Green has made efforts to drag itself upmarket, and it hasn't done badly: it's buzzing even on usually quiet weeknights, with the wide range of seating – booths, stools and sofas – all enthusiastically grabbed. But in reality, it still feels like a chain pub – albeit an ambitious one: the martinis are on the watery side (but they are only a fiver), the wine list is divided into categories such as 'dare to be different' and

South West

Cat's Back. *See p132.*

'sit back and relax', and the presence of extensive beer tasting notes on the menu feels downright weird. But the staff are warm and accommodating, the atmosphere is convivial, and the beer is well kept. Worth a peek.
Disabled: toilet. Tables outdoors (pavement, 11).

Waterside NEW

Riverside Tower, Imperial Wharf, SW6 2SU (7371 0802/www.watersidelondon.com). Fulham Broadway tube. **Open** 11am-11.30pm daily. **Food served** 11am-4pm, 6-10.30pm Mon-Sat; noon-10pm Sun. **Credit** AmEx, DC, MC, V. Pub
Are pubs responsible for the customers they attract? Maybe. This new Young's pub, housed in a recently built luxury waterside development, is so vast that even large office parties seem to think their racket goes unnoticed. The staff did their best to be polite and were utterly charming to us, but too many people were hooting, hollering and generally creating an uncomfortable atmosphere for customers not there on drinking marathons. Let's assume the maelstrom on our visit was just bad timing, and that you come on a quieter night. You then have a spacious, three-levelled, modern pub with great river views, an outside terrace and a selection of Young's excellent cask-conditioned ales. Good jazz acts are a draw on Saturday nights; otherwise, the Waterside provides an excellent opportunity to have a snoop around the ritzy Imperial Wharf development.
Bar available for hire. Music (jazz Sat eve; free). Restaurant. Tables outdoors (front terrace, 24; back terrace, 10). Wi-Fi (free).

White Horse

1-3 Parsons Green, SW6 4UL (7736 2115/www. whitehorsesw6.com). Parsons Green tube. **Open** 11am-midnight Mon-Thur; 11am-1am Fri, Sat. **Meals served** noon-10.30pm Mon-Fri; 11am-10.30pm Sat, Sun. **Credit** AmEx, MC, V. Pub
Referring to this pub as the 'Sloaney Pony' has become a cliché; in fact, it should be recognised primarily for its sumptuous, globe-trotting range of bottled beers, especially Belgian ones, from bruins and krieks to delicious Saison Dupont. The clientele is evenly split between hooraying poshos, bearded CAMRA members and lager-drinking Londoners wondering what on earth's going on. Aside from a well-appointed restaurant area, the pub is nothing flash; there are tables and benches rather than sofas and coffee tables, and the toilets are labelled 'Pistols' and 'Dolls'. A worthy pilgrimage for anyone even remotely interested in Belgian or British brews (draught offerings too).
Babies and children admitted. Disabled: toilet. No piped music or jukebox. Tables outdoors (30, garden).

Putney

Coat & Badge

8 Lacy Road, SW15 1NL (8788 4900/www.geronimo-inns.co.uk). Putney Bridge tube/Putney rail/14, 39, 74, 85 bus. **Open** 11am-midnight Mon-Sat; 11am-10.30pm Sun. **Food served** noon-3pm, 6-10.30pm Mon-Fri; noon-4pm, 6-10.30pm Sat; noon-4pm, 6-9.30pm Sun. **Credit** AmEx, MC, V. Pub

It's great when what is effectively a town-centre pub puts in a little effort and forces punters to try something different. To walk across the road from a shopping centre and be presented with Hook Norton, St Austell and Sharp's ales, and a large blackboard urging customers to 'forget merlot, try Chilean carmenère' is refreshing – especially when a large, garrulous crowd of twentysomethings seem to be taking those recommendations on board. Indeed, even in winter the throng often spills on to the paved area outside, kept warm by burning braziers. Aside from the ubiquitous TV that no one is watching, and mirrored pillars that give a Caesars Palace-style naffness to the decor, the Coat & Badge is a great old pub, bravely skiing off-piste. *Babies and children admitted (until 7pm). Disabled: toilet. Function room. Games (board games). Tables outdoors (25, terrace). TV.*

Duke's Head

8 Lower Richmond Road, SW15 1JN (8788 2552). Putney Bridge tube/22, 265 bus. **Open** 10am-midnight Mon-Thur; 11am-1am Fri, Sat; noon-midnight Sun. **Food served** 10am-10pm Mon-Sat; noon-10.30pm Sun. **Credit** AmEx, MC, V. Pub
This cavernous place on the banks of the Thames supposedly offers 'views of the river', but the vistas are only visible to diners, and are slightly compromised by drinkers spilling out of the pub with pints in hand and stumbling up and down the riverbank. Young's have once again made something of an attempt to tart the pub up for the middle classes, with menus in little folders, hilarious beer tasting notes and wines categorised in terms of their, er,

laid-back-ness. No one can deny the handsome character of the place, with its original Victorian features and gorgeously ornate glass screens, and it's always busy – but despite the ever-reliable Young's ales and eclectic wine list, it feels a bit like an upmarket Harvester. *No piped music or jukebox. Over-21s only. Tables outdoors (9, riverside patio).*

Half Moon

93 Lower Richmond Road, SW15 1EU (8780 9383/ www.halfmoon.co.uk). Putney Bridge tube/Putney rail. **Open** noon-11pm Mon-Thur; noon-midnight Fri, Sat; noon-11pm Sun. **Food served** 1pm-8pm Tue-Sat. **Credit** MC, V. Pub
If you're heading out for an evening to watch a few upcoming indie bands, you have a simple choice: either stand in a lager-sodden, slightly depressing fleapit in Camden or Kentish Town, or visit the Half Moon, where you'll be rewarded with swiftly pulled pints of Young's beer and upmarket lagers like Leffe, plus a fine choice of wine, among them a great white Rioja. And if you're peckish, they'll even order in Lebanese food from the takeaway across the road. The main pub is big and woody, but has a cosy vibe; the intimate back room is a cracking place to catch a band, with gigs nightly. Being slightly off the main London music circuit, the Half Moon has managed to avoid corporate takeover and continues to do what it has done since 1963 – offer cheap entertainment and decent booze to an alternative crowd. The wall of fame boasts a splendidly diverse array of performers, from Desmond Dekker to Kasabian and Carter USM.

Games (board games, fruit machines, pool, quiz machine). Music (bands 8.30pm nightly; from £2.50; jazz 2-5pm Sun; free). Tables outdoors (8, garden).

Putney Station
94-98 Upper Richmond Road, SW15 2SP (8780 0242/www.brinkleys.com). East Putney tube. **Open** 10am-midnight Mon-Sat; 11am-11pm Sun. **Food served** noon-11.30pm Mon-Fri; 11am-10.30pm Sat, Sun. **Credit** AmEx, MC, V. Wine bar
Owned by the Brinkley's group, which runs a host of other wine bars, including the Oratory in South Kensington, Putney Station is at opposite ends of the scale to that ode to bohemia. Instead it's bright and modern, with large plate-glass windows, pot plants and venetian blinds. The wine list is the same as at the Oratory, with commendably low mark-ups. It's generally good by the bottle but poor by the glass, Marqués de Cáceres 2002 Rioja being the exception – this was showing delicious, fresh, raspberry-tinted flavours. The food is pretty decent too, with a menu that ranges from thin-crust pizzas to thai curries and chunky burgers. Our large plateful of fish cakes, made of potato, smoked haddock and tiny prawns, were fried without breadcrumbs – and all the better for it. Chunks of tomato and red onion, with sorrel and lovely, earthy spinach, were good accompaniments. Located almost opposite Putney East tube station, this is a great place for a quick lunch without the crowds; in summer, you can retire to the sweet little paved garden.
Babies and children welcome: high chairs. Disabled: toilet. Separate room for parties, seats 40. Tables outdoors (3, pavement; 12, garden).

Whistle & Flute
46-48 Putney High Street, SW15 1SQ (8780 5437). Putney Bridge tube/Putney rail. **Open** 11am-11pm Mon-Thur; 11am-midnight Fri, Sat; noon-10.30pm Sun. **Food served** noon-4pm, 5-10pm Mon-Fri; noon-5pm, 6-10pm Sat; noon-5pm, 6-9pm Sun. **Credit** AmEx, MC, V. Pub
It can be tough to find anywhere on Putney High Street that's worth drinking in. But this place, converted from a branch of NatWest, has more to offer than you might expect. For starters, it's one of the few pubs in this part of town that isn't tied to Young's, so take the opportunity to down a pint of Fuller's ESB or London Pride, and if you peer over the bar there are bottles of Cruzcampo where you'd normally find a stash of alcopops. If you're lucky enough to grab the sofa at the back, you'll also see a large collection of ketchup bottles, which give an idea of the unpretentious grub on offer (steak and ale pie, goat's cheese omelette, burgers, sandwiches and the like). The Whistle & Flute's location doesn't help it to draw in discerning drinkers, but it's certainly worth a visit if you happen to be passing through.
Babies & children admitted (until 6pm). Disabled: toilet. Games (fruit machine, quiz machine). TVs (big screen, satellite).

Also in the area...
Eight Bells 89 Fulham High Street, SW6 3JS (7736 6307). Venerable boozer, its view of the river and Putney bridge sadly blocked by some of London's ugliest buildings. Fuller's ales on tap.
Jolly Gardeners 61-63 Lacey Road, SW15 1NT (8780 8921). Spacious pub with twelve beers on tap – including dark Budvar, Franziskaner and Paulaner.

Wandsworth

Alma
499 Old York Road, SW18 1TF (8870 2537/www.thealma.co.uk). Wandsworth Town rail. **Open** 11am-midnight Mon-Sat; noon-11pm Sun. **Food served** noon-4pm, 6-10.30pm Mon-Sat; noon-9.30pm Sun. **Credit** AmEx, MC, V. Pub
Its marvellous green-tiled façade the first sight to greet travellers alighting at Wandsworth Town train station, the Alma is the ever busy hub of an otherwise sleepy high street. Run for years by Charles Gotto (as was the nearby Ship), it's now under Young's management – but retains its popularity. Local tradesmen, commuters postponing their return home, rugger fans and sweaty amateur sportsmen make up most of the clientele, but the well-designed interior (antique carved wood, mosaics, painted mirrors) has more than enough room for everyone. From the elegant central bar, attentive staff serve the usual suspects alongside Young's ales and draught Peroni (£3.80 a pint!), while the cellar downstairs (peek in on the way to the toilets) shows that wine is taken seriously here. The swanky adjoining dining room serves epic portions of superior British grub (steak, ale and mushroom pie, sirloin steak with chips, poached lemon sole).
Babies and children welcome. Disabled: toilet. Function room. **Map p283 B2.**

★ Cat's Back NEW
86-88 Point Pleasant, SW18 1NN (8877 0818). East Putney tube/Wandsworth Town rail. **Open** 11am-midnight Mon-Thur, Sun; 11am-2am Fri, Sat. **Food served** 11am-10.30pm Mon-Fri; 10am-10.30pm Sat; 1-4pm Sun. **Credit** AmEx, MC, V. Pub
Stuck between building sites and glistening riverside apartments, the ancient, poky Cat's Back is crammed with an eclectic population of students, furry-chinned old-timers and boho aesthetes (and their dogs) every Friday and Saturday night. In candlelight and to a soundtrack that veers from Joy Division to 1970s disco, choose a pint from the range of frequently rotated and sometimes obscure ales (Slaters) or a fine glass of red from the ample wine list. The hugger-mugger decor – a wagon-wheel bench, Elvis memorabilia, a cupboard of golliwogs, wonky tables and barbers' chairs that spill out into the street – makes this an oddball gem. The Mediterranean-inspired dishes (mains from £8.50) served in the upstairs restaurant include the likes of steamed salmon with mash and grilled peppers in a wild garlic sauce, and a tasty Sunday lunch of roast lamb shank and cauliflower cheese.
Babies and children admitted. Disabled: toilet.

ditto
55-57 East Hill, SW18 2QE (8877 0110/www.do ditto.co.uk). Wandsworth Town/Clapham Junction rail. **Open** noon-2.30pm, 6.30-11pm Mon-Fri; noon-5pm, 6.30-11pm Sat, Sun. **Food served** noon-2.30pm, 6.30-11pm noon-11pm Sat; noon-9pm Sun. **Credit** MC, V. Bar/Restaurant
This bar-cum-restaurant has lost a little of its polish of late: the white-washed walls need a scrub, the leather sofas and stools seem a little too 'well loved' and the stacks of empty drinks boxes and washing-up in plain view suggest standards may be slipping. However, the staff are friendly and knowledgeable, and get on with what they do best: serving Modern European grub (mains around £14) to monied locals and their families (there's a crèche out back),

Hartley. *See p162.*

and mixing classic and innovative cocktails from the many premium spirits (including seven vodkas) loitering behind the bar. Try the bubbly and strawberry Ditto Fizz or the vanilla, mint, lime, cranberry and vodka East Hill (both £7.50). Beer drinkers don't fare so well: there's a choice of Grolsch, Coors and Carling on tap and a few bottled lagers, but no real ales.
Babies and children admitted (until 5pm in play area). Function room. Restaurant. TV (big screen, satellite).
Map p283 B2.

East Hill
21 Alma Road, SW18 1AA (8874 1833/ www.geronimo-inns.co.uk). Wandsworth Town rail. **Open** noon-11pm Mon-Wed; noon-midnight Thur-Sat; noon-10.30pm Sun. **Food served** noon-3pm, 6-10pm Mon-Fri; noon-9pm Sat, Sun. **Credit** AmEx, MC, V. Pub
The reward for conquering the steep climb from Wandsworth Town train station is this airy corner establishment, part of the Geronimo chain. A neighbourhood favourite, it appeals to a mixed crowd of ale aficionados, foodies and sports fans. Otter Ale, Adnams Broadside and Sharp's Doom Bar are among the offerings on tap, as well as Bitburger, Steinlager and Aspall Suffolk Cyder; meat-and cheeseboards stand temptingly on the bar, and a blackboard lists the day's specials, from hearty pastas to seafood and steak (£5-£17). And everything from motocross to Twenty20 county cricket gets a look-in on the moderately sized screens. The country-kitchen decor is a little clichéd, but the jumble of old tables, knackered seating and weathered rugs provides a fine setting for a quiet drink or a more rowdy get-together.
Babies and children admitted. Games (board games). Quiz (8pm Sun; £1). Tables outdoors (4, paved area). TVs (satellite).

Hope
1 Bellevue Road, SW17 7EG (8672 8717). Wandsworth Common rail. **Open** noon-11pm Mon-Thur; noon-midnight Fri, Sat; noon-11pm Sun. **Food served** noon-10pm Mon-Sat; noon-9pm Sun. **Credit** (over £5) AmEx, MC, V. Pub

The drink is clearly the thing at this smartly furnished pub on Wandsworth Common: the pumps dispense an impressive range of international beers (Früli, Sleeman, Paulaner, Peetermans, Hoegaarden, Küppers Kölsch) and obscure draught ales (on our last visit, seasonal Robinsons Dark Horse was deliciously dark and salty), and blackboards advertise bin-end wines. Indeed, the Hope seems almost embarrassed to stock the bog-standard lagers, serving them from minimalist, logo-free pieces of plumbing. There is food too, with exotic sausages (venison and sloe gin, anyone?) to the fore. Our pork chop came with cold mash and gravy; it was reheated with apologies, but no recompense. Despite the overly relaxed service (even on a quiet evening the food took an age to arrive) and too-loud hip hop soundtrack (possibly needed to drown out the traffic noise), the quality of the booze just about carries the Hope through.
Disabled: toilet. Games (retro arcade machine). Quiz (8.30pm Mon; £5/team). Tables outdoors (15, patio). TVs.

★ Nightingale
97 Nightingale Lane, SW12 8NX (8673 1637). Clapham South tube/Wandsworth Common rail. **Open** 11am-midnight Mon-Sat; noon-11pm Sun. **Food served** noon-10pm daily. **Credit** AmEx, DC, MC, V. Pub
The Nightingale is as much a community centre as a neighbourhood boozer: ten per cent of the price of every plate of sausage and mash goes to local charities, and an entire wall is taken up with pictures of the guide dogs the pub has sponsored. Punters young and old mingle quite happily, enjoying a game of darts or a pint from the range of Young's beers. The bar staff must be the smartest-dressed and politest in the borough, and the decor is satisfyingly staid (upholstered banquettes, rank carpet). With a sideline in flogging brewery paraphernalia (key rings, caps, a book, even a die-cast toy truck) and antique Young's bottles lined up along the bar, the Nightingale is a museum to drinking – but one still very much full of life.
Babies and children admitted (until 9pm). Games (board games, darts, fruit machine, quiz machine). Quiz (winter 7.30pm 1st Tue of mth; £1). Tables outdoors (12, garden). TV.

Ship
41 Jew's Row, SW18 1TB (8870 9667). Wandsworth Town rail. **Open** 11am-11pm Mon-Wed; 11am-midnight Thur-Sat; noon-11pm Sun. **Food served** noon-10.30pm Mon-Sat; noon-10pm Sun. **Credit** AmEx, DC, MC, V. Gastropub
Formerly run by farming couple Charles and Linda Gotto, the Ship (and its sister pub the Alma) are now under Young's management, but thankfully little else has changed. The pub still makes much of its riverside location – and so it should, even if the view's main features are a Currys and a Topps Tiles warehouse (and there's a bus garage next door). An outdoor barbecue smokes for most of the year, rustling up cheeseburgers (£9.95) or whole baby sea bass (£11.95) for the yummy mummies and hoodied, just-out-of-Oxbridge types who dominate the decked suntrap of a beer garden. The labyrinthine interior features two pleasant bar areas: one is for drinkers (with Young's beers all the way), the other is a conservatory-like space where free weekend papers are offered along with generous (but not cheap) plates of upgraded pub favourites rustled up in the adjoining open kitchen. A wood-burning stove keeps things cosy in winter.

South West

Fox & Grapes

9 Camp Road, SW19 4UN (8946 5599/
www.massivepub.com). Wimbledon tube/rail.
Open 11am-11pm Mon-Thur; 11am-midnight Fri,
Sat; noon-10.30pm Sun. **Food served** noon-3pm,
6.30-10pm Mon-Thur; noon-10pm Fri-Sun. **Credit**
AmEx, MC, V. Pub

This edge of Wimbledon Common is definitely still
London, but the sight of horse riders, muddy paths and
waxed jackets means you could be forgiven for thinking
you'd somehow strayed into the heart of the countryside.
The Fox & Grapes fits perfectly into this environment –
oozing simple rustic charm with its dark overhead beams,
a slew of real ales (Timothy Taylor Landlord, Deuchars,
Sussex Best, Tribute, Courage) and hearty traditional pub
grub (fish and chips, sausage and mash) plus a few more
modern dishes. With its huge ceiling and large tables, the
main room feels rather like a school refectory, but the L-
shaped bar area is warm and cosy. At midday on Sunday,
friendly Antipodean staff were greeting and seating customers, and the place was already beginning to fill up –
arrive early if you want to eat.
Babies and children admitted. Function room. Games
(board games). Quiz (8pm 1st Tue of mth; £1). TV
(big screen, satellite).

★ Leather Bottle

538 Garratt Lane, SW17 0NY (8946 2309/www.
leatherbottlepub.co.uk). Earlsfield rail. **Open** 11am-
midnight Mon-Sat; noon-11pm Sun. **Food served**
noon-10pm Mon-Sat; noon-8pm Sun. **Credit** MC, V.
Gastropub

Standing on a fairly uninspiring, traffic-heavy main road,
this bulky, detached building has an inviting, manor-house
feel. Inside, the spruced-up country theme continues with
plenty of dark mahogany wood, leather farm equipment
on the brick walls and beautiful brass beer pumps at the
bar, delivering a range of excellent ales (including Young's
and Bombardier). The separate dining area is small but
smart, serving succulent dishes such as wild boar steak
with sautéed potatoes and the house speciality of lobster
and chateaubriand. The mezzanine behind the bar acts
as a snug, where customers can cosy up amid the old
black and white photos. Best of all, though, is the utterly
enormous beer garden (standing capacity 450), with a useful covered section and what feels like an acre of farmland, dotted with tables in the shape of cows. An ideal
country retreat in the Big Smoke.
Babies and children admitted (if dining). Disabled:
toilet. Restaurant. Tables outdoors (50, garden;
11, patio). TV.

Suburban Bar & Lounge

27 Hartfield Road, SW19 3SG (8543 9788/
www.suburbanbar.com). Wimbledon tube/rail. **Open**
5-11pm Mon-Thur; 5pm-midnight Fri; 2pm-midnight
Sat; 5-10.30pm Sun. **Credit** AmEx, MC, V. Bar

Behind the exposed-brick bar, bright barmen effortlessly
twirl glasses while fixing reasonably priced cocktails for
a young, professional, after-work crowd. The raspberry
mojitos (£5.50) are sweet and refreshing, but a glass of
Beverly Hills (£7) – a potent mix of vodka, rum, gin, triple
sec and champagne – is guaranteed to get the party started
(or end it rather rapidly, depending on your capacity).
Customers mingle around the smattering of small tables,
or take to the two brown leather sofas at the back to bask
in the warmth of a stylishly raised open fire. Suburban it
may be, but there's none of the tackiness you sometimes

find in central London meat markets/cocktail bars. In fact,
this is the perfect spot for a night of getting slowly but
steadily trashed with a group of old friends – especially if
you make it in time for Happy Hour.
Disabled: toilet. Tables outdoors (8, garden).
TV (big screen).

Sultan

78 Norman Road, SW19 1BT (8542 4532). Colliers
Wood or South Wimbledon tube. **Open** noon-11pm
Mon-Thur; noon-midnight Fri, Sat; noon-11pm Sun.
Credit MC, V.

In south Wimbledon's backstreets lies an ale drinker's
nirvana, and it's called the Sultan (named after the famous
racehorse from the 1830s). Deserved winner of Time Out's
Best Pub award in 2005, it's still an absolute gem – and
the Wiltshire-based Hop Back Brewery's only London
pub. The 1930s suburban architecture may not be particularly striking, but inside it's a delightful den, characterised by its colourful locals, two bars (the Ted Higgins
bar is named after a beer-loving actor who once starred in
Radio 4's *The Archers*) and Hop Back's lovely ales. There's
GFB, Entire Stout and the much-acclaimed Summer
Lightning, priced from a bargain £2.05 a pint (carryouts
are also available), along with various bottled ales. Piped
music is banned, with darts being the only sport allowed
– unless you count beer swilling, or the quiz that takes
place here on a Tuesday night.
Beer club (6-9pm Wed). Disabled: toilet. Games
(darts). Quiz (8.30pm Tue, Sept-June). Tables
outdoors (8, garden).

Velvet Lounge NEW

394 Garratt Lane, SW18 4HP (8947 5954).
Earlsfield rail. **Open** 6pm-midnight Mon-Fri;
10am-midnight Sat, Sun. **Food served** 6-10.30pm
Mon-Fri; 10am-10.30pm Sat, Sun. **Credit** AmEx,
MC, V. Bar/Restaurant

The Velvet Lounge's purple exterior is a funky beacon
among Earlsfield's suburban drag of unspectacular
shopfronts. Inside, the shiny steel and black leather reek
of cool contemporary design – albeit with a decided 1980s
feel. But the 1970s is the decade that this small bar aims
to hark back to, with its range of well-presented retro
dishes. That tried-and-tested dinner party classic, the
prawn cocktail, is boldly revived for the 21st century with
three giant, freshly cooked tiger prawns with seafood
dressing and mixed leaves, all piled into a martini glass,
while mushroom stroganoff is brought up to date using
girolles, shiitake and a sweet and sour sauce. The shepherd's pie comes highly recommended, and the big portions fly in the face of today's size-zero eating habits.
Drinks include lagers, decent wines and well-rendered
cocktails. A brilliant venue for a party.
Babies and children welcome: high chairs, children's
menu. Bar available for hire (Mon-Thur, Sun). Tables
outdoors (3, pavement).

Also in the area...

Bar Café *153-163 The Broadway, SW19*
1NE (8543 5083). Branch of Jamies.
Colliers Tup *198 High Street, SW19 2BH*
(8540 1918). Branch.
Common Room *18 High Street, SW19 5DX*
(8944 1909). Branch of Jamies.
Eclipse Wimbledon *57 High Street, SW19*
5EE (8944 7722). Branch.

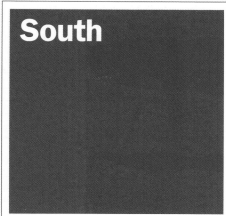

South

South

The well-heeled environs of Battersea and Clapham remain the focus for nightlife in south London. Pubs, gastropubs, bars, bar-restaurants – you'll find them all here, but discerning cocktail lovers, in particular, are spoilt for choice with the likes of **Dusk, Iniquity**, **Lost Society** and stylish newcomers **Alchemist** and **Frieda B**. Grown-up drinking and eating is to the fore at two other newbies, **Out of the Blue Bar & Kitchen** and **Westbridge Bar & Dining Rooms** (which seems to be making a success of a previously unlucky site). Brixton is the place for fun-lovin' party animals rather than grizzled real-ale fans, with DJs and cocktails in the ascendant at the likes of long-running **Dogstar, Living** and **Mango Landin'**.

Back towards the centre of town, Waterloo mixes commuter bolt-holes with more upmarket options for visitors to the cultural attractions around the South Bank. There's something for everyone here, including much-lauded gastropub **Anchor & Hope**, east European bar-restaurant **Baltic** and laid-back pubs the **Crown** and **King's Arms**. Newcomers such as cocktail specialist **Arch One** and tasteful **Cut Bar** add further variety.

Further south along the Thames, Vauxhall has long been a focus for gay nightlife in the capital – the grande dame of the scene is the **Royal Vauxhall Tavern**, home to drag shows, avant-garde cabaret and general naughtiness since World War II – but shiny new waterside developments are towing

shiny new drinking venues in their wake, including Young's purpose-built **Riverside** pub with its impressive river views.

The watering holes are more down-to-earth in nearby Kennington and Stockwell. Characterful, dog-eared, backstreet pubs dominate: the multifarious offerings at the **Dog House** pull in a youthful and arty crowd, while real-ale drinkers will find nirvana in the shape of the proudly old-fashioned **Priory Arms**. Or you can soak up the flavours (and super-cheap beer) of the area's Portuguese community at **Bar Estrela**.

As Balham gentrifies, so its drinking options improve; stylish Soho House offshoot **Balham Kitchen & Bar** has been joined by the **Balham Bowls Club**, an admirable conversion of, yes, an old-fashioned bowls club into a delightfully eccentric bar-cum-restaurant. There's less inspiration in adjoining Tooting, where dreary boozers still hold sway – though the conversion of one such operation into the friendly and civilised **Garden House** is a boost for locals.

Balham

★ Balham Bowls Club NEW
7-9 Ramsden Road, SW12 8QX (8673 4700). Balham tube/rail. **Open** 4-11pm Tue-Thur; 4pm-midnight; noon-midnight Sat; noon-11pm Sun. **Food served** 7-9pm Wed-Sun. **Credit** MC, V. Bar
A crusty bowls club goes into receivership, the old score cards, wall plaques ('Timber Traders Benevolence Society'!) and furniture are saved, and the place is opened

South

to the public. What a treasure the result is. The front half could be Sir John Mortimer's living room, replete with Victorian dressing-screens, leather sofas and bookcases, while the space at the back could be a Labour Club in Barrow c.1971 (we loved the plastic bingo hall seats). This area also doubles as the dining room. Dishes on the daily changing menu come in sizes meant for sharing; the fish pie was an unctuous treat, overflowing with prawns – but expensive at £14. Draught beers include Bitburger and Cruzcampo. Overall, a genuine London peculiar.
Babies and children admitted (until 7pm). Disabled: toilet. Quiz (8pm Tue; £2). Tables outdoors (10, garden; 4, terrace). TV.

Balham Kitchen & Bar
15-19 Bedford Hill, SW12 9EX (8675 6900/www. balhamkitchen.com). Balham tube/rail. **Open** 8am-midnight Mon-Thur; 8am-1am Fri, Sat; 8am-10.30pm Sun. **Food served** 8am-11pm Mon-Thur; 8am-11.45pm Fri, Sat; 8am-10.15pm Sun. **Credit** AmEx, MC, V.
Bar/Restaurant
Bringing a touch of the New York brasserie to Bedford Hill, this Soho House offshoot certainly looks the part with its imposing zinc bar, fold-back french windows, dark-wood tables and banquette seating (and some rather uncomfortable bar stools). There's plenty of choice on the drinks front: fruity cocktails, a global wine list, a wide array of premium spirits, a few bottled beers and continental lagers on tap (Leffe, Staropramen, Stella). And the food covers all the brasserie classics, from breakfast to after-dark, with brunch at weekends; we plumped for excellent gravadlax,

at a reasonable £7.50. Kids have their own menu, and the downstairs 'playroom' really does become a playroom on weekend afternoons.
Babies and children admitted. Disabled: toilet. Function rooms. Music (DJ 10pm Fri, Sat). Tables outdoors (6, pavement).

Bedford
77 Bedford Hill, SW12 9HD (8682 8940/www.the bedford.co.uk). Balham tube/rail. **Open** 11am-midnight Mon-Thur; 11am-2am Fri, Sat; noon-10.30pm Sun. **Food served** 7-10pm Mon; noon-2.45pm, 7-10pm Tue-Fri; noon-3.30pm, 7-10pm Sat; noon-5pm, 7-9.45pm Sun. **Credit** MC, V. Pub
An institution that steadfastly refuses to rest on its laurels. This gigantic corner boozer is best known for its weekend Banana Cabaret comedy nights, held in the balconied back room called the Shakespearean Globe Theatre, and drawing top circuit names including Brendan Burns and Milton Jones. The rest of the multitude of rooms in this hardy Victorian survivor are well used too. Classes in salsa, Argentine tango, pole-dancing and more all jostle for space in the schedule, alongside televised footie. The Bedford is no slouch in the beer and food stakes either, offering a decent line in real ale (Courage, Fuller's and 6X), plus a very popular menu that includes the frankly intimidating Homemade Balhamburger (£7.50).
Babies and children admitted (until 6pm). Comedy (9pm Thur, £3; 7.30pm Fri, £8-£12; 6.30pm Sat, £12-£15). Dance classes (line dancing 7.30pm Mon, £5; swing 8pm Tue, £8-£10; salsa 7.45pm Wed, £5;

Balham Bowls Club. *See p137.*

pole-dancing 7.30pm Thur, £8; tango 7.15pm Sun, £8). *Disabled: toilet. Function rooms. Games (fruit machines). Music (bands 9pm Mon, Tue, Thur, free; acoustic 9pm Wed, free). Nightclub (11.15pm-2am Fri, Sat; £5). Quiz (8.30pm Wed; £1). TV (big screen, satellite).*

Exhibit

12 Balham Station Road, SW12 9SG (8772 6556/ www.theexhibit.co.uk). *Balham tube/rail.* **Open** 11.30am-11pm Mon-Thur; 11.30am-2am Fri, Sat; 11.30am-midnight Sun. **Food served** noon-3pm, 7-10.30pm Mon-Sat; noon-4pm Sun. **Credit** AmEx, MC, V. Cocktail bar

An appalling location beside a Sainsbury's car park has not prevented this three-level operation from thriving. At the top is a small cinema space and a cocktail bar, which clearly has designs on being a match for Notting Hill's Electric Cinema. On the second floor, a spacious restaurant focuses on the gastro end of comfort food, with a popular weekend brunch menu (pan-seared lamb's kidney with portobello mushrooms, £5.50). But the action really takes place on the ground floor, where a young, straight-from-work crowd loosens its collars for the evening, against a backdrop of a giant tropical fish tank embedded in the wall. As well as wines, champagnes and cocktails, there's Grolsch and Guinness on tap, and a cluster of bottled beers (including Corona, San Miguel, Pilsner Urquell, Negra Modelo and Duvel). Look out for a new comedy night on Sunday and screenings in the cinema every Tuesday evening. Wi-Fi is on offer too.

Babies and children admitted (until 7pm). Comedy (8.45pm Sun; £5 after 9pm). Disabled: toilet. Film screenings (8.45pm Tue; £5). Function room. Restaurant. Tables outdoors (8, garden; 12, pavement). Wi-Fi.

Grove

39 Oldridge Road, SW12 8PN (8673 6531). *Clapham South tube/Balham tube/rail.* **Open** 11am-midnight Mon-Sat; noon-11pm Sun. **Food served** noon-10.30pm Mon-Sat; noon-9.30pm Sun. **Credit** MC, V. Pub

Located on a residential stretch between Balham and Clapham South, keeping itself to itself, the Grove looks like a fairly standard Young's pub both outside and in. But on a Sunday afternoon, the tinkling jazz soundtrack and large groups of bohos enjoying games of Trivial Pursuit (boxes of old-school games are available to the right of the bar) compelled us to stay for far longer, and to drink far more than was sensible from the full range of robust Young's ales. If you're not sure which beer to sample, the drinks menu has some useful tasting notes; otherwise, there are eleven wines of each colour to choose from (around half available by the glass). Food is fairly priced, with standard dishes of steak or sausages and chips clocking in at around a tenner. A comfy old trackie top of a pub, not easy to stumble across but all the better for it.

Babies and children admitted (restaurant). Games (board games). Quiz (8pm Sun; £2). Tables outdoors (9, terrace).

Green & Blue

What our customers say about us :

"Green & Blue take the notion of sampling the products to a new level - drink wine from the shop in the bar with great food from the deli counter"

◼

"Green & Blue - a bit like the Ambassador in the Ferrero Rocher advertisements - is spoiling us, with an exciting, diverse and eclectic range of wines"

◼

"My wine drinking life has changed entirely thanks to Green & Blue"

◼

"This is without doubt the best place to buy or drink wine in London - you can browse the shelves like a bookshop and the staff are brilliant. Makes you realise how much fun drinking wine can be'.

◼

"I can't get enough of this place - I just loved the atmosphere and complete lack of pretension"

Please note that all the above were written in a state of sobriety - at least we think so.

Please also note that although wine is our passion, we serve great beer as well (both on tap and in bottles), organic fruit juices and delicious wine cocktails, or great coffee and pastries during the day.

Have a look at our website for full details of our wine list and menu. If nothing on the latter appeals, you can bring your own food for a £3 a head cover charge - we call it 'chippage'!

36 - 38 Lordship Lane, London, SE22 8HJ, 0208 693 9250
Hours :   9am - 12am Monday to Saturday
12pm - 11pm Sunday

www.greenandbluewines.com

LOST SOCIETY

WINNER OF TIME OUT BEST BAR 2006/07

INTELLIGENT DRINKING WITHIN THE LIBRARY BAR

DELECTABLE DINING IN THE BLACK & WHITE ROOM   CHINESE WHISPERS IN THE ORIENTAL LOUNGE

BENDY BEATS PLAYING IN THE CRYSTAL BALLROOM   SUBLIME COCKTAILS IN OUR SECRET GARDEN

ALL HOUSED IN A TWO STOREY, 16TH CENTURY BARN

LOST SOCIETY
697 WANDSWORTH ROAD
CLAPHAM, LONDON
SW8 3JF
ALL ENQUIRIES CALL 0207 652 6526 OR EMAIL: INFO@LOSTSOCIETY.CO.UK
WWW.LOSTSOCIETY.CO.UK

menu is worth exploring; shared bites include top-quality feta parcels stuffed with spinach (Filo Phil, £6.50). The Mr Scruff soundtrack sums up the place perfectly: fun, clever and not willing to take itself too seriously. The crowd of crepuscular hedonists know, as do we, that Dusk is still way ahead of the pack in this part of town.
Dress: smart casual. Music (DJs 9pm Wed-Sat; free). Tables outdoors (10, terrace).

Fox & Hounds
66-68 Latchmere Road, SW11 2JU (7924 5483/ www.thefoxandhoundspub.co.uk). Clapham Junction rail. **Open** 5-11pm Mon; noon-3pm, 5-11pm Tue-Thur; noon-11pm Fri, Sat; noon-10.30pm Sun. **Food served** 7-10.30pm Mon-Thur; 12.30-3pm, 7-10.30pm Fri, Sat; 12.30-4pm, 7-10pm Sun. **Credit** MC, V. Gastropub
This tucked-away gastropub scores full marks for retaining the feel of an all-inclusive neighbourhood boozer. The large two-room space was packed on a Friday night, with chattering thirtysomething locals enjoying the daily changing Mediterranean menu prepared in the open kitchen. Offerings include the likes of grilled Italian sausages with fennel and braised borlotti beans (£9.50), and a fine choice of cheeses from Hamish Johnston. Ale lovers are well catered for, with London Pride, Deuchars and Harveys' exquisite Sussex Best pumped at the bar. Framed sepia photos of terraced Battersea streets of yore are a reminder of when pubs like this were full of cloth caps rather than ciabatta bread.
Babies and children admitted (until 7pm). Disabled: toilet. Tables outdoors (10, garden). TV. **Map p283 E1.**

Freemasons
2 Wandsworth Common Northside, SW18 2SS (7326 8580/www.freemasonspub.com). Clapham Junction rail. **Open** noon-11pm Mon-Thur; noon-midnight Fri, Sat; noon-10.30pm Sun. **Food served** noon-3pm, 6.30-10pm Mon-Fri; 12.30-10pm Sat; 12.30-9pm Sun. **Credit** AmEx, MC, V. Gastropub
This splendid, claret-painted gastropub on the north side of Wandsworth Common attracts a younger, trendier crowd than most in the area, and you'll have to fight for a seat by the bar, or else grab a table in the less frenetic back room. Despite the busy mood, rows of picnic tables out front provide a pleasant summertime setting for sipping a tall glass of Früli, Hoegaarden or Leffe (all on tap). Or ask the enthusiastic bar staff to recommend a wine to suit your budget (bottles range from £12.50 to £85). You can also taste the beers; the Everards Tiger and Timothy Taylor Landlord are served from ingenious taps fitted with a glass cylinder that lets you see the colour of your drink. The scrumptious, adventurous menu (mains cost £9.50-£12.95) offers the likes of pan-fried salmon, honey-roasted organic pork belly and fillet of lamb.
Babies and children welcome (restaurant): high chairs. Quiz (8pm Mon; £1). Tables outdoors (11, patio). **Map p283 C2.**

Frieda B NEW
46 Battersea Rise, SW11 1EE (7228 7676/www. frieda-b.co.uk). Clapham Junction rail/35, 37 bus. **Open** 5pm-midnight Mon-Thur, Sun; 5pm-2am Fri, Sat. **Credit** AmEx, MC, V. Cocktail bar
The tiny display boxes in the basement showcasing pairs of sumptuous Jimmy Choo's says a lot about this extremely assured new venture. The exterior has the air of a bespoke furniture shop of the kind you might find tucked

away in a Mayfair backstreet. The tiny front bar branches out into a couple of nooks perfect for canoodling, and a downstairs space filled with brown leather sofas and scatter cushions that certainly haven't come from Ikea. The mint walls, portraits of pouting chanteuses and a cocktail list that mixes brevity with imagination (try the 180 Biflora, with Mount Gay rum, Falernum, lime juice and bitters) are fast proving popular with raffish couples looking to avoid the more corporate drinking dens nearby. Recommended.
Bar available for hire. **Map p283 E2.**

Holy Drinker
59 Northcote Road, SW11 1NP (7801 0544/ www.holydrinker.co.uk). Clapham Junction rail/ 35, 37 bus. **Open** 4.30-11pm Mon-Wed; 4.30pm-midnight Thur, Fri; noon-midnight Sat; 1-11pm Sun. **Credit** MC, V. Bar
This pleasantly dingy veteran of Northcote Road continues to charm all who enter with its air of the slightly stoned, retired surfer. Beanie-clad barmen potter about, serving a relaxed crowd of former scenesters in their late twenties, who are now more preoccupied with kicking back than setting the pace. The soundtrack of laid-back funk, alongside unvarnished wooden tables, candles and a big screen that looks as if was made out of old sail (it was showing a variety of Evel Knievel stunts on our visit), make for a vibe conducive to lingering late to sample the impressive array of ales and lagers, including the little-known Hahn, Golden Promise and Schneider Weisse.
Babies and children admitted (until 7pm). Tables outdoors (4, pavement). TVs. **Map p283 E2.**

Iniquity
8-10 Northcote Road, SW11 1NT (7924 6699/ www.iniquitybar.com). Clapham Junction rail/35, 37 bus. **Open** 5-11pm Mon-Wed; 5pm-midnight Thur, Fri; 3pm-midnight Sat; 3-10.30pm Sun. **Food served** 5-10.30pm Mon-Fri; 3-9.30pm Sat, Sun. **Credit** AmEx, MC, V. Cocktail bar
A much-needed shot of class and imagination on a chain-sodden stretch of road, Iniquity is a magnet for Clapham plutocrats, with its incantation of leather, velvet, drapes and cocktails. And what fine cocktails they are. Mixologist Tim Oakley has created a vintage-to-contemporary menu that mixes the supine with the sublime. We feel compelled to warn you of the dangerously moreish Bramble (gin, lemon juice and crème de mure). The barmaids – a collection of FHM 'High Street Honey' wannabees – will bring drinks to your table. It all appears to be a rousing success with a buzzy crowd of well-heeled young careerists on the fast track at Goldman Sachs.
Disabled: toilet. Function room. Tables outdoors (12, terrace). TV (big screen). **Map p283 D2.**

Latchmere
503 Battersea Park Road, SW11 3BW (7223 3549). Battersea Park or Clapham Junction rail/44, 49, 344, 345 bus. **Open** noon-11pm Mon-Wed; noon-midnight Thur-Sat; noon-10.30pm Sun. **Food served** noon-3pm, 5-10pm Mon-Fri; noon-9pm Sat, Sun. **Credit** MC, V. Theatre pub
The pub downstairs from the esteemed fringe theatre is only one misplaced fruit machine away from resembling a provincial Wetherspoon's. But the Latchmere is an attractive-enough corner boozer that certainly has potential and is doing some things right: witness the good selection of real ales (6X, Young's and Adnams), the roaring fire and

South

midnight Fri; 10am-midnight Sat; noon-10.30pm Sun. **Food served** noon-3pm, 6.30-10.30pm Mon-Thur; noon-10.30pm Fri-Sun. **Credit** MC, V. Pub
Now here's a sight for sore eyes. Situated on the residential end of forlorn Battersea High Street, at first glance this looks like an uninspiring estate pub relic. But venture inside and you'll discover a tardis of a boozer, stretching back to a cute little garden space (ideal in summer). Billed as a 'new kind of traditional pub', the Woodman is a great place to plant yourself with some mates on a Sunday morning; sit at one of the big wooden tables in the long, attic-like back room and enjoy a respite from the dismal sprawl of ex-council blocks outside. They do a nice line in real ale too, with Badger Ale and Festive Pheasant on draught on our visit.
Babies and children admitted. Music (blues 8pm Tue; free). Quiz (8.30pm Mon; £1). Tables outdoors (10, garden). TVs (satellite).

Also in the area...

brb@the duck *110 Battersea Rise, SW11 1ET (7228 0349/www.barroombar.com).* Branch of Bar Room Bar. **Map p283 D2.**
Le Bouchon Lyonnais *38-40 Queenstown Road, SW8 3RY (7622 2618).* Branch of Le Bouchon Bordelais.
Eagle Ale House *104 Chatham Road, SW11 6HJ (7228 2328).* Welcoming pub with book-lined shelves and four real ales on tap. **Map p283 E3.**
Fine Line *33-37 Northcote Road, SW11 1NJ (7924 7387).* Branch. **Map p283 E2.**

Brixton

Brixton Bar & Grill
15 Atlantic Road, SW9 8HX (7737 6777/www.bbag. me.uk). Brixton tube/rail. **Open** 5pm-midnight Tue, Wed; 5pm-1am Thur; 5pm-2am Fri, Sat; 3.30-11pm Sun. **Food served** 6-10.30pm Tue-Sat; 4-10.30pm Sun. **Credit** MC, V. Bar/Restaurant
The Brixton Bar & Grill is located right next to Brixton overground station – and don't you know it. The venue occasionally rumbles with the vibration of trains going past, and the patchy plasterwork, arched ceiling and long narrow shape give it the feel of a converted tube tunnel. It attracts thirtysomething couples tucking into one of the grill meals or sharing a selection of tapas, as well as a smattering of pressed-shirted lads out on the pull, drinking pints of Bitburger. There's a huge range of spirits, and a long cocktail list offering a couple of more unusual choices, such as Ginger & Spice (Tuaca, muddled physalis, pear, lemon juice, ginger beer and nutmeg).
Disabled: toilet. Music (DJs 9pm Fri, Sat; free). Tables outdoors (4, pavement). **Map p284 E2.**

Dogstar
389 Coldharbour Lane, SW9 8LQ (7733 7515). Brixton tube/rail. **Open** 4pm-2am Mon-Thur; 4pm-4am Fri; noon-4am Sat; noon-2am Sun. **Food served** 5-10pm Mon-Fri; 1-10pm Sat, Sun. **Admission** £5 after 10pm Fri, Sat. **Credit** MC, V. DJ bar
The kind of experience you have in this legendary Brixton DJ bar depends entirely on when you visit. Go late and you can find yourself pushed against the bar by a heaving crowd, struggling to converse over the music, but at 8pm on a Friday it was comfortably empty. In times past

this would have been unheard of, and the state of the women's toilets hinted that standards have slipped a bit (of the three cubicles, one bore the legend 'out of order', another 'well out of order' and the third looked as if it had been sprayed with apple Tango). Nonetheless, the clientele of trendy-trainered hip-hop heads, shaven-headed males and indie girls remains loyal, sipping draught lager (the selection includes Leffe and Staropramen) under the opera-style curtains that hang above the bar, talking of days gone by.
Babies and children admitted (until 6pm). Disabled: toilet. Function rooms. Music (DJs 9pm daily). Tables outdoors (5, garden). TVs (big screen, satellite). **Map p284 E2.**

Effra
38A Kellet Road, SW2 1EB (7274 4180). Brixton tube/rail. **Open** 3-11pm daily. **Food served** 3-10pm daily. **No credit cards.** Pub
Welcome to a corner of SW9 that's yet to be touched by the Kronenbourg and cocktail revolution that has seen most of the area's watering holes trendying up their acts in the past few years. The interior is an exercise in fading Victorian splendour; while pretty gold cornicing adorns the ceiling, and domed glass lamps light the proceedings, the once-splendid golden curtains look like they've seen better days, and the patterned wallpaper has a distinctly sticky look to it. Still, the predominantly Afro-Caribbean crowd remains fiercely loyal. They don't worry about the random addition of garden furniture-style tables and chairs to the otherwise old-school pub fittings, but instead appreciate the excellent pints of Guinness (Red Stripe and Young's are also available on tap), big pull-down screen for sports matches and tasteful jukebox playlist.
Games (dominoes). Jukebox. Music (musicians 8.30pm Tue-Thur, Sat, Sun; free). Tables outdoors (3, garden). TV. **Map p284 E2.**

Far Side
144 Stockwell Road, SW9 9TQ (7095 1401). Stockwell tube/Brixton tube/rail. **Open** noon-11pm Mon-Thur; noon-3am Fri, Sat; noon-10.30pm Sun. **Food served** noon-3pm Mon; noon-3pm, 6-9pm Tue-Thur; noon-3pm Fri; noon-4pm Sat; noon-8pm Sun. **Credit** MC, V. Pub
There's an appealing community feel to this pub on the Brixton/Stockwell border, with our visit seeing the bar lined with regulars drinking pints of Guinness while ribbing the bar staff. No real ales are available, but there's a wide selection of bottled lagers, including Leffe Blonde, Brahma, Belle-Vue Framboise and, in a nod to the nationalistic make-up of the Stockwell community, popular Portuguese beer Super Bock. The back room is a dimly lit snug with leather sofas, a cosy fireplace and a 1950s-style gold-framed mirror creating the illusion that the space is bigger than it really is. The modernised pub grub menu, including Indian-style vegetable burger with ownmade fries (£6.50), goes down well with the locals.
Babies and children admitted (until 7pm). Bar available for hire. Tables outdoors (16, garden). TV (big screen, satellite). **Map p284 D1.**

Hive
11-13 Brixton Station Road, SW9 8PA (7274 8383/ www.hivebar.net). Brixton tube/rail. **Open** 5pm-midnight Mon-Wed; 5pm-2am Thur; 5pm-3am Fri; 10am-3am Sat; 10am-11pm Sun. **Food served** 6-11pm Mon-Fri; 10am-11pm Sat, Sun. **Credit** MC, V. Bar/Restaurant

Located above a restaurant, this chic, white-walled space isn't the most popular watering hole in Brixton, but that only makes it better for those in the know. It's usually easy to get a seat – even on a Friday night, when a smattering of pre-club thirtysomethings were rushing their way through the drinks list. The walls are lined with artworks for sale, there's a disco ball casting coloured lights across the room, and the Motown-y soundtrack provided by end-of-the-week DJs creates a relaxed atmosphere. The emphasis is on cocktails and wine, not beer – there are no draught options, which is a shame. *Babies and children admitted (restaurant). Bar available for hire. Music (DJ 8pm Thur-Sat; free). Tables outdoors (7, pavement).* **Map p284 E2.**

Hope & Anchor
123 Acre Lane, SW2 5UA (7274 1787). Clapham North tube/Brixton tube/rail. **Open** noon-11pm Mon-Thur, Sun; noon-1.30am Fri, Sat. **Food served** noon-3pm, 6.30-10pm Mon-Sat; noon-5pm Sun. **Credit** MC, V. Pub
It's a Young's pub, Jim, but not as we know it. The Hope & Anchor has recently undergone a refurb that's seen it move towards the contemporary bar style that dominates Brixton's drinking holes. The place is now painted a cool green, and there's a youngish clientele quietly sipping pints of continental lager (Leffe, Hoegaarden, Staropramen) as well as the usual selection of fine Young's ales, as a louche, dancey soundtrack plays. The pub is located in the no-man's land between Clapham and Brixton, so the move away from being a local boozer is a brave one, but there are still enough draws (jazz piano on Thursday nights, the pretty beer garden) to keep people rolling in. Sporting events are shown on a big screen in the corner; food is pub-standard – average but reasonably priced. *Babies and children admitted. Disabled: toilet. Function room. Music (jazz pianist Thur). Tables outdoors (40, garden). TV (big screen, satellite).* **Map p284 C2.**

Living
443 Coldharbour Lane, SW9 8LN (7326 4040/ www.livingbar.co.uk). Brixton tube/rail. **Open** 5pm-2am Mon-Thur, Sun; 5pm-4am Fri; noon-4am Sat. **Admission** £5 after 10pm Fri, Sat. **Credit** AmEx, MC, V. Bar
Come Friday evening, having a drink in this two-tiered DJ bar can make you feel like an extra in classic 1980s sci-fi movie *Tron*. Blue spotlights illuminate the faces of the Topshop-garbed clientele, as jerky retro graphics skitter over the big screens that hang from the ceilings. At other times, the atmosphere is more 1970s, thanks to the swirly, retro-patterned wallpaper and sprawling leather sofas. Drinks on tap include San Miguel and Scrumpy, two-for-one cocktails are on offer from Sunday to Thursday and there's an excellent programme of midweek events including film nights on Wednesday and sporadic pole-dancing courses, for those inclined. *Babies and children admitted (until 9pm). Disabled: toilet. Entertainment (film screenings and pole-dancing classes; phone for details). Music (DJs 9pm nightly). Tables outdoors (3, pavement).* **Map p284 E2.**

Lounge
56 Atlantic Road, SW9 8PX (7733 5229/ www.brixtonlounge.co.uk). Brixton tube/rail. **Open** 11am-11pm Mon-Wed; 11am-midnight Thur-Sat; 11am-6pm Sun. **Food served** 11am-10pm Mon-Sat; 11am-5pm Sun. **Credit** AmEx, MC, V. Café/Bar

This relaxed, yellow-walled café-cum-bar is one of Brixton's treats. Table service, low lighting and the gentle hubbub of conversation give the place a restauranty vibe – not surprising given that it's a café during the day. Elfin waitresses ferrying drinks squeeze around groups of funky Brixtonians sprawled on the black leather sofas. Local art (with price tags) lines the walls, staff are super-friendly, and beer on tap includes the relatively rare Dutch lager Gulpener. Don't dawdle towards the end of an evening, though. On a Saturday night, the shutters were pulled down at 11pm prompt, and we were ejected into the street shortly afterwards. *Babies and children welcome: high chairs. Bar available for hire. Disabled: toilet. Music (jazz 8pm Wed monthly; free).* **Map p284 E2.**

Mango Landin'
40 St Matthew's Road, SW2 1NL (7737 3044/ www.mangolandin.com). Brixton tube/rail then 2, 3, 133, 159 bus. **Open** 5pm-midnight Mon-Thur; noon-3am Fri, Sat; noon-11.30pm Sun. **Credit** AmEx, MC, V. Cocktail bar
They don't stand on ceremony in this yellow-painted, tropically themed bar, located behind a church on the corner of a housing estate. A request for a glass of wine saw a tumbler of the stuff thrust across the bar, full to the brim. And the bands that play this lively venue don't even get a stage: on our Friday night visit, the frontman was dancing with the front row of the middle-aged audience. Scrawled above the bar in multicoloured script is a long list of cocktails; in keeping with the decor, these tend towards the exotic – try the Original Red Rum Punch (Mount Gay, strawberries, blueberries and orange juice), a Mango Rising (Wray & Nephew rum with mango and strawberry juice), or a mojito topped with fresh mango, all £5.50. There's an organic food market on Saturday and occasional quizzes and film nights; weekend barbies attract a fair crowd. One of the more fun venues on Brixton's roster. *Babies and children welcome (until 8pm): high chairs. BBQ (noon Sat). Food market (Sat). Games (board games, chess, table football). Music (bands/DJs 9pm Thur-Sat, 6pm Sun; free). Tables outdoors (20, garden).* **Map p284 E3.**

Prince
467-469 Brixton Road, SW9 8HH (7326 4455/ www.dexclub.co.uk). Brixton tube/rail. **Open** noon-midnight Mon, Tue; noon-2am Wed, Thur; 11am-4pm Fri, Sat; 11am-midnight Sun. **Food served** noon-10pm Mon-Fri; 11am-10pm Sat, Sun. **Credit** AmEx, MC, V. Gastropub
Heavy red curtains and chandeliers, combined with varnished pine slatting behind the bar and bare bricks elsewhere, give the Prince a peculiar house-meets-sauna atmosphere. But the nattering young crowd that regularly packs the place barely seems to notice, distracted perhaps by the bassy hip hop lite soundtrack and low lighting. The selection of draught beers isn't the most inspiring (Timothy Taylor Landlord is the sole ale), but during the day it's a nice venue for a relaxed lunch, with a weekly changing gastropubby menu. A garden is there for warm-weather days; a fine Champagne list for those in celebratory mood. There's free wireless internet access too. *Babies and children admitted (until 9pm). Disabled: toilet. Music (DJs 10pm daily; £3 after 10pm Fri, Sat). Tables outdoors (12, garden). TV (big screen). Wi-Fi (free).* **Map p284 E2.**

South

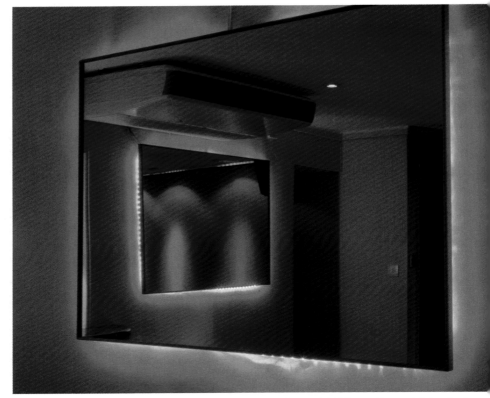

SW9

*11 Dorrell Place, SW9 8EG (7738 3116). Brixton
tube/rail.* **Open** 10.30am-11pm Mon-Wed; 10.30am-
midnight Thur; 10.30am-1am Fri, Sat; 11am-5.30pm
Sun. **Food served** 11am-10pm daily. **Credit** AmEx,
MC, V. Café/Bar

By day, a venue for recovering clubbers tucking into hearty
breakfasts; by night, a lively bar, offering about as wide a
selection of drinks as you're likely to get in Brixton. The
shelves behind the bar are lined with row upon row of spirits; Kirin, Red Stripe and Erdinger are available on tap. The
decor is unusual, with full-length glass windows next to
the paisley-printed bar, all presided over by a semi-porno-
graphic painting of jelly babies. At the weekend, it's not
unusual to find the pre-club crowd still sitting at the rickety metal tables come the 1am closing time, having gotten
too drunk to move on anywhere else.
*Babies and children admitted (until 5pm). Music
(jazz 9pm Fri, Sat; free). Tables outdoors (16, patio).*
Map p284 E2.

Trinity Arms

*45 Trinity Gardens, SW9 8DR (7274 4544).
Brixton tube/rail.* **Open** 11am-11pm Mon-Thur;
11am-midnight Fri; noon-midnight Sat; noon-11pm
Sun. **Food served** noon-3pm, 6-9pm Mon-Fri; 1-5pm
Sun. **Credit** MC, V. Pub

It's rare to find a pub in Brixton with a good choice of real
ales, but the Trinity Arms breaks the mould. It's a Young's
pub, so there's Young's Bitter and Special on tap, of course,
as well as Bombardier. On our visit, a CAMRA Pub of the
Year voting form was affixed to the wall. As a result, the
clientele tends to be older than at your average trendy
Brixton drinking haunt, although there's still the occasional group of dressed-down twentysomethings enjoying
the cosy bitter-and-dry-roasted ambience. The decor is
much as you'd expect – no-frills tables and chairs sit on a
fading patterned red carpet – but that's all part of the
place's down-to-earth charm.
*Babies and children admitted (until 7.30pm, garden
only). Games (fruit machine). No piped music or
jukebox. Tables outdoors (13, garden; 6, pavement).
TV.* **Map p284 D2.**

White Horse

*94 Brixton Hill, SW2 1QN (8678 6666/www.white
horsebrixton.com). Brixton tube/rail then 59, 118,
133, 159, 250 bus.* **Open** 5pm-midnight Mon-Thur;
4pm-3am Fri; noon-3am Sat; noon-midnight Sun.
Food served 5-10pm Mon-Fri; noon-9pm Sat;
noon-10pm Sun. **Credit** AmEx, MC, V. Pub

In keeping with the media types that it attracts, the White
Horse likes to be quirky. Jars of old-fashioned boiled sweets
are available at 40p a tumbler, the drinks list announces

Frieda B. *See p143.*

the availability of cigarettes by declaring that they have 'no poxy 16s', and George, the landlord's black labrador, roams around nuzzling customers. Big, saggy leather sofas, low lighting and carefully positioned candles can't hide the fact that it resembles a disused warehouse, with bare brick walls by the entrance and painted steel girders serving as pillars. Kronenbourg, San Miguel and London Pride are available on tap. It's a pleasant spot for a relaxed breakfast or Sunday roast, but come the evening, funk and soul DJs take to the central booth and the crowd hits the dancefloor, for one of the more enthusiastic party environments Brixton has to offer.
Babies and children admitted (until 9pm). Bar available for hire. Disabled: toilet. Games (board games, pool). Music (DJs 9pm Thur-Sat; jazz/DJ 5pm Sun; free). Tables outdoors (6, courtyard). **Map p284 D3.**

Windmill
22 Blenheim Gardens, SW2 5BZ (8671 0700/ www.windmillbrixton.co.uk). Brixton tube/rail then 49, 59, 118, 133, 159, 250 bus. **Open** 11am-midnight Mon-Thur; 11am-1am Fri, Sat; noon-11pm Sun. **No credit cards**. Pub
Anyone who's anyone within the world of indie will have played the Windmill at some point. There's such a constant stream of up-and-coming acts taking to the stage that they don't even bother to remove the drum kit on the rare night

when there are no performers. The pub has a youth-club-cum-student-bedroom feel, with chipped paintwork, trailing fairy lights and toilet doors plastered with stickers. A hand-drawn mural of the sun dominates one wall. The drinks selection is fairly limited; draught Red Stripe and San Miguel are the best options.
Babies and children admitted (until 7pm). Disabled: toilet. Games (fruit machine). Music (8pm nightly; £3-£4). Tables outdoors (4, garden; 4 pavement). TV (big screen).

Also in the area...
Bar With No Name 71 Atlantic Road, SW9 8PU (7738 6576). Style wins out over practicality at this newish cocktail bar with an ambient techno soundtrack; pizzas are available, as are Kirin and Budvar on tap. **Map p284 E2.**

Clapham

Bar Local
4 Clapham Common Southside, SW4 7AA (7622 9406/ www.barlocal.co.uk). Clapham Common tube. **Open** 5pm-midnight Mon-Wed; 5pm-1am Thur, Fri; noon-1am Sat; noon-midnight Sun. **Food served** 5-10pm Mon-Fri; noon-10pm Sat, Sun. **Credit** MC, V. Bar

This fashionable bar couldn't be further away in attitude from its location – on what becomes Clapham's drunken, shouting drag-strip on weekend evenings – if it tried. The space is long and narrow, and despite the crowds and lack of tables, the vibe is always laid-back. In the daytime, pashmina-wearing locals with cut-glass accents natter about what mummy and daddy earn, while the occasional dance fan sips pints of Staropramen or Cobra. There's a collection of music-based paintings, one of which gives the biggest clue to the bar's self-imposed outsider status: a blurry black and white depiction of Piccadilly Circus features a bright red individual in jeans and T-shirt on the outskirts of the scene, labelled 'Bar Local'. It would be easier to believe without the cut-glass accents, though.
Music (DJs 8pm Thur-Sun; free). **Map p284 A2.**

Bread & Roses
68 Clapham Manor Street, SW4 6DZ (7498 1779/ www.breadandrosespub.com). Clapham Common or Clapham North tube. **Open** noon-11pm Mon-Thur; noon-midnight Fri, Sat; noon-10.30pm Sun. **Food served** noon-3pm, 6-9.30pm Mon-Fri; noon-4pm, 6-9.30pm Sat; noon-6pm Sun. **Credit** MC, V. Pub
Run by the Workers' Beer Company, a funding organisation for trade unions and left-wing campaigns, this pub is named after a song sung by female textile workers during a 1912 strike over better working conditions (the lyric itself is daubed above the bar). They pride themselves on treating the staff well – and if friendliness is any indicator, they're doing a good job. There's a rotating selection of CAMRA medal-winning ales; Doom Bar, Cambridge and Woodford Wherry were available on our visit, along with draught lagers Erdinger, Budvar, Budvar Dark, Piretti, San Miguel, Leffe and a delicious Heller raspberry beer. Those in the know shun the raucous venues of Clapham High Street and come here for a sophisticated, politically right-on pint.
Babies and children admitted (until 9pm). Comedy (monthly; check website). Disabled: toilet. Entertainment (burlesque monthly; check website). Function room. Games (board games). Music (band monthly; check website). Tables outdoors (15, garden; 8, conservatory; 8, patio). **Map p284 B1.**

Clapham North
409 Clapham Road, SW9 9BT (7274 2472/ www.theclaphamnorth.co.uk). Clapham North tube. **Open** 11am-midnight Mon-Wed, Sun; 11am-2am Thur-Sat. **Food served** 11am-10pm Mon-Thur, Sun; 11am-9pm Fri; 11am-8pm Sat. **Admission** £2-£3 after 10pm Fri, Sat. **Credit** AmEx, MC, V. Bar
If you plan to spend an evening here, it's worth arriving early. The place might be big, but come 6pm on a Saturday it's hard to find anywhere to sit, thanks to the slew of reserved signs on tables, and the large number of party-happy girls flicking their poker-straight hair at the estate agent-y males. The narrow middle section of the bar can make standing a little awkward, but the low lighting and DJs playing loud house music mean that the crowd don't stand still for long. Spirits and cocktails dominate the drinking options. Food is available during the day and, in a bizarre 'plan your meal while you excrete' tack, menus are stuck to the back of toilet doors for those who put a lot of thought into choosing their grub.
Babies and children admitted. Disabled: toilet. Music (DJs 8pm Thur, 9pm Fri, Sat, 5pm Sun). Tables outdoors (5, terrace). TVs (big screen, satellite). **Map p284 C1.**

Coach & Horses
175 Clapham Park Road, SW4 7EX (7622 3815/ www.barbeerian-inns.com). Clapham Common tube. **Open** noon-11am Mon-Wed; noon-midnight Thur-Sat; noon-10.30pm Sun. **Food served** noon-2.30pm, 6-9.30pm Mon-Fri; noon-3pm, 6.30-9pm Sat; 12.30-5pm, 7-9pm Sun. **Credit** MC, V. Pub
True to form for Clapham, the rack of *TNT* magazines around the corner from the bar indicate the demographic of nationalities that frequent this traditional pub. To top it off, the stereotypical rugby-shirted Claphamites come here in force at the weekend, shouting over the selection of Top 40 hits that plays on the jukebox. Things are a touch more sedate during the week and in the day at the weekend, with a two-for-one Sunday afternoon offer on Bloody Marys drawing a quieter, broadsheet-reading crowd. The same offer applies to burgers on Monday. There's a monthly quiz night too; London Pride, Spitfire and Bombardier are available on tap.
Babies and children admitted (until 8.30pm). Disabled: toilet. Function room. Games (board games). Jukebox. Quiz (8pm 1st Mon of mth, £1; 7pm Sun, free). Tables outdoors (8, enclosed terrace). TVs (big screen, satellite). **Map p284 B2.**

Gigalum [NEW]
7 Cavendish Parade, SW4 9DW (8772 0303/ www.gigalum.com). Clapham South tube. **Open** noon-11pm Mon-Thur; 11am-midnight Fri, Sat; 11am-11pm Sun. **Food served** noon-3pm Mon-Fri; 11am-7pm Sat, Sun. **Credit** AmEx, MC, V. Pub
There's an exotic look to the exterior of this Clapham South newbie, with the palm tree and year-round garden heaters on the terrace putting the barren, litter-strewn expanse of Clapham Common to shame. Sadly, the interior doesn't follow suit. Our Friday evening visit saw a predictable crowd of Magners-swilling, besuited gents being eyed up by glammed-up women in their twirties. Later on, the low white leather sofas, big mirrors, marbled panelling and palm trees are swathed in an orangey glow, as DJs play 'bar house' (too plodding to be funky, too tuneless to be uplifting). During the day a gastro-menu is on offer, including a good range of breakfast/brunch options. The drinks selection is extensive, including cocktails, a vast selection of spirits, Leffe Blonde and Brun and Brahma in bottles – but only one real ale (Flowers IPA).
Babies and children admitted (until 6pm). Music (8pm Fri-Sun; free). Tables outdoors (12, garden). TVs. **Map p284 A3.**

Grafton House
13-19 Old Town, SW4 0JT (7498 5559/ www.graftonhouseuk.com). Clapham Common tube. **Open** 11am-11pm daily. **Food served** Bar noon-4pm Mon-Sat; noon-6pm Sun. Restaurant 7-11pm Mon-Sat; noon-4pm Sun. **Credit** AmEx, MC, V. Bar/Restaurant
With its slick, streamlined design and no-expense-spared fixtures and fittings, this spot is unsurprisingly popular with Clapham's young, monied professionals. Sultry lighting, marble floors and tropical hardwoods ooze understated opulence – even the beer taps are more akin to the kind you'd find in a five-star hotel bathroom than your average boozer. The on-tap lager is König, accompanied by a changing guest lager – though there's Guinness for the traditionalists. In the evening, a funky house soundtrack competes with the buzz of conversation, and a big pull-down screen appears for weekend football and rugby fixtures. The restaurant at the back is breathtakingly

South

ornate, with coloured lighting setting off a plethora of attractive sparkling glass.
Babies and children admitted. Disabled: toilet. Music (DJs 7pm Fri, Sat; free). Restaurant. TVs (big screen). Map p284 A1.

Landor
70 Landor Road, SW9 9PH (7274 4386/ www.landortheatre.com). Clapham North tube. **Open** noon-11.30pm Mon-Thur; noon-midnight Fri, Sat; noon-10.30pm Sun. **Food served** noon-2.30pm, 6-9.30pm Mon-Fri; 1-8.30pm Sat; 1.15-5pm Sun. **Credit** MC, V.
Theatre pub
Landor Road might once have been known as the place where the yoof of the adjoining estate attempted to pass off bags of oregano as a slightly stronger herb to naïve students – but times have changed. Though not much has altered at this chintzy theatre pub, which has been presenting an array of work (notably musicals) in the downstairs theatre space since 1995 (plus a monthly comedy night on Sundays, occasionally interspersed with a cabaret act). The decor is an eccentric mish mash: canoes and hammocks dangle from the ceiling, old lobster pots perch on top of the bar, and black and white photos of old maritime scenes adorn the walls. A local crowd comes to play pool and sample the wide selection of real ales (permanent fixtures London Pride and IPA, plus two regularly changing guest ales). Otherwise there's the monthly quiz, or Sky Sports on the big screen showing the big games.
Comedy (8pm 3rd Sun of mth; £6-£10). Entertainment (cabaret 8pm 2nd Sun of mth; £6-£10). Games (fruit machines, pool). Quiz (8pm 1st Sun of mth; £2). Tables outdoors (16, garden). Theatre (7.30pm Tue-Sat; £7-£10). TVs (big screen, satellite). Map p284 C1.

Mosquito Bar
Indian Flavours, 5 Clapham High Street, SW4 7TS (7622 4003/7622 2060/www.theindianflavours.com). Clapham North tube. **Open/food served** *Bar* 5pm-5am Mon-Thur, Sun; 5pm-6am Fri, Sat. *Restaurant* 5pm-midnight daily. **Admission** £5 after 12.30am Fri, Sat. **Credit** MC, V. Bar/Restaurant
Restaurant Indian Flavours by day, bar by night, the main draw of Mosquito is its 5am licence. The place remains empty until near 11pm, at which point it kicks progressively, until closing time sees a boisterous crowd picking its way through puddles of vomit. On our Wednesday night visit, the crowd varied between hoodie-wearing Rastafarians holed up in the gents making hasty repairs to their bags of cannabis, ageing bikers in leather, and young IT workers. Despite the exorbitant level of inebriation, the revelry remains good-natured. While the drinks selection is nothing special, the atmosphere – as well as the schizophrenic collection of celebrity photos from Elephant and Castle sister restaurant/club Ivory Arch (a photo of Cherie Blair stands side by side with Bobby Brown and Heather Smalls) – make this possibly the most entertaining place to visit in Clapham.
Babies and children admitted (restaurant, until midnight). Restaurant available for hire. TVs. Map p284 C1.

Prince of Wales
38 Old Town, SW4 0LB (7622 3530). Clapham Common tube. **Open** 5-11pm Mon-Wed; 5pm-midnight Thur; 5pm-1am Fri; 1pm-1am Sat; 1-11pm Sun. **Credit** AmEx, MC, V. Pub

Booze talking
Lost Society

You are?
Mark Banks, co-owner of Lost Society, Wandsworth Road, SW8.
Tell us about the concept behind the bar.
We [Mark and co-owners James Parfitt and Fiaz Iqbal] felt that Clapham was in need of a venue that was first-rate in three regards: good food, good drinks and good music. Often you go for a night out and end up moving from place to place because nowhere is good for *everything*. We wanted this to be a place people could come for their entire evening and not have to leave.
The holy trinity...
Exactly. We're off the beaten track and competing with Clapham High Street, so we knew that we had to offer something better than everything there. Lost Society's not a pub, but it's relaxed and serves 35 bottled beers; it's not a restaurant, but it has great food and dining areas; and it's not a bar, but it has fantastic cocktails and a dancefloor. We're lucky that we've got the space to do all of those things.
Why this particular spot?
It was the first place we heard about after deciding to launch our own place, and we said yes without even visiting. We knew of its reputation for individuality as the Tearooms des Artistes so we grabbed the opportunity straightaway. It's so unique – full of character and history. This place has been everything from a barn to a tie shop. With its two-leveled layout and garden out the back, we couldn't have asked for a better venue.
And the decor?
We wanted a subtle, old-school, manor-house feel – like the Hudson Hotel in New York, with an English twist. We were quite superficial about it; we knew the moment the customer walks in is critical and wanted to create a place that would surprise them.
You won Time Out's Best Bar award in 2006. Have you been surprised by Lost Society's rapid success?
It's strange to see people queuing around the block to come to something that we've created. It's a huge surprise – we never thought it would get so popular that we'd have to open seven days a week – especially after only a year. We were shocked and flattered by the award, especially as we have such respected rivals like Annex 3 and Gilgamesh. That was a big night of celebrating, I can tell you.
What's next for the team?
We're looking at other ventures in the area, but it will have to be something different because we'll never be able to replicate Lost Society. It's too unique.

South

From the outside, a bland-looking, white-walled pub; from the inside, a cornucopia of eccentric clutter. The curio-strewn interior features a set of traffic lights suspended above the cigarette machine, a full-size soap-wagon hooked up to an inflatable bottle of milk, stuffed animals in glass cases and a plate commemorating a 1970s NUS strike. There's an easy-going atmosphere, and geeky indie kids in square glasses happily rub shoulders with off-duty City boys arguing about the technicalities of deals they've signed off. The selection of ales (Adnams Bitter, Timothy Taylor Landlord and a rotating guest ale) add an air of authenticity to a venue that could otherwise border on the overly wacky.
Babies and children admitted (until 9pm). Quiz (8pm Thur; free). Tables outdoors (4, pavement). TV. **Map p284 A2.**

Royal Oak
8-10 Clapham High Street, SW4 7UT (7720 5678). Clapham North tube/Clapham High Street rail. **Open** noon-11pm Mon-Thur; noon-midnight Fri; noon-1am Sat; noon-10.30pm Sun. **Food served** noon-10pm daily. **Credit** MC, V. Pub
Not one for ale fans. Despite stocking draught Adnams and a guest beer, the flat-capped barman could barely suppress a snigger when we asked what real ales they had. With a trendier crowd than some of the other establishments in the area, this contemporary, white-walled pub isn't afraid to break with Clapham High Street's funky-house solidarity and play some fun pop tunes. On a Saturday night you might find table pressure relegating you from the bar proper to the garage-like backroom area (via a door that is misleadingly labelled as the men's toilets); while nice and airy in summer, in winter it's rather like having a furtive pint in a chilly carport.
Babies and children admitted (until 6pm). Tables outdoors (4, pavement). TV (big screen, satellite). **Map p284 C1.**

Tim Bobbin
1-3 Lilleshall Road, SW4 0LN (7738 8953). Clapham Common tube. **Open** noon-11pm Mon-Wed; noon-midnight Thur-Sat; noon-10.30pm Sun. **Food served** noon-3pm, 7-10pm Mon-Fri; noon-10pm Sat; noon-9pm Sun. **Credit** MC, V. Pub
With its wooden beams, old-fashioned lampshades and collection of young blonde barmaids serving pints of ale (Bombardier, London Pride and Harveys Bitter) to old codgers propped up at the bar, it's the country-pub feel of places like this that explains why Clapham is referred to as a 'village'. And there's definitely a nod to the area's oval ball and gastro fixations: on our Saturday afternoon visit, rugby-shirted girls sat at the bar drinking pints of snakebite and black, while families sat at stripped-down wooden tables in the restaurant at the rear, tucking into the Modern British food. And the pub's name? Tim Bobbin was the pen-name of an 18th-century school teacher and caricaturist John Collier, whose lewd drawings cover the walls. Those with delicate sensibilities should stare straight at their drink.
Games (darts). Restaurant. Tables outdoors (11, garden). TVs. **Map p284 A1.**

Vinifera NEW
20-26 Bedford Road, SW4 7HJ (7498 9648). Clapham North tube. **Open** 6pm-1am Mon-Fri; noon-1am Sat, Sun. **Food served** 6-10pm Mon-Fri; noon-10pm Sat, Sun. **Credit** MC, V. Wine bar

This little wine bar, stuck in an awkward site behind Clapham North tube, hasn't taken off yet. It doesn't help that the clinically white-walled interior is lacking in atmosphere, particularly when empty. The wine list is badly laid out, so it took a lot of time to find the ten wines by the glass – and these were the least interesting options. A shame, as the list includes novelties such as white Georgian and English wines, and unusual grape varieties such as the leafy, rustic grolleau and the dry, slightly bitter teroldego rotaliano. Positive points are eager, attentive staff, and a fair pricing policy. You can drink well for under £15 per bottle, and the wines from southern France are well chosen; for oenophiles, the 'Inner Cellar' is the place to look. Nicca socca – little chickpea flour pancakes with pizza-like toppings, originally from Nice – made a good accompanying snack.
Babies and children admitted. Function room. Wine tastings (phone for details). **Map p284 C1.**

Windmill on the Common
Windmill Drive, Clapham Common Southside, SW4 9DE (8673 4578/www.windmillclapham.co.uk). Clapham Common or Clapham South tube. **Open** 11am-midnight Mon-Sat; noon-11pm Sun. **Food served** noon-10.30pm Mon-Sat; noon-10pm Sun. **Credit** AmEx, DC, MC, V. Gastropub
This pub-cum-hotel's recent makeover typifies Young's current renaissance. Primary-coloured lighting illuminates the bottles behind the bar, where three varieties of champagne take pride of place. Alongside the usual suspects of Young's ales (Ordinary, Special and Winter Warmer), there's draught Bombardier and Peroni, plus two varieties of Pimm's. The quirky decor differs from room to room. In the dining area, groups of middle-aged bearded gents play chess amid faux-medieval wood panelling, wall-mounted antlers and an ornately carved bacchanalian motif. The centrepiece, though, is the lounge area, where green leather sofas sit alongside a postmodern collection of art and low-hanging red tubular lampshades – all set to a funk soundtrack. For once, Young's lives up to its name.
Babies and children admitted (conservatory, restaurant). Disabled: toilet. Function room. Games (fruit machine). Quiz (8pm Sun, winter; £1). Restaurant. Tables outdoors (12, garden). TV (big screen, satellite). **Map p284 A3.**

Also in the area...
Bierodrome *44-48 Clapham High Street, SW4 7UR (7720 1118).* Branch. **Map p284 B2.**
Fine Line *182-184 Clapham High Street, SW4 7UG (7622 4436).* Branch. **Map p284 B2.**
Revolution *95-97 Clapham High Street, SW4 7TB (7720 6642).* Branch. **Map p284 B2.**
Rose & Crown *2 The Polygon, SW4 0JG (7720 8265).* Pub with attractive tiled frontage and ales such as Morlands and Hardys & Hansons on tap; shame about the bus garage view. **Map p284 A2.**

Kennington

Beehive
60-62 Carter Street, SE17 3EW (7703 4992). Kennington tube/12, 68, 68A, 171, 176, P5 bus. **Open** 11am-11pm Mon-Sat; noon-10.30pm Sun. **Food served** noon-3pm, 5.30-10pm Mon-Fri; noon-10pm Sat, Sun. **Credit** MC, V. Pub

South

As with the best backstreet pubs, there's a real community feel to this charming boozer. On a Friday night, there was a noticeable absence of music; instead, the soundtrack was provided by the buzz of chattering middle-aged couples enjoying the pleasant food (lamb curry, burgers, pan-fried salmon – for under a tenner – and roasts on Sunday). The walls are lined with large canvasses by a local artist, who we found propping up the bar, setting the world to rights with the landlord. There's a vast selection of whiskies, alongside London Pride and Directors on tap. With a warm light given off by the candle-filled wine bottles on the tables, and a collection of antiquated objets d'art lining the shelves, this cosy local is perfect for those looking for a low-key, friendly night out.
Babies and children admitted (until 7pm). Tables outdoors (30, patio). TV.

Dog House
293 Kennington Road, SE11 6BY (7820 9310).
Kennington or Oval tube. **Open** noon-midnight Mon-Thur, Sun; noon-1.30am Fri, Sat. **Food served** noon-3pm, 6-10pm Mon-Fri; noon-10pm Sat, Sun. **Credit** MC, V. Pub
There's a certain scruffy charm to this Kennington Road watering hole. With its no-frills decor, dog-eared board games piled up in the corner, sporadic performances by local bands, an impeccable selection of dancey music during the day, a Saturday afternoon knitting club and late opening times at the weekend, it's popular with an arty young crowd. Local celeb Stephen Merchant has been spotted enjoying Sunday lunch here; the gastropub-style menu is a particular forte. The draught selection includes Black Sheep, Bombardier and Abbot Ale, plus a host of lagers from Leffe to Red Stripe. Staff can be rather vague (trying to order an orange juice turned into a farce of Woosterian proportions), but this only seems to add to the place's character.
Babies and children admitted (upstairs). Function room. Games (board games). Music (jazz/latin 8.30pm alternate Tue; DJs 9pm Sat; musicians 6pm alternate Sun; free). Tables outdoors (20, pavement). TV.

Prince of Wales
48 Cleaver Square, SE11 4EA (7735 9916).
Kennington tube. **Open** noon-11pm Mon-Sat; noon-10.30pm Sun. **Food served** noon-2.30pm, 6-9pm Mon-Thur; noon-2.30pm Fri, Sat; noon-3pm Sun.
Credit AmEx, MC, V. Pub
Set in a square cluttered with flashy sports cars and Chelsea tractors with blacked-out windows, it's hardly surprising that this small local is filled with a clipped-tone buzz. The crowd mixes sugar daddies with blonde trophy girlfriends on their arms, rangy posh youths in pinstriped blazers enjoying the selection of Shepherd Neame's Spitfire, Kent's Best and Porter ales, and the odd, confused-looking indie kid. The walls are lined with black and white photos of 19th-century cricketers and, in a nod to the pub's 1901 origins, the signs for the toilets are in a deliberately olde worlde style. Don't take the heritage factor as an indicator of a relaxed vibe, though; on our visit, the staff almost shoved us out of the door in their eagerness to close up.
Tables outdoors (3, pavement).

White Hart
185 Kennington Lane, SE11 4EZ (7735 1061/
www.thewhitehartpub.co.uk). Kennington tube/196 bus. **Open** noon-11pm Mon-Wed; noon-1am Thur-Sat; noon-10.30pm Sun. **Food served** noon-3pm, 6-10.30pm

Mon-Fri; noon-4pm, 6-10.30pm Sat; noon-9pm Sun. **Credit** MC, V. Pub
With a selection of beers on tap that includes Bombardier, San Miguel and Baltica (from Russia), this homely, open-plan pub is a relaxed spot for a quiet pint – but the food is the real crowd-pleaser, and a cut above what's available elsewhere in the neighbourhood. Bar snacks feature mini cocktail sausages and plates of whitebait while, come Saturday evening, half the tables are booked by well-heeled locals sampling the main menu of Modern European/ British fare (porcini and potato ravioli in spinach and taleggio sauce, £9). The wine list is decent too. A big screen upstairs shows sporting events, and free wireless internet access is available.
Babies and children admitted. Function room. TVs (big screen, satellite).

Also in the area...
brb@kennington *111 Kennington Road, SE11 6SF (7820 3682).* Branch of Bar Room Bar.
Greyhound *336 Kennington Park Road, SE11 4PP (7735 2594).* Popular with cricket fans and local students; plasma screens dotted around the interior make this a good pub for TV sport. Looks out for the signed bats and sweaters on the walls.
Old Red Lion *42 Kennington Park Road SE11 4RS (7735 3529).* Medieval-style boozer with beer garden, dartboard and giant TV screen, and Bass, Bombardier and Toby Bitter on the taps.

Stockwell

★ Bar Estrela
111-115 South Lambeth Road, SW8 1UZ (7793 1051).
Stockwell tube/Vauxhall tube/rail. **Open** 8am-midnight Mon-Sat; 10am-11pm Sun. **Food served** 8am-11pm daily. **Credit** AmEx, MC, V. Bar
It's a wonder Stockwell residents spend money going on holiday with this charmingly exotic bar in the locale. Above the counter hangs a Portuguese sign bearing the legend 'if you drink to forget, pay before you drink'; higher up there's a collection of scarves from Portugal's major football teams. The black-waistcoated staff natter to the ruddy-faced locals, who vary in age but are united by the fact that they're almost all Portuguese speakers. A restaurant adjoins, so the glass counter below the bar is stocked with bowls of parsley-flecked mussels, chocolate éclairs and custard tartlets. As you'd expect, the drinks are predominantly Portuguese, with the most popular choice being bottles of Super Bock lager (only £1.30), which are served with a freshly poured bowl of nuts.
Babies and children admitted. Tables outdoors (10, pavement).

Canton Arms
177 South Lambeth Road, SW8 1XP (7587 3819).
Stockwell tube. **Open** noon-11pm Mon-Wed; noon-midnight Thur-Sat; noon-10.30pm Sun. **Food served** noon-3pm, 6-9.30pm Mon-Fri; noon-9pm Sat, Sun.
Credit MC, V. Pub
Depending on which door you enter, you're likely to end up with contrasting first impressions of the Canton Arms. Stepping into the back section – with its humidor, black and white tiled floor, 1950s dresser stacked with cutlery, and a bookcase filled with antiquated tomes – is a little like stepping into an old-fashioned scullery. Here, customers

South

Vinifera. *See p152.*

range from after-work media types to pairs of mates catching up over a pint (Deuchars, Timothy Taylor Landlord) on the leather sofas. The front area sees a more animated crowd relishing the pub's more contemporary touches: watching the big-screen TVs, playing table football and taking advantage of various drinks offers, such as two-for-one Bloody Marys on Sundays.
Babies and children admitted (until 8pm). Games (table football). Tables outdoors (8, patio). TV (big screen, satellite).

Priory Arms
83 Lansdowne Way, SW8 2PB (7622 1884). Stockwell tube. **Open** 11am-11pm Mon-Sat; noon-10.30pm Sun. **Food served** noon-9pm Mon-Sat; 12.30-5pm Sun. **Credit** MC, V. Pub
One of the most overtly proud bastions of old-fashioned pub culture that London has to offer. The lights are bright, the decor is set staunchly in the old-school red carpet mould, the fruit machine occupies pride of place by the door and there's even a Young's brewery clock. In keeping with the Priory's pride in its craft, the beer selection is the stuff of CAMRA members' wet dreams. Harveys Sussex Best, Hop Back Summer Lightning and Adnams are permanent fixtures; there are also three guest ales, five kinds of Belgian fruit beer and 15 or so types of fruit wine. Above the bar are more than 200 pump labels from guest beers served in the past. The most impressive range of drinks in this part of London, no question.
Children admitted (Sun lunch only). Function room. Games (fruit machine; backgammon club, Sun afternoon; chess club, Wed afternoon). Quiz (9pm Sun; free). Tables outdoors (4, patio). TVs (satellite).

Royal Albert
43 St Stephen's Terrace, SW8 1DL (7840 0777). Stockwell tube. **Open** noon-11pm Mon-Thur, Sun; noon-midnight Fri, Sat. **Food served** 6-10pm Mon-Thur; 6-11pm Fri; noon-10pm Sat, Sun. **Credit** MC, V. Pub
Set on one of Stockwell's quieter side streets, this old boozer turned funkyish bar has twinkling fairy lights in wave patterns across the windows, high-backed leather chairs, Ikea-style shelving stuffed with books, and large leather sofas piled high with mohair cushions next to a lit fireplace. At times, it tries a little too hard to be young and trendy – the menu of flavoured vodkas is headed 'flavad vodkas', and the toilets are labelled 'berts' and 'berties' – and yet the crowd is predominantly middle-aged, making it the David Brent of the Stockwell pub scene. Nonetheless, with a rotating selection of three ales, plus Weston's Cider, Amstel and San Miguel on tap, it's a decent choice for a quiet pint.
Babies and children welcome (until 7pm Mon-Fri): high chairs. Disabled: toilet. Games (board games, golf machine, table football). Music (jazz 8pm Thur; free). Tables outdoors (16, garden; 3, pavement). TV (big screen, satellite).

Surprise
16 Southville, SW8 2PP (7622 4623). Stockwell tube/Vauxhall tube/rail. **Open** 11am-11pm Mon-Sat; noon-10.30pm Sun. **Food served** noon-3pm Mon-Fri, Sun. **Credit** MC, V. Pub
This Young's pub is very much a local boozer, complete with dartboard and weather-worn tables. The back room is lined with caricatures of the regulars (done by Dave, the ex-Marvel Comics illustrator turned labourer who fre-

South

quents the pub) and, on our visit, the clientele consisted mainly of those self-same regulars nursing pints of ale at the bar (Young's Bitter and Special, plus one guest ale). No surprises then, but there's a nice community feel; our presence was called upon to settle a debate about Michael Jackson's suitability as a child minder, and one local happily took us through all the caricatures. The place gets a lot busier during the week than it does on a Friday evening, but this little hinterland of community charm is an enjoyable drinking experience at any time.
Games (board games, boules pitch, darts, fruit machine). Tables outdoors (12, patio). TV (satellite).

Also in the area...
Circle *348 Clapham Road, SW9 9AR (7622 3683/www.circlebar.co.uk).* Bar-cum-pub with a reasonable food menu. During happy hour (5-9pm daily), two house cocktails cost £5.50.

Tooting

Garden House NEW
196 Tooting High Street, SW17 0SF (8767 6582/ www.gardenhousetooting.com). Tooting Broadway tube. **Open** noon-11pm Mon, Tue, Sun; noon-midnight Wed-Sat. **Food served** noon-3pm, 5-10pm Mon-Thur; noon-10pm Fri-Sun. **Credit** MC, V. Pub
After a botched launch, when a mailshot was sent before they'd got themselves in gear, the Garden House is slowly bringing some decorum and civilisation to the southern end of Tooting. The mismatched furniture, brick walls, displays of local art and an eclectic soundtrack are slowly wooing a sparse but friendly crowd – a far cry from the lager-soaked fleapit of this large corner pub's previous incarnation. Staropramen, Grolsch and 1664 sit alongside a couple of real ales, including London Pride; add a few decent wines by the glass and some reasonable bar grub, and everyone's more than happy. Oh, and there's a nice little courtyard at the back – although they're somewhat optimistic in calling it a garden.
Babies and children welcome (until 9pm): high chairs. Disabled: toilet. Games (board games). Music (DJ 8.30pm Sat; musicians 6pm Sun; free). Tables outdoors (9, garden). TV.

★ Selkirk NEW
60 Selkirk Road, SW17 0ES (8672 6235/ www.theselkirk.co.uk). Tooting Broadway tube. **Open** noon-midnight daily. **Food served** noon-3pm, 5-10pm Mon-Fri; noon-10pm Sat; noon-9.30pm Sun. **Credit** MC, V. Pub
Lying a few hundred yards off Tooting's main drag, the Selkirk has slowly established itself as the best pub in SW17 by quite a long chalk. It feels like a real local: the kind of place where you can sink a good few crisis-driven pints with your mates, but also bring your parents on a weekend night without being embarrassed for, or indeed of, them. IPA and Directors, Leffe and Artois Bock on tap, a healthy wine list, food with pretensions to gastro fare but not excessively so, a bar billiards table, very amiable staff – they all add up to a welcome alternative to the cheap-booze-and-widescreen establishments that are prevalent nearby.
Babies and children admitted. Function room. Games (bar billiards, games machine). Music (jazz 6pm Sun). Tables outdoors (20, garden). TV.

Trafalgar Arms
148 Tooting High Street, SW17 0RT (8767 6059). Tooting Broadway tube. **Open** noon-midnight Mon-Wed, Sun; noon-1am Thur-Sat. **Food served** noon-9.30pm daily. **Credit** MC, V. Pub
Situated a stone's throw from St George's Hospital, this much-loved pub is often packed with doctors and nurses attracted by the prospect of stress-relieving drinks after another day of NHS belt-tightening, and a 20% discount on food. It's a cheap and cheerful place, with a solitary Spitfire ale, and lagers that occupy the cold, colder and coldest categories – but it's the oddities that attract: perhaps a DJ wedged into a corner behind a bookshelf, drag queen bingo on Tuesdays, or the sprawling mass of people sat out on the front courtyard in summer, enjoying bracing fumes from the A24. The Trafalgar has recently become a little tatty around the edges, but locals still have a lot of affection for it.
Babies and children admitted (until 9pm). Entertainment (bingo Tue). Games (fruit machines). Music (DJs 9pm 1st Fri of mth; free). Tables outdoors (20, pavement). TV.

Also in the area...
smoke bar diner *14 Trinity Road, SW17 7RE (8767 3902/www.smokebardiner.com).* Bar with a retro 1970s feel; very busy at weekends.

Vauxhall

Fentiman Arms
64 Fentiman Road, SW8 1LA (7793 9796/ www.geronimo-inns.co.uk). Vauxhall tube/rail/Oval tube. **Open** noon-11pm Mon-Thur; noon-midnight Fri, Sat; noon-10.30pm Sun. **Food served** noon-3.30pm, 7-9.30pm Mon-Fri; noon-4pm, 7-10.30pm Sat; noon-4pm, 7-9.30pm Sun. **Credit** MC, V. Gastropub
There is some corner of distant Vauxhall that is forever Chelsea, and it's called the Fentiman. Here, foppish young City types rub shoulders with, well, foppish young City types in a gastropub that seems to be multi-tasking capably. Part of the small Geronimo Inns chain, it serves hearty, foodie fare, as well as fine – if pricey– bar snacks (we paid £5.50 for a small bowl of scampi) and a selection of draught booze that ranges from Budweiser (but who ever orders that?) to Bombardier. The interior has some witty flourishes, including a massive James Dean screen, and the landscaped garden (designed by a Chelsea Flower Show winner, no less) is a world away from the mean streets of SW8. The regular Tuesday quiz night, as hosted by the Falstaffian Jim, is packed.
Babies and children admitted. Function room. Quiz (8pm Tue; £1). Tables outdoors (15, garden). TV (satellite).

Riverside NEW
5 St George's Wharf, SW8 2LE (7735 8129/ www.riveridelondon.com). Vauxhall tube/rail. **Open** 11am-midnight daily. **Food served** 11am-10.30pm daily. **Credit** MC, V. Pub
Part of the glossy, glass-walled St George Wharf development, the Riverside opened in summer 2006. As its name would suggest, the main draw is the location; in summer, you can take your bottle of El Coto Rioja rosé (£15.50) outside and sun yourself on the sizeable Thameside terrace. Inside, the decor is modern but rather

South

Getting saké

Ten years ago, London-based saké fans had to fly off to Japan to sample the subtleties of saké. Here in the capital, they might have been able to find expense account sakés in the sort of Japanese restaurants frequented by oriental businessmen, or warmed-up, low-grade saké in Japanese cafés, but that was it. All's changed. Now, several London restaurants have gone as far as installing 'saké sommeliers' to guide increasingly interested customers through ever-expanding selections.

Sayaka Wanatabe, a trained expert from Tokyo, was London's first saké sommelier when she started work at Zuma restaurant (5 Raphael Street, SW7 1DL, 7584 1919, www.zuma restaurant.com) in March 2003. Here, they stock around 40 sakés. 'When I started two years ago,' she says, 'I found that most non-Japanese customers didn't even know what saké was. But things have changed – I even get customers coming in asking for specific brands or styles.'

Saké comes in many guises, with styles ranging from light and refreshing to aged and slightly oxidised; there are also unpasteurised sakés that are milky in appearance. In general, the most popular sakés are delicately aromatic and resemble white wines, but with a different spectrum of aromas – broadly similar to light sauvignon blancs. They also vary from slightly sweet to very dry. 'It's not wine,' says Wanatabe,

'but it's the simplest way of explaining it to customers. In alcoholic strength (typically 14-15%) it's closest to wine, and the subtleties of flavour are similar.'

Wanatabe trained in Japan, but the majority of London's saké sommeliers are French wine waiters who have discovered an appreciation of the spirit through wine. 'The style and character of wine and saké are similar,' says Matthiu Garros, wine sommelier turned saké sage at Umu (14-16 Bruton Place, W1J 6LX, 7499 8881, www.umurestaurant.com). 'We even use the same words to describe them: punchy, dry, fruity, lively. If you understand wine, you can understand saké.'

Though most of us outside of Japan are used to drinking saké warm, to appreciate the complex flavours of premium saké it is best served cold. 'Warm sakés tend to be poorer grades,' says Morgan Selva, manager of Japanese restaurant Sumosan (26B Albemarle Street, W1S 4HY, 7495 5999, www.sumosan. com). 'We serve three warm sakés and even flavoured versions because there is such demand for them, but our saké sommelier, Jean-Louis Naveilhan, tries to encourage people towards the better quality chilled sakés, served in proper wine-tasting glasses. We have around 30 of these, and people tend to pay the same amount as they might for a great bottle of wine, between £22 and £45.'

bland – although floor-to-ceiling windows maximise its natural assets. Service is charming and there's a good range of draught beer, including Young's Bitter, Peroni, Bombardier, Leffe Blonde and a monthly changing guest ale, plus Pimm's on tap. It tries hard – a little too hard, perhaps, when it comes to the menu. Forget simple fish 'n' chips; here, it's gussied up to become hake fillet in tempura batter, accompanied by pea velouté and own-made tartare sauce. Crikey.
Babies and children admitted. Bar available for hire. Music (funk/soul band 6pm occasional Thur, Fri; free). Tables outdoors (35, terrace). TV (plasma).

Royal Vauxhall Tavern
372 Kennington Lane, SE11 5HY (7582 0833). Vauxhall tube/rail. **Open** 9pm-2am Sat; 2pm-midnight Sun. **No credit cards.** Pub
A Victorian boozer that proclaims itself to be the beating heart of Vauxhall, and would you know, it's bang on. A key influence on London's gay scene since World War II when returning servicemen would show up for the cross-dressing performances and rub shoulders with local homosexuals – so very underground and risqué back then. The numerous tables and raised platform hark back to the pub's music hall roots, while the stage gets trod most nights of the week with the much-adored avant-garde club every Saturday, called Duckie, and Vauxhall, a spit and sawdust cabaret every Thursday.
Bar available for hire. Music (cabaret Thur; DJs 9pm Sat; 2pm Sun; £5-£6).

Waterloo

★ Anchor & Hope
36 The Cut, SE1 8LP (7928 9898). Southwark or Waterloo tube/rail. **Open** 5-11pm Mon; 11am-11pm Tue-Sat; 12.30-5pm Sun. **Food served** 6-10.30pm Mon; noon-2.30pm, 6-10.30pm Tue-Sat; 2pm sitting Sun. **Credit** MC, V. **No credit cards.** Gastropub
The no-booking policy at this deservedly celebrated gastropub means many would-be diners have to while away time before getting a table. Thankfully, the bar side of the operation works as more than just a waiting room to the adjoining dining space. It's dark and buzzy, made dimmer still by aubergine walls and a dark wooden floor. The tables are set a little too close together for comfort, especially when the place is packed with waiting diners, but drop in when the foodies aren't around and it's all very convivial. The beer choice – Bombardier and Young's – may not be as fabulous as the retro British food, but you can't have everything. A shame, too, that the piano by the door never gets played.
Babies and children admitted. Bookings not accepted. Tables outdoors (4, pavement). **Map p282 N8.**

Arch One [NEW]
1 Mepham Street, SE1 8RL (7401 2329/www.arch-1.com). Waterloo tube/rail. **Open** noon-1.30am Mon-Sat. **Food served** noon-3pm, 5-10pm Mon-Sat. **Credit** MC, V. Cocktail bar
If you fancy something classier than bog-standard wine or a pint, Arch One could be for you. The 30 or so cocktails (around £7) include the likes of coriander mojito and various takes on the martini, with nothing too tacky and stupidly named to lower the tone. The space is similarly unfussy, created out of a railway arch whose exposed

brickwork curves high above polished wood tables and red leather banquettes. The huge glass frontage gives a fine view of Waterloo rail station's grandest entrance, especially if you can bag a table in the tiny mezzanine space above the door. The food – pasta, salads and grills – could be more ambitious, but it's a better bet than many other options nearby.
Babies and children admitted (until 9pm). Bar available for hire. Music (DJs 8pm Thur-Sat; free). Tables outdoors (20, pavement). TV (big screen). **Map p282 M8.**

L'Auberge
1 Sandell Street, SE1 8UH (7633 0610). Waterloo tube/rail. **Open** noon-11pm daily. **Food served** noon-10.30pm daily. **Credit** AmEx, MC, V. Wine bar
Though less popular than it was a few years back as the tides of fashion move on, L'Auberge has stuck to its guns with its take on a French-Belgian bistro. Wood dominates the light, high-ceilinged main bar, which can be dispiritingly quiet during the day but perks up greatly at night (there's also a restaurant upstairs). The bar menu offers decent, reasonably priced fare – haddock and salmon fish cakes, perhaps, or steak frites – but most of the thirtysomething office set are here to drink. There's plenty to enjoy, from an above-average wine list (eight whites and reds are available by the glass), complemented by fruit beers, Trappist ales and Duvel, alongside more familiar Flemish offerings such as Hoegaarden and Leffe.
Babies and children admitted. Restaurant (available for hire). Tables outdoors (15, roof terrace). **Map p282 N8.**

Baltic
74 Blackfriars Road, SE1 8HA (7928 1111/ www.balticrestaurant.co.uk). Southwark tube/rail. **Open/food served** noon-11pm Mon-Sat; noon-10.30pm Sun. **Credit** AmEx, MC, V. Bar/Restaurant
A discreet, classy, east European-influenced bar and restaurant. No light or sound spills out from the dark curtained entrance and blackened windows. Inside, low-level lighting shows off the colours in the gorgeous amber-covered bar. Having some of the highest bar stools in London may not be a good idea, mind, when you boast a 40-strong vodka list. Tyskie and Lech beers maintain the Polish influence, though there's an enticing list of cocktails (£6-£7) and London Pride and Breton cider for Western decadents. The latter will also love the food, whether they go for the costly but top-notch fine dining in the restaurant at the back or stick to the tempting east European bar snacks (around £7), such as veal and pork dumplings, Polish sausages with sour cream, or kamchatka salad (crayfish, crab, egg, mustard, dill).
Babies and children admitted. Disabled: toilet. Function rooms. Music (jazz 7pm Sun). Tables outdoors (4, terrace). **Map p282 N8.**

★ Crown
108 Blackfriars Road, SE1 8HW (7261 9524/ www.thecrownbarandkitchen.co.uk). Southwark tube/rail. **Open** 11am-11pm Mon-Fri. **Food served** noon-3pm, 5-10pm Mon-Fri. **Credit** MC, V. Pub
Despite its location on a fairly bleak stretch of road away from the main action around the Cut, the Crown is well worth the short walk down Blackfriars Road. It's a lovely T-shaped space lent a period feel by worn floorboards, vintage wallpaper, antique clocks and cut-glass light shades throwing pretty patterns on to the wall. A cluster of tables

at the front gives way to a cosier rear section with suitably distressed sofas, while low-level beats add to the languid mood. Great too to see the likes of Bishops Finger on offer alongside Bombardier, while whisky lovers can choose from around 20 malts. A decent selection of wines is chalked on the board above the open kitchen, which knocks out an array of tempting dishes (sage and pancetta risotto, top-quality steaks). Top place.
Babies and children admitted. Bar available for hire. Function room. Tables outdoors (4, pavement). TV. **Map p282 N9.**

Cubana

48 Lower Marsh, SE1 7RG (7928 8778/ www.cubana.co.uk). Waterloo tube/rail. **Open** noon-midnight Mon, Tue; noon-1am Wed, Thur; noon-3am Fri, Sat. **Food served** noon-3pm, 5-11pm Mon-Fri; 5-11pm Sat. **Credit** MC, V. Bar
While Fidel himself grows increasingly careworn, this joint is still going strong after a decade or so of unswerving dedication to Cuban booze and food. As well as bottled beers (Sol, San Miguel, Budvar), various takes on the classic triumvirate of mojito, daiquiri and margarita are well priced for £5. A fiver also buys into a tapas selection featuring the likes of prawns with mango-chilli salsa or chorizo and sweet-potato croquettes. The two-course lunch for £5.95 is a great local bargain. It's an engagingly higgledy-piggledy space too, with different levels offering a variety of nooks, unified by rough yellow stone walls, battered wooden seats and Cuban knick-knacks. It may take a couple of drinks before it begins to look anything like Havana, but by then you'll probably be having too good a time to care.
Disabled: toilet. Music (bands 11pm Wed-Sat; £5 after 11pm). Tables outdoors (4, pavement). **Map p282 N9.**

Cut Bar NEW

66 The Cut, SE1 8LZ (7928 4400/www.thecutbar.com). Southwark or Waterloo tube/rail. **Open** 8am-1am Mon-Fri; 10am-1am Sat; 11am-midnight Sun. **Food served** 8am-11pm Mon-Sat; 11am-9pm Sun. **Credit** AmEx, DC, MC, V. Bar
Though attached to the Young Vic, the Cut Bar operates in its own right rather than as just a place for pre- or post-theatre snifters. The design eschews obvious theatricality in favour of clean-lined, spacious tastefulness: dark wood, stone floor and big windows to watch the world go by. A decent wine list, 20 or so cocktails (£6-£6.50) and chilled music help attract more women than many of the other drinking dens nearby, though there's a wide selection of bottled beers for the boys, including Negra Modelo, Budvar and fruity Framboze. Guinness, Red Stripe and Kirin are on tap, but there are no real ales. The nicest spot is upstairs, where an L-shaped mezzanine bar offers an eyrie with slouchy sofas and a slightly more boho vibe.
Babies and children admitted. Bar available for hire. Function room. Games (board games, poker). Tables outdoors (20, roof terrace; 5, pavement). **Map p282 N8.**

Fire Station

150 Waterloo Road, SE1 8SB (7620 2226). Waterloo tube/rail. **Open** 11am-11.30pm Mon-Sat; noon-10.30pm Sun. **Food served** Bar 11am-10.30pm Mon-Sat; noon-9.30pm Sun. *Restaurant* noon-3pm, 5.30-11pm Mon-Fri; noon-11pm Sat; noon-9.30pm Sun. **Credit** AmEx, MC, V. Pub

Thirtysomething office workers and assorted Waterloo dossers have replaced the fire crew who laboured here until its conversion into a bar/restaurant in the 1990s, but the large 1910 building is still an imposing presence with its wide façade and glowing red sign. The vast interior splits into two, with a dining area at the back, and an expansive, high-ceilinged bar at the front that looks good with its dark stone floor, big steel lights, hanging fire buckets and industrial ironwork to remind you of its working past. A large curved bar dispenses Marston's Pedigree and London Pride alongside the now ubiquitous continental offerings of Staropramen and Paulaner; a wine list is chalked above. Benches outside get packed come summer. While it's all perfectly serviceable for the after-work crowd, the atmosphere lacks anything distinctive enough to really set things alight.
Babies and children admitted. Disabled: toilet. Function room. Restaurant. Tables outdoors (4, pavement). TV (big screen, satellite). **Map p282 N9.**

Hole in the Wall

5 Mepham Street, SE1 8SQ (7928 6196). Waterloo tube/rail. **Open** 11am-11pm Mon-Thur; 11am-11.30pm Fri, Sat; noon-10.30pm Sun. **Food served** noon-9pm Mon-Sat; noon-4pm Sun. **Credit** MC, V. Pub
This landmark seems to have been offering 'one for the rail' since the age of steam. Tucked beneath a railway arch opposite the main entrance to Waterloo station, it's a place designed to concentrate the minds of its clientele – geezers in trainers alongside suits with cigars – on their beer. There isn't even a window in the main bar to distract from the arched ceiling of exposed brickwork, faded yellow walls and old pub mirrors. You can trade space for light by squeezing into the miniature front bar, where a window looks out on to a little lane and the mood is slightly less blokey. An excellent and well-kept ale selection offers old troupers such as Greene King IPA, Adnams Broadside and Bombardier as well as various guest beers. Leffe, Staropramen and Paulaner add a nod to the continent. One of the few places left with a pinball machine too.
Babies and children admitted (until 8pm). Games (fruit machines, quiz machine, pinball). TV (big screen, satellite). **Map p282 M8.**

★ King's Arms

25 Roupell Street, SE1 8TB (7207 0784). Waterloo tube/rail. **Open** 11am-11pm Mon-Fri; noon-11pm Sat, Sun. **Food served** 11am-3pm, 6-10.30pm Mon-Fri; 6-10.30pm Sat; noon-4pm Sun. **Credit** AmEx, DC, MC, V. Pub
If you had to choose just one pub in the area, this is probably it. Hidden away amid the tiny dark brick Victorian terraces on one of London's most atmospheric streets, it's a marvellous warren of a boozer. At the front, a sepia-lit saloon bar and tiny public bar pull in the bearded CAMRA brigade, drawn to the fine selection of ales (Adnams, Bass, London Pride, Greene King IPA) served at the old horseshoe-shaped bar. A fire warms the beautifully cosy rear bar, where a riot of old posters and quirky objects look down on a dark stone floor. There's a couple of battered sofas in one corner, which get quickly snapped up, forcing most punters towards corner seats or the benches running along the long wooden table in the middle. A fine Thai menu rounds things off very nicely, with roasts adding even more appeal at the weekend. Certainly worth seeking out.
Function room (available weekends only). **Map p282 N8.**

South

Laughing Gravy

154 Blackfriars Road, SE1 8EN (7721 7055/ www.thelaughinggravy.com). Southwark tube/rail. **Open** noon-11pm Mon-Fri; 7-11pm Sat. **Food served** noon-10pm Mon-Fri; 7-10pm Sat. **Credit** MC, V. Bar
Named after a slang term for booze used during the US Prohibition era (and also the mischievous name Laurel & Hardy gave their dog), this teams up with the Crown opposite as a point of solace on an otherwise desultory stretch of road. The room is long and thin, with the light, glass-roofed rear section operating as a restaurant when not providing spillover space for the darkier, cosier front bar. The mood is one of casual refinement, with a mish mash of modern art and old prints overlooking wooden tables and dark flagstones. A short but well-chosen wine list is complemented by the area's most intriguing bottled beer selection – including such rarities as Barbār Honey Ale from Belgium and Bravara from Brazil – as well as St Peter's Organic, Hoegaarden and Peroni on tap.
Babies and children admitted. Booking advisable. Disabled: toilet. Restaurant available for hire. Tables outdoors (2, pavement). **Map p282 O9.**

Ring

72 Blackfriars Road, SE1 8HA (7620 0811). Southwark tube/rail. **Open** 11am-11pm Mon-Wed; 11am-midnight Thur-Sat; noon-10.30pm Sun. **Food served** noon-3pm, 6-10.30pm Mon-Sat; noon-5pm Sun. **Credit** AmEx, MC, V. Pub
Pint and a fight? Don't worry, the punch-ups are all in the past at this surprisingly smart former boxing pub (a training gym operated upstairs until a few years ago). Memories are kept alive, though, thanks to the dozens of monochrome pugilistic prints covering the dark purple walls, paying homage to such local legends from the Blackfriars Ring across the road as Ted 'Kid' Lewis and promoter Ted Broadribb. At weekends, the Ring gets crowded enough to make you want to throw a punch or two yourself to get to the bar, but during the week there's a pleasanter vibe as (mainly male) office types enjoy a quiet pint and something from the Thai menu. The drinks choice is far from knock-out, however, with only London Pride as an alternative to lager, Guinness or house plonk.
Babies and children admitted (lunch Sat, Sun). Tables outdoors (8, pavement). TV. **Map p282 N8.**

Three Stags

67-69 Kennington Road, SE1 7PZ (7928 5974). Lambeth North tube/159 bus. **Open** 11am-midnight daily. **Food served** noon-7.30pm Mon; noon-10pm Tue-Sat; noon-9pm Sun. **Credit** MC, V. Pub
This small but sturdy corner boozer, located diagonally opposite the Imperial War Museum, attracts a mix of tourists and office workers. Once the pub in which Charlie Chaplin's father drank himself to death as his young son worked in the nearby poorhouse, it's now a more upmarket affair. (A rear booth, with etched and coloured glass, is named Chaplin's Corner – in honour of either hard-working son or hard-drinking dad.) The ceiling, supported by five columns, is hung with ornate chandeliers and old-fashioned lamps; a raised area next to the piano has some splendid chesterfields. All very posh. The wine list is less so, but all bottled options are available by the glass too. Three draught ales (Greene King IPA, Abbot and Old Speckled Hen) improve on a dull selection of lagers.
Babies and children admitted (until 8pm). Disabled: toilet. Games (fruit machine). Music (jazz 8pm Mon; free). Tables outdoors (10, pavement).

Wellington

81-83 Waterloo Road, SE1 8UD (7928 6083). Waterloo tube/rail. **Open** 11am-11pm Mon-Wed, Sat; 11am-11.30pm Thur, Fri; noon-10.30pm Sun. **Food served** noon-9pm daily. **Credit** (over £5) MC, V. Pub
Located on one of the busiest corners in the area, this big boozer hoovers up passing workers who can't be bothered hunting out better venues in the backstreets. Its size means it's large enough to cope with a busy Friday night crowd, crammed into a space that neatly splits into two – the bit below the painting and the bit that's not. The painting in question is a vast panoramic rendition of the Battle of Waterloo, augmented by old army boots and other military paraphernalia in homage to the eponymous Duke. It's pearls before swine, though, as the office lads focus on a clutch of games machines, while the ladies enjoy an uninspired selection of Hardy's wine.
Babies and children admitted (until 5pm). Bar available for hire. Games (fruit machine, quiz machine). TVs (big screen). **Map p282 N8.**

White Hart

29-30 Cornwall Road, SE1 8TJ (7401 7151). Waterloo tube/rail. **Open** noon-11pm Mon, Sun; noon-midnight Tue-Sat. **Food served** noon-10pm Mon-Sat; noon-9.30pm Sun. **Credit** MC, V. Pub
It may be small, but this excellent pub is a beacon of excellence set amid an atmospheric surrounding of dark brick terraces and railway arches. Popular with creative types from nearby South Bank or IPC Magazines' HQ, it's a dark, cosy space, with neat design flourishes such as retro 1960s lights over the little central bar. With an impressive 21 beers on draught, it has fair claim to offer the best beer selection in SE1, whether you fancy London Pride, one of several wheat beers or maybe a Kriek. Bar food includes burgers made with combos like stilton, peppers and pesto (£7). A trio of tables outside provides welcome overspill from the happy throng inside.
Disabled: toilet. Tables outdoors (4, pavement). **Map p282 N8.**

Also in the area...

Albert Arms *1 Gladstone Street, SE1 6EY (7928 6517).* Living room-sized pub; alongside Greene King IPA, a guest ale is great value at £1.75. **Map p282 N10.**
Archduke *Concert Hall Approach, SE1 8XU (7928 9370).* Split-level bar under Waterloo's railway arches; an impressive array of wines pleases the chatty, mixed clientele. **Map p282 M8.**
Doggett's Coat & Badge *1 Blackfriars Bridge, SE1 9UD (7633 9081).* Spacious riverside boozer set over four floors with a games room and a garden terrace; four ales on tap. **Map p282 N7.**
Film Café *National Film Theatre, Belvedere Road, SE1 8XT (7928 3535/www.bfi.org.uk/nft).* Glass-fronted bar-café that's expensive, but gets away with it thanks to a first-rate location under Waterloo Bridge, in the heart of the South Bank redevelopment. **Map p282 M7.**
Founders Arms *52 Hopton Street, SE1 9JH (7928 1899/www.foundersarms.co.uk).* Young's pub notable for its stunning riverside location next to Tate Modern. **Map p282 O7.**
Stage Door *30 Webber Street, SE1 8QA (7928 8964).* Pub with Adnams ales at the bar, live music at weekends, retro pinball machine and dartboard. **Map p282 N9.**

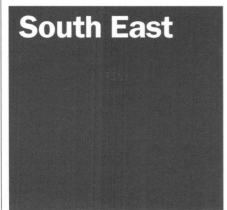

South East

Even disregarding the tourist crowds drawn by its maritime sights, Greenwich is host to some of south-east London's finest pubs. **Greenwich Union**, flagship outlet of Alastair Hook's Meantime Brewing Company, is still our fave place in the area for a pint; boho-leaning **Gipsy Moth** is worth a look for a livelier night. In Bermondsey you'll find boozers that sent the Pilgrim Fathers on their way to the New World (the **Mayflower**), those that serve fine wine and cocktails to the area's loft-dwelling media yuppies (**Village East**, **Hide**) and those that defy categorisation altogether (the wonderfully bizarre boat-pub **Wibbley Wobbley**).

Camberwell has recently been improved by the addition of fine gastropub **Dark Horse**, while East Dulwich has garnered a lovely one of its own in the **Herne Tavern**. In Dulwich Village, the pace is more stately at wonderful old pub the **Crown & Greyhound**. Similarly cosy (though drawing a younger crowd) is Peckham's flawless **Rye Hotel**. Despite Elephant & Castle's cast-iron nightlife rep (courtesy of Ministry of Sound), good pubs are thin on the ground. Likewise, the only pubs worth visiting in Lewisham (unless you like fighting) are those at a decent remove from the centre, such as the homely **Dacre Arms**. In Blackheath, however, it's a different story: of the many fine boozers, the centuries-old **Hare & Billet** and the Mitchell Brothers-refurbed **Princess of Wales** are the nicest. **Zerodegrees**, meanwhile, impresses with its microbrewed beers.

To the west, Deptford has the real ales, good Sunday lunches and unpretentious charm of the **Dog & Bell** to recommend it; newcomer the **Royal Albert** has asserted itself on to the area's pub scene too. In New Cross, live music pulls 'em in at the kitsch **Montague Arms**. Lastly, don't forget London Bridge and Borough – places such as the family-run **Lord Clyde** and the real-ale paradise of the **Royal Oak** are among the best pubs in London. Also excellent is **Wine Wharf**, the oenological bar attached to Vinopolis wine museum.

Bermondsey

Garrison
99-101 Bermondsey Street, SE1 3XB (7089 9355/ www.thegarrison.co.uk). London Bridge tube/rail.
Open 8am-11pm Mon-Fri; 9am-11pm Sat; 9am-10.30pm Sun. **Food served** 8-11.30am, noon-3.30pm, 6.30-10pm Mon-Fri; 9-11.30am, 12.30-4pm, 6.30-10pm Sat; 9-11.30am, 12.30-4pm, 6-9.30pm Sun.
Credit AmEx, MC, V. Gastropub
This bustling place is more like a bistro than a gastropub, with the floorspace so full of tall rickety tables and chairs there's no real standing room. Hops are strung along the etched glass windows as if to remind you there's booze available, but it's the Modern British food and 50-strong wine list (ranging from a medium-bodied Terres de Truffes Côte du Ventoux at £20 all the way up to a fine Château Troplong Mondot St-Émilion Grand Cru at £60) that catch the eye. The interior is a quirky assortment of country-kitchen scrubbed wood in grey-green, old Chinese inkwork wallpaper and pictures of World War I soldiers. The little downstairs cinema room is used for overspill (and private parties) and has its own jukebox.
Babies and children admitted (lunch Sat, Sun). Booking essential. Disabled: toilet. Separate room for parties, seats 25. Vegan dishes.

South East

Hartley
64 Tower Bridge Road, SE1 4TR (7394 7023/
www.thehartley.com). Borough tube/London Bridge
tube/rail. **Open** noon-midnight Mon-Thur; noon-2am
Fri; 11am-2am Sat; noon-10.30pm Sun. **Food served**
noon-3pm, 6-10pm Mon-Fri; 11am-4pm, 6-10pm Sat;
noon-6pm Sun. **Credit** AmEx, DC, MC, V. Gastropub
Named after the now obsolete jam factory, the Hartley has
picture windows and a raised seating area at the front.
Large old lamps are suspended above the zinc-topped bar,
and the bare brick walls are adorned with modern art and
black and white photos of the factory. Appetising aromas
waft across the flower-topped wooden tables from an open
kitchen that is surrounded by ceramic tiles. There's free
internet access, board games and racks stuffed with the
daily papers, and live music on Tuesdays and alternate
Fridays; the bar has recently added Adnams Spindrift on
draught. Bottles include Bass, Old Peculiar, Leffe and
Baltika. The small wine list has some excellent choices,
such as the Gravitas sauvignon blanc (£25) and Domaine
du Grand Tinel Châteauneuf-du-Pape (£32.50).
Babies and children admitted: children's portions;
high chairs. Games (board games). Music (musicians
8pm Tue, alternate Fri). Separate room for parties,
seats 50. Wi-Fi (free).

Hide Bar NEW
39-45 Bermondsey Street, SE1 3XF (7403 6655).
London Bridge tube/rail. **Open** 10am-11pm Mon;
10am-midnight Tue; 10am-1am Wed, Thur; 10am-2am
Fri; 4pm-2am Sat; noon-8pm Sun. **Food served** noon-
9.30pm daily. **Credit** AmEx, MC, V. Cocktail bar
'We really like drink' is the proud boast of this cocktail bar.
A good start, and a promise it lives up to: Hide has a drinks
list made in bar heaven. It stocks all the premium spirits
you've ever heard of, plus quite a few you haven't. And the
staff are happy to make anything; they even have a library
of historic cocktail books you can leaf through, and pick
what you fancy. There's also a decent selection of wine,
draught beers from the Meantime Brewery in Greenwich
and bottled beers from Belgium and beyond. Some gripes:
the staff appeared inexperienced at dealing with customers
(we kept being forgotten) and the slightly gloomy interior
lacks liveliness and a sense of fun. Hide is the only good
cocktail bar for miles, and is worth a special journey if you
care about what you drink – but it's also an illustration
that it takes more than just a great drinks list to make a
truly great bar experience.
Bar available to hire. Drink tasting (7pm Tue; free).
Function room. Wi-Fi (free).

Mayflower
117 Rotherhithe Street, SE16 4NF (7237 4088).
Rotherhithe tube. **Open** *Winter* 11am-3pm, 5.15-11pm
Mon-Thur; 11am-11pm Fri-Sun. *Summer* 11am-11pm
daily. **Food served** *Winter* noon-2.30pm, 6-9.30pm
Mon-Sat; noon-9pm Sun. *Summer* 11am-11pm daily.
Credit MC, V. Pub
Restored and renamed in 1957, the Mayflower tells its tale
on a manuscript-style menu, starting in 1620 with the
Pilgrim Fathers setting sail from a quayside near the pub,
then called the Shippe. Dark wood panels and oak beams,
gold-painted olde English rhymes ('a warm hearth and fine
wine soothes the soul and passes the time') and nautical
artefacts play the history card hard to riverside walkers
and tourists. An upstairs dining room overlooks the
Thames, which laps against an outside decked area.
Draught options include Abbot, Old Speckled Hen and

Greene King IPA, alongside nitro-keg lagers. For entertainment there's a popular quiz night on Tuesdays and,
on our visit, an incongruous soundtrack of Boney M hits.
Babies and children admitted (restaurant). Quiz
(8.30pm Tue; £1). Restaurant. Tables outdoors
(25, riverside jetty).

Village East NEW
171-173 Bermondsey Street, SE1 3UW (7357 6082/
www.villageeast.co.uk). London Bridge tube/rail.
Open noon-11.30pm Mon-Thur; noon-1.30am Fri,
Sat; 11am-10.30pm Sun. **Food served** noon-3.30pm,
6-10pm Mon-Sat; 11am-8pm Sun. **Credit** AmEx, MC, V.
Bar/Restaurant
Village East is a modern-chic joint with a New York vibe
and Scandinavian design, run by the same people as the
nearby Garrison. The front bar has full-length windows
covered by beige drapes and a long narrow counter
adorned with large white tiles; seating is on a series of long
leather benches, and there are exposed ventilation pipes
overhead. Next come the zinc-topped tables of the dining
area, with an open kitchen on a raised platform. Another
dining area is hidden downstairs, with a gnarled wooden
column in the middle; media and fashion industry types
recline in comfy leather chairs in a lounge bar upstairs. The
main bar dispenses Staropramen and Hoegaarden, but it's
the wine list that impresses, with over 130 choices including a Lebanese Château Musar for £38. Food – from a
superbly designed one-sheet menu – is the likes of braised
rabbit leg in a beer and mustard sauce (£14.60).
Bar available for hire. Function room with
plasma screen. Restaurant.

Wibbley Wobbley
Greenland Dock, Rope Street, SE16 7SZ
(7232 2320). Canada Water or Surrey Quays tube.
Open 11am-11pm Mon-Sat; 11am-10.30pm Sun.
No credit cards. Bar
The late Malcolm Hardee, a major force in British alternative comedy in the 1980s, co-owned this floating gem, so
we're glad to see the comedy nights being restored to their
proper place every other Thursday. The atmosphere within is low-key, with a broad clientele of locals and people
from further afield, drawn by the place's eccentricity. The
decor of red bench seats, portholes and seafaring knick-
knacks is a tad worn, but nobody would want it any other
way. In addition to the comedy, there are quiz nights on
Tuesday and wine and cheese evenings on Friday. There's
also a video jukebox. Old Speckled Hen, Greene King IPA
and Hoegaarden on draught help the bobbing to start.
Babies and children admitted (until 8pm).
Comedy (alternate Thur). Jukebox. Games
(quiz machine). Quiz (8pm Tue). Restaurant.
Tables outdoors (12, pontoon).

Blackheath

Crown
47-49 Tranquil Vale, SE3 0BS (8852 0326).
Blackheath rail. **Open** 11am-11pm Mon-Sat;
noon-10.30pm Sun. **Food served** noon-9pm
daily. **Credit** AmEx, DC, MC, V. Pub
In its various guises, the Crown has been central to
Blackheath since its days as a staging-post inn more than
200 years ago. Appealing to the rugby fraternity and
young professional couples, the pub has left its history

written on a plaque outside and gone for a comfortable modern makeover. A low bar counter in the open-plan main room serves Young's, Deuchars, Bombardier and Spitfire, and 16 wines by the glass and bottle. None costs more than £13 a bottle, apart from the Wolf Blass Yellow Label shiraz (£3.65/£14.10) – so if you're celebrating, splash out on a bottle of bubbly, perhaps Lanson (£27.50) or Veuve Clicquot (£32.45). Food is of the 8oz rump steak variety, with burgers and jackets ensuring a nice post-heath scoff. *Babies and children admitted (until 8pm). Games (fruit machines, video games). Tables outdoors (8, pavement). TV (satellite).*

Hare & Billet

1A Elliot Cottages, Hare & Billet Road, SE3 0QJ (8852 2352). Blackheath rail. **Open** 11am-11pm Mon-Thur; 11am-midnight Fri, Sat; noon-11pm Sun. **Food served** noon-3.30pm, 5.30-9pm daily. **Credit** MC, V. Pub
This landmark pub on the edge of the heath has been satisfying visitors since the 1600s – but probably not with crayfish and crab-claw salad or bottles of Ropiteau Frères Chablis (£17.45). Although they've upped the ante on the food, throwing in a few choice wines for good measure, most customers are just here for an after-stroll pint. Draught options include Flowers, Greene King IPA, Old Speckled Hen, Abbot, Heineken, Hoegaarden, Strongbow and Guinness, with a couple of Leffes and other popular Belgian labels by the bottle. If it's just a standard glass of wine you're after, a L'Emage sauvignon blanc or merlot (£3.10/£12.45) should suffice.
Babies and children admitted (lunch only). Games (darts, quiz machine). TV (big screen). **Map p285 E3.**

Princess of Wales

1A Montpelier Row, SE3 0RL (8297 5911). Blackheath rail. **Open** noon-11pm Mon-Sat; noon-10.30pm Sun. **Food served** noon-9pm Mon-Fri; noon-9pm Sat, Sun. **Credit** MC, V. Pub/Bar
Another Mitchell Brothers' revamp of a pub into a bar bright with exotic beer taps, the PoW hasn't completely forgotten its history. It was here that England players gathered before rugby's first international match in 1871, commemorated with a modest corner of mementoes. That, though, is in one alcove. The rest – main bar, corridor of tables and back area in pub-cum-lounge-bar style – has been given over to a twirties clientele slurping and sipping to a student-rock soundtrack. Kirin, Paulaner, Spitfire, Old Speckled Hen, Bombardier and London Pride are the highlights of the extensive draught options. Wines, 30 by the bottle and nearly all by the glass, include a Stopbanks Marlborough sauvignon blanc (£3.75/£16) and an Argentine Alamos malbec (£3.65/£14.50).
Babies and children admitted (until 5pm). Conservatory available for hire. Disabled: toilet. Games (darts, fruit machine, golf machine). Quiz (8.30pm Tue: £1). Tables outdoors (30, garden).

Railway

16 Blackheath Village, SE3 9LE (8852 2390). Blackheath rail. **Open** noon-11pm Mon-Wed; noon-midnight Thur-Sat; noon-10.30pm Sun. **Food served** noon-10pm daily. **Credit** AmEx, MC, V. Pub/Bar
One of the Mitchell Brothers' first transformations from standard pub to well-stocked and therefore busy bar, the Railway by Blackheath station does a roaring trade. The beers, lined down a long bar counter that links a spacious front area to an intimate back one, are one of the reasons

for this success – Liefmans Framboizen, Franziskaner, Maredsous, Früli, Erdinger, Belle-Vue Kriek, Schneider Weiss, Budvar, Peroni, Leffe, Beck's Vier and Hoegaarden, plus Weston's Vintage and Addlestones ciders and Guinness. Behind, fridge shelves heave with Chimay, Cusqueña and Singha and a dozen other labels. Extensive chalked-up wine lists are augmented by bin-end specials such as a Mexican LA Cetto Petite syrah (£13.50). Civilised chatter midweek gives way to heaving hedonism from Thursday, with a DJ spinning on Friday nights.
Disabled: toilet. Music (DJ 8pm Fri; free). Tables outdoors (5, garden).

★ Zerodegrees

29-31 Montpelier Vale, SE3 0TJ (8852 5619/ www.zerodegrees.co.uk). Blackheath rail. **Open** noon-midnight daily. **Food served** noon-11pm Mon-Sat; noon-10.30pm Sun. **Credit** AmEx, MC, V. Bar
Blackheath's microbrewery, bar and pizzeria has expanded from its base (at zero degrees longitude) between the Village and the heath, and now has outlets in Reading and Bristol. The name also nods at the brewing process taking place in the vast vats by the entrance, producing four categories of beer for a buzzy young clientele. They arrange themselves around an open-plan, two-floor bar. Black and pilsner lagers are made to Czech specifications, pale ale is of American provenance, while the wheat ale has German and Belgian influences. All are tasty and cost £2.50 a pint (£9.25 for a take-home four-pint keg). Prices drop to £1.90 during happy hour (4-7pm weekdays). Many customers also partake of the thin-crust pizzas of intriguing variety, served in an adjoining sunken dining area.
Babies and children admitted. Restaurant (available for hire). TV (big screen, satellite).

Camberwell

Castle

65 Camberwell Church Street, SE5 8TR (7277 2601). Denmark Hill rail. **Open** noon-midnight Mon-Thur, Sun; noon-2am Fri, Sat. **Food served** noon-10pm Mon-Sat; noon-9.30pm Sun. **Credit** MC, V. Gastropub
The infectious enthusiasm of its owners and staff ensure the Castle remains a winner with thirtysomethings out for some fun, despite the gloominess of the stuffed animal heads on the walls (look out for an especially melancholy bull above the open fire). Stark white walls contrast with dark pews, comfy red chesterfields and candle-lit wooden tables. Draught options are Adnams Explorer, Flowers IPA, Grolsch and Kronenbourg Blanc; a 30-strong wine list includes D'Arenberg Hermit Crab viognier (£19.50) and a Kloovenburg Swartland shiraz (£25). Extra fun arrives in the form of wine tastings with jazz on Tuesday and salsa classes on Thursday, but the place really takes off at the weekends when DJs spin disco and party classics.
Babies and children welcome: high chairs. Booking advisable. Entertainment (wine tastings Tue; salsa classes Thur). Music (DJs 10pm Fri, Sat). Separate room for parties, seats 30.

Dark Horse NEW

16 Grove Lane, SE5 8SY (7703 9990). Denmark Hill rail. **Open** 11am-11pm Mon, Tue, Sun; 11am-midnight Wed-Thur; 11am-1am Fri, Sat. **Food served** noon-10pm Mon-Fri; 11am-5pm Sat, Sun. **Credit** AmEx, DC, MC, V. Gastropub

South East

Part of the Black Sheep stable, the Dark Horse welcomes a happy mix of young locals and medical staff from nearby King's College. The handsome frontage is dated 1826, but an interior makeover has left things looking swish in dark-red and cream, with a large wrought-iron chandelier hanging from the high ceiling. Heavy purple velvet drapes partition off a separate dining area, where the Modern European menu seems to be well received. The music is modern indie rock (think Queens of the Stone Age), but not played overbearingly loudly. At the bar there's Black Sheep Bitter, Addlestones cider, Staropramen, Leffe and Hoegaarden on draught; early bird promotions (5-7pm Monday and Tuesday) brings two-pint jugs of cocktails for £8.95 and house wine for £9.
Disabled: toilet. Function room. Outdoor tables (6, pavement).

Funky Munky
25 Camberwell Church Street, SE5 8TR (7277 1806).
Denmark Hill rail. **Open** noon-midnight Mon-Wed, Sun; noon-2am Thur; noon-3.30am Fri, Sat. **Food served** noon-10pm Mon-Fri; noon-6pm Sat, Sun. **Credit** MC, V. Bar
Funky Munky is still the liveliest venue in this part of south-east London. The decor is Mexicana, which means lots of orange. Weekdays have a somewhat chilled vibe, but things heat up at the weekends when the Sambalanco crew play an eclectic mix of Afro-Latino, funk, disco and hip hop. Not all the seating is comfortable – it's best to try to nab one of the chesterfields – but there's a club upstairs (free before 11pm) if sitting down wasn't the intention in the first place. Beer-wise, there's Kronenbourg Blanc and San Miguel, but cocktails are popular too, especially when priced as low as £3.50 during happy hour. A dozen wines, five of them sparkling, round things off nicely.
Art exhibitions. Babies and children welcome. Film screenings. Function room. Games (board games). Music (DJs 9pm Wed-Sun; £3 after 11pm; bands 8pm Sun; free). Tables outdoors (6, pavement).

Hermit's Cave
28 Camberwell Church Street, SE5 8QU (7703 3188).
Denmark Hill rail. **Open** 10am-midnight Mon-Wed; 10am-2am Thur-Sat; noon-midnight Sun.
Food served noon-4pm daily. **No credit cards.** Pub
The sign outside says: 'Best beer round here'. It's a justifiable claim, given that old-school boozers are a dying breed in these parts. Day or night there's a diverse and friendly crowd of local chancers. Wall-mounted oddities include an eerie figurine above the bar that resembles a young Pope John Paul, a moose's head sporting various football hats and, on ground level, a brass tube with a small gorilla's head plonked on top. The rest is a pleasant-enough jumble of etched glass, dark wood, flock wallpaper and open fires. The range at the pumps includes Gravesend Shrimpers Bitter, London Pride, Weston's organic cider, Leffe, Staropramen and Hoegaarden.
Babies and children welcome (lunch only). Tables outdoors (3, pavement). TV (big screen, satellite).

Sun & Doves
61-63 Coldharbour Lane, SE5 9NS (7733 1525/www.sunanddoves.co.uk). Denmark Hill rail.
Open noon-11pm Mon-Thur, Sun; noon-midnight Fri, Sat. **Food served** noon-10.30pm Mon-Sat; noon-5.30pm, 6.30-10pm Sun. **Credit** MC, V. Gastropub
This independently minded corner gastropub delivers three things – food, drink, art – and delivers them well. The

local art college crowd are always colourfully represented through regularly changing art exhibitions; indeed, they're often here in person, sampling the booze on offer with equally local medical students. The fiercely lit bar airy single room hosts a variety of entertainments: film classics on Tuesday, a quiz on Wednesday, bands on Sunday. At the zinc-topped bar, Adnams Bitter, Old Speckled Hen, Kronenbourg Blanc and San Miguel are pulled by chummy staff. Cocktails are also poured (£4.50-£6), backed by a basic wine choice. Out back is a popular beer garden.
Art exhibitions. Babies and children welcome. Film screenings (8pm Tue; free). Music (musicians 8.30pm Sun; free). Quiz (8pm Wed; £1). Restaurant. Tables outdoors (20, garden; 6, pavement).

Catford

Blythe Hill Tavern
319 Stanstead Road, SE23 1JB (8690 5176).
Catford or Catford Bridge rail. **Open** 11am-11pm Mon-Sat; noon-10.30pm Sun. **No credit cards.** Pub
Cheery barmen who serve a cracking pint of Guinness? Yep, this is an authentic Irish pub. The interior is divided into three: the front bar is full of golfing paraphernalia, the back section concentrates on Lester Piggott and the sport of kings, and the side bar celebrates Irish writers. You're never far from a TV, tuned to Gaelic games or horse racing, but there's no shortage of other entertainment – from Irish folk music on Thursday to a Monday-night quiz whose popularity is assured by free entry and a traditional first prize of a crate of beer. As well as Guinness, the bar parades London Pride, Adnams Broadside, Courage Best and guests from the Westerham brewery (Black Eagle SPA on our visit), plus the usual lagers.
Babies and children welcome (until 7pm). Games (fruit machine). Music (Irish traditional 9pm Thur; free). Quiz (9pm Mon; free). Tables outdoors (20, garden). TV (big screen, satellite).

Crystal Palace

Bluebottle
79 Westow Hill, SE19 1TX (8670 0654). Crystal Palace rail. **Open** 5pm-midnight Mon; noon-midnight Tue, Wed; noon-1am Thur, Sun; noon-2am Fri, Sat. **Credit** MC, V. Pub/Bar
A large-fronted building, Bluebottle is set back on the corner of Westow Hill's long stretch of restaurants, theme pubs and run-down boozers. It's one of the better options in the area. From a roadside beer garden you enter the roomy front bar, with its high ceiling and ornate chandeliers. There's a scattering of wooden tables and chairs, some comfortable leather sofas and an enormous open fire. At the back lurks a quieter, dimly lit area that is transformed into a pulling paradise and packed dancefloor at weekends, with DJs spinning old-school classics on Friday or funk and disco on Saturday. To drink, there's draught Hoegaarden, Leffe, Staropramen and Peetermans Artois, as well as Adnams Spindrift, Belle-Vue Kriek and Früli by the bottle.
Babies and children admitted (until 4pm). Function room. Games (table football). Music (DJs 8pm Thur-Sun; free). Tables outdoors (12, garden). TV (big screen).

Deptford

Bar Sonic NEW

1 Deptford Broadway, SE8 4PA (8691 5289). Deptford Bridge DLR. **Open** noon-1am Mon-Sat; noon-midnight Sun. **Food served** 2pm-12.30pm Mon-Sat; 2pm-11.30pm Sun. **No credit cards.** Bar
The striking blue logo of this new venture fronts an ambitious cross of West African diner and DJ bar. As the Centurion, whether West Indian (first) or Irish (later), this venue always relied on music for its custom. What it now also has (along with garage, R&B and soul downstairs on Thursday and Saturday) is a well-priced menu, served throughout the day, of goat-meat kebabs, pepper soup, plantain with white or jollof rice, and other dishes. If formality is preferred, there's a 30-cover restaurant below. At street level, the bar ticks over nicely, punters chatting over the carefully sourced dance rhythms or Premiership commentary, supping Carlsberg Export or Guinness on draught, Gulder, Star or imported Guinness by the bottle. *Bar available for hire. Games (pool, fruit machines). Music (DJ 9pm Thur; bands 9pm Sat; free). Restaurant. Tables outdoors (10, pavement).* **Map p285 C2.**

★ Dog & Bell

116 Prince Street, SE8 3JD (8692 5664/www.thedog andbell.com). New Cross tube/rail/Deptford rail. **Open** noon-11pm Mon-Sat; noon-10.30pm Sun. **Food served** noon-2pm, 6-10pm Mon-Fri; noon-10pm Sat; noon-7pm Sun. **Credit** AmEx, MC, V. Pub
This CAMRA-favoured landmark has come on leaps and bounds since the arrival of chef Adam and his wife

Anmolia in 2005. There's still a reasonably priced and carefully sourced selection of ales, illustrated by the mosaic of beer-mats over the bar; Dark Star Old Ale, Hop Back Elf & Hoppiness and Sharp's Atlantic IPA featured on this visit. There are 30 bottled Belgian beers too. But this place is far more than a real-ale retreat tucked down a dark street beyond the Greenwich end of Deptford High Street. The daily changing menu attracts a lunchtime and less blokey crowd, a favoured starter being the speciality salad of beetroot, horseradish and mackerel smoked on the premises. Wine sales have boomed, but without any loss in character: artists and artisans still gather in the side room, bookended by a pre-war bar billiards table and embellished by regularly changing exhibitions. *Bar available for hire. Disabled: toilet. Quiz (9pm Sun). Tables outdoors (4, garden).* **Map p285 C1.**

Royal Albert NEW

460 New Cross Road, SE14 6TJ (8692 3737). New Cross tube/rail. **Open** 4pm-midnight Mon-Thur; 4pm-1am Fri; noon-1am Sat; noon-midnight Sun. **Food served** 6-10pm Tue-Thur; 5-9pm Fri; noon-7pm Sat; noon-5pm Sun. **Credit** AmEx, MC, V. Pub
Reopened in autumn 2006, this corner pub has quickly asserted itself on to the Deptford scene. The relaxing chesterfields and padded brown banquettes, the tassled lampshades and decorative remnants of yesteryear (bay windows, frosted glass, carved mahogany back bar) lull locals into a genuine sense of security. The Paradise Bar previously on this site was late-night and sometimes lary; the original Albert was a spit-and-more-spit dive. Now one of seven venues in the Antic group, it is run by genial Brazilian Amadeo, whose smiling staff dispense draught

South East

Dark Horse. *See p163.*

Timothy Taylor Landlord, Grolsch and Gulpener Korenwolf wheat beer, plus a selection of ten wines by the glass and bottle, none over £16. A back area of red Formica tables and framed art accommodates lunchtime diners. *Babies and children admitted (until 5pm). Tables outdoors (9, garden).* **Map p285 B2**.

Dulwich

Crown & Greyhound
73 Dulwich Village, SE21 7BJ (8299 4976). North Dulwich rail/P4 bus. **Open** 11am-11pm Mon-Wed, Sun; 11am-midnight Thur-Sat. **Food served** noon-10pm Mon-Sat; noon-9pm Sun. **Credit** AmEx, MC, V. **Gastropub**
In the old days, this large Victorian boozer was two pubs: the Crown for gentry and the Greyhound for the proles. Things are more democratic now: the only pub in the village, it hosts film, wine and chess club meetings, and has a licence to perform civic weddings. The three front rooms have unusual hexagonal ceiling mouldings and beautifully ornate wooden bench seats. At the back, the lovely dining area has an adjoining conservatory that looks out on to a large two-tier beer garden that's crowded come summer. There's an impressive range of draught wheat beers (Schneider Weisse, Franziskaner, Erdinger), fruit varieties (Früli, Belle-Vue Kriek), a couple of guest cask ales and a seasonal ale. Bottled beers include Kirin and Maredsous. *Babies and children admitted. Disabled: toilet. Entertainment (film screenings; wine club; call for times). Function room. Games (chess). Restaurant. Tables outdoors (50, garden).*

East Dulwich

Clock House
196A Peckham Rye, SE22 9QA (8693 2901). East Dulwich or Peckham Rye rail/12, 197 bus. **Open** 11am-midnight daily. **Food served** noon-3pm, 6-9pm Mon-Fri; noon-4pm, 6-8pm Sat, Sun. **Credit** MC, V. **Pub**
The smaller front bar of this pleasant Young's boozer, situated directly opposite Rye Park, was playing host to as many dogs as people on a recent visit. The bar is subdivided into distinct areas, with a raised quiet section holding just a couple of tables. The decor includes a large pike above an open fire and stuffed birds in glass cases, while a horological theme runs to a selection of antique timepieces, including a fine grandfather clock. An additional section to the rear (formerly a no-smoking pit) is more spacious, with emerald green walls and daylight pouring in through a large skylight. To drink, there are the usual Young's ales and nitro-keg lagers, complemented by bottles of Ramrod, Oatmeal Stout, Waggledance and St George's. A roadside terrace looks towards the park. *Babies & children admitted (patio). Disabled: toilet. Tables outdoors (20, patio).*

East Dulwich Tavern
1 Lordship Lane, SE22 8EW (8693 1316). East Dulwich rail. **Open** noon-midnight Mon, Wed, Thur, Sun; 11.30am-midnight Tue; noon-1am Fri, Sat. **Food served** noon-6pm daily. **Credit** MC, V. **Pub/Bar**
The EDT takes extraordinary pains to cater for the needs of local residents. We arrived on a Tuesday afternoon at the end of a chaotic parent and child club; the pub also holds film screenings on Wednesday, DJs on Friday and Saturday, and plans are afoot to relaunch its comedy club. Sunday is titled rather ambiguously 'drag night' (cars or queens?). The two main bars share harlequin floor tiles; our favourite is the one to the left, with its 1970s-style clocks and wallpaper, and table football. The large screening room is great for watching a big match; on non-football days a comfy area within can be closed off with curtains. On tap there's Black Sheep, Young's Bitter and Bombardier, plus Leffe, Hoegaarden and Grolsch. *Babies and children welcome (until 6pm). Disabled: toilet. Entertainment (film screenings, Wed). Games (darts, quiz machine, table football). Music (DJs, Fri, Sat). Restaurant. Tables outdoors (5, pavement). TVs (big screen, satellite). Wi-Fi.*

Franklins
157 Lordship Lane, SE22 8HX (8299 9598/ www.franklinsrestaurant.com). East Dulwich rail. **Open** noon-11pm Mon-Wed; noon-midnight Thur-Sat; noon-10.30pm Sun. **Food served** noon-4pm, 6-10.30pm Mon-Sat; 1-10pm Sun. **Credit** AmEx, MC, V. **Gastropub**
Franklins remains popular with a thirtysomething local crowd. The frontage and busy, compact bar are bare wood; the larger rear area, with open kitchen, has a three-quarter brick wall adorned with an enlarged photograph of diners taken from the 1924 British Empire exhibition at Wembley. An unremarkable choice on draught (Young's Bitter is the best) is saved by decent bottle options, including Leffe, Budvar, Hoegaarden and Estrella Damm. The 30-strong wine list offers Macon Charney Dom Jean Manciat '04 at £29.50 or a 2004 Cuvaison pinot noir from the Napa Valley at £33. *Babies and children welcome: high chairs. Disabled: toilet. Separate room for parties, seats 30. Tables outdoors (3, pavement).*

★ Green & Blue NEW
38 Lordship Lane, SE22 8HJ (8693 9250/www.green andbluewines.com). East Dulwich rail. **Open/food served** 9am-11pm Mon-Sat; 11am-10.30pm Sun. **Credit** MC, V. **Wine bar**
There have been big changes at this outstanding wine bar, one of a wave of new places in the capital to combine a sit-down area and shop. Next door has been knocked through to form a deli counter and shelving for more wines, while an expanded bar is now packed, even on a lazy Sunday afternoon. It deserves the increase in business, a shabby-chic look being the backdrop for 150 carefully chosen wines, each accompanied by intelligent tasting notes and divided according to flavour. Although few wines are priced under £10, this isn't a place setting out to rip you off. £1 will bring you a one-litre bottle of filtered water, and for £3 you can take in your own food (they'll provide the plates and cutlery). These are remarkable concessions to what customers might want, and the most imaginative wine list of any shop or bar in London adds to the appeal. *Bar available for hire. Babies and children admitted (until 7pm). Wine shop.*

Herne Tavern NEW
2 Forest Hill Road, SE22 0RR (8299 9521). East Dulwich or Peckham Rye rail/12, 197 bus. **Open** noon-11pm Mon-Thur; noon-1am Fri, Sat; noon-10.30pm Sun. **Food served** noon-2.30pm, 6.30-9.45pm Mon-Fri; noon-3pm, 6.30-9.30pm Sat, Sun. **Credit** MC, V. **Gastropub**

Now under the same ownership as the nearby Palmerston, this former Courage pub has had the familiar gastropub makeover (and serves standard gastro fare). On our visit, the ex-public bar, now a perfectly pleasant dining room, was completely empty, whereas the saloon bar, which retains a semblance of its previous existence, was filled with locals. A small conservatory at the back looks out over the new owners' greatest improvement: a newly landscaped beer garden and children's play area (look out for *Tellytubbies*-style grass walls). A reasonable wine list offers nearly two dozen choices, among them a spicy Domaine Les Charmetts cabernet sauvignon (£17.50) and a peachy Domaine Piquemal viognier (£16). Real ales are Deuchars IPA and Adnams Bitter, while draught lagers run to Staropramen and San Miguel.
Babies and children admitted. Function room. Tables outdoors (25, garden).

Inside 72
72 Lordship Lane, SE22 8HF (8693 7131). East Dulwich rail. **Open** 5pm-midnight Mon-Fri; noon-midnight Sat, Sun. **Food served** noon-4pm Sat, Sun. **Credit** MC, V. Bar
This great little retro bar is a refreshing change from the norm. It looks like the plasterer went on a tea-break from which he never returned and the owner decided to stick whatever he could find on the walls instead. Witness an impressive collection of toy robots, a Soviet propaganda poster and an old map mounted beside a horned cow skull. Leather sofas and rickety wooden chairs are lined besides full-length windows. Regulars are a lively, local mix who enjoy a soundtrack of 1970s rock 'n' roll played loud enough to be enjoyed, but quiet enough for conversation. The draught selection disappoints, but bottled options include Erdinger, Duvel, Chimay and London Pride.
Games (board games, cards).

Liquorish
123 Lordship Lane, SE22 8HU (8693 7744/www.liquorish.com). East Dulwich rail. **Open** 6pm-midnight Mon-Thur; 6pm-1am Fri; 10.30am-1am Sat; 10.30am-11.30pm Sun. **Food served** 6-10.30pm Mon-Fri; 10.30am-9.30pm Sat, Sun. **Credit** AmEx, MC, V. Cocktail bar
Liquorish crams two distinct functions into a slender space: sleek cocktail bar and simple diner. Things are quiet during the day – couples mooch and kids play their parents at Connect 4 – but resident DJs on Friday and Saturday liven things up for a younger set. Bare bulbs hang at various lengths above the bar, illuminating primary-coloured walls and cube-shaped bar stools. An excellent cocktail list features house creations such as Dulwich Genie (Miller's gin and cassis, shaken with fresh mint and topped with champagne, £6), while wine ranges from reasonable examples by the glass (Castillo de Montblanc tempranillo, £3.60) to fine examples by the bottle (Premier Cru Montmain Chablis, £25). Beer comes only in bottles, Kirin and Amstel being the pick of the bunch.
Games (board games). Music (DJ 9pm Fri, Sat; free). Tables outdoors (8, terrace).

Palmerston
91 Lordship Lane, SE22 8EP (8693 1629/www.the palmerston.co.uk). East Dulwich rail. **Open** noon-11pm Mon-Thur; noon-midnight Fri, Sat; noon-10.30pm Sun. **Food served** noon-2.30pm, 7-10pm Mon-Fri; noon-3pm, 7-10pm Sat; noon-3.30pm, 7-9pm Sun. **Credit** MC, V. Gastropub

Many original features remain from its original incarnation as the *Lord* Palmerston – an illuminated Watneys beer sign and all the attractive wood panelling, for example – but under its current ownership, the Palmerston is more gastro than pub. Indeed, pop in for a quick pint and you might well find the tables are all booked for diners. The upside is an imaginative menu of high-end food, the likes of line-caught wild sea bass with champagne, broad bean and mint butter sauce (£15.75) catching the eye. The excellent 50-strong wine list stretches from a Le Marquis syrah (£12) to a Cobaw Ridge shiraz viognier (£60). Appeasing the pub fan, though, is the beer selection on draught: Timothy Taylor Landlord, Bombardier and Adnams Bitter, plus Kronenbourg Blanc, Leffe and Peetermans Artois. Lovely.
Babies and children welcome: children's portions; high chairs. Booking advisable. Restaurant available for hire. Tables outdoors (6, pavement).

Forest Hill

Dartmouth Arms
7 Dartmouth Road, SE23 2NH (8488 3117/www.the dartmoutharms.com). Forest Hill rail/122, 176, 312 bus. **Open** noon-midnight Mon-Sat; noon-11.30pm Sun. **Food served** noon-3.30pm, **Credit** MC, V. Gastropub
This fine gastropub continues to thrive on a shabby, traffic-choked street of takeaways and run-down boozers. The rectangular front bar, done up in sepia tones with 1960s-style silver dome lights with red bulbs, opens on to a smaller square bar, with red walls covered in work by local artists. The dining area and open kitchen at the back provide good, reasonably priced food, and ale lovers are as well catered for as the gastronomes, with London Pride, Adnams Broadside and Brakspear on offer alongside Hoegaarden and Staropramen. The wine list is extensive, including a smooth Les Fumées Noires pinot noir for £18.70 and a nicely balanced white Rioja at £22.50.
Babies and children welcome: high chairs. Disabled: toilet. Restaurant available for hire. Tables outdoors (10, garden).

Also in the area...
Railway Telegraph 112 Stanstead Road, SE23 1BS (8699 6644). Shepherd Neame pub, starkly lit but boasting a large pool table and a competition thereon every Tuesday.

Gipsy Hill

Mansion
255 Gipsy Road, SE27 9QY (8761 9016). Gipsy Hill rail. **Open** noon-11pm Mon-Thur, Sun; noon-midnight Fri, Sat. **Food served** noon-4pm, 6-8pm Mon; noon-4pm, 6-10pm Tue-Thur; noon-4pm, 6-10.30pm Fri; noon-5pm, 6-10.30pm Sat; noon-9.30pm Sun. **Credit** MC, V. Gastropub
Reincarnated a couple of years back, this impressive black-fronted gastropub reigns supreme in the area. Not many pubs have a grand piano – and this one doesn't look at all out of place among the gilt mirrors and elaborate candelabras. The 1970s-style brown wallpaper stops things getting too gothic. On tap there's Young's Special and a frequently changing guest ale (Archer's Pride on our visit), plus Peetermans Artois, Leffe, Hoegaarden and Weston's

Plume of Feathers NEW
*19 Park Vista, SE10 9LZ (8858 1661). Cutty Sark
DLR/Maze Hill rail.* **Open** 11am-11pm Mon-Thur;
11am-midnight Fri, Sat; 11am-10.30pm Sun. **Food
served** noon-3pm Mon, Sun; noon-3pm, 7-9.30pm
Tue-Sat. **Credit** MC, V. Pub
Along a quiet residential street next to Greenwich Park but
away from the tourist beat, the Plume is a popular, cosy,
traditional pub filled with locals of all generations.
Horsebrasses line the fireplace, naval and regimental
iconography abounds, and Churchill and Montgomery are
honoured on the display of dinner plates. A small bar dispenses Old Speckled Hen, Adnams Bitter and Broadside
and Fuller's London Pride, and standard lagers to chatty
customers – the Plume is a place for a natter. At the back,
a restaurant serves quality pub grub; you can tuck into
your Sunday roast in the bar area as well. A small square
of courtyard beside the attractive tiled exterior serves as
a modest beer garden.
Outdoors table (30, garden). Quiz (9pm Wed; £1).
Map p285 E1.

Powder Monkey NEW
*22 King William Walk, SE10 9HU (8293 5928).
Cutty Sark DLR.* **Open** noon-1am Mon; 3pm-1am Tue-
Thur; 3pm-2am Fri; noon-2am Sat; noon-midnight Sun.
Credit AmEx, DC, MC, V. Bar
On the prime former site of ale pub the Cricketers, a street
corner full of tourists between the sights and Greenwich
Park, Powder Monkey has assumed the mantle of key gay
venue in the area. Three floors are comprised of a main bar,
disco and lounge bar in ascending order. The ground floor
– a simple open space of bar and reddish interior – attracts
a mixed crowd, drawn by the late hours. No gaudiness here
– instead, there's a little disco ball, an inconspicuous spread
of wallpaper showing the Greenwich skyline, a stack of
gay press by the door and bar stools. At the bar are taps
of Beck's Vier, Staropramen, Hoegaarden and Strongbow,
plus Budvar and Breezers in the fridge.
Music (DJs 9pm Thur-Sat; free). **Map p285 E1.**

Richard I
*52-54 Royal Hill, SE10 8RT (8692 2996). Greenwich
rail/DLR.* **Open** 11am-11pm Mon-Sat; noon-10.30pm
Sun. **Food served** noon-3pm, 6-9.30pm Mon-Sat;
noon-9pm Sun. **Credit** MC, V. Pub
Adjoining the Greenwich Union, this cosy, two-bar
Young's pub hasn't felt the need to trendify. In fact, its very
old-school approach has encouraged loyalty in a conservative clientele more interested in a pie and a pint than
Rwandan coffee or Czech bottom-fermented beer. The photographic souvenirs of hop-field outings either side of the
war – images of a long-lost England – set the tone. Still,
along with the staunchly British Young's range and
Bombardier, you can find Bitburger, Corona, Tiger and
Peroni by the bottle, plus platters and baguettes as well as
steak and chips from the newly designed menu. Wines provided by Cockburn & Campbell, now responsible for the
Young's group, come in an attractive range.
*Babies and children admitted (garden). Chess club (6pm
Tue; free). No piped music. Quiz (8pm Sun; £1). Tables
outdoors (15, garden). TV.* **Map p285 E2.**

Trafalgar Tavern
*Park Row, SE10 9NW (8858 2909/www.trafalgar
tavern.co.uk). Cutty Sark DLR/Maze Hill rail.* **Open**
noon-11pm Mon-Thur, Sun; noon-1am Fri, Sat. **Food**
served noon-10pm Mon-Sat; noon-5pm Sun.
Credit MC, V. Pub
Everyone knows the Trafalgar. Now marked by a statue
of Nelson (erected outside in 2005 to mark the bicenten-
nary of the Battle of Trafalgar), this Thames-lapped venue
isn't as historic as the stern portraits inside would have
you believe – it was built in 1837 – but it draws boatloads
of tourists, locals, loners, lovers and ale aficionados. The
main room adjoins a restaurant and two other seating
areas, the outer one newly open-plan. Flowers, Timothy
Taylor Landlord, Boddingtons and Adnams are on tap, as
are Beck's Vier and Hoegaarden. Bottles of Trafalgar bitter are also available, the house theme extending to the
Trafalgar whitebait (£6.95) and sirloin steak (£11).
*Babies and children welcome (until 7pm). Function
rooms. Restaurant. Tables outdoors (20, riverside).
TV (big screen, satellite).* **Map p285 E1.**

Also in the area...
Davy's *161 Greenwich High Road, SE10 8JA (8858
7204). Branch.* **Map p285 D2.**

Herne Hill

Commercial
*210-212 Railton Road, SE24 0JT (7501 9051).
Herne Hill rail.* **Open** noon-midnight daily. **Food
served** noon-3pm, 5-10pm Mon-Fri; noon-10pm Sat;
noon-9pm Sun. **Credit** MC, V. Pub
Formerly a down-at-heel railway boozer, the Commercial
is proof that an extensive chain makeover (by Mitchells &
Butler, in this case) doesn't have to mean the loss of all
character. This is by far the best and most popular pub
hereabouts. Both bars are blessed with snug little micro
living rooms complete with comfy household furniture
around open fires. Thought has gone into the detail: customised lighting, unusual artwork, restored old tiling. Even
better is the selection on tap: Bombardier, Greene King IPA,
Black Sheep and Marston's Pedigree, with Küppers Kölsch
and Leffe nestling beside an excellent wheat beer selection
(Paulaner, Franziskaner, Schneider Weisse and
Hoegaarden). A mixed clientele and friendly staff complete
the appealing picture.
*Babies and children welcome. Disabled: toilet.
Games (board games). Tables outdoors (5, garden).*

Half Moon
*10 Half Moon Lane, SE24 9HU (7274 2733/www.half
moonpub.co.uk). Herne Hill rail.* **Open** noon-midnight
Mon-Thur; noon-1.30am Fri, Sat; noon-10.30pm Sun.
Food served 6-10.30pm Mon-Fri; 12.30pm-1.30am
Sat; 12.30-10.30pm Sun. **Credit** MC, V. Pub
From the outside nothing has changed at the Half Moon,
its wonderful old Victorian frontage continuing to grow
old gracefully. Inside, refurbishment was afoot at the time
of review. The blokes in the carpet-and-no-trimmings front
bar must feel like an endangered species in Herne Hill these
days. Not that unreconstructed means ugly – there's still
a high ceiling, dark wood panels, etched glass and some
beautiful painted glass in the rear snug. Things have
already improved at the bar: the nitro-kegs have been
enhanced by the addition of Adnams Broadside and Bitter,
plus Peetermans Artois.
*Function room. Music (bands 8pm Thur-Sat; £3-£5).
Quiz (8pm Tue; £1). Tables outdoors (12, terrace).
TV (big screen, satellite).*

Number 22

22 Half Moon Lane, SE24 9HU (7095 9922/www.
number-22.com). Herne Hill rail. **Open** noon-11pm
Mon-Sat; noon-10.30pm Sun. **Food served** noon-4pm,
6-11pm Mon-Sat; noon-11pm Sun. **Credit** MC, V. Bar
This chic little tapas bar is building an excellent reputation locally for great food and service. The brown and blue
decor features interesting photographs of south-east
London; it's warmed by an open fire. At the front, the small
lounge area has L-shaped, brown leather bench seating.
There you can try Cruzcampo on draught or Vedett,
Paulaner or Innis & Gunn by the bottle, or select from a
30-strong, mainly European wine list. The terrific sherries
run to a Fernando de Castilla Pedro Ximenez Antique (£36)
and the dozen cocktails include a Gin Apple Crush of lemon
and mint with Bombay Sapphire. Space is at a premium
here, but an area near the tiny back garden has been ear-
marked for an extension.
Babies and children admitted. Tables outdoors (16, patio).

Prince Regent NEW

69 Dulwich Road, SE24 0NJ (7274 1567). Herne Hill rail.
Open noon-11pm Mon-Wed; noon-midnight Thur-Sat;
noon-10.30pm Sun. **Food served** noon-3pm, 7-10pm
Mon-Sat; noon-6pm Sun. **Credit** MC, V. Gastropub
The all-wood interior at the Regent is nicely set off by an
abundance of fresh lilies and oil-burning lamps, while second-hand books lying around for sale (all proceeds to the
Green Party) mark another sensitive touch. To one side is
a partitioned dining area with a stack of board games and
lots of old pictures and paintings; in the main bar are some
semi-sectioned booths. On tap you'll find Spitfire, Black
Sheep and a guest ale (on our visit, Lone Wolf), plus
Hoegaarden, Leffe and the ordinary lagers. The soundtrack
of languid funk is superceded on a Tuesday by a popular
quiz. Dishes from the light menu (fishcakes, salads) are
excellent; a main menu lists the likes of cod and lamb.
Babies and children welcome (until 7pm): high chairs.
Disabled: toilet. Games (board games). Separate room
for parties, seats 50. Tables outdoors (12, pavement).

Pullens

293-5 Railton Road, SE24 0JP (7274 9163). Herne Hill
rail. **Open/food served** 8.30am-11pm Mon-Fri; 9am-
11pm Sat; 10am-10.30pm Sun **Credit** MC, V. Bar/Bistro
You'd think this double-fronted bar and bistro had sprung
up in line with SE24's recent gentrification, but Pullens has
been around since its main competitors were greasy spoons
and dusty boozeholes. The busy and compact drinking
space has a chunky wooden bar, a blue ceiling and red
walls adorned with work by local artists. The dining area
bears the same colour scheme, but is more spacious. You
wouldn't expect there to be anything on draught, but
there's a half-decent range of bottled beer (Whitstable Bay,
Estrella Damm, Hoegaarden) and a 20-strong, predominantly French wine list from which you can sample a spicy
Côte du Roussillon Villages (£19.95) or a fruity
Bellefontaine sauvignon blanc (£12.95).
Babies and children admitted. Restaurant.
Tables outdoors (10, pavement).

Also in the area...

Escape Bar & Art *214-216 Railton Road, SE24 0JT*
(7737 0333/www.escapebarandart.com). Large
open space combining an art gallery with a modern
café. Come the evening, trendy youngsters move in
for banging DJ sets.

Booze talking
Lord Clyde

You are?
Michael Fitzpatrick, landlord of the Lord Clyde,
Clennam Street, SE1.
Your pub's very much a family affair, isn't it?
Absolutely – the Fitzpatricks have run it for 50
years now. My son, Martin, is in the process of
taking over, which will make it a third-generation
pub. My parents brought me here when I was
nine and I used to help stoke up the coal fire.
I didn't want to become the landlord at first –
I couldn't stand the thought. But I came to help
out one day in 1974 when my father was ill
and I've been here ever since.
It's very well preserved...
We've always been very conscious about
keeping the pub as it was when we got here.
When the windows blew out in World War II
we made sure that we replaced them exactly
as they were before, the same etchings and
everything. Our customers are just as
protective of the look as we are; there
would be uproar if we tried to change anything.
Who drinks here?
We get a real mix in the pub: CAMRA men,
office workers, trade from the nearby theatres,
stallholders and shoppers from Borough
Market... People come in at the weekend
laden with bags of food, gasping for a drink.
**How does it feel to be handing the reins
to your son?**
I'm getting used to it, but I'll always be
involved because it's my home. It's my
favourite pub to come for a drink too. Of
course, I can't relax when I do come in,
because I'm always looking around noticing
ashtrays that need emptying.
Is Martin planning any changes?
He feels the same way as me – why mess
with a good thing?

South East

Also in the area...

Walpole Arms *407 New Cross Road, SE14 6LA (8692 2080).* Former grizzly boozer turned student pub with a front terrace that's useful in summer. Map p285 A2.

Peckham

Bar Story

213 Blenheim Grove, SE15 4QL (7635 6643/ www.thesassoongallery.co.uk). Peckham Rye rail. **Open** 3pm-midnight Mon-Fri; noon-11.30pm Sat, Sun. **Food served** 4-9.30pm daily. **Credit** AmEx, DC, MC, V. Bar

Bar Story feels like one of those legalised squat bars you come across in mainland Europe. In front is an outdoor bar that uses railway sleepers for seats. Enter the white-walled main room by a glass sliding door and sink into the convivial, communal atmosphere. There's an open kitchen beside a bar that rests on fridges of bottled Duvel, Erdinger, Zywiec, Leffe, Pilsner Urquell and London Pride. The 16 wines offer four organic options, and a blackboard list of 32 cocktails includes a decent £6 mojito. Lap-tops on wooden tables at the rear provide internet access and a soundtrack of indie rock, funk and hip hop, while a separate building houses the Sassoon Gallery, a showcase for local artists that also screens short films.

Babies and children admitted. Function room. Music (DJs 7pm Thur-Sun; free). Tables outdoors (8, patio).

Gowlett

62 Gowlett Road, SE15 4HY (7635 7048/www.the gowlett.com). East Dulwich or Peckham Rye rail/12, 37, 40, 63, 176, 185, 484 bus. **Open** noon-midnight Mon-Thur; noon-1am Fri, Sat; noon-11.30pm Sun. **Food served** 6.30-10.30pm Mon; 12.30-2.30pm, 6.30-10.30pm Tue-Fri; 12.30-10.30pm Sat; 12.30-9pm Sun. **Credit** AmEx, MC, V. Pub

This prize-winning local (it won awards from CAMRA and, er, LBC radio in 2005) on a residential side street is maintaining standards. The real ale is top-notch, with Adnams and three guests always available; a long list displays what's coming next. Most of the wine is Fairtrade and organic, with ten options by glass or bottle. The pub itself is relaxed but fairly plain: wooden floor and tables, some opaque glass tiling, green leather banquettes beneath three-quarter wood panelling that shows off beer mats of former guest ales. Activities include a Monday quiz, knockout pool on Tuesday and laid-back guest DJs on Sunday.

Babies and children welcome (until 9pm). Disabled: toilet. Games (pool, tournament Tue). Quiz (8.30pm Mon). Music (DJs 6pm Sun). Tables outdoors (3, heated terrace; 4, pavement).

Page 2

57 Nunhead Lane, SE15 3TR (7732 5366). Peckham rail. **Open** 3pm-midnight Mon-Thur; 3pm-2am Fri; noon-2pm Sat; noon-midnight Sun. **Food served** 5-10pm Mon-Fri; noon-10pm Sat, Sun. **Credit** MC, V. Pub

This cosy local pub doesn't seem to have taken off yet, perhaps because it lies in the shadow of the neighbouring Rye Hotel. Yet it deserves to be better frequented. There are snug corners, open fires and comfy furniture, and a relaxed and relaxing welcome is extended by the staff. The chefs run an unusual rotation system that means the appealing menu changes daily and dramatically: in the past, we've had Jamaican jerk tuna one day, an authentic Ulster fry-up another. Up at the bar things aren't so rosy: the draught options are just Staropramen, Leffe and Hoegaarden, although Erdinger is available by the bottle, and the only wine is the house. A Thursday quiz, bands on Friday and DJs on Saturday keep things busy, while an arcade classics game offers further distraction.

Babies and children admitted (until 8pm). Function room. Games (board games, retro arcade machine). Music (blues/jazz band 9pm Fri; DJ 9pm Sat; free). Quiz (9.30pm Thur; £1). Tables outdoors (4, pavement). TV (big screen, satellite).

★ Rye Hotel

31 Peckham Rye, SE15 3NX (7639 5397). Peckham Rye rail. **Open** noon-11pm Mon-Thur, Sun; noon-midnight Fri, Sat. **Food served** noon-4pm, 6-10pm Mon-Fri; noon-5pm Sat; noon-9pm Sun. **Credit** MC, V. Gastropub

Easily the most popular gastropub in these parts, the Rye Hotel is the kind of place where you can chat with friends or read alone without fear of disturbance. It sparkles of an evening, with fairy lights, an open fire and dim candlelight caught in the gilded mirrors; fresh flowers and local art brighten the daytime. At the bar are pints of Wadsworth 6X, Exmoor Hound Dog, Hoegaarden, Staropramen and Leffe, while the wine list is reasonably priced, with most available by the glass – try a white Viura David Moreno NV Rioja (£16.50) or a Pieters Drift pinotage (£15). Outside are a covered and fenced area and another spot decked out like a Bedouin tent, heated in winter.

Babies and children admitted (until 6pm). Games (board games). Separate room for parties, seats 40. Tables outdoors (40, garden).

Sydenham

★ Dulwich Wood House

39 Sydenham Hill, SE26 6RS (8693 5666). Sydenham Hill rail/63, 202 bus. **Open** 11am-11pm Mon-Wed; 11am-midnight Thur-Sat; noon-10.30pm Sun. **Food served** noon-10pm Mon-Sat; noon-9pm Sun. **Credit** AmEx, DC, MC, V. Pub

This large and peculiar-looking building was constructed in the mid 19th century as a private residence by Joseph Paxton, architect of the Crystal Palace. It's a bit of gem, with a clutch of wood-panelled rooms adorned with cracked old portraits and Victorian cricket scenes. Paxton, primarily a gardener, might well have enjoyed the large beer garden that runs around the pub; it has a heated and covered area of decking that also serves as a stage for jazz sessions starting each spring. The usual Young's ales (Bitter and Special) are enhanced by some from co-brewer Charles Wells (Bombardier) and reinforced by nearly a dozen ales and stouts by the bottle, among them tasty delicacies like Wells Banana Bread Beer and Young's Double Chocolate Stout. Missed dessert? Come here for a beer...

Games (darts, fruit machines, quiz machine). Music (jazz every spring). Restaurant. Tables outdoors (50, garden). TV.

Also in the area...

Oceans Apart *152 Portland Road, SE25 4PT (8663 8881).* Music-driven bar at the forefront of South Norwood's limited nightlife scene.

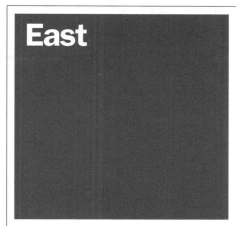

East

Yes, the fins, mullets and bangs that once defined the area have long been cut, with many of the über-cool moving on entirely, but Shoreditch is arguably still the focal point of nightlife in the east. We find **Bar Kick** near perfect, with its authentic table football tables and unceasingly upbeat vibe; funky dim-sum-and-cocktail bar **Drunken Monkey** is also a delight. Round the corner, newcomer club-cum-bar-cum-restaurant **Favela Chic** is turning heads with its shanty town aesthetic and wild theme nights; boldly decorated pub **Commercial Tavern** is equally kitsch, while the subdued drinker might prefer a trip to the **Wenlock Arms**, specialist in real ales.

The theme in Bethnal Green seems to be the gentrification of old man-boozers – no bad thing when it turns up beauties like the **Camel**. Locals can also gloat over first-class **Green & Red**, excelling in its bid to treat tequila as a proper, sippable drink. South to Brick Lane, the laid-back ambience (and year-round barbecues) continue to draw in punters at the **Big Chill Bar**; the **Pride of Spitalfields** is a more homely place for a pint and a pie. Further east, drinking options in Clapton aren't quite so appealing, though **Eclipse** offers promise for the future.

South again to Limehouse and Wapping are a smattering of riverside pubs, many that have existed in some form or another for centuries: the **Grapes** in Limehouse (built 1720) and the **Prospect of Whitby** in Wapping (built 1520) are prime examples;

new this year is Gordon Ramsay's entry into the gastropub market, **Narrow Street Pub & Dining Room**. Though considered the netherland between the fashionable East End and the wilder expanses of east London, Mile End and Bow contain some decent joints: gastro-leaning **Morgan Arms** for a relaxed pint, the fabulously raucous **Palm Tree** for anything but. The Docklands nightscene is dominated by chain wine bars; the lack of imagination is depressing. Still, highlights are local's fave the **Ferry House** and classy gastropub the **Gun**.

Bethnal Green

Approach Tavern
47 Approach Road, E2 9LY (8980 2321). Bethnal Green tube/rail. **Open** noon-11pm Mon-Thur, Sun; noon-2am Fri, Sat. **Food served** noon-2.30pm, 6-9.30pm Mon-Fri; noon-9.30pm Sat; noon-5pm Sun. **Credit** MC, V. Pub
This classic East End boozer has been something of a barometer for Bethnal Green's rapidly changing social demographic over the past decade: additions such as an upstairs gallery championing YBAs, ironic advertising signs on the walls and good-quality grub reveal a lot about its target clientele these days. Yet despite the patronage of a younger crowd, longstanding features (mahogany pillar-backed bar, heavy black velvet drapes, glass case displaying stuffed pheasant) ensure the place remains comfortably time-worn. Old soakers that have clung on to the place don't seem to mind the changes much – they're pleased enough with a healthy range of Fuller's ales on tap. The large patio space is pleasant in summer, heated toastie-warm in winter.
Art gallery (noon-6pm Wed-Sun). Babies and children admitted. Jukebox. Quiz (8.30pm Tue; £1). Tables outdoors (6, garden; 9, heated terrace). TV. **Map p278 U3.**

Bistrotheque Napoleon Bar
23-27 Wadeson Street, E2 9DR (8983 7900/
www.bistrotheque.com). Bethnal Green tube/rail/
Cambridge Heath rail/55 bus. **Open** 5.30pm-midnight
Mon-Sat; 1pm-midnight Sun. **Credit** AmEx, MC, V.
Cocktail bar
The path that leads to Bistrotheque – an unlit and rather
forbidding side street off Cambridge Heath Road – makes
it clear that this is a bar out of the ordinary, even before
you enter the (unsigned) building. The dimly lit ground-
floor bar (so-named because of its association with
Courvoisier cognac, allegedly the Petit Corporal's
favourite), with its grey-blue walls and retro carpet, has an
industrial feel that echoes the building's previous incarnation as a clothing factory. Classic cocktails are served at
the antique mahogany bar, expertly mixed by white-shirt-
ed staff and served to groups of arty thirtysomethings who
appreciate the 1970s and 80s music. Many are on their way
in or out of the excellent French bistro upstairs. If you time
your visit correctly you can catch a performance in the
adjoining cabaret room.
Babies and children admitted. Booking advisable.
Disabled: toilet. Music (cabaret dates vary; pianist
noon-4pm Sun). Separate room for parties, seats 50.

★ Camel
277 Globe Road, E2 0JD (8983 9888). Bethnal Green
tube/rail. **Open** noon-11pm Mon-Sat; noon-10.30pm
Sun. **Food served** 1-9.30pm daily. **Credit** MC, V.
Gastropub
The flock wallpaper, black and white photos, espresso
machine and gourmet pies might enrage those soapbox
drinkers, forever complaining about the gentrification of
London's old boozers. But wait – only the most cynically
minded could fail to appreciate Matt Kenneston and Joe
Hill's thoughtful, stylish refit of the Camel, purchased
derelict two years ago after the building was saved from
demolition by a local campaign. Drinks at the carved wood-
en bar are sourced from all over: you'll find Adnams
Broadside and Southwold real ales alongside Bitburger,
Amstel and Guinness, plus an excellent range of spirits
and wines (several available by the glass). Outdoor tables
give punters a chance to admire the brown-tiled exterior.
Gentrification done well.
Babies and children admitted. Tables outside
(4, pavement). **Map p278 U3.**

Florist
255 Globe Road, E2 0JD (8981 1100). Bethnal Green
tube/rail. **Open** 2.30-11pm Mon-Sat; noon-10.30pm Sun.
Credit MC, V. Pub/Bar
Lying somewhere between a down-at-heel boozer (blokes
with dogs, ancient patterned wallpaper) and a trendified
bar (battered leather sofas, candlelit fireplace, DJs stepping
up the pace from raggae to funk), the Florist is most popular with ironic student types who pack the dimly lit one-
room space at weekends. These hedonistic Friday and
Saturday nights involve blaring music, spilled drinks and
much jollity – dancing on tables is by no means unheard
of. Beers, served from a central wooden bar, are Heineken,
Bitburger and Cruzcampo; surprisingly elegant cocktails
(given the clientele) contain high-end spirits such as
Ketel One. Come summer, you can sit on a bench-shelf
along the outside wall. An acquired taste, maybe, but certainly worth a gander.
Games (board games). Music (DJs Mon, Fri, Sat; open
decks 6pm Sun; free). Tables outdoors (2, pavement).
Map p278 U3.

★ Green & Red
51 Bethnal Green Road, E1 6LA (7749 9670/
www.greenred.co.uk). Liverpool Street tube/rail.
Open 5.30pm-midnight Mon-Thur; 5.30pm-1am
Fri, Sat; 5.30-10.30pm Sun. **Food served** 6-11pm
Mon-Sat; 6-10.30pm Sun. **Credit** AmEx, MC, V. Bar
Well conceived and well run, Green & Red has an almost
evangelical commitment to fine tequila: only 100% agave
tequila is stocked, and the huge selection includes a large
range of exceptional 'private reserve' tequilas for sipping
neat. Latin bottled beers and cocktails round out the menu
(we enjoyed a delicious watermelon margarita, £6.70, made
with Jose Cuervo tequila, fresh watermelon and lime). DJs
play upbeat music in the basement area at weekends, but
with a kitchen that produces great Mexican grazing food
(soft own-made tacos, chilli-roasted pumpkin seeds, fresh
salsas and proper guacamole), G&R works equally well
whether you're boozing, dancing, eating or just killing time
with the papers.
Babies and children welcome: high chair.
Disabled: toilet. Music (DJs 9pm-1am Fri, Sat).
Tables outdoors (6, terrace). **Map p278 S4.**

Redchurch
107 Redchurch Street, E2 7DL (7729 8333). Liverpool
Street tube/rail. **Open** 5pm-1am Mon-Thur; 5pm-3am
Fri; 11am-3am Sat; 11am-1am Sun. **Food served**
noon-5pm Sat, Sun. **Credit** AmEx, MC, V. Bar
A busy wee bar open till the busy wee hours. There's a
global choice of drinks: by the bottle there's Brooklyn
Lager, Boston Lager, Lindeboom, Samuel Adams, Anchor
Steam, Coopers IPA, Orval and Goose Island IPA; on tap
there's Sierra Nevada pale ale and Maisel's Weisse.
Whiskies and tequilas are something of a speciality, with
a sizeable selection of both. Unusual cocktails include New
Orleans Milk Punch (buffalo trace bourbon, milk, cream,
vanilla and nutmeg). The uncontrived decor encompasses
retro neon-tube lighting and chrome swivel bar stools, and
weeknights have an easy aural ambience of slouchy reggae. Weekends welcome funky grooves with DJs spinning
funk, Latin, northern soul, hip hop, jazz and rock tracks. A
fine late-night option.
Babies and children admitted. Disabled: toilet.
Music (DJs 9pm Thur-Sat; music 8-11pm Sun; free).
Film screenings (noon, 3pm Sat; free). **Map p278 S4.**

Royal Oak
73 Columbia Road, E2 7RG (7729 2220/www.royal
oaklondon.com). Bethnal Green tube/Old Street tube/
rail/26, 48, 55 bus. **Open** 6-11pm Mon; noon-11pm
Tue-Thur; noon-midnight Fri, Sat; noon-10.30pm Sun.
Food served 6-10pm Mon; noon-4pm Tue-Sat; noon-
4pm, 6-9pm Sun. **Credit** AmEx, MC, V. Gastropub
This is a classic Bethnal boozer that's retained its original
(inter-war) features, updated for contemporary tastes.
Original wood panelling throughout and a lovely low, central bar are the first of its attractive features you'll notice;
settle in and you'll appreciate the yellow glazed ceiling and
original art-deco wall lamps too. The beer choice is fine –
Adnams Bitter, Timothy Taylor Landlord, Hoegaarden,
Leffe, Guinness – while the extensive wine list contains
plenty of options by the glass. It's busy on Sundays, of
course, when shoppers at the flower market reward themselves for getting up early with a mighty roast (£13).
Babies and children welcome: high chairs.
Booking advisable. Restaurant available for hire.
Tables outdoors (4, yard). **Map p278 S3.**

East

Camel

Also in the area...

Albion 94 Goldsmith's Row, E2 8QY (0871 984 3403). Football pub popular with West Bromwich Albion fans. Three real ales, a Thursday evening quiz and a dartboard provide distractions for those who hate the Beautiful Game. **Map p278 T3.**

Fleapit 49 Columbia Road, E2 7RG (7033 9986/ www.thefleapit.com). Laid-back, arty café-bar and event space offering Freedom organic beer, veggie food and free internet. **Map p278 S3.**

Pleasure Unit 359 Bethnal Green Road, E2 6LG (7729 0167/www.pleasureunitbar.com). Former pub turned music venue that plays host to music events, plus a club night or two (see website for listings). Maximum capacity is 150, so expect to queue on big nights. **Map p278 T4.**

Sebright Arms 34 Coate Street, E2 9AG (7729 0937). Unreconstructed boozer known for its (free) music nights on Friday and Saturday. A three-course Sunday lunch also draws. **Map p278 T3.**

Brick Lane

★ Big Chill Bar

Old Truman Brewery, off Brick Lane, E1 6QL (7392 9180/www.bigchill.net). Aldgate East tube/Liverpool Street tube/rail. **Open** noon-midnight Mon-Thur; noon-1am Fri, Sat; 11am-11.30pm Sun. **Food served** noon-11pm Mon-Sat; noon-10.30pm Sun. **Credit** MC, V. DJ bar
The Big Chill franchise can do no wrong: its annual summer festival continues to increase in scale, while the Big Chill House in King's Cross opened to great acclaim in 2006.

This outlet – its original foray into the bar scene – is now firmly etched into the Brick Lane drinking landscape, drawing easy-going punters from London and beyond. Nightly changing DJs spin an enticing medley of laid-back tunes, and there's plenty of room to kick back on the brown leather sofas while sipping a freshly mixed mojito or raspberry caipirinha (£6.75). The trippy decor – beige curtains, bird-shaped mirrors – isn't easy on the eye, and the low concrete ceilings can feel claustrophobic (especially late on Saturday, when it gets very busy), but sweet sanctuary comes in the form of picnic tables on the outside terrace. There's a decent enough lager selection (Budvar, Amstel), plus Kingstone Dry Cider on tap, but ale drinkers get just bottled Old Speckled Hen. The glass-tossing bar staff can be a bit lackadaisical.
Babies and children admitted (until 6pm). Disabled: toilet. Music (DJs 7pm Tue-Sat; noon-11.30pm Sun). Tables outdoors (4, patio). **Map p278 S5.**

Exit

174 Brick Lane, E1 6RU (7377 2088). Liverpool Street tube/rail. **Open** 4pm-2am Tue-Thur; 2pm-2am Fri; 11am-2am Sat; 10am-2am Sun. **Food served** 4.30-10pm Tue-Thur; 2.30-10pm Fri; 11.30am-10pm Sat; 11am-10pm Sun. **Credit** (over £10) MC, V. DJ bar
In a word: loungey. Retro 1970s lamps and stools, incense smells and contemporary kitsch wallpaper adorn the small space; Air's Moon Safari album was even pumping out of the stereo on our afternoon visit. But don't let that put you off. The leisurely, almost Mediterranean vibe is the perfect antidote to the cluttered vintage shops and grime of the street outside. Exit's spacious leather sofas and amiable bar staff further accommodate you – but expect a change

East

10.30am-midnight Sat; 10.30am-11pm Sun. **Food served** 10.30am-2pm Sat; 10.30am-12.30pm Sun. **Credit** MC, V. Pub

The maligned residents of Clapton deserve the Eclipse, a top pub that lies between fierce council estates and gentrified housing. The flower baskets and Charringtons sign outside suggest trad boozer, but the place has broader appeal. The interior is a beauty, from the 1930s bar that weaves gracefully through both rooms, to a reclaimed fireplace with turquoise tiles to match the ceiling details. Drinks do more than cover the basics – cask ales (London Pride, Harveys Sussex Best, Adnams Broadside, Timothy Taylor Landlord), Staropramen and Pilsner Urquell sit alongside the usual lagers, plus there are eight well-chosen wines of each colour and even a few aged whiskies. Food is more limited, but includes an excellent full English. The piano is caressed by Dom Pipkin each Thursday.
Games (board games, cards, dominoes). Music (pianist Thurs; free). Tables outdoors (10, pavement).

Princess of Wales
146 Lea Bridge Road, E5 9RB (8533 3463). Clapton rail/48, 55, 56 bus. **Open** 9am-midnight Mon-Sat; noon-10.30pm Sun. **Food served** 9am-3pm, 6-9pm Mon-Sat; 9am-6pm Sun. **Credit** AmEx, MC, V. Pub

This big Young's pub is a bit characterless, but has a wonderful lockside location and plenty of outdoor tables. Even if the weather's bad, there are good views of the River Lea from a sort of interior conservatory in one corner of the main bar. The draught options are decent, if unremarkable (Young's Special, Waggledance, Bombardier), or you could sate yourself with house doubles at £3 each. Otherwise, there are fruit machines, a dartboard and several TVs for sport, plus live music on a Saturday. A blackboard advertises industrial tucker: beef, pork, lamb and nut roasts, greek salad, lasagne, salad and chips – all £5.95.
Games (darts, fruit machines). Music (bands/musicians 9pm Sat). Quiz (8.30pm Wed; free). Tables outdoors (15, patio). TV (big screen).

Docklands

Ferry House
26 Ferry Street, E14 3DT (7537 9587). Island Gardens DLR. **Open** 2pm-midnight Mon-Fri; 11am-midnight Sat; noon-11pm Sun. **Credit** MC, V. Pub

A mile to the north stands priapic, nouveau Docklands. To the south, just across the water, lies tourist-packed Greenwich. The Ferry House, though, is a defiantly old-school corner of the Isle of Dogs, where the dartboard is London Fives, the Sunday lunch bar food includes not £14 pies but Mini Cheddars, and 'fuck' is pronounced with an 'a'. The oldest pub on the island' lives up to its billing: the paintwork is peeling, the air is smoky and the ale is good old Courage Best. The locals have long since ceased to notice the vintage photographs that decorate the walls and the tabletops, but it's less nostalgia and more a simple desire for preservation that led them to be placed there in the first place. An evocative place.
Games (London Fives dartboard). Music (karaoke 9pm Fri; free). Tables outdoors (3, pavement).

★ Gun
27 Coldharbour, E14 9NS (7515 5222/www.thegun docklands.com). Canary Wharf tube/DLR/South Quay DLR. **Open** 11am-midnight Mon-Fri; 11.30am-midnight

Sat; 11.30am-11pm Sun. **Food served** noon-3pm, 6-10.30pm Mon-Fri; 11.30am-4pm, 6-10.30pm Sat; 10.30am-4pm, 6-9.30pm Sun. **Credit** AmEx, MC, V. Gastropub

An immaculately maintained gastropub with enough space to retain an equilibrium between bar and kitchen. Drinkers should head to the right of the central bar, to either the chesterfield-lined, fire-warmed snug or the large, heated riverside terrace overlooking the Millennium Do… sorry, the O2. You can eat outside, but diners wanting to enjoy the full menu (excellent, but pricey) should look for the white tablecloths to the left. Bar snacks (pints of prawns with mayonnaise, roast beef sandwiches) are also available. The broad drinks selection include Adnams Broadside, Young's Ordinary, Greene King IPA and Hoegaarden on tap, plus an extensive wine list, an array of premium spirits, rums, ports and sherries and a smattering of classic cocktails. Nelson once drunk here; these days, it's mostly new-school Docklanders with expensive haircuts and perfect table manners.
Babies and children welcome: high chairs. Disabled: toilet. Separate rooms for parties, seating 14 and 24. Tables outdoors (11, terrace).

Via Fossa
West India Quay, E14 4QT (7515 8549). West India Quay DLR. **Open** 11am-11pm Mon-Wed; 11am-midnight Thur, Fri; 11am-1am Sat; noon-10.30pm Sun. **Food served** 11am-10.30pm Mon-Wed; 11am-11.30pm Thur-Sat; noon-10pm Sun. **Credit** AmEx, DC, MC, V. Bar

It may be housed in a 200-year-old dockside warehouse, but Via doesn't seem interested in playing up to its history. The capacious, cave-like interior is potentially cosy, the outdoor patio is understandably popular when the sun's out, and the beer selection includes such novelties as Budvar Dark and Kirin on tap. Still, there's something naggingly corporate about the whole place, from the jaunty menus and the five-quid cocktails to the understaffed bar. And then there's the soundtrack – on our visit, made up of a disagreeable selection of I ❤ 1987 drivetime classics by the likes of Michael Jackson and Bruce Hornsby & the Range. That's just the way it is.
Disabled: toilet. Function rooms. Music (DJ 7pm Sat; free). Restaurant. Tables outdoors (45, quayside).

Waterman's Arms
1 Glenaffric Avenue, E14 3BW (7093 2883). Island Gardens DLR. **Open** 11am-11pm Mon-Sat; 11am-10.30pm Sun. **Food served** noon-3pm, 6-10.30pm Mon-Sat; noon-4pm, 6-10pm Sun. **No credit cards.** Pub

Longtime Londoners may remember when this sizeable corner pub was run by Daniel Farson, a renowned broadcaster, fine author, entertaining bon viveur and catastrophically hopeless businessman, who lost his shirt after trying to revive music hall here in the early 1960s. Lucky punters back then could have rubbed shoulders with Judy Garland or Shirley Bassey, both of whom sung here; entertainment these days is limited to big-screen football, a pool table and a London Fives dartboard. To drink, there's Young's Ordinary, Adnams and London Pride, plus Guinness and the usual lagers.The menu includes Indian nosh of the chicken tikka masala variety; the sizeable beer garden is a boon in summer.
Babies and children admitted (restaurant). Games (bowling machine, London Fives dartboard, fruit machine, pool, quiz machine). Restaurant (available for hire). Tables outdoors (15, garden). TV (big screen).

East

Also in the area...

Brodies *43 Fisherman's Walk, E14 5HD*
(7719 0202). Branch of Jamies.
Cat & Canary *1-24 Fisherman's Walk, E14 4DH*
(7512 9187). By-the-book Fuller's pub with the
usual staples on tap (London Pride, Discovery,
ESB) plus a few more exotic bottles, such as
Maredsous and Duvel from Belgium.
Corney & Barrow *9 Cabot Square, E14 4EB*
(7512 0397). Branch.
Davy's *31-35 Fisherman's Walk, E14 4DH*
(7363 6633). Branch.
Fine Line *29-30 Fisherman's Walk, E14 4DM*
(7513 0255). Branch.
Jamies *28 Westferry Circus, E14 8RR*
(7536 2861). Branch.

Limehouse

Booty's Riverside Bar

*92A Narrow Street, E14 8BP (7987 8343). Limehouse
or Westferry DLR*. **Open** noon-11pm Mon-Thur;
noon-midnight Fri, Sat; noon-10.30pm Sun. **Food
served** noon-9.30pm Mon-Fri, Sun; noon-7.30pm Sat.
Credit AmEx, DC, MC, V. Pub/Wine bar
On a bright summer's day or a quiet evening, Booty's
ersatz charms are strangely beguiling. It's a mixture of pub
and suburban wine bar, with London Pride and Greene
King IPA on tap, plus a dozen wines of each colour, as well
as fizz and a couple of rosés. The food is regionally inde-
cisive (jacket potatoes, burritos, Sunday roast, decent looking ploughman's) and often reheated in the microwave,
although the fresh fish from Billingsgate advertised for
Fridays is a real temptation. With gingham tablecloths, a
telly at the front beside the games machines, a camp
conglomeration of flamingos and racoons outside the
broad window overlooking the Thames, and Saturday
jazz sessions, it seems to please all-comers: witness signed
photos from the likes of Ian McKellen, Bob Hoskins and,
er, Lawrence Dallaglio.
*Babies and children admitted. Games (fruit machine,
quiz machine). Music (jazz 9pm Sat; free). Tables
outdoors (2, pavement). TVs (satellite).*

Grapes

*76 Narrow Street, E14 8BP (7987 4396). Westferry
DLR*. **Open** noon-3pm, 5.30-11pm Mon-Thur; noon-
11pm Fri, Sat; noon-10.30pm Sun. **Food served**
noon-2pm, 7-9pm Mon-Fri; noon-2.30pm, 7-9pm Sat;
noon-3.30pm Sun. **Credit** AmEx, MC, V. Pub
The Grapes isn't large, but it is lovely. The roadside front
is all greenery and etched glass, the interior has the
requisite dark wood, beams and open fire, and there's a
sweet, rickety balcony overhanging the Thames. The current premises date to 1720 and there's a pretty solid
Dickens connection (the pub was the model for the Six Jolly
Fellowship Porters of *Our Mutual Friend*). But the Grapes
isn't about plastic heritage: lively (if not always youthful)
locals enjoy pints of Marston's Pedigree, Timothy Taylor
Landlord and Adnams on draught, or snifters of wine,
alongside grandad-style Sunday roasts and trimmings.
Follow the narrow stairs up to an equally cosy dining room.
The Grapes may have to contend with heavyweight new-
comers like the Narrow, but it seems ready for battle.
*Booking advisable (restaurant). No piped music
or jukebox.*

★ Narrow Street Pub & Dining Room

*44 Narrow Street, E14 8DQ (7265 8931). Limehouse
DLR*. **Open** noon-11pm Mon-Sat; noon-10.30pm Sun.
Food served noon-10pm daily. **Credit** AmEx, MC, V.
Gastropub
No longer just the Narrow Street, this first Gordon Ramsay
gastropub (to be followed by the Warrington in Maida
Vale) is a real good 'un. Excellently located on the Thames
near Limehouse Basin, the large terrace has lost its bench
seating for more intimate table sets. On the pumps are perfectly kept London Pride and Deuchars IPA (although –
naughty – the vaunted seasonal guest was also Pride), as
well as Meantime's wheat beer and lagers (from Peroni to
Foster's). There are also three dozen fine bottled beers –
excellent British, reasonable Belgians – plus 40 wines, premium spirits and intriguing cocktails for £7. Try a Cider
& Black (vodka, apple, lime juice, blackberries and chambord, topped with cider). Bar snacks include cockles and a
soup, served in a striped mug, but the real food is served
in the adjoining former boathouse: affordable dishes such
as devilled kidneys on toast (£4.50), or pig's cheek and
bashed neeps (£9). Gordo's done well.
*Babies and children admitted. Disabled: toilet.
Restaurant. Tables outdoors (36, riverside terrace).*

Mile End

L'Oasis

*237 Mile End Road, E1 4AA (7702 7051/www.loasis
stepney.co.uk). Stepney Green tube*. **Open** noon-11pm
Mon-Sat; noon-10.30pm Sun. **Food served** noon-
9.30pm Mon-Thur; noon-10pm Fri, Sat; noon-9pm Sun.
Credit MC, V. Gastropub
L'Oasis is a well-established favourite, thronged by the
classier kind of student and a mishmash of locals. The
ground floor is a narrow room with stripped floors and
solid teak tables, enhanced by a listed green-panelled ceiling. Adnams Bitter and Timothy Taylor Landlord cater to
the beer drinker (we applaud the promise of a new range
of real ales), but Addlestones cider, a well-priced wine list
and an army of spirits (including a mighty array of
whiskies) lined up under the purpose-made mirror would
keep anyone happy. Those ascending to the dining room
are serenaded by a Betty Boop figure at the forefront of a
jazz band; not to everyone's taste, but there'll be no complaints about the food – baked ham with colcannon and
swede mash, or sardines with excellently judged parsley
and caper salad. Mains ring in at just over a tenner.
Disabled: toilet. Function room. **Map p278 U5.**

Morgan Arms

*43 Morgan Street, E3 5AA (8980 6389/www.
geronimo-inns.co.uk). Mile End tube*. **Open** noon-
11pm Mon-Thur, Sun; noon-midnight Fri, Sat.
Lunch served noon-3pm daily. **Dinner served**
7-10pm Mon-Sat. **Credit** AmEx, MC. V. Gastropub
If you don't know Bow, this relaxed but affluent gastropub from the Geronimo stable will come as a surprise –
until, that is, you take note of the broad splendour of nearby Tredegar Square. You can sup a good pint of draught
Adnams or Timothy Taylor Landlord, perhaps sample
something Chilean from the blackboard, or settle down to
top-notch nosh in the dining area with its conservatory
extension. The bar area is crammed with furniture, but
there's a good buzz and the place is never unbearably busy.
A refurb, approaching completion when we last visited,

doesn't seem to have changed the Morgan much: modern art still adorned the walls, pretty interior-decorator touches still softened the familiar gastro aesthetic. So much the better, says us.
Bookings not accepted. Disabled: toilet. Restaurant available for hire. Tables outdoors (4, pavement; 3, garden).

★ Palm Tree
127 Grove Road, E3 5BH (8980 2918). Mile End tube/8, 25 bus. **Open** *noon-midnight Mon-Thur; noon-2am Fri, Sat; noon-1am Sun (last admission 10.45pm).* **No credit cards.** Pub
Isolated beside the canal in Mile End Park, this is a classic East End boozer. There is gorgeous old bronze-patterned wallpaper and, above the bar, publicity pics of forgotten crooners, while drums and a covered piano wait in the corner for the evening's trad jazz session. A second room, complete with a rare London Fives dartboard, can be entered only via the external doors. The landlady looks a little severe in her specs, but is thoroughly charming, pulling great pints of Timothy Taylor Landlord and changing guest ales (Hop Back Spring Zing on our last visit) or patrolling the usual spirits. Handwritten signs barring large bags after 8pm indicate the place's popularity with suit-and-sovereign East End oldies and younger incomers.
Games (London Fives dartboard). Music (jazz 9.45pm Fri-Sun; free). Tables outdoors (4, summer park).

Also in the area...
Bow Bells *116 Bow Road, E3 3AA (8981 7317).* Pool table, dartboard and CD jukebox are well used at this cheerfully unreconstructed boozer. Brakspear Bitter and London Pride on tap, and there's an Elvis impersonator on the last Saturday of every month.

Plaistow

Black Lion
59-61 High Street, E13 0AD (8472 2351). Plaistow tube. **Open** 11am-11pm Mon-Sat; 11am-10.30pm Sun. **Food served** noon-2.30pm, 5-7.30pm Mon-Fri. **Credit** MC, V. Pub
The exterior of this former coaching inn has had a crisp tart-up, but inside nothing has changed: low beams, yellow plaster and the action centring around the wiggly counter of the narrow saloon bar. Most of the punters are men armed with Guinness, but Courage Best is joined at the pumps by fine guest beers (Archers Arctic Blonde and Saucy Mare, Mighty Oak Simply the Best) and there are three types of Bushmills whiskey on optic. The wine – a red, a white, a rosé – is still democratically priced (around £3 a glass) and the plight of the drinking man is further eased by one TV tuned to football, the other to cricket. The 'quiet bar' is resplendent in classic purple-red velour; there's also an underused beer garden beneath a tower block to the rear.
Babies and children admitted (until 7pm). Function room. Games (fruit machine, quiz machine). Tables outdoors (10, garden). TVs (satellite).

Shoreditch

Anda de Bridge
42-44 Kingsland Road, E2 8DA (7739 3863/ www.andadebridge.com). Old Street tube/rail. **Open** 10am-midnight Mon-Sat; 10-11.30pm Sun. **Credit** AmEx, DC, MC, V. Bar
A haven of Jamaican cool under the railway bridge on Kingsland Road, Anda da Bridge is a bar that should work better than it does. There's Amstel, Grolsch, Red Stripe and

Commercial Tavern. *See p187.*

Guinness on tap, bottled Carib lager and a menu of hearty Caribbean meals and snacks (jerk chicken, goat curry, ackee and saltfish). You'll also find great reggae tracks on the sound system, decent DJs at weekends and enough fairy lights to deck out a small forest of Christmas trees. However, the blandly decorated back room, dodgy photo montages next to the DJ booth and decidedly chilly concrete floors are a let-down during daylight hours. It's definitely best approached as darkness falls, when the unpretentious vibe works well for drunken revelry and you won't notice the cracks in the decor.
Babies and children admitted. Disabled: toilet. Music (DJs, times vary). Separate room for parties, holds 200. **Map p276 R3**.

★ Bar Kick

127 Shoreditch High Street, E1 6JE (7739 8700/ www.cafekick.co.uk). Old Street tube/rail. **Open** noon-11pm Mon-Wed, Sun; noon-midnight Thur-Sat. **Food served** noon-3.30pm, 5-10pm Mon-Wed; noon-3.30pm, 5-11pm Thur, Fri; noon-midnight Sat; noon-10pm Sun. **Credit** AmEx, MC, V. Bar
Football is the focus at Bar Kick, sister to the smaller Café Kick on Exmouth Market. Spacious and purposefully laidback, Kick attracts local hipsters with its loungey seating and haphazard decor, and besuited office types with the boss-thrashing potential of a table footy tournament. The football crowd are kept happy with big screens aplenty; for key games the downstairs bar becomes a makeshift footy theatre, with neat rows of mismatched plastic chairs and a respectful hush for tense free kicks. Happy hour (4-7pm) is worth the early start, with a selected bottled beer (Chimay Rouge, Duvel, Super Bock, Leffe and the like) coming in at just £1.80. Whether you're watching the game or just watching the world go by through the massive windows, this is a bright and breezy bar in which to sink a few.
Disabled: toilet. Function room. Games (table football;

tournaments 7pm last Thur of mth; from £3). Tables outdoors (4, terrace). TVs (big screen, satellite). **Map p276 R4**.

Bar Music Hall

134 Curtain Road, EC2A 3AR (7729 7216). Old Street tube/rail. **Open** 10am-midnight Mon-Thur, Sun; 10am-2am Fri, Sat; 11am-midnight Sun. **Food served** 9am-5pm, 6-10pm Mon-Fri; 10am-5pm, 6-10pm Sat; 11am-5pm, 6-10pm Sun. **Credit** (over £10) MC, V. DJ bar
The huge central bar takes centre stage here, serving a decent selection of draught lagers (there's also usually a guest ale), bottles and cocktails, as well as freshly squeezed fruit juices for the health conscious. There's plenty of seating, though this is largely ignored at weekends when a top-notch roster of DJs – and pleasing lack of door tax – sees the place rammed with dancefloor-hogging club kids. During the week, things are much more sedate: gossipy office groups sprawl across the black leather banquettes, while laptop-wielding creatives nap in the quiet corners. The large windows offer a Curtain Road streetscape that makes for hours of people-watching potential – handy on jazzy Monday nights when there's sometimes no one to look at on the inside but the barman.
Babies and children welcome. Disabled: toilet. Music (jazz 8pm Mon; bands/DJs 8pm Tue-Sun). Tables outdoors (12, pavement). **Map p276 R4**.

Barley Mow

127 Curtain Road, EC2A 3BX (7729 3910). Old Street tube/rail. **Open** noon-11pm Mon-Sat; 4-10pm Sun. **Credit** MC, V. Pub
A fine place to escape the Shoreditch bar scene and relax with a proper pint of ale (Fuller's ESB and London Pride, among others). Soak up the airy, done-up boozer vibe on the ground floor – stripped wooden floor, small tables and

East

CAMRA's top ten beers

We asked the beer experts for their pick of the pints to look out for in London's pubs.

Adnams Broadside
Grainy and dark brown, with a rich, fruity hop flavour and aftertaste (4.7 per cent abv).

Batemans XXXB
A brilliant blend of malt, hops and fruit on the nose with a bitter bite over the top of a faintly banana maltiness. A russet-brown classic (4.8 per cent abv).

Everards Sunchaser
Brewed with ingredients usually used in lager, this golden ale has soft and subtle malt and hop flavours, with a hint of lemon and a pleasing long, sweet finish (4 per cent abv).

Fuller's Discovery
A golden beer with an aroma of citrus and perfume. The taste is citrus fruit complemented by malt and a dry bitterness (3.9 per cent abv).

Fuller's London Pride
A fruity, sweet malt nose with a hoppy edge that is also present on the palate and aftertaste (4.1 per cent abv).

Hook Norton Hooky Dark
A chestnut-brown, easy-drinking mild. Complex malt and hop aromas give way to a well-balanced taste and a long, hoppy finish that is unusual for a mild (3.2 per cent abv).

McMullen Country Best Bitter
A full-bodied beer with a well-balanced mix of malt, hops and fruit (4.3 per cent abv).

Meantime Grand Cru Raspberry
A vibrant red colour, with a fine white head. Brewed with malted barley and malted wheat, and fermented with a rare, warmth-loving yeast. The secondary fermentation of the sugars in the raspberries gives the beer a refreshing tang (6.5 per cent abv).

Young's Bitter
A light brown bitter, well balanced by fruity citrus hop notes, finishing with a refreshing dryness (3.7 per cent abv).

Zerodegrees Black Lager
A light, east European-style black lager brewed with roasted malt that has a refreshing coffee finish (4.8 per cent abv).

For more information, visit www.camra.org.uk.

church-like pew seating – or venture up a flight of stairs to a small, snug-like room. On our visit, this was eerily silent and unadorned but for a lone mirror ball and a book-shelf stuffed with abandoned reading material; it looked like the room that time and (given the tables strewn with empty glasses) the bar staff forgot. Ideal for staging a dramatic break-up away from the main action, but an unsettling place to sup an ale. Still, this is a great pub.
Babies and children admitted (until 6pm). Function room. Quiz (9pm Mon; £1). **Map p276 R4.**

Bavarian Beerhouse
190 City Road, EC1V 2QH (7608 0925/www.bavarianbeerhouse.co.uk). Old Street tube/rail. **Open** noon-11pm Mon-Thur; noon-1am Fri; 1pm-1am Sat. **Food served** 11am-10pm Mon-Sat. **Credit** AmEx, MC, V. Bar
This low-rent homage to Bavaria looks like it was cobbled together yesterday with the contents of someone's student flat (unpolished pale wood panels, a cheap Ikea lamp, rickety bench seating). Though expense was definitely spared on the decor, there's enough within this basement to keep the City boys coming back for more. Dirndl-wearing damsels escort you to your table, smile obligingly and happily talk you through the menu's beer options. And beer is, of course, the whole point: Paulaner, Erdinger, Löwenbräu, Warsteiner and Küppers Kölsch are among the offerings. Food is less spectacular (goulash and endless variations of sausage), but this isn't somewhere you come to wine and dine. It's a place to gather a crowd of your most annoying work colleagues together for loud banter, big-screen sports and the comedy value of ordering a 'Porno half meter' of schnapps shots.
Babies and children welcome. Function rooms. Music (DJs 7.30pm Fri, Sat; free). Restaurant. TV (big screen, satellite). **Map p276 P3.**

Cantaloupe
35-42 Charlotte Road, EC2A 3PD (7613 4411/ www.cantaloupe.co.uk). Old Street tube/rail. **Open** 11am-midnight Mon-Fri; noon-midnight Sat; noon-11.30pm Sun. **Food served** 11am-midnight Mon-Sat; noon-11.30pm Sun. **Credit** AmEx, DC, MC, V. Bar
Way back when EC2 was da hood, Cantaloupe was one of just three local watering holes. Everyone else soon caught on, but the legacy remains. One of a handful of Shoreditch bars that are as full in the week as they are at the weekend, Cantaloupe is invariably packed with arty old-timers, big office groups and gregarious gangs of students. They come for the good food (quesadillas, burgers, massive sharing platters of charcuterie, dips and cheeses), upbeat music (DJs play a funky Latin-inspired mix at weekends) and unpretentious vibe. There's plenty of space between the loungey sofas and sturdy wooden benches for dancing, and the cocktails (£6) are potently good. Best of all, there's no charge to get in. A must-visit Hoxton original.
Bar available for hire. Disabled: toilet. Music (DJs 8pm Fri-Sun; free). Restaurant available for hire. **Map p276 R4.**

Casita NEW
5A Ravey Street, EC2A 4QW (7729 7230). Old Street tube/rail. **Open** noon-11pm Mon-Sat; noon-10.30pm Sun. **Credit** MC, V. Cocktail bar
This tiny street-level bar brings a South American holiday vibe to a shabby Shoreditch side street. Ditch all but your inner circle (seriously, there's barely room to swing a small gerbil) and assemble yourselves on the high bar stools for an evening of expertly mixed cocktails (great caipirinhas,

margaritas and daiquiris come in at around £6), South American bottled beers (Cuban Cristal, Columbian Aguila, Argentinian Quilmes – there's also Sagres on tap) and high spirits. By the end of the night you'll be on first-name terms with the staff, the regulars and anyone else who happens to drop by. And not just because it's small, but because it's that kind of place: friendly, thoughtful and that little bit different. Shoreditch needs more bars like Casita.
Bar available for hire. **Map p276 Q4.**

Catch
22 Kingsland Road, E2 8DA (7729 6097/www.thecatch bar.com). Old Street tube/rail. **Open** 6pm-midnight Tue, Wed; 6pm-2am Thur-Sat; 6pm-1am Sun. **No credit cards.** DJ bar
Towards the end of the week, Catch comes into its own, with a roster of quality nights (anything from indie to electro to 1960s garage) that attract an up-for-it, rock 'n' roll crowd. Earlier in the week, though, things are quieter, with a pool table taking up dancefloor space, gigs upstairs and a smattering of frock-rocker girls eyeing up boys in eyeliner. Still, regardless of the time of day or night, there's something about Catch's unadorned decor, orangey glow and fuss-free drinks list that makes it feel eternally 2am. The booths tucked away on the raised area to the left of the bar are perfect for conducting a clandestine affair, gossiping or warming up with a beer (Grolsch, Carling and Bitburger on tap) before the end-of-week mayhem begins.
Function room (club upstairs). Games (pool table). Music (bands/DJs Tue-Sun; free-£5). **Map p276 R3.**

Charlie Wright's International Bar
45 Pitfield Street, N1 6DA (7490 8345). Old Street tube/rail. **Open** noon-1am Mon-Wed; noon-4am Thur, Fri; 5pm-4am Sat; 5pm-2am Sun. **Admission** £4 after 10pm Fri, Sat; £3 Sun. **Credit** MC, V. DJ bar
Charlie Wright's was dishing out late-night pints round these parts when most of the area's current bar owners were still doing their A-levels. It remains much as it always was: laid-back, friendly and slightly shambolic (on our most recent visit, half the impressively wide range of draught beers were off). Still, it's ideal for a taste of the Hoxton of old, and the kind of worn-in local vibe that newer bars can't hope to compete with. There's a pool table, great Thai food and a multicoloured disco ball above the dancefloor. And if that doesn't swing your night out in the direction of Pitfield Street, the late, late licence (never earlier than 1am, 4am at weekends) and opportunity to make the acquaintance of the amiable ex-weightlifter owner should.
Babies and children admitted (until 7pm). Games (darts, fruit machine, pool tables). Music (DJs 8pm Thur-Sun). Restaurant. TV (big screen, satellite). **Map p276 Q3.**

★ Commercial Tavern
142 Commercial Street, E1 6NU (7247 1888). Aldgate East tube/Liverpool Street tube/rail. **Open** 5-11pm Mon-Sat; noon-10.30pm Sun. **Food served** 5-10pm daily. **Credit** MC, V. Pub/Bar
Like the long-lost love child of Tiffany's and GAY, the Commercial Tavern leaves no corner unadorned (walls are painted delicate duck-egg blue or plastered in old covers of *Interview* magazine, sparkly umbrellas adorn the outside tables) and no punter unwelcomed. And, fittingly, its motley crew of skinny rockers and Edie Sedgwick wannabes are more than willing to shove up, share tables and give you a shout when the pool table is free. Drinks run the usual boozer gamut, with some excellent ales

(Black Sheep, London Pride) thrown in for good measure. The upstairs space is beautiful, with candlelight, plenty of seating and huge double-aspect windows overlooking Commercial Street. It's grown out of its fresh-faced refurb into a Spitalfields stalwart well suited to the area's fussily cool crowd.
Disabled: toilet. Function room. Games (pool). Tables outdoors (3, pavement). **Map p276 R5.**

Dragon
5 Leonard Street, EC2A 4AQ (7490 7110). Old Street tube/rail. **Open** noon-11pm Mon; noon-midnight Tue, Wed; noon-1am Thur; noon-2am Fri, Sat; noon-11pm Sun. **Credit** (over £10) MC, V. DJ bar
Far enough from the beaten track to have retained the buzz of its early-noughties glory days, the Dragon is a great place to sample a taste of old-school Shoreditch. It whispers rather than screams cool, with subtle gold letters on a doorstep the only indication of the entrance, lots of exposed brickwork and an arty-shabby decor. The upstairs bar, decked out in fairy lights and Eine graffiti art, dispenses standard lagers while DJs play a mix that includes everything from dancehall to electro-clash. The place is a roadblock at weekends, and busy enough during the week to make a Tuesday night pint feel hardcore. Service can be painfully slow, however, and the graffitied toilets are endlessly confusing (note: it's girls to the right).
Babies and children admitted (until 6pm). Music (DJs 8pm nightly; open mic 7pm 3rd Sun of mth; free). Tables outdoors (1, pavement). **Map p276 Q4.**

dreambagsjaguarshoes
34-36 Kingsland Road, E2 8DA (7729 5830/ www.dreambagsjaguarshoes.com). Old Street tube/rail. **Open** 5pm-midnight Mon; 5pm-1am Tue-Sat; 5pm-12.30am Sun. **Credit** MC, V. DJ bar
Dreambagsjaguarshoes has become the ultimate Shoreditch poster-bar. Thoughtfully shambolic, with massive floor-to-ceiling windows, a grungey cellar and an experimental music policy, it's a fast-track education in Shoreditch cool. And remember, one man's terrifyingly trendy freak show is another's Bohemian love-in of like-minded souls. Find out which side of the fence you sit on over a well-pulled pint (Hoegaarden, Leffe, Staropramen and Guinness are all on tap) and a plate of fantastic bangers and mash (from Bang, a few doors down). You'll be draped over a battered sofa discussing the graffiti walls with an exchange student called Nico before the night is out. And, you know what? You'll probably like it.
Bar available for hire. Music (DJs 8pm Wed-Sat; 4pm Sun; free). **Map p276 R3.**

★ Drunken Monkey
222 Shoreditch High Street, E1 6PJ (7392 9606/ www.thedrunkenmonkey.co.uk). Liverpool Street tube/rail. **Open** noon-midnight Mon-Fri; 6pm-midnight Sat; noon-11pm Sun. **Food served** noon-11pm Mon-Fri; 6-11pm Sat; noon-10.30pm Sun. **Credit** AmEx, DC, MC, V. Cocktail bar
One of the pioneers of the drinking-and-dim-sum trend, Drunken Monkey is a sophisticated yet unpretentious space. Moody lighting, potent cocktails (Monkey mojito, £6.50) and an excellent sound system give it a clubby feel that's spot-on for weekend debauchery, but it works just as well during the week. This is one of very few Shoreditch bars that can claim a proper buzz on a Monday night; a reservation is advised if you want to sample the dim sum

East

(£3-£4.50). Lager drinkers have bottled (Brooklyn Beer, Corona, Tiger) and draught (Kronenbourg, San Miguel) options, but there's no real ale on tap. Happy hour operates early evening during the week and all day Sunday. The Chinese-style design – heavy wooden tables, red lanterns strung above the bar, huge mirrors edged with gilt latticework – is appealing and atmospheric, and ideal for dates (there's a tiny, secluded side room that fits just two tables). Service is excellent.
Babies and children admitted. Function room. Music (DJs 8pm Tue-Sun; free). Restaurant. **Map p276 R4.**

★ Favela Chic NEW
91-93 Great Eastern Street, EC2A 3HZ (7613 4228/ www.favelachic.com/london). Old Street tube/rail. **Open** 6pm-1am Tue-Thur, Sun; 6pm-2am Fri, Sat. **Food served** 7-10.30pm Tue-Sun. **Credit** AmEx, MC, V. DJ bar/Restaurant
Sister to the über-cool Parisian bar of the same name, Favela Chic brings a touch of louche glamour to London's East End. There's a definite carnival feel to the place, with bric-a-brac-strewn around the tatty, lived-in interior (intended to bring to mind a real Brazilian favela) and funky Brazilian beats on the sound system. The big bar serves decent (though small, considering the £7 price tag) mojitos and caipirinhas alongside fairly standard draught lagers. The theme extends to the food (Brazilian classics such as black bean and pork feijoada), but it's the music that really pulls in the crowds. An eclectic policy sees DJs spin everything from electronica to hip hop, leaving plenty of room for fun nights like Swap-A-Rama Razzmatazz, a monthly booze-fest where everyone swaps clothes when a klaxon sounds.
Music (DJs 8pm Fri, Sat). Restaurant. **Map p276 Q4.**

Foundry
84-86 Great Eastern Street, EC2A 3JL (7739 6900/ www.foundry.tv). Old Street tube/rail. **Open** 4.30-11pm Tue-Fri; 2.30-11pm Sat; 2.30-10.30pm Sun. **No credit cards.** Bar
A giant art installation with a bar tagged on, the Foundry is freakily surreal. Amputee dolls hang from the ceiling and brassiered cotton-wool torsos compete for space with old shoes and piles of defunct PCs. At the bar, Pete Doherty lookalikes order pints of Boddingtons with an enthusiasm that defies their moody muso credentials, while grungey girls in eyeliner drain bottles of Sol at a fast pace. The Foundry doesn't look like much from the outside (it's usually partially obscured by the giant advertising banner above), but on the inside it's a living, breathing museum of the Hoxton of old. Head on down for a night of laid-back boozing, arty shenanigans and performance poetry. The basement gallery is worth checking out too.
Art exhibitions (free). Games (chess). Music (pianist 6pm Tue; free). Poetry readings (9pm Sun; free). Tables outdoors (5, pavement). **Map p276 Q4.**

George & Dragon
2 Hackney Road, E2 7NS (7012 1100). Old Street tube/rail. **Open** 5-11pm daily. **No credit cards.** Bar
It's cash only at this edgy, rather shambolic boozer, so stuff your pockets with fivers before you head out. Every corner of the G&D is put to use, with tightly packed tables, maximal decor and a DJ booth, though there's enough space (surprisingly) for impromptu gigs and happenings. Walls are strung with fairy lights, and surfaces are scattered with glittery ornaments, broken dolls and oddball lamps; the mechanical horse's head above the entrance to

the loos is slightly disturbing after a few drinks. Heavy curtains block out the outside world, allowing the crowd within to kick back to retro sounds, spontaneous poetry or anything else this creative hub might throw up. Don't get excited about the bar menu – it's standard draught lagers and bottles all the way – but prepare for the kind of night you'll definitely regret in the morning.
Disabled: toilet. Music (DJs 8pm nightly; free). **Map p276 R3.**

Great Eastern
54-56 Great Eastern Street, EC2A 3QR (7613 4545/ www.greateasterndining.co.uk). Old Street tube/rail. **Open/food served** Ground-floor bar noon-midnight Mon-Fri; 6pm-midnight Sat. *Below 54 bar* 7.30pm-1am Fri, Sat. **Credit** AmEx, DC, MC, V. Bar
The Great Eastern offers a classy take on Shoreditch boozing, with an elegant ground floor decked out in sleek dark wood and muted creams and greys. Turn left as you enter and head straight for the bar where attentive staff craft quality cocktails (£6) from one of two lists: 'contemporary' or 'classic'. Order carefully, though – this is the kind of grown-up space better suited to a quiet linger over a good bottle of red than a raucous tequila-downing session. There are pan-Asian bar snacks (edamame, dim sum, sushi, sashimi) to line the stomach, and similar but more substantial options in the adjoining restaurant. Below 54 caters to a younger, clubbier set on Friday and Saturday nights with its late-opening cellar bar.
Babies and children admitted (restaurant only). Bar available for hire. Music (DJs 9pm Fri, Sat; free). Restaurant. **Map p276 R4.**

Hoxton Grille NEW
81 Great Eastern Street, EC2A 3HU (7739 9111/ www.grillerestaurants.com). Old Street tube/rail. **Open** noon-midnight daily. **Credit** AmEx, MC, V. Bar
Inoffensive, spacious and formulaically stylish, this new addition to the Hoxton drinking scene is a goodie. Join the lively crowd of suits and out-of-towners for well-crafted cocktails (£5.50-£7) and bog-standard draught lagers, and feel the life-force slowly drain from your soul. Service is seamless and there's a very pleasant atrium for outdoor drinking, smoking or both. The adjoining brasserie offers bistro classics at a price (caesar salad, eggs benedict, steak sandwich). Watch the glass doors on your way out – they don't mix well with tequila.
Disabled: toilet. Function rooms. Music (DJ 7pm Sat, Sun). Restaurant. Tables outdoors (courtyard). **Map p276 Q4.**

Hoxton Square Bar & Kitchen
2-4 Hoxton Square, N1 6NU (7613 0709). Old Street tube/rail. **Open** 11am-1am Mon-Thur, Sun; 11am-2am Fri, Sat. **Food served** noon-11pm daily. **Credit** MC, V. Bar
A Hoxton 'heritage' bar that's lived to tell the tale, Hoxton Square Bar & Kitchen attracts local workers with its flame grills and great cocktails, the weekend rent-a-crowd with its on-the-square location, and hip young things with its late nights and innovative music policy. The space itself is sleekly industrial, with huge windows either end of the main bar and ample outside space. There's a separate restaurant area and a dark, windowless back room that becomes one giant dancefloor at weekends. This is a bar that pulls a crowd throughout the week, but talk of the town is Sunday night's BoomBox. Be prepared to dress up (admission is free, but the door policy verges on fussy) and

feel like death come Monday morning. And get down there fast before the fickle nu-rave kids leave it for dust. *Babies and children admitted (until 6pm). Disabled: toilet. Film screenings (phone for details). Music (bands/DJs 9pm Thur-Sun; free-£5). Restaurant. Tables outdoors (4, patio).* **Map p276 R3.**

Legion
348 Old Street, EC1V 9NQ (7729 4441/4442). Old Street tube/rail. **Open** 5pm-midnight Mon-Thur; 5pm-2am Fri, Sat. **Credit** AmEx, DC, MC, V. DJ bar
Drinking and dancing are the priorities at this long, thin Old Street bar. There are plenty of large, picnic-style tables and benches, but come Saturday most of the them lie abandoned and strewn with coats and bags, while the dancefloor (and every other corner besides) is packed, courtesy of the DJs' funky, sometimes rocky, playlists. During the first half of the week, Legion is either empty or packed with hipster muso types attending one of the many niche DJ nights and gigs (the recent karaoke sessions have been going down a storm). At the bar you'll find a decent array of draught beer (Belle-Vue, Leffe and Hoegaarden, as well as standard lagers) and a fairly substantial wine list. Genuinely friendly doormen – incredible! – complete the laid-back picture.
Disabled: toilet. Games (board games). Music (karaoke 9pm Tue; DJs 8pm Fri, Sat; free). **Map p276 R4.**

Light Bar & Restaurant
233 Shoreditch High Street, E1 6PJ (7247 8989/ www.thelighte1.com). Liverpool Street tube/rail. **Open** noon-midnight Mon-Wed; noon-2am Thur, Fri; 6.30pm-2am Sat; noon-10.30pm Sun. **Food** served noon-10.30pm Mon-Fri, Sun; 6.30-11pm Sat. **Admission** (upstairs bar) £2 Thur-Sat. **Credit** AmEx, DC, MC, V. DJ bar
If good bars were all about good buildings, this stunning venue on the edge of the City would have Shoreditch sewn up. Instead, the former railway power station spends much of the week with the voices of sparsely dotted suited types echoing off its exposed brick walls. The Light is a bar that can take a crowd – and doesn't really work without one. Things do, however, heat up come the end of the week when the party hordes descend. The upstairs bar is a fine place for a birthday celebration (call ahead and ask to put yourself and some friends on the guestlist) with its outdoor terrace and upbeat vibe. Cocktails come in at a decent £5.50, there's a well-priced wine list and standard lagers on draught (but no ales), plus a few interesting bottled options (Sleeman's Honey beer, Paulaner, Duvel, Fruli). *Babies and children admitted (restaurant). Disabled: toilet. Dress: no suits in upstairs bar. Function room (Mon-Thur, Sun only). Music (DJs Thur-Sat; free). Restaurant. Tables outdoors (9, courtyard).* **Map p276 R5.**

Loungelover
1 Whitby Street, E2 7DP (7012 1234/www.lounge lover.co.uk). Liverpool Street tube/rail. **Open** 6pm-midnight Mon-Thur, Sun; 6pm-1am Fri; 7pm-1am Sat. **Food served** 6-11.30pm Mon-Fri, Sun; 7-11.30pm Sat. **Credit** AmEx, DC, MC, V. Cocktail bar
Loungeloving is a popular pastime in these parts: Shoreditch loves this bar's OTT approach to glamorous, cocktail-swilling bonhomie. The luxe junkshop decor does much to impress: giant champagne glasses filled with flowers, palm-tree chandeliers, huge stage lights and glittery stag's horns cover every inch of available space. And the cocktails (£7.50-£11) are utterly fabulous. But there's something about the neat, ordered service that makes it hard to relax. For a venue that looks like it was made for chandelier-swinging excess, there isn't much scope for spontaneity (you need to book tables in advance, for a start). Still, it's well worth joining the upmarket in-crowd for a blowout drink and a gawp.
Booking advisable. Disabled: toilet. Music (DJs 7pm Fri, Sat). **Map p276 R4.**

Mother Bar
333 Old Street, EC1V 9LE (7739 5949/www.333 mother.com). Old Street tube/rail. **Open** 8pm-3am Mon-Wed; 8pm-4am Thur, Sun; 8pm-5am Fri, Sat. **Credit** MC, V. DJ bar
Even if you're not half-cut as you ascend Mother's narrow staircase, there's something about the retro-seedy decor and pumping bass that makes you feel like you are. This is the kind of late-night institution that great night-out stories are made of, the type of place where you find yourself dancing to Donna Summer next to Alexander McQueen or swapping trilbies with a Russian exchange student in the toilets. Cocktails are only £4 before 11pm, but if you arrive before then you've missed the point entirely. This is an after-party venue par excellence. Whether it's 2am on a Tuesday or 5am on Saturday morning (you can keep drinking, but have to buy your drinks before 2am), Mother is rammed and loving it. Weekend queues are an endurance. *Music (DJs 10pm daily; free).* **Map p276 R4.**

Pool
104-108 Curtain Road, EC2A 3AH (7739 9608/ www.thepool.uk.com). Old Street tube/rail. **Open** noon-1am Mon-Thur; noon-2am Fri; 5.30pm-2am Sat; noon-midnight Sun. **Food served** noon-3pm, 5.30-10.30pm Mon-Fri; 5.30-10.30pm Sat; 1-10.30pm Sun. **Credit** MC, V. Pool bar
The original Shoreditch pool bar has not only stood the test of time, but survived the menace of a better-equipped Elbow Room just across the street. Despite having just three tables, Pool draws a loyal crowd who'd rather wait their turn than join the hordes opposite. A late licence throughout the week attracts up-for-it, boisterous custom, while Sunday offers free pool all day to help stave off the resulting hangover. The vast downstairs area is dimly lit and clubby, with faux-leather seating and beanbags, and a DJ policy that tends towards hip hop at weekends. Great happy-hour deals (two-for-one cocktails, shooters and bottled beers) pull in the after-work gang, and the decent Thai food offers ample fuel to keep them there. *Babies and children admitted (until 5pm). Games (pool tables). Music (DJs 8pm Tue-Sun; free).* **Map p276 R4.**

★ Prague
6 Kingsland Road, E2 8DA (7739 9110/www.bar prague.com). Old Street tube/rail. **Open/food served** 9am-midnight daily. **Credit** MC, V. Bar
Prague makes no grand gestures and no bold claims, yet somehow this small, slightly ramshackle bar at the bottom of Kingsland Road manages to pull off a rare feat for this part of town. It feels neither jaded nor try-hard, and there's not a gimmick in sight. In fact, you could transplant its exposed brick walls, subtle folky background music and smoky candlelit vibe on to any street in Europe and it would attract the same laid-back jumble of art students, local workers and melancholy barflies. There's a lengthy menu of cocktails (£4.95-£5.50), Czech lagers, decent cheap wine and quirky bar snacks such as plaited sheep's cheese

or roll-mops (80p-£2.50). A great space for relaxed drinking, hot dates or pretending to write poetry on your laptop while browsing with free Wi-Fi.
Babies and children admitted (until 6pm). Bar available for hire. Disabled: toilet. **Map p276 R4.**

★ Princess
76-78 Paul Street, EC2A 4NE (7729 9270). Old Street tube/rail. **Open** noon-11pm Mon-Fri; 5.30-11pm Sat; 12.30-5.30pm Sun. **Food served** 12.30-3pm, 6.30-10.30pm Mon-Fri; 6.30-10.30pm Sat; 1-4pm Sun. **Credit** AmEx, MC, V. Gastropub
Though generally rammed during the week, this grand gastropub was refreshingly peaceful as the clock nudged last orders on a Saturday evening. The fact that it's tucked away behind warehouse conversions and office buildings probably helps (the mammoth queue to nearby ghetto-fabulous Favela Chic is oblivious to this delightful boozer's existence), but the Princess's grown-up crowd seems content with keeping it that way. For daytime drinking, its corner site ensures plenty of natural light from the sizeable latticed windows. Arty landscape pictures and decorative wallpaper offset the stained floorboards and wrought-iron furnishings – including the head-spinning spiral staircase, which leads to a more refined dining room. Downstairs, it's classic gastropub fare (wild boar sausages and mash, beer-battered cod and chips). Draught beers include Timothy Taylor Landlord, London Pride, Hoegaarden and Staropramen, and there's an impressive wine list.
Babies and children admitted. Restaurant available for hire. **Map p276 Q4.**

Red Lion
41 Hoxton Street, N1 6NH (7729 6930). Old Street tube/rail. **Credit** MC, V. Pub
A swift pint at the tiny Red Lion is rarely complete without the uneasy feeling that you've accidentally gatecrashed a private fancy dress party. But you haven't. The hot girl in 80s clothing dancing to the *Flashdance* soundtrack with the chap in the smoking jacket is just kicking back after a hard week at the office. The girl at the bar with the 'doughnut' hat is the DJ. An old-school boozer of many makeovers, the Red Lion has settled on wooden floors, gaudy wall lights, a DJ booth and a proper fire. The bar – while generally well stocked with draught and bottled beers – has been known to run out of wine, but the upbeat vibe and off-the-beaten-track location just about compensate. Thai food is served in the restaurant upstairs.
Bar available for hire. Music (DJs 8pm Fri-Sun; free). Restaurant. Tables outdoors (2, yard). **Map p276 R3.**

Reliance
336 Old Street, EC1V 9DR (7729 6888). Old Street tube/rail. **Open** noon-11pm Mon-Thur, Sun; noon-2am Fri, Sat. **Food served** noon-9pm daily. **Credit** DC, MC, V. Pub
The perfect bar-pub compromise, the Reliance caters for a grown-up Shoreditch crowd more interested in a quality drink and a chat than largeing it until the sun comes up. A worn-in drinking hole, it has two airy floors, plenty of seating and a laid-back, uncontrived feel. Bottled Belgian beer is the speciality, with just under a dozen brands on offer, including Duvel, Westmalle and Liefmans, alongside draught Hoegaarden, Litovel, London Pride and Adnams Bitter, and an array of modern and classic cocktails. The hearty Sunday lunches are well worth getting out of bed

for, and there's a substantial menu of pies, sandwiches and big salads to work your way through during the rest of the week. Tuck yourself into a corner – the dark alcove at the back of the ground floor or the raised area by the windows upstairs are prime positions – and enjoy fuss-free Old Street drinking at its best.
Disabled: toilet. Jukebox. **Map p276 R4.**

Sosho
2 Tabernacle Street, EC2A 4LU (7920 0701/www. sosho3am.com). Moorgate or Old Street tube/rail. **Open** noon-midnight Tue; noon-1am Wed, Thur; noon-3am Fri; 7pm-4am Sat; 9pm-6am Sun. **Food served** noon-10.30pm Tue-Fri; 7-11pm Sat. **Admission** £3-£10 after 9pm Thur-Sun. **Credit** AmEx, DC, MC, V. Cocktail bar
Its dubious attempt at a new name for the City fringes (SOuth of SHOreditch) never quite caught on, but Sosho's clubby cocktail credentials are still a hit with the Square Mile crowd. Join them for deftly mixed cocktails (pint fans should make an 180° turn at the entrance), booze-soaking bar snacks (fries, onion rings, sharing platters) and a late-night fumble on the downstairs dancefloor. It's perfect if you want an excuse to get dressed up and party hard, regardless of the looming menace of work the following morning. Service is excellent and very accommodating: the bar is happy to take table/area reservations, even at short notice. A great choice for all kinds of celebrations and to escape from the grungier side of Shoreditch drinking.
Babies and children admitted (until 6pm). Disabled: toilet. Music (DJs 9pm Wed-Sun). Separate room for parties, seats 150. **Map p276 Q4.**

T Bar
56 Shoreditch High Street, E1 6JJ (7729 2973/www.tbar london.com). Liverpool Street or Old Street tube/rail. **Open** 9am-midnight Mon-Wed; 9am-1am Thur; 9am-2am Fri; 8pm-2am Sat; 11am-midnight Sun. **Food served** 9am-4pm Mon-Fri. **Credit** MC, V. DJ bar
The sign outside this vast, industrial space within the Tea Building counts down the seconds to last orders. Inside, the young, clubby crowd are far too busy dancing to care about such minor details. The decor divides the space into zones – a louche red velvet den, monochrome 1960s space, corduroy-clad chillout zone – but is definitely best viewed after dark (dried-on chewing gum features heavily). Bottled beers and wine are available, but the emphasis is on classy and original cocktails (£6.50-£7.50); try a Flirtini, perhaps, or an earl grey margarita. Though this isn't much of a daytime or weeknight space (things only really hot up from Thursday), there's a caff-style menu that's popular with local workers. Be prepared for the trek to the toilets and to be accosted by at least one wide-eyed 19-year-old who, like, 'really, really loves the DJ, man' and wants to tell the world.
Booking advisable. Disabled: toilet. Games (table tennis, call for details). Music (DJs 9pm Thur-Sat). Separate room for parties, seats 60. **Map p276 R4.**

Three Blind Mice NEW
5 Ravey Street, EC2A 4QW (no phone). Old Street tube/rail. **Open** 7-11pm Tue-Thur; 7pm-midnight Fri, Sat. **No credit cards.** Bar
Three laid-back mates set up Three Blind Mice in summer 2006, retaining much of what made its predecessor (Smersh) one of the area's favourite hidden bars. The decor hasn't changed much: the subterranean space still looks like the haphazard party venue you might create on the fly once mum and dad leave town for the weekend. There's no

East

Favela Chic. *See p188.*

sign outside, while low ceilings and deep red walls give the place an unpretentious, low-key feel. If you're after gaudy cocktails, the latest imported beers or draught offerings, head straight back up the stairs, but for a large glass of red, a reggae-to-hip hop soundtrack and a dark corner to hide in for the night, this place hits the spot.
Bar available for hire. Music (DJs 8pm Thur-Sat).
Map p276 Q4.

★ Wenlock Arms

26 Wenlock Road, N1 7TA (7608 3406/www.wenlockarms.co.uk). Old Street tube/rail. **Open** noon-midnight Mon-Wed, Sun; noon-1am Thur-Sat. **Food served** noon-9pm daily. **No credit cards**. Pub
Despite its no man's land location, the Wenlock packs 'em in for fine ales, doorstep sarnies (£2-£3.50) and good-natured banter at the bar (if you prefix your drink order with the words 'Can I get…' you'll be accused of bastardising the English language – and quite right too). This is a pub of the old school: gaudy carpet, friendly mutts and a rough-around-the-edges vibe. There's a cricket team, a football team, a Thursday night quiz, live music and a hotchpotch crowd of fiercely loyal regulars. Ales are the Wenlock's main USP. You'll find a changing menu of up to ten speciality brews: the fantastically named Oakham Asylum and Northern Soul Time were among the options on our recent visit; the website lists up-to-date incumbents.

Babies and children admitted. Function room. Games (darts). Music (blues/jazz 9pm Fri, Sat; 3pm Sun; free). Quiz (9pm Thur; free). TV (satellite).

★ William IV NEW

7 Shepherdess Walk, N1 7QE (3119 3012). Old Street tube/rail. **Open** noon-11pm Mon-Wed; noon-midnight Thur-Sat; noon-10.30pm Sun. **Food served** noon-3pm, 6-10pm Mon-Sat; 1-4pm, 6-9pm Sun. **Credit** MC, V.
Gastropub
You know you're in business when a pub has a cat, and this one – a ginger and white specimen called Harry – warrants his own section on the venue's website and his own armchair by the fire. There's plenty of room for human loungeing too, with massive painted wood tables and tons of seating. The decor takes a break from the stripped wood norm, with a light, bright paint job, tasselled standard lamps and heavy curtains. The dining room upstairs serves top-notch gastro grub, and there's also a short but exciting bar menu (rabbit and white bean pie, Cornish mussels, sausage sandwiches). Wash it all down with a glass of the decent house red or a pint – Black Sheep, London Pride, Hoegaarden, Leffe and Guinness are among the beer options.
Disabled: toilet. Function room. Games (board games). Tables outdoors (4, yard).

Also in the area...

Bedroom Bar *62 Rivington Street, EC2A 3AY (7613 5637).* A double iron bed in the corner gives this DJ bar its name. Expect Euro-house from the speakers and a reasonable choice of draught lagers and cocktails from the bar. **Map p276 R4.**

Bricklayer's Arms *63 Charlotte Road, EC2A 3PE (7739 5245/www.thebricklayersarmspub.com).* Shabby but popular boozer; undergoing a refurb at the time of going to press. **Map p276 R4.**

Cocomo *323 Old Street, EC1V 9LE (7613 0315).* Moroccan themed bar with Red Stripe on tap and a decent choice of wines. Weekends are livened by free DJs. **Map p276 R4.**

Elbow Room *97-113 Curtain Road, EC2A 3BS (7613 1316/www.theelbowroom.co.uk).* Branch. **Map p276 R4.**

Griffin *93 Leonard Street, EC2A 4RD (7739 6719).* Blokey boozer with big-screen football, real ales (Old Speckled Hen, Pedigree, London Pride), doorstep-sized sarnies, pool table and dartboard. **Map p276 R4.**

Medicine Bar *89 Great Eastern Street, EC2A 3HX (7739 5173).* Branch. **Map p276 Q4.**

Pulpit *63 Worship Street, EC2A 2DU (7377 1574).* Branch of Davy's. **Map p276 Q4.**

Tabernacle *55-61 Tabernacle Street, EC2A 4AA (7253 5555/www.tabernaclegrill.com).* Upmarket ground-floor bar and restaurant; clubby basement drinking den. **Map p276 Q4.**

Stratford

★ King Eddie's
47 Broadway, E15 4BQ (8534 2313/www.kingeddie. co.uk). Stratford tube/rail/DLR. **Open** noon-11pm Mon-Wed; noon-midnight Thur-Sat; noon-11.30pm Sun. **Food served** noon-10pm daily. **Credit** MC, V. Gastropub

Still the King of Prussia to regulars, this has been King Eddie's (or the Edward VII) since a fit of patriotism overtook the owner in World War I. It's now Grade II-listed, with all the dark wood, open fires, etched glass and low ceilings that implies. There's a fine selection of beer (highlights include Woodforde's Wherry and Archers IPA on draught, Innis & Gunn Edinburgh ale and Samuel Smith Organic Cherry by the bottle), half a dozen each of red and white, and high-end spirits. The same food is served in each of three rooms: generous under-£10 portions of excellent ham knuckle and duck terrine, haddock and chips, or rock oysters at £1 each. In the saloon bar grizzled blokes sup with young professionals under the gaze of a mounted motorbike-riding stoat.

Babies & children admitted. Music (acoustic/open mic, 9pm Thur). Separate room for parties, seats 32. Tables outdoors (7, yard).

Theatre Royal Bar
Theatre Royal Stratford East, Gerry Raffles Square, E15 1BN (8534 7374/www.stratfordeast.com). Stratford tube/rail/DLR. **Open** 11am-11pm Mon-Sat; noon-10.30pm Sun. **Food served** 12.30-9.30pm Mon; 12.30-8.30pm Tue-Sun. **Credit** MC, V. Bar

The tables are slapped together next to the french windows at the entrance to the bar of the Theatre Royal Stratford,

giving the punters a good view of a small stage and a minor ocean of bare floor. Indeed, entertainment is as important here as drinking or troughing down the Jamaican food: there's a full nightly programme of comedy, poetry and music, and a preponderance of family groups in the afternoons. To sup, choose from draught Bombardier and the usuals, or four of each colour of wine, plus a couple of opening-night champagnes. The interior is a rather dramatic red, with black and white photos of productions past, among them a nightie-clad Babs Windsor on compelling form in *Fings Ain't Wot They Used T'Be*. Cor.

Babies and children welcome. Comedy (8pm Mon; free). Disabled: toilet. Music (bands/solo musicians 6-9pm Mon-Fri, 1-4pm Sat, Sun; free). Poetry (7pm Sun; free). Restaurant. Tables outdoors (4, heated terrace).

Wapping

Prospect of Whitby
57 Wapping Wall, E1W 3SH (7481 1095). Wapping tube. **Open/food served** noon-11pm Mon-Wed, Sun; noon-midnight Thur-Sat. **Credit** AmEx, MC, V. Pub

With impressive views south and east (most notably of Canary Wharf), this ancient riverside pub's top outdoor terrace is some setting for a quiet tipple. Inside, there's more to distract the eyes, with local historical memorabilia scattered throughout and reminders that this is 'London's oldest riverside pub' (est 1520) – though we could have done without the similarly emblazoned rugby shirts and tankards. It's no surprise, then, that the tourists arrive in droves (Charles Dickens and Samuel Pepys both drank here); a minor refurbishment in 2006 has, sadly, only added to a slightly tacky museum mood. Things improve markedly upstairs, with bright wooden panelling and cosy seating easily trumping the gloomy walls and dark stone floors downstairs. The beer selection isn't too shabby either: Greene King IPA, Timothy Taylor Landlord and London Pride, as well as Leffe and Staropramen.

Babies and children admitted. Function room. Tables outdoors (7, garden). TV.

Town of Ramsgate
62 Wapping High Street, E1W 2PN (7481 8000). Wapping tube. **Open** noon-midnight Mon-Sat; noon-11pm Sun. **Food served** noon-9pm daily. **Credit** AmEx, MC, V. Pub

In a pretty soulless and often eerily quiet part of town, this old pub, festooned with nautical bric-a-brac and historic manuscripts, serves as a welcome reminder of Wapping's rich past. The staff and loyal local customers also demonstrate that the area hasn't been completely taken over by monied, warehouse-dwelling City and Canary Wharf workers. The long corridor of an interior and shabby carpet are brightened up by a large front window and vases of flowers, while a small TV and backgammon, cards and chess are on hand if conversation palls. Honest pub food (think burgers and a roast on Sunday) is available, and beers on tap include Adnams, Young's, London Pride, Hoegaarden and Leffe. Weather permitting, nestle down on the cute riverside terrace and drift away to the sound of the Thames lapping at the stones below.

Babies and children admitted (until 7pm). Games (backgammon, board games, cards, chess). Quiz (8.30pm Mon; £1). Tables outdoors (12, riverside garden). TV.

East

North East

The trendification of Hackney continues apace, with more and more boozers going gastro. As the likes of the splendid **Empress of India** prove, change is not always for the worse. Still, those in search of a simple pint and bag of crisps can rest assured that one old stalwart is still standing firm; step forward the **Prince George**. Also going from strength to strength is the effortlessly hip **Dalston Jazz Bar**, another local institution.

Down Leyton and Leytonstone way, welcoming locals like the **Birkbeck Tavern** are much more peaceful – unless there's a match on, that is. Meanwhile, the Stoke Newington scene is still buzzing, with quality gastro fare to be had at the likes of the **Three Crowns** and the **Alma** – though a thrifty ploughman's and London Pride at the **Rose & Crown** takes some beating. The gastropub revolution hasn't reached as far as Walthamstow yet, even in the leafy surrounds of Walthamstow Village – though as you nod along to a Sunday jazz session and sup a glass of wine at the **Nag's Head**, it doesn't seem like it can be too far off.

Hackney

Cat & Mutton
76 Broadway Market, E8 4QJ (7254 5599/www.cat andmutton.co.uk). London Fields rail. **Open** 6-11pm Mon; noon-11pm Tue-Thur, Sun; noon-midnight Fri, Sat. **Food served** 6-10pm Mon; noon-3pm, 6-10pm Tue-Sat; noon-5pm Sun. **Credit** AmEx, MC, V.
Gastropub

The best time to visit this venue (all bare-brick walls, squashy sofas and battered tables) is during the week – at weekends it's a moshpit. Not that that stops hordes of party people heading over from Shoreditch for a pre-big night out; pork-pie hats, skinny jeans, patent leather shoes and *Ugly Betty* and Russell Brand lookalikes abound. Mismatched tables fill the downstairs space, while upstairs there's lovely red and gold wallpaper, more seating and a pool table. Food is good (though pricey, especially the Sunday breakfast at £8.95) and there's a decent wine selection too; Italian house red and whites are £12. There are also sherries and champagnes. The pump selection isn't great (San Miguel, Staropramen, Guinness) though they were all off on our visit anyway – a problem with the gas apparently. A final draw (for some, at least) is the fact that the Cat is dog-friendly. Unlikely, hey?
Babies and children welcome (until 8pm): high chairs. Disabled: toilet. Games (snooker). Music (DJs 7.30pm Sun; free). Separate room for parties, seats 50. Tables outdoors (5, pavement).

Dalston Jazz Bar
4 Bradbury Street, N16 8JN (7254 9728). Dalston Kingsland rail. **Open** 5pm-3am Mon-Thur; 5pm-5am Fri, Sat; 5pm-2am Sun. **No credit cards.** Bar
It's been around for a while, but the DJB still has a temporary, 'put up overnight' feel to it. Glass-walled on three sides and plonked in the middle of a car park in a Dalston side street, it might not seem to have much to recommend it. But something about the place – maybe it's the cocktails, maybe it's the up-for-it crowd – works. The interior is dotted with battered sofas and low tables, interspersed with eclectic tat (an old dentist's lamp, a cycling road sign, a bookshelf that gives a clue to the owner's varied reading tastes), while at the makeshift-like bar there are five beers on tap (Erdinger the highlight), plus plenty of bottles in the fridge. Come Saturday and Sunday it's essential to sample what might be the cheapest cocktails in London (£4.50 before midnight, £5 after); try a sour apple martini or 'razberi' cosmopolitan. The place packs out as the wee hours approach.
Bar available for hire (Mon-Fri). Music (DJs 10pm daily; free).

North East

North East

Dolphin

165 Mare Street, E8 3RH (8985 3727). London Fields rail. **Open** 11am-2am Mon-Thur, Sun; 11am-4am Fri, Sat. **No credit cards.** Pub

It might not look like much from the outside (or from the inside for that matter, apart from the cool tiled dolphin mural), but come Friday and Saturday everyone heads to the Dolphin for an East End knees-up – Hoxton-style. Expect punters with bad, mad haircuts, plenty of hats, gold lamé leggings and 1970s retro mixing it with the Turkish and Vietnamese locals. And the draw? The karaoke machine is cranked right up and it's not unusual to see 50 or more funsters crammed on the 'dancefloor' singing their hearts out. During the week, things are much more sedate. There's no karaoke but the jukebox holds 5,000 tunes and at 50p a pop (three for £1) you can still exercise your vocal chords. The drinks choice is pretty mundane: Foster's, Strongbow and 1664 on tap. If you're peckish, it's pork scratchings or crisps. You might even get offered a dodgy DVD. The Dolphin: we love it.
Games (fruit machine, pool). Music (DJ 8pm Fri; karaoke 8pm Sat, Sun; both free). TV (big screen, satellite).

★ Dove Kitchen & Freehouse

24-26 Broadway Market, E8 4QJ (7275 7617/www. belgianbars.com). London Fields rail. **Open** noon-11pm Mon-Thur, Sun; noon-midnight Fri, Sat. **Food served** noon-3pm, 6-10pm Mon-Wed; noon-11pm Thur-Sat; noon-10pm Sun. **Credit** MC, V. Gastropub

This is beer heaven. Lit by candles, with a number of cosy nooks, this atmospheric drinking hole, all dark wood and burgundy walls, offers more than 100 Belgian beers and 17 beers on tap (including De Koninck, Belle-Vue Kriek and Timothy Taylor Landlord); there are always at least four real ales including guest beers. The wine list is sound and the excellent food menu includes own-made burgers, sausages and mash, and pint glasses of chips. The place packs out on Sunday, so booking for full roasts (including a veggie option) is recommended. Thankfully, the loos have been refurbed (frosted glass and marble) and there's now a baby-changing area. You'll also find friendly staff, a good supply of board games and a welcoming vibe, which is why the Dove retains a loyal, local following. Top.
Babies and children admitted (until 6pm). Games (board games). Music (jazz 8.30pm Wed, Sun; free). Restaurant. Tables outdoors (6, pavement).

Empress of India NEW

130 Lauriston Road, E9 7LH (8533 5123/www.the empressofindia.com). Mile End tube then 277 bus. **Open/food served** 8am-11pm Mon-Sat; 9am-10.30pm Sun. **Credit** AmEx, MC, V. Gastropub

The owners (who also run the Gun in Docklands, the White Swan in the City and the Well in Clerkenwell) have refurbed this fine old boozer with glorious wallpaper featuring views of Moghul India, and splendid chandeliers fashioned from strings of mussel shells. It looks a treat. The emphasis is on eating rather than drinking, though: most of the large space is devoted to dining tables. Still, the range of drinks is pretty impressive: there's a top-drawer selection of beers, including Timothy Taylor Landlord, Greene King IPA and a couple of Greenwich Meantime brews on tap, an appealing wine list and an excellent selection of juices and smoothies. Seafood makes a big showing on the solidly British menu, from oysters to a pint of prawns; mains feature roasts, game or fish pie; puddings are school-dinner classics. The Empress also does

North East

Old haunts

North East

It's no great surprise that so many of London's haunted buildings are pubs. There's nothing quite like an evening of boozing to leave you convinced you've seen something you haven't.

One of the more intriguing spectres is the chap who sits at the bar of the **John Snow** (39 Broadwick Street, W1, 7437 1344), said to be a victim of the area's cholera epidemic in the 19th century. The **Dolphin Tavern** (44 Red Lion Street, WC1, 7831 6298) boasts a haunted clock (*pictured*), rescued from piles of rubble after the pub was flattened in a Zeppelin raid in 1915. It is said that it sometimes emits the whistling sound of an incoming bomb.

The City has a fair few haunted pubs, but the best story is attached to **Ye Olde Cock Tavern** (22 Fleet Street, EC4, 7353 8570), where in 1984 an Aussie barmaid (natch) was confronted with a floating disembodied head. She was consoled by the landlady, only to scream once more when she saw the same face in a portrait on the wall. It belonged to 18th-century writer Oliver Goldsmith, who is buried nearby.

Other haunted pubs include the **Rising Sun** (Cloth Fair), where two Brazilian barmaids once had their bedclothes removed by an, ahem, 'invisible' presence, and the **Anchor** (34 Park Street, SE1, 7407 1577), where a ghostly pooch is said to roam in search of its severed tail. One of London's celebrity spectres is Dick Turpin, who can be seen riding in the vicinity of the **Spaniards Inn** (Hampstead).

But perhaps the best story concerns the **Gun** (Docklands), once frequented by Nelson and Lady Hamilton and where, in 1970, an author decided to test local gullibility by inventing a tale about a departed vicar who haunted the pub, a fiction that was promptly supported by a number of witnesses who claimed to have seen the ghost. Conclusive evidence, it seems, that exposure to spirits can have unforeseen effects.

breakfast, morning pastries and coffee, and afternoon tea. Service is professional (something of a rarity in these parts). The most recent addition to the group, the Prince Arthur, opens in London Fields in summer 2007.
Babies and children welcome: changing room, children's menu, high chairs. Disabled: toilet. Tables outdoors (terrace, 8).

Pembury
90 Amhurst Road, E8 1JH (8986 8597/www. individualpubs.co.uk/pembury). Hackney Central or Hackney Downs rail. **Open** noon-11pm daily. **Food served** noon-3pm, 6-9pm Mon-Sat; noon-9pm Sun. **Credit** MC, V. Pub
Refurbished in 2006, the massive Pembury has lost its former rough-and-ready charm. It now has a pretty soulless community-hall look and a smattering of drinkers who variously play cards, bar billiards or board games, or coo over kids in buggies (it's been no-smoking since it reopened). There's no music, and precious little atmosphere either. On the plus side, the real ale selection is faultless. You'll find 16 ever-changing pump ales, many from the Milton Brewery (including Pegasus, Sparta, Jupiter and Minotaur), a healthy array of bottled German and Belgian beers, the usual spirits and a reasonable wine selection. The food's not bad either, with pâtés, ploughman's, sandwiches, sausages and roasts (including veggie options). We're glad to see the place up and running again – a shame it's so dull. Things probably liven up during the annual real ale festival (call to find out when the next one's due).
Babies and children admitted. Disabled: toilet. Games (bar billiards, board games, pool). No piped music or jukebox.

Prince George
40 Parkholme Road, E8 3AG (7254 6060). Dalston Kingsland rail/30, 38, 56, 242, 277 bus. **Open** 5-11pm Mon-Fri; 2-11pm Sat, Sun. **Credit** MC, V. Pub
The George has always prided itself on the fact that it doesn't do food. It's a pub. And a much-loved one at that, drawing a loyal local following years before the latest Hackney upstarts arrived. The drinks selection is perfectly respectable, with well-kept London Pride, Flowers Original and Litovel on tap and a decent wine range (from £10.40 a bottle), plus the usual spirits. On Monday, friendly but focused locals pack in for one of the best pub quizzes around, and the jukebox offers an excellent range of tunes from the likes of Neil Simon and Nina Simone. The decor is strictly period Victorian: stuffed birds and fish, a bust of Brunel above the bar, and one of those old-school wall maps where England is the same size as France (and almost a quarter the size of India). In winter the fires blaze, but the welcome is warm year-round. And if you're hungry? Well, there's posh biltong or crisps.
Babies and children admitted (until 8.30pm). Games (board games, pool table). Quiz (9pm Mon; £1). Tables outdoors (8, heated forecourt). TV.

Royal Inn on the Park
111 Lauriston Road, E9 7HJ (8985 3321). Mile End tube then 277 bus. **Open** noon-11pm Mon-Sat; noon-10.30pm Sun. **Food served** 12.30-3.30pm, 6.30-10pm Tue-Sat; noon-4pm Sun. **Credit** MC, V. Pub
There is little to fault at this wonderfully located old boozer on the edge of Victoria Park. With its high ceilings, original central bar, heavy drapes and muted lighting, it's a perfect place for meeting mates, having a meal or enjoying the jukebox offerings (Lou Reed, Nina Simone, Stevie

Wonder). The superb selection of draught beers includes Fuller's Organic Honeydew, London Pride, Porter, Festival and Chiswick, as well as Litovel, Hoegaarden, Leffe, Früli, Paulaner and Scrumpy Jack. There's a decent list of red and white wines from £11. Food is a big draw, especially at Sunday lunch, when you can have slow-roasted pork with crackling and all the trimmings (£11) or baked stuffed aubergine, chickpea and pepper stew (£8.50). Dogs and babies are welcome (there's a family room, and a play area across the road) and there's a large outdoor area with heat lamps and summer barbecues.

Babies and children admitted (restaurant). Disabled: toilet. Function room. Quiz (8.30pm Tue; £1). Restaurant. Tables outdoors (30, garden).

Spurstowe

68 Greenwood Road, E8 1AB (7249 2500). Hackney Central rail. **Open** 4.30-11pm Mon, Tue; noon-11pm Wed, Thur; noon-midnight Fri, Sat; noon-10.30pm Sun. **Food served** 5-10pm Mon, Tue; noon-10pm Wed-Sun. **Credit** MC, V. Pub
One of a clutch of tatty Hackney boozers that are now gastropubs, the Spur is a fabulous local that's always buzzing, with a mainly thirtysomething crowd. Sensitively refurbished, it's got the requisite bare-brick walls, battered sofas and mismatched tables and chairs, but also has a lovely deco-ish glass-backed bar and a small back garden decorated with mirrors and heat lamps. Food ranges from kippers on toast (£6) to shearer stew with mash and greens (£12), but it's the drinks that really impress. How about Abbot, Tetley's, Black Sheep, Brakspear, Hoegaarden, Leffe and Staropramen on tap, plus a good selection of wines, champagnes and spirits, a host of cocktails and shooters, and specialities of tequilas, absinthe and bourbons (including the award-winning 20-year-old Pappy Van Winkle's Family Reserve). The music is low, funky and conversation-friendly, and the service is great too. Recommended.

Babies and children admitted (until 6pm). Tables outdoors (18, garden).

Also in the area...

Fox *372 Kingsland Road, E8 4DA (7254 4012).* A welcome pub addition to Dalston, serving reasonable gastro grub and a range of ales.

Leyton

Birkbeck Tavern

45 Langthorne Road, E11 4HL (8539 2584). Leyton tube. **Open** 11am-11pm Mon-Thur; 11am-midnight Fri, Sat; noon-11pm Sun. **Credit** MC, V. Pub
This former hotel is the favoured haunt of discerning Leyton Orient fans, trying to forget their team's latest woes with a pint or two of Rita's Special – named after a previous landlady – or one of a rotating line-up of guest beers from the likes of Mighty Oak, Archers, Weltons and other microbreweries. Indeed, the *Football and Real Ale Guide* voted it their divisional pub of the year for 2006/7. You don't need to be a footy fan, though, to enjoy its large lounge and smaller saloon at the front, while the beer garden comes into its own when the sun shines. There's not much in the way of food other than rolls and pickled eggs, and the place can be noisy when the jukebox and TV are blaring. The bar staff cope with practised good humour, especially on busy Saturday nights when the O's have won.

Entertainment (karaoke 8.30pm; free). Function room. Games (darts, fruit machine). Quiz (8.15pm alternate Sun; £1). Tables outdoors (18, garden). TV.

William IV

816 Leyton High Road, E10 6AE (8556 2460). Leyton tube/Walthamstow Central tube/rail. **Open** 11am-11pm Mon-Sat; noon-10.30pm Sun. **Food served** noon-3pm, 5-10pm Mon-Fri; noon-10pm Sat, Sun. **Credit** MC, V. Pub
The fondly remembered Sweet William microbrewery seems to have closed for good, but this handsome boozer at the Bakers Arms end of Leyton is still worth the ten-minute trek from the nearest tube station. The distinctive red-brick Victorian exterior is adorned with hanging baskets and greenery, while there's a relaxed, old-time atmosphere to the two rooms, with cosy fires, papers to read, attentive staff and a cosmopolitan clientele. The front bar can be noisy when there's a big match on telly. Fuller's London Pride, ESB and Discovery, plus Leffe and occasional guest ales, are the main drinking attractions, making this the best pub in an area that has plenty of pubs but few of any quality.

Babies and children admitted (until 7pm). Games (board games, fruit machines). Music (blues 8.30pm Sun; jazz 8.30pm last Thur of mth; free). Tables outdoors (7, garden). TV (big screen, satellite).

Leytonstone

North Star

24 Browning Road, E11 3AR (8989 5777). Leytonstone tube. **Open** noon-11.30pm Mon-Sat; noon-10.30pm Sun. **No credit cards.** Pub
Surrounded by early Victorian cottages, this small, two-bar local is an unexpected gem. It's the focal point of the Browning Road Conservation Area, and was created in the 1850s by two of the dwellings being knocked together. Behind the etched-glass saloon door and half-net curtains, the place has an appealingly tatty feel, with tongue-and-groove panelling, photos of olde E11 and a cast of middle-aged regulars and dog walkers attracted by the excellent draught beer and friendly service. Three well-kept ales, perhaps Deuchars IPA, Bombardier and Broadside are always available. Sit on the suntrap forecourt and imagine you're miles (rather than just 50m) from grubby Leytonstone High Road. The pub has put up for sale shortly after our last visit, so phone to check it's still open.

Games (darts, fruit machine). Tables outdoors (4, garden; 2, pavement). TV.

Sheepwalk `NEW`

692 High Road Leytonstone, E11 3AA (8556 1131). Leytonstone tube. **Open** 1pm-midnight Mon-Fri; noon-2am Sat, Sun. **No credit cards.** Pub
The garish blue and yellow livery does this straightforward, male-dominated east London boozer no favours. Nor does the name – it's a long time since there were shepherds on Leytonstone High Road – and many locals still think of it as the Crown. However, most of the Victorian fittings and Irish regulars survived the revamp, only to be swamped by country pub furniture, a pool table and two big screens. Real ale fiends should also give the place a miss, as it's fizz all round. What makes the Sheepwalk worth a visit is the terrific What's Cookin' club, which dishes out country, blues, rock 'n' roll, cajun and pub rock every Saturday in the main bar, and every Wednesday in the

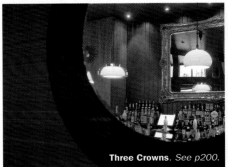

Three Crowns. See p200.

Leytonstone Ex-Servicemen's Club just round the corner (at least while the surreally decorated upstairs ballroom is out of action). What's more, almost all the gigs are free. *Babies and children admitted (until 6pm). Games (darts, fruit machine, pool, table football). Jukebox. Music (bands 8pm Sat; free).*

Stoke Newington

Alma

59 Newington Green Road, N1 4QU (7359 4536/ www.the-alma.co.uk). Highbury & Islington tube/rail/ Canonbury rail. **Open** 5-11pm Mon-Thur; noon-11pm Fri, Sat; noon-10.30pm Sun. **Food served** 7-10.30pm Mon-Thur; 12.30-3pm, 7-10.30pm Fri; 1-4pm, 7-10.30pm Sat; 1-4pm, 7-10pm Sun. **Credit** MC, V. Pub
The Alma was refurbed and relaunched by Caroline Hamlin and Kirsty Valentine two years ago, at which point 'the dartboard was swapped for a blackboard menu'. One thing the new owners didn't change, thankfully, was the vast bay windows that dominate the front of the bar, looking out onto Newington Green. On a sunny afternoon the result is arresting: light pours through like a hazy, golden big-budget beer commercial. The pub, then, is best suited to lazy afternoons spent flicking through the broadsheets or discussing the cricket. Courage and Director's are on draught, while the kitchen churns out the likes of roast pork belly with apple risotto (£11). This can be washed down with one of ten wines of each colour, half of which are available by the glass.

Babies and children admitted. Bar available for hire. Games (board games). Tables outdoors (4, pavement; 8, courtyard).

Auld Shillelagh

105 Stoke Newington Church Street, N16 0UD (7249 5951). Stoke Newington rail/73, 393, 476 bus. **Open** 11am-11pm Mon-Sat; noon-10.30pm Sun. **Credit** AmEx, DC, MC, V.
Crammed between two off-licences, the claret exterior of this slimline pub is barely bigger than its door. Inside, a skinny bar stretches towards a seated area and a beer garden at the back, frosted glass keeps curious passers-by at bay, and bantering Irish regulars swill Guinness to a man. Some claim the black stuff here is the best in London; it's certainly served with panache, poured by pint-proud staff who'll bring it to your table unbidden. Entertainment is limited (with no space elsewhere, a dartboard used to hang on the door to the gents' toilet – we don't like to speculate why it was taken down), but music sessions on alternate Friday nights pull in a fair crowd.

Babies and children admitted (until 7pm). Games (fruit machine). Music (musicians 8pm alternate Fri; free). TV (big screen, satellite).

Fox Reformed

176 Stoke Newington Church Street, N16 0JL (7254 5975/www.fox-reformed.co.uk). Stoke Newington rail/73, 393, 476 bus. **Open** 5pm-midnight Mon-Fri; noon-midnight Sat, Sun. **Food served** 6.30-10.30pm Mon-Fri; noon-3pm,

6.30-10.30pm Sat, Sun. **Credit** AmEx, DC, MC, V.
Wine bar/Restaurant
As evinced by the mountains of corks in the windows, the
emphasis at the Fox is on wine, with some adventurous
varieties complementing a menu of French bistro food (a
steak sandwich, perhaps). The exterior is classically
British, painted telephone-box red, and the front room
screams Taunton B&B, with toby jugs and a ticking grandfather clock. Behind the bar are the Fox's hosts, Robbie and
Carol Richards, who have run the place since 1981. A loyal
Stokey crowd come to play backgammon, Scrabble and
chess, attend the regular wine club, or sample one of the
30 bottles on offer (around a third are available by the
glass). The name, by the way, is in honour of the joint's
original moniker, 'Fox's Wine Bar'; the building was also
once Edgar Allan Poe's schoolhouse.
*Games (backgammon, board games). Tables outdoors
(5, heated garden). Wine-tasting club (7pm alternate
Thur; £30 a year).*

Londesborough
*36 Barbauld Road, N16 0SS (7254 5865). Stoke
Newington rail/73, 476 bus.* **Open** 4.30-11pm
Mon-Thur; 4.30pm-midnight Fri; noon-midnight Sat;
noon-10.30pm Sun. **Food served** 5-10pm Mon-Fri;
noon-4.30pm, 5-10pm Sat, Sun. **Credit** MC, V. Pub
A shining example of what's possible when it comes to gen-
trifying an old boozer. The chalkboard wine list covers all
of the grape bases and the draught is diverse enough –
Sidestreet, Pedigree, Adnams and Harveys on one side,
Staropramen, San Miguel and Hoegaarden on the other – to
satisfy most tastes. (A fiendish house bloody mary sits in a

jug on the counter at weekends, for those who dare.) The
backyard is equipped with some swanky garden furniture;
when the sun shines it can often feel like a chic private party.
The downside (for the child-free) is the proliferation of
toddlers who seem to invade every Sunday afternoon; the
young and fancy-free get their own back thanks to blaring
DJs at the weekends.
*Babies and children admitted (until 6pm). Music
(DJs 8pm Fri, Sat; 7pm Sun; free). Tables outdoors
(12, garden).*

Prince
*59 Kynaston Road, N16 0EB (7923 4766/www.prince
pub.com). Stoke Newington rail/73, 393, 476 bus.*
Open noon-11pm Mon-Thur; noon-midnight Fri, Sat;
noon-10.30pm Sun. **Food served** noon-2.30pm, 5-10pm
Mon-Fri; noon-4pm, 5.30-10pm Sat; noon-4pm, 6-9pm
Sun. **Credit** MC, V. Gastropub
The Prince's narrow L-shaped room – elegantly decorated
in dark gothic shades, with an industrial-looking zinc bar
– gives up over half of its floor space to well-heeled diners
(a mixture of couples and families). When there's a run on
dishes from the kitchen (roasts cost about £12), you might
find yourself standing near the fireplace, tucked up by the
piano or edged into the small garden. Nevertheless, service
is always friendly and there's a decent range on draught:
Stella, Carlsberg, Guinness, Staropramen, Hoegaarden,
Leffe, San Miguel, London Pride, Bass and IPA, in addition to a solid wine list. Despite being somewhat incongruous with its upmarket image, the Prince's weekly pub
quiz is great, hosted by a pint-swilling gal who knows how
to keep the chatty rabble focused.

Babies and children welcome (until 7pm): high chairs. Disabled: toilet. Function room. Quiz (8.30pm Tue; £1). Tables outdoors (8, garden). TV.

Rose & Crown
199 Stoke Newington Church Street, N16 9ES (7254 7497). Stoke Newington rail/73, 393, 476 bus. **Open** 11.30am-midnight Mon-Sat; noon-midnight Sun. **Food served** noon-2.30pm Mon-Fri; noon-3.30pm Sat, Sun. **Credit** MC, V. Pub
While other pubs have refurbed and reworked the word gastro into their designation, the R&C stays much as it has always been: a matey room with a wood-panelled interior, its seats fashioned from beer barrels and its floors scuffed with much use. It certainly wouldn't benefit from any licks of modernity – on the contrary, it revels in handsome '30s fustiness. There's a coal fire, an unobtrusive TV for match days and a dining area that offers overwhelmingly generous and tasty grub like own-made steak pie (£8) and pâté ploughman's (£5.50). As befits a beer lovers' pub, there is a fantastic and well-tended selection of draught, including Budweiser, Holsten Export, Martin's Pedigree, Fuller's London Pride, Theakston XP and IPA, as well as one guest ale. The landlord is a dedicated Gooner – enter into a football discussion at your peril.
Babies and children welcome (until 7pm): high chairs. Games (fruit machine, quiz machine). Quiz (8.30pm Tue; £1). Tables outdoors (2, pavement). TV (satellite).

Shakespeare
57 Allen Road, N16 8RY (7254 4190). Dalston Kingsland rail/73, 141, 476 bus. **Open** 5-11pm Mon-Fri; noon-11pm Sat; noon-10.30pm Sun. **Credit** MC, V. Pub
Tucked away in a residential enclave off Shakspeare (sic) Walk – a variation on the name that must be horribly familiar to A-Level examiners – the nicotine-stained Shakespeare is a gastro-free, kid-free, honest-to-goodness boozer. There's church-pew seating around a horseshoe bar, a free jukebox humming out everything from the Clash to Elvis or the Arcade Fire, and a jar of pickled eggs behind the counter. The decor might be a touch theatrical, but it conjures up fantastic character – you almost expect to feel sawdust underfoot. Regulars are from the half of eastern Stokey that doesn't work for Endemol; instead, the clientele tends to be raffish, lefty, vaguely Bohemian and ultra-keen on getting another round of Discovery, HSB or London Pride in at last orders.
Babies and children admitted (until 7pm). Games (board games, cribbage, darts). Jukebox. Quiz (9pm Mon; £1). Tables outdoors (12, covered garden). TV (satellite).

Three Crowns NEW
175 Stoke Newington High Street, N16 0LH (7241 5511). Stoke Newington rail/73, 76, 141, 393, 476 bus. **Open** noon-11pm Mon-Thur; noon-1am Fri, Sat; noon-10.30pm Sun. **Food served** noon-3pm, 6-10pm Mon-Fri; noon-4pm, 6-10pm Sat; noon-4pm, 6-9.30pm Sun. **Credit** MC, V. Gastrobar
An awkward L-shaped space is put to good use at the Three Crowns: the smaller right for dining at tightly-packed tables, the larger left for boozing and chatting on leather sofas. As a spot from which to survey the curious cash divide that splits Stoke Newington, it takes some beating. Eat peering out at the unreconstructed edginess of Stoke Newington High Street, where Anatolian restaurants and cab firms predominate; drink looking out on the moneyed-media families on Stoke Newington Church Street, where the pushchair and *Tracy Beaker* books are boss.

Pumps of Harveys Sussex Bitter complement Timothy Taylor Landlord at the bar; the kitchen churns out enormous sharing platters such as rib of beef for two (£38). A wine list includes 14 bottles of each colour, half of which can be ordered by the glass.
Babies and children admitted (until 6pm). Disabled: toilet. Music (DJs 9pm Fri, Sat; free).

Also in the area...
Daniel Defoe *102 Stoke Newington Church Street, N16 0LA (7254 2906/www.thedanieldefoe.com).* Cosy pub with three real ales on tap.
Lion *132 Stoke Newington Church Street, N16 0JX (7249 1318).* Landmark corner pub with a small garden offering escape from the big-screen footie.
Mercado *26-30 Stoke Newington Church Street, N16 0LU (7923 0555/www.mercado-cantina. co.uk).* Laid-back Mexican cocktail bar.

Walthamstow

Flower Pot
128 Wood Street, E17 3HX (8520 3600). Walthamstow Central tube/rail. **Open** noon-11pm Mon-Wed; noon-12.30am Thur-Sat; noon-11.30pm Sun. **Credit** MC, V. Pub
Traditional pleasures prevail at this resolutely unreconstructed boozer, with Sky Sports on the telly and regular crowd-pleasing performances from 1960s and 1970s tribute bands. As you'd expect, the pumps boast plenty of trusty stalwarts: Bass, John Smith's and Guinness, two guest ales and a proliferation of less inspiring lagers are all present and correct. But that's not all; with Peetermans on tap and a fruity array of Belgian bottled beers, including strawberry Früli and cherry-flavoured Floris Kriek, there's something for everyone here. Old-fashioned hospitality from the bar staff, a quiz on Thursday nights and the odd race evening add to the unpretentious charm.
Babies and children admitted (until 7pm). Games (board games, cribbage, darts, retro arcade machine). Music (tribute bands 8.30pm Fri-Sun; free). Quiz (8.30pm Thur; £1). Tables outdoors (10, garden). TV (big screen, satellite).

Nag's Head
9 Orford Road, E17 9LP (8520 9709). Walthamstow Central tube/rail. **Open** 4-11pm Mon-Fri; 2-11pm Sat; 2-10.30pm Sun. **Credit** MC, V. Pub
Set in the unexpectedly leafy surrounds of Walthamstow Village, the Nag's Head is a pub with aspirations – note the velvet tablecloths and black and white movie stills on the walls. Drinks offerings are a cut above the ordinary too, with Belgian fruit beers, real ales and a nicely-chosen selection of wines. Sink into one of the sofas by the bar, or retreat into the courtyard beer garden – a popular spot on balmy afternoons. If you think things can't get much more laid-back than this, try popping in for pilates classes on a Thursday evening or jazz sessions on a Sunday afternoon.
Life drawing classes (7.30pm Mon; phone for details). Music (jazz 4-8pm Sun; free). Pilates classes (7.30pm Thur; phone for details). Tables outdoors (8, heated patio; 20, heated garden).

Also in the area...
Village *31 Orford Road, E17 9NL (8521 9982).* Traditional pub with four real ales on tap.

North

Beyond its dosser- and junkie-filled pubs, Camden hosts some first-rate drinking dens: including the **Lord Stanley** for a quiet pint of real ale and decent indie pubs the **Dublin Castle** and the **Hawley Arms** for a head-bang and a pint of Guinness. Nearby, the unassuming **Crown & Goose** draws a crowd with great food. Up the road, Kentish Town has charming boozers **Pineapple** and **Abbey**; Primrose Hill pulls an often celeb-studded crowd with superb gastropubs like **Queens**, the **Lansdowne** and the **Engineer** (worth a visit just for the beer garden).

In Islington, Upper Street is a focal point for bars – smart **Keston Lodge**, or trendy **Medicine Bar** – but the best of the area's drinking options are elsewhere. Miniature wine bar **Colebrookes** and ace boozer **Island Queen** offer quiet delights; for a livelier evening, check out the **Old Queen's Head** or DJ bar the **Warwick** opposite it. Islington's also home to some of London's best gastropubs: the **Duke of Cambridge** and the **Marquess Tavern** are among the big-hitters, but we prefer the **Charles Lamb**.

North to Stroud Green and Tufnell Park choice is more limited, but try eccentric boozer **Faltering Fullback** in the former and gastropub **Lord Palmerston** in the latter. If you're after gastropubs, **St John's** and the fine **Landseer** make Archway worth a visit; for a proper locals' local, Haringay's **Haringay Arms** is a delight. The **Salisbury Hotel** is also a pleasant surprise, given its unpromising location amid the Green Lanes kebab shops.

Archway

★ Landseer

37 Landseer Road, N19 4JU (7263 4658/www.the landseer.com). Archway or Holloway Road tube/17, 43, 217 bus. **Open** noon-11pm Mon, Tue, Sun; noon-midnight Wed-Sat. **Food served** noon-3pm, 5-10pm Mon-Fri; noon-4pm, 5-10.30pm Sat; noon-5pm, 6-9.30pm Sun. **Credit** AmEx, MC, V. Gastropub

Appropriately, given its name, this place is top dog when it comes to Archway gastropubs. Nestled at the junction of two residential streets, and within easy shouting distance of a well-maintained playground, its popularity with nicely dressed families is hardly surprising – particularly in summer, when there's a no-nonsense barbecue stationed outside. Friday night used to be New York Night, but this has recently been ditched (Archway being nothing like Manhattan) in favour of a more conventional happy hour, with two-for-one cocktails from 4pm. The conventional gastropub food, best consumed in the airy, glass-ceilinged dining area, rarely disappoints, although our enthusiastic waiter did refer to the chocolate pudding as 'the shit' (we gave it a miss, unsurprisingly). Draught ales on offer include Timothy Taylor Landlord and Pedigree.
Babies and children welcome: high chairs, smaller portions. Games (board games). Restaurant. Tables outdoors (15, terrace).

St John's

91 Junction Road, N19 5QU (7272 1587). Archway tube. **Open** 5-11pm Mon-Thur; noon-11pm Fri, Sat; noon-10.30pm Sun. **Food served** 6.30-9.30pm Mon-Thur; noon-3.30pm, 6.30-9.30pm Fri; noon-4pm, 6.30-11pm Sat; noon-4pm, 6.30-9.30pm Sun. **Credit** AmEx, MC, V. Gastropub

Resist the gauntlet of kebaberies running from Archway tube station down Junction Road, and you'll be rewarded with this fine gastropub. St John's stocks a wide selection of grog, including Grand Union Bitter and wines from a pleasingly descriptive blackboard, but the main event is the food, served throughout the minimalist front room and theatrical back restaurant. The latter, with its high ceilings and vast collection of paintings by owner Nick Sharp, is the nicer place to be in colder months, when the bar can feel slightly austere. We ordered a pricey tart from the starters menu (garlic, artichoke and spinach, £6.95) but instantly regretted it upon spying the mountain of meringue and forest fruits being devoured nearby. Next time, next time…

Babies and children welcome: high chairs. Booking advisable. Restaurant available for hire. Tables outdoors (6, patio).

Settle Inn

17-19 Archway Road, N19 3TX (7272 7872). Archway tube. **Open** noon-1am Mon-Sat; noon-midnight Sun. **Food served** noon-3pm, 6-10pm Mon-Fri; noon-9.30pm Sat, Sun. **Credit** MC, V. Pub

In gusty weather, the attentive bar staff of the Settle Inn spend half their time dashing over to slam shut the pub's corner door: this one-room boozer is as welcoming as the Archway Road is inhospitable, and the cosiness must be kept in at all costs. The maroon and cream decor is tasteful, but avoids crossing into identikit gastropub territory through the inclusion of random prints and some quirky, throne-like seating. The ramshackle kitchen out back serves delicious Thai food from £5.50 for a main course, and the lone chef was rushed off his feet when we visited on a Tuesday. The energy from our huge starter platter (£9.50) came in handy when the pub quiz required us, literally, to vote with our feet to answer questions. The bar serves the usual lager suspects plus ales like Flowers IPA.

Babies and children admitted (dining only). Games (board games, quiz machine). Quiz (8.30pm Tue; free). TV (satellite).

Swimmer at the Grafton Arms

13 Eburne Road, N7 6AR (7281 4632). Holloway Road tube/Finsbury Park tube/rail. **Open** 5-11pm Mon; noon-3pm, 5-11pm Tue-Thur; noon-11pm Fri, Sat; noon-10.30pm Sun. **Food served** 6-9pm Mon, Wed; 1-3pm, 6-9pm Thur, Fri; noon-4pm, 6-9pm Sat; noon-4pm Sun. **Credit** MC, V. Pub

Sometimes it feels as if the Holloway Road, like the Great Wall of China, is so vast it must be visible from space. Thank goodness, then, for cosy havens like the Swimmer, where the weary can take the weight off. Free Wi-Fi is evidence that this refurbished Victorian gastropub is servicing a very different crowd to the neighbouring Hercules; fortunately, there's far too much fun stuff here for anyone to bother with their emails for long. There's the legendary, lucrative quiz on Mondays, a jukebox, board games and an open kitchen serving the best chips in the area (and there are lots of chips in the area). A well-heated outdoor space means you can enjoy an alfresco Litovel Premium (£3.20) or one of three real ales even after the sun goes down.

Games (board games). Jukebox. Quiz (9pm Mon). Tables outdoors (15, garden). Wi-Fi (free).

Also in the area...

Coronet *338-346 Holloway Road, N7 6NJ (7609 5014/www.jdwetherspoon.co.uk).* Impossible-to-miss pub housed in a 1930s cinema. More than half a dozen real ales at the usual (low) Wetherspoon prices.
Winchester Hotel *206 Archway Road, N6 5BA (8374 1690).* Spacious traditional pub pumping London Pride, with a dartboard and beer garden.

North

Camden Town & Chalk Farm

At Proud NEW
Proud Galleries, Stables Market, Chalk Farm Road, NW1 8AH (7482 3867/www.atproud.net). Camden Town or Chalk Farm tube. **Open** 11am-1am Mon-Wed, Sun; 11am-3am Thur-Sat. **Admission** £3 after 7.30pm Mon; £5 after 7.30pm Tue, Thur, Fri; £7 after 7.30pm, £10 after 10pm Sat; free Wed, Sun. **Credit** (over £10) MC, V. Bar
The bar at Proud Galleries is housed in a giant marquee in the colder months, giving it a rather temporary feel – and rather odd wedding reception overtones. A 'Vladibar' winter makeover meant that, on our visit, the interior had a ski chalet vibe, complete with stag heads on the walls – though heaven knows where the life-sized plastic horses fitted in. One wall is lined with mattresses, and there are alcoves lined with fairy lights; here, the clientele swig bottled beers and studiously ignore the smattering of local celebrities (Noel Fielding is a regular). In summer, the marquee is packed away and hip Camdenites sprawl on deckchairs on the terrace. An eclectic line-up of gigs and club nights attract a varied, youthful crowd.
Bar available for hire. Function room. Music (jazz/DJs 7.30pm Mon; DJs 7.30pm Tue-Thur; band/DJs 7.30pm Fri-Sun). Tables outdoors (20, terrace). TVs (big screen). **Map p286 H26.**

Bar Solo
20 Inverness Street, NW1 7HJ (7482 4611/www.solobar.co.uk). Camden Town tube. **Open** 8am-1am Mon-Thur, Sun; 8am-2am Fri, Sat. **Food served** 8.30am-11.30pm daily. **Happy hour** 5-7pm daily. **Credit** MC, V. Bar/Restaurant

Service is unfailingly friendly, if erratic, at this Spanish bar/restaurant – we were brought bread and olives before our glasses of wine, which were left languishing on the bar for an inordinately long time on a quiet night. Despite its name, this place feels more geared towards diners than drinkers, with a small bar out front and a much larger candlelit restaurant section at the back. The bar area is pleasant enough, with a long leather sofa running the length of the wall, but possibly best for convivial daytime drinking and tapas; of an evening, the strip lighting certainly isn't conducive to romance. Disappointing too is the fact that just two red and three white wines are offered by the glass (£3-£4.50). Happy hour (5-7pm daily) includes two-for-one deals on a range of cocktails, spirits and bottled beers.
Babies and children admitted (until 7pm). Function room. Tables outdoors (2, terrace). **Map p286 H1.**

Bar Vinyl
6 Inverness Street, NW1 7HJ (7681 7898). Camden Town tube. **Open** 11am-11pm Mon-Thur; 11am-midnight Sat, Sat; 11am-10.30pm Sun. **Food served** noon-9pm Mon-Thur, Sun; noon-8pm Fri, Sat. **Credit** (over £10) AmEx, MC, V. DJ bar
Squeezed into narrow premises midway along bar-filled Inverness Street, Bar Vinyl exudes urban attitude. A DJ mixes pounding beats in the background, while the trendy clientele perch on cube seats opposite the dimly lit bar, or devour stone-baked pizzas at the bigger tables towards the rear. Graffiti-scrawl murals and digital artwork adorn the walls, and laid-back bartenders banter with the regulars as they mix cocktails from a battered, record-shaped list. A Barry White (vanilla-flavoured Stoli, apple, mint, lime, brown sugar and apple juice) went down a treat, but the barman's attempt to make a Blueberry Hill with raspberries

At Proud

North

instead of blueberries was less than successful – safer, perhaps, to stick to the draught Staropramen and Grolsch, or ample selection of bottled beers. Downstairs, hip Vinyl Addiction peddles breakbeat, electro trash and house. *Babies and children welcome (until 5pm). Music (DJs 8pm Tue-Fri, daytime & evening Sat-Sun). Record shop (11.30am-7.30pm daily). Tables outdoors (2, pavement).* **Map p286 H1.**

Bartok
78-79 Chalk Farm Road, NW1 8AR (7916 0595/ www.bartokbar.com). Chalk Farm tube. **Open** 4pm-3am Mon-Thur; 3pm-3am Fri; noon-3am Sat; 1pm-3am Sun. **Food served** 5-9pm Mon-Fri; 1-9pm Sat, Sun. **Admission** £4 after 11pm Fri; £5 after 11pm Sat. **Credit** MC, V. Cocktail bar
With its deep red walls, low leather sofas, dark wood tables and minimalist flower arrangements, Bartok exudes grown-up sophistication. Tea lights and chandeliers cast a sultry glow, along with a red neon art installation. Bartok is particularly popular with couples, who've cottoned on to the fact that this is an excellent spot for a date, thanks to well-spaced tables, seductively dim lighting and cocktails starting at a very reasonable £5.50. Why Foster's and Stella are the chosen on-tap lagers, alongside Guinness and Hoegaarden, remains a total mystery – though there's a reasonable array of bottled beers. The wine list is also fairly disappointing, with just two reds and two whites available by the glass. Despite an avowed classical music manifesto, it's always been contemporary sounds on our visits, courtesy of nightly DJs and bands. *Babies and children admitted (until 6pm Sat, Sun). Music (DJs 8.30pm Mon, Tue, Fri, Sat; bands 6pm Wed, Thur, Sun). Tables outdoors (3, pavement).* **Map p286 G26.**

Bullet
147 Kentish Town Road, NW1 8PB (7485 6040/ www.bulletbar.co.uk). Camden Town tube/Kentish Town tube/rail. **Open** 7pm-midnight Mon-Wed; 7pm-1am Thur; 7pm-2am Fri, Sat; 6pm-midnight Sun. **Admission** £3-£5 Mon-Fri; £5 after 9pm Sat; free-£3 Sun. **Credit** MC, V. Cocktail bar
There's something quite surreal about Bullet. With its deep red walls, chrome bar stools, black leather sofas and (slightly '80s) cocktail lounge-feel, it doesn't seem to belong at the seedy end of Kentish Town High Street, huddled next to Costcutters. The space too is a surprise – this place is vast. On our last visit, a guitar-strumming trustafarian was signally failing to pull in the crowds for the Sunday night music session; the nearby Abbey Tavern, by contrast, was packed. New management bodes well for the musical offerings, however; the charming, shaggy-haired Armenian owner has big plans for the place, including more European jazz. Although this is primarily a cocktail joint, the choice of beers is pretty decent, though the wine list offers just two reds and two whites by the glass. *Disabled: toilet. Music (bands 7pm Mon, Tue, Thur, Fri; acoustic/open mic 7pm Wed; DJ 7pm Sat; musicians 7pm Sun; free). Tables outdoors (5, garden).* **Map p286 J26.**

Camden Arms
1 Randolph Street, NW1 0SS (7267 9829/www.the camdenarms.com). Camden Town tube. **Open** noon-11pm Mon, Tue, Sun; noon-11.30pm Wed, Thur; noon-

midnight Fri, Sat. **Food served** noon-3pm Tue; noon-3pm, 6-9pm Wed-Fri; noon-5pm Sat, Sun. **Credit** AmEx, DC, MC, V. Pub
The purple lights illuminating the Camden Arms' black and silver façade provide a welcome beacon for intrepid drinkers who make the effort to seek it out – this place marks the furthest outpost of the pub-bar scene in this part of Camden. From the quote-etched tables exhorting you to kick back and relax ('I believe we were put on earth to fart around' – Kurt Vonnegut), to the giant hexagonal bar stocked with spirits, it's a relaxed spot for a tipple or two. Seating could be more comfortable, however, while San Miguel is the most adventurous beer you'll get on tap. Food has improved considerably since our last visit, and there's a pleasant beer garden for summer day lounging. Historically minded drinkers may wish to ask about the pub's claim that it was the site of Britain's last fatal duel in 1843. *Disabled: toilet. Function room. Restaurant. Tables outdoors (14, garden; 6, pavement).* **Map p286 J26.**

★ Crown & Goose
100 Arlington Road, NW1 7HP (7485 8008). Camden Town tube. **Open** 11am-1am Mon-Thur, Sun; 11am-2am Fri, Sat. **Food served** noon-3pm, 6-10pm Mon-Sat; noon-9pm Sun. **Credit** MC, V. Gastropub
On a quiet side street off Camden High Street, this lovely little pub feels deliciously out of the way. With dark green-painted panelling, glimmering candlelight and an open fire on chilly nights, it's delightfully old-fashioned and romantic – especially when bar staff close the shutters towards the end of the evening. To the rear, the tiny kitchen prepares simple but seriously good food, including very superior steaks, sausage and mash and tapas-style sharing plates. You'll find Caffrey's, Heineken, Kronenbourg, San Miguel, Leffe, Aspall Suffolk Cyder, Guinness and Guinness Extra Cold on tap. The wine list, meanwhile, offers four reds and fours whites by the glass, all under £3.40. What's not to like? *Babies and children admitted (until 9pm, dining only). Function room. Tables outdoors (4, pavement).* **Map p286 J1.**

Cuban
Unit 23, Stables Market, Chalk Farm Road, NW1 8AH (7424 0692/www.thecuban.co.uk). Camden Town or Chalk Farm Road tube. **Open/food served** 10am-1am Mon-Thur; 10am-2am Fri, Sat; 10am-midnight Sun. **Credit** MC, V. Bar
The obligatory portrait of Che Guevara gazes out over Cuban's cavernous, bare-brick interior – though what he makes of the more eccentric design touches (random pink flamingos and empty birdcages) is anyone's guess. There's time to ponder the question as you wait for your drink – cocktail-mixing is taken seriously by the attentive, black-clad barmen, and can be on the slow side. No complaints about the quality of the finished article, though, and there's a commendable choice of classic cocktails and more outré fruity concoctions, as well as a varied selection of tapas and main courses to accompany them. Wicker chairs and wooden tables add a vaguely colonial feel, while diner-style red booths line the wall; in summer, the doors are thrown open and the party spills on to the outdoor tables. *Babies and children welcome. Bar available for hire. Disabled: toilet. Music (bands 4pm Sun; DJ 7pm Fri, Sat; both free). Tables outdoors (11, pavement). TVs.* **Map p286 H26.**

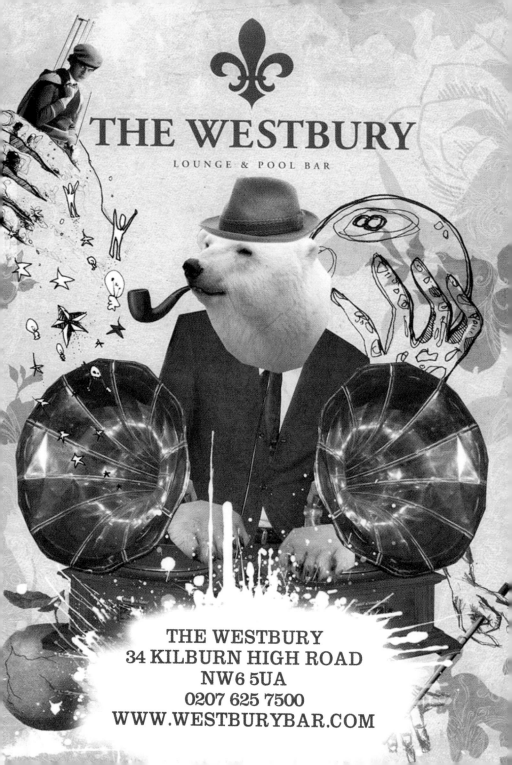

THE WESTBURY

LOUNGE & POOL BAR

THE WESTBURY
34 KILBURN HIGH ROAD
NW6 5UA
0207 625 7500
WWW.WESTBURYBAR.COM

Dublin Castle

*94 Parkway, NW1 7AN (7485 1773/www.bugbear
bookings.com). Camden Town tube.* **Open** noon-1am
Mon-Thur; noon-2am Fri-Sun. **No credit cards.**
Music pub

The Dublin Castle pulls off a good impression of authentic
dinginess – if you don't look too closely you really feel like
you're in a sleazy rock joint. Actually, on closer inspection,
it's clean, neat and thoroughly respectable. But don't let that
put you off: this Parkway institution has genuine cachet in
these parts, putting on a packed roster of up-and-coming
bands in its back room. While it can boast about having been
a springboard for Blur and Madness and owns a heroically
rock-heavy jukebox, it's the new blood that punters come
for; more recent acts include the View and Little Man Tate.
Don't come expecting a seat – the bands and loyal locals
ensure a busy night every day of the week.
*Babies and children admitted (until 6pm). Games
(fruit machine). Jukebox. Music (indie/rock bands
8.30pm nightly; admission £4.50-£6).* **Map p286 H1.**

Enterprise

*2 Haverstock Hill, NW3 2BL (7485 2659). Chalk Farm
tube.* **Open** 11am-11pm Mon-Sat; noon-10.30pm Sun.
Food served noon-8pm daily. **Credit** MC, V. Pub

With its battered wooden panelling, beat-up tables and
nicotine-yellow walls, the decor here is best described as
lived-in. It's the perfect antidote to anodyne gastropubs,
resisting the usual gilt mirrors and leather sofas in favour
of a comfortable clutter of seemingly random bric-a-brac:
model ships and fiddles, old pots and portraits, plus a statue
of Oscar Wilde. Large groups of twentysomethings and
lone older drinkers seem equally at home here; fuelled by
Caffrey's, Früli, London Pride and Carling, a hum of chat
rises above the familiar strains of the Beatles and the Arctic
Monkeys. The back area is the cosiest spot, with its open
fire, bookshelves and fairy lights; upstairs, there's a lively
line-up of comedy nights.
*Babies and children admitted (until 7pm). Comedy (8pm
Mon, Wed, Sun, closed Aug; £4-£5). Function room.
Tables outdoors (4, pavement). TV.* **Map p286 G26.**

★ Fifty-Five NEW

*31 Jamestown Road, NW1 7DB (7424 9054/www.
fiftyfivebar.co.uk). Camden Town tube.* **Open** 5pm-
12.30am Mon-Fri; noon-12.30am Sat, Sun. **Happy
hour** 6-8pm daily. **Credit** MC, V. Cocktail bar

Do keep up! Bar guides need to be published annually just
to stay abreast of the comings and goings at 31 Jamestown
Road, Lush having recently gone the way of Blakes
before it. Independent outfit Fifty-Five has now grasped
the poisoned chalice, and has had the sense to fill this space
to the brim with 150 expertly mixed cocktails: a point of
difference in an area famed for scuzzy pubs. Perhaps the
misleading name (it's not at No.55) is a way of distancing
the bar from its predecessors. Whatever, Fifty-Five thoroughly deserves to succeed; it's worth digging out a shirt
just to spend happy hour (6-8pm daily) here. If this is the
Manhattanisation of London, we like it.
*Bar available for hire. Function room. Tables outdoors
(13, pavement).* **Map p286 H1.**

Gilgamesh NEW

*Stables Market, Chalk Farm Road, NW1 8AH (7482
5757/www.gilgameshbar.com).* **Open/food served**
6pm-2.30am Mon-Thur; noon-2.30am Fri-Sun. **Credit**
AmEx, DC, MC, V. Bar

Flask. *See p212.*

Inspired by the Babylonian epic of King Gilgamesh, this
is an opulent, theatrical temple to excess. The scale is
breathtaking, from the splendid mosaic-inlaid bar to the
huge sphinxes that stare implacably out on the embossed
or embellished surfaces: intricate hand-carved wall panels
depict ancient battles, pillars are inset with polished stones,
and the immense carved tree that stretches around the
sweeping entrance staircase has to be seen to be believed.
The adjoining eating area is equally extravagant, with a
retractable glass ceiling for open-air dining in summer. It feels
a world away from the market below – grab a table by the
floor-to-ceiling windows to enjoy the surreal contrast. Eye-
wateringly expensive cocktails are blended with consum-
mate skill and taste as divine as they look.
Function room. Music (DJs 7pm Sat; free).
Map p286 H26.

Grand Union NEW

*102-104 Camden Road, NW1 9EA (7485 4530/www.
grandunioncamden.co.uk). Camden Town tube/Camden
Road rail.* **Open** noon-11.30pm Mon-Thur; noon-1.30am
Fri, Sat; noon-11pm Sun. **Food served** noon-3pm, 6-
10pm Mon-Sat; noon-8pm Sun. **Credit** AmEx, MC, V. Bar

Formerly the Mac Bar and now part of a small chain, the
Union fulfils every aspirational north London pub cliché:
battered second-hand furniture, dark floorboards, chocolate-
brown walls, mismatched bric-a-brac-chic lamps and table
football are all here. Yet it manages to be a warm, inviting
and loungey drinking hole, and the location is great – just

good sign when the staff have beer bellies, and there are a fair few behind the bar here. But most importantly there are smiles.
Babies and children admitted (before 7pm). Jukebox. Tables outdoors (4, patio and roof terrace). **Map p286 H26**.

Lock Tavern
35 Chalk Farm Road, NW1 8AJ (7482 7163/www.lock-tavern.co.uk). Chalk Farm tube. **Open** noon-midnight Mon-Thur; noon-1am Fri, Sat; noon-11pm Sun. **Food served** noon-3pm, 5-10pm Mon-Fri; noon-5pm, 6-9pm Sat, Sun. **Credit** MC, V. Pub/DJ bar
The beautiful people of north London continue to flock to this self-proclaimed 'Tarted Up Boozer'. Whether they come for the impressive DJ line-up, all-engulfing black leather sofas or delicious Square Pies we don't know, but come they do, either to stay for the duration or as a stop-off en route to the Barfly. Inside, bare-brick walls are lit by unexpectedly imaginative lighting (check out the fireplace) and there's ample alfresco drinking space – enjoy your pint of Staropramen, Amstel or Früli in the garden-patio out back, or up on the balcony area with views across to Camden Market. It's a fashionable joint, and yes, the bar staff dress like a cross between Dickensian street urchins and the Clash – but there isn't an inch of attitude.
Music (DJs 7pm Thur-Sat; 3pm Sun; free). Tables outdoors (4, roof terrace; 12, garden). TV (projector). **Map p286 H26**.

Lockside Lounge
75-89 West Yard, Camden Lock Place, NW1 8AF (7284 0007/www.locksidelounge.com). Camden Town tube. **Open** noon-midnight Mon-Thur, Sun; noon-1am Fri, Sat. **Food served** noon-9pm daily. **Credit** AmEx, MC, V. Bar
To see this place at its best, drop in for a Pimm's or a beer or two on a sunny afternoon. The tables and wooden decking overlooking Camden Market's West Yard and canal are the perfect place to loiter while day turns into night, watching backpack-toting tourists, rainbow-clad hippies and multi-pierced punks milling below. Inside, the bar is narrow but lofty, with a boathouse-meets-attic feel; it's let down by bland, slightly contrived decor (Ikea-esque furniture and uninspired artwork) and, on our last midweek visit, relentlessly pounding dance music. Thankfully, the drinks menu is more inventive, with a tremendous range of draught and bottled beers that includes Kronenbourg Blanc, Duvel and Old Speckled Hen.
Babies and children admitted (until 7pm). Disabled: toilet. Games (arcade machine). Music (DJs 7pm Fri-Sun; free). Tables outdoors (10, terrace). **Map p286 H26**.

★ Lord Stanley
51 Camden Park Road, NW1 9BH (7428 9488). Camden Town tube/Camden Road rail then 29, 253 bus. **Open** 10am-11pm Mon-Thur; 10am-midnight Fri, Sat; 10am-10.30pm Sun. **Food served** noon-3pm, 6.30-10pm Mon-Thur; noon-3pm, 6.30-10.30pm Fri; noon-4pm, 6.30-10.30pm Sat; noon-4pm, 6.30-9.30pm Sun. **Credit** AmEx, DC, MC, V. Pub
Once you're ensconced at a ramshackle wooden table – or better still, on one of the tatty but much coveted leather sofas – this is the kind of place where day segues into evening with dangerous ease. There's a convivial buzz: beardy intellectuals rub shoulders with vintage-chic girls and louche youths in skinny cords, while regulars hold

up the road from the tube, but removed from the hustle and hassles of the main drag. It's ultra-urban, with huge windows overlooking a busy junction, but excellent soundproofing ensures that as you sip a glass of wine (from the five reds and six whites available by the glass) or glug back a bottle of Budvar or pint of Kronenbourg while watching car lights swooping past, you feel blissfully removed from the ebb and flow of city life outside.
Babies and children admitted (until 7pm). Bar available for hire. Music (DJs 9pm Thur-Sat). Tables outdoors (18, pavement). TVs (big screen). **Map p286 J26**.

Hawley Arms NEW
2 Castlehaven Road, NW1 8QU (7428 5979). Camden Town tube. **Open** noon-midnight Mon-Thur, Sun; noon-1am Fri, Sat. **Food served** noon-8pm Mon-Sat; noon-6pm Sun. **Credit** MC, V.
Turn off Chalk Farm Road at the giant poster of Pete Doherty and you risk bumping into the real thing at this towering Camden boozer topped off with a snug roof garden. But don't let that put you off; the Hawley Arms is as homely as it is trendy, with nostalgic childhood tat (Tomy robots, mammoth jars of liquorice allsorts) nestled alongside dedications from the likes of Razorlight and Pelé. Football and music are the pub's twin preoccupations, but there's a strong selection of draught ales (Old Speckled Hen, Olde Trip, Abbot) and enough carb-laden comfort food to tackle the most stubborn hangover and still leave you change for the jukebox. It's always a

North

court at the gleaming, horseshoe-shaped bar over a wordlessly replenished pint. Despite a preponderance of good shoes and directional haircuts among the trendier clientele, this remains an unpretentious neighbourhood boozer, so there's minimal posing and preening. Draught offerings range from Adnams to Staropramen and the wine list is nicely chosen; the food is great, if pricey. Get here early if you can – latecomers invariably end up at the tiny table by the gents.
Babies and children admitted. Function room. Tables outdoors (10, garden; 5, pavement).

Monkey Chews
*2 Queen's Crescent, NW5 4EP (7267 6406/www.
monkeychews.com). Chalk Farm tube.* **Open** 5-11pm Mon-Thur; 5pm-1am Fri; 3pm-1am Sat; noon-10.30pm Sun. **Food served** 5-11pm Mon-Sat; noon-10pm Sun. **Credit** MC, V. Pub
'Happy Lounging' is the message printed at the bottom of receipts here, and that's exactly what you'll find all week in this endearingly ramshackle drinking den. Try and pretend you're a local as you sink into one of the careworn chesterfields – Monkey Chews is one of the area's best-kept secrets, with a cunning frosted-windows-and-bouncer-combo doing little to recommend the place to the outside world. Inside, things couldn't be more cosy: the womb-like decor and friendly staff make it an ideal rainy day hideout, although the toilets could do with a new loo brush (actually, a door would be a start). There's Grolsch, Red Stripe and Leffe on tap, and those wishing to explore the bar's vague kung fu theme can sample a Hong Kong Bong cocktail. Acoustic bands liven midweek evenings; DJs move in at weekends.
Babies and children admitted (until 9pm). Function room. Games (quiz machine). Music (acoustic band 9pm Wed, Thur; DJs 9pm Fri, Sat; free). Tables outdoors (5, pavement). TV (big screen, satellite). **Map p286 G25**.

Quinn's
*65 Kentish Town Road, NW1 8NY (7267 8240).
Camden Town tube.* **Open/food served** 11am-midnight Mon-Wed, Sun; 11am-2am Thur-Sat. **Credit** AmEx, MC, V. Pub
You can't miss Quinn's: it has a lurid blue and yellow paintjob that closely resembles Leeds United's away kit. Fortunately, the drinks selection is every bit as dazzling: there are approximately 20 German and 50 Belgian beers (for £6 we shared a 75cl bottle of Belgian L'Angelus, recent winner of a gold medal in Paris, apparently). That's before you've even started on the draught ales, which include Titanic and Kookaburra. Given the bewildering choice, it's helpful that the epic handwritten menu divides grog into Lambic (dry, cidery beer from the Pajottenland region of Belgium), Blonde, Red and Dark. It's testament to the enduring quality of the Quinn's experience that a fair proportion of its customers are resolutely grey-haired.
Babies and children admitted. Tables outdoors (20, garden). TV (big screen, satellite). **Map p286 J26**.

Torquil's Bar NEW
Roundhouse, Chalk Farm Road, NW1 8EH (0870 389 9920/www.roundhouse.org.uk). Chalk Farm tube. **Open/food served** 11am-11pm Mon-Sun. **Credit** MC, V. Bar
Before being converted into a theatre in the 1960s, Chalk Farm's Roundhouse was a gin store. Appropriate, then, that with the opening of Torquil's Bar, the relaunched arts space should have an impressive watering hole. Despite sounding like something out of *Jeeves and Wooster* (it's

actually named after the philanthropist who kick-started the venue's reinvention), Torquil's is an uncompromisingly modern affair, occupying the first floor of the building's new glass and steel outer rim. The view from the massive patio-cum-car park is classic north London, from the distant serenity of Primrose Hill to the flashing neon of Marathon Kebabs across the street. Compulsory plastic tumblers feel a bit naff, but the bar is intended primarily to service a sudden influx of interval drinkers. It's too good to be kept just for them.
Babies and children welcome: high chairs. Bar available to hire. Disabled: toilets. Function room. Tables outdoors (15, terrace). **Map p286 G26**.

Also in the area...
Camden Tup *2-3 Greenland Place, NW1 0AP (7482 0399).* Branch. **Map p286 J1**.
Cottons *55 Chalk Farm Road, NW1 8AN (7485 8388/www.cottons-restaurant.co.uk).* This cosy restaurant-attached bar stocks over 150 rums and is invariably packed. **Map p286 H26**.

Crouch End

Aanya Wine Bar NEW
29 Park Road, N8 8TE (8342 8686/www.aanya.co.uk). Finsbury Park tube/rail then W7 bus. **Open/food served** noon-3pm, 5.30-11pm Mon-Thur; noon-3pm, 5.30pm-midnight Thur, Fri; noon-midnight Sat; noon-10.30pm Sun. **Credit** MC, V.
Inside Aanya, there's little to suggest its speciality is tapas-style Indian snacks. With red rattan sofas set along cream walls and pebble-dashed panels, the interior is pure chic wine bar, though we were puzzled by some of the decorative flourishes – notably a set of giant test tubes filled with corks. The wine list is a tad under-ambitious, and most offerings are only available by the bottle – though the owners assured us that the by-the-glass count was soon to be upped to 30. Such quibbles aside, the food is good; well-off thirtysomethings happily devoured plates of grilled swordfish, lamb keema biriyani and tandoori prawns. The sleek black slab of a bar sports a respectable selection of spirits and bottled beers (Leffe, Tiger, Peroni, Asahi).
Babies and children admitted (daytime). Booking advisable dinner Thur-Sat. Restaurant available for hire.

Banners
21 Park Road, N8 8TE (8348 2930/www.banners restaurant.co.uk). Finsbury Park tube/rail then W7 bus. **Open** 9am-11.30pm Mon-Thur; 9am-midnight Fri; 10am-midnight Sat; 10am-11pm Sun. **Food served** 9am-11.30pm Mon-Thur; 9am-midnight Fri; 10am-4pm, 5pm-midnight Sat; 10am-4pm, 5-11pm Sun. **Credit** MC, V. Bar
Its cluttered Tex-Mex interior, dotted with rams' skulls, flags, movie posters and branded T-shirts, may recall Planet Hollywood, but there's nothing corporate about this sweet little bar and eaterie. The kooky young professionals all seemed to be having a blast, munching on a global array of dishes (Malay pumpkin curry, jerk chicken) – the licence dictates that if you want to drink something alcoholic, you must spend at least £3.50 on food. A delightfully diverse drinks menu includes bottled beers from Brazil, Lapland and, er, Lancashire, as well as Cruzcampo and Leffe on tap, along with an extensive

Charles Lamb. *See p214.*

cocktail menu (£5.25). If you're venturing in during the day, be prepared to dodge the kids, as the venue becomes a yummy mummy hangout and informal crèche. *Babies and children admitted. Booking advisable. TV.*

★ Harringay Arms
153 Crouch Hill, N8 9QH (8340 4243). **Open** noon-1am Mon-Sat; noon-midnight Sun. **Food served** noon-3pm Mon-Fri. **Credit** MC, V. Pub
There are local pubs, and then there are *local* pubs. This wee treat of a boozer falls into the latter category, thanks to its pre-gentrification crowd – who no doubt can all remember Crouch End before the advent of yummy mummies. The 1950s-era decor helps too. Flimsy tables topped with plastic ashtrays, a stone-rimmed gas fire and wood-panelled walls resplendent with china plates and photos of Irish literary greats form the perfect stamping ground for the throng of old lags and scruffy intellectuals vociferously putting the world to rights. They're mainly supping ales (Courage and Bombardier), while the unexceptional lager options includes Foster's and Kronenbourg. And this being an Irish-run pub, they pour a mean Guinness.
Games (darts, fruit machine). No piped music or jukebox. Quiz (9pm Tue; £1). Tables outdoors (4, garden). TV (satellite).

Queen's
26 Broadway Parade, N8 9DE (8340 2031). Finsbury Park tube/rail then W3, W7 bus. **Open** 11am-midnight Mon-Sat; noon-midnight Sun. **Food served** noon-10.30pm daily. **Credit** AmEx, MC, V. Gastropub
The mammoth size of Queen's could easily make it an unwelcoming prospect, but it has enough personal touches to ensure its well-heeled local customers have a gastropub they can be proud of. A tasteful makeover in 2005 scrubbed up the ornate plasterwork ceiling, wood panelling and beautiful stained-glass windows, and left the wrought-iron shutters and tiled entrance intact. The mostly cheery staff dole out Bombardier, Eagle IPA and guest ales, as well as gastropub staples Erdinger and Leffe, from the large central wooden hub of a bar. There's also a helpfully descriptive wine menu and a mix of traditional cocktails starting at £5.50 (non-alcoholic concoctions are £3.50). The rather grand dining room serves tarted-up renditions of pub-food favourites from its shiny open kitchen.
Tables outdoors (10, garden).

Harringay

Oakdale Arms
283 Hermitage Road, N4 1NP (8800 2013). Manor House tube. **Open** noon-11pm Mon-Sat; noon-10.30pm Sun. **Credit** MC, V. Pub
The second-hand books lining the window ledges at the Oakdale probably don't get read very often, due to the myriad entertainments on offer. Air-hockey in the main bar might be a lively way to start, followed by pool, darts, chess or table football in the spacious games room at the back. For those traditional souls who prefer to simply stick to the beer, there's Pegasus and Mammon from the Milton Brewery, and usually four other real ales on tap. And there's the beer garden to retreat to in summer – which is perhaps when the paperbacks might come in handy.
Games (air hockey, board games, chess, darts, pool, table football). Quiz (8.30pm Thur; free). Tables outdoors (8, garden). TV (big screen, satellite).

★ Salisbury Hotel
1 Grand Parade, Green Lanes, N4 1JX (8800 9617). Manor House tube then 29 bus. **Open** 5pm-midnight Mon-Wed; 5pm-1am Thur; 5pm-2am Fri; noon-2am Sat; noon-11.30am Sun. **Food served** 6-10.30pm Mon-Fri; noon-11pm Sat; 1-7pm Sun. **Credit** MC, V. Gastropub
Once upon a time the Salisbury was a fairly rough and ready affair, but a makeover has enabled this majestic Victorian boozer to finally realise its potential. Worn carpets and tired fittings have been replaced with black and white floor tiles, stripped wood, potted plants and plush drapes, which complement the period wall frescoes and cut-glass mirrors nicely. At the back, the marble-clad exposed kitchen affirms the pub's new-found gastro credentials, dishing out upmarket pub grub along the lines of bangers and mash and own-made beefburgers (£6.95 upwards). Here too are black leather sofas to lounge on (on Sundays this area is often given over to jazz musicians). There's ESB, London Pride and Discovery at the handsome bar, alongside Litovel Czech lager and Fuller's Organic Honey Dew on tap. Long may it continue.
Babies and children admitted. Disabled: toilet. Function room. Music (jazz 8.30pm Sun mthly; phone to check). Quiz (8.45pm Mon; £1). TV.

Highgate

Angel Inn
37 Highgate High Street, N6 5JT (8347 2921). Archway or Highgate tube. **Open** noon-midnight Mon-Thur; 11am-midnight Fri, Sat; 11am-11pm Sun. **Food served** noon-4pm, 5-10pm Mon-Fri; 11am-10pm Sat; 11am-9pm Sun. **Credit** MC, V. Pub
Perhaps the headless angel statue perched above the doorway is a posh Highgate signal for the punters to join in by getting legless. If so, this is clearly a popular spot in which to make the effort, given the boisterous throng of (Highgate) Village People inside. The decor is a contemporary pick 'n' mix of influences – dark wood panelling, stylishly outsized tassled lampshades, calming fish tank, jar of pickled eggs as retro nod. So, looking good on the surface. Shame, then, about the lousy dance music played just loud enough to be irritating, and beer (both the Wychwood guest beer and an Adnams) so bad as to be undrinkable. Best perhaps to stick to the continental draught offerings like Schneider Weisse and Früli or bottled lagers (Peroni, Becks and Tiger). Or perhaps try the excellent Flask nearby.
Disabled: toilet. Quiz (9pm Wed; £1). Tables outdoors (3, pavement). TV (big screen).

Boogaloo
312 Archway Road, N6 5AT (8340 2928/www.the boogaloo.org). Highgate tube. **Open** 6pm-midnight Mon-Wed; 6pm-1am Thur; 6pm-2am Fri; 2pm-2am Sat; 2pm-midnight Sun. **Credit** MC, V.
The jukebox is excellent and the irregular DJ nights are an understandable draw, but this music-themed boozer has built its reputation on the B-list indie celebs who drink in it. Shane MacGowan props up the bar nightly when he's in London, while the roster of live music occasionally features Pete Doherty, mumbling indistinctly into a microphone before toppling headlong into the gutter. Both are old pals of owner Gerry O'Boyle from his days running Filthy McNasty's, a pub that managed to retain a more democratic vibe than this less characterful but by no means

North

Once a simple local boozer, situated opposite a picturesque square, the Albion was snapped up by new owners last October, and those popping in for a half of Mild and a few games on the Bandit will now be forced to take their business elsewhere. Going straight for the monied Islingtonite jugular, this place is now a posh gastropub with cushy armchairs, pale-green walls and hulking oak tables. The outside seating and delightful beer garden remain, but the drinks menu focuses more heavily on wines and cocktails than the lagers and bitters of yore. Typical British gastro fare adorns the menu, albeit with the curious addition of a whole suckling pig, which must be ordered 48 hours ahead, costs £195 and feeds ten. Yum.
Babies and children admitted (weekends). Disabled: toilet. Tables outdoors (5, patio; 20, garden). **Map p287 N1.**

Anam
3 Chapel Market, N1 9EZ (7278 1001/www.anambar. com). Angel tube. **Open** 6pm-midnight Tue, Wed; 5pm-2am Thur-Sat; noon-11.30pm Sun. **Credit** MC, V. DJ bar
Tucked away on Chapel Market, this swish little DJ joint prides itself on being London's first Irish cocktail bar. It's a dizzying proposition, but rest assured – it's not a case of Guinness and cream soda with an umbrella on top. The cocktail list is, in fact, a thing of real beauty, divided into two subsections which speak for themselves: Heaven and Hell. While the eclectic mix of music played on the many DJ nights puts it in competition with the nearby Salmon & Compass, Anam offers a slightly more grown-up, refined atmosphere, with its crepuscular deep-red interior, comfy furniture and large fish tank. There are two small but perfectly formed floors, and just the right amount of room for those looking to have a bit of a jig. Bouncers will insist on smart-ish dress come the weekend.
Basement bar available for hire. Disabled: toilet. Dress: smart casual. Music (DJs 8pm Thur-Sat). **Map 9 N2.**

Angelic
57 Liverpool Road, N1 0RJ (7278 8433). Angel tube. **Open** noon-midnight Mon-Thur, Sun; noon-1pm Fri, Sat. **Food served** noon-10pm Mon-Sat; noon-9.30pm Sun. **Credit** MC, V. Pub
There's much to enjoy at this charming, airy pub, which is a relaxed spot to hang out in by day or night. The decor has an artful shabby-chic feel – you can almost imagine they'd employed people to age the tables that perfectly scuffed look, with similarly battered sofas and bookshelves dotted about the bar. Bombardier and San Miguel are on tap, and a decent wine list starts at £13 for a bottle of house plonk. Staff are generally attentive and pleasant, even down to the permanently ensconced doorman, who'll turf you out at the end of the evening in the most courteous way imaginable. And whoever came up with the idea of playing live comedy in the loos – buy that man a drink.
Babies and children admitted (until 6pm). Disabled: toilet. Games (board games). TV (big screen). **Map p287 N2.**

Bull
100 Upper Street, N1 0NP (7354 9174). Angel tube. **Open** noon-midnight Mon-Wed, Sun; noon-1am Thur, Fri; 11am-1am Sat. **Food served** noon-10pm Mon-Fri; 11am-10pm Sat; noon-9.30pm Sun. **Credit** AmEx, MC, V. Pub/Bar
Slap bang in the centre of Upper Street, the Bull is a great place for a quick-one-on-the-way as well as for a relaxed afternoon's drinking (especially when the in-house DJ is

spinning jazz tunes on Saturday). As testament to the cheerful, constant bustle of the place, there's always someone running to the door so they can hear their mobile. The menu offers the usual array of gastro comfort food, including a mean Sunday roast, while the bar serves an impressive range of continental lagers and ales. The spiral staircase that famously sits in front of the entrance is the cause of many a drunken head-thwacking injury, but this is mere nitpicking.
Disabled: toilet. Games (board games, chess). Music (DJ 11am-3pm Sat; free). **Map p287 O1.**

Camden Head
2 Camden Walk, N1 8DY (7359 0851). Angel tube. **Open** noon-11pm Mon, Tue; noon-midnight Wed, Thur; noon-1am Fri, Sat; noon-10.30pm Sun. **Food served** noon-7pm daily. **Credit** MC, V. Pub
Just off the beaten track, amid the bijou trappings of Camden Passage, lies this popular local boozer, which attracts a predominantly alternative crowd. With its large, oval-shaped bar in the centre of the main saloon, manoeuvrability can sometimes be a little strained, with the constant refrain of 'could you just move your chair in a little?' echoing over the indie-rock jukebox. While the interior is a little grimy (the carpets look as if they've soaked up a few gallons of weak lager in their time), there's plenty of outside seating, regular comedy nights and an exceedingly cheap drinks menu (pint of lager: £2.90, bottle of house white: £11) in comparison with surrounding venues.
Babies and children admitted (until 6pm). Comedy (8.30pm nightly; £3-£5). Function room. Games (fruit machines, quiz machines). Jukebox. Tables outdoors (12, heated garden). TVs. **Map p287 O2.**

★ Charles Lamb NEW
16 Elia Street, N1 8DE (7837 5040/www.thecharles lambpub.com). Angel tube. **Open** 4-11pm Mon, Tue; noon-11pm Wed-Sat; noon-10.30pm Sun. **Food served** 6-9pm Mon, Tue; noon-3pm, 6-9pm Wed-Sat; noon-6pm Sun. Main courses £8-£12. **Credit** MC, V.
A gem of a pub consisting of two small rooms decorated in a down-home fashion, with fairy lights around the fireplace, framed maps and a notice saying 'Don't feed Mascha' (the cute, neckerchief-wearing pub dog). As a gastropub, it's at the no-nonsense end of the spectrum, with hearty food (fish pie, pork rillettes on toast) and plenty of bar snacks, ranging from crisps and pork scratching to jars of cockles and sausage rolls. A good selection of world beers (from the US and Belgium in particular) is sold alongside ales such as Fuller's Honey Dew, and a very decent selection of wines is sold by the glass, carafe and bottle. Staff are lovely, the atmosphere relaxed and the clientele a nicely varied bunch. Oh – and the loos are a cut above most pub facilities too.
Babies and children admitted. Bookings not accepted. Tables outdoors (6, pavement). **Map p287 O2.**

★ Colebrooke's
69 Colebrooke Row, N1 8AA (7226 7517/www. colebrookes.co.uk). Angel tube. **Open/food served** 11am-midnight Mon-Wed, Sun; 11am-1am Thur; 11am-2am Fri, Sat. **Credit** AmEx, MC, V. Wine bar
This teeny weeny wine bar tucked away off Essex Road is a very grown-up affair. Opened at the latter end of 2005, the living room-sized bar sits on the site formerly occupied by a pizzeria. There are some bottled beers, spirits and classic cocktails on offer, but the bulk of the drinks menu is made up of 30 or so wines – ranging in price from £15 to £45 a bottle – that complement two draught lagers

North

(Kronenbourg and San Miguel) and the antipasti-inspired sharing platters also served. Colebrookes is a very sweet and honest proposition, well suited to a quiet glass over a game of Scrabble or a romantic bottle-for-two. The only flaw we can see is the rather changeable nature of staff – sometimes falling over themselves to be helpful, at other times too concerned with their knitting to attend the bar. *Babies and children admitted (until 6pm). Bar available for hire. Games (board games). Music (classical solos 7pm Sun; DJs 8pm Sat; jazz band 8pm Wed; all free). Tables outdoors (4, pavement).* **Map p287 O2.**

Crown
116 Cloudesley Road, N1 0EB (7837 7107). Angel tube. **Open** noon-11pm Mon-Sat; noon-10.30pm Sun. **Food served** noon-3pm, 6-10pm Mon-Fri; noon-10pm Sat; noon-9pm Sun. **Credit** AmEx, MC, V. Gastropub
A pleasant Islington gastropub, with possibly more of an emphasis on the pub than the gastro. Still, there's a big open kitchen just off to the side where you can see your food being prepared, with a varied menu that changes daily and a mean roast dinner on Sundays. Mains hover around the £11 mark, with some imaginative veggie options. The atmosphere is convivial enough, with patrons mainly of the young professional sort snuggled into the trad interior. Beer-wise, there's well-kept Fuller's on tap, with a strong range of guest ales and some more unusual lagers (Kirin). Massive banqueting tables and lots of outside seating make this a good bet for larger parties. *Babies and children admitted (until 8pm). Games (board games). Tables outdoors (6, patio).* **Map 9 N1.**

Drapers Arms
44 Barnsbury Street, N1 1ER (7619 0348/www.the drapersarms.co.uk). Angel tube/Highbury & Islington tube/rail. **Open** noon-11pm Mon-Sat; noon-10.30pm Sun. **Food served** noon-3pm, 7-10pm Mon-Sat; noon-3pm, 6.30-9.30pm Sun. **Credit** AmEx, MC, V. Gastropub
While the peach walls, surfeit of flowers and some decidedly dodgy blown-up art prints would have traditional Pub Landlord types up in arms, there is a pleasingly genial, friendly feel to the Drapers. An impressive garden to the rear, lots of tables and huge windows in the front that let in plenty of daylight add to its allure. The daily-changing food menu, with an emphasis on fish and seafood dishes, is slightly on the expensive side for this type of place, averaging out at about £7 for starters and £15 for mains, but a good range of wines starts at £12 a bottle. There's a decent selection of beers and ales on tap too, including Speckled Hen and Courage Best, plus rotating guest ales. *Babies and children admitted (until 7pm unless dining). Tables outdoors (20, garden).* **Map p287 N1.**

Duchess of Kent
441 Liverpool Road, N7 8PR (7609 7104/www. geronimo-inns.co.uk). Highbury & Islington tube/rail. **Open** noon-11pm Mon-Thur, Sun; noon-midnight Fri, Sat. **Food served** noon-3pm, 7-10pm Mon-Thur; noon-3pm, 7-10.30pm Fri; noon-4pm, 7-10.30pm Sat; noon-4pm, 7-10pm Sun. **Credit** MC, V. Gastropub
This sleek gastropub really captures a snug living room atmosphere, with its low-slung velvet sofas positioned around roaring coal fires and a bar that's tucked away behind a menagerie of old-fashioned ornaments and plants. It's refreshingly clean as well, dispensing of that film of grime which other, lesser pubs seem to wear as a badge of honour. Friendly staff serve a good range of continental

lagers, weisse beers and bottled ales, with Adnams on draught. TV screens are unobtrusively dotted about the bar, showing rugby every Sunday. The food menu isn't huge, but with dishes like fish pie, veggie risotto and mini pasties, offers something for everyone, and is complemented with a well-above-average wine list. Dining tables are sparse though, so reservations are recommended. *Babies and children admitted (until 9pm). Booking advisable (dining). Disabled: toilet. Tables outdoors (13, pavement). TVs.* **Map p287 N25.**

★ Duke of Cambridge
30 St Peter's Street, N1 8JT (7359 3066/www.duke organic.co.uk). Angel tube. **Open** noon-11pm Mon-Sat; noon-10.30pm Sun. **Food served** 12.30-3pm, 6.30-10.30pm Mon-Fri; 12.30-3.30pm, 6.30-10.30pm Sat; 12.30-3.30pm, 6.30-10pm Sun. **Credit** AmEx, MC, V. Gastropub
Is it a pub or is it a restaurant? That's the question on everyone's lips. In our humble opinion, it triumphs as both, with a delicious choice of lagers and ales (from the St Peter's brewery), wines and food – all organic. At the front is a large, atmospheric saloon; to the rear, a traditional dining room. The crowd here tends to be on the mature side, and staff can be slightly snotty; it wasn't a pretty sight when we saw someone (shock horror!) try to order a pint of Grolsch. That's more than made up for by the quality of the beer, however. The refurbishment that occurred last March seemed to be little more than a new lick of paint – but really, why mess with a winning formula? *Babies and children welcome: children's portions; high chairs. Tables outdoors (5, pavement).* **Map p287 P2.**

Filthy McNasty's
68 Amwell Street, EC1R 1UU (7837 6067/www.filthy macnastys.com). Angel tube. **Open** noon-11pm Mon-Sat; noon-10.30pm Sun. **Food served** noon-3pm Mon-Fri. **Credit** MC, V. Music pub
This scuffed-up backstreet boozer is a haven for hard-drinking boho types, with bands playing Libertines-style alco- pop and plenty of spoken word and poetry events. Indeed, it's a place that seems to have been purpose-built for you to sit there in a tweed hat looking bummed out with a half of Red Stripe in your hand. Although there are lots of varieties of cheap beer, with revolving guest ales on tap and a distinct bias towards the Black Stuff, Filthy's is probably best known for its comprehensive selection of whiskies (it's a self-dubbed 'Whiskey Bar'). Many rare and expensive brands are finished off swiftly by the visiting musos and weathered locals, so act fast. *Children admitted (over 14yrs, until 6pm). Disabled: toilet. Function room. Music (bands, call for dates; free). Poetry readings (call for dates; free). Tables outdoors (7, pavement). TV (big screen).*

Hemingford Arms
158 Hemingford Road, N1 1DF (7607 3303). Caledonian Road tube/rail. **Open** 11am-11pm Mon-Sat; noon-10.30pm Sun. **Food served** noon-3pm, 6-10.30pm Mon-Fri; 6-10.30pm Sat; 12.30-4pm, 6-10pm Sun. **Credit** MC, V. Pub
Hidden behind a thick wall of ivy, this gorgeous little pub gains full marks for resisting the urge to tart itself up into yet another identikit gastropub. Instead, garishly painted mannequins and rusty old bikes hang from the ceiling, and a genial, unpretentious atmosphere prevails. It gets packed out in the evenings and at weekends, although there's plenty of seating around the edges; that said, it's

North

Colebrooke's. *See p214.*

the sort of place where standing up and rubbing shoulders with your fellow drinkers is all part of the experience. There's IPA, Adnams, Broadside and Brakspear Special, plus rotating guest beers and a staggering selection of lagers and bitters on draught. By sticking to the basics, the Hemingford Arms achieves a goal that many other pubs have left well and truly by the wayside: it's a fantastic place to get pissed in. Decent bands play here too. *Babies and children admitted (until 6pm). Games (fruit machine). Music (bands 9pm Mon, Fri-Sun; free). Quiz (9pm Thur; £1). Tables outdoors (6, pavement). TVs (satellite).*

Hen & Chickens Theatre Bar
109 St Paul's Road, N1 2NA (7704 7621/www. henandchickens.com). Highbury & Islington tube/rail. **Open** 5pm-midnight Mon-Wed; 5pm-1am Thur; noon-1.30am Fri, Sat; noon-midnight Sun. **Credit** MC, V. Theatre pub

As a destination for a spot of fringe theatre or some superlative stand-up comedy, the Hen & Chickens cannot be faulted. As a place to go for a quiet drink and a natter, it arguably doesn't measure up quite so well, with its slightly cramped saloon, foliage overkill and, on the night we visited, loud funky house blasting out from the speakers – perhaps a little inconsiderate, seeing as there were only about five people in there. On the plus side, beer is relatively cheap for the area, and there's a small and reasonably priced food menu (pizzas, panini, nachos and the like for a fiver). In short: if you're planning a trip to the Hen & Chickens, be sure that you're wearing your party shoes, or that you've bought a ticket to move on to the theatre upstairs.

Comedy (8pm Mon, Sun; £6-£7). Games (quiz machine). Theatre (eves Tue-Sat, box office 7704 2001; £6-£10). Tables outdoors (3, pavement). **Map p287 O25.**

Hope & Anchor
207 Upper Street, N1 1RL (7354 1312). Highbury & Islington tube/rail. Ground floor **Open** 11am-11pm Mon-Wed; 11am-1am Thur-Sat; noon-10.30pm Sun. **Food served** noon-4pm daily. *Basement* **Open** 8.30pm-1am Mon-Sat; 8pm-midnight Sun. *Both* **Credit** MC, V. Pub

The Hope & Anchor is the gentrified Islington equivalent of places like the Monarch or the Barfly. A great venue for bands looking to score their first gig, it's lovingly decorated with old vinyl and concert posters – and is distinctly less scuzzy than its Camden counterparts. The selection of beers and wines is somewhat rudimentary, however, with Speckled Hen on draught and a few unexciting lagers (Foster's, Grolsch). The fact that it gets rammed on weekends, coupled with a jukebox that is constantly pumping out late '90s indie rock, means it's not the greatest place to hold a conversation. But to test-run those new skinny jeans and look elegantly wasted with a pint of weak lager in your hand, it's near darn perfect. *Disabled: toilet. Games (fruit machines, pool, video games). Jukebox. Music (bands 8.30pm nightly; £4.50-£6; DJs 11pm Thur-Sat; free).* **Map p287 O26.**

House
63-69 Canonbury Road, N1 2DG (7704 7410/www.in thehouse.biz). Highbury & Islington tube/rail. **Open** 5-11pm Mon; noon-11pm Tue, Wed; 5pm-1.30am Thur-

Sat; noon-10.30pm Sun. **Food served** 6.30-10.30pm
Mon; 12.30-2.30pm, 6.30-10.30pm Tue-Fri; 12.30-3.30pm,
6.30-10.30pm Sat; 12.30-3.30pm, 6.30-9.30pm Sun.
Credit MC, V. Gastrobar
With its discernibly un-ergonomic bar stools, shiny white
walls and stock 'modern art' hanging on the walls, House
feels as if it's been constructed from the same blueprint as
the type of place you'd find in a club-class airport lounge.
A very classy cocktail menu (Tom Collins, yes; Slippery
Nipple, no) and the added option of munching oysters at
the bar makes this the kind of place you'd go to celebrate
a promotion or, indeed, inheritance. The vast wine list is
categorised by taste instead of country, and starts at £13.50
for a bottle of *vin de pays*, hurtling up to a cool £125 for
what's described as an 'extravaganza wine'. Food-wise,
the focus is well-executed classics (shepherd's pie, pan-
fried skate), with steeply priced breakfasts at the weekend.
*Babies and children admitted. Disabled: toilet. Music
(DJs 10pm Thur-Sat; free). Restaurant available for
hire. Tables outdoors (4, garden). TV (big screen).*
Map p287 O26.

★ Island Queen

87 Noel Road, N1 8HD (7704 7631). Angel tube.
Open noon-11pm Mon, Sun; noon-11.30pm Tue, Wed;
noon-midnight Thur-Sat. **Food served** noon-4pm,
6-10pm Mon-Thur; noon-10.30pm Fri, Sat; noon-10pm
Sun. **Credit** MC, V. Pub
An absolute gem of a pub, buried in an anonymous row
of terraced houses near the canal. Huge front windows
showcase the welcoming, high-ceilinged Victorian saloon,
complete with delicately etched glass and heavy velvet
drapes. Comfy sofas occupy the back room, and an
upstairs section can accomodate larger parties. With its
hum of indie rock and cheery buzz of conversation, the
Island Queen is a supremely relaxing spot. Staff are
super-attentive and knowledgeable, and there's a fine
selections of speciality beers (Früli, Leffe, Deuchars) and
well-kept guest beers on draught. The food menu isn't
vast, but what there is tends to be above-average pub
grub – roasts, fish and chips and the like. Tuesday's quiz
night is a hotly contested but genial affair.
*Babies and children admitted (until 7pm). Function room.
Quiz (8pm Tue; £1). Tables outdoors (4, pavement). TV.*
Map p287 O2.

Keston Lodge

*131 Upper Street, N1 1QP (7354 9535/www.
kestonlodge.com). Angel tube/Highbury & Islington
tube/rail.* **Open** noon-midnight Mon-Wed, Sun; noon-
1am Thur; noon-2am Fri, Sat. **Food served** noon-3pm,
5-10pm Mon-Fri; noon-10pm Sat, Sun. **Admission** £3
after 10.30pm Sat. **Credit** MC, V. DJ bar
With an aspirational clientele and exceedingly attractive
bar staff, you'd probably do well to scrub up a bit before
venturing into Keston Lodge. Decor is industrial chic: the
two-level space as shiny as the hair-dos of its monied
crowd. A wide selection of continental and speciality lagers
makes up for the lack of draught ales, and there's a decent
food menu, including Pie Minister pie dishes and a good
range of burgers. Arrive early if you're thinking of spending the evening here and want to secure a seat; you'll be
rewarded with some very pleasant table service. DJs raise
the volume from Thursday onwards.
*Babies and children admitted (until 6pm).
Disabled: toilet. Music (DJs 9pm Thur; 9.30pm
Fri, Sat; 8.30pm Sun). Tables outdoors (2, garden).*
Map p287 O1.

King's Head

*115 Upper Street, N1 1QN (7226 0364/www.kings
headtheatre.org). Angel tube/Highbury & Islington
tube/rail.* **Open** 11am-1am Mon-Thur; 11am-2am
Fri, Sat; noon-1am Sun. **Food served** *(pre-booked
theatre dinner only, £16 3 courses)* 7-8pm Tue-Sat.
No credit cards. Theatre pub
This is easily the most rowdy (in a good way; no sports on
TV or background music) pub on Upper Street – just try
walking past without attempting to peep through its constantly steamed-up windows to see what all the commotion
is about. Venture inside and you'll find old thesps propped
at the bar with customised pint pots, discussing the finer
points of Strindberg while the lively serving staff gamely
grind at a rickety old till to obtain their change. With a theatre upstairs and mugshots of the great and good adorning
the homely deep-red walls, many would argue that it's the
best place in the neighbourhood for a late drink, especially
with a good selection of modestly priced ales (Adnams,
Tetley and Wadworth among them) and a bargain three-
course dinner menu.
*Babies and children admitted (until 9pm). Bar
available for hire. Disabled: toilet. Function room.
Music (bands 10pm nightly; £3 after 10pm Fri, Sat).
Tables outdoors (2, pavement). Theatre (box office
7226 1916).* **Map p287 O1.**

Marquess Tavern

*32 Canonbury Street, N1 2TB (7354 2975).
Angel tube/Highbury & Islington tube/rail.* **Open**
noon-11pm Mon-Thur, Sun; noon-midnight Fri, Sat.
Food served noon-3pm, 6-10pm Mon-Fri; 12.30-
4pm, 6.30-10pm Sat; 12.30-5pm, 6.30-9pm Sun.
Credit AmEx, MC, V. Gastropub
Since winning Time Out's Best Gastropub award in 2006,
the Marquess has had an up-and-down year. Accolades
from some quarters have been countered by negative
reports elsewhere. We find it a charming place to drink:
the front bar has a warm caramel hue, with comfy seating and a preserved Victorian fireplace complementing
the grade II-listed horseshoe bar. Here, old men and
Islington twirties choose from the usual selection of
Young's draughts, plus around 40 bottled beers and an
impressive selection of whiskies. To the rear is a dining
room: dark oak tables, bright walls, a high ceiling and a
meat-heavy food menu that will send carnivores doolally.
This is where problems have occurred, erratic service and
repeatedly scored-out menu items being frequent complaints. Perhaps these are teething troubles, to be cor-
rected as the Marquess enters its second year. We hope so.
*Babies and children admitted (until 6pm). Restaurant
available for hire. Tables outdoors (6, patio).*
Map p287 P26.

Medicine Bar

*181 Upper Street, N1 1RQ (7704 9536/www.medicine
bar.net). Angel tube/Highbury & Islington tube/rail.*
Open 4pm-midnight Mon; 4pm-1am Tue-Thur;
4pm-2am Fri; noon-3am Sat; noon-midnight Sun.
Food served 4-11pm Mon-Thur; 4pm-9pm Fri, Sat;
noon-11pm Sun. **Admission** £4 after 10pm Fri, Sat.
Credit MC, V. DJ bar
Big velvet drapes cloister the front of Medicine Bar, while
its dimly lit interior is dominated by the ornate, rococo
decor. Being long and thin, the bar can be hard to navigate,
especially when DJs are playing (every night except
Monday and Tuesday). Back in the day, when it was
pitched as a non-commercial alternative to the chain pubs,

it stuck out as a true original. But now, with its hip crowd, loud funky beats and pricey drinks menu (Beck's, San Miguel and Guinness are on tap), it's hard to see what all the fuss is about. It can get painfully crowded of a weekend so be prepared to queue; a 'no ties' policy might be there to filter out Upper Street's (many) estate agents. *Function room. Music (DJs 8.30pm Wed-Sat). Tables outdoors (10, pavement).* **Map p287 O26.**

Mucky Pup
39 Queen's Head Street, N1 8NQ (7226 2572/ www.muckypup-london.com). Angel tube. **Open/food served** 4-11pm Mon-Thur; 4pm-1am Fri, Sat; noon-11pm Sun. **Credit** MC, V. Pub
This earthy, unpretentious boozer has a decent selection of beers, with Greene King IPA on tap alongside the usual lagers. Low, cushy sofas perfectly complement the predominantly laid-back clientele (and, often, their dogs – as the name would suggest, canine companions are very welcome here). There's a separate room for darts and pool, free Wi-Fi and a dinky courtyard out back for lazy summer afternoons. Another highlight is the pleasingly outré jukebox, well-stocked with 1970s avant rock and free of charge (so get in there early to hog some tunes). A nice bolt-hole from the somewhat frenetic pace of Upper Street. *Games (board games, darts, pool). Jukebox. Quiz (8.30pm Wed; £1.50). Tables outdoors (3, garden). Wi-Fi (free).* **Map p287 O2.**

Narrow Boat
119 St Peters Street, N1 8PZ (7288 0572). Angel tube. **Open** 11am-midnight Mon-Sat; noon-midnight Sun. **Food served** noon-3pm, 5-10pm Mon-Fri; noon-10pm Sat, Sun. **Credit** MC, V. Pub
A pub located on the edge of a canal sounds like fun – although the management has (probably quite sensibly) tempered the potential for waterside high jinks by only letting you enter the establishment at street level, and banning outside drinking after 10pm. Head inside and you'll find a fine pub with a quasi-nautical theme, lovely views over the canal and towpath, and an extremely welcoming atmosphere. Steaks and burgers make up the food menu, with some interesting beers on tap (Cruzcampo and Stiegl) as well as Adnams. If an acquaintance seems to be spending a long time in the loo, they're probably gripped by the hard-to-resist *Beano* comic strips pasted on the wall. *Babies and children admitted (until 8pm). Function room. Games (board games, chess, fruit machines). Music (Irish band 8.30pm Thur; free). Quiz (8.30pm Sun, £1). Restaurant. TV (big screen, satellite).* **Map p287 P2.**

New Rose NEW
84-86 Essex Road, N1 8LU (7226 1082/www.new rose.co.uk). Angel tube. **Open** noon-midnight Mon-Thur; noon-2am Fri, Sat; noon-10.30pm Sun. **Food served** noon-10pm Mon-Sat; noon-9pm Sun. **Credit** MC, V. **No credit cards.** Pub
Aesthetically, you'd struggle to pick the New Rose out of a line-up with its local rivals – it's the familiar melange of pale-green walls, exposed brickwork, oak furniture, leather seating and tea candles. Yet the pub has retained a swagger from its previous incarnation as 'proper' old man's boozer, the Half Moon. Divided into tiny subsections, it has plenty of alcoves and annexes to hide away in, while the bar dispenses a decent range of beers, including Staropramen and London Pride on tap. The food menu offers a splendid selection of pizzas and a great Sunday

roast. It gets packed on match days, but there is evidence of attempts to offset the laddish vibe – they were advertising a ladies' night when we visited. *Babies and children admitted (until 5pm). Music (DJs 7pm Fri, Sat; free). Tables outdoors (6, pavement). TVs (big screen).* **Map p287 P1.**

Northgate
113 Southgate Road, N1 3JS (7359 7392). Essex Road rail/21, 76, 141 bus. **Open** 5-11pm Mon; noon-11pm Tue-Thur; noon-midnight Fri, Sat; noon-10.30pm Sun. **Food served** 6.30-10.30pm Mon; noon-3pm, 6.30-10.30pm Tue-Fri; noon-4pm, 6.30-10.30pm Sat; noon-4pm, 6.30-9.30pm Sun. **Credit** MC, V. Gastropub
From its moderately scuzzy frontage, you might expect the Northgate to be a bit salt-of-the-earth inside. In fact, it's a smart gastropub, attracting well-heeled types who enjoy reading the *Independent* with a pint of ale and dish of gourmet nuts for company. The reliance on small four-seater tables heightens the feeling of being in a restaurant, as does a sprawling, nicely chosen wine list that ranges from £12.50 house wine up to £30 bottles. A chandeliered and white-walled dining room is elegantly sectioned off with a thick red velvet curtain, and attracts a loyal local following. Young, sprightly staff inject the place with a bit of pep, and the outdoor area is a pleasant spot on balmy evenings, with gas burners to take off the chill. *Babies and children admitted (patio, restaurant). Tables outdoors (10, patio).*

Old Queen's Head
44 Essex Road, N1 8LN (7354 9993/www.theoldqueens head.com). Angel tube. **Open** noon-midnight Mon-Thur, Sun; noon-2am Fri, Sat. **Food served** 6-11pm Mon-Thur; noon-7pm Sun. **Credit** MC, V. Pub
Queues often snake out of this popular Essex Road boozer and down the road, so popular it's become since being taken over and relaunched last year. Witness: even though there are two large bars over two floors (not to mention picnic tables at the front and a beer garden behind), it was too busy for us to nab a seat on a Wednesday night. The bar sells mainly lagers and spirits (the barmaid didn't know what a hand pump was), with a few speciality beers in bottled form and a workable wine list and food menu. It's difficult to put your finger on exactly what makes the Old Queen's Head such a hit – perhaps it's the twice-monthly bands, or the perverse fact that people love to join a queue. Either way, if it's an atmosphere you're after, this is the place. *Art exhibitions. Babies and children welcome (until 6pm). Function room. Music (acoustic band twice monthly; £2; DJs 9pm Fri, Sat; £4 after 10pm Fri, £4 after 9pm Sat). Tables outdoors (7, garden; 3, pavement). TV (satellite).* **Map p287 O1.**

Old Red Lion
418 St John Street, EC1V 4NJ (7837 7816/www.oldred liontheatre.co.uk). Angel tube. **Open** noon-midnight Mon-Thur; noon-1am Fri, Sat; noon-11pm Sun. **Food served** noon-3pm Mon-Fri. **Credit** MC, V. Theatre pub
Combining a laid-back and friendly local boozer with a 60-seat fringe theatre, this bustling Islington luvvie den is a great place to eavesdrop on stories about fallen stars of the stage and screen. The piano next to the bar has, we suspect, seen many a late-night, post-theatre singsong, but this place isn't geared solely towards arty types – a huge projection screen is brought out for major sporting events. An etched glass partition separates the saloon from the public bar, and there's a nice range of beers,

North

including Abbot Ale, London Pride, Adnams Broadside, Staropramen and Peetermans. A place worth turning your back on Upper Street for.
Babies and children admitted (if dining). Games (board games, fruit machine). Tables outdoors (4, patio). Theatre (Tue-Sun; £6-£12). TV (projector, satellite).

Rosemary Branch
2 Shepperton Road, N1 3DT (7704 2730/www. rosemarybranch.co.uk). Old Street tube/rail then 21, 76, 141. **Open** noon-midnight Mon-Thur; noon-1am Fri, Sat; noon-10.30pm Sun. **Food served** noon-3pm, 6-9.30pm Mon-Sat; noon-6pm Sun. **Credit** MC, V.
Theatre pub
In this era of super-sanitised gastropubs, a lick of grime will send many well-to-do folk bolting for the saloon doors. Not so with the Rosemary Branch, a spacious, bright and bustling boozer where grime equals character that you just can't put a price on. Scale models of fighter planes hang from the ceiling, flowers on the window sills add a touch of colour, and bench seating encourages friendly conversation. The beer selection is nicely skewed in favour of Czech and Belgian lagers, but there's also Früli and Leffe as well as a very decent wine list. If that wasn't enough, there's a 60-seat theatre, awesome jukebox and two weekly quizzes. Add in above-par pub grub from £6, and what more could you want?
Babies and children admitted. Function room. Games (board games). Jukebox. Quiz (9pm Tue, Thur; £1). Theatre (7.30pm Tue-Sat; £8-£10). Tables outdoors (6, patio). **Map p287 P1**.

Salmon & Compass
58 Penton Street, N1 9PZ (7837 3891/www.salmon andcompass.com). Angel tube. **Open** 4pm-2am Mon-Thur, Sun; 4pm-4am Fri, Sat. **Food served** 4-10pm daily. **Happy hour** 5-9pm Mon-Fri. **Admission** £3 after 9pm, £5 after 11pm Fri, Sat. **Credit** AmEx, MC, V. Bar
From the outside, you'd be forgiven for dismissing the Salmon & Compass as a stock old man's boozer, with its beige tiling, traditional nameplate and 'We sell Courage Ales' sign (they don't) on the front wall. The interior, however, is a different story, with its sleek, black lacquered tables, moody lighting and expensive-looking art deco wallpaper. At the far end of the bar lies a mammoth DJ stack, from whence a range of eclectic (mainly dance-oriented) music emanates on the regular club nights (Thursday to Saturday). Drinks are also a polished act, with mainly high-end lagers on tap (Staropramen, Beck's Vier), a large range of bottled speciality beers and a generous wine list. The crowd is generally young, clubby and raring to dance.
Function room. Games (board games). Music (DJs 8pm daily). Tables outdoors (5, pavement). TV (big screen, satellite).

25 Canonbury Lane
25 Canonbury Lane, N1 2AS (7226 0955/www.25 canonburylane.co.uk). Highbury & Islington tube/rail. **Open** 5-11pm Mon-Thur; 4-11pm Fri; noon-11pm Sat, Sun. **Food served** 6-10pm Mon-Thur. **Credit** MC, V. Bar
Tucked away just off Upper Street, this supremely trendy bar claims to have 'redefined Islington bar culture with its eclectic combination of old and new', while offering an 'understated atmosphere of decadent chic'. It all sounds a bit try-hard to us – though it is an undeniably elegant,

Marquess Tavern. *See p217.*

220 Time Out | Bars, Pubs & Clubs

intimate little spot for a drink and a spot of tapas. The cocktails and shooters menu is extensive, although draught offerings are more limited (Stella, Grolsch, Hoegaarden). With its opulent decor (gilded mirrors, extravagant flower arrangements and crystal chandeliers) and unfeasibly beautiful clientele, it can all seem slightly intimidating – and please, someone tell these people that wearing sunglasses inside is a definite faux pas.
Babies and children admitted (until 6pm). Tables outdoors (5, conservatory). **Map p287 O26.**

★ Warwick

45 Essex Road, N1 2SF (7688 2882/www.thewarwick bar.com). Angel tube. **Open** 5pm-midnight Mon-Thur; 5pm-1am Fri; 3pm-1am Sat; 3pm-midnight Sun. **Credit** MC, V. Pub

Purely because it doesn't have pale-green walls and stripped leather furniture (like every other pub on Essex Road), it could be argued that the Warwick is the best bar on the strip. There is a certain charm to the retro interior, which features miscellaneous movie ironica on the walls and chairs, tables and sofas that look as if they've been lovingly saved from the dump. There's also a 'world famous' pop quiz and a jukebox that doesn't only rotate the same two Kasabian and Killers albums. The selection of beers is fairly standard, though Baltika, Paulaner and San Miguel stand out, but an adventurous cocktail list offers some consolation. At the rear, a great space with its own bar is perfect to hire for private parties.
Bar available for hire. Disabled: toilet. Function room. Jukebox. Music (DJs 7pm Thur-Sun; free). Quiz (call for details). Tables outdoors (2, pavement). **Map p287 O1.**

Winchester

2 Essex Road, N1 8LN (7704 8789/www.thewinchester bar.co.uk). Angel tube. **Open** noon-midnight Mon-Wed; noon-2am Thur, Fri; 10am-3am Sat; 10am-11pm Sun. **Food served** noon-9.30pm Mon-Fri; 10am-9.30pm Sat; 10am-8.30pm Sun. **Credit** AmEx, DC, MC, V. Gastropub

Although it used to be more of a raucous joint, with DJ nights and drink deals, the Winchester (née Bar & Dining House) now shows little sign of its uncouth past. Neatly positioned tables, (purposely) dog-eared leather sofas and tea candles on every table see the venue stake its claim as a proper gastropub. Drinks now play second fiddle to a great food menu, which places the emphasis on sharing by proferring various styles of platter (meat, seafood, Greek). However, even though the Winchester's newfound classiness makes it very much a venue suited to couples looking to share a bottle of decent wine, there's still a DJ bar in the basement should the romance turn sour.
Babies and children admitted (until 6pm). Function room. Music (DJs 9pm Thur-Sat; free-£3). **Map p287 O1.**

Also in the area...

Bank of Friendship 224 Blackstock Road, N5 1EA (7288 9891). Time-worn, traditional pub with open fires, a dartboard, Pride and Courage on tap – and, inevitably, a fair number of Arsenal fans. Gets busy on match days.
Barnsbury 209-211 Liverpool Road, N1 1LX (7607 5519/www.thebarnsbury.co.uk). Above average locals' pub offering very decent sharing platters, draught ales and a fine choice of whiskies and other spirits.

North

Bar Lorca. *See p226.*

Bierodrome *173-174 Upper Street, N1 1XS (7226 5835).* Branch. Map p287 O26.
brb@the arc *Torrens Street, off City Road, EC1V 1NQ (7837 9421).* Branch of Bar Room Bar. Map p287 N2.
brb@the junction *2A Corsica Street, N5 9LP (7226 1026).* Branch of Bar Room Bar. Map p287 O25.
Elbow Room *89-91 Chapel Market, N1 9EX (7278 3244/www.theelbowroom.co.uk).* Branch.
Elk in the Woods *39 Camden Passage, N1 8EA (7226 3535).* Attractive gastrobar with a line in meaty platters. Map p287 O2.
Embassy Bar *119 Essex Road, N1 2SN (7226 7901/www.embassybar.com).* Stalwart N1 party venue with ground floor bar area and basement dancing den. Worth a look. Map p287 P1.
Grand Union *153 Upper Street, N1 1RA (no phone/www.gugroup.co.uk).* Branch, due to open at time of going to press. Map p287 P1.
Green *74 Upper Street, N1 0NY (7226 8895/ www.the-green.co.uk).* Sparsely-decorated gay bar.
Lord Nelson *100 Holloway Road, N7 8JE (7609 0670).* Popular pub with live music every night.
Mother Red Cap *665 Holloway Road, N19 5SE (7263 7082).* Run-down pub with plenty of worn Victorian charm; draught Guinness, pool, darts and live music at weekends keeps loyal locals happy.
North Star *188-190 New North Road, N1 7BJ (7354 5400).* Reasonable gastropub, struggling on despite hot competition in the area; an enclosed garden is appealing in summer. Map p287 P1.
Social *33 Linton Street, N1 7DU (7354 5809).* Branch. Map p287 P2.

Kentish Town

Abbey Tavern
124 Kentish Town Road, NW1 9QB (7267 9449/www. abbey-tavern.com). Kentish Town tube/rail. **Open** noon-midnight Mon-Wed, Sun; noon-1am Thur-Sat. **Food served** noon-3.30pm, 6-10pm Mon-Thur; noon-3.30pm, 6-10.30pm Fri; noon-10.30pm Sat; noon-10pm Sun. **Credit** MC, V. Gastropub
The Abbey Tavern has managed to carve out quite a niche for itself, by dint of its regular live music events and competent gastropub fare. Sunday's acoustic music sessions are particularly lively, with enthusiastic punters clambering on the tables to dance, and roaring their appreciation of the acts. The decor mixes industrial chic (exposed silver pipes and stripped-down brickwork) with more mellow touches (red leather banquettes to lounge on, soft globe lights hanging from the ceiling). An excellent range of bottled Belgian beers, including Liefmans, Chimay and Kwak, supplement the standard on-tap lagers. In summer, the sprawling, multi-level outdoor area is a suntrap, and the perfect spot to linger over a leisurely weekend brunch (we'd highly recommend the eggs benedict).
Babies and children admitted (until 9pm). Disabled: toilet. Function room. Music (bands 8pm Tue, 7.30pm Sun; free). Restaurant (available for hire). Tables outdoors (20, garden; 6, terrace). Map p286 J25.

Assembly House
292-294 Kentish Town Road, NW5 2TG (7485 2031). Kentish Town tube/rail. **Open** noon-11.30pm Mon-Thur; noon-midnight Fri, Sat; noon-10.30pm Sun.

North

Food served noon-3pm, 6-10pm Mon-Fri; noon-10pm Sat, Sun. **Credit** MC, V. Pub
Victorian pubs may be ten a penny in north London, but the cavernous, grade II-listed Assembly House is really rather splendid. The scale is impressive, with a double-height ceiling and acres of floor space. Generously spaced tables are dotted around the suitably stately interior, with its elaborate plasterwork ceiling, carved bar and original etched-glass mirrors. For a more homely feel, retreat to the sofas by the fireplace in the bookshelf-lined side room – a favoured spot for a game of Monopoly or Scrabble, requisitioned from the bar. Abbot Ale and Greene King IPA are on draught, alongside Scrumpy Jack and Budvar. The North American bar menu promises a host of freshly made dishes and fine ingredients, but prices are disconcertingly high.
Babies and children admitted. Games (board games). TVs (big screen, satellite). **Map p286 J24.**

Junction Tavern
101 Fortess Road, NW5 1AG (7485 9400/www. junctiontavern.co.uk). Tufnell Park tube/Kentish Town tube/rail. **Open** noon-11pm Mon-Sat; noon-10.30pm Sun. **Food served** noon-3pm, 6.30-10.30pm Mon-Fri; noon-4pm, 6.30-10.30pm Sat; noon-4pm, 6.30-9.30pm Sun. **Credit** MC, V. Gastropub
Maroon walls, randomly sourced chairs, natty chandeliers and huge mirrors: decoratively, the Junction has all the stock-in-trades of a north London gastropub. It also happens to have a particularly beautiful conservatory. But what makes this place truly remarkable is the calibre of its staff – all of them competent, charming individuals who seem very clued up about the local area. One of the waiters managed to be genuinely witty on the subject of toast. Such warmth of service means that despite a pricey-ish dinner menu (£10.50 for vegetable lasagne), old-timers aren't put off the place; for every brash media type, there's a bloke with his dog, enjoying a solitary pint of Deuchars.
Babies and children admitted (restaurant). Booking advisable. Tables outdoors (15, garden). **Map p286 J24.**

Oxford
256 Kentish Town Road, NW5 2AA (7485 3521/www. realpubs.co.uk). Kentish Town tube/rail. **Open** 11pm Mon-Thur; noon-midnight Fri, Sat; noon-10.30pm Sun. **Food served** noon-3.30pm, 6-10pm Mon-Fri; noon-5pm, 6-10pm Sat; noon-9pm Sun. **Credit** MC, V. Gastropub
On a summer's evening, the pavement tables outside the Oxford are a popular rendezvous for Kentish Towners. It's a fine urban alfresco drinking spot; with the odd pop star mooching past and occasional fisticuffs on the high street, who needs riverside beer gardens or greenery? Bar staff pour a very generous glass of wine, and real ales include Timothy Taylor and Brakspear. In colder months drinkers retreat inside, where retro floral lampshades cast a cosy glow over the scuffed floorboards and mismatched wooden tables and chairs. A few theatrical flourishes – a baroque gilt mirror, chandeliers – complete the look. Past the bar, a sleek open kitchen offers a short menu of gastropub fare – the likes of pork chop with parsnip mash, kidney with mushrooms or beef and ale pie, all priced under a tenner. These are enjoyed in a candlelit dining room occupying the rear of the pub.
Booking advisable. Children admitted. Disabled: toilet. Function room. Music (jazz 8.30pm Mon). Tables outdoors (6, pavement). **Map p286 J25.**

★ Pineapple
51 Leverton Street, NW5 2NX (7284 4631/www. thepineapplelondon.com). Kentish Town tube/rail. **Open** noon-11pm Mon-Sat; noon-10.30pm Sun. **Food served** 1-3pm, 7-10pm Mon-Sat; 1-4pm Sun. **Credit** MC, V. Gastropub
Testament to the Pineapple's charms is the fierce loyalty of its regulars – among them Jon Snow and Roger Lloyd-Pack – who rallied round to stop developers from turning it into flats a few years ago. Raise a glass to their victory in the snug front bar, with its battered red velvet banquettes, comfortable clutter and pineapple-etched mirrors (indeed, the eponymous fruit is honoured throughout, with paintings, carvings and even pineapple-shaped coat hooks). If the bar's packed out – a given on Monday quiz night – the conservatory offers more supping space, with rickety basket chairs and William Morris wallpaper. The walled garden is a splendid spot to sample the excellent and ever-changing menu, with Pedigree, Young's, Hoegaarden and Leffe on tap to wash it all down with.
Babies and children admitted (until 7.30pm). Function rooms. Games (backgammon, cards, chess, darts). Quiz (8.30pm Mon; £1). Tables outdoors (9, garden; 16, pavement). **Map p286 J24.**

Torriano
71-73 Torriano Avenue, NW5 2SG (7267 4305). Kentish Town tube/rail. **Open** noon-11pm Mon-Sat; noon-10.30pm Sun. **Food served** noon-10.30pm Mon-Sat; noon-10pm Sun. **Credit** MC, V. Pub
Although the cream-and-grey-painted exterior looks very smart indeed, the Torriano's stripped-down, diminutive interior is slightly tatty round the edges – and all the better for it, we say. On cold nights an open fire crackles by the bar, while candles and a string of fairy lights twinkle in the dim back area. Food options are simple but sustaining, with toasted sandwiches and barbecues in the sunken garden on summer weekends. The Croatian landlord keeps a fine line-up of beers and real ales, including Hoegaarden, Pedigree, Guinness and London Pride, and a good choice of wines are chalked up on the blackboard. The music's a winner too, with tracks from the Byrds and Spencer Davies Group providing a suitably laidback soundtrack to our last midweek visit.
Babies and children admitted (until 7pm). Quiz (8.30pm Mon; £2). Tables outdoors (6, garden). **Map p286 J24.**

Vine
86 Highgate Road, NW5 1PB (7209 0038/www.the vinelondon.co.uk). Tufnell Park tube/Kentish Town tube/rail. **Open** noon-11pm Mon-Wed; noon-midnight Thur-Sat; noon-11pm Sun. **Food served** noon-3pm, 6-10pm Mon-Sat; noon-10pm Sun. **Credit** AmEx, DC, MC, V. Gastropub
There's something of the Edwardian seafront hotel about the Vine's proud white façade – which is odd, seeing as this place is a gastropub on the Highgate Road. Venture beyond the forecourt picnic tables, however, and things take a dramatic turn for the contemporary. There's a zinc-topped bar, Matthew Williamson-designed wallpaper, imposing photographic prints and designer lighting. This is less humourless than it might sound: the staff are cheery, a log fire burns and a friendly atmosphere prevails. Leffe, Hoegaarden and Addlestones cider are on tap.
Babies and children welcome. Function rooms. Tables outdoors (22, garden). **Map p286 H24.**

North

Muswell Hill

Phoenix

Alexandra Palace Way, N22 7AY (8365 4356). Wood Green tube/Alexandra Palace rail/W3 bus. **Open** *Winter* 10.30am-8pm Mon-Thur; 10.30am-11pm Fri, Sat; 10.30am-10.30pm Sun. *Summer* 10am-11pm daily. **Food served** 11.30am-5pm daily. **Credit** MC, V. Pub
If you make it to the top of the steep hill where Ally Pally stands in state, you'll no doubt be in need of a sit down and a spot of light refreshment. The light-filled bar area and narrow conservatory of the Phoenix provide a very welcome pit-stop, serving London Pride on tap, bottles of Spitfire and Magners cider, and basic but hearty pub grub. That said, the plastic glasses and uncleared tables do give the place a slightly makeshift feel. The palm court area, with its huge columns, sphinxes and shady palms, is impressive, but for a truly splendid view over the capital, to Canary Wharf and beyond, head for one of the picnic tables outside.
Babies and children admitted (garden only). Disabled: toilet. Function rooms. Tables outdoors (50, garden terrace). TV.

Victoria Stakes

1 Muswell Hill, N10 3TH (8815 1793/www.victoria stakes.co.uk). Finsbury Park tube/rail then W3, W7 bus. **Open** 5-11pm Mon-Wed; 5pm-midnight Thur; noon-midnight Fri, Sat; noon-10.30pm Sun. **Food served** 6-10.30pm Mon-Thur; noon-4pm, 6-10.30pm Fri, Sat; noon-9pm Sun. **Credit** AmEx, DC, MC, V. Gastropub
Webster's Green label is the lone real ale among a slew of draught lagers that includes the unusual, tasty Artois Bock, though a decent range of bottled beers and ciders features Kopparberg apple and pear ciders, Duvel and Leffe. The wooden tables and leather lounge sofas in the dark wood bar area play host to a genial crowd of thirty-something, graphic designer types, who all seem to know each other. A narrow staircase curls up to the civilised dining room, which is filled with light from the big bay windows, while nondescript ambient music plays on a loop in the background. Staff are exceptionally polite and convivial, the waiter even throwing in a few fancy moves with the pepper mill. The gastro fare (steak sandwiches, thai fishcakes and an array of tapas; the restaurant upstairs serves some excellent meat and fish mains) is what you'd expect, and care goes into the three-course Sunday lunch (£16.50) – the potatoes were nice and crispy, and the beef tender. Make a beeline for the garden at the first hint of sunshine.
Babies and children admitted. Games (board games). Music (acoustic band 8pm 1st Mon of mth; free). Restaurant. Tables outdoors (20, garden).

Primrose Hill

★ Engineer

65 Gloucester Avenue, NW1 8JH (7722 0950/www.the-engineer.com). Chalk Farm tube/31, 168 bus. **Open** 9am-11pm Mon-Sat; 9am-10.30pm Sun. **Food served** 9-11.30am, noon-3pm, 7-11pm Mon-Fri; 9am-noon, 12.30-4pm, 7-11pm Sat; 9am-noon, 12.30-4pm, 7-10.30pm Sun. **Credit** MC, V. Gastropub
The Engineer's huge, square townhouse of a building strikes an imposing sight from afar, but up close it's hard to walk past the inviting windows without getting drawn to the reverie inside. Chatty young locals settling in for the night would surely concur. The odd snatch of trendy wallpaper, antique mirrors and assorted chandeliers freshens up the worn wood of the tables, floorboards and cocktail-ready bar, where the taps dispense ales (Bombardier, Hooky Bitter, Caffrey's) and lagers (Erdinger and Leffe, among others). A similar but slightly more sedate theme continues in the three dining rooms, which serve highly rated gastro fare (such as chargrilled organic sirloin steak for £16.75). If it's not too chilly, the roomy back yard, with sturdy furniture, plentiful heaters and healthy plants, serves as a lesson on how to do a beer garden right.
Babies and children admitted. Disabled: toilet. Function rooms. Tables outdoors (15, garden). **Map p286 G1.**

Lansdowne

90 Gloucester Avenue, NW1 8HX (7483 0409/www.thelansdownepub.co.uk). Chalk Farm tube/31, 168 bus. **Open** noon-11pm Mon-Fri; 9.30am-11pm Sat; 9.30am-10.30pm Sun. **Food served** noon-3pm, 7-10pm Mon-Fri; 9.30-11.30am, 12.30-3.30pm, 7-10pm Sat; 9.30-11.30am, noon-4pm, 7-9.30pm Sun. **Credit** MC, V. Gastropub
You'll be greeted with accents of a decidedly rummy tone upon entering this fine gastropub, opened in 1992 and owned by the same group as the Lord Stanley in Kentish Town. But the spread-out wooden tables and chairs, overflowing white candles and lavender sprigs create an easygoing French barn restaurant ambience, counterbalanced somewhat by the low ceiling and small fireplaces. Dishes such as slow-roasted Cornish mackerel, ribeye steak with chunky chips and pork chops with lentils are displayed on the blackboard (there's also an upstairs dining room); the wine selection scribbled above the bar is quaff-tastic, with bottles starting at around £14 and plenty of red and whites available by the glass. At the bar, draughts include Grolsch, Staropramen, Hoegaarden and Guinness, and a guest ale (the heady 6.9% Jaipur bitter on our visit). Alternatively, relive memories of Glastonbury Festival with Burrow Hill Cider, also on tap. And be sure to take a few moments to admire the marvellous antique brown and cream tiles of the exterior.
Babies and children admitted. Booking advisable (restaurant). Disabled: toilet. Restaurant available for hire. Tables outdoors (5, pavement). **Map p286 G26.**

Pembroke Castle

150 Gloucester Avenue, NW1 8JA (7483 2927). Chalk Farm tube/31, 168 bus. **Open** 11am-11pm Mon-Sat; noon-10.30pm Sun. **Food served** noon-3pm, 6.30-9.45pm Mon-Fri; noon-8pm Sat; noon-7pm Sun. **Credit** AmEx, MC, V. Pub
The small arty photos and free Wi-Fi signs aren't fooling anyone: this is a common or garden large British pub. A mix of blokes (in jeans and suits), couples and the odd literary loner populate the wooden chairs and comfy leather cocooned seats, while the low-level lighting, piped-in pop music and general airiness add to the clean, inoffensive vibe. Beer-wise, it's not bad (Castlemaine XXXX, Stella, Hoegaarden and Leffe), but the only real ale is Greene King IPA. The main draw is undoubtedly the sizeable and very well-kept beer garden, with decent outdoor furniture, tastefully exposed brickwork and assorted leafy plants. Heaters ensure its use is not just confined to the summer months.
Babies and children admitted (until 7pm). Function room. Games (fruit machine). Tables outdoors (25, heated terrace). TVs. Wi-Fi (free). **Map p286 G26.**

North

Princess of Wales

22 Chalcot Road, NW1 8LL (7722 0354). Chalk Farm tube/31, 168 bus. **Open** 11am-11pm Mon-Wed; 11am-midnight Thur-Sun. **Food served** noon-3pm, 7-9.30pm Mon-Sat; noon-5.30pm Sun. **Credit** MC, V. Pub
'Less is more' is certainly not an adage this old man's boozer lives by. Obligatory faded historical pictures of the area and old china fill most available wall space, while random plants, lamps and bits of furniture are spread throughout. Even the wood-panelled bar in the middle houses an array of different-shaped glasses, charity tins… and a worryingly un-PC statuette of black and white minstrels. Indeed, the only concessions to modernity seem to be a few fancy lagers (Hoegaarden, Peetermans Artois and Staropramen) and a couple of young foreign bar staff who look mildly bemused. A gentle crew of old gents mumble 'those were the days' platitudes, while happily supping their ales (Adnams, Slater's Supreme and London Pride). The perfect antidote for those jaded by nearby gastropubs.
Babies and children admitted. Function room. Music (jazz, 8.30pm Thur; noon Sun; free). Quiz (9pm Tue; £1). Tables outdoors (10, patio garden; 5, pavement). TV. **Map p286 G1.**

Queens

49 Regent's Park Road, NW1 8XD (7586 0408/www.geronimo-inns.co.uk). Chalk Farm tube/31, 168, 274 bus. **Open** 11am-11pm Mon-Thur; 11am-midnight Fri, Sat; noon-10.30pm Sun. **Food served** noon-3pm, 7-10pm Mon-Thur; noon-3pm, 7-10.30pm Fri, Sat; noon-6pm Sun. **Credit** MC, V. Gastropub
The Queens is perfectly situated to draw in park visitors at the bottom corner of tourist and celeb mecca Primrose Hill. Despite its location's constant passing trade this gastropub retains a distinctly local feel thanks to its loyal regulars – a friendly bunch of old lags usually found propping up the long bar – though 'Primrose Hill's answer to Walford's Queen Vic' (as the website helpfully states) is perhaps a bit wide of the mark. The splendid stained-glass windows, deep tartan sofas, fireplace (gas, unfortunately) and pleasant service help ensure younger, trendier folk are made to feel welcome. You also can't imagine Peggy Mitchell taking orders for food like butternut squash and sage risotto or eggs benedict (with even more options available in the majestic dining room upstairs). Ale-wise, Young's Ordinary and Special, and Bombardier are available (Young's has run the pub since 1991), and the lager options include Hoegaarden and Red Stripe.
Babies and children admitted (restaurant). Tables outdoors (3, balcony; 3, pavement). **Map 8 G1.**

Also in the area…

Albert *11 Princess Road, NW1 8JR (7722 1886).* This laid-back pub has a distinctly standard drinks selection, but a lovely beer garden and pavement tables at the front; there are board games behind the bar. **Map p286 G1.**

Stroud Green

Chapter One

143 Stroud Green Road, N4 3PZ (7281 9630/www.chapteronebar.com). Finsbury Park tube/rail/210, W3, W7 bus. **Open** noon-2am daily. **Food served** 3-11pm Tue-Sun. **Credit** AmEx, MC, V. Bar

There may be a picture of Che Guevara on this bar's charity collection boxes, but the revolution has yet come to Chapter One – and that's something to be grateful for. While other bars in the area have become dispiritingly tasteful, this place has real cosy charm, with a vibe that's half Greek taverna, half Costa del Sol English bar. Our disappointment at finding that happy hour applied only to house wines and spirits (we were in the mood for draught San Miguel) evaporated on sampling the World Tapas menu – £10.95 for three generous, flavoursome plates. It's no surprise that lots of the drinkers seem to know the staff well; once found, this is the kind of place you return to time and time again.
Disabled: toilet. Music (DJs 9.30pm Fri, Sat; latino band 9.30pm occasional Sun; free). TV (big screen).

Faltering Fullback NEW

19 Perth Road, N4 3HB (7272 5834). Finsbury Park tube/rail. **Open** noon-11pm Mon-Thur; noon-midnight Fri, Sat; noon-10.30pm Sun. **Food served** 6.30-10.30pm Mon-Sat; 6.30-10pm Sun. **Credit** MC, V. Pub
Housed in a dramatic corner building, covered from top to bottom with ivy, the Fullback is so well camouflaged you half expect armed commandos to lunge forth at the sound of approach. Once you're safely inside, the front bar is a warren of dinky rooms and hanging bric-a-brac, following the curve of a meandering bar where London Pride on tap complements Leffe, Beck's Vier, Guinness and the usual brand lagers. Good value Thai food (curries with rice for around a fiver) is served in a cavernous back room that, but for the aroma of coriander and coconut, is pure scout hut. Picnic tables seat the cheerful, chatty diners, while a pool table keeps the competitive occupied.
Disabled: toilet. Games (fruit machine, pool, quiz machine). Jukebox. Quiz (9pm Mon; £1). Tables outdoors (8, garden). TVs (plasma).

Old Dairy

1-3 Crouch Hill, N4 4AP (7263 3337). Finsbury Park tube/rail/Crouch Hill rail. **Open** noon-11pm Mon-Wed; noon-midnight Thur; noon-1am Fri, Sat; noon-10.30pm Sun. **Food served** 6.30-10.30pm Mon; noon-10pm Tue-Fri; noon-4.30pm, 6.30-10.30pm Sat; noon-9pm Sun. **Credit** MC, V. Gastropub
There must have been room for quite a few Friesians here, because this impressive building dwarfs almost everything in its vicinity. Although the cavernous, pared-down interior is undoubtedly classy, the emphasis on black can make it feel rather joyless in parts. Those feeling sinister had best stay near the snazzy wallpaper of the lofty, open-plan dining area, where oversized blackboards list pub grub and adventurous gastro fare (venison wellington with juniper sauce, steamed mutton with orange and thyme pudding). Elsewhere, a trendy young crowd squeezes on to the black leather sofas to enjoy the Addlestones, Old Stockport and Spitfire on draught. If your date doesn't turn up, there's always Pac-Man or bar billiards to keep you busy.
Babies and children welcome. Disabled: toilet. Games (bar billiards, retro arcade machine). Music (DJ 8pm Fri; free). Restaurant. TV (plasma).

★ Triangle

1 Ferme Park Road, N4 4DS (8292 0516/www.the trianglerestaurant.co.uk). Finsbury Park tube/rail then W3 bus/Crouch Hill rail. **Open/food served** 6pm-midnight Tue-Fri; 11am-midnight Sat, Sun. **Credit** MC, V. Bar/Restaurant

'You'll come here again,' smiled the manageress, as she led us to a table at the back of this highly unusual Moroccan den. Given the heady surroundings (Arabic music, hookah pipes and candles everywhere), this seemed more like prophecy than sales patter. Either way, she was right: Triangle is a gem. It's really a small restaurant rather than a bar – with cowhide-covered menus detailing dishes from all over the globe, not just North Africa – but there's no obligation to eat. The atmosphere is beguilingly intimate, with dimly glowing lanterns and a beautifully tiled open fire. Book 'the top' (a cosy, cushion-strewn enclave at the back), order a round of Casablanca beers or a bottle of Moroccan merlot (£18.50) and prepare to forget all about London.
Babies and children admitted. Disabled: toilet. Function room. Games (board games). Tables outdoors (5, garden; 7, pavement).

Tufnell Park

Bar Lorca NEW
156-158 Fortess Road, NW5 2HP (7485 1314). Tufnell Park tube. **Open** 4pm-midnight Mon-Thur; 4pm-1am Fri; noon-1am Sat; noon-midnight Sun. **Food served** 5-11pm Mon-Fri; noon-11pm Sat, Sun. **Credit** MC, V. Bar
If you look carefully, you'll see that the windows are stacked with beautifully packaged Spanish ingredients, but, aside from that, Bar Lorca's grey façade reveals little of the Iberian treasures within: posters of love god Julio Iglesias, a shrine to Lorca crafted from oyster shells and, for those wishing to expand their linguistic horizons, a Spanish word of the day on the blackboard behind the bar. (On our visit it was 'boquerones' – anchovies – and we were offered some in demonstration.) Bar Lorca does a little bit of everything, and does it well. There are Spanish cocktails (the Bloody Maria, £6, is a nice touch), beers (Negra Modelo, Cruzcampo) and delicious meaty snacks prepared before your eyes at the bar. Paella for Sunday lunch is a fiver, plus there's salsa every Tuesday.
Babies and children admitted (until 7pm). Bar available for hire. Music (8.30pm Fri, Sat; free). Salsa classes (Tue, call for details).

Bull & Last
168 Highgate Road, NW5 1QS (7267 3641). Gospel Oak rail. **Open** 11am-11pm Mon-Thur; 11am-midnight Fri, Sat; 11am-10.30pm Sun. **Food served** noon-3pm, 6.30-10pm Mon-Fri; noon-10pm Sat; noon-7pm Sun. **Credit** MC, V. Gastropub
Like neighbouring Hampstead Heath, this pub varies wildly depending on the time of year. In winter, it's all roaring fires and church candles; the perfect place to sink into a sofa, read a broadsheet and fill up on hearty fare such as sausage of the day (£7.95). In milder weather, the massive windows and pavement tables mean you won't have to miss any sunshine as you sup. The wine list (five reds, five whites) covers some nice territory, and all bottles cost £12.50 – which may or may not be a good thing, depending on how you look at it. Don't be dismayed by the usual lager staples at the bar – there are surprises too, including delicious bottled Tapio (rum, apple and ginger, £3) and Addlestones cider. Greene King IPA, London Pride, Pilsner Urquell and bottles of Weston's organic cider also feature.
Babies and children admitted. Function room. Tables outdoors (5, pavement).

Dartmouth Arms
35 York Rise, NW5 1SP (7485 3267/www.dartmouth arms.co.uk). Tufnell Park tube/Gospel Oak rail. **Open** 11am-11pm Mon-Fri; 10am-11pm Sat; 10am-10.30pm Sun. **Food served** 11am-3pm, 6-10pm Mon-Fri; 10am-10pm Sat, Sun. **Credit** MC, V. Gastropub
Those who fear they may have overdosed on Cath Kidston tastefulness at the nearby Lord Palmerston should consider rolling down the Chetwynd Road to the Dartmouth, an altogether more spit-and-sawdust affair. That's not to say it's uncouth – the night we visited, a 30-strong wine tasting was going on in the back bar. Aspall Suffolk Cyder or Adnams are the grog of choice, and it's very homely (if your home happens to feature a stag's skull); indeed, there's nothing to stop you from curling up with one of the fireside paperbacks (Dick Francis is well represented) and staying all day. A dining area at the back serves quality staples, as well as hosting special mussels nights on Thursday: 1lb of mussels and a pint of Hoegaarden for £10.
Babies and children admitted (until 8pm). Comedy (8pm Thur; £4). Quiz (8pm alternate Tue; £1). Restaurant (available for hire). TV (big screen, satellite).

★ Lord Palmerston
33 Dartmouth Park Hill, NW5 1HU (7485 1578/ www.geronimo-inns.co.uk). Tufnell Park tube. **Open** noon-11pm Mon-Sat; noon-10.30pm Sun. **Food served** noon-3pm, 7-10pm Mon-Sat; noon-9pm Sun. **Credit** AmEx, MC, V. Gastropub
There's a copy of *Elle Decoration* perched on the bar here, and it's clearly been well thumbed by the management – the Lord Palmerston is immaculately turned out. Fairy lights and muted greens create a pleasantly feminine vibe, and the bar looks more like a Smallbone kitchen than a boozer's backbone. Pub purists should hold back their scorn, however: for every design flourish (the gents' loos have mock-croc flooring), there's a well-chosen ale or wine (Otter Bitter, Adnams, Gran Hacienda sauvignon blanc) to demonstrate that the place has substance as well as style. The food is imaginative and decently priced, and, for summer, there are picnic tables and a garden at the back.
Babies and children admitted. Bookings not accepted. Function room. Tables outdoors (7, garden; 13, pavement).

Tufnell's NEW
162 Tufnell Park Road, N7 0EE (7272 2078). Tufnell Park tube. **Open** noon-midnight Mon-Thur; noon-3am Fri, Sat; noon-1am Sun. **Food served** noon-6pm daily. **Credit** MC, V. Pub/Restaurant
The name may have changed (this used to be Progress Bar), but the uninspiring exterior remains – it's mystifying that so many publicans these days opt for a dingy grey outside paint job reminiscent of an undercoat. Inside, things are funkier: glitter-strewn walls and platinum discs bring a touch of Studio 54 to Tufnell Park Road, and there's an impressive white grand piano in the restaurant upstairs. Lamentably, the billiards tables have disappeared and real ales on tap are no more, but the atmospheric skyline mural remains and the beer garden is soon to be decked – a sign that gentrification is in full flow.
Babies and children admitted (until 7.30pm). Disabled: toilet. Tables outdoors (20, garden).

Also in the area...
Boston Arms *178 Junction Road, N19 5QQ (7272 8153).* Stately-looking boozer with a pool table.

North West

Despite a close proximity to raucous Camden and Kentish Town, Belsize Park is a place more suited to a quiet drink and a meal than DJs and shouting; nevertheless, cavernous pub **Sir Richard Steele** is ever lively. Up the hill to Hampstead, smart public houses beckon, most of them offering good food, decent ales on tap and well-chosen wines. The warren-like **Holly Bush** is our favourite, but newcomer **Horseshoe** deserves praise for its cellar microbrewery; the ancient **Spaniards Inn** has been worth a visit since the days of Dick Turpin. Kensal Green's **Paradise...** is a pretty place to sit with a beer and a book (there's a lending library at the back); over in Kilburn, gastropub **Black Lion** feeds stomachs rather than minds with its cracking pub grub. In St John's Wood, the **Clifton** makes a fine bucolic retreat.

Belsize Park

Hill
94 Haverstock Hill, NW3 2BD (7267 0033).
Belsize Park or Chalk Farm tube. **Open** noon-11pm Mon-Wed, Sun; 11am-midnight Thur-Sat. **Food served** noon-3pm, 6-10pm Mon-Fri; noon-10pm Sat; noon-9pm Sun. **Credit** MC, V. Gastropub
This former Geronimo Inns pub – bought in the last year by Joe Developments – is a world away from the nearby Sir Richard Steele. While the Steele is raffish and rambunctious, this casual, appealing spot is very much a product of its time. Indeed, on some nights, it doesn't even feel like a boozer at all; the 'gastro' part of the equation is every bit as important as the 'pub' bit, especially on quieter weeknights. Cast aside thoughts of mismatched furniture and

over-prominent blackboards: the old Victorian space has been modified with grace and elegance uncommon in such conversions. The food too is a cut above normal gastropub fare (guinea fowl, pork medallions), albeit priced accordingly (around £13 for mains). Drinks-wise, the emphasis is firmly on wine; there are no real ales.
Babies and children admitted. Games (board games). Separate rooms for parties, seating 25 and 60. Tables outdoors (20, garden).

★ Sir Richard Steele
97 Haverstock Hill, NW3 4RL (7483 1261).
Belsize Park or Chalk Farm tube. **Open** 11am-midnight Mon-Sat; noon-11.30pm Sun. **Food served** noon-3pm, 6-10pm Mon; noon-3pm, 6-10.30pm Tue-Fri; noon-10.30pm Sat; noon-10pm Sun. **Credit** MC, V. Pub
Named after the man who co-founded the *Spectator* three centuries ago, this local landmark is a huge place, even larger than it looks from the outside. It's also a cracking pub, an unashamedly old-fashioned boozatorium crammed with purposeless knick-knacks, and popular with everyone from red-nosed old scoundrels to the neighbourhood's nouveau riche newcomers. The front bar is usually pretty busy, but there's a variety of snugs around the corner and an upstairs room that, if it's not hired out, makes a nice retreat, perhaps to sample the Thai menu. However, it's really all about the chaos downstairs, with all and sundry getting soaked on real ale (London Pride, Flowers IPA and Spitfire) and talking nonsense to anyone who'll listen and plenty who won't. Jazz groups and other musicians – plus a weekly quiz – provide further diversions.
Games (fruit machine). Music (Irish music 9pm Sun; trad jazz 9pm Mon; acoustic blues/rock 9pm Wed; free). Tables outdoors (16, patio). TVs (big screen, satellite).

Washington
50 England's Lane, NW3 4UE (7722 8842).
Belsize Park or Chalk Farm tube. **Open** noon-11pm Mon-Thur; noon-midnight Fri, Sat; noon-10.30pm Sun. **Food served** noon-3pm, 5.30-10pm Mon-Fri; noon-10pm Sat; noon-9.30pm Sun. **Credit** AmEx, MC, V. Pub

North West

Sir Richard Steele. *See p227.*

Operated by the Mitchells & Butlers group, ever careful not to brand their pubs too heavily while simultaneously steering clear of any nasty surprises, the Washington is a perfectly civilised corner local that fits hand in glove into the perfectly civilised neighbourhood in which it sits. M&B did the sensible thing and left a fair chunk of the grand old 1890s interior intact, but also scrubbed the place up a bit to suit 21st-century tastes; it's all a little pub-by-numbers, but no less pleasant for it. The drinks selection is fine enough (Beck's, Amstel), and the menu of not-quite-gastropub classics serves as useful sustenance. Ivor Dembina's long-running Hampstead Comedy Club is staged here on Sundays, and a Monday night quiz gets the week off to a flying start.
Function room. Games (board games). Quiz (8pm Mon; £1). Tables outdoors (4, pavement). TV.

Hampstead

★ Holly Bush
22 Holly Mount, NW3 6SG (7435 2892/www. hollybushpub.com). Hampstead tube/Hampstead Heath rail. **Open** noon-11pm Mon-Sat; noon-10.30pm Sun. **Food served** noon-10pm Mon-Sat; noon-9pm Sun. **Credit** AmEx, MC, V. Pub
Tucked away on a tiny lane amid some gorgeous NW3 piles, the Holly Bush is a gem of a place. It's a warren of little rooms, each offering their own distinctive historic patina alongside shared elements (burnished wood panels, low ceilings, sepia lighting). Only the rear dining room bucks the trend: it feels distinctly modern with its white painted walls and brighter lights. Adnams, Harveys and

London Pride do the business on the pumps, though a lot of people check in for the food: quality nosh such as quails' eggs, smoked duck with fig and mint salad or a substantial organic rump steak. A few outdoor tables beckon from out front in summer, though keep the noise down if you don't want to gain the ire of local residents, who keep a wary eye on the place.
Babies and children admitted. Function room. Games (board games). Restaurant. Tables outdoors (3, pavement).

Horseshoe NEW
28 Heath Street, NW3 6TE (7431 7206). Hampstead tube. **Open** 10am-11pm Mon-Sat; 10am-10.30pm Sun. **Food served** 12.30-3.30pm, 6.30-10pm Mon-Sat; noon-4.30pm, 6.30-9.30pm Sun. **Credit** MC, V. Gastropub
This big corner bar just off the High Street has quickly found favour among the Hampstead set, exuding the kind of confidence that comes from being well thought out and well run. Huge windows and white painted brickwork create a light, airy space in which to enjoy the alluring food – confit of duck with red cabbage, perhaps, or grilled sardines – washed down with something from the extensive wine list. Adnams plus guest ales are pumped from a bar that is artfully lit by a quartet of lights shrouded in big geometric shades. Bonus points too for the microbrewery housed in the cellar – a bit of a surprise in the heart of Hampstead. On our trans-seasonal visit, winter brews complemented a fragrant McL Summer Ale. The Horseshoe's clean, modern aesthetic may veer too close to Ikea for some, but they should like the quirky tables shaped from old floorboards.
Babies and children welcome: high chairs.

King William IV

77 Hampstead High Street, NW3 1RE (7435 5747). Hampstead tube. **Open** 11am-11pm Mon-Thur; 11am-midnight Fri, Sat; noon-11pm Sun. **Food served** noon-9pm daily. **Credit** MC, V. Pub

A lonely standard bearer for Hampstead's gay scene for decades – curious, perhaps, given the Heath's reputation as a cruising hotspot – refurbishment has removed much of this pub's charming former shabbiness. In place of period oddities and a welcome as warm as the open hearth, there's now an uninspired colour scheme and a lowering of standards all round; poorly kept beer (Theakston, Greene King IPA) is a common complaint. The music too has gone down a grade as the volume has gone up. Only the pleasant beer garden offers much enticement. Little wonder that discerning types – whatever their persuasion – seem to have moved on, leaving the KW to unaware tourists or shoppers too tired to drag themselves the short distance to the Holly Bush.
Bar available for hire. Function room. Games (fruit machines). Quiz (9pm Wed; £2). Tables outdoors (15, garden).

Magdala

2A South Hill Park, NW3 2SB (7435 2503). Hampstead Heath rail. **Open** 11am-11pm Mon-Sat; noon-10.30pm Sun. **Food served** noon-2.30pm, 6-10pm Mon-Fri; noon-10pm Sat; noon-9.30pm Sun. **Credit** AmEx, DC, MC, V. Gastropub

Just down from the lower end of the Heath, the Magdala presents an unprepossessing exterior to the world with its plasticky name board and undistinguished brickwork. The brickwork does have a claim to fame, mind you – scarred to this day by bullet holes fired by Ruth Ellis when she killed her lover, an act for which she became the last woman to be hanged in Britain in 1955. For a former crime scene, the interior is comfortingly serene. Pastel walls and big windows combine to create a light, airy dining area, while the adjacent bar is full of nice touches: gorgeous 1950s patterned carpet, a pretty bench covered with vintage fabric and stained glass details in the windows. Amid all this, liberal Hampstead types rail against the wrongs of the world. The beer choice (London Pride, Greene King IPA) and wine list could be widened, but the Magdala is a reasonable gastropub to rival the friendly Wells.
Babies and children admitted. Function room. Games (board games, cards). Restaurant. Tables outdoors (4, patio).

★ Roebuck

15 Pond Street, NW3 2PN (7433 6871). Belsize Park tube. **Open** noon-11pm Mon-Thur; noon-midnight Fri, Sat; noon-10.30pm Sun. **Food served** noon-3pm, 5-10pm Mon-Fri; noon-4pm, 5-10pm Sat; noon-9pm Sun. **Credit** AmEx, DC, MC, V. Bar

Never judge a book by its cover. From the outside, this looks like a rather uninspired utilitarian drinking hole, as ugly as the monstrous Royal Free Hospital across the road. Inside, it's rather fabulous. A clutch of classic 1960s seats vie for attention with a huge pale sofa and old brown armchairs. Vintage lamps and globe lights illuminate a space wrapped in the sort of geometric wallpaper you might have seen in Biba. A pretty conservatory, meanwhile, offers diners a view of the beer garden along with decent food (burgers and the like) and a good wine selection. An equally lovely downstairs lounge (tiled floor, exposed brickwork) is there to soak up overspill from the main room. What impresses us most, though, is the beer

choice – an incredible 17 on tap by our count. This includes lagers Kirin and Paulaner, fruit beer Früli and three rotating ales (Timothy Taylor Landlord, Black Sheep and Abbot Ale when we visited).
Babies and children admitted (until 7pm). Function room. Games (board games). Tables outdoors (16, garden).

Spaniards Inn

Spaniards Road, NW3 7JJ (8731 6571). Hampstead tube/210 bus. **Open** 11am-11pm Mon-Fri; 10am-11pm Sat, Sun. **Food served** 11.30am-10pm Mon-Fri; noon-10pm Sat, Sun. **Credit** AmEx, MC, V. Pub

Perched on one of Hampstead's highest points, Spaniards Inn is one of the capital's most historic pubs, outside the Square Mile, at least (it's the reputed birthplace of highwayman Dick Turpin). There's been a pub here since the 1580s, a fact that's particularly easy to believe in the fascinating upstairs room with its wonky floorboards and misshapen doors. The downstairs bar is surprisingly small given the number of punters, though in summer most just order then scuttle out to the sizeable courtyard, spread beneath an expansive centrepiece tree. In winter, the back room is a dim, cosy hideaway, as is a tiny private snug beneath the stairs. The draught options are good – Adnams, Harveys, Marston's Pedigree and Deuchars – with a decent complement of bottled Belgians. Keats reputedly composed 'Ode To A Nightingale' in the courtyard; maintaining tradition, the pub hosts poetry readings on Tuesday evenings.
Babies and children admitted. Entertainment (poetry 8pm Tue; free). Function room. Tables outdoors (90, garden).

Wells

30 Well Walk, NW3 1BX (7794 3785/www.thewells hampstead.co.uk). Hampstead tube. **Open** noon-11pm Mon-Sat; noon-10.30pm Sun. **Food served** noon-3pm, 6-10pm Mon-Fri; noon-4pm, 7-10pm Sat, Sun. **Credit** MC, V. Gastropub

Though a pub first sprang up here in 1701 – taking advantage of the alleged therapeutic properties of the long-gone Chalybeate spring – the modern Wells has had a modern makeover that's turned it from a yoof's drinking den to an urban sophisticate's watering hole. The dark brick exterior fits neatly with the surrounding residences, a theme continued by the black and brown decor inside. Customers are a mix of thirty-plus locals and savvy tourists, most enjoying a bite to eat from a snack menu offering the likes of salt beef or fish cakes. Posher nosh is available in the upstairs dining room. It hits the 'relaxed and classy' note well enough, but there's a slight characterlessness about the place that almost makes you long for the days when it hosted 'Court ladies and Fleet Street sempstresses'.
Babies and children welcome: children's menu; colouring books; high chairs. Disabled: toilet. Music (musicians 8.30pm alternate Mon, winter only). Quiz (8pm alternate Mon; £2). Separate room for parties, seats 12. Tables outdoors (8, patio).

Ye Olde White Bear

Well Road, NW3 1LJ (7435 3758). Hampstead tube. **Open** 11am-11pm Mon-Sat; noon-10.30pm Sun. **Food served** noon-9pm daily. **Credit** MC, V. Pub

This is a fine old backstreet boozer, not far from the Heath yet off the radar of the daytripping hordes. So it's a locals' haunt, with worn parquet floor and mishmash of old prints scattered around the wood panelling. Defiantly untrendy

Darting about

Darts is said to be related to a 19th-century pub sport called Puff and Darts, which involved blowpipes and sounds like terrific fun. In its modern form, though, it really took off in the UK in 1937, when the King and Queen were touring a social club in Slough and casually lobbed a couple of arrows at a dartboard by way of amusing the locals. The press picked up on it, and darts became a hit across the UK; the number of pubs with boards is said to have tripled over the next couple of years. Incidentally, London's place in darts history is assured every time you look at a board: the standard design is called the London Board, because it was in the capital that it proved most popular. Other types of board are used in the UK, including the London Fives (or East End) board, which is smaller, with a different numbering system, and can be found in the **Ferry House** and **Waterman's Arms** in Docklands, and Mile End's **Palm Tree**.

London's premier darts league, the Greater London Darts Organisation (www.londondarts. org.uk), was formed in 1966, with men's and women's teams from all over the capital competing in the Super League. The standard is high: 'To be a Super League player you need to average 501 in around 18 to 20 darts for men, and 22 to 26 darts for women,' says GLDO vice-president Allan Fuller.

If you're looking to up your average, you need to find a decent pub in which to practice. Most Sam Smith's pubs, with their impressive eye for detail, have dartboards; we like the sports-themed **Champion**. Otherwise, the **Scarborough Arms** (35 St Mark Street, E1, 7481 3070), the **Queens Arms** (23 Burrage Road, SE18, 8854 0540), which used to be run by Andy 'Viking' Fordham, and the **Prince Arthur** (49 Brunswick Place, N1, 7253 3187) all have boards. The City Darts – the name says it all – was recently rechristened the **Princess Alice** (40 Commercial Street, E1, 7247 5371), but still packs a decent dartboard if you're looking for a game.

(how many places would choose Peter Gabriel-era Genesis for their background music?), the White Bear shows a similar independence in its beer selection: guests like Butcombe stand alongside Bombardier and Ruddles. A TV in one corner silently chronicles the day's sporting news, but everyone seems perfectly happy to burrow deep into their own conversations. A log fire keeps things warm in winter; outdoor seats do their job in summer.
Babies and children admitted. Games (board games). Quiz (9pm Thur; £1). Tables outdoors (6, courtyard). TV (satellite).

Also in the area...
brb@hampstead *48 Rosslyn Hill, NW3 1NH (7431 8802).* Branch of Bar Room Bar.
No.77 Wine Bar *77 Mill Lane, NW6 1NB (7435 7787).* Cavernous yet undeniably stylish wine bar; 40 wines, most available by the glass.
Tabby Cat Lounge *765 Heath Street, NW3 1DN (7794 5450).* New cocktail bar with intriguing, multi-levelled interior complete with a 1960s-style hanging basket seat. The cocktail list is brief but well realised by bar staff.

Kensal Green

Greyhound
64-66 Chamberlayne Road, NW10 3JJ (8969 8080). Kensal Green tube/Kensal Rise rail. **Open** 6.30-11pm Mon; noon-11pm Tue-Thur; noon-midnight Fri, Sat; noon-10.30pm Sun. **Food served** 6.30-10pm Mon; 12.30-3.30pm, 6.30-10.30pm Tue-Sat; 12.30-7pm Sun. **Credit** AmEx, MC, V. Gastropub
Think Portobello without the pretence in this long, dark pub. There's a bit of a tribute to all things fab and British on the walls, with greyhound portraits, Player's cigarettes ads and a *Get Carter* poster. Take your pick from the large menu of comforting grub, which has earned this place a fine reputation with thirtysomething locals over the last few years. We washed down our braised Suffolk pork belly with bubble and squeak in a cider sauce (delicious, and keenly priced at £9.50) with some Aspall Suffolk Cyder. There's a good wine selection too, and Adnams on tap, plus a 30-strong collection of liqueurs, vermouths and aperitifs that would put many a West End hotel bar to shame. DJs liven up Sunday nights.
Babies and children admitted. Disabled: toilet. Music (DJs 7.30pm Sun; free). Restaurant. Tables outdoors (7, pavement; 15, garden).

Paradise by Way of Kensal Green
19 Kilburn Lane, W10 4AE (8969 0098). Kensal Green tube/Kensal Rise rail. **Open** 12.30pm-midnight Mon-Thur; 12.30pm-2am Fri, Sat; noon-11.30pm Sun. **Food served** 12.30-4pm, 7.30-11pm Mon-Sat; noon-9.30pm Sun. **Credit** MC, V. Gastropub
Now here's a gastro conversion that's a little more original than the norm. Situated at the bottom of the characterful Kilburn Lane, Paradise ticks the usual boxes with its mismatched furniture and threadbare cushions – but there's more to it than that. Ivy sprouts everywhere, modern art hangs on the walls and the whole place has the air of a country manor gone to seed. One that has now been taken over by very well-read squatters – note the fine lending library in the back room, which is low on JK Rowling but included a dog-eared copy of *The Ballad of the Sad*

North West

Café. On our visit, the splendid restaurant in the back room was serving up pricey lamb shanks and Italian sausages. Only two real ales (Adnams Broadside and Spitfire), are offered on tap, mind. *Babies and children admitted. Function room. Restaurant. Tables outdoors (10, garden). TV (widescreen).*

Kilburn

Black Lion
274 Kilburn High Road, NW6 2BY (7624 1424/ www.blacklionguesthouse.com). Kilburn tube/ Brondesbury rail. **Open** 11.30am-midnight Mon-Thur; 11am-1am Fri, Sat; 11am-11.30pm Sun. **Food served** noon-3pm, 6-10pm Mon-Fri; 11am-10pm Sat; noon-9.30pm Sun. **Credit** MC, V. Gastropub
Dating from 1898, this glorious, ornate Victorian corner boozer is a homage to friendly service, superb decor and cracking food – oh, and did we mention the decor? Ludicrously over-the-top gold embossed ceiling panels, an island back bar, etched glass and a lovely cornice to boot. The former billiards room to the side has been turned into a restaurant serving carefully sourced, quality British grub. At the bar, ales include Bombardier and Adnams Broadside; snacks are fine too (tasty thin-crust pizza, £8-£9). If you really can't tear yourself away from the relaxed crowd and conversational buzz around the candlelit tables, there's a guesthouse upstairs with rooms for around £35 a night. An absolute delight of a pub. *Babies and children admitted (until 6pm). Restaurant. Tables outdoors (6, garden).*

Kilburn Pub & Kitchen
307-311 Kilburn High Road, NW6 7JR (7372 8668/ www.thekilburn.com). Kilburn tube/Brondesbury rail. **Open** noon-11pm Mon-Wed, Sun; noon-midnight Thur-Sat. **Food served** noon-3pm, 5.30-10pm Mon-Thur; noon-9.30pm Fri-Sun. **Credit** AmEx, MC, V. Gastropub
Owner John Donnelly has overseen a spectacular overhaul of this formerly old-school Irish establishment. Half of the pub remains unchanged; it's a fantastically atmospheric

Horseshoe.
See p228.

North West

boozer with walls plastered with hurling, rugby and football photos from yesteryear. The main bar, however, has become something of a homage to that dream diner you'd expect to stroll into in downtown Memphis. The sofas and booths were all taken on our late afternoon midweek visit, with a crowd of laptop-browsing boys and stylishly attired girls somehow blending in nicely with the portraits of old bluesman and shots of gigs from the award-winning Luminaire music venue upstairs. Food is Delta meets Dagenham, with baby back ribs and cheeseburgers mixing it with toad in the hole and bangers and mash, all for under a tenner. A Kilburn Classic from the cocktail menu, with champagne, chambord and orange bitters, slipped down a treat.
TV (big screen, satellite).

North London Tavern
375 Kilburn High Road, NW6 7QB (7625 6634).
Kilburn tube. **Open** noon-11pm Mon-Wed, Sun; noon-midnight Thur-Sat. **Food served** noon-10.30pm Mon-Sat; noon-9.30pm Sun. **Credit** MC, V. Pub
The huge black frontage on an unsavoury stretch of Kilburn High Road makes this old boozer look slightly forbidding. All fears are banished when you step inside, however, as this is a very smartly maintained pub that's adapting to the 21st century without losing any of its original character. The blood-red ceilings and simple Victorian decor of brown wood and mirrors provide a classy backdrop beloved by a boho, literary-inclined crowd, many enjoying their espressos as much as draught Timothy Taylor Landlord. The large dining room to the rear serves some interesting fishy options, but it's the outstanding value of the bar menu that catches the eye. A comforting selection of dishes includes eggs benedict, linguine Genovese and chargrilled ham steak with fried eggs – all a fiver, available all day. Tasty.
Babies and children welcome. Disabled: toilet. Function room. Restaurant. Tables outdoors (5, pavement). TV.

Power's Bar
332 Kilburn High Road, NW6 2QN (7624 6026).
Kilburn tube/Brondesbury rail. **Open** noon-11pm Mon-Sat; noon-10.30pm Sun. **No credit cards.** Bar
Dark and resolutely blokey, this den of a pub belies its smart, brasserie-style frontage. The gently sozzled crowd on our early evening visit seemed to be content with the dire range of beers (Foster's and Staropramen being about your lot). Still, there's a spoken-word open mic night on Wednesdays, which is proving very popular; a cupboard-like alcove to the back is handy if you want to escape Kilburn's beginner-bards. On other nights, the preference is to just enjoy the bare-brick walls, scuffed wooden tables and odd bit of Irish paraphernalia. The jukebox plays Dylan, the Band and Bryan Ferry to an amiable collection of fellas who probably think the Kooks is the name of a TV show about chefs.
Babies and children admitted (Sun afternoons only). Jukebox. Music (acoustic 9pm Tue, Wed; DJs 8.30pm Thur-Sat; Irish band 4-7pm Sun; all free). Tables outdoors (pavement). TV.

Salusbury
50-52 Salusbury Road, NW6 6NN (7328 3286).
Queens Park tube/rail. **Open** 5-11pm Mon; 10am-11pm Tue-Thur; 10am-midnight Fri, Sat; noon-11pm Sun. **Food served** 7-10.30pm Mon; 12.30-3.30pm, 7-10.30pm Tue-Sun. **Credit** MC, V. Gastropub

The exterior of this pub – with its small frosted-glass windows – looks like the kind of building into which Tiny Tim might peer on a cold winter's night. And so he should – inside, the Salusbury is a most welcoming boozer, with a roaring fire by the bar and a snug, intimate atmosphere. It blends in nicely with the organic foodshops that are creeping into the area. Tables are artfully mismatched in true gastropub fashion; many are scattered around an incredibly dark dining area. There are a couple of ales on tap (generally Adnams); the local media crowd, stopping off from the voiceover studio up the road, prefers to plunge into the decent-enough wine list.
Babies and children welcome (until 7pm): high chairs. Restaurant. Tables outdoors (4, pavement).

St John's Wood
....
★ Clifton
96 Clifton Hill, NW8 0JT (7372 3427). St John's Wood tube. **Open** noon-11pm Mon-Sat; noon-10.30pm Sun. **Food served** noon-3pm, 6-9pm Mon-Sat; noon-4pm, 6.30-9pm Sun. **Credit** MC, V. Pub
A pub in a Georgian villa – just what you'd expect in these parts. Tucked away down a residential side street off Abbey Road, the Clifton is a bucolic hangout with a collection of distinctive rooms that appeal to a broad demographic. A century ago, it was even good enough for royalty – Edward VII conducted trysts with his mistress Lillie Langtry here. These days, a large rear room adorned with classical murals and other traditional touches suits posher locals, while the more down-to-earth customers convene by the old fireplace in a snug, red-trimmed section. Beer lovers are blessed with Adnams Explorer and Hogs Back ales, alongside Greene King or London Pride; Hendrick's gin used in G&Ts shows similar thoughtfulness. A lovely, leafy front terrace beckons in summer; borrow a board game from the bar and while the day away.
Babies and children admitted (until 7pm). Games (board games). Tables outdoors (12, garden).

Ordnance
29 Ordnance Hill, NW8 6PS (7722 0278). St John's Wood tube. **Open** noon-11pm Mon-Sat; noon-10.30pm Sun. **Food served** noon-2pm, 6-9pm Mon-Thur; noon-2pm, 6-9.30pm Fri, Sat; noon-5pm Sun. **Credit** MC, V. Pub
An air of muted restraint emanates from this popular NW8 hostelry. Decor is of a brown hue: a dash of sepia here, some chestnut there. Tree branches have been cunningly adapted for use as lighting fittings (appropriate for a pub in a Wood); they hang over well-worn wooden tables and scuffed floorboards. A roaring fire warms winter nights, while a little patio provides a welcome retreat when the mercury rises. The inside space is open and spacious; a rear room stretches away from the main bar, where you'll find the usual Samuel Smith's options, with bottled Taddy Porter and Oatmeal Stout freshening up the choice. Food is average, with steak, fish cakes, scampi and the like to the fore.
Babies and children admitted. No piped music or jukebox. Tables outdoors (9, garden).

Also in the area...
Salt House *63 Abbey Road, NW8 0AE (7328 6626).* Refurbed (and now rather snooty) gastropub, popular with a monied clientele.

North West

Outer London

The *rus in urbe* allure of its vast parks and Thameside wetlands makes Richmond and Kew a beacon for active, wholesome Londoners, who like their pubs to be equipped with such things as real ale and picturesque views. The **Cricketers**, in the former, and newcomer the **Botanist on the Green**, in the latter, are prime examples. Kingston, a chunk of suburbia focused on a busy but unlovely shopping area, lacks the cachet of its neighbours, but boasts some fine pubs away from the city centre. The **Canbury Arms**, in particular, stands out.

Kew, Surrey

Botanist on the Green NEW
3-5 Kew Green, Kew, Surrey TW9 3AA (8948 4838/ www.thebotanistonthegreen.com). Kew Gardens tube/ rail/65, 391 bus. **Open** noon-midnight Mon-Sat; noon-10.30pm Sun. **Food served** noon-3pm, 6-10pm Mon-Fri; noon-10pm Sat; noon-8pm Sun. **Credit** AmEx, DC, MC, V. Gastropub
Once a Brown's restaurant, the site was bought out by the company that runs the Firkin pub chain. It refrained from rebranding the place under the 'F-word & Firkin' banner, settling instead on this rather lovely title, a homage to neighbouring Kew Gardens. Indeed, the pub's dark-green exterior, spaciousness and elegant wooden furniture echo that calm oasis rather well. A pretty chandeliered walk-way divides the polished main bar and two-level dining space. On one side, diners enjoy the likes of tortilla-wrapped burgers, paella and, oddly enough, bison. On the other, beer fans mourn the choice of just one real ale (Adnams Broadside). Still, Kirin lager might be appropriate after a visit to Kew's Japanese garden. An outdoor courtyard awaits its first summer.
Bar available for hire. Tables outdoors (6, courtyard).

City Barge
27 Strand-on-the-Green, Kew, Surrey W4 3PH (8994 2148). Gunnersbury tube/rail/Kew Bridge rail. **Open** 11am-11pm Mon-Sat; noon-10.30pm Sun. **Food served** noon-3pm, 6-9pm Mon-Sat; noon-8.30pm Sun. **Credit** AmEx, DC, MC, V. Pub
The tiny front door and cave-like downstairs bar may make loftier drinkers feel that they've ventured into the land of hobbits. But appearances can be deceptive, and the split-level City Barge is larger than it looks. If you're feeling claustrophobic, head for the roomier but less atmospheric upstairs bar – or better still, nab a table on the waterside terrace. Quaff a pint of real ale (Fuller's London Pride, Adnams and Young's) in the sunshine, and make your selection from the decent, if entertainingly eclectic, selection of grub on offer, including red Thai chicken curry, bacon and eggs, and salmon and crayfish risotto. It's a sublime spot to while away a summer's afternoon – and not a hobbit in sight.
Babies and children admitted (until 9pm). Games (quiz machine). Tables outdoors (6, riverside terrace).

Inn at Kew Gardens
292 Sandycombe Road, Kew, Surrey TW9 3NG (8940 2220/www.theinnatkewgardens.com). Kew Gardens tube. **Open** 11am-11pm Mon-Sat; 11am-10.30pm Sun. **Food served** noon-3pm, 6-10pm Mon-Fri; noon-4pm, 6-10pm Sat; noon-4pm, 6-9pm Sun. **Credit** AmEx, DC, MC, V. Pub
Situated below the Kew Gardens Hotel, the Inn is an ambitious proposition. Downstairs is occupied by a tasteful clutter of big tables and easy chairs, with flock wallpaper adding a quaintly old-fashioned touch. A smart separate dining area lies at the back, serving up enticing, well-executed gastropub fare (braised lamb shank, pan-fried calf's liver and the like). Up the spiral staircase is yet another area: a slick, loft-style room where you can lounge in front of a rugby-showing TV under dark wooden beams. Real ales are bountiful: Adnams, Ruddles County, London Pride and Twickenham Original.
Babies and children welcome: children's portions. Disabled: toilet. Separate room for parties, seats 40. Tables outdoors (2, pavement; 8, terrace).

Also in the area...

Coach & Horses *8 Kew Green, Kew, Surrey TW9 3BH (8940 1208/www.coachhotelkew.co.uk).* Former coaching inn near Kew Gardens, now a smart Young's pub/ hotel/restaurant.

Isleworth, Surrey

London Apprentice
62 Church Street, Isleworth, Surrey TW7 6BG (8560 1915). Isleworth rail. **Open** 11am-11pm Mon-Fri; 11am-midnight Sat; noon-11pm Sun. **Food served** noon-5pm, 6-9.30pm daily. **Credit** AmEx, DC, MC, V. Pub
This large, old-fashioned riverside pub offers a fine choice of real ales (Bombardier, Landlord and London Pride), making it a popular stop-off for the rugby crowd, who like to sink a few here before heading on to Twickenham. This can cause headaches for staff and customers, as the backlog of unwashed glasses soon builds up – be prepared to wait a while at the bar on match days. Having said that, the beer is well kept and food arrives promptly. The riverside terrace is the perfect spot for watching the Thames wildlife, albeit to the rumbling soundtrack of overhead Boeings on the Heathrow flight path.
Babies and children admitted (until 9.30pm, if dining).

Function room. Games (fruit machine, video games, darts). Tables outdoors (10, riverside terrace). TV (big screen).

Red Lion
92-94 Linkfield Road, Isleworth, Surrey TW7 6QJ (8560 1457/www.red-lion.info). Isleworth rail. **Open** noon-11pm Mon, Wed, Sun; noon-11.30pm Tue, Thur; noon-midnight Fri, Sat. **No credit cards.** Pub
The rickety gables and cracked paintwork may not look promising, but don't let initial appearances put you off. Not an obvious looker, then, but beneath its faded green tiles, forlorn hanging baskets and barren side bar is a seasoned pro, with bucketloads of character and effortless charm. Its appeal is backed up by quality cask ales (Pedigree, Landlord, Young's) and myriad Belgian beers. Homely sofas invite you to settle in for the duration, with a regular programme of live music providing uproarious entertainment. The beer garden, with its bright mural, curls round a corner, and hosts lively barbecues in the summer. In short, it's that rarest of London beasts – an unpretentious local.
Beer festivals (live music and family events, call for dates). Games (backgammon, board games, cards, chess, darts, pool, table football). Music (rock, blues, jazz 9pm Sat; free. Open mic 9pm Tue; free). Quiz (9pm Thur; £1). Tables outdoors (20, garden). TVs.

10am-10.30pm Sun. **Food served** 9.30-11.30am, noon-4pm, 6-10pm Mon-Sat; noon-4pm, 6-9pm Sun. **Credit** AmEx, MC, V. Gastropub
Located opposite a cluster of drab, unassuming local shops, the Canbury Arms' monolithic white premises loom like an iceberg in the light drizzle. The interior is equally unexpected; stripped light wood, magnolia walls, an open fire and a buzzy, enthusiastic atmosphere promise much. The food doesn't disappoint – our burger and chips oozed taste (and no grease), while the roasted salmon special was a triumph. An extensive wine list features delightfully meticulous descriptions, and there are some interesting ales (Hook Norton Old Hooky and Harveys Sussex Best on our visit). The airy, heated marquee-like annex is perfect for large parties. As we left, a rainbow curled over the roof – which says it all really.
Babies and children admitted (separate room). Games (board games). Tables outdoors (8, forecourt; 12, garden).

Isha Lounge Bar NEW!
43 Richmond Road, Kingston upon Thames, Surrey KT2 5BW (8546 0099/www.ishalounge.com). Kingston rail/65, 111 bus. **Open** 6pm-1am Tue-Thur, Sun; 6pm-2am Fri, Sat. **Credit** MC, V. DJ bar
A rather grubby exterior belies the trendy, intimate atmosphere of this DJ bar, which has become a popular spot in an area not renowned for its small and stylish haunts. The over-25s door policy is arguably slightly snooty, but intended to ensure a more discerning clientele. Once inside, drinkers can huddle in the dimly lit leather booths, while sipping a global selection of beers (Brazilian, Belgian, Russian and Spanish) or sampling the expansive range of premium spirits. There's a VIP suite for the high-rollers and the resident DJs keep things funky, without drowning out the conversation too much. A fun tandoori menu helps fuel partygoers until the wee hours.
Function room. Music (DJs 9pm Fri, Sat; £5. Jazz 8.30pm Sun; free.). Salsa (8pm Wed; £7).

Botanist on the Green. *See p233.*

Kingston upon Thames, Surrey

Boaters Inn
Canbury Gardens, Lower Ham Road, Kingston upon Thames, Surrey KT2 5AU (8541 4672/www.jazzatthe boaters.co.uk). Kingston rail. **Open** 11am-11pm Mon-Sat; noon-10.30pm Sun. **Food served** noon-9.30pm Mon-Sat; noon-6pm Sun. **Credit** AmEx, MC, V. Pub
Location is the prime draw here – smack bang on the waterfront, on a tranquil, tree-lined swathe of grass. You can watch the swans glide past from the warm comfort of a table inside or, weather permitting, from one of the many outdoor benches. An added enticement throughout the year is the long-running jazz night on Sunday. The cabin-style interior remains resolutely unfancy, as does the traditional pub grub (chicken wings, steak and kidney pie). There's Greene King IPA, Abbot and Broadside on tap plus a monthly changing guest ale, but on hot summer days the people's choice is undoubtedly Pimm's and lemonade.
Babies and children admitted. Games (board games, fruit machines). Music (jazz 8.30pm Sun; free). Restaurant. Tables outdoors (30, riverside patio). TV.

★ Canbury Arms
49 Canbury Park Road, Kingston upon Thames, Surrey KT2 6LQ (82559129/www.thecanbury arms.com). Kingston rail. **Open** 9am-11pm Mon-Sat;

Wych Elm
93 Elm Road, Kingston upon Thames, Surrey KT2 6HT (8546 3271). Kingston rail. **Open** 11am-3pm, 5pm-midnight Mon-Fri; 11am-midnight Sat; noon-11pm Sun. **Food served** noon-2.30pm Mon-Sat. **No credit cards.** Pub
Thick pile carpet, slightly chintzy furnishings and a dartboard are all telltale signs that the gastropub revolution has passed this place by – thankfully so. The fixtures and fittings may be pure English town pub circa 1970, but here-in lies the charm of this down-to-earth, family-run affair. The quiet location is worth seeking out to discover what pubs were like before stripped pine floors and goat's cheese burgers took over the world – and, more importantly, to partake of some seriously good, properly kept real ales. It's a Fuller's pub, so there's Discovery, ESB and Chiswick to choose from; no wonder it's a regular CAMRA award winner. The regulars are bright and friendly, and don't seem to mind the odd stray dart thrown by inexperienced players.
Babies and children admitted (dining area only). Games (darts, fruit machine). Tables outdoors (8, garden). TV.

Also in the area...
Kingston Tup *88 London Road, Kingston upon Thames, Surrey KT2 6PX (8546 6471).* Branch of Tup.

Outer London

Index

Index

1 Wood Lane, W12 7DP (8743 9593/www.gonumber. com/albertine).

42-44 Kingsland Road, E2 8DA (7739 3863/ www.andadebridge.com).

EC2R 8AY (7628 0001/ www.ballroom.uk.com).

(7608 0925/www.bavarian-beerhouse.co.uk).

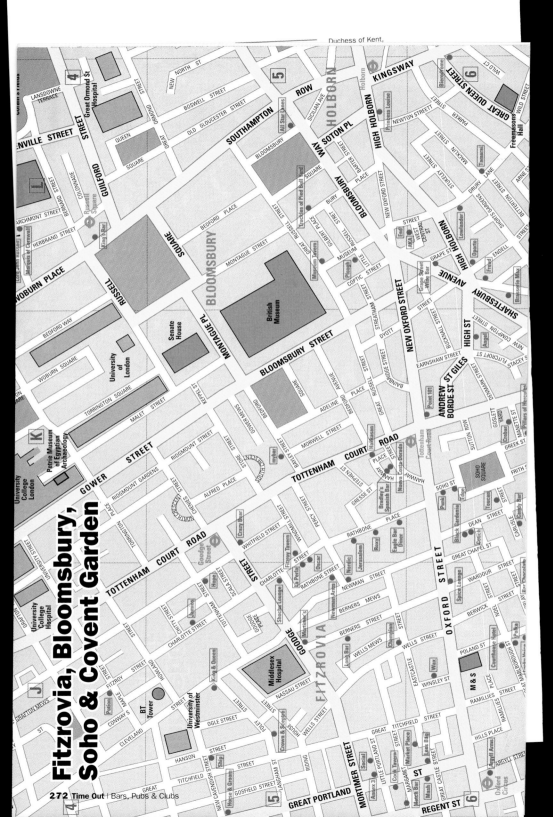

Fitzrovia, Bloomsbury, Soho & Covent Garden

Index

Index

A-Z index

Index

Index

Lockside Lounge p207
75-89 West Yard, Camden
Lock Place, NW1 8AF
(7284 0007/www.lockside
lounge.com).
Londesborough p199
36 Barbauld Road, N16 0SS
(7254 5865).
London Apprentice p234
62 Church Street, Isleworth,
Middx TW7 6BG (8560
1915).
Long Bar p41
The Sanderson, 50 Berners
Street, W1T 3NG (7300
1400).
Lonsdale p112
44-48 Lonsdale Road,
W11 2DE (7727 4080/
www.thelonsdale.co.uk).
Lord Clyde p173
27 Clennam Street, SE1 1ER
(7407 3397).
Lord Palmerston p226
33 Dartmouth Park Hill,
NW5 1HU (7485 1578/
www.geronimo-inns.co.uk).
Lord Stanley p207
51 Camden Park Road,
NW1 9BH (7428 9488).
Lost Society p145
697 Wandsworth Road,
SW8 3JF (7652 6526/
www.lostsociety.co.uk).
Lots Road Pub
& Dining Room p124
114 Lots Road, SW10 0RJ
(7352 6645/www.thespirit
group.com).
Lounge p147
56 Atlantic Road, SW9 8PX
(7733 5229/www.brixton
lounge.co.uk).
Loungelover p189
1 Whitby Street, E2 7DP
(7012 1234/www.lounge
lover.co.uk).
Low Life p50
34A Paddington Street,
W1U 4HG (7935 1272/
www.lowlifelounge.com).
Lowlander p38
36 Drury Lane, WC2B 5RR
(7379 7446/www.
lowlander.com).
Lucky Voice p69
52 Poland Street, W1F 7NH
(7439 3660/www.lucky
voice.co.uk).

m
Mad Bishop & Bear p97
Upper Concourse, Paddington
Station, Praed Street, W2 1HB
(7402 2441).
Madame Jo Jo's p244
8-10 Brewer Street, W1S 0SP
(7734 3040/www.madame
jojos.com).
Magdala p229
2A South Hill Park, NW3 2SB
(7435 2503).
Mahiki p55
1 Dover Street, W1S 4LD
(7493 9529/www.mahiki.
com).
Mandarin Bar p46
Mandarin Oriental Hyde Park,
66 Knightsbridge, SW1X 7LA
(7235 2000/www.mandarin
oriental.com).
Mango Landin' p147
40 St Matthew's Road,
SW2 1NL (7737 3044/
www.mangolandin.com).

Mansion p167
255 Gipsy Road, SE27 9QY
(8761 9016).
Maple Leaf p38
41 Maiden Lane, WC2E 7LJ
(7240 2843).
Market Place p41
11-13 Market Place, W1W
8AH (7079 2020/www.
marketplace-london.com).
Market Porter p173
9 Stoney Street, SE1 9AA
(7407 2495/www.themarket
porter.co.uk).
Marquess Tavern p217
32 Canonbury Street, N1 2TB
(7354 2975).
Mash p42
19-21 Great Portland Street,
W1W 8QB (7637 5555/
www.mash-bar.co.uk).
Mason's Arms p50
51 Upper Berkeley Street,
W1H 7QW (7723 2131).
Masons Arms p145
169 Battersea Park Road,
SW8 4BT (7622 2007).
Mass p244
St Matthew's Church,
Brixton Hill, SW2 1JF
(7738 7875).
Match Bar p42
37-38 Margaret Street,
W1G 0JF (7499 3443/
www.matchbar.com).
Match EC1 p30
45-47 Clerkenwell Road,
EC1M 5RS (7250 4002/
www.matchbar.com).
Mawson Arms p99
110 Chiswick Lane South,
W4 2QA (8994 2936).
Mayflower p162
117 Rotherhithe Street,
SE16 4NF (7237 4088).
Medcalf p30
38-40 Exmouth Market,
EC1R 4QE (7833 3533/
www.medcalfbar.co.uk).
Medicine Bar p217
181 Upper Street, N1 1RQ
(7704 9536/www.medicine
bar.net).
Met Bar p55
Metropolitan Hotel, 18-19
Old Park Lane, W1K 1LB
(7447 1000/www.
metropolitan.co.uk).
Metropolitan p120
60 Great Western Road,
W11 1AB (7229 9254/
www.realpubs.co.uk).
Mews of Mayfair p55
10-11 Lancashire Court,
W1S 1EY (7518 9388/
www.mewsofmayfair.com).
Microbar p145
14 Lavender Hill, SW11 5RW
(7228 5300/www.microbar.
org).
Milk & Honey p71
61 Poland Street, W1F 7NU
(7292 9949/www.
mlkhny.com).
Millbank Lounge p61
City Inn Hotel, 30 John Islip
Street, SW1P 4DD (7932
4700).
Ministry of Sound p244
103 Gaunt Street, SE1 6DP
(7740 8600/www.ministry
ofsound.com).
Mitre p127
81 Dawes Road, SW6 7DU
(7386 8877/www.
fulhammitre.com).

Mitre p98
24 Craven Terrace, W2 3QH
(7262 5240).
Mocoto p47
145 Knightsbridge,
SW1X 7PA (7225 2300/
www.mocoto.co.uk).
Mokssh p129
222-224 Fulham Road,
SW10 9NB (7352 6548/
www.mokssh.com).
Monkey Chews p209
2 Queen's Crescent, NW5 4EP
(7267 6406/www.monkey
chews.com).
Montague Arms p175
289 Queens Road, SE15 2PA
(7639 4923).
Montgomery Place p112
31 Kensington Park Road,
W11 2EU (7792 3921/
www.montgomeryplace.co.uk).
Moose p50
31 Duke Street, W1U
1LG (7224 3452/
www.vpmg.net).
Morgan Arms p183
43 Morgan Street, E3 5AA
(8980 6389/www.geronimo-
inns.co.uk).
Morpeth Arms p61
58 Millbank, SW1P 4RW
(7834 6442).
Mosquito Bar p151
Indian Flavours, 5 Clapham
High Street, SW4 7TS
(7622 4003/7622 2060/
www.theindianflavours.com).
Mother Bar p189
333 Old Street, EC1V 9LE
(7739 5949/www.333
mother.com).
Mucky Pup p219
39 Queen's Head Street,
N1 8NQ (7226 2572/
www.muckypup-london.com).
Museum Tavern p21
49 Great Russell Street,
WC1B 3BA (7242 8987).
mybar p21
11-13 Bayley Street,
WC1B 3HD (7667 6050/
www.myhotels.com).
Mô Tea Room p55
23 Heddon Street, W1B
4BH (7434 4040/www.
momoresto.com).

n
Nag's Head p200
9 Orford Road, E17 9LP
(8520 9709).
Nag's Head p19
53 Kinnerton Street,
SW1X 8ED (7235 1135).
Narrow Boat p219
119 St Peter Street, N1 8PZ
(7288 0572).
Narrow Street Pub
& Dining Room p183
44 Narrow Street, E14 8DQ
(7265 8931).
Nectar p124
562 King's Road, SW6 2DZ
(7326 7450/www.
nectarbar.co.uk).
Negozio Classica p112
283 Westbourne Grove,
W11 2QA (7034 0005/
www.negozioclassica.
co.uk).
Neighbourhood p244
12 Acklam Road, W10 5QZ
(7524 7979/www.
neighbourhoodclub.net).

Nell Gwynne p78
1-2 Bull Inn Court, WC2R 0NP
(7240 5579).
Nell of Old Drury p38
29 Catherine Street,
WC2B 5JS (7836 5328/
www.nellofolddrury.com).
New Cross Inn p175
323 New Cross Road,
SE14 6AS (8692 1866).
New Rose p219
84-86 Essex Road, N1 8LU
(7226 1082/www.
newrose.co.uk).
Newman Arms p42
23 Rathbone Street, W1T 1NG
(7636 1127/www.newman
arms.co.uk).
Nightingale p133
97 Nightingale Lane,
SW12 8NX (8673 1637).
93 Feet East p244
150 Brick Lane, E1 6QN
(7247 3293/www.93feet
east.com).
Nordic p42
25 Newman Street, W1T 1PN
(7631 3174/www.nordic
bar.com).
Norfolk Arms p39
28 Leigh Street, WC1H 9EP
(7388 3937/www.norfolk
arms.co.uk).
North London Tavern p232
375 Kilburn High Road,
NW6 7QB (7625 6634).
North Pole p169
131 Greenwich High Road,
SE10 8JA (8853 3020/www.
northpolegreenwich.com).
North Star p197
24 Browning Street, E11 3AR
(8989 5777).
Northgate p219
113 Southgate Road, N1 3JS
(7359 7392).
Notting Hill Arts Club p244
21 Notting Hill Gate, W11 3JQ
(7460 4459/www.notting
hillartsclub.com).
Nueva Costa Dorada p42
47-55 Hanway Street, W1T
1UX (7631 5117/www.
costadoradarestaurant.co.uk).
Number 22 p171
22 Half Moon Lane,
SE24 9HU (7095 9922/
www.number-22.com).
Numidie p168
48 Westow Hill, SE19 1RX
(8766 6166/www.numidie.
co.uk).

o
06 St Chad's Place p46
6 St Chad's Place, WC1X
9HH (7278 3355/
www.6stchadsplace.com).
Oakdale Arms p211
283 Hermitage Road, N4 1NP
(8800 2013).
L'Oasis p183
237 Mile End Road, E1 4AA
(7702 7051/www.loasis
stepney.co.uk).
Occo Bar & Kitchen p51
58 Crawford Street, W1H 4NA
(7724 4991/www.occo.
co.uk).
Ochre p85
2-3 Creed Lane, EC4V 5BR
(0871 223 5106).
Old Bank of England p85
194 Fleet Street, EC4A 2LT
(7430 2255).

Index

Index

Advertisers' Index

Please refer to relevant sections for addresses /
telephone numbers

Index

Maps

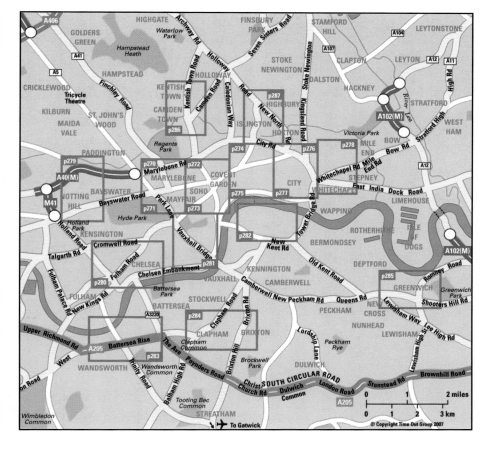

© Copyright Time Out Group 2007

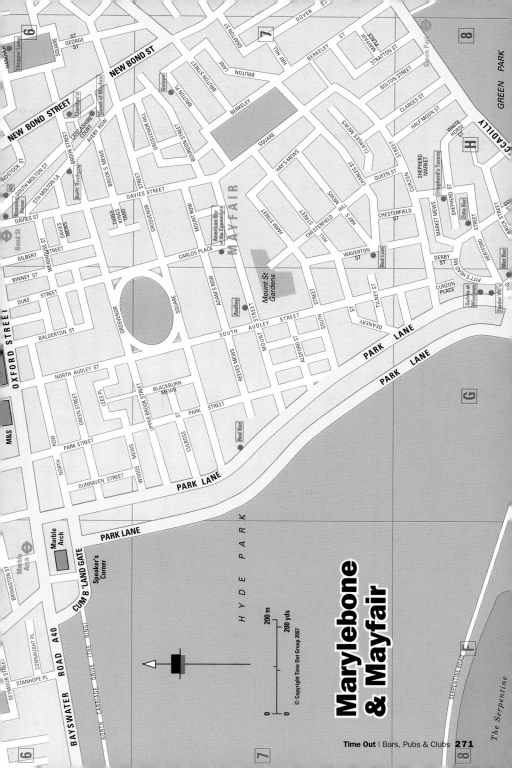

Fitzrovia, Bloomsbury, Soho & Covent Garden

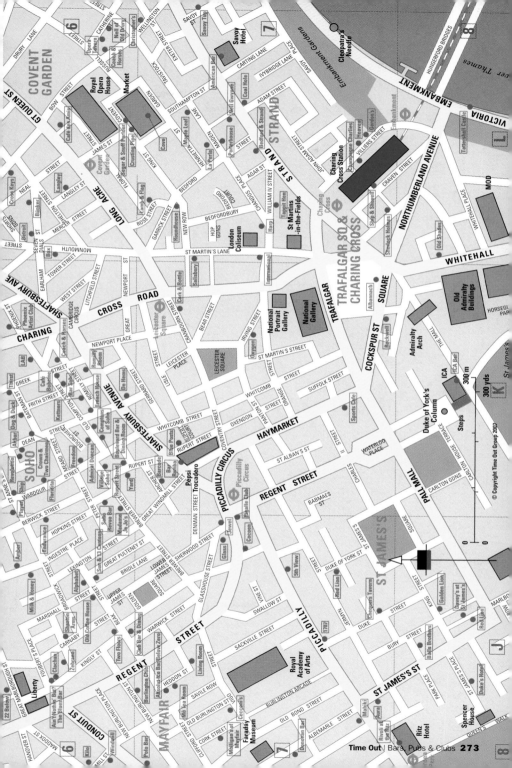

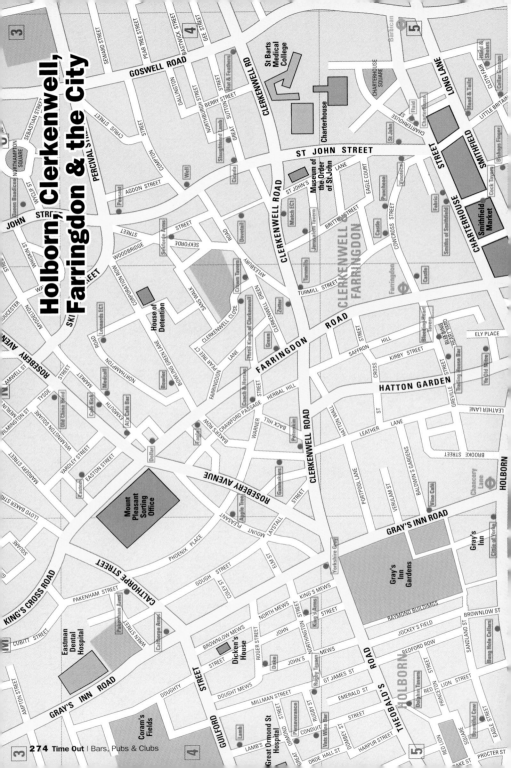

Holborn, Clerkenwell, Farringdon & the City

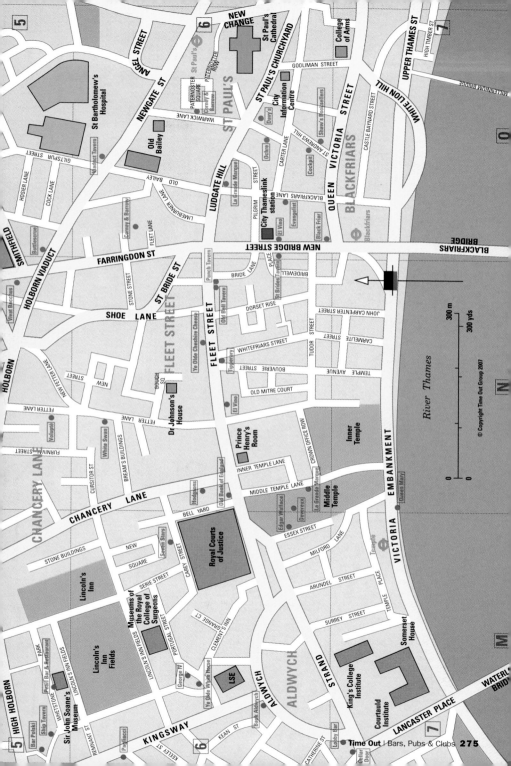

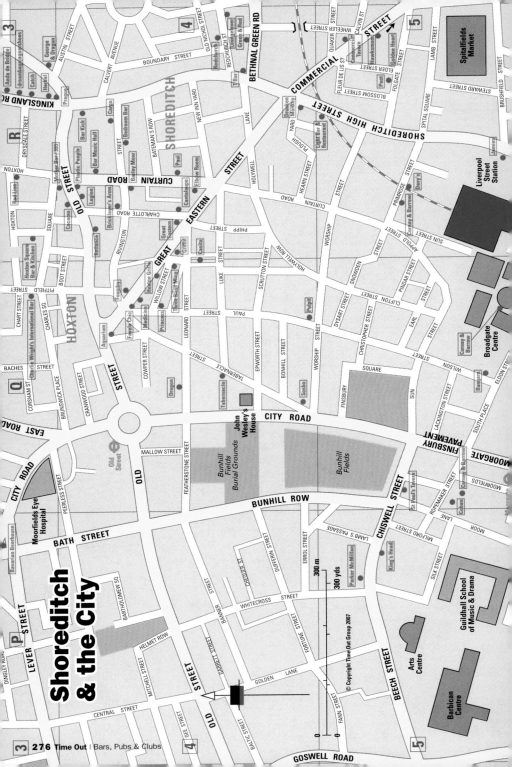

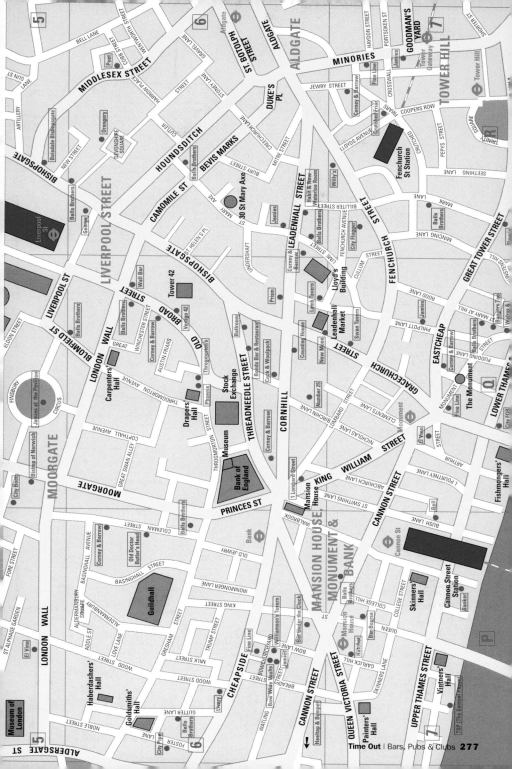

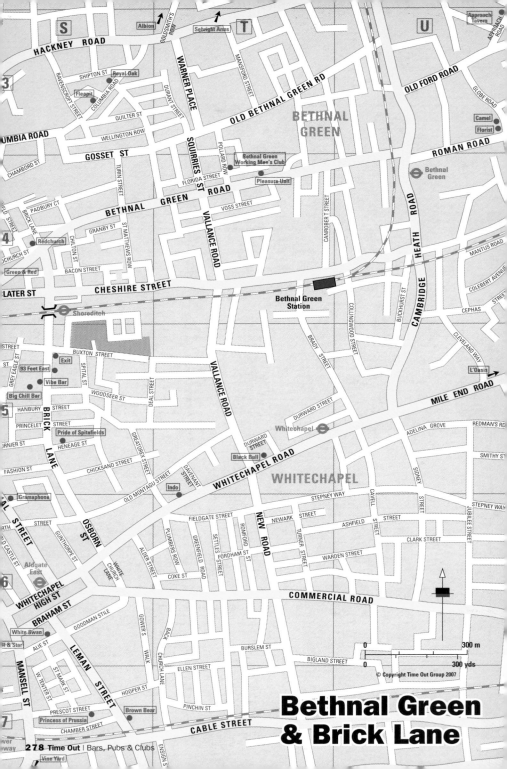

Bethnal Green & Brick Lane

Notting Hill

© Copyright Time Out Group 2007

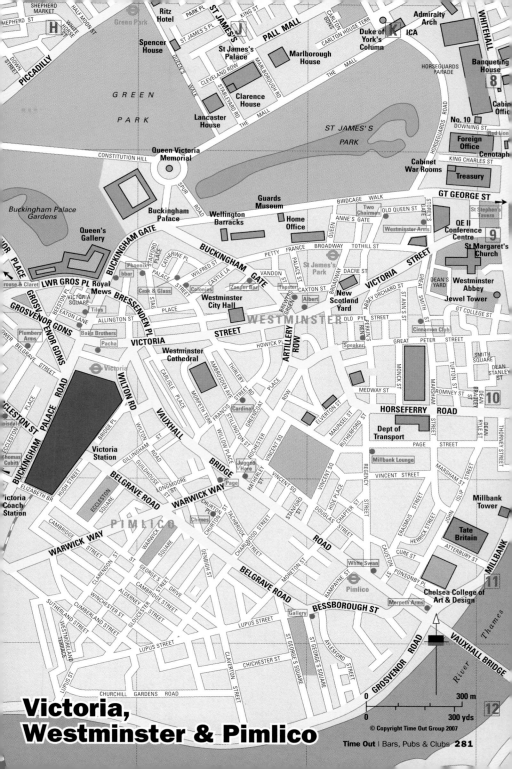

Victoria, Westminster & Pimlico

© Copyright Time Out Group 2007

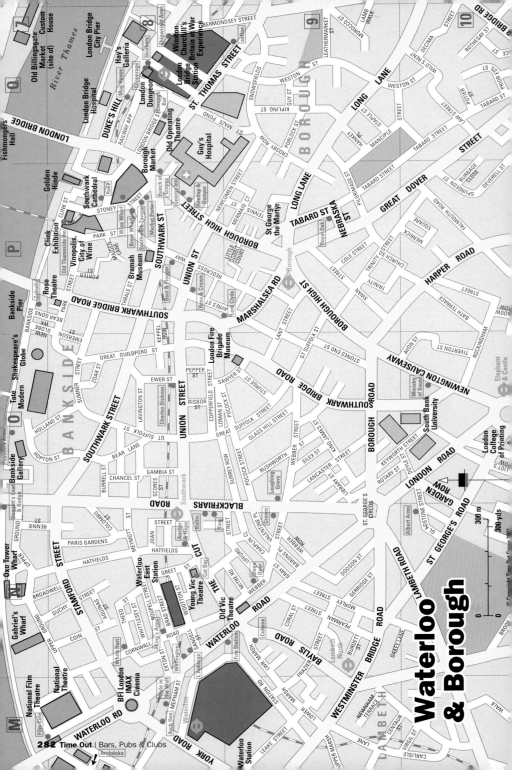

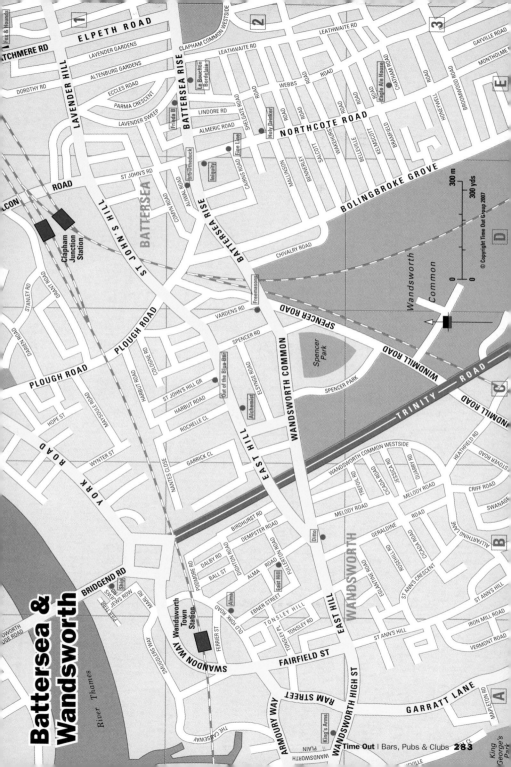

Battersea & Wandsworth

ELPETH ROAD

LAVENDER HILL

BATTERSEA RISE

BATTERSEA

ST JOHN'S HILL

ST JOHN'S RD

ROAD

LCON

NORTHCOTE ROAD

BOLINGBROKE GROVE

PLOUGH ROAD

PLOUGH ROAD

YORK

ROAD

BATTERSEA RISE

CHIVALRY ROAD

SPENCER ROAD

WANDSWORTH COMMON

EAST HILL

Wandsworth Common

Spencer Park

WINDMILL ROAD

TRINITY ROAD

WINDMILL ROAD

WANDSWORTH COMMON WESTSIDE

WANDSWORTH

EAST HILL

BRIDGEND RD

Wandsworth Town Station

SWANDON WAY

FAIRFIELD ST

RAM STREET

GARRATT LANE

ARMOURY WAY

WANDSWORTH HIGH ST

River Thames

King George's Park

Latchmere Rd, Lavender Gardens, Altenburg Gardens, Eccles Road, Parma Crescent, Lavender Sweep, Dorothy Rd, Clapham Common Westside, Leathwaite Rd, Leathwaite Rd, Webbs Road, Road, Road, Road, Eagle Ale House, Chatham Road, Gayville Road, Montholme, Road, Road, Road, Road, Road, Road, Honeywell, Broomwood Road, Lindore Rd, Shelgate Road, Cairns Road, Wakehurst Road, Mallinson, Bennerley, Salcott, Belleville, Kelmscott, Bramfield, Almeric Road, Eccles Rd, Comyn Road, Aliwal Road

St John's Rd, Vardens Rd, Spencer Rd, Elsynge Road, St John's Hill Gr, Harbut Road, Rochelle Cl, Garrick Cl, Cologne Rd, Harbut Road, Nantes Close, Stanley Rd, Grant Road, Darien Road, Falcon Road, Wandsworth Bridge Road, Hope St, Wynter St

Birdhurst Rd, Dempster Road, Dalby Rd, Ball St, Podmore Rd, Dighton Road, Fullerton Road, Alma, Road, Melody Road, Geraldine, Cicada Road, Dujardin Rd, Cicada Road, Road, Swanage, Criff Road, Trefoil Rd, Jessica Rd, Cicada Road, Rosehill Rd, Eglantine Road, Allfarthing Lane, Heathfield Rd, Stover Road

Poydmore Rd, Ebner Street, Tonsley Pl, Tonsley Hill, Tonsley Rd, Ferrier St, Old York Road, St Ann's Crescent, St Ann's Hill, St Ann's Hill, Iron Mill Road, Vermont Road, Mapleton Rd

King's Arms, King's Head, Smugglers Way, Pier, Bell Lane Cl, Jews Row, The Causeway, Fairfield St

Frieda B, Le Bouchon Bordelais, Holy Drinker, Iniquity, Breadtheduck, Eagle Bar, Freemasons, Out of the Blue Bar, Alchemist, Dino, East Hill, Alma, Shop

Clapham Junction Station

300 m

300 yds

© Copyright Time Out Group 2007

Clapham & Brixton

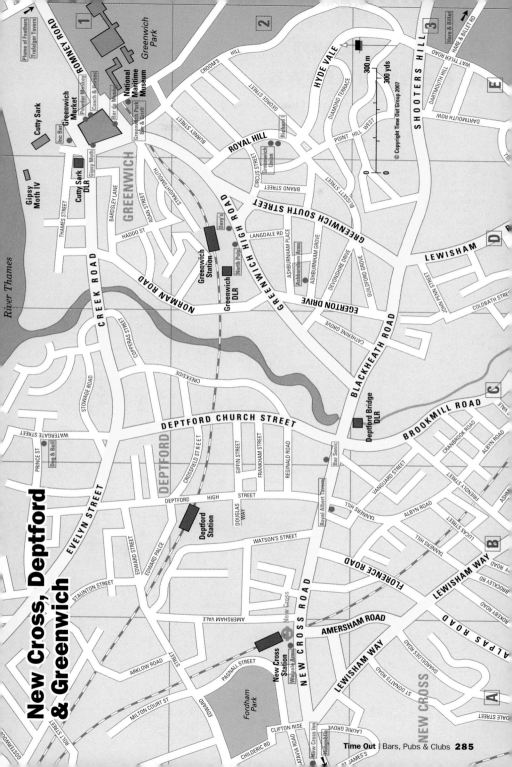

New Cross, Deptford & Greenwich

River Thames

Plume of Feathers
Trafalgar Tavern

Cutty Sark

Gipsy Moth IV

Greenwich Park

ROMNEY ROAD

Powder Monkey
Coach & Horses
Inc Bar
Bar du Musée
Greenwich Market

National Maritime Museum

Cutty Sark DLR

Gipsy Moth

GREENWICH

THAMES STREET

CREEK ROAD

STRAIGHTSMOUTH

ROAN STREET

BARDSLEY LANE

HADDO ST

COPPERAS STREET

STOWAGE ROAD

NORMAN ROAD

Greenwich Park Bar & Grill
Richard I
Greenwich Union

ROYAL HILL

CIRCUS STREET

BURNEY STREET

GEORGE STREET

CROOM'S HILL

HYDE VALE

Diamond Terrace

POINT HILL WEST

SHOOTERS HILL

WAT TYLER ROAD

Hare & Billet
Hare & Billet RD

DARTMOUTH ROW

DARTMOUTH HILL

© Copyright Time Out Group 2007

300 m
300 yds

BRAND STREET

BLISSETT STREET

GREENWICH SOUTH STREET

Davy's
North Pole
Greenwich Station
Greenwich DLR

LANGDALE RD

GREENWICH HIGH ROAD

Ashburnham Place
Ashburnham Arms
ASHBURNHAM GROVE

DEVONSHIRE DRIVE

GUILDFORD GROVE

EGERTON DRIVE

CATHERINE GROVE

LEWISHAM

JOHN PENN STREET

COLDBATH STREET

BLACKHEATH ROAD

Deptford Bridge DLR

BROOKMILL ROAD

VALE

CRANBROOK ROAD

ALBYN ROAD

ALBYN ROAD

FRIENDLY STREET

DEPTFORD CHURCH STREET

DEPTFORD

CROSSFIELD STREET

GIFFIN STREET

FRANKHAM STREET

REGINALD ROAD

Bar Sonic

VANGUARD STREET

TANNER'S HILL

Royal Albert Tavern

LUCAS STREET

TANNERS HILL

LEWISHAM WAY

BROCKLEY RD

WATERGATE STREET

PRINCE ST

Dog & Bell

EVELYN STREET

EDWARD STREET

EDWARD PALCE

STAUNTON STREET

DEPTFORD HIGH STREET

Deptford Station

DOUGLAS WAY

WATSON'S STREET

FLORENCE ROAD

AMERSHAM ROAD

LEWISHAM WAY

ALPAS ROAD

ROKEBY ROAD

ARKLOW ROAD

PAGNALL STREET

EDWARD

MILTON COURT ST

Fordham Park

AMERSHAM VALE

New Cross Station
Walpole Arms

NEW CROSS ROAD

St DONATTS ROAD

STARBOARDS ROAD

NEW CROSS

CLIFTON RISE

CHILDERIC RD

LAURIE GROVE

DALE STREET

New Cross Inn
Hobgoblin

James's

Time Out | Bars, Pubs & Clubs **285**

Camden Town
& Kentish Town

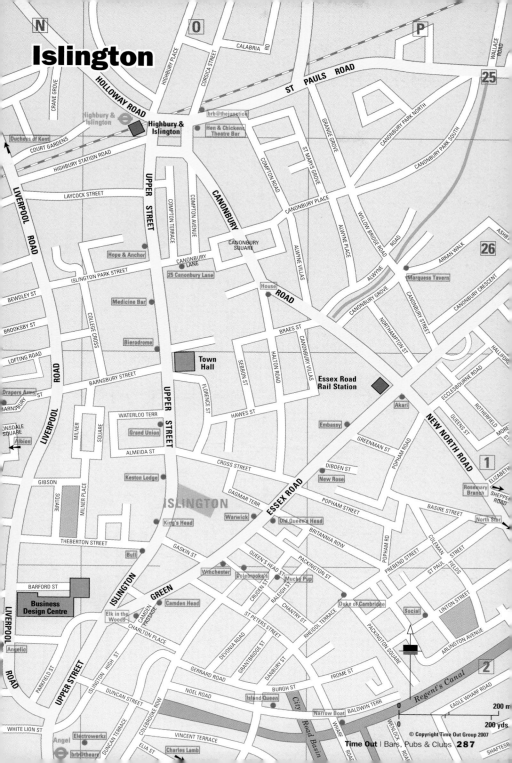

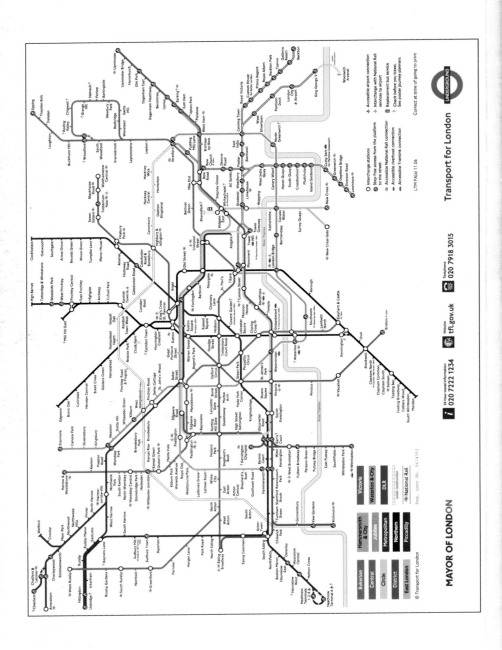

TIM DEE

A birdwatcher for fifty years and a radio producer for thirty, for the last ten years Tim Dee has written on nature and landscapes. His first book, *The Running Sky*, was published by Jonathan Cape in 2009 and described his encounters with birds across Britain. His second book, *Four Fields*, described more deeply his ideas of the pastoral. He collaborated with the poet Simon Armitage on the anthology *The Poetry of Birds*, and his most recent book is *Landfill* (Little Toller), a study of gulls and people.

Ground Work

Writings on Places and People

EDITED BY
Tim Dee

VINTAGE

1 3 5 7 9 10 8 6 4 2

Vintage
20 Vauxhall Bridge Road,
London SW1V 2SA

Vintage is part of the Penguin Random House group of companies whose addresses can be
found at global.penguinrandomhouse.com

Penguin
Random House
UK

CONTENTS

INTRODUCTION

We are living – many believe – in the Anthropocene, an epoch where everything of Earth's current matter and life, as well as the shape of things to come, is being determined by the ruinous activities of just one soft-skinned, warm-blooded, short-lived, pedestrian ape.

How, then, to live on our planet in the mess that we have made? And how to do that in harmony with the rest of the world that we have permitted to remain?

Places are anthropogenic creations called into being by the meeting of humans and their environment. They are prominent among our contributions to our times and our space. We make what has been called patterned ground. Place-making is a signal of our species. We make good ones and bad ones, and plenty of neither-here-nor-there ones. Good, bad or indifferent, they operate on all their constituents.

This is a book of writing about places. The personal geographies come from as many acres as people. The writing about them shares one constant: every description and every thought arises from someone being detained – by views, buildings, sculpture, weather, chairs, churches, trees, streets, people, memories. It seems, broadly, good to be stopped by a place. And this is one way a place comes into being. Our attention to them makes places significant. They are inhabited. Seen this way, these places are all cultural landscapes of one sort or another. Seen this way, they are vital for life. What follows, therefore, are various relief maps: they show what places might look like to themselves, but also how places work on us.

There is succour here. And this is important because most of the time most of us are *unplaced*. Even when we live somewhere that we can call home, we spend much of our time away. We traffic along roads, through airports, in offices, hospitals, supermarkets – all non-places where the most we can hope for is a relatively frictionless passage. The success of these zones is measured by their throughput, their flow, their footfall. The sinuous path many airports have imposed around their entrances and exits via their duty-free shopping areas might define this world. I want nothing to do with it, yet here I am joining the conga.

An oblong of flat glassy space is now our most common go-to place. Young children, scrolling their fingers, attempt to enlarge images in books as they can on a screen. I've seen that. Digits working the digits. Some might try the same outdoors. Why not? Unfold the clouds. Bring me my bow. Mediation is not new. Magnification has long assisted birdwatchers. Ted Hughes's killer thrushes in his poem were, I am sure, seen through binocular lenses. But optics can distort as well as enlarge. The very tools that take us in close are also keeping us, ultimately, from any happily muddying contact with the hard matter of the world. Objects, as it says on North American car mirrors, are closer than they appear. We fail to notice this when mediation is all.

One of the most depressing places I have been in recent years is Bellaghy in County Londonderry. Seamus Heaney is buried there near his childhood home: the great poet of the personal omphalos, the navel stone that might mark the centre of the world, hence the most important place of all. His grave was young when I was there, still bare and earthy. The town was something else. A flesher's survived, J. Overend & Sons, and I shivered at the name and the family's tasks, but many of the other shopfronts were boarded up, or rather blinded with window-sized stickers of garish leafy scenes, manipulated images of healthiness and happiness, screens of greenery elsewhere.

To talk about trees in dark times, Bertolt Brecht wrote, is almost a crime. As more and more people in the world seem to have no place of their own, it has got harder, rightly, for the fortunate to linger in any sort of sacred grove. The Jungle at Calais was certainly a place. And in the knowledge of such places, to extol Birnam Wood or

Burnham Beeches or any other sylvan spot would seem like an escapist romance, an umbrageous avoidance of the issue, that few can afford. Masking economic and social collapse and failure with digitised verdancy seems comparably culpable. Natural beauty once guaranteed the status of a place. Not now.

The threat to our understanding and valuing of place is not, then, the heaped-up world of the built environment. That is our habitat and has been for thousands of years, perhaps, as Mark Cocker has suggested, ever since we shared caves with swallows where their 'procreant cradles' gave us an idea for mud bricks. As long as we've been settlers we have been place-makers. We've made *pied-à-terre*, we've lived *in situ*. What saps the possibilities of rooted or detained or placed life is the untextured places we increasingly live among: the unmuddy world of the depthless screen and the sealed space. How many accumulated years have I lived in a car? Even before virtual life threatened lived life, the *place-ness* of place was under threat in this way: specificities have been dulled, local habitations and names globalised, the instress or haecceity of every street or field driven from common memory. It was house martins, the swallows' cousins, that King Duncan saw breeding on the battlements of the Macbeths' castle. It seemed propitious to him that the birds shared a home with his hosts. But it wasn't good news for Duncan, and now the martins too are struggling on British houses where the eaves are so made these days that there is little purchase. The birds' mud nests cannot stick.

*

Two thoughts – on the forecast end of places and on their observed persistence:

> This ... is less a warning than a prophecy of doom: the prophecy that if what is called development is allowed to multiply at the present rate, that by the end of the century Great Britain will consist of isolated areas of preserved monuments in a desert of wire, concrete roads, cosy plots and bungalows. There will be no

real distinction between town and country. Both will consist of a limbo of shacks, bogus rusticities, wire and aerodromes, set in some fir-poled fields.

Ian Nairn, from 'Outrage', Architectural Review, 1955

I live in a community whose members are scattered piecemeal around London (some of them live outside the city altogether); the telephone is our primary connection, backed up by the Tube line, the bus route, the private car and a number of restaurants, pubs and clubs. My 'quarter' is a network of communication lines with intermittent assembly points; and it cannot be located on a map.

Yet place is important: it bears down on us, we mythicise it – often it is our greatest comfort, the one reassuringly solid element in an otherwise soft city. As we move across the square to the block of shops on the street, with pigeons and sweet papers underfoot and the weak sun lighting the tarmac, the city is eclipsed by the here-and-now; the sight and smell and sound of place go to make up the fixed foot of life in the metropolis. Place, like a mild habitual pain, reminds one that one is; its familiar details and faces – even the parked cars which you recognise as having been there in that spot for months – assure us of a life of repetitions, of things that will endure and survive us, when the city at large seems all change and flux. Loyalty to and hunger for place are among the keenest of city feelings.

Jonathan Raban, from Soft City, 1974

*

Places, 'An anthology of Britain', edited by Ronald Blythe (and made for Oxfam), was published in 1981. It is rich in fine writing about beautiful places. There are poems and essays from, among others, Ruth Pitter, John Betjeman, Susan Hill, Alan Sillitoe, R. S. Thomas, Jan Morris, Dirk Bogarde and John Stewart Collis. Its prevailing mood is wistful and elegiac. Almost everywhere described is either no longer fully there or is remembered from childhood. It seems twentieth-century life has sent place-writing adrift. In one memorable formulation the historian Richard Cobb, writing about his Essex childhood, describes how he has always preferred facing backwards when travelling because the world appears more honest as it is disappearing. It's a rationale for a historian's methodology (the ghost of Walter Benjamin's Angel of History is perhaps hovering nearby), but it also describes the myopia about the present that is common to many of the contributions in the book. Throughout its soft-spoken pages the writing intimates its underlying subject: the long and continuing impact of industrialisation, the severance from the perceived sustenance and verities of the rural past, and the alienation of urban life. There is some writing about London, but it seems that in general today's places – cities and towns and all the living zones – are not places to be written. It is as if something isn't working, as if Britain, estranged from itself, couldn't make places any more.

The injuries continued, and another book looked to staunch some wounds and advance an argument. In 1984 Jonathan Cape published *Second Nature*, a 240-page collection of essays and illustrations edited by Richard Mabey (with Sue Clifford and Angela King). The book was made for the charity Common Ground, and its jacket declared the organisation's then purpose as being to stem the tide of destruction of much that was wild and natural in Britain, by providing a fusion between the arts and nature conservation.

The editors assembled an impressive collection of words and images, and divided the contributions into three sections headed Personal Landscapes, Nature and Culture, and Beyond the Golden Age. Among the writing commissioned were pieces from John Fowles, Ronald Blythe, Fay Weldon, Peter Levi, Norman Nicholson and Kim Taplin. Intersecting the essays were illustrations of artworks by, among others, Henry Moore, Elisabeth Frink, Richard Long, David Nash, Norman Ackroyd, Andy Goldsworthy and Fay Godwin.

Common Ground was looking forward, but most of the writing in *Second Nature* still looked back. The historical analysis in essays by John Barrell, John Berger and Raymond Williams reframed the past. But the book stood, as it declared, at the end of things, beyond a golden age. The ancient continuities were still just about graspable, but the incoming tide of destruction was running high. The old natural world was dying and, although imminent, the new man-made world, which had killed it off, had yet satisfactorily to be born, at least in prose. It is more than a collection of elegies, but most of the book's literary efforts were put into accounts of what had been lost. Common Ground was only a year old and much of the writing in the book (the visual arts are less constrained) makes for sunset songs, or requiems for the end of the long, lived-in (and perceived as mostly benign) entanglement of a people and their (mostly rural) places.

The poem isn't in the book, but much of what is there has the same odd tense of the pressingly posthumous of Philip Larkin's 'Going, Going':

> And that will be England gone,
> The shadows, the meadows, the lanes,
> The guildhalls, the carved choirs.
> There'll be books; it will linger on
> In galleries; but all that remains
> For us will be concrete and tyres.

How the value of place-writing has shifted, and what, more generally, has happened to ideas about place since the 1980s is, I hope, evident in this book. Concrete and tyres, the man said. We now understand that the paved world can be as articulate as the vegetated. Philip Larkin's poems themselves announced that. What has changed is that we are now prepared to consider as meaningful habitat places previously ignored or written off. Modernity has shattered our world like never before, we are more deracinated than ever, but because we feel most places to be *nowhere* we have also learned that *anywhere* can be a *somewhere*. All of our habitat is relevant: not just the pretty bits. It turns out, counter to prime-ministerial sound-bites, that we are all at once citizens of nowhere and citizens of the world. In one extraordinary essay in Ronald Blythe's collection, Russell Hoban questioned what a place might be: 'Place itself may not be possible at all ... all the place ... is may well be no more than the moving point of consciousness in us.' Whether we call this place doesn't matter (Heidegger and Merleau-Ponty's ideas are stalking somewhere about Hoban), but, whatever it is, it 'provides a cross-over between the seen and the unseen, between the potential and the kinetic energies of that space we move in which is not simply space: perhaps it is the soul of the universe; and perhaps we are the organ of perception required by that soul'.

A place, then, as ever, might be a hollow tree or the dark end of a street, a childhood bedroom, a roundabout, a refugee camp or a sewage farm. In the last thirty years all sorts of *anywheres* were promoted in the collective consciousness and could be written as places. Despite this, none of them were secure. All places are challenged by modern times, yet none will go quietly, even those hedged with simulacra or trampled under real feet. Places, meetings of people and world, remain stubbornly *there*, itchy, palpable, determining. Good or bad, they are felt on our skin and get under it too. Time, the deer, is in Hallaig wood, said Sorley MacLean (as translated by Seamus Heaney). Birmingham is what I think with, said Roy Fisher.

Among the pieces collected here, the art of Richard Long and Greg Poole does some place-holding for me. All three of us are Bristol people. Greg and I have birdwatched together for more than thirty years. We don't do so much now, and the place we most often meet is just behind his garden where his micro-meadow is up and coming. He tries again and again to get my non-bird naming – flowers, butterflies, moths, dragonflies, bats – up to scratch. I stake a claim to Richard Long's work. The polished stone behind his text here is the product of generations of Bristol bottoms sliding down a smoothing slope of rock between the old observatory and camera obscura on the top of the Downs and the approach-way to the Clifton Suspension Bridge (subject of Patrick McGuinness's piece here). For an hour of most Sundays for years of my youth my sister and I would add our shine.

A green city, Bristol has been called these past years, a green capital even. Green capital is what it has. One of the reasons I like the place is because from almost anywhere locked within its streets and buildings, you can see beyond to a green rim, where the city ends. It talks to its opposite in this way. My grandfather was a clerk in the old Fry's chocolate factory in Keynsham. From his desk he could see a summit ring of trees on a round hill south towards Bath. They kept him going, he would say. And the green belt fed Romanticism too. The poems of the *Lyrical Ballads*, first set in type in Bristol, were for Coleridge and Wordsworth made *out of* that West Country green.

At its simplest or starkest the effect of a cultural landscape is expressed in a poem fashioned from another west. Seamus Heaney, in his last book, *Human Chain*, translated 'A Herbal' by Guillevic, the great twentieth-century poet from Brittany, who was also a civil servant in the French Ministry of Finance. Towards the conclusion of the poem, which lists the grasses and flowers of a western headland, is this simple, somewhat stony, couplet:

> I had my existence. I was there.
> Me in place and the place in me.

It is striking how few of the places described here might be thought special other than to their describers. There are no grand houses, no Georgian cities, no national parks, no demarcated nature sanctuaries. Beauty spots – remember those? Preserved territory or reservations like these perhaps lose the quintessence of place, the co-evolved mutuality of people and surroundings, which many of the writers notice here. Places are better unplanned, when thay are feral spaces where things and lives can get on, more on less, like the entangled bank where life thrives, that Darwin described in the last paragraph of his *Origin*. Calculated attempts to make places often show only the dead hand of management. New public spaces often suffer in this regard; public art, too.

Striking, too, is how ugly and broken many telling places are. We paint with distemper when, as now, the time is felt as out of joint. In much of Britain everyone navigates what Ian Nairn called *subtopia*. The *drosscape*, Alan Berger's American term for the *splurge*, is perfectly at home in the UK, and extends for many miles in most directions.

Topographical phenomenologists and cultural geographers have found things to say in the non-places – those zones where we, unwittingly, spend much of our lives, where indeed we mostly live, but where no one feels at home. There are books on shopping malls, the M25; there is Jean Baudrillard's *America*. But it is scant fare. Recently the leftovers, the ends of places, have been more arresting and have offered better nourishment. W. G. Sebald was an unlikely tour guide, but showed many readers some ways back into the richness of rot, the humus of memory meeting an evanescent world.

But long before Eeyore walked East Anglia, Richard Mabey (the presiding genius of this book, its own spirit of place, and the only writer common to this and the other two place books I've mentioned here) had directed our attention to *The Unofficial Countryside*. Following him, Patrick Wright botanised on asphalt in *A Journey Through Ruins* and Paul Farley co-wrote *Edgelands* and re-launched a habitat. Ken Worpole studied suburban cemeteries and paved-over front gardens. The whole of Essex seemed brought to book. J. A. Baker's *The Peregrine*, like a radioactive pellet, the product of a sick man tracking a sick species in a sick place, became a holy text. Werner Herzog teaches it. Things fall apart and many of us like it that way. Analogue scratches on vinyl speak of a relationship between sound and listener as no digital dead air can. Ghost walks, hauntings, landfill, the draw-down of silting tides – all have made for copious place-based literary deposits. Edward Thomas has steered Matthew Hollis; the Thames estuary flooded Rachel Lichtenstein; Hayden Lorimer is excavating a pet cemetery on the North Sea shore. A kind of grit, the granulated ordinary past, has become a common currency. Copper pennies on the tongue are obols for many a traveller. Julia Blackburn, just out of Essex, knows the old money. David Matless mapped made-up landscapes and our inherited fantasy localisms in his *Landscape and Englishness*. Tim Ingold read into the lines on the land. We learned to call the scuffed marks that we've footed into a place desire paths. These have been Richard Long's *arteries*, ever since he created *A Line Made by Walking* fifty years ago in Wiltshire.

Places call up the places they were; that is part of what makes a place. Aside from Milton Keynes (which feels olde worlde these days, as old futuristic sci-fi films do, or the words *Betamax* or *escalator* or even *sci-fi*), is there any city in Britain that is more twentieth century than nineteenth? I can't think of any. But we have new ideas for these old places. Ruin lust is one of them. Entropy tourism. I recently joined the pilgrims to the modern ruin of a 1960s seminary at Kilmahew on the Clyde: as striking a place now as it falls down as it was when built up. Jonathan Meades made a tremendously *ferocious* TV film about rust. A recent book by Caitlin Desilvey is called *Curated Decay*.'Nothing in his life / Became him like the leaving it' – so Malcolm describes the death of the Thane of Cawdor in *Macbeth*. We might say the same of most of our places today. The ones that matter to us are still often going or gone. Ozymandias truncated says more than the whole man would. We don't want to know how the garish Greeks painted their palaces. Filters on our phone cameras will age an image before our eyes. But modern life has always done this. These fragments, quoted T. S. Eliot, I have shored against my ruins. W. H. Auden was drawn to old human junk in rocky places. Rimbaud liked trash and kitsch. We laughed at a president for fixing a new marble penis on a dismembered Mars. The broken place speaks louder than the perfect place. Even the National Trust finds visitors more interested in the kitchens of the great house than their ballrooms. Downstairs tells more truth than up.

There are many places noted here, many other conversations with natural places as well as nurtured places, with other people, and with other animals: Michael Viney has been writing dispatches from a shifting Irish shore for decades; Fiona Sampson moves house; Tessa Hadley looks outdoors from inside on a new view; Helen Macdonald accesses her *girlitude* in western Surrey; Andrew Motion goes fishing; Richard Holmes gets drenched; Peter Davidson raises the ghost of one of the first in Britain to consciously notice and capture an ordinary place; Marina Warner remembers being ushered into a landscape by Peter Levi; Andrew McNeillie digs over his allotment and thinks of his plot; Sean Borodale goes underground; Alexandra Harris sets out to learn about a place and asks where it leads her; Hugh Brody maps his British childhood onto his adult life in Arctic Canada; John Burnside stops at some wayside shrines; Sean O'Brien plays out; Adam Thorpe lets a muddy puddle take a cast of his mind; Nick Davies wonders what birds make of their places; Barbara Bender logs how communal memories can be preserved; Adam Nicolson digs up his own; Philip Marsden passes down river; Phillip Hoare goes out to sea; Dexter Petley asks what the salt water gives back.

*

In the summer of 1801, Coleridge often went walking in the Lake District. On 18 June he found a rest stop:

> A Hollow place in the rock like a Coffin – a Sycamore Bush at the head, enough to give a shadow for my Face, & just at the Foot one tall Foxglove – exactly my own Length – there I lay & slept – It was quite soft.

Before the tide ebbs a grazing limpet heads home … to its home scar: the shape of its shell can grow to precisely match the contours of the rock it fixes to. The limpet has marked the rock; the rock has marked the limpet. Jen Hadfield has written poems about the home scar of a limpet. It's a nice term for a nice idea. Richard Pearce has been counting the same in north Cornwall ever since the oiling disaster that followed the sinking of the *Torrey Canyon* in 1967. He showed me Porthmear beach where there are, he has counted, one million home scars.

*

This collection of new writing about places draws on the ideas and ideals of Common Ground. Common Ground gave Britain the concept of *local distinctiveness*, and this book is made for the organisation that has worked since the 1980s to revive, preserve and celebrate the diverse, local and intimate connections that people and communities have had, and might yet have, with the landscape that surrounds them.

Thirty years ago, Sue Clifford and Angela King set up Common Ground to help us understand where we are vis-à-vis nature in Britain: both to acknowledge our footprint, the tyre tracks, a paved country, its concrete overcoat, and to encourage some repairs, interventions, preservations and some newfangledness, and to do this in the belief that a relationship with our local outdoors environment – even as we have clobbered it to within an inch of its natural life – remains fundamental to human health and happiness.

The genius of Common Ground is precisely its understanding that *genius loci* is all important: that, in our ever-more internationalised, corporatised, mediated and de-individualised world, the spirit of a place, the sum of the meeting of people and land, remains of vital importance. Crucially, as Common Ground saw and sees it, place pertains and operates most and best at a local level, and on a scale we still might call human. Consequently, their efforts were not about restoring the wolf, or rewilding by managing facilities for nature: they were about looking at and growing a feeling for those less dramatic times in our lives when we cross the path of our own community; moments when old ways seem still operative; times when dormant traditions wait to be woken; times when our lives mesh with those of others who share the same weather; moments of intense and personal response to familiar corners.

The strong *presence* of both Common Ground's directed projects and the spontaneous manifestations of the same ethos elsewhere, their tang and their *multum in parvo* feel – a great deal in a small space, much in little – is even more important today in our vastly accelerated and denatured times. When Common Ground began no one anywhere in the world knew of the internet. But throughout its life the organisation's engine has been and remains the creation and inspiration of site-specific work for what it recognises as site-specific lives. Most, though not all, Common Ground projects have happened away from metropolitan centres. While it is fully understood that rural Britain is as man-made as urban, the parish scale has proved to be the most fruitful ground for the organisation's ideas. Where this scale can still can be felt in the big towns and cities, projects that promote local distinctiveness can be as life-enhancing there as anywhere.

Common Ground's work (art commissions, community projects, practical assistance) is made with an understanding that people and place are entangled at all levels – functionally (e.g. the built infrastructure of the country and farming and food); emotionally (novels, painting and music, flower arranging); intellectually (planning and philosophy); physically (walking, knitting, hang-gliding and working the land); and genetically (the home phenotype). Giving *a local habitation and a name*, Common Ground repeatedly declares, is neither yesterday's thing nor just a job for poets ...

Common Ground is still at work. In the last few years Sue Clifford and Angela King have handed over to Adrian Cooper. The rich archive of the charity's accomplishments to date is being prepared for study and exhibition, but its energies are still current, with its intentions little changed.

It has mostly failed, of course. As all our best-laid plans will. The world is still, substantially, to win. But its successes are many and have also been writ large into the wider world. One of the reasons why nature writing is resurgent today is because of Common Ground's steadfast belief in the value of exploring what the natural world – even the broken-down, rubbish-dump world – means to us. One of the reasons why almost every poet in Britain has written a blackbird poem is because Common Ground has reminded the country that local looking is as valuable as any panoptical survey – that the imaginative work that will address climate change, say, will come not from windy pieces blowing vatically around the planet, but from attending to what is close at hand.

There is still much to worry at. That tide is even higher, with the sea level rising, and lapwings, skylarks, even starlings and house sparrows, depleted beyond the imaginings of 1984. Larkin's concrete and tyres are even more in the ascendant. But to answer this has come passionate and articulate energy born of new ways of seeing that are less wistful and more animated, that demonstrate that fallen man can, by understanding his fall, be more vital than any heavenly body; that, for example, the edgelands might come to the centre of our lives and mean as much to us as any wilderness ever might have done.

We are on the far side of the river now, and no amount of looking back is going to help the guildhalls. A kind of singing in the dark times has begun. It says that the state we are in is worth as much attention as the world we have lost; that there is masses to do, and many struggles and obstacles ahead, but also that a renewed diligence and attention to what remains, and what it means to us, can help us live more fully, happily, healthily, wisely, more humanly, and better placed to know why we should step back from finishing off our planet in our own cracked image.

My thanks go to all those who have written here. The idea of writing something for Common Ground made many say yes very willingly. Some wouldn't, and I also failed to find anything other than white contributors. There are lots of gaps, and there are countless other places. But I hope something of how we live now is ahead.

Tim Dee
2018

NOTES FROM A DEVON VILLAGE

Barbara Bender

Until recently I lived in Branscombe, a small seaside village in East Devon. I lived there for nearly thirty years, which is the longest I've ever lived anywhere. As the child of German refugees who arrived in London in 1939, I never felt much at home, or that I really belonged. My mother did her best, but I always seemed to wear the wrong clothes, never seemed to know the right way to use a soup-spoon or fork, and, longing to conform, was mortified by my school friends' remarks about my mother's accent. My suburban childhood was, in retrospect, very lonely. Things got better, of course, as I got older. But Branscombe is the nearest I'll ever get to 'belonging' or being in place. I'll never be an 'insider': for that you'd have to be born in the parish, or have married in, but that's all right.

What's it like, this place? A tucked-away 'picturesque' landscape. Small streams from three steep valleys flow together a mile or so from the sea, meander through a narrow flood plain, skirt a high shingle bank that almost blocks the valley mouth, and peter out amongst the pebbles on the beach. The bay is a wide-open scoop with tricky currents that makes fishing difficult. To the east of Branscombe Mouth, chalk and sandstone cliffs rise steeply above an almost sub-tropical undercliff created in 1792 when a large stretch of land slipped down. You can take a narrow path through the undercliff lined in May with gentian-blue gromwell flowers, and if you're lucky watch peregrine falcons and ravens disputing the crags overhead. In contrast, to the west, the cliffs are dark red marl with a thin topping of chalk and sandstone. During the great gales of 2014, slides of red mud came down and glistening bands of pink gypsum suddenly appeared.

Inland, the valley slopes are parcelled into small odd-shaped fields. It's pasture land, and the slopes are so steep that there's never been a reason to uproot hedgerows or enlarge fields. On the higher slopes, and along much of the cliff top, the grass gives way to unkempt woodland. Only the segments of plateau between the valleys have larger fields – now, more often than not, slobby pig-lands.

Once upon a time five hamlets dotted the main valley, but over the centuries they were stitched together by small rows of terraced houses. Even so, there's still a strong distinction – if you live 'up' Street your pub is the Fountain Head; if you live 'down' Square, it's the Masons Arms.

These words don't begin to describe what season or weather does to this place – a dusting of snow with footprints of birds or foxes, moon paths across the sea, long winter shadows sharpening tump and hollow, low sun haloing sheep. It is heart-wrenchingly beautiful. And yet, a couple of years ago, we moved over the hill to the next village. Why? Partly because, as we got older, the hills got steeper and the garden larger. More acutely, there was a sense of malaise. Branscombe had been 'discovered'; in estate agents' parlance it had become 'iconic'. The kiss of death. More and more houses have become second or third homes or holiday lets. Thirty-five per cent of the houses are unoccupied for most of the year. Come the winter, most of the cottage windows at Street are dark, the lanes eerily quiet. It feels as if the village is hollowing out.

Finally, two years ago, the Post Office was sold. The old owner had wanted to find a buyer who would take it on; the new owners said they would. But they'd just wanted a cheaper house, and after six months they closed it. It was the end of a long, drawn-out process. Talk to the old villagers and they'll tell you stories about half a dozen small shops:

Wynne Clarke & Rita Saunders: Mrs Hopkins, she used to wear a shawl around her shoulders and a little sort of hat. She didn't use to walk like we do; she was more of a shuffler. She'd go out for the paraffin, then come in – didn't wash her hands – for the cheese. She'd cut the bacon with the knife, she'd dig the sweets out of the bottle with the same knife ...[1]

Shops and front-room tea rooms, a bakery, blacksmiths and cobblers, carpenters and coffin makers, fishmonger and market gardeners. By the time we arrived, in the late 1980s, they'd mostly gone, but the Post Office-cum-shop, hub of the long, straggling village, where you met and caught up with the news, where, alongside pensions and stamps, tickets were sold for village entertainments, was still there. Now a visiting post office sets up in the Village Hall for a couple of hours once a week.

One of the reasons the place is 'iconic' is because it appears 'timeless', and that's because much of it is 'owned' by the National Trust. They've preserved it, and pickled it. They say that they want to work with, and for, the community, which may once have been true, but isn't now. They used to let their cottages to villagers, but the rents have soared far beyond the range of local people. They used to house their warden in the village and pay local people to do conservation work. Proposals that they might offer – at a reasonable rent – a small building to serve as Post Office or farm shop or exhibition space are brushed aside. Time, energy and money is spent stamping their corporate image on their properties and, by extension, the village, but contact and consultation are minimal (and, more often than not, bad-tempered). Not good for them, nor us.

So we decamped to the neighbouring village of Beer – less tidy, more mixed, much busier, with shops, a doctor's surgery and a Post Office.

Beer is a good place to live, but Branscombe is still *my* place. Partly, of course, it's about knowing people. Partly because my heart still lifts when, taking the steep road down into the village, I catch a first glimpse of the hillside and hedgerows rearing up on the far side of the valley, or, swinging seaward, wait for the moment when the sea – and our old house – comes into view. But more, it's because I *know* so much about this place. My Branscombe landscape is a *depthy* place ingrained with stories that go back thousands of years.

Twenty-five years ago, a group of us set up the Branscombe Project. We were aware that the old villagers were getting older and that their children had often moved away. When we started there were at least forty people who had lived in the village all their lives; now, perhaps, there are ten. Alongside the affluent incomers, they have often seemed marginalised.

We began to record their voices and memories. Lillie Gush, the first person I ever recorded, was born in 'an hundred and one' (1901). With no teeth and a strong Devon accent, she wasn't easy to understand, but it was clear she was very angry. She'd lived in the village all her life, she'd looked after her family. Now there was no one left and no place for her, and she'd been sent to a care home some distance away. Not really anyone's fault, but still she felt it was unjust. She knew all about inequality and village class divisions. She remembered when the first water pipes were laid and how, though they passed through her parents' garden, 'they didn't even give we a tap. But', she added, 'they'll get their deserts where they've gone now!'

We wanted to do more than just siphon people's memories into cassettes. So we began to unwind their stories into annual exhibitions, wrote and published booklets, and ended up with a capacious website.[2] We also host well-attended winter talks.

Some of the best moments come as we pore over old photographs or postcards, or manipulate a digitised map[3] so that people can mark their favourite places or landscapes and wonder at each other's choices:

John Marchant: Pits, School Lane – the view to the sea and the sea of wild garlic flowers in the spring.
David Strange: South end of Stockhams Hill – a fantastic spot for star-gazing.
Betty Rowson: Goosemoor, where I lived as a child. I was happy there.
Mike Fielden: Up at Weston – as a kid going there. My father used to launch his glider up there – with an elastic band and a Jag.

Other good times are spent walking the landscape, stopping and poking around, old villagers and incomers talking with one another, remembering things they'd quite forgotten, often contradicting each other. Moments of communal gathering-in; theoretical or techy know-how twining with people's intimate local knowledge.

After we'd transcribed the old gravestones in the churchyard we put on a performance. Masked ghosts (old villagers and new) emerged from behind the gravestones to recount the life-stories of the deceased. At one point, Ralph Cox suddenly stopped, swept out his arms to embrace the graves – 'Thirty-five of them, thirty-five, all my relatives!'

We went on from oral history to working in the archives, and to field-walking. We pieced together stories that went back 700, even 5,000 years. Where the chalk-lands of southern England come to an end, on the east side of Branscombe Mouth, you can see the bands of flint nodules in the cliff face. It's a beautiful black flint highly prized by prehistoric people; they would have scavenged the beach and scaled the cliffs for it. Inland, you find spreads of waste flakes, cores, scrapers and points. Once, when I was walking with a fellow archaeologist on Bodmin Moor, he pulled out a flint point from the side of the path – Branscombe flint! Even 5,000 years ago, people and things moved long distances.

Working with maps is another way of exploring time and space. Recently we ran workshops[4] with about thirty people in which we compared the 1840 tithe map, an early Ordnance Survey map and a current map, and plotted changes in the social and economic landscape. For example, on the 1840 and 1880 maps every farmstead was surrounded by orchards. In spring the parish would be flushed with sweet-smelling apple blossom. But, until the beginning of the twentieth century, the farmers turned the apples into fairly gut-rotting rough cider which then formed part of the farm workers' wages. Not great news for the household economy. By the 1960s farmers were being subsidised to grub up old orchards.

We also used maps to trace the changing fortunes of footpaths and tracks. They leave the best traces of past generations of men and women going about their daily business. Paths taken by the farm workers as they walked to and from the farms and fields, climbed the hills to the quarries and lime kilns, or made their way down the zig-zag paths to the cliff-plats or beach. The five shutes[5] that mark the spring-line along the lane through the village were where the women came to fetch water and gossip. Other paths took them to work in service in the big houses, or to Barnells where John Tucker, the mean-spirited entrepreneur who enforced a monopoly on their Honiton lace-making, lived. He paid them a pittance, and made them buy their goods at his overpriced truck shop.

Although many of these paths have gone and those that remain are often deserted, it's still true that the best way to get a feel for the topography of a place, what was in view and out of view, the activities that went into the making of landscape, is by walking the footpaths. If you take the coast path from the beach, up the steep west hill to the cliff top, you're following the donkeys that carried the coal landed from Welsh colliers up to the Berry lime kilns. Further along the cliff top the path broadens out into Kiln Lane and you'll find huge flint spills, debris from the old lime quarries, or occasional pieces of coal or brick from one of the long-dismantled kilns. Eventually Kiln Lane meets the lane by which farmers 'from away' came by horse and cart to fetch the lime.

Most of the old zig-zag paths down the cliff to east and west of the Mouth have fallen away or become overgrown, but a few remain. At Littlecombe Shoot you're walking smugglers' paths that date back to the eighteenth century. 'Littlecombe Shoot', wrote a Customs officer in 1807, 'is a good landing place, and a road [Kiln Lane] leading up to the head of Branscombe Village. The fences in general very indifferent, so that the smugglers may cross them in any direction that best suits their purpose to avoid the Officers.'

An old smuggler recounted this story late in the nineteenth century:

> My brother was landing tobacco at Littlecombe, when the coast-guard boat rowed out gently from the shadow of the cliff ... The three men hearing the noise turned round & rowed smack out

to sea. That was Friday night, & by Sunday afternoon they had rowed to Jersey and sent the goods back to the consigners. I call that acting honest.[6]

Some of the smugglers, and many others as well, put these same paths to more legitimate use. On the cliff faces where the land had slipped, there were patches of soil which, aided by sea breezes and the sun on the cliff face, and manured with seaweed from the shore, produced very early crops. Farm workers renting the plots could grow early potatoes, vegetables and flowers. They called themselves cliff farmers and used their donkeys to carry the produce up the cliff and off to market. It gave them a modest, but much prized, independence. But it was hard work, and by the mid twentieth century the plats were abandoned.

But not quite. Some of the stone linhays the cliff farmers had built for their donkeys were turned into holiday huts. When these new cliff-dwellers were asked to mark their favourite places on our map, it was nearly always 'their hut':

Flo Pearson: It's our hut – it's been part of my life always and is my favourite place in the world. My dad's ashes are there, plus years of plants we've tried to protect from the brambles.
Adrian Symons: Recently my mother and my sister counted about thirty or forty different types of wild flowers.

And that's not the end of it. In 2007 a startling bit of Branscombe history was made when a huge container ship, the *Napoli*, breaking up in the channel, was beached at Branscombe below Littlecombe. Overnight the wind came up and nearly 200 containers slipped into the sea, many washing up on the shore. They contained an eclectic assortment of BMW engines, motorbikes, cosmetics, personal belongings, oak barrels, nappies, dog food and Xhosa Bibles. A microcosm of world trade.

The popular press castigated the white-van people 'from away' who arrived a couple of days later, for the wild scenes on the beach. Before that, however, the local lads had already appropriated most things of value. They easily avoided police cordons and guards by using the same old cliff paths. One night, Jamie Lambert and his mate were scouting the containers at Littlecombe when they suddenly saw the guards:

'Run!! Let's get the hell out of here!' The search lights were going and the people were chasing us. Pulled ourselves up the rope, started going up the cliff. We didn't use torches and we managed to run zig-zag all the way up the path. But, obviously, those security guards ain't local, they would struggle to believe that anyone could negotiate those cliff paths without a torch, so they spent the next twenty minutes ripping apart the chalets, going through the hedgerows. We were long gone!

Same footpaths; different histories.

Final story: not long ago we took an inland walk with a group of villagers. We were walking in the footsteps of Harry Layzell, village blacksmith-cum-chimney-sweep-cum-postman. Sometimes he'd deliver the post by bike, but mainly he walked, and sometimes it was a good eight miles. Jenny Newton, now in her seventies, used to ride on his shoulders, and as they went along he'd be singing Methodist hymns at the top of his voice. So, with Jenny, we walked part of his round. Down the steep hill to Hole Bottom where the owner of the former mill came out to tell us about the ghost of a lady in a red cloak, another man showed us the millstone that marks his threshold, and Angela Lambert brought out a polished chert axe found in the stream-bed behind her house. Then up the steep hill to the disappeared farmhouse at Hooknell. Ross Wilmington, the farmer's son from up the road, remembered that his grandma had lived here and that, each day, she'd walk up to the farm to fetch her bread. We stopped at another disappeared cottage – faint traces of wall foundations, different sorts of vegetation where the postman's path was barely visible – then trudged up to Hill Arrish for tea and buns.

Hill Arrish is a grand new house built on the footprint of a 1930s Indian-style bungalow. Pulling down the bungalow revealed a cache of newspapers. Copies of the *Black Shirt* and *Action* dating from 1935 to early 1940. Sitting out in the sun, reading these obscene anti-Semitic rags, the hairs rose on the back of my neck. The then owners of Hill Arrish, Rafe Temple-Cotton and his mother, Lucy, had been ardent fascists, and Rafe was chief south-west organiser for Mosley.[7] He ran a large market garden and was considered a good employer, but his innocuous white delivery van also served as a grandstand for him to spout his fascist views – in Sidmouth and Hyde Park. Villagers still remember him and some at least were not unsympathetic. In Sidmouth the locals threw him in the river.

It's a truism that history's always in the making and that we're part of the making. Sometimes, being on the spot, you can offer small interventions.

In 2014 came gales so fierce you couldn't stand up, a sea so wild that spume from the waves topped the Sea Shanty café. The waves took out the foundations of the beach chalets to the east and tore away the trackway to the west. Natural England and the National Trust showed little sympathy. For them, the wooden chalets were a blot on the landscape. Far better, and all part of the national Shoreline Management Plan, to allow cliff and beach to revert to their 'natural' state. The owners of the chalets and café offered to pay the costs of reinstatement. To no avail: the pebbles were not to be moved because they might disturb the elusive scaly cricket (which, it seems, had not been much disturbed by the beaching of the *Napoli* or the heavy clean-up operation that followed). No 'foreign' stone could be imported to shore up the trackway. They envisaged that as sea levels rose and breached the pebble bank, a fine estuarine habitat would be created. In the longer term they may well be right, but in the meantime the chalets are part of the landscape, much loved, and they and the café are important to the local economy.

Moreover, just as we recognise that the gale and its aftermath are not 'natural' but are caused by climate change due to human activity, so the notion that the cliffs should be returned to a pre-chalet 'natural' state is nonsense. So we have helped make the case for a *cultural* landscape. Had they not noticed, for example, the stands of white buddleia that mark the old cliff plats? Or the remains of a donkey linhay and lime kiln. Permission has reluctantly been given for 'temporary' repairs.[8]

That's it. For me love of place comes with the detail, and in trying to understand the stories and histories that go to make a living landscape; comes, too, with a sense of belonging.

Bringing this piece to a close, I realise that I've hardly cited any significant landscape literature. And thinking about it, I find myself wanting to bypass more recent writings, to return to the people who first fired my imagination and helped form my understanding of place and scape. To W. G. Hoskins[9] for his pleasure and skill in explaining why a road takes a particular bend, or what a faint field trace might mean. For insisting that 'Any small tract of England [makes] a marvellous study under the microscope of the local historian'. And to Raymond Williams[10] for teasing out the way cultural perceptions and social and economic relations play off one another, and for shifting easily between micro and macro: 'history active and continuous: the relations are not only of ideas and experiences, but of rent and interest, of situation and power; a wider system'.

And John Berger for not only insisting on how subjective our understanding of the world is, and how caught up in unequal social relations, but for his ability to 'hold things dear', to feel gratitude, and to engage with other people.[11]

Perhaps, before we uprooted from Branscombe, we should have reminded ourselves that history *is* always in the making. Our sombre assessment of parish and community is already open to question. For example, it's noticeable that, being able to work from home, and with the council making efforts to rent out council houses to local people, there are now more young people in the village. The primary school begins to look less like a basket case. The young ones have successfully fudged traditional events – Apple Pie Fayre, Harvest Festival – with new ones to create a Harvest Fair that's re-enthused the community. New stewardship schemes have begun to address environmental and social issues. A local environmental group is in the making, wanting to talk within the community about climate change, bio-diversity and sustainable energy. 'Bad times' spur new energies.

Notes

1. Barbara Farquharson and Joan Doern (eds), *Branscombe Shops, Trades & Getting By* (Branscombe Project, 2000). In the context of village and Project I use my married name, Farquharson. It seems more comfortable than Bender, my professional maiden name.
2. www.branscombeproject.org.uk
3. The digitised 'Favourite Places, Favourite Landscape' map, and a discussion of what it was that people chose, and why, is posted on the Project website.
4. This project, undertaken in conjunction with the East Devon AONB and English Heritage, was known as the HEAPS project – Historic Environment Action Plan.
5. The shutes are pipes let into the roadside banks to tap the spring-line water.
6. Ephraim Perryman, talking to J. A. Morshead in 1893.
7. Todd Gray, *Blackshirts in Devon* (Mint Press, 2006).
8. These issues are taken up in the last chapter of *Cliff and Beach at Branscombe* by Barbara Farquharson and Sue Dymond (Branscombe Project, 2014).
9. W. G. Hoskins, *The Making of the English Landscape* (Pelican, 1955).
10. Raymond Williams, *The Country and the City* (Chatto & Windus, 1973).
11. John Berger, *Ways of Seeing* (BBC & Penguin, 1972); with Jean Mohr, *A Fortunate Man* (Canongate, new edition 2016); with Jean Mohr, *A Seventh Man* (Penguin, 1975).

A Box of Old Shells

Julia Blackburn

I was walking along the beach. Sunshine and a cold wind. Nobody, and then a couple sitting very still side-by-side on the upturned concrete bunker close to the water's edge. Two dogs milling softly around them, and I was sure I had seen exactly this scene before long ago, but I couldn't remember when.

I had a slight sense of hurry because the tide was coming in and it was possible to get cut off, with the steep cliffs at my back and the waves biting at my toes. Stepping quickly over sand and pebble and the shiny expanses of exposed clay, I sometimes looked out towards the mirage of distance, but mostly I looked down, hoovering the solidity of surface with my eyes.

I noticed a man walking towards me from out of the distance. He was also looking down, and stopping every so often to pick something up. He was carrying two bright-green plastic shopping bags that appeared to be rather heavy. As we passed each other I said, 'Treasure?'

'No,' he replied, as if this was not an odd question: 'lead' – and he opened one of the bags to reveal a tangle of lead piping. 'I get fifty quid a week, some weeks,' he said.

'Ever find fossils, bones?' I asked.

''Undreds of 'em. Got me garage full. Three years back, under the forest bit of the cliff, it was all bones, scattered on the sand. I got a vertebra as big as a table top' – and he put down both his bags to define the size of the vertebra. 'Sold it on eBay for two hundred quid. Gave a lot of stuff away a few weeks back – a young girl who's interested in fossils, and now she's studying 'em at college, and I reckon she'll become a palaeowhatsit.'

I told him I was writing a book about Doggerland and all the lands that came before it, and he turned his head vaguely towards the soupy grey of the North Sea as if he was looking at the country I had just referred to.

I felt bold and said I'd love to see his collection, and he said, 'Come any time! You can 'ave what you want from it. It's no use to me.' I wrote his phone number into my mobile. His name was Ray. He lives in Pakefield, not far from the Pontin's Holiday Park.

I phoned him a couple of days later and his wife answered. 'Ray! It's that lady you met!' And so I arranged a visit.

They live in a little bungalow in a loop of little bungalows, shoulder-to-shoulder like biscuits in a tin. The people in the house next door had a life-sized black panther in their garden, sitting upright. I think it must have been made of fibreglass: it was too smooth and shiny to be the painted cement of garden gnomes.

There was no bell on the front door, so I followed a concrete path round the side. The two of them were in the kitchen, close to the window, and they looked up and waved as if we were old friends. Ray opened the back door with the front-door bell in his hand. 'It's broke,' he said.

'Making a noise all night,' she said.

He is not very tall and has a nice quiet manner to him, like an old-fashioned idea of a bank clerk. She – Gail – is round and jolly, like an old-fashioned idea of a schoolteacher. I had brought them a book and a packet of biscuits. 'That looks nice – I like reading,' she said. 'Ray will eat the biscuits. He'll eat anything sweet. Me, I eat crisps. Crisps are my downfall.'

We went into the sun room and Gail brought us mugs of coffee. I sat in a big upholstered armchair with flower patterns on it. A smattering of polite conversation, and then Ray pottered off to his garage in the garden and returned with a little pile of plastic ice-cream boxes. He pulled the lids off and lifted out small objects he thought might interest me, each one in its own sealed pocket.

'All this lot's from Covehithe – the beach, the cliff and the private land behind the lake. I've permission to go there from the lady of the house.' We started with medieval seals and then moved on to Anglo-Saxon buckles. I paused to admire a broken bit of worked metal: some kind of belt clasp, on which the crude outline of a running dragon had been scratched, or maybe etched is a better word. Unmistakably a dragon, and done with a sort of familiarity as if from life. I said how lovely it was.

'Have it,' said Ray. I was rather taken aback, but I thanked him and put the dragon on the side table next to my mug of coffee.

Now lots of Roman coins. The faces of emperors, one after the other. Hadrian, with the word *Aegyptus* on the reverse side, and a naked female form which I thought might have been Cleopatra. And then a really tiny coin that would balance comfortably on the tip of my little finger, and very shiny as though it had just been polished, holding the perfect image of a round-faced and rather insecure-looking emperor, but I couldn't find his name.

Ray gave me a broken clay pipe. 'There you are,' he said, and I put it next to the dragon.

He kept going out and coming back with more stuff and saying how much he had given away or sold. 'There's a good market for the seals. I gave stuff to the Norwich Museum, but when I went to have a look, they said they'd lost it. Lent them stuff to be identified and now they can't find that either.'

His collecting began when he was given a metal detector forty years ago. The first thing he found with it was a gold coin. He brought out the coin from its plastic bag. He keeps it in a box lined with red imitation-velvet. It looked as fresh and beautiful as a wild flower still growing in a field, thin and delicate, and it seemed impossible it could have survived undamaged for so long. On one side there was a rather snaky-looking boat riding some rather snaky waves, and a king was standing in the middle of it, almost as tall as the central mast. He had a pronged crown upon his head and a kingly, or perhaps a saintly, expression on his face I could distinguish the Latin letters that circled the king and his boat, but I couldn't read them because my Latin wasn't up to it.

'1362,' said Gail. 'Edward III.' She paused and then said, 'You hold it in your hand and you think, it's not people like us who ever owned something like this. We took it to the coroner, but he gave it back. He didn't want it, so we kept it.'

I wanted to ask about the nature of finding – the compulsion of it, perhaps, or the quiet that comes from looking without knowing what you are looking for, but Ray wasn't interested, and all he would say was, 'If conditions aren't right you still got to go, because you don't know, do you … When I find something that's been in the ground all that time, it's a marvellous feeling. But the thrill for me is the finding of it. I don't need to keep the stuff.'

Ray's father was one of seventeen children. They all grew up in Covehithe, but Ray moved to Kessingland later, which I think was something to do with his mother dying. It was in Kessingland that he met Gail and became a slaughterman.

He spoke of Covehithe as if he could see its past history from having found so many traces of what had been, and perhaps also because his family had lived there for generations and it was still the place where they all belonged, dead or alive.

He explained that in medieval times Covehithe had been very wealthy: lots of rich people, traders; there was a port there, and he was shown an aerial photo in which you could make out a sort of square shape in the sand. 'You can see where it was if you know what you're looking for. You follow the little path past the pigs; through the narrow bit, and then there's that notice board and a bent tree, and you look across towards the reeds and there's a sort of dip, almost an outline. Boats came right in at high tide, and they'd unload when the tide went out.'

Ray kept going to the garage and returning with more boxes, more talk, more little gifts for me to add to my heap. He did have a Papal seal from 1100: Pius I, he thought it was, but he sold that, and some years ago, after a storm, he found a medieval well. 'A circle as big as that' – and he held his arms out as if he was embracing the air – 'lying there on the sand, just the base of it, and it was made of wood, and there were black things all the way round the sides, and at first I thought it was a bear trap.'

That had been the day before Christmas, and he'd contacted his friend Paul Durbridge and together they'd dug the well out. 'A bell-well it were. Double layer of wood nailed together and made from parts of barrels. The mouth of it was at the top of the cliff, but of course the edge was much further back in those days. The people who made it had dug all the way down, fifty feet or so, until they reached the water level, and the well ended in a point at the bottom. There were pots in there, some of 'em near-perfect, and the wood was as good as new, and you must be talking six or seven hundred years. It was a work of art.' Ray wondered why they'd dig a well there in the first place, because surely it must have been filled with salty water. There was no answer to that.

While he went to get more boxes, Gail told me she wasn't really interested in his treasure hunts, but they kept him happy, and anyway she and an old school friend went out quite regular to a place called Potters for a girlie weekend. They laughed a lot. So she has her fun too.

Ray returned with some worked flints. He said the lake at Covehithe, which is known as Benacre Broad, was once a stream, and an archaeologist told him the stream was a tributary of the Thames. 'Archaeologists are a bit like zoo keepers,' he said then, remembering the conversation: 'they think that because they're paid by the taxpayer and have got stuff, it all belongs to them. They take over. They don't like it if a member of the public gets in the way and knows more than they do.'

We were moving back in time. The flints were followed by a cardboard box filled with clam shells, all of them stained in gentle shades of cream and ochre and a sharp yellow like clear honey. Some were filled with a coarse-grained sand, packed in tight. 'After a really big storm the sand can go right down, and there's scouring at the base of the cliff and you get about four foot of these shells. You only see them for a while and then they're gone.' He said these ones were 2 million years old, and they were soft when he first got them, but he dried them out and now they were hard.

'There was a chap came with sacks and a sack barrow, and he'd collect the shells and dry 'em out and go through 'em with a magnifying glass, and he found some teeth of a mouse that was unknown and he named it after his wife. He was big in fossils, he was – he had a bone that came out from the sea and he thought it were a pelvis, but it were the top vertebra from a giant deer. D'you want 'em?' – and the box came to sit beside my chair.

Then he told me that once he was walking at Covehithe and on that day the layer of grey pink marl that is part of the old riverbed was smooth and flat, lovely it was, and he noticed these white markings in the clay, and that was an animal, about six foot long and four foot wide, and it was complete, but he couldn't tell what sort it was. The white markings were the lines of its skeleton, like a beautiful drawing, and as he watched it was erased by the incoming tide.

He went out one last time and came back with a cardboard box filled with mammoth bones. 'These any use to you?' he said, and I said they were. 'There you are then' – and he set the box down beside the box filled with shells.

There was a final rush of giving, and I received a bit of mammoth tusk, dark brown and shiny, and he explained how you could tell what it was by the texture of it; two belemnites; a lovely piece of pale fossilised wood, and a sea urchin that had been partly crushed, maybe trodden on by some heavy beast, before it was transformed into a lump of golden-coloured flint. He'd had it for years.

'You don't mind if I give her this, do you, dear?'

'No, dear, it's been on the side of the sink long enough.'

They called each other dear, very sweetly, with a tenderness floating in the word.

I said my goodbyes and they accompanied me outside, the dragon and the broken clay pipe in my pocket and all of us carrying everything else in cardboard boxes. There was something odd about my car, and we saw that the back wheel was flat. I'd only had the thing for a couple of months and didn't even know where the spare tyre was hidden.

'Don't worry – Ray will do it, won't you, dear?' said Gail. And so she read the instruction manual to him, while he crouched on the pavement and did the practicalities of removing the wheel and fitting its replacement. I looked on and felt foolish. 'Me and Ray are a good team,' said Gail.

'She reads books,' he said, struggling to undo a nut. 'All I ever read is the *Metal Detector* magazine.'

Before I drove off, Ray promised he'd let me know when he next hears from his friend Fred, who has lots of worked flints, beautiful ones. He's sure Fred would like to show them to me: we can meet him together.

When I got home I laid out the shells on a long pale table in my husband's studio and they looked like music, or a story without the need of words.

I Am Still Yesterday

Sean Borodale

The moment when a feeling enters the body is political.
This touch is political.

Adrienne Rich

House

Rain like a fog. River pounding. Scent of blossom smashed up. I surprise
a deer; it bounds away under the fence into the boggy corner of the
field where the flag iris grow. Stack wood in the woodshed for it to dry.
Bring dry logs into the house. The slightly fermented smell of cherry
as the dampness dries off. In this wet, tangible land whose sour earths
are the decay of meadowsweet, scabious, knapweed, the windfall of
apples, the sloe leaves when they turn yellow, how does a beehive occupy
site? I look at the bleached boards of the box on its stand to the north
of the house. A point of dissonance: its assemblage of stackable supers
reminds me of Le Corbusier's vision for a new Paris.[1] A modernist tower
block, endlessly repeatable, honed to the right angle, aligned to the
vertical. BS1300: 1960 is the 'Modified National' endorsed by the
Ministry of Agriculture in the 1920s. The 1920s: when Rudolph Steiner
warned that modern apiculture might be devastating to the honeybee.

The terrain here is rough, unkempt; but I can see invisible fields and
points of attention that echo Le Corbusier's 'relational lines' – the hidden
geometry that connects distinct elements in the architectural scheme.
'Relational lines' inhabit the footprints of ancient settlements.

Architecture has lifted them into the vertical as regulators in the organisation of facades. These relational lines of architecture haunt stage-craft,
too, as they are worn into my theatre of writing across site. Repetition,
tangible forces, worked and reworked like glances between actors on
stage; honed through revisiting sites (the walk from the house to the
beehive, or the entry into the confines of a particular cave), becoming
paths of assertion as force-fields, gravities, 'spots of time'.[2] The place is
actor: we perform together. I try language to X-ray the earth and the
air. Writing live is like working with wood; a mobile joinery of motion
respective to grain of moment attempted. Writing almost quiet; a mime
bound to earth's substance through exertion, the labouring body in the
field of its work is collaborative: unit of footstep, angle of turn, reach
of arm, capacity of ear.

Cave

I have gone into the dark; entered the mouth of the cave uphill taking
Sophocles' *Oedipus at Colonus* with me as torchlight and guide; as equipment for seeing darkness.[3] The process of recovery has been in the field
of language. The poetic voice. All that is dark, coveted, hidden by the
earth, in state of burial or decay, is brought to exposure in the flickering
wings and poetic speech of the dimension of light. Insects metamor-
phosing in darkness unfold wings and take flight. Flowers sing or scream.
The air into which speech is given broadcast is where bees fly. Speedier
than the slow-urn of burial-time. Working boots of children rise from
scoured river-silts and are lit: enigmatic as the keeping of bees.[4] What
lies in the dark is darkness itself; rare as a mineral; bones, teeth, bodies,
toxins. The river is metaphor for the direction of transport. Time is
transport, but convoluted here: an alliance with the anticline on which
this valley rests.

Cell

The bees hatch from cells built by bees. In *Krapp's Last Tape*,[5] the
cell is the closed apartment in which Krapp hears the memory of
himself. His only actual location: 'a late evening in the future'.[6]

I imagine a locked apartment in a tenement or tower. The load-bearing of the singular voice in isolation is an audio honey; memories of a springtime. The voice which meets its own ghost-echo, isolation. This is the voice that steps out, as it moves towards the beehive and finds its singularity tested in what is modular. The beehive stands as the pragmatic symbol and principle of the cell's multiplicity. Memories and formative sensations locked in combinations that – by simply walking through a site – parts of the lock align and open into emotion. How does honey encrypt time? How does language transform itself? How does the terminology of beekeeping diminish a symbiosis? Why am I forced to say: 'national hive', 'queen bee', 'colony', 'worker'?

Asylum

The honey in the stacked supers and brood frames can be taken as a microfiche for the data of a locality, environment, weather, flora, pollen, meteorological condition. The river silt here is not nearly as nutritious as it looks: leaves grow with difficulty; roots remain shrunken and woody; beans aspire to grow but are most often severed at the root by earthen mice and wilt suddenly. What am I made of eating this landscape? A place of repetitions that equivocate the bearings of continuity. Tonight, I took peelings out to the compost, then up to the beehive to cut the long grasses away from the entrance. Grasses gone mad, everything on bowing stilts. Apples in this valley taste of coal tar: sour and vinegary, blotchy red, a black lichen growing over them like coal dust.

Everything has happened in this ground; the place is a physical archive of caves, quarries, swallets, mines, Neolithic burials, Mesolithic cave cemeteries, Bronze Age barrows, Cold War bunkers. What am I in? A thirty-mile ridge in north Somerset, twenty miles south of Bristol, running in an east–west direction with a northern trend towards the west where it falls into the Bristol Channel at Brean Down. In the east the karst landscape of the Mendip high plateau breaks up into the hills of the coalfields between Frome and Radstock. 'Mendip' is cognate with the Welsh *mynydd* (hill), echoing *mine deep* and *men dip*'.⁷ I hear in the word *asylum* the refuge of archive; collecting voice-prints from sites of darkness into accession for a future unknown, for a use not yet recognised. Recording the instant of lyric unconscious: the edge of the unheard, recording incidentals of noise, action; decay, generation.

Riverbed

The bees hum in their box as I lower down fully into the river water, neck-deep, cold gripping me, a whole skin-suit of prickles like nettles stinging. Immersed at the lowest point of the valley, I watch the black river flow below the level of everything. Bits of moon: what else was there underneath flowing past, crouching in the unseen where otter have been and in water which flows from a pike pond four miles upstream? Too alert to fingers and toes numbing in the depths of crayfish and all other imaginings, I step back onto the soft land.

Deciphered scrawl I made in the near-full moonlight, but darkened by trees, rough writing I can barely read. I remember smelling mint, water mint – I must have crushed it underfoot. Contingent essence. How can I write the smell of water mint?

Presence

I kept busy to evade the calm which shows up absence: I took a wall apart, baked a cake with coconut and sultanas, made popcorn for a 'makeshift' cinema with the children. I made a lunch of bread, cheese and a grated celeriac-and-apple salad, I made a chicken stock, I cooked a supper, mowed lawns, read. At midnight a white moth was upside-down in the bath tub. I took it out and put it on the side of the bath. Watching it being still, a barn owl in miniature, brown flecks and freckles along its wings; a furry head, large feathered antennae. Pure white. The dips of its eyes glinting, tiny inverted rubies shone back at me when I rotated it in my hands and looked in. I thought it was dead. I took it with me on a piece of paper. When I woke there was only the page, no moth; the absence of it a greater statement.

Time-Exposure

Late summer. I hope to take some honey out of the hive. Blue scabious in the two fields nearby – a haze of blue not unlike the blue of eyes – somewhere between the knee and the ankle, in the afternoon sunlight; wading perfect seawater but airy and field-borne. Look up the steep hill into the air full of aslant sun, thousands of insects, crane flies; like being underwater, thick with life, deep and gelatinous air of living flight. A steep scarp rises from the bee field: once a cave holding a Neolithic teenage couple hunched before a hearth: burnt hazelnut shells, elder twigs, pointy-jawed faces whose bone fragments are boxed, numbered, archived in Wells Museum today. How does time run in such a world? Like Beckett's 'hold about five seconds' as I find myself looped into this evening, trying to cross its mire …

And the sun risen, white and flaring and brilliant, at that waiting spot, the only level, where the cows steam, like a damp chorus on a hillside threshing floor in ancient Greece. So they waited for the sun: all night they stood vigil and sculptural and waited, perhaps believing in its arrival, trusting the minute it would sear up and create the pasture again, and now it hangs in cobwebs and grasses laden with dew barely able to stand up, and the pools of white fog absorbing all organisms.

Mask

Incident carries a rhyming meaning; a constellation of harmonics across language in modulation. Transcript: a tower block of text. The lyrigraph on its printed pages scattered over the floor of the attic; Borges' map of the world. Its ratio 1:1 text to lyric-kinetic time and place. How does the field of text differ to the field of spoken voice? When I put on the beekeeper's 'costume' and mask, I earth myself into being something here. When I put on the role and voice of Hestia at the stove, I ground myself in function.[8] I exist as a shadow otherwise. The lyrigraph is born of a shadowy set of instruments – in my records of this place are the experience of a shadow.[9]

The road twists downhill, its A-road banking and hard verge rubbish-strewn. It will always be the road on which I caught the swarm of bees; it will always be the road from which I picked up the dead black cat stiffened with rigor mortis. The road snakes around the line of the Fosse Way, the Roman road which cuts through the coalfields of the valley. Deaths of forests under the stone and grass and worms of the present country. It is the landscape where I have tried most to formulate a physical poetics not of poetry but of the experience of writing poetry – the *lyrigraph*. How writing on location is set up, how it happens live through the presence of body: the task which is also the play, the game which is the art, the act of uttering which is writing …

Faucet

A tap in the corner of the kitchen is bound up like a wounded hand. A small well which I pass each day overflows quietly and runs under the track, under the garden, a hole keeps opening. There was once a leaning apple tree, its apples were huge black with light, frothy flesh. I never found the name of it. It fell one spring after a heavy rain, most was burnt in the fireplace. They burnt slowly, its limbs often a whole day's fire, putting an aromatic smoke into the air above the place which gathered the light and grew them first. I have a damp notebook which I left out where I was clearing the tree, now retrieved and to be deciphered. I left it where I'd crouched down to watch a leatherjacket laying her eggs in the grass. A clock ticks. A Black Forest clock from the 1930s with a pendulum which swings and runs fast. Here, time is always out. Darkening along the rill which ran from the ground close to its roots and calciferous water, anything which dropped in it or grew near (nettle roots, leaves, twigs, coins, toys, left for months) encrusted with a grubby white stone. Roots thick with the bone-white scale, twigs inside it rotting away to hollow negative spaces like pieces of old clay pipe if snapped. The road crackles with cars, like a great long twisted aerial laid down over the valley floor. Rolling marbles down a metal sheet, tyre noise and wake of sound falling in pitch …

Duende

Digging out the bank to rebuild the wall, black granular soil down to the ochre clay which lies in bands of colour, black roots of horsetail; a copper slow worm, a bracelet bent open. A badger came out at dusk and spoke its strange language to me: rough and like a radio from France drifting badly over the Channel. Going back to my own excavation: five centimes from 1997 and a dark yellow rib, the corner of a plate with a piece of flight on it, perhaps a bird, its wings up, like an angel's; blue wings. A plate. What else do I have from the ground here? A gold locket with two locks of hair, a jet ring-stone, a small porcelain dove, a lead songbird, small blue bottle, a bone paper knife. Memory and digging. I go down. The spade cutting neat slices, until I have the bank re-defined, a foot back from where it's to be. Notebooks are like batteries; full of charge. Lorca: 'Whatever has black sounds, has *duende* ... a power, not a work ... a struggle, not a thought.'[10]

Blitz

Quarry workings within earshot. 13.01. The air-raid siren; Gurney Slade or Stoke St Michael quarry. It is permanent sound, pitch winding and braiding, but also as it moves the wind rises, hushes, whines. I feel it. A thing across my face and neck. The wind brings the sound closer and further. A variant on the unchanging. The noise of wartime. People rushing down into dark underground spaces, shelters, terrors, some irritated, some frightened, some mourning, some feeling the random community of possible survivors they might become, all feeling uncertainty. Or perhaps it has become normal. Seventy or more years ago. It is 13.06. Five minutes have passed. Trespass through sound into the shudder of time. Underground of time. A song of the air-raid siren. I remember what I cannot remember. Fragments of readings, takings, gleanings into a composite imagining. It phases, the sound, made of two twisting notes of exactly the same pitch but not quite synchronised. The siren falls, drops, empties of itself. 13.08. I do not feel the blast.

Honey

Honey dripping off my hands as I walked back to the house away from the hives. Bees circling around me; and I so calm the bees could barely 'see' me. Sentences moving around. The wind moaning through wire fencing, a refracted wind.

On the old midsummer: noise at the river, otters, a two-week-old fawn running, trying to swim out. Thoughts of Albion, Avebury, Blake, turfs brought to Bronze Age barrows from elsewhere. Such places at this time of year. All those lives and our lives. Here now. The grass grows ... bright sward from the jaundiced, fragile grass-coat on winter's muds. The house a machine for living in, yes; the theatre of place a machine for writing in. I woke to quarry noise at Gurney Slade; they used to burn stone to send down to Torbay sewage works. A use for limestone. They make tarmacadam for B-roads now. Roadstone. Aggregate for concrete. The water runs into the low stream of the little steep valley, milky water, barely any direct sun, frost all winter, ill-looking grass. Small, hunched houses on a steep track. A single brown pony. The sound: aching joints.

Opened the hive. The bees looked very fine; feisty and so many. I had to improvise a smoker. Packed with honey, packed like a battery; some from the winter too, still in the comb: a red, dark, sticky clump of cells in the middle of the clear, bright, new summer's honey. A light-emitting-diode display of honey; matrix of rooms brightened variously. A metropolis of power. Five frames out, and a big operation in the kitchen with the children helping but mostly licking fingers and spoons, closed doors, scraping the honey off, straining and bottling. About nine jars. Most left for the bees in the hive. Thankful for flowers, nectar; had Turner's *god is sun* in my head, we melt the bee's-wax down into a pristine buttery-yellow block.

A closed-down pub by the main road; a man always with his back to the sky in a nearby field, bent over the scratchings of his chickens; no lefts or rights but meanderings between changeable obstacles and allures and creatures at various stages of their cycles and lives. Trying to hear stars, seeing a fish leap in the dark flow of the river swirling its

lace shapes, its tension and contortions; a gauze woven of swirling flies.
I go in from the damp field. I am a piece of the grass and the failing
last colours of a dusk reflected in the north. Saw a coppery iridescent
moth: midnight creatures all disappeared into grass from the heatwave
of day.

Nkisi

A hornet flew into the room and onto the table. I tried to catch it
under the table lamp with a glass and a card. It died, struggling
slowly and heavily, almost as big as my hand. The dream precipitated
by a queen wasp crawling out of logs in the wood stove that had
been lit, and then falling headfirst into flame as I rushed to find a
glass to catch it, and of course perishing; we listened to it hiss. Then
a huge ashen hornet fell out onto the ash pan, long dead. I took it
up to the attic on a piece of paper to observe later – I think its
kinship absorbed the energy of the dying wasp, and ran into my
hands and pursued my dreams like one of those African sculptures.
What are they called? With iron nails in their heads, glass mirrors
in their stomachs.

Changed into thick thorn-proof clothes and went out with a wool
hat on my head and gloves on: into the green chemistry of the overgrown. Struggling with nettles I revealed an earth world of tiny bright
insects and caterpillars with copper heads and one dying comma
butterfly so slowly interposed between the morning and afternoon that
I couldn't tell what state it was in. A spider crawled across its underwing.
I find myself trying to use – not write – an autobiography to cast pieces
of my study of them – the insects – against a roughly human scale of
need; to set it at an odd, vague old, imagined or dream-held state. Made
notes in the damp air on notebook pages. More earth than words.

Insulation

Typing slowly today. Centipede words, centipede sentences that struggle:
pale, soft, not fully alert. Not fully born. Insects that are dead or are

dying. Most of them that I encountered, however: wayside stragglers, seeking refuge, or failing mid-step, or shaking near the place where they will drain of consciousness.

A dandelion growing from the pedal of a child's bike. I started to transcribe a moth. I move about aching in time, aching in time like the body aches in certain positions: is it positions of time I ache in? Mary Wordsworth: 'Left William in bed hurting with a sonnet.' I was thinking of insects, wondering how I will make the transition of them as remains of bodies and expressions of being into images that are theatrical, held, uncovered, inside out, performed. The small radio in the head will attempt to tune into the thoughts of insects. Quiet under the stars, under the pantiles of the roof. Tiles made in Bridgwater a hundred years ago. Every tile I put back up on the roof of this house: hung on batons I nailed down on roof felt I unrolled and chalk with a taut chalked string snapped against it to mark a line straight. Inherent warmth. Sheep's wool insulates the roof, big grey sections of it, like Joseph Beuys' felt.[11]

There is nothing rehearsed here, nothing that comes with a script; only the damp stones, mud, dead grass, river silt, deer, badgers, the stag running heavily up and down in the dark close to me breathing shortly, withholding my presence. Scrolls of ice oozed from split hemp agrimony stems. I stand on the creaking of ice and hear the faint signal of bees pulsing like a star; near *and* distant. The hive is a tower. The bees are ions, electrons, magnetism. Flux in a society of units of repetition. Their wild organisation has entered the machine of the house. Hive walls symbolic of improvement, advancement: 'the plan is the generator'.[12] I think of Beuys' *Honigpumpe am Arbeitsplatz*, its tubes of pumped honey: machine as symbol of creative intellect in society.[13] Here it is: the beepump sucking nectar from the flowers and concentrating it here for use more slowly. It makes a sound and the boards of the hive smell of its sound. At night in this valley it is heard more easily, like the incandescent lights of rooms seen through windows. It enters my body.

Notes

1. Le Corbusier, *Towards A New Architecture* (John Rodker, 1931).
2. William Wordsworth, *The Prelude*.
3. Sophocles' play, *Oedipus at Colonus*; the cave is Cockle's Wood Fissure.
4. 'Perhaps you noticed something about the entire nature of beekeeping, something, I would say, of the nature of an enigma.' See Rudolph Steiner, *Bees: lectures; with an afterword on the artistic alchemy of Joseph Beuys* (Anthroposophic Press, 1998).
5. Samuel Beckett, *Krapp's Last Tape and Embers* (Faber, 1960).
6. Stage direction preceding *Krapp's Last Tape*.
7. Robin Atthill (ed.), *Mendip: a new study* (David & Charles, 1976).
8. Hestia is a persona lying at the back of the voice in Sean Borodale, *Human Work* (Jonathan Cape, 2015).
9. 'Lyrigraph', a word I coined from the Greek *lyric*, concerning the lyre, and *graphos*, writing. The lyrigraph is a counter-poetics to the closure of a finished poem, in which the moment of writing is an intentional performance. The writing itself *is* the live performance. The text is its record; a transcript of live experience *of* the performance of writing. The performance of writing the lyrigraph is not the same as the latent performance in a playscript. I made (and printed) texts which scripted the attempt to write about place, in situ or on location. I felt a need, in creating this term *lyrigraph*, to move away from the deadweight of making the poem appear *fait accompli* and into the moments when I felt most alive as a writer. See also Introduction to Sean Borodale, *Bee Journal* (Vintage, 2016).
10. '*Duende* climbs up inside you, from the soles of the feet ... it is ... a question ... of spontaneous creation ... It brings to old planes unknown feelings of freshness, with the quality of something newly created ... All arts are capable of *duende*, but where it finds greatest range, naturally, is in music, dance, and spoken poetry, for these arts require a living body to interpret them, being forms that are born, die, and open their contours against an exact present.' Federico

García Lorca, *Teoría y juego del duende* (Theory and Play of the *Duende*), (Maurer, 1998) pp. 48–62.

11. Joseph Beuys, artist, for whom felt was an important element in his art and theory of social sculpture.

12. Le Corbusier, *Towards a New Architecture*.

13. 'Honeypump in the Workplace', *Documenta* 6 (Kassell, 1977). I discuss this work in more detail in 'Unity in Diversity', *Tate Etc.* issue 38, Autumn 2016.

A Story of Arctic Maps

Hugh Brody

There's no place like home. No other territory that can remind you of childhood feelings – of belonging, and of constriction and loss; nowhere else defines the forces that shape you, and that you need to get away from; the landscape that is both wonderfully familiar and rich in primitive heartbreak. The place that can make you long for elsewhere.

*

Peoples who live by hunting and gathering do not leave much evidence of their occupation and use of their lands. The Inuit of the Canadian Arctic lived in houses built with stone and whale-bone insulated with chunks of sod, or in the famous igloo, shaped in a spiral of blocks of wind-packed snow; and, in summer, in tents made from animal skins. They did not build monuments or mark the boundaries of their territories with any kind of wall or fence. Apart from the delicate evocations of a figure in the landscape, the *Inuksuk*, that was put up as a marker of a trail or used to divert migrating caribou towards waiting hunters, they left almost nothing on the land to show they had been there. And they did not want to change the land itself. Hunting peoples need their world to stay the same – knowledge of it is their most valuable tool. They did not have a way of writing down this encyclopedia of knowledge – their histories and experience – but passed these on in what they said, through the stories they told. Theirs was the life of the mind and the voice.

Minds and voices leave indelible marks on the next generation, but not on the land itself. There are hints of occupation – a ring of stones shows where a tent had been pitched, the broken circle of rocks and sod where a winter house was made, a curve of boulders across the shallows of a river where a weir had been for trapping migrating fish, and the *Inukshuit*, small piles of stone that, in the words of one Arctic traveller, redeemed the empty wastes of their loneliness. Empty and lonely; Arctic wastes. These are terms, a way of evoking the north, that suggest that people have made no difference to it and, indeed, are absent or irrelevant.

The Inuit claim to these empty wastes had to deal first of all with that stereotype, and then with the overarching problem of evidence. They could say this was their land, but could they prove it? Could they show that they were more than perched at the edges of the vast expanses of tundra, wild fjords, and winter ice? No one would deny that the Inuit were the people of the north, but how much of it? Where in truth had their way of life given them a basis for making a claim? Which bits of the Arctic could be said to be their homeland? What areas of this forbidding landscape could be shown to be a territory that had supported life 'since time immemorial'? This was the legal requirement: the Inuit must show that they had a way of life, an economic system, that linked them to specific lands, and that all this had been in existence for many generations, and at least since well before any southerners arrived. What was their way of owning their world?

The attempt to answer these questions, to find the evidence, to make the invisible visible, began in the Arctic in 1974. The Canadian government funded a project that would set out the nature and extent of Inuit use and occupation of their lands. Milton Freeman, a British-born biologist turned anthropologist who had lived in Canada all his adult life, and had done extensive research in the far north, was given the job of coordinating this work. It was to be an independent study, aiming to give definitive answers to the questions raised by the Inuit claim to the Arctic. Lawyers were asked to give their advice: what did they need to know in order to develop the legal basis for a claim? Their answer was simple enough: everything – they needed every possible fact about Inuit ways of using their lands. Freeman decided that the way forward was to make maps of every Inuit hunter's life history – a biography that would show on a map, or a set of maps, all the places he or she had been and all the hunting and gathering he or she had done there. Freeman set out the objectives of the study: as close to 100 per cent coverage of the population, with a map biography for every person who had used the land.

Through all its history as a nation, Canada had been calling for the assimilation of its 'Native Peoples' into society as a whole, or into some idea of a single Canadian society. There had been repeated declarations, as at so many colonial frontiers, that 'Native' people at the margins, 'primitive' peoples, must somehow be absorbed into the body politic, or at least protected against their inherent ignorance and 'lack of development'. Maps would refute these notions – they would make the wealth and sophistication of Inuit life visible and undeniable. They would show that the Inuit, like all the indigenous peoples of Canada, lived at the centre of their worlds. To see the extent and nature of their ways of life would show strength, not weaknesses; riches, not poverty.

The Arctic was divided into regions. A list was made of every creature and plant that could have been hunted, caught or gathered. This list would be used as the basis for the mapping: each hunter and gatherer would be asked to mark on a map where every resource had been found. Older hunters would be asked to make separate maps for earlier times – the era before there was a trading post, the time when there was a trading post but not a school, and then the time since the school came. These are the phases of modern Inuit history. Three different ways of relating to the place where they continued to live. The maps would show how the way and extent of using the land had been affected by these historic changes brought from far to the south.

The project also aimed to make maps of cultural sites – the graves of ancestors, an area that figured in important stories, trails and travel routes, ancient villages, the bays and headlands where the distant ancestors of the Inuit had lived, reaching back several thousand years. This understanding of ancient history was also part of Inuit knowledge, of their links to their lands. This would be done on another set of maps. As if this were not enough, maps would also be made to show how the people understood the biological and environmental relationships that their system depended upon. Routes and patterns of caribou migration; areas where polar bears would make their dens to give birth; ways in which the structures and movements of ice explained patterns of seal hunting; connections between movements of walrus, narwhal and killer whales. This level of information – the ethno-scientific – would emerge in ways and with details that could not be foreseen; but as it did emerge, further maps should be made to show as much of this as possible.

I was given responsibility for the mapping in the North Baffin region. The first task was to put together the topographical map sheets that would include the widest possible extent of the land use of the Inuit of the communities of Pond Inlet and Arctic Bay. I had an idea of this from my time in North Baffin, both listening to accounts of hunting and travel across the region, and being taken out on trips at each time of year with some of the most active hunters. I knew it was a large area: when I came to put the map sheets together, I discovered that we would have to map onto a base that extended over 450 miles from east to west, and 400 miles from north to south. This area was made all the more extensive, with all kinds of possible travel, by its fractured topography: multitudes of bays, inlets, islands and mountains meant that those who used this land would be travelling routes that twisted and turned, headed out across spans of open water and far inland along both dramatic fjords and long river valleys. I knew that many families often had travelled to hunt with or visit relatives and neighbouring settlements that were 150 miles away; and one family I knew had made an extended journey of over a thousand miles, moving from one Inuit community to another, all the way to the edge of the tree line, far to the south-west. Putting together this extent of land use meant making a set of base maps that was five feet across.

In house after house people squatted and crouched around this great area of virtual territory. We went through the list: can you mark all the places you have hunted for ring seal, bearded seal, harp seal, walrus, narwhal? And the places you hunted for caribou, hare, polar bears? And trapped foxes? And fished for arctic char, trout, cod, sculpin? And gathered clams and sea urchins? And hunted eider ducks, snow geese, tundra swans; or collected the eggs of Arctic terns, murres, gulls, black guillemots? And found blueberries, cranberries? Show us all this for when you were living out on the land before the school was set up. Now all the places since the school. And where were the graves of your ancestors, the camp sites you used, the places you put your tents? Then the ecological knowledge: the bears' dens, the way cracks formed in the ice and meant that seals and narwhal could be hunted in open water. Which way did the caribou move in spring and autumn; where did they have their calves; where was their favourite summer grazing? Someone mentioned spiders – were there many in this particular place? Or butterflies? Someone had picked mushrooms – where were they usually found? And a journey – to trade one year, to visit a sick relative another, to travel for the fun of travelling. Along this shoreline, across that mountain pass, then down the coastline there. These were the places we stopped. Here there was a bad storm, and across that headland the ice was always piled high in early spring so it was slow and difficult to use that route. And here is where you can find the bones of my grandparents, or the grave of a southerner who came to trade, or the wreck of an old whaling ship ...

One map biography could take two days, and then be added to with extra visits, more stories, another set of memories. We worked and worked, all of every day, for weeks on end. The maps became filled with circles, lines, notes; and the maps piled up. To our surprise, everyone was able to find themselves on these maps – they could see their world in these representations from above, as if the bird's-eye view, which they could have had only in flights of the imagination, was as easy for them as any other way of seeing their lands; and the setting-out of all this experience and knowledge was to discover what it had meant to be a hunter and gatherer in these territories. For all their clutter or information, crossings-out and corrections, lines going in all directions in many different colours, the maps were astonishing, compelling and beautiful creations. They showed just how intense, extensive and rich the Inuit relationship to their world had been, and still was.

The people of North Baffin revealed this to me, the outsider who had brought this inquiry into their homes. They also showed it to one another. No one did their mapping in solitude: members of the family sat and watched, neighbours who were visiting joined in. This was work that celebrated experience and skill. Everyone was delighted to show, tell, share. Everyone took pride in what was being revealed. Each group had its set of hunting, fishing, trapping and living sites. Inuit life had been built around a seasonal round, with winter seal-hunting areas out on the sea ice where a number of households would gather; then a scatter to spring hunting places; a further scatter to summer caribou hunting inland or coastal hunting where kayaks and skin boats could be used; then a move to autumn fishing places at a river the char would be migrating up; and back to the winter seal hunting. Each group had a set of such places. In winter some groups might overlap; for much of the year each group would move between its particular set, along its distinctive seasonal round. As we made the maps, everyone could see that between them they had created a large and widespread system of interconnected patterns of hunting, fishing, gathering and trapping. And of culture. Each family would only speak for its particular part of the large pattern; but to see the pattern as a whole was to understand the brilliance and completeness of Inuit use of their lands and their stories about their lives. When all the maps were put together, every possible harvesting area and living site had been used; everywhere and everything seemed to be known and understood. Stories became maps; maps turned into a new kind of story.

*

During the years I worked and lived in the Arctic I went home, or parts of home, for long visits. I did my writing there. I was in my thirties. My parents were in the north of England; my girlfriend lived in London, where we shared a small flat in Bayswater, at the edge of Hyde

Park. I had new friends in Ottawa, and old friends in England. All the sources of life, all the things that make up the contexts and circumstances of home, were far away and scattered. But when living in the Canadian north I felt alive, or felt that I was able to be who I wanted to be or to experience myself as I really was. I would have the use of a bunk bed in the house of Inuk and Inuya, the family where I always stayed, in a row of low-cost government housing in Pond Inlet, looking out at the mountains and glaciers of Bylot Island, across the wide inlet where I would be taken hunting, moving in winter and spring across the sea ice on a sledge pulled by skidoo or dogs, and in small, open boats in summer and autumn. I was taken to rivers and lakes to fish, and up onto the tundra to look for caribou or geese. By the time the mapping project got under way I was able to live and work in Inuktitut, speaking the language of everyday without too much difficulty, able to learn about most aspects of hunting without needing an interpreter, dreaming in the language; and able to wear the clothes, eat the food, share the routines of my adoptive family without making too much of a fool of myself. I was sometimes miserable with cold or with fear when out on the land. But when I was there, immersed in being there, I did not want to be anywhere else.

The mapping was the most pleasing and, at times, exciting work I had ever done. There was clarity and a fundamental simplicity to the task. We helped people to show on paper what they had done and what they knew. It was obvious what to ask, and it made perfect sense to those who answered. Every map produced surprises: no one had ever known the extent of each family's use of the land; there was a spread of long journeys that people had made that had never been recorded; and I had never seen the systems and patterns of life across an immense area of the eastern Arctic. The work led to real, material results: map after map covered with facts, names, bits of stories, history, culture. The invisible made visible. It was possible to make journeys across it all without going beyond a room where I laid out a set of map sheets.

So I did not give much thought to elsewhere, to the people or places that were 'home'. I never imagined that I would live all the time in the Arctic. It was as if I had no home; or could find enough of a home in a form of homelessness – in being immersed in the Inuit idea of home, and by taking intense issue with the ways in which I could disregard the extent to which I might be homeless. I did not have a phone; there was no such thing as email; the post came in once every two weeks, weather permitting. I could have found ways to be in touch: the radio-phone at the government office could be used, and there was a postal service. I did write occasional letters, with descriptions of what I had been doing or, at times, with expressions of loneliness and missing – these being the times, the states of mind, when I would want to write a letter. But they were few and scant. I gave little thought to the difficulty this might cause to those who had wanted to make homes for me.

I am not sure if anyone worried about me: they never said they did. And there was nothing to worry about. I did not look for danger; every day was an adventure, but I was given the safety and comforts that came from this being a home to the people who took me out onto their lands. Part of their sense of place, and my discovery of the north, came from it being shaped by knowledge, by stories, and not by any remodelling of the physical world. In this sense it was a wild place; though, for the Inuit, and for anyone who followed them into their territories, everything was shaped by their voices and knowledge and a way of living that gave everyone the same kind of connections to the world. A place that took sharing and equality for granted; and where no one staked an individual claim, but all individuals shared in the system as a whole.

When I returned to England, and went again to the Derbyshire hills where I had grown up, or to the London where I continued to be based, I looked out at a world that was shaped and built and understood through private ownership, permanent sites of all kinds, and exclusion. Even the open spaces of the north of England were caught in this net of transformation and class. The walls and hedges marked where land had been worked into fields, and where boundaries had been set up. Bare slopes, moorland and bracken, were the result of deforestation and grazing of the farmers' sheep. The intricate mazes of property.

These were landscapes of social and economic exclusions, the basis and expression of great inequity.

I would look out at this, my childhood home, and understand a bit more about why I had needed to leave it; and what I had experienced in that other way of being human, in the Canadian Arctic. At times as I walked in England, aware of its particular kinds of beauty, I would have a sense of a screen between my eyes and all that I saw; and I would imagine onto this another kind of place. Having been immersed in the lands and the lives of hunters, I needed to see, at least in my mind's eye, a land unmarked by boundaries, open to all, rich with names in a very different kind of language.

IN ARIZONA

John Burnside

Wayside Shrines

On the hard shoulder of Highway 86, halfway between Tucson and the Tohono O'Odham Indian reservation, you might come across a simple wooden cross decorated with trinkets, dusty Valentine hearts, scraps of faded tinsel and a single, magically untarnished Dr Pepper can. It will not be dissimilar to the wayside shrines you have seen in other parts of the world, home-made memorials to the casual dead in Mexico or rural Italy, strangely poignant in spite, or perhaps because, of their crude construction, and as transient as the lives they commemorate. Yet what distinguishes the shrines of southern Arizona is the way in which they differ, not only in number (and they are painfully common sights on this stretch of 86), but also in their remarkable inventiveness, their elaborate decoration and – most of all – in their oddly haunting beauty.

The shrines are not a new phenomenon in this landscape, but their construction has evolved, over years, into a local art form. More often than not, what began as a simple marker has developed into a thing of beauty: ringed around with blue, or red, or yellow painted stones, or draped with Christmas-tree lights and ornaments, a stark white cross gradually becomes a local description of home – a home both real and imagined, drawn, as all American homes are, from television, popular magazines and the myth of a better time, where the deceased may be sensed as continuing in the usual way, his can of Dr Pepper or an old-fashioned Coke bottle in pride of place amongst the knick-knacks, as if he might come back at any time to finish it off. Some of the crosses bear heartbreaking messages – 'Killed by a Drunk Driver', or 'We Love You Daddy' – but most are silent, anonymous, a private treaty between the one who has passed and those who are left behind. Yet even as those unnamed dead continue, they are also magically transformed, like the dead of prehistoric times. The roadside shrines are not official, they have no orthodox function, yet they are the true focus of the region's most authentic funeral rites: better than Church, better than anything the state can provide. Here, mourning, and the process of regeneration, are home-made, just, and true to the dead they honour.

It must be admitted that many, if not most, of these shrines have fairly banal histories. In this part of Arizona drunk-driving is commonplace, especially on the reservations, where poverty, humiliation and boredom are the banal facts of life. The standard vehicle is the old and painfully dilapidated pick-up: a vehicle which should seat three at most in the cab, but which is often used to transport whole gangs of reckless partygoers, men, women and children perched in the back of the truck as it cannons along an empty road in the dark, the driver out of his head on cheap liquor, or exhausted after days of celebration. It's part of the culture, anyhow, to be fearless: life is too poor, too dull and too little prized by the outside world to be overly careful about, consciously at least. A short drive through reservation land confirms it: even the police here are careless road-users, and they sometimes tolerate the drunk-driver who meanders blindly along the empty highway at dawn, weaving from lane to lane or sliding off into the chaparral to sleep it off, if he is lucky, in the shadow of a tall saguaro. If he is lucky.

The unlucky ones kill themselves, or others, or both and, equals in death, are marked by wayside shrines tended by their wives and children, or their parents, or their workmates, through feast days and holidays. The shrines are painted red and decked with hearts on St Valentine's Day, draped with the Stars and Stripes for foreign wars and days of remembrance, twined about with tinsel and hung with tiny coloured bells at Christmas. On birthdays and special occasions, the families drive out with cakes and sweets and canned drinks, yet nobody ever sees them, just as nobody ever sees the careful relatives and friends as they tend the shrines, making them, with each short visit, ever more beautiful and elaborate.

The stores and service stations that line Highway 86 have caught onto this grave culture. Here, the gas stations have a wide selection of plastic flowers and decorations, everything from tinsel to coloured ribbon to Christmas-tree baubles, alongside the car accessories and snacks. Yet – and this really is spooky – nobody is ever looking at these displays when my friends and I stop in for road supplies, and the locals we encounter, the thin old grandfathers in cowboy shirts and hats, the obese children in sweatshirts and cutaway pants, are both shy and suspicious when we loiter at the plastic flower stall to stare, with surprising reverence, at the unacknowledged grave goods. Oddly enough, notwithstanding the very exposed nature of the wayside shrines, death, and the honouring of the dead, is not a public matter here.

In a strange way, the shrines are just as private. This is a country where nobody stops on the road unless death or chance intervenes. As my friends and I pull over to look at one particularly beautiful shrine, I feel awkward, somehow blasphemous, as if I am about to rip open one of those sacred Dr Pepper cans and steal precious liquid from the memorialised father, or son, whose death marks this particular spot. It is hard not to feel that I am being watched, as I hunker down to read the message – a simple 'We Miss You' – on a red, white and blue painted crucifix. When I look up, however, nothing is there, not even a passing car. Only the desert, stretching away as far as the eye can see. This stretch of Arizona is a land of ghosts, a land of those who have died violently, but for as long as I watch it stays silent, empty, utterly peaceful. For a moment I allow myself to hope – perhaps even to pray – that this silence, this peace, gives the unseen mourners who built this shrine some kind of solace. Then I stand up and hurry back to the car, relieved, and disappointed, to be on my way.

Place, or, something there is that doesn't love a wall

Where, or what, is Arizona? For that matter, what is *place*, anyway? How do we know where one place ends and another begins? Where is America? Mexico? Do we find place, or do we make it? Perhaps both: we find a place, we give it a name – our name – and we begin to change its intrinsic nature, more often than not transforming it into property. We plant a flag. We draw up deeds. A man says, 'This is mine,' and does not even consider the absurdity of such a position. One of the main reasons for changing a place is to facilitate this process of acquisition. Our first relationship to place, then, is a betrayal. After that, the only question is: where do we build the wall?

Though non-native (whatever that means here), my Arizona friends do not belong to that species known as 'snow-birds' – town people from the north, usually elderly, who drive south in the winter to save money on heating and other bills. No – they live in the desert all the year round, working from home and accommodating themselves to their various neighbours, with a strong sense that they are newcomers there, and ought to practise respect for those older inhabitants. I still recall the first night with them when, exhausted after my long journey, I headed off to their spare room, only to be offered some advice about the morning schedule that involved a little more than where to find my favourite cereal. Knowing my penchant for rising early and getting out of doors as soon as I can (especially in perennially overheated America), my friends advised me that, if I did go out early, I should remember to put my boots on first. 'That way, the rattler won't catch you barefoot,' they said, with a grin.

It was true: they had a rattlesnake as their closest neighbour, a sizeable fellow who often climbed onto their porch to catch the morning sun. Other locals included coyotes and roadrunners, straight out of those old Chuck Jones Wile E. Coyote cartoons that satirised not only our insane love affair with technology, but also the absurd pace at which we choose to live. Meanwhile, there were bigger and scarier critters to be avoided further afield (diamondbacks, bobcats, mountain lions). The real beauties of the desert, however, are its birds, from tiny hummingbirds to red-tailed hawks to the strange, and oddly cartoonish, burrowing owl, a creature that seems to live in a constant state of wide-eyed surprise, and the only owl species known to live underground. My friends tended a large garden, and I saw a huge variety of birds just by sitting on their porch and waiting for what passed through each day, but they told me that, if I really wanted to see birds, the place to go was Arivaca.

Arivaca. The town itself is nothing much, but the nearby *cienaga* (a marshy area at the edge of grassland where, in this case, several waters meet) was like a dream of heaven. Yellow-billed cuckoo, Swainson's hawk, Lucy's warbler and black-bellied whistling duck breed here, along with thick-billed kingbirds, rufous-winged sparrow and the rare buff-collared nightjar. When we think of desert, we tend to picture mono-tones – sand, rock, dry arroyo, scree – but wherever water is present the daily round turns miraculous. At the same time, when birds find water, they tend to linger, and they are easier to watch for longer periods of time. So many bird encounters are teasing and elusive – walking a rocky trail, I have heard the song of the canyon wren (to my mind, one of nature's most beautiful sounds), but that doesn't always mean I have seen it, while far too many warblers have passed by like restless spirits, filling my head with song, but flitting away into the reeds or the shadows before I quite caught sight of them. Though I have to admit that part of the reason for this is that I am not one of those patient souls who spend whole days in well-camouflaged hides with binoculars and photo-graphic equipment that makes space travel look amateurish. I'm not a real birder; I prefer to saunter.

I should be more disciplined. For stillness offers rare treats now and then: like the day I sat, alone, utterly still, at the edge of a dry arroyo and watched as a passing roadrunner gave me a curious, but far from fearful look, before moving on along the muddy track. It was a good moment, a rare instance of proximity, even a kind of intimacy, and I was about to store it away and carry on my walk, but something held me there and, a few minutes later, a not very wily-looking coyote appeared, obviously trailing the bird, albeit in rather nonchalant fashion. It wasn't like the cartoons at all: speed was not a factor, or wouldn't be, at least, until much later in the game, and it reminded me, once again, of the patience of animals – and of how impatient we are. Then, without further ado, I stood up, and walked back to the point where my world began, a realm that all at once seemed endlessly frenetic, for reasons I was no longer so sure I understood.

Songbirds of Pima County

I am glad you love the blossoms so well. I hope you love
birds, too. It is economical. It saves going to Heaven.

Emily Dickinson

With so many ways for them to fall,
there are days when I cannot bear
to hear them singing.
Yet I look up and, always, the light
is larger than my gaze,
making of each cottonwood a house
of many mansions, where they come and go
from this world to the next.

If, once, I could not raise my hand to stop
the older boys from emptying a nest
and pinning each cowlicked chick
to the bars of a gate,
I still couldn't run for safety, crying
murder, there was too much happening
and, whether by choice or not,
I was involved.

Later the bunting's song would lead me
out into the dark viridian
above a stream, where willows huddled in
so close, it seemed a room in which the mind
could lose itself, the way the heart was lost
in love, when love
was still that kind
of story.

Now love is mostly song
and song

is mostly reminiscence: not
a true account, but something writ
in cypher, like the local
dialects of vireo, or towhee, or a secret
history of mourning dove
and shrike, it speaks to us

in ways we do not care
to understand.
Yet I would understand them, if I could,
the red-tailed hawk sucked
clean into the wheels
and dragged for fifty yards along this desert
road, its last cry
drowned out by the screaming of the tyres,

or later, when we pull in by the creek,
a full moon in the giant
cottonwood, where who knows what
is roosting
and the voice out in the dark
is one part whippoorwill and three parts
grief for something
none of us could name –

though grief is natural, where there is time,
and time is in the music, when we hear
the canyon wren
at daybreak, or the raven
quartering the land, the cottonwood
expanding into light, a red-winged blackbird
calling from the reeds in the *cienaga*:
insistent and lusty, persisting and passing away

as we drive across town to the sun-tiled
diner, where a local is telling the usual

story of how, in the old days (and this is true),
the fishing was good, and the birds
more numerous; while, somewhere, out in back,
a radio is playing to the sunlit
kitchen, and the waitress sings along
so lightly, you could almost love again.

Florida

'Is there a brick wall getting in your way? Fine. That happens. But you have a choice. You can walk away from the wall. You can go over the wall. You can go under the wall. You can go around the wall. You can also obliterate the wall. In other words, don't let anything get in your way. Get a balance, and then let the positive outdistance the negative.'

Yes. That *is* Donald Trump, in his 2010 book, *Think Like a Champion: An Informal Education in Business and Life*. I don't imagine the boys my friend met in the Sonora Desert had read that book, but they had surely absorbed something of its aspirational thinking, or why would they be standing there, in the middle of nowhere, with little or no supplies to speak of, when my friend arrived (her work involves travelling around the remoter corners of this wide country)? Asked where they had come from, they did not reply. Asked what they were doing there, they said they were 'waiting for a friend'. Offered water and a little food, they accepted warily. Then, opening up somewhat, they expressed the concern that their friend might not be coming – they had been waiting for two days. Finally, as my friend made to leave, she asked if she could help them in any way, maybe drive them somewhere, or make inquiries about their lost companion. They shook their heads in unison, and then one boy, the shorter of the two, asked her to point out which direction they should take for Florida.

A few days after I heard this story, I spent a day in the Gila Desert, wandering amongst vast stands of organ pipe cactus. Then, when nightfall came, my companions and I made our way to a small motel on the edge of Ajo, not far from the Mexican border. Given my aforementioned aversion to overheating, I do not linger in hotel rooms easily; more often than not, I am up and about by daybreak – and that overnight stay was no different. After a long dinner at the local Chinese restaurant, I had gone to bed fairly late, but I was out of my cabin by six the next morning, sitting on the tiny porch area and staring off across the yard, towards the desert beyond. A few feet away, an unhappy-looking dog turned and looked at me wearily, but he didn't bark, or come to see if I had anything to offer him, he just lifted his head for a moment, checked what manner of beast I was and then, clearly disappointed, settled back into the dust. It was more or less day already. The yard was partly separated from the desert beyond by a row of parched, twiggy shrubs, and though I knew that makeshift hedge for what it was – one of the *thin places* known to the Celts as borderlines between this world and the other – I let it be and stayed on my porch, feeling the morning cool on my skin and enjoying the fact that, for once, my mind was empty of noise. Twenty paces would have taken me through that invisible borderland into the mystery beyond, but I stayed put and studied to be quiet, and it was a long moment before I realised that I had grown apprehensive of something, though even then I didn't know what. And, of course, it was nothing major: for a local, I later discovered, it was even a commonplace, but to me it was both magical and tragic. At first, I had no idea what was going on, but as I stood gazing into space, I became aware of movement, and then, of a line of people, maybe fifteen or more, coming through one of the many gaps in the hedge and hurrying across the yard: men, women and children, clutching bundles to their chests, following a tall, very thin man who looked no better-off or sure of himself than they were, but who must have been a coyote, nevertheless, one of those professional guides who lead bands of migrants across the border and up to *El Norte*, where the money lives. When they saw me, some of the people in that line looked startled, not because they were afraid I might be a border guard or a busybody, but because I would have looked like an apparition to them (apparitions being common in the thin places). Nevertheless, most of them kept their eyes fixed on the man who was leading the way, hoping they could trust him, possibly wondering where they were and how far it was to safety – and I understood, suddenly, that while apparitions might be a source of fascination for me, for them, hurrying from nowhere to nowhere, and hoping for work and such dignity as life affords, such things were a needless luxury. Some of them would make it (or so I hoped), but most would be forcibly returned, sent back across a border no more real than that straggling line of dusty shrubs at the edge of the motel yard, to begin the journey again. Those who did stay would be confined to other forms of borderland, where someone like me would not linger and, when they stood at the edge of their world, gazing out, their eyes would be turned, not towards the desert, but to the streets and houses that, able as I am to take them for granted, I am always a little too eager to leave behind.

Spring Gentians

Mark Cocker

I'd long heard about Upper Teesdale in County Durham. For botanists, for almost 400 years, it has been a holy grail. The pre-eminent story of the place is the chance it offers to see the ancient plant life of this country at a point when its great carapace of ice had finally begun to slip off. It is the early Holocene at its most tender and pristine. In truth, I was moved to visit when I chanced on pictures of its totem flower. The spring gentians looked like strange, furled tongues of ocean blue bulbed out of the Earth from who knows what depths.

On a whim I set off, but not all wildlife excursions are successful. Yet none is ever wasted. On the drive to the car park at Cow Green I stopped briefly in Langdon Beck. The weather seemed too brutal and the river too swollen with run-off even to get out. Instead I sat and watched a scrap of black plastic – the defining foliage of the oil age – that had somehow escaped the farmer's control. It had snagged across eight tines of a barbed-wire fence.

While its iron-claw grip anchored that sheet down, the gusts wanted to take it and I was mesmerised by the physics of their contest. Minute corrugations in the fabric relentlessly rippled across the surface so that it resembled molten lava freshly setting, or perhaps the black motile liquid from which it was originally made. With each lull the sheet's ragged edge slumped under gravity. Then battle resumed and the plastic bellied out and heaved, and I noticed how its upwelling dark shapes momentarily resembled the wider contours of Cronkley Fell immediately beyond. It was strange to reflect how that rippling crag was made from the same kind of elemental arguments, but over a period of 295 million years.

From the Cow Green car park there were just two small receding eyes of snow somewhere on the high slopes of Great Dun Fell. At 2,782 feet it is the second highest hill in the entire Pennines, and the average May temperature is the same as London's in January. Then the cloud mass rolled steadily down from those northern English vertebrae and the snow eyes were obliterated and the light fell.

I braced myself for the walk while the wind snuffled at the car's underside. I could feel the whole vehicle rock with quiet violence on its axles, but I had not thought through the angle at which I had parked, so when I finally opened the door it was snatched from me and there was a hideous crunch as it whanged against the hinges. Then I got out and my hat flew off 50 feet before coming to Earth. I raced after, having almost to fight for each in-breath against the pull of the wind.

I retrieved the cap and set off along the track by the spot where the gentians are seen. I found it hard to conjure anything so rare or so colourful in this landscape. In fact it was hard to imagine any plant, of any description, in flower today in this vile weather, when there were just the leached sand tones of dead grass and the leached russet of dead rush and the long dark cloud brood passing east.

Cow Green Reservoir was on my right as I headed towards the dam head. The westerlies scoured the down slopes and jack-knifed off the water, sending clean white mare's tails across the surface. The rain never stopped until I got back to the car two hours later, and with each gust it clattered at the surface of my waterproof. I dragged the hood down, but the wind found a way to squeeze in and prise it off my head so that rain could sleet full in my face and coat my spectacles in blobs of water. When I arrived at the vehicle all down one side, sleeve and trousers, was slathered cold and wet onto bare skin.

In between the blur I picked out this handful of details: the way the elements had hollowed out the wooden fence posts until only the hardest lignin cores remained. Yet each post top had its own headful of grey lichen, and between the skeletal uprights were strands of barbed wire, buckled and snapped with rust. In my notebook I wrote:

> There were few flowers but probably dried remnants of last year's bog asphodel and sundew without their fly-trap stems. Withered and desiccated lichen and drab heather, but no fresh green anywhere: only winter recoil. Spring was not here. The single sign of recent human was an apple core crushed to the path. Cow Green was entirely free of vertebrate life, aside from two curlews blown slantwise and silent across the cloud race. And me.

You realise that while this has been a site of constant human traffic – the old adits of the lead mines and the reservoir's 1,700-foot concrete dam were proof of that – the elements test everything to destruction. Cow Green admits of nothing that is not weighted to the place. And you are always aware of wind: either its imposing, even brutal, presence or, occasionally, its momentary lack. It affects the grand – the clouds over the Pennines – and the trivial – stray wool strands wittering at snags in the wood posts. Like a tongue in a tooth cavity it is incessant and erosive. All is shaped and made fit to meet it, gravity and mass holding everything to the landscape – stone, water, tree, plant – until it is entirely true. Temporarily.

A few weeks later

As I head for Cow Green at dawn, with the sun at my back, the whole landscape is cleanly engraved by low-angled soft light. Below and immediately above Middleton-in-Teesdale is that stock northern blend of cattle and sheep pasture segmented by drystone wall or stout wind-slanted thorn hedge. The River Tees flows by the town and at intervals bends close to the road as I climb west, all shallow blue shimmer and white-flecked stone. Then it is lost to view in the valley; the cattle fall away; so too the ash and the sycamores towering over the fields, while the lime-washed white cottages grow more distant from their neighbours. I pass the High Force Inn, where botanists have stayed since the 1840s, and just after the turning for Force Garth Quarry I ride out on to the upper reaches of the dale and the grandeur of it all seizes me.

Even as I absorb the panorama, a lapwing in full display blusters like a wind-slewed cloth just in front of the car, and even through the glass and engine drone I can pick out the ecstatic sweet ache of its song. A pair of pied wagtails flushes up from the road edge, and the cold dawn glow fringes all their feathers so that the two birds look as if they had just been freshly minted from bright light.

But nothing equals the impact of the marsh marigolds. In the roadside fields, which weeks ago had been the pastel shades of snow-burnt grass, they are spread in such profusion that they embody the ideal of the colour yellow. I'm heading for Widdybank and Cow Green, but the flowers immediately unravel my programme. I fling the car door wide open. Within a minute the knees of my jeans are swollen with ground water (despite a plastic sheet I roll out to lie on), but there is also the joy of photography: forcing you to get on eye-level terms with flowers.

Our friend Polly Monroe (partner of Richard Mabey) calls the same species by their old Norfolk name – 'molly blobs' – which evokes the way that the stems and leaves of her local plants rise up with robust, water-filled, lily-like fleshiness. Here in Upper Teesdale, marsh marigolds are wind-sculpted creepers. I find a patch that has grown just high enough to meet my wide-angle lens, and behind their crisp detail is the blurred lustre of the yellow pool; beyond, a whitewashed gable end to a farm and, blurrier still, the Whin Sill plateaux of Cronkley and Widdybank Fells. The smothering of flowers reminds me of what has been lost with the destruction of 4 million acres of herb-rich meadow, of which this is such a singular, breathtaking example.

I have never seen its like before, and I am pitched into an elevated state of mind so that when I arrive, a few moments later, at a flower-lined trickle just by Langdon Beck it feels nothing to stop again. Weeks ago this very spot was a foam-flecked torrent, and the sound of angry water had been obliterated by the insane skitter of black plastic snagged in barbed wire.

Now I am straight across the brook and flat on my front before bird's-eye primroses. I saw the basal leaves last time – star-like rosettes of pale waxy green, prostrate to the ground – but here the plants are a spring song of exquisite colour. The petals are gently notched in their outer fringes so that a central yellow eye, formed by the cluster of pollen-bearing stamens, is encircled with five hearts of deepest pink. Almost without end they quiver in the breeze, and it is more than an hour before I align everything to my satisfaction: the blood pulse of my own hands, the detail of the flowers, a lull in the wind and then May sunshine coming and going between white cloud. As I lie to attend to this scarce resident of Upper Teesdale, I can listen to the sky songs of its most abundant bird neighbours – the lapwings and snipe, whose displays are fletched higher and higher by the morning's warmth and sunlight.

That hour with the primroses reflects how the whole day goes – a seven-mile distracted meander right around Widdybank Fell, which occupies me until seven in the evening, entirely alone, through scenes of overwhelming beauty punctuated with moments of absolute joy: the five-bar gates mottled white and grey and crusted along their upper beams by intricate gardens of fruticose lichens; the weathered slabs of Whin Sill, so empathetically curved to the human rear you would swear they were hand-cut stone benches (yet the upper planes of the dolerite are entirely smothered in a lichen cartography. My favourite, which I photograph over and over and later select as screen saver for my computer, is a Rothko-like blend of desert sand with islands of black-flecked ginger or grey).

I have my lunch sitting on such a stone with the white rush of Cauldron Snout boiling down beside me and my senses immersed in its force-drenched music; and despite its power, a dipper, nesting in the crag above where I sit, manages to pierce the heart of all the water noise with song.

Around teatime a short-eared owl, wafting like some kind of finned sea creature from the depths, performs a slow-savoured display that makes it seem larger than it truly is. I notice as it passes over the outcrops of sugar limestone, which are the colour of an Aegean shore, how the whole of the owl's underwing acquires its own calcareous glow. Then it swims away with the breeze and across the predominant rust-infused straw of Widdybank's wider vegetation, and in direct sunshine the bird is oat-white like setting steel.

This is all preparatory to the gentians. In a sense it has taken more than 300 million years to create the conditions for this flower. The decisive element is the Whin Sill itself, which began as lava from deep within our planet's core around 295 million years ago. On its journey through the crust it met strata of Carboniferous limestone, sand- and mudstones, which had been laid down around 33 million years earlier when this part of England lay near the equator.

The magma extruded through faults in the older sedimentary rocks and, as it rose, so it cooked the adjacent limestone layers to a coarse crystalline marble. When the latter weathers it acquires the consistency of fine sand or, according to geologists, of white sugar granules; hence the name: 'sugar limestone'. The surface outcrops of it are found only on Cronkley and Widdybanks Fells, and it is these that in large measure give rise to the botanical significance of Upper Teesdale.

The special nature of the flora was noted by the late seventeenth century, when the pioneer botanist John Ray published records of shrubby cinquefoil, which grows in Upper Teesdale and in only one other English location, the Lake District. By the early nineteenth century botanists had found most of the famous Teesdale plants, including alpine bartsia, alpine bistort, alpine cinquefoil, alpine meadow-rue, alpine penny-cress, bearberry, bird's-eye primrose, bog orchid, hair sedge, hoary rock-rose, hoary whitlow grass, holly fern, another fern called kobresia, mountain avens, Scottish asphodel, sea plantain and three-flowered rush.

On paper the most special of all is a tiny tufted, glabrous perennial called Teesdale sandwort *Minuartia stricta*. Yet the five-millimetre flower is entirely insignificant. Were it not for the fact that the species grows on just two isolated patches here at Widdybank, and nowhere else closer to these islands than Norway, it would be hard to be aroused.

Not so the gentians. And I find them eventually in good numbers. And I know, instantly, exactly what they are. Here's one. Quite soon, they surround me. I am routinely amused by the way in which a naturalist sets off with a long-brewed sense of longing for some rare organism – a bird or a flower – which one dreams to see; and then the ever-so-casual manner in which that anticipation confronts reality. There is no drum roll. No climax. Not even fumbling excitement. You simply pass quickly, efficiently almost, from one existential state to another.

With the gentians there may be no dramatic transformatory moment, but there is indubitably the life-lasting star-like beauty of them. It is not hard to see why they are the ultimate botanical symbol for Upper Teesdale. It is the colour. Of her own Californian gentians, the writer and pioneer feminist Mary Austin, a woman seldom lost for the exact word, could only pile up the one hue for added impact: 'blue–blue–eye-blue, perhaps'. One is not surprised to learn, she added, 'that they have tonic properties'.

It is a blue so much more striking than the sky, or the sea – as blue perhaps as the Earth when seen from outer space. The gentians are eyes of intense happiness in a brown and wind-troubled place. I drop to my knees to meet them.

Bodleian Library, Oxford; Aubrey Manuscript 17, Folio 12r

Peter Davidson

I am writing about a place which I have never seen and which I know by heart: gently sloping parkland falling to a stream, with the fields on the other side of the valley bright with new grass. It is one of the coloured drawings (technically limited, even amateur, but eloquent in their love and sorrow) which John Aubrey (1626–97) made of his family house, grounds and farmland at Easton Piers, near Kington St Michael in Wiltshire. He may have begun by testing a perspective device for landscape drawing, at some point before-and-after fantasies of an Italianate recasting of house and garden entered the series, but the sequence of drawings seemed to change purpose and atmosphere about halfway through. The change almost certainly came at the point when Aubrey realised that his inheritance was going to be dispersed because of the lawsuits which had ruined him at the age of forty-four. Once he knew that everything was going to be sold, his purpose altered to the making of a series of tender records of the estate as is was in reality, a series of captured moments and places from the April of the year 1670.

This loss called forth from him an intensity of identification with place. Depth of feeling is embedded in these coloured drawings, a sense of devotion to the sheep-cropped slopes and small, stream-scoured upland valleys. Memory inhabits their coppices, stone shelters and field gates, as well as their grand, cloudy Wiltshire distances, recessions of wooded ridges seen at evening from the high ground behind the house. There is an intensity here which transcends aesthetic limitations: a fragile, personal set of notations set down in the pocket drawing book – a portable memory book for a landless, migratory future. This can be felt in Aubrey's notes in the margins: 'my grandfather Lyte's chamber wherin I drew my first breath', 'a thin blew landscape'. What is recorded by his careful, unsophisticated work is a kind of memoir of youth and young manhood, a history of walking the fields, dog at heel, year after year, combined with an exceptional degree of natural observation.

It is this passion and closeness of observation which are extraordinary, seeming to belong less to the era when the drawings were made, than to the intense relation to English place which marks the years after the 1780s. Some of the drawings even speak to times and moods nearer to our own, wholly unlike the formalities of the estate and prospect poems which were the seventeenth-century ways of writing about landscape. The last drawing is sepia monochrome, a haunting prospect eastwards across fertile, well-wooded land towards the spire of Kington St Michael, the church school where Aubrey had his first education. A spring rain shower is passing over from the south, the trees and hedges are in leaf. The little figure of Aubrey is walking away from his lost inheritance, a stick over his shoulder. His dog Fortune, running ahead of him, turns back to look up at his master. *Mine now, his tomorrow, after that nobody knows whose*, is the English version of the motto which Aubrey wrote on the title page of this little book of drawings.

On this overcast late-winter afternoon, the sheets of paper which Aubrey carried around the Wiltshire field paths in the blue spring days of 1670 lie on the table in front of me in the Weston Library, part of the Bodleian Libraries in Oxford, the university which Aubrey attended until the civil wars put an end to his studies. He remained associated with Oxford all his life, and is buried somewhere in the church of St Mary Magdalene, at the other end of Broad Street from the Library, four minutes away. Little of his work was printed in his lifetime, so the manuscripts now in Oxford are his real legacy. In their varying degrees, all of these manuscripts of Aubrey's are beguilingly unfinished – a disordered, mysterious and poetic world of jottings about people and places and inventions and anecdotes and rumours and hauntings and antiquities. Inevitably every reader is sooner or later seduced by the feeling that if only these fragments could be deciphered (the hand is difficult, the papers dishevelled) and set in order, then the past would somehow be all but tangible and the voices of the dead would speak at the frontiers of our hearing, their shadows linger at the other door as we come into the room. You don't know Aubrey as a writer: you are drawn into knowing him as a collaborator in his great unfinished, unfinishable work. In a curious sense, he remains our contemporary, as though he is in some way still alive, out there in the green south-western quadrant of England, kept in being by the seductive incompleteness of his work. Thus, reading him makes you somehow his contemporary, or him yours. It is a strange, satisfying, sleep-troubling, dream-invading, unique relationship. (Part of the success of the recent, peerless edition of Aubrey's *Brief Lives* is its subtle assent to this process.)

The manuscript is on the table in front of me, the grey and white stripes of my shirt cuff are beside it where Aubrey's own hand must often have rested. I work with such things regularly, and have grown almost insensitive to the way that manuscript brings you into physical contact with the past and its inhabitants, the way that the individuality of a script long outlives the hand which shaped it. But Aubrey's works, and especially this manuscript, where he has dared to commit such defenceless love to the page, is an exceptional object which compels you to think of its paper as a contact with Aubrey, paper which has rested on his knee at the end of a field path. We are still aware of his hand under-drawing the scenes in the brownish ink of the seventeenth century, then setting the colours of coppice and sky, his brush hand hovering carefully just where my hand is now above the page as I turn to the twelfth leaf of the little bound book.

I gaze long and carefully at the saddest and most powerful of the drawings: we are looking down a sparsely wooded slope to a small stone building with a mono-pitch roof – some sort of cattle shelter or 'sheep house'. A hedge runs along the bottom of the valley, hinting at the presence of a stream. Another hedge divides the coppice from a field of grass to the right, entered by a wooden field gate. At the bottom of this field here are shadings and monochrome brushstrokes which outline small rocks breaking the surface of the grass.

Green slopes rise gently on the other side of the water. The more you look the more you see: a strong line of vertical light lies on the right-hand side of the tree trunks as if the sun is now low in the sky, shooting light along the valley. I think that it is growing cold as evening draws on. The tree shadows are strongly patterned on the ground. The under-drawing is in sepia ink, which shows through now-fading watercolour almost like the prefiguration of the autumn which will follow the partings to come. The brownish colouration dominates the page, for all that the sky is very blue. A green pigment must have faded from the sloping field on the other side of the valley, which once must have been bright with new grass. As the colour has gone, the hedgerows have dimmed and umbered. It is spring on the page, but the day is ending, and the shadows cast by the trees grow very long. You half catch Aubrey's murmur: *Nunc mea, mox huius, sed postea nescio cuius*. He must have gathered up his brushes and colours as the sun dipped below the horizon and, calling his dog to him – *Fortune, Fortune* – set off up the hill.

I take a last look at the sloping field in the westering sun, and turn the pages gently for one more glance at the sepia drawing of Aubrey and Fortune walking away into the green April evening. I close the manuscript, put on my jacket, hand the little oblong book in at the issue desk, then go downstairs and out through the peaceful, enormous hall. It is dark now and the evening air strikes with a chill like water on the skin. Bicycles whisper swiftly through the dusk. Opposite is the golden stone ensemble of theatre, museum and the endearing provincial baroque of the stone piers crowned by giant heads of the Roman emperors (I wish I could have seen this 'ragged regiment' in their 'wonderful state of decomposition' in the mid twentieth century[1]). These contrast with the stark grandeur of Hawksmoor's Clarendon building, which is tough and melancholy and belligerent all at once. Blackened lead statues of the Muses patrol the roofline – pitiless executives of success and genius and fame. *Fortune, Fortune.*

I start to walk home along Broad Street, past the closed gates and the concert posters. I glance across to Trinity, Aubrey's college, sitting far behind its screen of railings, beyond lawns and trees, like a country house. I turn south into Turl Street – in the panelled front room of the Turl Street Kitchen the first customers are eating an early supper by candlelight. Streetlamps and college windows shimmer dimly on damp flagstones. Now the smart shops pass: jeweller, bootmaker, dandy's tailor, whisky shop with its window full of names from the uplands around the house where I once lived in Aberdeenshire. Light strikes upwards to the brass chandeliers and high stucco ceiling of the church turned library on the corner. *Fortune, Fortune.*

I cross the High Street at the lights. Then down bricky Albert Street, round the corner by the Bear, where the lamplight is playing on the polished wood in the bar. Out into St Aldate's and threading through the crowds at the bus stops – the buses for Wantage and Abingdon, setting off into the damp night and through the lighted villages. I walk down past the front of Christ Church, Wren's Gothic tower high above me, through the breath of wood smoke from the pizza van at the college gate, and across the wide road. Brewer Street is dim, sheltered by the bulwark of the old city wall, by Pembroke's high buildings. The main road falls behind with every step, more removed still as I push open the outer door of Campion Hall and slide the tab against my name to IN.

I think that only in this college are there three choices: IN or OUT or AWAY. (Given the early history of the Jesuits in Britain it is hard not to associate AWAY with phrases like *gone beyond the seas*, or *fled to his kinsfolk in the North*.) *Fortune, Fortune.* A smell of polish and flowers and good, careful cooking. Past the great polychrome and gold carving of Ignatius and his companions, through the dim dining room (with habitual glances at the weekly menu, and at Augustus John's nervous, brilliant portrait of Fr Martin D'Arcy). Through the lobby with its paintings from Flanders and Peru, and into the library. Panelling above the broad stone fireplace, books from floor to ceiling, pools of light under the standard lamps. The room is profoundly still, and this quiet house grows quieter at evening. It is almost as though it grew more remote, when the lamps are lit in the library and the fire in the common room. It becomes like a manor house, silent at evening, remote and westerly and enfolded by wooded hills. The buds of the birch tree rustle in the dark like the gentlest rain. And I am thinking of John Aubrey, still walking away northwards through the green land, the shower over, the drops glistening on new hawthorn leaves, dog Fortune dancing at his heels down the green lane.

Note

1. The state of the Emperors before renovation is described by Nikolaus Pevsner in Jennifer Sherwood and Nikolaus Pevsner, *The Buildings of England: Oxfordshire* (Penguin, 1974) p. 256. He borrowed the phrase 'ragged regiment' from William Morris who borrowed it in turn from the traditional description of the royal waxworks in Westminster Abbey.

FROM THE OLD TOWER HIDE ON WICKEN FEN

Nick Davies

From the top of this old tower hide, I have a cuckoo's-eye view of Wicken Fen. My horizon is encircled by waving reeds. Nine miles to the south-west lies my home city of Cambridge where, as a young student nearly 200 years ago, Charles Darwin eagerly awaited the barges that brought the reed and sedge harvest from the Fens, for among the debris he found many rare species of beetles. When I was a Cambridge student in the early 1970s I too sought fenland treasures, but my passion was birds, and not collecting but watching. As often as I dared, I escaped lectures and laboratories and cycled out to Wicken, and here, in the reeds fringing the waterway right below this hide, I saw my first cuckoo chick. It was in the nest of a reed warbler, the cuckoo's favourite host in the fens, and the foster-parents seemed to risk being devoured themselves as they bowed deep into the enormous orange gape to feed a chick that was five times their own weight. Why, I wondered, were these little warblers being so stupid?

That memory remained fresh, so when I returned to Cambridge six years later to teach and do research I was drawn back to Wicken to try to solve the puzzle of how cuckoos trick their hosts. I have always felt at home out in the Fens, perhaps because I imprinted on a flat landscape during my childhood days on the Lancashire coast, where wide skies and skeins of pink-footed geese calling over the marshes seemed to me then, as they do now, the most wonderful sight and sound there could ever be. Young cuckoos also imprint on the habitat where they were born and on the host species that raises them. It pleases me to think that we are both drawn here by the same impulse to become watchers on the fen.

This wooden tower has been a focus for my watching and wondering ever since my student days. The narrow windows invite me to look out on the world rather than in on myself, and I now often come here to plan my experiments. Many biologists begin by wondering, having been inspired by new theory; then they find a suitable study animal to watch in order to test their ideas. For me, it is always the watching that comes first; whenever I see a bird doing something interesting, I then wonder why. As I survey the fen, I think of the female cuckoo sitting in the treetops beside me, also hiding and watching to plan her summer of trickery. Perhaps this is a good place for me to plan precisely because of my cuckoo's-eye view. From this height I am better able to see the fen through her eyes and to imagine the problems she faces as she looks down on the reed warbler nests below: how to monitor their progress, so she can time her egg-laying, and how then to slip unnoticed past host defences. As my mind plays the part of the cuckoo, I imagine the costs and benefits of her alternative options, and I wonder what might be the best way for her to trick her hosts. These thought experiments simulate just what natural selection does over the generations, favouring the most effective behavioural strategies. Perhaps this is why imagining oneself as your study animal often provides insights into evolution.

The first adult cuckoos arrive on the fen towards the end of April, just as reed warblers are arriving and setting up territories for the summer, and their departure in early July coincides with the time when most reed warblers cease to start new nests. So the cuckoos' visit matches exactly the period when there are opportunities for parasitism. During their first few weeks here in May, I watch the fen become transformed from winter's canvas of yellows and browns to one of bright green, as the stems and leaves of new reeds come to dominate and provide cover for reed warbler nests. In the bright reflected light from this green and watery landscape, splashes of colour come as a surprise: on the banks there are patches of pink marsh orchids, yellow iris and creamy meadow rue, and then sudden flashes of red and blue as dragonflies dart across the water. The reeds provide a uniform soundscape too; against their gentle whispering in the wind other sounds are magnified and catch you unaware: a burst of chattering song from a reed warbler hidden in the reeds, or a loud and haunting chuckle cry from a female cuckoo in the bushes nearby. All senses are on alert out here in the fens.

For a female cuckoo, every bush provides a hidden perch for observing reed warblers from above, but it is harder for a human to remain concealed here, and in any case my power of observation can never match that of a cuckoo, so I look for nests by walking along the banks and parting the reeds with a stick. Along the best stretches, there is a nest every twenty metres or so. Those nearest bushes are most likely to be parasitised, and my view from the tower shows why, because they are the ones that the female cuckoo can most easily find and watch from her secret look-out perches.

She has wonderful natural camouflage: her contrasting dark upper-parts and pale, barred underparts enable her to blend in with the vegetation and to avoid detection. I have often sat in this hide and watched her sitting motionless on a high branch as visitors walk by, unaware that Nature's most notorious cheat is just a few metres away. The cuckoo might sit for an hour or more as her egg passes down her oviduct in readiness for laying, and then she awaits a perfect moment to parasitise the nest. It is an agonising wait for me, too, and I dare not look away for fear of missing the action because it takes her just ten seconds to glide down to the nest, remove a host egg, lay her own in its place and fly off. Her egg is greenish in colour and spotted, just like the reed warbler's eggs. So when the warblers return to their nest, nothing seems amiss; there are the same numbers of eggs as before and all are similar in appearance. But they are now sitting on a bomb set to explode in eleven days' time, one that will destroy their chances of reproduction. For the cuckoo chick will hatch first; then, just a few hours old, and still naked and blind, it balances each of the other eggs on its back, one by one, clambers up the inside of the nest to the rim and, with a flick of its tiny wing stumps, heaves them overboard.

It is only a short flight of fancy from imagining you are a cuckoo to becoming one yourself. My colleagues and I soon realised that the best way to test how the cuckoo fools her hosts was to play the part of the female cuckoo by placing model eggs in host nests. Our experiments revealed that the cuckoo's egg mimicry is vital for fooling the reed warblers, because they are on the look-out for any egg unlike their own. When we 'parasitised' a nest with a model egg that we had painted to be different in colour and pattern from the reed warblers' own eggs, most were quickly ejected. Only model eggs painted like their own were likely to be accepted. However, the female cuckoo's speed and secrecy is important too: when we alerted the warblers by placing a stuffed cuckoo on their nest, they were more likely to reject even a good-matching model egg. So to succeed, the female cuckoo not only needs to hide her egg, she needs to hide herself too.

Adult cuckoos return to the same territory each year. Perhaps getting to know a particular area well enables them to exploit it better; they learn where the hosts' nests are, the best food sources and the local dangers. This is surely why I, too, return here each year: as I learn the best places for my observations and experiments, I work the fen better and so become more attached to this place. Repeated visits also create my personal songline of treasured memories, woven into the landscape as firmly as any reed warbler's nest. Whenever I pass a particular bush or patch of reeds, I thrill once more to the replay of special moments: a male Montagu's harrier, Britain's rarest bird of prey, sailing close by on a surprise visit one day in May; a flock of black terns hawking insects over the mere and then rising high into billowing white clouds to continue east on migration; and one spring dawn a nightingale singing with a cuckoo calling close by, when, for a magical few minutes, they were accompanied from the heavens by the melancholic bugling cries of a pair of cranes soaring overhead.

Attachment to a particular place also alerts you to change. Since I first visited Wicken Fen in 1971, some new birds have arrived: as a student, I hitchhiked to southern Europe to see my first little egrets, but these have now spread north throughout Britain and are common residents here. Other species have increased in numbers: populations of resident Cetti's warblers and long-tailed tits now flourish because of better survival in our milder winters. But there have been many losses too, especially among our summer migrants. In the 1980s I brought my two young daughters, Hannah and Alice, to this tower hide to show them their first cuckoo. I cupped my hands to make a sound chamber, blew a loud '*cuck-oo*', and to their delight a male cuckoo immediately flew in and circled close by, uttering a '*kwow-wow-wow*' in annoyance at the unseen intruder. He then landed in a treetop right next to us, his tail cocked and wings drooping, the characteristic posture of a territorial male, and he called continuously for several minutes as if in triumph.

Today, my calls are often met with silence, for in the last thirty years we have lost two-thirds of our English cuckoos. In the early years of our studies, in the mid 1980s, about 20 per cent of the reed warbler nests on Wicken Fen were parasitised; since 2005 this has plummeted to 5 per cent or less. There are just as many reed warblers now as in the old days. It is cuckoos that are disappearing.

Satellite tagging by the British Trust for Ornithology has revealed that this decline is linked to increased mortality in southern Europe during their migration to winter quarters in the Congo rainforests. Our studies have shown the challenges cuckoos face during the breeding season, as they try to overcome host defences in a continuing evolutionary arms race. But cuckoos face equally tough challenges at other times and in other places. We often think of cuckoos as 'our' birds that go to Africa for the winter. But their visit here to breed is brief, just a couple of months each year, and they spend most of their lives elsewhere. Their dramatic decline is a potent symbol of our diminishing natural world, and a stark reminder that events on this little patch of fen, and indeed everywhere, depend on the health of a wider world.

The season has turned. In the low winter light, colour drains from the fen and the landscape becomes silver as the fluffy seeds of the old reed tops blow in the wind. The soundscape is starker, too: the clacking of flocks of frosty fieldfares in the hawthorns and the whistling of wigeon from the grey waters of the mere.

My winter visits to the tower are often at dusk, and now I am marvelling at new wonders in the reeds as starlings fly in to roost. From all directions they come, and in silence except for the rush of wings as they speed past my hide. They arrive in small groups of a hundred or so, and then gradually the flocks begin to merge into one, so soon tens of thousands of individuals begin to wheel over the reed bed like a giant amoeba flowing gracefully across the sky in ever-changing shapes. They are reluctant to descend, and with good reason, for there are sparrowhawks waiting, hidden in the bushes below. Whenever a hawk dashes out towards the flock, starlings retreat from the point of attack and an invagination forms, as if the amoeba had been wounded. But it heals quickly as surrounding individuals also rise up, and the flock regroups to become a sphere. The starlings rise higher still, but as they gain safety from attack by surprise from below, they now face attacks by speed from above, as first a peregrine and then a merlin dive down towards them. Any starling on the edge of the flock that fails to keep up becomes an easy target. As individuals rush to escape and yet still maintain contact with the group, the flock constantly changes formation, elongating to a ribbon as it flows away in retreat, twisting and turning, before it re-forms and continues its sweeps across the sky.

As dusk falls, the starlings at last begin to descend, and they swoop lower over the reeds. Small groups begin to peel off and plunge down towards the roost, but if there are not sufficient followers the birds return in apparent panic to join the main group again. Eventually, sufficient voters begin their descent for all to follow, the momentum shifts suddenly, and for a thrilling few seconds the entire flock pours out of the sky, like liquid from a jug, into the safety of the reeds below.

Cuckoos and reed warblers play a game of hide-and-seek in their battle of trickery and defence. But in the open skies, as starlings fly in from the surrounding farmland, there is nowhere to hide. These murmurations before they roost are the outcome of another game, one of safety in numbers, and the scientific explanation, first suggested by Bill Hamilton in 1971, is beautiful in its simplicity. If there are birds of prey at large, an individual starling will be safer if it joins others, because this dilutes its risk of attack. If it is alone, clearly it is at risk if a predator comes along. If it is in a group of a thousand, it now has a one-in-a-thousand chance of being the victim. A larger group might attract more predators, but as long as a group of a thousand does not attract a thousand times more attacks – which is unlikely as there are usually far fewer predators than prey – an individual will still be safer in a group. Therefore individual prey should selfishly join others, in the hope that someone else gets attacked rather than them. The safest place is in the middle of the group, hiding behind a barrier of companions. So the flock is in constant motion as individuals jostle for the best places.

How can a large flock behave so synchronously, as if it was one organism? Early philosophers imagined that there must be a leader to orchestrate the movements, or perhaps such rapid changes in shape and direction involved 'thought transference' among individuals or other mystical powers. However, computer tracking of individuals has shown how waves of movements can spread rapidly through the group simply by local responses to neighbours. There can be sudden cascades of behavioural change in a group as just a few informed individuals flee and others follow.

Darwin likened the complexity and diversity of the natural world to an entangled bank where, even in a constant physical environment, natural selection forever leads to evolutionary change as individuals battle to beat their predators, parasites and social competitors. To human eyes, these games can lead to cruel outcomes, as female cuckoos plunder host nests and cuckoo chicks evict host eggs and young. But the dances of starling flocks against an evening sky remind us that the outcome of competition can seem extraordinarily beautiful, too. For me, watching the natural world is enriched by scientific wondering, and I hope to be inspired by many more spring dawns and winter dusks in this old tower hide.

TIPPING BUCKETS

Paul Farley

First, you need to Google 'tipping buckets' and 'Liverpool'. There. This'll make a lot more sense with an image to hand. In the last years before the invention of place, they built a fountain in the city, near the site where the old Goree Piazza and warehouses had once stood. It's a miracle it's survived. It was officially named Piazza Waterfall, but everybody I knew called it the Tipping Buckets, a piece of kinetic sound-sculpture designed by Richard Huws, which was installed in a small concrete square off Brunswick Street in 1967. If you happen upon it when it's working, the chances are you'll hear it first: the effect is of coming across an unexpected maritime sloshing and sluicing. The Mersey can be seen beyond the bottom of the street – all roads here lead down to the waterfront – but the sound still comes as a surprise: a little Atlantic enclosure, or the boom of a sea cove. When you see what's making the noise, the fountain's appearance sustains this maritime mood: in profile, there are echoes of topsails and mizzens, like in those diagrams of a ship's rigging. Each steel bucket fills slowly with water, the smaller ones upending when they reach their tipping points to empty into larger buckets, which in turn send a final excerpted waterfall crashing into the main pool. It's as automated as a set of traffic lights, and as mysterious as a machine from the *Book of Ingenious Devices*. I've seen it when it was new, as a child, from my father's shoulders. I've seen it derelict, the buckets seized up, its empty basin a pan of rusty silt littered with broken glass. I've seen it aged fifty, re-fitted and in full flow again. Because we're roughly the same age, it seems to abide, a thing that has always been there. It provides metaphor on tap. It's a living pool. It's a constant bailing-out, a spectacle of credit and debit. On parched and dusty city afternoons in summer, it's an oasis. On overcast days when it isn't switched on, it can ironise the drizzle. It's a piece of public art but a private curiosity, a rumour engine and unpredictable cascade in earshot of office blocks. One thing leads to another.

The A5036 dual carriageway cuts across the bottom of Brunswick Street, following the line of the old Dock Road, which along this section is still briefly known as the Goree. Or just Goree, like on the street sign at the base of the George's Dock Building, a huge, pale ventilating tower built so the Mersey Tunnel can breathe. That name fascinated me when I was younger. Maybe it was simply the homophone, the way 'gory' might catch the ear of a boy. I don't remember. Maybe I first heard my father say it. Or maybe I read the plaque, in the shape of an African shield, at the base of the Piazza Waterfall, and discovered how another place name was stowed away inside this place name. Gorée Island lies off the Senegalese coast near Dakar, and, as I came to understand it, was one point on the big Atlantic triangle that stretched between Liverpool, Africa and the Americas, home of the Maison des Esclaves, the House of Slaves, with its Dantean 'Door of No Return', a valve through which slaves passed on entering the 'Middle Passage', never to see Africa again. From then on, the word Goree filled me with a complicated dread. It was local and secretive, unwilling to come out into the light, or hiding in plain view: GOREE L2. It was shifty, losing an accent and taking or leaving the definite article. It was worse than gory. It became a dungeoned, shackled, bullwhipped, pustular, maggoty word, printed in slightly wonky eighteenth-century serif type on a colonial press. The Tipping Buckets become pails of seawater, washing down the decks of a Guineaman sailing west, rinsing the boards clean and running through gratings to fall into a dark, stifling hold where hundreds of human beings lay packed on plank beds.

Looking down Brunswick Street towards the river, I remember grasping the idea of offices, and being attracted to the sense of all that paper inside them, stacked right up to the water's edge. A few bills of lading and ledgers always managed to slope away to sea, but the vast and hidden paperscape of finance, insurance, investment and banking that the port relied upon seemed to increase in density and layers as it came closer to salt water, then stopped. The ecosystem of any city used to rely on paper: processed rag and cotton fibre, then wood pulp, circulating information around the whole biomass like xylem in the deepest forest. Even though the paperless office has never really (de)materialised, I like to think my father and I walked these streets in the twilight years of paper, an age that had begun when the earliest writing took shape next to water, the recording and control of material goods set down in hieroglyphs, made with plants of the water margin, the reeds and papyrus that grew along the fertile flood plain of a river. The Tipping Buckets become a fantasia on a theme of the shadoof or swape, one of the very earliest water-raising tools for irrigation.

One of the conditions of the new and rapidly expanding city was its gathered dryness, an environment for the stable storage of goods. Imagining all of this tindery space on the edge of salt water seems to be ignoring an element: fire. Much of today's square footage of office space was once bonded space, and many of Liverpool's warehouses went up in smoke. Even into the nineteenth century, plenty of storehouses were still being constructed using inflammable materials. The Albert Dock, towards the river beyond the Goree, was notable for its new-fangled fireproof construction. The Goree Warehouses themselves caught light in September 1802. Thomas De Quincey, frequent visitor to picturesque Everton Brow, described how

a prodigious fire occurred at Liverpool; the Goree, a vast pile of warehouses close to one of the docks, was burned to the ground. The huge edifice, eight or nine stories high, and laden with most combustible goods, many thousand bales of cotton, wheat and oats in thousands of quarters, tar, turpentine, rum, gunpowder, &c., continued through many hours of darkness to feed this tremendous fire. To aggravate the calamity, it blew a regular gale of wind; luckily for the shipping, it blew inland, that is, to the east; and all the way down to Warrington, 18 miles distant to the eastward, the whole air was illuminated by flakes of cotton, often saturated with rum, and by what seemed absolute worlds of blazing sparks, that lighted up all the upper chambers of the air.

The Tipping Buckets become an infernal human chain, drawing water from wellheads and standpipes and the river itself, an organised but frantic pumping and dowsing and dampening, an attempt to contain fire in the city.

My father occasionally smoked King Edward or Tom Thumb cigars, a quick and cheap machine-cut smoke in the dry Dutch style. If I catch the smell of one now – rarely these days – I think of him lighting up. He would dock the cigar with his teeth and spit away the end. After the whitewater of the Tipping Buckets would come the slowed-down, green-grey ancient river water, drawn from its mainstream and disappearing into huge arches and tunnels, trapped between sluice gates at the Canning Half-tide Dock, running in veinous gutters through deep silt at the Albert Dock. Visiting the latter was like being in a vast, gloomy mud bath for giants, a sump surrounded by brooding ruins. As an art student in the early 1980s, I came here to sketch it, a storehouse of the sublime that cried out to be rendered in charcoal. But I also imagined the inland sea of tea, the cloud forest of tobacco, the glacier of sugar that had passed through. I visited the Port of Rotterdam a few years ago, and was surprised by how you could tell which goods were being moved or stored, even in its closed steel world. To the eye, everything was a geometric Mondrian of stacked sea containers, but my nose knew when we'd entered the spice dock, pungent and unmistakable. In the ruins of the fireproof Albert Dock, even this weightless cargo of smells had long been dismantled, and all I can recall is the tang of salt water, the mud with its sheen of algal bloom, the cold damp of stone passageways, empty except for the odd tray of rat poison, and wafts of a Tom Thumb. My father has sparked up once more, making a shell of his hands to guard the flame, taking a few exploratory puffs to check it's caught. This isn't a film noir featuring a smoking man, collars pulled up against a biting river wind, keeping to the shadows of the derelict arcades. But my father is a complete mystery to me, and that waft of tobacco smoke in the huge and deserted dock rises like a memory, floating up from nowhere in a mind gone blank. The Tipping Buckets become synaptic, a cold firing sequence, a charge circulating through the closed system of a backwater.

These walks with my dad were bound to have happened on either a Saturday or Sunday. He worked as a window cleaner, and his firm was contracted to buildings and firms all over the city centre. The Piazza Waterfall might easily have fallen on one of his weekday rounds, its pool and concrete observation deck overlooked by workers in the office buildings that surround it. I find it difficult to imagine the Tipping Buckets on weekends in the past, toiling away with hardly anybody around to witness their display, especially on Sundays. Sundays in the past are switched off, closed and unbearable. Then again, the last time I visited the fountain, just a few days ago on a busy Monday afternoon, I found everything silent and still, the basin dry and empty except for a film of dark silt speckled here and there with wished-on coins (a meagre deposit compared to the deep coffers of Italian banking you'd find in the Trevi Fountain). I was standing in an enclave of Sundays, a concentrated emptiness, and I didn't hang around for long. In a bar round the corner, I considered who or what governs a fountain's operation, whether simple calendrical observances or occult lunar tables might be involved, and if some modern incarnation of the lamplighter or lighthouse keeper came to turn it on and off, somebody who carried a cruciform stopcock key about their person on a lanyard or belt loop; or if it was worked remotely, activated by a switch somewhere in a secret Bureau of Ornamental Street Furniture. The Tipping Buckets become the difference between life and death, day and night, Saturday and Sunday.

Because they're an early memory, the Tipping Buckets seem to loom over my childhood, but revisiting the Buckets now, I'm thinking it's entirely possible that my father might only have taken me on *one* walk, a single tour of the city around James Street, Brunswick Street and Water Street, the old Mann Island bus terminus and the Pier Head docks. Maybe I've replayed this scenario and gone over this ground so many times, it's crowded itself out, become a regular fixture, a place in the mind where me and my dead dad can meet and spend some quality time. The Tipping Buckets become a window cleaner's sculpture, a static pageant of ladders with pails of soapy water emptying and filling, a mechanical window cleaning round on the spot, just for show, a lathering of the air.

There's a way I can count the rings and carbon-date this memory, and that's by using the music that must have been in the air. When I hear 'Dedicated to the One I Love' by the Mamas and Papas, 'Can't Take My Eyes Off You' by Andy Williams, 'Do You Know the Way to San José?' by Dionne Warwick or – especially – 'Wonderful World' by Louis Armstrong, I'm transported very quickly to the greens of old Corporation buses, whitewashed shop windows, the sound of the ferry funnel being blown, doughnut oil at smoking point, rare earth smells (once common and abundant) like putty, solder, ozone in the underground station at James Street, the warm and vaguely electrical scents blowing up from street gratings choked with litter, and the Tipping Buckets' sea-spray generator … So this is the late spring or summer of 1968. I'm three years old. Part of the recent mythology of Liverpool involves the entry of American Blues and R'n'B records into the city via these docks, but we all carry around our own iconographic hit parades. The Tipping Buckets are a bunch of strange instruments, a steel section, where water is lifted high into the air through valves and pistons that bring each gurgling metal calyx to life; then taking their final bows as the big drums empty, and everything falls to earth as white noise.

Nathaniel Hawthorne had an office nearby, in the old Washington Buildings overlooking Goree Piazza. Somewhere in the air above that dual carriageway, I'd guess. He was US Consul in Liverpool for a few years in the middle of the nineteenth century, and was visited here by a fellow American novelist, the younger Herman

Melville, passing through the city on his way to the Holy Land. His whale had stranded, and by this point Melville was also on his way to oblivion. There's a famous account of the two men – recorded by Hawthorne – taking a walk a few miles up the coast at Southport, where the Consul was living, and there in the desolate sand hills, wearing their stovepipe hats and smoking their cigars, Melville told Hawthorne he had 'pretty much made up his mind to be annihilated'. Whenever I take a walk around this waterfront patch, I think of Melville doing the same as a sailor on his first trip to Liverpool. In his partly autobiographical novel *Redburn*, the eponymous hero consults an old guidebook that his own father had used on an even earlier visit to the city, made long before he was 'included in the census of the universe'. The son finds an arch where he imagined his father had stood, the same bronze Nelson Memorial (still standing in Exchange Flags) whose four manacled figures round the pedestal remind him of four African slaves in the market-place. But in large part his father's guidebook only creates confusion. The Old Dock has vanished completely, long since filled in and built on. 'This world, my boy, is a moving world,' he reflects, 'and its sands are forever shifting.' Forget guidebooks: we might be better following our noses. In the way everything changes here, nothing has changed. This old city built on sandstone is still a work in progress, and I'm taken by surprise, blindsided or stopped in my tracks by something new or missing or unexpected every time I visit. A lot of my ancestral, familial Liverpool has been bulldozed, or changed beyond recognition, and cities, like language, don't stand still. Not even the Tipping Buckets, chugging away in their backwater. They now become an Arte Povera version of that Nelson monument, the water-bearing vessels themselves styled on the grabbing and digging heads of plant machinery, all mounted on a rig of scaffolding.

A couple of centuries ago, the river would have run a lot closer to where the Tipping Buckets now stand, its bank being nearer the bottom of Brunswick Street; the docks beyond stand on reclaimed land. The Pool that Liverpool takes its name from, the inlet that was turned into the Old Dock, would have lain just south of here, roughly where the new Liverpool One shopping development and Paradise Street stand today. But the whole thing was almost anni- hilated, reduced to nothing, in my father's lifetime. During the early years of the Second World War, Merseyside was heavily bombed. There's a photograph of the devastated city hereabouts, navigable only by the Victoria Monument that somehow remained standing at the top of James Street. As a teenager I crossed this debris field without realising it. In summer, we'd often take the Southport line up to Crosby or Freshfield, and walk through the turpentine scent of the pinewoods that stand on the approaches to the dunes along that coast. Once, I found the Brick Beach at Hightown, the shoreline underfoot suddenly and entirely made from rubble. This was where much of blitzed Liverpool had ended up, as infill to prevent erosion, a shattering of red Accrington 'bloods', floor tiles, grey masonry, ashlar, granite, sometimes a carved word or a numeral, smoothed and worn by the sea like soaps on the sink edge of the world. 'Sous les pavés, la plage!' the striking students over in Paris wrote on the walls when I was first brought to see the Tipping Buckets. Along the shoreline to the north of here, the cobbles and paving stones became a beach! But I didn't realise any of this as a teenager, clacking my way along the Brick Beach, and 'May 1968' was insignificant to me. I think now of something I would have known, something else from the same period, a film called Planet of the Apes, and that final scene where Charlton Heston – in loincloth, on horseback – finds the wreck of the Statue of Liberty on a beach, and realises he is not on some distant planet but has been here all along, at home, on a ruined Earth.

If this is only so much botanising on asphalt, or covering of water- front, it still feels like returning to a source. Even within my timeframe, my lifespan, the ground has constantly shifted, flown even. Maybe I'm grateful for the Tipping Buckets, which stand for many things but remain rooted, plumbed-in, fixed to the same spot. I try to look in on them when I'm in town, to see how they're doing, to check the time on an old clepsydra. I can't be sure why I do it, and can only say it's something I've always done. They oxygenate me. I'm reminded that the imagination in early life doesn't need much, and can subsist on the simplest of things, and that even if my dad did only bring me here once, for a few minutes fifty years ago, something poured into me, and through me, and is still flowing.

A City Pastoral

Tessa Hadley

We moved to live in London five years ago, when I was in my mid fifties. I liked it that the move ran counter to imagining ageing as a centrifugal force – as you grow older you're supposed to move out from the humming centre to the calm periphery. There was a perversity in moving closer in. And I'm still besotted with the perversity. The air is filthy here, it's true – even though it's often clear and bright, because the pollution isn't as manifest as in the days of coal fires and fogs. And there aren't many stars in the London sky. Four or five, most nights? In Somerset the sky can seem almost dirty with its swathes of stars, like a sublime cosmic pollution. The metropolis has a compromised relationship with emptiness, or even openness. Everywhere you look, the vista is crowded beyond ever counting or knowing. You could never have been everywhere in London. You feel the absurdity of the weight of the built fabric pressing down, the pointless agglomeration of lives, the endless urgent movement replicating itself over and over and never ceasing, even at the lowest ebb of the night. Individuality drowns in the sheer mass, the impersonal huge politics and economics of the place. You're aware of yourself as an atom, carried along in great rivers of atoms. You can't be known here; the city can't know you.

But that's also a liberation. And a reality, anyway: you are an atom! All these people exist – they have to live somewhere! No point in pretending you're alone in a desert. And it's such a miracle of civilisation, a triumph of ingenuity and resourcefulness, that a vast city functions at all. All those complex clunky systems, imperfect but functioning, delivering our nourishment and energy, carrying our communications, transporting us around, taking off our sewage and material waste, nursing us when we're sick, burying or cremating us when we're dead. Millions of people move around the arterial routes of London and mostly don't break out into violence, mostly don't kill one another, mostly even respect one another's property.

Our transience inhabits the shells of a built environment which changes at a slower speed than individual lives, so that we move around inside the forms of the past. In an old city like London tradition isn't an idea; it's in the shapes of our parks and streets and rooms, giving form to the shapelessness of our present. We redeem our ever-present collective stupidity through the persistence of the best things that have been made, the wisdoms of the past. Our built environment is the consequence of innumerable unrolling gestures of adaption and conservation, which are our version of ancestor worship. And we live, too, among monuments to our most complex art and thought and science. Not that the past was pretty. It was bloody – just like the bloody present, or worse. London is beautiful-ugly, heaped up with the leftover spoils of empire, brute power, ill-gotten greatness. It's as encrusted with history, as cumbersome with it, as – let's say – Rome or Istanbul or St Petersburg. And that's another miracle – that the new generations walking round inside the shapes of empire are also, so many of them, the children of the subjects of empire. Is it too romantic to think that London's population nowadays represents in its heterogeneousness some kind of redress, some rebalancing, from the days when the English deluded themselves that they lived inside a closed system all their own?

In the first months after we came I used to feel as if, through some sleight of hand, I'd been given two incompatible opportunities both at once. There was the chance to live somewhere exotic, with all the high colour and historical drama, the rich otherness, that one might move abroad for – to Istanbul or Rome or Barcelona. And yet at the same time, in the deep foundations of my imagination, this exotic place was home. I belonged in it; I wasn't an ex-pat. Perhaps in London no one's an ex-pat: that category simply isn't open. You might be displaced, exiled, marginalised, alienated, homesick – definitely. But not an ex-pat, not set apart – you're in the crowd, participating in the great global heterogeneous flow. My feeling of being at home must have something to do with language – my good luck that the first language of this world city is also my language: capacious, baggy English, which can be accented every which way and absorb every new idiom – a bastard creation in itself, out of the ancestral collision of its Teutonic and Romance origins.

There's more sleight of hand. We have got away with something. When we first moved to London – needless to say, selling a big family house in Cardiff only paid for half of our two-bedroomed London flat – we expected to be crowded, to have to put up with an intensification of the urban bleak environment. It was worth it, we thought. We were used to that; we were fine with it. In Cardiff the gardens tend to be small yards, so that our vistas were closed in by the fronts of the houses opposite, the backs of the houses in the next street. There wasn't much room for green, and the back garden next door had been concreted over by the housing association that owned it. The garden on the other side – the house rented to students – was concreted too, though at least the weeds grew through in that one. I was passionately attached in Cardiff, it's true, to the hornbeams that lined our street at the front, and to a massive rogue ash tree at the back which strewed its saplings bounteously across several gardens, filled our bedroom window with its grace. Last to get its leaves in spring, it was the first to shed them – they would lie like supplicant hands, palm upwards, on our mossy scrap of lawn. Because the ash was in the garden of a house of rented bedsits no one cherished it, and I was always afraid that it would be cut down; I said that I'd have to move away if it ever was. Our window without the tree filling it would have been too desolating, the scruffy house-backs opposite too rawly exposed, unmitigated. In the end, anyway, we went first: the tree outlasted us. I expect it's still there.

The irony is, living in the immediate environment of our new London home feels almost as if we've moved to the country, by contrast with that Cardiff street we came from, and where we'd lived for almost thirty years. London's a green city: you can see that when you fly into it – all those magnificent famous central parks saved somehow from past developers, all those scraps of lesser suburban ones – and all the private gardens, cherished and neglected, and the allotments, and the roof gardens, the little corners of wasteland and canalside. Our flat, only twenty minutes' Tube ride from the centre, two minutes' walk from the roiling A5 main road, takes up one half of the first floor of a red-brick detached Victorian villa, in an estate of such villas; the street at the front is very wide and lined with plane trees, and at the back the houses in the next street are almost remote, the distance of two very long gardens away. It's like looking out onto fields, or woods. Emotionally it's like that, like a country view. We don't have any garden ourselves, but that's fine with me: I'm not much of a gardener. I'd rather look out over gardens than be responsible for them.

And I do look out. We watch out of the windows sometimes with the same interest as if it were television, or art – call each other over to admire a sunset, or a cloud formation, or the moon, or a fox asleep on the back lawn, curled up like a cat, nose tucked into its tail. We survey this secret nook of nature's growth and respite, which seems to exist not in spite of the great thrumming brazen machinery of the city which lies all around it and never ceases from its striving, but because of it: it's the other side of the same life. People made these gardens as a conduit for all the rest of life, which isn't human. With big sash windows at front and back, and living elevated on the first floor, we feel as if we live inside the air. The sky takes up as much room inside our flat as the walls do, so that it matters: when we pull up the blinds in the morning and open the curtains, what's outside is such a presence, setting its mark on the day, colouring it. There's no such thing as ugly weather. You might not want to go out into the rain, but it always falls interestingly, differently. Earlier this afternoon there was a lemony-yellow watery sun and the watercolour clouds were flossy with light, smoke-grey against an effulgent, brilliant yellow-white. The slim silver pencil of a distant aeroplane drew its line, apparently noiselessly, across the tops of the roofs opposite; the winter trees seemed poised, in this late-January moment before spring begins, in extreme stillness. And the movement of the clouds was almost imperceptible at first, then giddying once you were aware of it – the slow inexorable drift of the whole sky towards us, then over our heads over the roof. Gleaming, the sun peeked through its veil of cloud, then withdrew and sulked, then burned through again.

The gardens stretch as far as we can see to right and left out of our back windows; our horizon is closed in with trees. We can see easily into the garden immediately below us and the ones adjacent. Between them these compose a comically varied spectrum of garden aesthetics. The one directly below isn't used much by our nice down-stairs neighbour – he's very busy. Someone comes to cut the grass and water things, and at some point a few ornamental trees and dumpy evergreen shrubs were planted uninspiringly down either side of the long strip of grass, half a villa wide, where the traces of old paths, and of what was perhaps once a fishpond, show up as yellower and mossier against the green. I'm grateful for its empty plainness, its polite non-statement, its absences ripe for filling up with thought. A ceanothus fills our view with its brilliantly vulgar blaze of blue in the spring. A fox pushes through the trees at the far end and scarcely bothers to check whether the coast is clear before he comes trotting casually down the middle of the strip as if he owns it, nose down, business-like, his haunches so superbly muscled and fluent, insolent. He does own it. He's out there far more often than our neighbour is. We've sometimes seen two or three foxes out there all at the same time. Once there were three of them curled up asleep. And then there are the grey squirrels, the dull wood pigeons browsing like fat cattle, jays, cats, rats, blackbirds, parakeets.

The other half-strip belonging to our house is prettier, with curvy vistas and seats and flowers, and the one next door again is positively the pampered baby among these gardens – planted, manicured, clipped, topiary-ed, adored, with solar-powered lights sunk in the beds and an extant fishpond. The man who owns it – a civil servant made redundant, someone said – is often out there at work: strimming and mowing, pruning and spraying, taping up tender shrubs and garden furniture in bubble-wrap for the winter. In summer he hosts an open-garden afternoon with a brass band and refreshments – we ought to have gone along, but we haven't yet. Something's touching in how that garden's cherished and he's put everything into it – but I'm so glad all the same that it's not underneath us, unsettling us, all that titivating and perfecting. That kind of garden is used up, exhausted, somehow, as a mental space. If you were a child, it wouldn't be any good for playing in – there's nowhere to hide, nowhere that hasn't been thought through already, nowhere not known. That conception of gardening is as an extension to interior decorating: the garden as another space to make-over, eliminating what's accidental, imposing a design.

He's out there now, using his noisy leaf blower. I loathe the leaf blowers – and the strimmers, for that matter. I grieve for the old swish of brooms, for rakes stuttering across wet grass, for the soothing, vacuous conversation of a pair of shears. It's because I'm not a labouring gardener hard at work, of course – only a watcher from the window. My favourite garden is the one next door the other way, to the left. It's generously wide – and it's almost a wild garden, but not quite. Apparently the flats in that house are social housing, or were, or some of them still are, and families seem to come and go: at present there's a Portuguese woman who comes out sometimes to talk on her phone, a man with long grey hair who potters with a plastic carrier, a Francophone African family with an angry teenage daughter who practises her singing. There's a municipal-sized trampoline, black rubber strung on a steel frame; girls lie on it to sunbathe, and whenever there are children in the house they love it. They talk companionably in pairs or threes while bouncing, or bounce in meditative solitude to the rhythmic accompaniment of the squeak of springs – which sound as sweet as the leaf blower is offensive.

No one who lives in those flats at the moment has taken any possession of the garden or has plans for it – although this must have happened periodically in the past, because there are three sheds in different corners, and in different stages of disrepair. Two vast pear trees have grown beyond the point where anyone could ever prune them: to the size of oaks, almost. In spring they're a bridal dream of white blossom, which blows across to our side like a spatter of snow; and in autumn the pears fall into the grass – I've never seen anyone pick them up, though I suppose they do. The beautiful grass in the garden grows waist-high and golden blonde and then droops its heavy seed-heads; two Polish men came at the end of last summer and cut it down with scythes, talking together in their language from time to time. I did not dream that episode of Mickiewicz pastoral: it actually happened. They also pulled down the dense bindweed which had grown over one of the sheds and down the side of the L-shaped back extension of the house, uncovering items we'd forgotten ever having seen before, because they'd been smothered for so long: an abandoned moped, a trailer for pulling a boat – minus the boat, with only an old garden umbrella in it. And a resplendent Victorian tiled floor, patterned in brown and black and cream, partly concreted over and partly grown with grass. Was it once the floor for a conservatory, perhaps? It's as eloquent of past grandeurs as a Roman mosaic.

The weather's changed again outside the windows while I've been writing. At the front of the flat now the clouds are slate-grey, and there's a lurid late light, almost coppery, on the thin young branches, straight and taut as whips, grown up from the knuckles of the plane trees pollarded by the council two years ago. The last single leaves clinging on in these trees look like small brown birds, only too still. Tiepolo clouds meanwhile are banked up at the end of the street, resplendent pink and gold against a pale blue. A magpie falls with drama, tail fanned out, through the tracery of a winter tree. I feel as if I belong here in this place, at this rich intersection between the made world and the found world, culture and nature: trying and failing to catch it in my language.

THE MARSH AND THE VISITOR

Alexandra Harris

Slip down between the general stores and the pet shop in Pulborough, West Sussex. Barn House Lane narrows from a track to a steep-sided path as it runs downhill. Then there's a gate, and you're out onto the Brooks, a great expanse of grazing marsh stretching away to where the Downs rise in the distance. The flood plain is flat, but the flatness is shaped and parcelled by raised banks and causeways. So the view in each direction is built up in strata: in summer there's the glint of water deep in a rush-lined ditch, reeds above it, the still, rough turf of a bank where a few clumps of ragwort stick up like bunches of shabby chrysanthemums, and meadow grass blowing in clouds beyond. A dark line of trees marks the point where the land turns from low clay to higher sandy heath. And then, always, smooth and spacious, steady parent of the land below, there is the long grand slope of the Downs.

The slope visible here is Amberley Mount: a yellow-green cliff, scalloped where it rounds into caves and swells out again, lime-bright in the sun, with a luminosity that comes of the chalk beneath. Woods grow up into the hollows, outlining the bareness between. And it's the bareness by which you know this Down, distinct from the hangers to either side, its turf closely nibbled by centuries of sheep. The few scattered trees have individual identity, each exaggerated by the shadow it throws. Sometimes they have a childish look: model trees stuck to felt; toys on a baize card table. Then the hill turns adult: muscle rounding over bone, flesh stretching and creasing. Mostly the Down is remote and ancient and impersonal. It loses its solidity as the evening fades, turning sage-grey to an elusive purple-blue. For a moment it is a low cloud on the horizon.

The path from the village follows the Arun as it runs between deep banks grown over with grasses, ragged robin, and meadowsweet in summer. From the east, the Stor comes to join it; where they meet, there's a clanging metal footbridge and a willow. Beyond the bridge, you can walk low down by the water, chin-high in grass, or up on the causeway built by the Romans to get across the marsh from the posting station at Hardham to the settlement with its bath house at Wiggonholt, which now lies under the nettles of a roadside verge.

From this high path, part of the Greensand Way, the network of drainage ditches and dykes becomes visible, cutting purposefully across the meadows. In summer, it's not the drains themselves you see, but the rushes that grow up from them. So there'll be purple clouds of fine-eared grass, and then a column of dense green. In autumn the ditches will be full, a kind of water-writing appearing on the flat. And then, as the floods rise, the humming grassland will become an inland sea. Most of the path is too wet to walk in winter, so I know the view only from a distance, from the village looking down over the pale floods reflecting low white skies. Even on summer days, when damselflies flap in the rushes and the high paths are cracked with dryness, the place holds the memory of winter like a basin. It is winter that makes it the shape it is.

This was the landscape I loved when I was growing up, and it's still my secret standard for understanding other places. There's nowhere like it; I've looked. But trying to describe it I feel a strain. I don't know the names of the sedges I thought I liked so much: why had I never looked them up? To describe a place you're meant to know it intimately, to have lived with it, to have kept vigil through seasons and through years; better, to have been its active cultivator and guardian. The tradition of English place-writing, which flourished in the eighteenth century, and which has today expanded beyond all bounds, espouses slow, patient looking. It projects an ideal: that the writer of a scene will be as familiar with it as Gilbert White was familiar with the hanger at Selborne, and that he or she will have an expert understanding of the ecology. It has little truck with holders of a return ticket via London. The nature writer does not go out with the Dorling Kindersley book of wild flowers in order to check that those big plants by the river are Himalayan balsam (invasive; disapproved of) and not a rare Sussex orchid. Quite right too in many respects, but not, perhaps, in all. It's a common thing to be a visitor in one's most loved places, and to learn about them has its own kind of value. My own way of looking has an urgency about it. I must stow away all I can in the short time before leaving again.

I grew up near Pulborough without knowing much about it in the naturalist's sense. The regular walk from home was over the golf course, a routine that seems to have left me with a lifelong aversion to gorse and sand. But going into the village was a pleasure. When we parked in the village car park, it was to go over the road for a prescription, or into the solicitors' to drop off an envelope at the polished front door with an equally shiny magnolia growing beside it. I knew every shop along Lower Street and the times of the trains that would take me to the shopping mall in Horsham, and these things were inseparable from the view of the Downs. The council tip came to the car park one week in four. The omni-guzzling machine alarmed me – its actions were so frighteningly irrevocable – but I liked to go along with my father so I could stand and look out over the Brooks. Behind me the lorry ate another box of defunct cassette tapes, and before me lay what seemed the very contours of peace.

I wasn't conscious of being 'in the country' until I came back to it in university vacations. I found a leaflet in Tesco's advertising the South Downs National Park and was astonished. There was a map showing all my familiar places marked as visitor attractions. Visitors! Never had it struck me that one might travel to the Arun Valley especially to see it. I had been for years a dedicated visitor to other places. My shelves were piled deep with saved-up leaflets from rural churches and guide-books from many hundred country houses. They were mostly from the

West Country, which was, as I knew from my family and from Daphne du Maurier novels, an area worth visiting. Sussex had always been the ordinary home we left behind on annual trips to real country, where there were red cliffs or moors. Now, suddenly, I wanted to look at the place from which we started.

As an adult, then, I became a visitor to this part of Sussex where the Arun cuts through the chalk. What had been background became foreground. The Downs acquired names and were sorted into scarp slopes and dip slopes. 'The path on the bank' became the Greensand Way. I sat making notes in churches, then put my coins in the slot for all the leaflets available, and postcards too. If there were no leaflets in the marked place on top of the prayer-book shelf by the door, I trespassed anxiously behind vestry curtains for further supplies.

I studied the Ordnance Survey map and saw with delight the profusion of italic lettering: Roman road (course of), priory (site of), Roman villa, cross-dyke, barrow, barrow, camp. I have never had much capacity for cynicism about italics on a map – not like Evelyn Waugh, for example, who was sceptical about old England in the 1920s. 'When I see Gothic lettering on the Ordnance Survey map,' he said, 'I set my steps in a contrary direction.' I am hopelessly unstylish in this regard. I can't accept that 'site of' means 'nothing to see here'; I'm stubbornly concerned to stand in the place, to look out from that spot. So I loiter on the verge among the ragged grass and pineapple weed as the cars go by on the A283, magnetised by the idea that somewhere under me, somewhere behind me, there's another language, a quite different way of life, and a frigidarium leads to a hot bath.

My shoe boxes of antiquarian knowledge are increasingly well stocked these days. Yet I'm still only a visitor. My work is in cities (Birmingham, London, Oxford) and, however vividly I dream of a small open window under a low tiled roof, I'm not in the market for second homes. How valid, then, is my feeling about Sussex? And in what possible capacity can I write about it?

I wonder about the difference in perception between an enthusiastic church visitor and an all-year-round parishioner. It's a difference much more pronounced if one shifts it back into the nineteenth century, or earlier, when a shepherd or the rector's wife, say, would know Wiggonholt church and two or three nearby, but nothing beyond that. I look at the font and recognise it as Sussex marble, I enjoy the plainness of the smooth arcades carved in low relief, and place it among the other eleventh- and twelfth-century fonts I know. I'm moved by its simplicity in contrast with grander carvings, its silence in comparison with the dragons and saints elsewhere. I touch its cool Norman sides with pleasure. But for the local farmer this is not one font in a whole inexhaustible language of fonts; it is *the* font. It is what a font is. Would I like it so much if I had no choice, if I could not – next month – be off to the great churches of North Norfolk where painted angels hold up gilded lyres in the rafters?

Then, and it feels related, there's the problem of cows. Cows have a tendency to bring things to a head for the visitor. Their giant stillness arouses a strong sense of permanence. The faint low sound of their munching, or moving over the grass, sharpens the ear to the quiet. Or in the evening, when sound carries, perhaps a cough is audible several fields away and reminds one of the herd still outside, and there for the night. But a footpath that leads into a busy grazing field is a worry. There is the possibility of turning back, but it is probably a long way, you will probably get caught out by the approaching dusk if you risk it, and you may well already have come through a field of cows, so that going back is on a par with going forward.

They look thoroughly absorbed and contented, the cows this afternoon. Most of the herd are grazing intently a little way to the left, but three cows have settled down around the stile which is the exit from the field. I set off calmly, and wait to catch the eye of a nearby grazer, not wanting to disturb her. I smile encouragingly, feeling ridiculous. She looks up and, very slowly, swinging her bulk from side to side, wanders towards me. Her movement is a show of both casualness and determination, which I return in kind – until I'm stopped short by disaster. There's a calf tucked into the hedge on my right, and its mother is on my left. I can't walk between them so must walk round, thereby going straight through the herd.

What matters about this typical incident, aside from the fact that I was not trampled or squashed that afternoon, is that it makes me feel so stupid. I bring myself to tell it only because I discover how many otherwise practical and competent people feel the same. The cow problem bars me from places I would otherwise love. It's worse than a 'Private Property: No Entry' sign: it's a no-entry sign put up by myself. My maternal ancestors were dairy farmers in Cornwall, continuously, hundreds of them, for about four centuries. And now I can barely walk across a field.

Then again, my ancestors didn't have a library card, and I don't think I'd relinquish mine for any level of familiarity with cows. All sorts of knowledge make a difference to the path down the side of the marsh, be it inherited or learned-up, gleaned through daily necessity or sporadic enthusiasm. So, for example, I'm starting to learn about local building stones. Lavant stone, Bargate stone, Wisborough sandstone, Upper Greensand: a whole new landscape. The names, which I read in long lists in conservation documents, suggest a geological tour of the area, some of it deep below ground and other parts shaping the familiar surface topography. The lists constitute a geological itinerary, but they are also a course in architecture. Reading the names I think of certain church walls and the differences in colour and erosion start to emerge, amazingly various, requiring attention. It's the overwhelming sharpness of new prescription glasses, which makes you feel giddy for a morning because there are so many bricks in the walls. Here, there are so many stones.

In the grand buildings not far away – Chichester Cathedral, Boxgrove Priory – the best materials were used for the job and no efforts spared. Fine-grained Caen stone was shipped over from Normandy – tonnes of it transported by human ingenuity and labour. It could be intricately carved, holding the true curve of a trefoil or a smooth ribbed vault. In the little hamlets on the edge of the marsh – Wiggonholt and Hardham – the churches were achieved with stones readily to hand. The Hardham walls are mostly rubble, which is not to say haphazard or made from rubbish (the word now suggests broken cement blocks piled into skips), but built from stones that had already been used elsewhere, shaped for the wall of a barn or a house. Particularly strong materials were reserved for the church quoins, and there they still are. One of the big quoin blocks is a group of Roman clay tiles, set into Roman cement that dried around them two millennia ago. A later builder thought – why not? And with a good slathering of his own fresh-made mortar, he set the whole lot of tiles into the wall. He must have known a bit about those old Roman people who had left their remains all over the land; he gleaned odd bits of knowledge, like rubble. There's an Anglo-Saxon poem about a Roman wall, which refers to proud builders, long lost, now held in the earth. The medieval builder knew there was a long history of life around these marshes.

Over at Wiggonholt I peer at the church walls, trying to identify the stones for myself. It's like looking for clues in a painting to identify the hand – a connoisseurial kind of looking that moves from hunch to analysis, from a first impression to an up-close reading of an inky line. Except that here it's nothing like that, for me, as yet. I don't know nearly enough about stones for the grain and the ridge lines and the kinds of lichen to be meaningful. Resorting to the internet, and the excellent *Building Stone Atlas* produced by Historic England, I discover that I am looking at Pulborough sandrock. To know your stones you have to know the character of every quarry ever dug within in a radius of a hundred miles. I am content to realise that, though I'll never know those quarries, there is a common store of hard-won knowledge to which I can turn.

For the first time, I see the dials on the south wall. There's a rough dial incised into a high quoin stone, and a finer, larger dial a few blocks below. All the twenty-four-hour lines and numerals are just about legible. Since the sun is out, I rummage for a biro and hold it in place as a gnomon. The shadow falls, and yes it falls precisely: seven o'clock. The sun hasn't changed its orbit and the dial hasn't moved, so on this bright evening the dial still tells the right time.

Seven o'clock in a crowded café on the Cowley Road in Oxford and I readjust my earplugs as two small boys wail distractedly into their milkshakes. The tall man next to me is reading Cervantes while swaying his crossed feet to music I can't hear; the glossily dressed student on the other side is explaining her thesis to her laptop camera with professional confidence. I can see the shadow falling on a dial scratched in sandstone on a church wall a hundred miles away.

Holding my coffee cup, I'm cross-legged in the long grass by the river. The sun is lowering behind me, sending a raking light over the meadow and the willows. It picks out bronze in the rusting spires of curly dock. Every hummock of grass casts a shadow. Yard by yard, as the sun moves, fields are lit up for examination. The light gives substance to each ear of grass and measures the thickness of sedge. For a moment the meadowsweet is luminously bright: creamy lace curling above red stems. Sappy buds move against hairy nettles.

The light begins to be more forgiving; the examination has been passed. Evening walkers come out along the path from the village in ones and twos, their dogs racing round me and then bounding into the water. The bare Down in the distance is smoothly aloof from it all.

Behind me, the roofs of Pulborough have joined together. The estate on the hill and the retirement flats and the old barns and the controversially prominent village hall are now all one, an ancient settlement on the edge of the flatland. There's a light coming on here and there. Later the wind will rise as the temperature drops; in the houses up the hillside people will look out at the black trees moving and pull their windows to on the way to bed. The marsh, now, is the visitor. It's come to Oxford. I'm glad of it here.

THE UNFINISHED WORLD

Philip Hoare

For part of my childhood – a rather conflicted part – I shared the three-bedroom, semi-detached, suburban house in which I grew up with eight other people. My personal space was reduced to the width and length of a bunk bed. There was no common ground; or perhaps, there was too much of it. I felt like the peeled potatoes in the huge pan of water my mother had to prepare: bare, bobbing there, crowded like carp in a pool.

To escape, I lived in one long fantasy. I imagined, as I walked to school on dark winter mornings, the layers of other worlds beneath my feet, the strata of histories laid down below. I invested the reliquary green space of a strange, semi-village area that had been swallowed by the greater city of Southampton with the power that confinement lends. Everything was heightened by normality; nothing was what it seemed.

Our suburb was where the city petered out; that which the city had yet to drown. It was gravelly, hilly and drained, built on a former soft-fruit-growing area; but also one where troops had trained since medieval times, and where travellers had traded. There was a sense of no-man's-land to it. Gypsies lived in caravans in a sub-section known as Botany Bay, separated from our quiet road by a residual wooded valley, muddy and dark and traversed by a narrow overgrown path that dipped up and down, crossing a desultory stream, usually embellished with an upturned supermarket trolley.

On other sites around here, pockets of green that the developers had somehow overlooked, Victorian houses stood empty, gently crumbling into the Hampshire heathland, where gorse and bracken still sprouted, given half the chance, re-appropriating, as if they'd been there all the time and were only waiting to take their chance. These were the places where I dawdled. They scared and excited me, because of the freedom that they offered.

This eastern side of Southampton Water was nicknamed Spike Island – a reference, I would later discover, to the vast convict depot on Inis Pic in Cork Harbour where men made criminal by the Great Famine were deposited in what was the largest prison of its time. The epithet presumably imputed that the Irish navvies and dockers who were here, in exile, in Southampton were themselves prison fodder. (Spike Island in Bristol – a city physically connected to Cork by steamer – may have been similarly named.) It was a migratory pattern which, had I but known it, also applied to my own family: my father's ancestors had come over from Dublin and Limerick to the north of England, as strangers in a strange land. Their identities too were regarded as suspect and other, until they learned to conform.

The openness of the heaths on which our 1920s semi-detached house was built – just one of many that marched across the heathland – was associated in my mind with some archaic image of dolorous transportees chained up ready for prison hulks and their transition to other penal colonies. Now dull-eyed ponies chained to concrete blocks grazed these left-over fields. Herons perched over a forgotten mill pond that froze solid in winter. I remembered a story my mother had told me, about a boy who had walked out on the ice and never came back.

Returning to my childhood home after an adult life spent in London, I found myself reclaiming those spaces, even as they ran out. A housing estate now occupies the gravel pit where I used to play, and from where I'd occasionally see a badger lumbering across the path like a stubbly tank. Front gardens yield to the tyranny of the car; you can barely see the houses now. Even walking on suburban streets now seems a kind of subversion.

I opted out of that process. I do not drive. I don't operate a mobile phone, or wear a watch. I cycle, like the boy I was, negotiating streets I could (and do) ride in the pitch-dark, I know them so well. They are part of my neural network, just as my body is hard-wired to my bike. These are my escape routes, and wherever I go, they lead me to the sea.

I can't see the sea from my house. But I can see, through the trees and over the roofs, the red lights that stud the power-station chimney which stands sentinel over the waterway. It is a piece of modernist industrial architecture, solid and block-like. But peregrines circle its summit, and it summons me.

In the winter I find myself drawn there even in the middle of the night, rising with the full moon at spring tide at 2 or 3 a.m., riding down the streets with my arms open wide like a bird, daring the traffic lights not to change. Skidding through the shingle down at the shore, I watch roe deer launch out of the undergrowth; rabbits run in my lights. I prop up my bike by a sea wall reduced to rubble by the storm surges that have ravaged this soft southern coastline in recent years, a physical casualty of the 'managed retreat' of bureau-crats' terminology. A testament to our abandonment of nature. The future.

Then I tip myself into the inky black water, align myself to Orion's grid as it wheels over the vast refinery on the far side of the shore; its spires and silos are lit up as a simulacrum of some future city. Once the space station prowled overhead as a shooting star fell in the other direction. In the darkness, the cold becomes comforting, a reassurance of my physical self and intimation of my mortality. Climbing out, I cling to my hot-water bottle, shivering like a dog as I tug my clothes back on.

My love of the water – that most fluid of common grounds, the thing that connects us even as it separates us – has always been problematic. Although I grew up within sound of dolorous fog horns, and although I felt the sea close by, its presence intimidated me. Not least because I could not swim, and had no way of engaging with or entering the alien element. I'd look at the birds that scrabbled their living out of the blackened wasteland at low tide – Southampton Water has a remarkably *full* relationship to the swell and sway of the moon-tugged tides, its daily double tide a result of the Atlantic Pulse that surges up and down the English Channel – and I'd wonder at their loyalty to this scrubby shore.

The oystercatchers and the brent geese that occupied the suburban beach; the crows that hovered and flickered in the nearby car park; the gulls that overflew it all like a white blur: they didn't feel part of my world, any more than I felt part of theirs. They made their space, negotiated it; occupied their liminal place. I didn't even register them, then.

But as I grew up and felt more of a stranger in the human world – informed by that world that I was *unnatural* – so the natural world seemed more of a solace, since nature itself is queer. Its solitude and escape has always attracted the other, to those who claimed the common ground for its utopian prospects, proposing a future world in which their desires, like those of the rest of creation, were not proscribed. During the nineteenth century, Walt Whitman and Edward Carpenter realigned their lives to different rhythms, at a time before their desires had been diagnosed or pathologised. Their otherness and their 'back-to-nature' impulses – partly invested with the sensuality of the noble savage – would earn them the scornful and euphemistic epithet, 'nature-lovers'; partly because no one else had a name for them yet. In the same way that, as it has been observed, a blackbird doesn't know it is a blackbird, so their identities were not defined by human judiciaries and the relentless categories of capitalism, imposed to sustain its own brutal progress.

Perhaps that's what drew me, aesthetically and emotionally, to the shore: some non-genetic memory, a subvert culture, passed from hand to hand. The porous, shifting shingle of Southampton Water, overlooked by its industrial installations – petro-chemical simulacra of the New Forest on whose edge it stood – also reflected the way that Derek Jarman colonised his Dungeness beach, repurposing its stones, plants and debris in a post-nuclear vision of a garden-wilderness. For Jarman, nature elided with sensuality: for him common grounds were cruising grounds, like Hampstead Heath, another city-contained wilderness.

Like some contemporary Thoreau – his tar-painted seaside hut set, not like Thoreau's Walden next to the new railroad, but in the shadow of a nuclear reactor – Jarman recorded his sojourn in *Modern Nature*, his ironically titled journals, alongside the development of the virus that would soon take his life. His shore proposed another kind of mortality. His writing spoke to a queer nature, as well as being a natural history of his infection in the way that Kathleen Jamie's essay 'Pathologies' treats cancer cells under a microscope in a Dundee hospital as an equally valid subject for 'nature writing'. Questioning what is natural, and frustrated by 'the foreshortened definition of "nature"' ('It's not all primroses and otters'), Jamie looks to 'our own intimate, inner natural world', a mirror of ourselves.

I thought too of Denton Welch's writing, which I discovered in a copy of his novel-memoir, *A Voice Through a Cloud*, that I found in a local jumble sale when I was a teenager. Welch had the same visionary ability to evoke queer suburbia and the southern England of the 1940s, and to observe so minutely the mix of the natural and human history with which most of us live. When I picked up the book, I knew nothing of the author. I just liked the slender feel of it in my hand, the putty-grey-green cloth cover – the same colour, I imagined, as Welch's greenish tweed suit – blocked with what Wilde would call 'tired' bronze lettering.

Even more enticing were the endpapers and drawings inside, spiky illustrations of semi-human, semi-animal, semi-botanical images: curling shells and blank-eyed statues, spouting cornucopia and moonish faces, all done in spidery, scratchy ink, precise and internalised, like his words. They were mythic and naturalistic in the style of other neo-romantic artists of the period; both contemporary yet retrospective, referring to a land which had already been lost. For me, Denton's writing provided a counter-version of the mid century into which I was born; another history, pages passed from hand to hand.

In *A Voice Through a Cloud*, Welch is injured in a serious bike crash while riding from Greenwich to his uncle's house in Surrey. Chronically ill, he is taken from his London hospital to the desultory resort of Broadstairs, at southern England's most easterly edge, to recuperate within sight and sound of the beach. His bed is pulled up to the window, looking out to sea; he describes feeling surrounded on three sides by sea and sky, and how his bay window shakes in the high winds.

The expanse of sea becomes an extension of his terror and loneliness, its emptiness 'the negation of everything living. The suck and mumble of the waves on the beach, licking and slithering and eating, filled me with a wry, fearful pleasure.' He invents words to echo its relentless rhythm, its 'everlastingly industrious, hopeless music', singing to himself not so much in consolation as in despair. At night he resigns himself to the 'washing and whining' waves, which had by now become an extension of his own body: 'the wonderful, booming, wriggling skin of the sea', a phrase which recalls Melville's image of 'the ocean's skin' – the sea as a body of water, a transgressive place, in its own fluid state.

Later, as a semi-invalid, Welch lived in a kind of blur of rural-suburbia, contained by war and fitful peace. England, always a place of ruins, had been ruined anew, destroyed to save itself. In the spaces the destruction created, Welch's imagination flourished like opportunistic weeds on a bombsite, in the shocking pink and purple of buddleia and rosebay willowherb. A place in which beauty might be preserved, and yet slowly decay; where what one used to be and what one had become were one and the same thing. When he watches, voyeuristically, young men with pale flesh diving in the river and lying on the grass, the scene might come from Ovid, or a Powell–Pressburger film, while his description has the distance of anthropology and the intense observation of a 'nature-lover':

The first boy lay flat on his back and half shut his eyes. He looked charmingly coarse and young-animalish now, with thick brown neck, smooth arms and hairs round each brown-red nipple … 'He dives too deep,' I said to the friend.

Welch's writing gave me a new way to look at suburbia. A generation after him, I lived in the lee of the Second World War. Common ground, in a blitzed city such as Southampton, was what the bombs had left behind. Like Welch, the neo-romantics of the 1940s such as John Piper or Graham Sutherland (with his 'unfinished world', as seen by George Shaw, the great contemporary artist of abandoned spaces of modern Britain) created sublime landscapes out of this destruction, just as their predecessors – from Turner to Constable and Palmer to writers such as Horace Walpole and Thomas Gray – had romanticised ruined Gothic abbeys and overgrown ancient sites as a reaction to the lumbering inevitability of the Industrial Revolution and the enclosures that John Clare protested, a slower sort of destruction.

It was another way of reconfiguring common ground with the other; the recreation of an imaginative or even an imagined landscape. In those lonely, dark places, the natural world of plants and animals inevitably adopted – or were invested with – anthropomorphic identities, assimilated by the human need for narrative. Another kind of imposition.

That is exactly what I, in my teenage manner, did to the empty spaces where I lived, the unfinished world in which my imagination could thrive.

One of the wildest places I knew was the cut that ran along the end of our garden, ostensibly connecting the backs of the semi-detached houses. About three foot wide, it had long since lost its navigability, like some overgrown jungle path into the heart of the suburban darkness. In the process it became a conduit for wildlife, a runway for foxes, hedgehogs and grass snakes that crept and crawled and slithered, protected by a tangle of high privet hedges and haphazard brambles. George Shaw's paintings, created using the ultimate teenage medium, Humbrol paint usually reserved for model kits, encapsulate that sense of the reliquary world in which he and I both grew up. To an imagined soundtrack from Joy Division or the Smiths, his work – superficially glossy, three-dimensionally dark with the adolescent imagination – sees what is at stake in the edges of things. The end of the twentieth century. What the future had left behind.

If common ground means anything, it means freedom. And yet to some what they regard as common *good* reduces the individual to a body in pursuance of political or even totalitarian aims. In his book, *What a Fish Knows*, Jonathan Balcombe refuses to call his subjects 'fish', collectively, since the plural is reductive of what he regards as sentient, social animals; rather, he insists on calling them 'fishes'. Anyone accused of turning their back on the human world, the better in order to study the natural, can, in these times, retort that the abuse of the animal is directly analogous to, and intimately connected with, the abuse of the human.

The ultimate denial of common ground – the control of everything, the development of all land and even sea towards total human dominion – is the terrible future dream which we must resist and subvert as it denies our identities. Our common ground is our commonwealth: the shared resource of a fragile planet. In the microcosmic is the macrocosmic. To Thoreau, Walden Pond was an ocean. Whitman, walking with his 'electric self' on the beach at night alone, saw 'All souls, all living bodies though they be ever so different, or in different worlds / ... / All identities that have existed or may exist on this globe, or any globe'.

I learned to swim in a dank, echoing Victorian baths in east London when I'd washed up in the city unemployed. And when my widowed mother needed me, and I needed to escape, I came back to this shore, substituting my life in underground nightclubs for the nocturnal allure of this interzone. The darkness, far from an absence, is itself a reclamation: an intimation of what was, a seceding to primeval rhythms. Even though the sodium street lights prompt blackbirds to sing through the night.

Now I feel more at home here than I do almost anywhere else; unless that anywhere else is the sea. Shifting, shaping the land, constantly re-inventing itself, the sea doesn't care about me. It leaves me behind, even as it bears me up. But it, and this grubby, desolate, lovely shore, overlooked by a petro-chemical refinery, by container ships and the rumbling of the docks, has become my common ground. It is everything and nothing.

And I like it here.

An Elemental Education

Richard Holmes

1

There is a brass outdoor tap in our garden in the little village of St Hippolyte de Caton, on the edge of the Cévennes hills. It is mounted in a circular metal casing, die-cut in the shape of a heraldic southern sun, and screwed into the back of the small stone arbour at the foot of a mulberry tree. When first installed, this tap was bright, sharp-edged and industrial, with gleaming threads that could cut the thumb. But it is now oxidised to a soft, blurred verdigris green, as if it had somehow grown directly out of the mulberry. The tips of its butterfly handle have been re-polished to a dull glow by seventeen years of human use. They remind me of the bright brass toes of the bronze goddess at the entrance to the Hofgarten in Munich, which are traditionally touched for good luck by passers-by on the way to work. That is how I have come to feel about the water tap.

On some days the tap has a slight drip, beloved of lounging wasps and beetles. Here we keep a green 15-litre watering can, and our three-year-old grandson, who can only just reach the top, grips the sides and peers down into it with intense concentration, as if he were examining a new world.

He reaches down into the dark of the can, and grabs the water with one hand as if it were an animal, making it splash and swirl, and then bursting into puzzled laughter. More laughter when we attach the lawn sprinkler, le tourniquet. It is a powerful agricultural one, made of metal, and sits on triangular legs, throwing out a high, turning helix of water. The child dances in and out of this ever-shifting rain-storm, trying to judge its approach and retreat, leaping in and out with shrieks of delight. I have seen the same water-dance in pre-war photographs of children in London's East End, or the Bronx in New York, or the back streets of Calcutta.

Here water is a universal cause of laughter, as well as mock terror and secret reverence. It is also a cause of early metaphysics, when later that evening, tucked up in bed, the boy compares the flying water spray to ordinary falling rain in England. After a long pause he asks, 'And does it *know* it's raining?' I thought I could answer that question easily, but now I'm not so sure.

2

At the western end of the garden, by the herb and tomato bed, is the stone well. It is a monument to water: an impressive, looming beehive shape of Cévenol limestone, about two and a half metres tall, with a waist-high sill and an iron grille made by a local *ferronier*. The grille takes the form of a Gothic gateway, with two wings and bars like arrowheads, which can be swung open like an altar piece, and then shut and locked again with a central bolt. Obviously this grille is to keep live creatures, and notably children, *out*; but I sometimes wonder if it is also to keep other things *in*.

Inside, a tin bucket waits on its chain in its niche. It suggests rituals, offerings, immersions, not always benevolent. My face, looking back up from the reflection thirty feet below often startles me, especially at midday when the sun casts *contrajour* shadows. There is an M. R. James ghost story, 'The Treasure of Abbot Thomas', which involves something hidden in the walls of a deep medieval well, down which the innocent treasure-hunter looks, only to find the face reflected in the water at the bottom is not his own.

My measuring rope, with its iron plummet, indicates that the well water itself goes down another two or three metres, but its blackness and its echo suggests unfathomable depths. It reminds me of all the great underwater beasts slumbering in the abyss: Tennyson's Kraken, Melville's Moby-Dick, Spielberg's Jaws, Ted Hughes's pike ...

The bucket can be hard on the hands, when trying to water the nearby herb garden. So we have installed a submerged electric pump, with a black hosepipe that kicks like a snake when it's turned on, and spews a thick rope of water over five metres as far as the two olive trees. This hissing curve of water, stippled with air-bubbles, is itself curiously alive and snake-like, and seems to attack the ground where it lands with a sudden white thump, and slithers away.

The actual snake I met there one morning, slithering out of the wall and along under the ivy, I assumed had appointed itself as the guardian of the water hole. We have since established an uneasy relationship, and I think of D. H. Lawrence's Sicilian poem, 'Snake':

> A snake came to my water-trough
> On a hot, hot day, and I in pyjamas for the heat,
> To drink there ... And truly I was afraid, I was most afraid,
> But even so, honoured still more
> That he should seek my hospitality
> From out the dark door of the secret earth ...

There is also a small black scorpion that likes to live in the cool space under the flat Roman brick, where I keep the key to the well grille. Every time I pick up the brick it is waiting for me, a black tattoo on the stone, and I briskly crush it with a special cube of rock kept there for the purpose. But it is always back there the next time I pick up the key, the small black triangle of menace. I assume its malevolence, but in fact it has never done me harm, and I wonder why we have not yet found a ground for peaceful co-existence.

So the well seems both sacred and sinister. Here in the Cévennes one is never far from the history of the early eighteenth-century Camisards, the Protestant peasants who in spring 1702 revolted against the authority of the French Catholic king, and murdered the local bishop who had been persecuting them for heresy. They expected help from a British fleet commanded by Sir Cloudsley Shovel, but it never arrived. They were eventually suppressed with much cruelty by squadrons of the Royal Dragoons sent down from Paris. The standard punishment for a captured Camisard was simply to throw him – or her, or their child – down the nearest well.

3

Beyond the garden wall to the east, is a small stream, the Troubadour. It gushes a foot deep over the stone ford leading into the vine fields where the farmer grows merlot grapes. Further down the valley, beneath the small hill known as Le Caton, it feeds into a larger stream called La Droude, which in turn runs into a real river, called Le Gardon. The Troubadour has a silver crown of foam in April, then suddenly dries up overnight, usually in the first three days of May.

Severe summer droughts in July and August have always been indigenous to the region, but they have got steadily worse. Temperatures can reach forty-two degrees Centigrade, and when a *canicule* is officially declared, drought regulations are strict: no hose pipes, no *tourniquets*, no car-washing, no hand-watering of the garden between 8 a.m. and 8 p.m. The bans are announced on the board in front of the Mairie. Our grass becomes straw. The big soft leaves of the tomato plants droop. The fields of sunflowers go from yellow to black. Even the water in the well slowly drops away. Up in the Cévennes, above Le Martinet, the rivers shrink inside their white sleeves of shingle.

The sudden summer storms and downpours are received sceptically by Monsieur Hugues, the vine farmer next door: 'Cela suffit pour arroser la poussière,' he will say after an hour's driving rain – just enough to settle the dust. (*Arroser* is the same word used for drinking wine with a meal. There is no good English translation of it – 'washed down with' will do for beer, but not for wine.) Nature's brief waterings can give endless pleasure during drought. Sitting on two white wooden chairs, side by side in the stone arch above our front door, we indulge in the great St Hippo spectator sport of simply watching the rain fall, and smelling that strangely exotic perfume which rises from hot flagstones.

The winter floods (*les crues*) of the Cévennes are infamous, and go back to ancient times. Major inundations are recorded from the thirteenth century onwards, about once every fifty to seventy years, with catastrophic ones occurring in 1403, 1604, 1768 and 1846. But they have become more severe. The most recent ones occurred in 1958 and 2002, the latter causing 1.2 billion euros of damage and leading to the building of a new raised motor road, the A106 between Alès and Nîmes. On its way this flood reached knee-high in our kitchen, carried our fridge out into the garden, and the wooden gate out into the vine field.

To this day the bridges on the country D-roads and narrow lanes around us carry a warning sign: '*Attention! Pont Submersible*'. The surrounding vine fields are classed as '*innondable*', floodable, and consequently they cannot be built on by law. To celebrate this fact we formed a society known as 'Les Innondables', and families from the other five houses at this end of the village (the whole village consists of some two hundred souls) used to have an open-air lunch together every August. Beatrice, the *maire-adjoint*, wrote a song to celebrate this. The *déjeuner* began at midday and ended about 6 p.m., by which time we were all ready to sing. Very little water was consumed.

When he lived at nearby Uzès as a young man in the 1650s, the poet Jean Racine wrote a chant against flooding. It begins roughly along these lines: 'Let no wild waters come unto these pastures, let every stream lie quiet in its bed, let the lovely Naiads be pleasant and peaceful, let the torrents of springtime abstain from the flood ...' One day we are going to have it carved on a tablet and set on the front of the well.

It was the Romans in the first century AD who first seriously addressed the regulating of the flood/drought problem in the Gard department. They planned, surveyed and built in a mere twenty years a fifty-kilometer canal from the springs at nearby Uzès to their regional capital Nîmes. Their engineering genius included six aqueducts to carry the water, of which the huge Pont du Gard is still standing. It is built of local limestone, in three tiers of fifty-two arches, standing 160 feet high. The canal itself, often underground, is little more than a stone conduit a metre wide and two metres deep, but it is a miracle of civil engineering. To flow smoothly and steadily, relying on the force of gravity alone, it had to have a precise fall of thirty centimetres every kilometre, over its whole fifty-kilometre length, and to move at an average speed of two kilometres an hour. Once successfully completed, it delivered 200,000 cubic metres of fresh water every day to the fountains, public baths and private houses of Nîmes, and remained in working order for over 300 years. Yet no one knows the names of the engineers who designed and built it.

Today, the rivers are being managed by a newly created regional water board, sometimes known as 'Le Petit Parliament de l'Eau'. This operates a policy known by the convenient acronym of SAGE (Scheme for the Improvement and Management of Water Resources (Aménagement et Gestion des Eaux). It declares with a flourish five main aims: balanced water consumption, prevention of flooding, control of water quality, improvement of river banks and the study of underground water reserves. It publishes a small campaigning magazine, Le Journal des Gardons, and has certainly cleared many sections of overgrown riverbank and blocked riverbed, and encourages the trout.

But not all these water policies are popular. Over the last decade there have been rumours of a plan to construct a huge reservoir up in the Cévennes hills, somewhere above Saint-Jean-du-Gard. This was a project on a Roman scale, and with a Roman logic, intended to control and preserve the winter flood-water with a huge dam in one of the valleys somewhere near the beautifully named village of Saint-Etienne-Vallée-Française. With the vast inland lake thus created, it would be possible to release a steady supply of fresh water during the parched summer months to the thirsty towns and villages on the plains below. But the mountain spirit of the eighteenth-century Camisards is still alive in those remote communities. Popular village protests against the flooding of any Cévenol valley, with its remote wild life symbolised by the golden eagle, have been stiffened by visiting environmentalists and ornithologists, preaching like the illuminated pasteurs du Désert three centuries before them. Whether it has been their objections, or technical engineering problems, or simply shortage of regional cash funds, no reservoir has yet appeared in these wild hills. Up there the old water gods (and the Naiads) still exercise their ancient powers.

4

I'm not sure the Naiads don't also influence the swimming pool at the eastern end of the garden, with its remarkable transformations. At dawn it has a placid, unbroken, gleaming presence: a Zen statement of calm. But its appearance alters at different times of day with infinitely subtle reactions to changes in wind and weather and the angle of the sunlight. It has sudden evaporations (often caused by the drying wind of the Mistral), or mysterious pollutions and 'turnings', from lucid turquoise to hazy green. It has brown dustings from the vine fields, and occasional red dustings from the sands of the Sahara. And then there are all its visitors: the wasps, dragonflies, butter-flies, snakes, flying ants, beetles, hornets, a mouse (saved), a wild boar (rumoured), and the heartbreaking swallows, with their cries and aerobatics overhead, and their sudden dramatic dives downwards to drink on the wing.

No one can observe the dynamic life of a swimming pool without beginning to take its measurements, and learn some of its physics. Though the basin is comparatively small, some seven metres by nine, it contains about eighty cubic metres which take over twenty hours to fill from scratch with a hose. This only has to be done once every three or four years, but in summer, because of evaporation, it has to be topped up weekly, sometimes with about 250 litres (three bathfuls of 85 litres), but sometimes, when the Mistral blows, as much as twice that. I started to record these figures from the household water meter, and this first made me aware of domestic water consumption figures in general.

Most European households consume 150 litres of fresh water per head per day, and surprisingly 30 per cent of this goes on flushing toilets. Showers can of course be more economical than baths, but brushing your teeth while the tap runs can consume six litres, as also running the cold tap to produce acceptably cool drinking water. Washing machines with their new eco-cycles have become less spendthrift, but then most European households wash clothes more often than before. In the eighteenth century most well-to-do households had only one 'washday' a month – as for example in the memorable opening chapter of Penelope Fitzgerald's masterpiece, *The Blue Flower*. Water consumption around the world has also become a measure of comparative wealth. American East Coast households can consume up to 300 litres per head per day, though restrictions are starting to operate on the West Coast, since the great Californian drought began in 2015. Meanwhile many Third World households still do not use – or have access to – more than ten litres of fresh water a day.[1]

Prompted by these thought-provoking statistics, I began to wonder what water actually consists of. The H_2O we all learned in school chemistry sounds familiar and reassuring: two hydrogen atoms arm in arm with an oxygen atom, thus forming a single friendly water molecule. Yet the necessary bonding or ganging-up of many water molecules, to form the continuous flowing stuff we all recognise, depends upon a quite strange and complicated five-part structure, and this too changes when it hardens into ice, or expands into vapour. I learned some of this theory from Philip Ball's wonderful science classic, H_2O: A Biography of Water, and also the fact that water has a history.[2]

It was the eighteenth-century French chemist Antoine Lavoisier who first showed experimentally that water is not a 'prime element', any more than earth, air or fire. He proved that in reality it is an elastic compound of hydrogen and oxygen, in a public demonstration performed in Paris in 1783, also attended by Charles Blagden of the Royal Society, and published in his Traité élémentaire de Chimie of 1789. He showed that it is an unique substance which occurs naturally in three different states; liquid, solid (crystalline as ice) or gas (water vapour) out of which fog, frost and snowflakes are all formed. This was followed in 1800 by William Nicolson's experiment in London, using the newly invented voltaic battery, proving that the hydrogen–oxygen chemical bond could be broken with an electric charge (electrolysis). Yet to this day its structure and bonding remain ultimately mysterious, producing such anomalies as 'surface tension'.

The complex content of water is also surprising, even in its supposedly purified state. On the side of a bottle of San Pellegrino there is a list of minerals and sulphates: 'Silico, Nitrate, Strontium, Potassium, Fluoride, Sulphate, Bicarbonate, Calcium, Magnesium, Chloride and Sodium'. The pool also shows me that its acid level is permanently fluctuating. The human tear drop has an acid pH of 7.6, which is thought to be a perfect environmental balance. But the misapplication of 'purification chemicals' to pools can raise this by ten per cent, and around the globe so-called 'acid rain', caused by man-made pollution of sulphur dioxide and nitrogen oxide (mostly from burning coal), can rise to levels high enough to begin to destroy such vast and ancient structures as the Great Barrier Reef.

When it comes to water even physics has its limitation. Philip Ball writes at the close of his strictly scientific study that he has not covered everything, and notably he has omitted the magic: 'In the end it seems to me that the "magical" properties attributed to water – an inexhaustible fuel, a universal remedy – derive from psychological and emotional correspondences.'[3] I wonder about these.

The problem of water 'magic' is illustrated by Richard Dawkins's critique of the parable of the Marriage Feast at Cana. This is the New Testament story of how 'a wandering Jewish preacher called Jesus' (as Dawkins puts it) miraculously turns the jugs of water prepared for the wedding guests into delicious wine. In his study for young people, *The Magic of Reality*, Dawkins points out that on the molecular level this transformation from water to wine is simply not possible. 'Molecules of pure water would have to have been transformed into a complex mixture of molecules, including alcohol, tannins, sugars of various kinds, and lots of others.'[4] The 'miracle', he concludes, was either simply 'a conjuring trick' or, more likely, 'a piece of fiction that somebody made up'. In short, it is nothing more than a piece of religious nonsense, comparable to the fairy tale of 'the pumpkin being turned into a coach'.[5]

Yet this supposedly scientific analysis completely overlooks the possible meaning and symbolism of such a parable of water. *Why* should somebody make up such a story? Clearly, it is intended to express a universal truth about the need for human generosity and hospitality, and these are not nonsense or superstition. The marriage feast represents a transformation of human lives into something richer and more fruitful. What happens is just 'like' water being transformed into wine. The 'miracle' is not a trick, but a metaphor, a parable of generosity and communal hospitality ('the best wine until last', as Dawkins remarks). Moreover, the parable has universal roots in folk tales from many other cultures, telling of bottomless urns or 'unemptiable' jugs of water, wine or oil, all celebrating the vital principle of generosity and largesse.

5

The physics of water leads naturally on to its poetry. I have begun to collect a little anthology of water, as a sort of poetical reservoir or prayer book, for times of dry inspiration. It begins with D. H. Lawrence's 'Snake', then Philip Larkin's brief and enigmatic 'Water', in which he considers how 'to construct a religion' from a liturgy of fording and sousing, and a 'furious devout drench'. Both these poems find, in their own way, the sacred element in water, though from quite different sources. With Lawrence the snake-god is drinking from a dark pagan subterranean one, 'from the burning bowels of this earth'. While in Larkin the sacred is located in a bright, sunlit space, as simple as a clear glass of water, raised ceremoniously towards the east, 'Where any-angled light/Would congregate endlessly', a brilliant joyful image of a whole worshiping community of dancing water molecules.

My anthology has become especially rich in the Romantics poets, who make use of images of water in so many different ways. Who can forget Wordsworth's lakes, or Shelley's clouds, or Coleridge's rivers and seas?

Water always had magic powers for Coleridge, and often connected with memory. The whole of 'The Rime of the Ancient Mariner' can be seen as a study in the effects of water, and also the traumatic memories it can release. By contrast, in his beautiful early poem on his own native river, 'Sonnet to the River Otter', he transforms water into blessed memories of childhood:

> Dear native brook! wild streamlet of the West!
> How many various-fated years have passed,
> What happy and what mournful hours, since last
> I skimmed the smooth thin stone along thy breast,
> Numbering its light leaps! Yet so deep impressed
> Sink the sweet scenes of childhood, that mine eyes
> I never shut amid the sunny ray,
> But straight with all their tints thy waters rise,
> Thy crossing plank, thy marge with willows grey,
> And bedded sand that, veined with various dyes,

Gleamed through thy bright transparence! On my way,
Visions of childhood! oft have ye beguiled
Lone manhood's cares, yet waking fondest sighs:
Ah! that once more I were a careless child!

Here 'bright transparency' is both the peculiar, bright, magnifying
clarity of water, and also that of earliest memories and recollections.
Coleridge's Notebooks are full of such water observations, drawing
constantly unexpected similes and metaphors from both its appearance
and its movement. In the Lake District he found 'a whole new world
of Images in the water!' He wrote detailed prose studies of the water-
falls at Moss Force, Scale Force and Lodore, and compared the latter
at twilight to 'a vast crowd of huge white Bears rushing, one over the
other, against the wind – their long white hair shattering abroad in
the wind'.

In the stripling River Greta, behind his future house, he spotted a tiny
whirlpool of water forming and re-forming in the lee of a large flat rock
in the midst of the fast-flowing current, and made it first into a flower,
and then into a metaphysical image of recurrence and human hope itself:
'The white Eddy-rose that blossom'd up against the stream in the scallop,
by fits and starts, obstinate in resurrection – It is the *Life* that we live.'[6]

By contrast, Shelley's poem 'The Cloud' turns out to be based on
an accurate meteorological description of the workings of the convec-
tion cycle. Yet its form is dazzlingly musical, light and rapid, carried
on dancing dactyls and quick internal rhymes, making it seem more
like a child's song than a scientific treatise. Throughout the Cloud itself
(herself?) speaks, another kind of pagan sprite, full of laughter and
mischief. In the last stanza the identity of the Cloud takes on a series
of surreal transformations, becoming a pure pagan symbol of death
and resurrection, endlessly repeated or recycled.

... I am the daughter of Earth and Water,
And the nursling of the Sky;
I pass through the pores of the ocean and shores;
I change, but I cannot die.

For after the rain when with never a stain
The pavilion of Heaven is bare,
And the winds and sunbeams with their convex gleams
Build up the blue dome of air,
I silently laugh at my own cenotaph,
And out of the caverns of rain,
Like a child from the womb, like a ghost from the tomb,
I arise and unbuild it again.

6

For me, too, water has many ghosts, and has become associated with my early dreams of freedom and adventure in France. I have never forgotten the primal mountainside spring from which I drank, fifty years ago, as a lonely eighteen-year-old walking with an ex-army backpack and sleeping bag, over Mount Lozère, as later described in my book *Footsteps*. I now see how many other 'furious drenchings' there are in that secret autobiography.

For instance, there was a memorable starlight swig from my metal water flask when I woke during my first night 'à la belle étoile' on a remote Lozère hillside following Robert Louis Stevenson's walk and, looking up into the glimmering southern night, felt 'I was falling upwards into someone's arms'. But whose arms? I now wonder. Then there was my endless search for fresh water in each tiny Cévenol village I came down to out of the hills, sweating. My first question would always be: 'Bonjour, où est la fontaine qui coule?'

This was a pilgrim's question, which is not remotely rendered by the English version: 'Excuse me, is there a fresh-water supply somewhere in this village?' In those days there always was one. Usually it was a simple brass or iron spigot, coming directly out of a piece of stone, either in the main square (if there was such a grand place), or sometimes on a roadside bank at the entrance or exit to the village. I would often hear this water tinkling long before I could find it. No tap or switch, simply a thin steady stream of continuous water from some local spring, always icy cold and clear and free.

Sometimes, but not always, there would be a plaque: *'Eau potable'*. I think I read this as: 'Holy water', and all my Catholic childhood would rush back to me as I drank and drank. Now these blessed little fountains are mostly disused and silent. Although there is a restored one in Uzès, in the little square above the Hôtel d'Entraigues, not far from that original Roman spring which fed the distant city of Nîmes. I last used it fifty-two years ago, in summer 1964.

In those days I invented many brief water chants as I went along. But more recently I wrote a song – or rather, what Byron used to call 'a versicle' – about the shrinking of the River Gardon in high summer: 'Song for the Thirsty Gardon'. It was originally dedicated to the farmer's teenage son Maxim, a passionate fisherman in the local pools with his grandfather, until he was sent off to train as an accountant in distant Montpellier. It was partly designed as a farewell gift, and also to remind Maxim of some English words. The only two French words included in the poem were local ones – *apéro* and *pression*, meaning the evening drinks hour (aperitif), and a cold lager drawn from the keg in a café – which were words he naturally honoured.

Chanson pour le Gardon Assoiffé

Deep beneath the shingle
And hidden from all eyes
The Water Gods are working
And another river lies.

Silently and swiftly
A current dark and strong
Wells up from distant Lozère
And southwards snakes along.

Where Gardon lies a-gasping
As dry and white as bones
His subterranean sister
Uncoils beneath his stones.

She rises up at Alès
And makes the fountains leap,
Then sinks again for ages
As if she's gone to sleep.

At Pont de Ners she wakens
When *apéro*'s on hand,
And bubbles up like *pression*
And quenches all the land.

7

There is an old white wooden seat under the cherry tree in the centre of the garden, which we have christened the Philosopher's Bench. Sitting here over many evenings, as the shadows lengthened, I found myself trying to formulate an inclusive and hopeful philosophy of water. This became '*le philo d'eau*'. It was eventually condensed, or crystallised, into this formulation: 'All things would go much better in the world if we had three elements that were both cheap and universally available: *education, solar power and water.*' I haven't greatly improved on this formulation since.

A genuine philosopher, the ancient Greek Thales of Miletus, who 'flourished' in the fifth century BC, said simply that everything in the world came from water. It was the foundation of all matter, the beginning and end of all life on earth. It strikes me that this beautiful naïve theory would now make complete sense to modern cosmologists who, in their search for any signs of life on the exoplanets (the first only discovered in 1997), are looking essentially for signs of water.

Water would be the unique cosmological signature of extraterrestrial life anywhere in the universe (or at least in this universe). Hence the excitement about the new exoplanet recently discovered by a telescope in Chile in August 2016 orbiting Proxima Centauri, the closest star to our sun, a mere 4.24 light years away. This planet, not yet named, is thought to be small and rocky, like the Earth, and in the 'Goldilocks position', that is, neither too hot nor too cold, where liquid water – and therefore life – may be possible, and what's more, discoverable. I hope there may be a garden like ours up there.

Notes

1. See WaterAid *www.wateraid.org.uk*
2. Philip Ball, *H₂O: A Biography of Water*, Phoenix, 2000, pp. 134–5
3. Philip Ball, p. 310
4. Richard Dawkins, *The Magic of Reality: How we know what's really true*, Bantam, 2011, p. 253
5. Richard Dawkins, p. 239
6. *The Notebooks of Samuel Taylor Coleridge*, edited by Kathleen Colburn, Routledge, 1957, vol. 1, entry 496 (1799)

SOMEWHERE IN NORTHERN KARELIA

Tim Ingold

Somewhere in the woods of northern Karelia there lies a huge boulder. If you could count such boulders, it would be one of thousands. But my boulder cannot be counted. I do not know whether it is one, two, three or four. Once it rode a glacier as a wandering erratic, having been torn from granite bedrock by the force of moving ice. Then, when the ice melted, it was unceremoniously dumped on a steep incline. It has remained there ever since, ever about to roll down the hill but never quite doing so, as soil, moss, lichen, shrubs and trees have grown up all around it. The boulder has become its own environment, providing shade and shelter for plants on the lower side, and surfaces for other plants to grow; there is even a pine sapling rooted in a fissure near the top. Deep in the forest, you have to pick your way over rocks and wade through a carpet of vegetation to find it. Standing some four metres tall, with an equivalent girth in all directions, what meets your eyes is about 200 tonnes of rock, not settled flat on the ground but falling down the slope with a velocity of zero. Only a precarious balance of forces holds it there.

But at some time in the past – possibly thousands of years ago – it was rent asunder. It is likely that water penetrated a crack, expanded when it froze and, with immense force, split the boulder from top to bottom, breaking off a massive slab that at the same time shifted some seventy centimetres to the side. The wedge-shaped crack remains open at the top, and a small block of stone has fallen into it, where it remains jammed, about a third of the way down. Another shard of rock has slid from the cracked face and rests on the block exactly as it fell, supported on its sharp edge. All this must have happened in a split second, and in the stillness of the forest I try to imagine the explosive sound it must have made, and how it must have echoed through the landscape. Looking at the precariously balanced assembly, of shard on block, of block in crack, of crack in boulder, of boulder on incline, I have the feeling that I inhabit a silence on the inside of the explosion. It is as if nature, in this boulder, were forever holding its breath. One day it will give way, and the boulder will tumble down. We cannot know when that will be. Best not to be beneath it when it comes!

Somewhere in these woods is a special tree. If you could count trees, it would be one of millions. But my tree cannot be counted. It is not large, nor has it grown to any great height. At its foot, its roots are tightly wrapped around an outcrop of glacier-smoothed rock, from which a thick, gnarled trunk coils out like a snake, eventually inclining towards the vertical as it thins into more recent growth, dissolving into a spray of needle-covered branches and twigs. The tree is a pine and, thanks to its location on the shore of a great lake, it has known extremes of wind and cold from which its larger inland cousins are somewhat protected. Its twisted trunk bears witness to early years of struggle against the elements, when once it was but a young and slender sapling. Deep inside, that sapling is still there, buried beneath decades of further growth and accretion. Within every tree hides a younger version of itself. Now hardened and gnarled with age, my tree can hold out against anything that nature might throw at it.

What for me is so special about this tree, however, is the way it seems to establish a sort of conversation between rock and air. At base the wood has all but turned to stone. The roots, following the contours of the outcrop and penetrating its crevasses, hold the rock in an iron grip. But up above, delicate needles vibrate to the merest puff of wind and play host to tiny geometrid caterpillars that measure out the twigs in their peculiar looping gait. How is it possible for such ageless solidity and ephemeral volatility to be brought into unison? This is the miracle of my tree. Through it, the rock opens up to meet the sky, while the annual passage of seasons nestles within what seems like an eternity. To spend time with this tree, as I have done, is at once to be of the moment and to sink back into a reverie of agelessness.

Here in these woods, forest ants are at work, building their nest. From a distance the nest reveals itself as a perfectly formed mound, circular in plan and bell-shaped in elevation. Observe it closely, however, and it turns out to be seething with movement as legions of ants jostle with one another and with the materials they have brought back – mostly grains of sand and pine needles. From the centre, ant-roads fan out in all directions. You have to peer at the ground to see them. Often they are more like tunnels, boring their way through the dense carpet of mosses and lichens that covers the earth. If you were the size of an ant, the challenges of the passage would be formidable, as what to us are mere pebbles would present precipitous climbs and vertical drops, while tree roots would be mountain ranges. Yet nothing seems to deter the traffic as thousands upon thousands of ants march out and back, the outward goers often colliding with returnees laden with materials of some sort to add to the heap. Wandering alone in the forest, it is odd to think that beneath one's feet are miniature insect imperia, populated by millions, of unimaginable strangeness and complexity.

In the woods the wind is blowing. If you could count gusts, you would never finish, as fresh ones always come along. But the wind cannot be counted. You can hear it coming from a long way off, especially through the aspen trees. Each tree hands it on to the next until, for a moment, their leaves are all singing to the same tune. Every leaf is aquiver, even though the trunks sway only a little. Then all is quiet again. The gust has moved on. On the waters of the lake the surface is disturbed into ripples which focus the reflected light into little suns that flash first double and then single. As the ripples reach the lake shore the reeds bend over, rustling in unison, until they in turn fall silent. Do trees create the gust of wind by waving their leaf-draped limbs? Does water create wind by rippling? Do reeds create wind by rustling? Of course not! Yet surely the clarinettist needs a reed to turn his breath into music. So if, by wind, we mean it's music to our ears, or it's sun-dance to our eyes, then yes – leaves, ripples and reeds do make the wind. For when I say I hear the wind, or see it in the surface of the lake, the sounds I hear are made by leaves just as much as is the light I see made by ripples.

Once I was flying a kite out on the field, where the grass had recently been cut. As I played on the string, it seemed to me that my kite, like the leaves of the trees, was also an instrument for turning aerial gusts into music in motion. However, the string, often entangled on previous flights, had been repaired at many points by cutting and retying. An unusually strong gust overwhelmed one of the knots and my kite broke loose. Off it went, sailing over the treetops, buoyed up by the wind. I imagine the kite having relished its new-found freedom. 'Watch me,' it would have crowed. 'I am a creature of the sky. Field and forest, they are all the same to me!' But its dreams were to come to an ignominious end as it drifted down to earth. Most likely it was snagged on an angling tree branch as it fell. I never found it again. But I am sure it is there, somewhere in the woods, draped forlornly from the branch, utterly lost.

I too, in straying from field to forest, have risked becoming lost. I know an old path that runs through the woods, though I am not sure where it begins, and it ends in the middle of nowhere. Long ago, however, it was made by the passage of many feet as people, year in year out, would go with rakes, scythes and pitchforks from the farms around the lake to cut the hay in far-flung meadows. The hay would be stored in field barns and brought in by horse and sledge over the winter to feed the cattle in their stalls. But that was in the past. First the horses went, as every farm acquired a tractor. Then the outfields were abandoned, as forestry became more profitable than dairy production. Then the cows were sold off, and finally the people left. Few farms remain inhabited year-round.

And so the path fell out of use and is gradually fading. In places it has completely disappeared. Trees have fallen across it or are even growing in its midst. I can tell the path is there only by following a line of subtle variation in the leaf mould on the ground, a gap in lichen cover, a thinning of soil on rock. So long as I am on it, I can discern the path by running my eye along the line. But I know that if I move to one side or the other, the line will disappear. Indeed, this has happened to me on more than one occasion: having deviated from the path in one direction – my attention drawn by an anthill or by luscious bilberries to pick – I have crossed right over it on the return without even noticing, and strayed too far in the opposite direction. How then should we think of this path, which is visible only as you go along it? It is a line made by walking; an inscription of human activity on the land. Yet while one can distinguish the path from the ground in which it is inscribed – albeit only faintly, and with an eye already tuned to its presence – it is not possible to distinguish the ground from the path. For the ground is not a base upon which every feature is mounted like scenery on a stage set. It is rather a surface that is multiply folded and crumpled. The path is like a fold in the ground.

Somewhere in northern Karelia there are still cows. But here there are none. The fields fell silent many years ago. Once we would row across the lake with a churn to fetch milk, warm and fresh, from the dairy. But these days, it doesn't pay to look after a few head, and anyway, who will do the milking when the old folk retire? No girl wants to follow her mother into the cowshed; no boy aspires to what has always been seen as women's work. Nowadays cattle are concentrated in big production facilities, whose managers rent the fields once used for grazing to provide a year-round supply of fodder. Sometimes I imagine that the cows are still there, wandering the fields like ghosts. I think I see them staring asquint with their doleful moon-eyes, and hear them lowing, chewing the cud, crashing through undergrowth. Then silence falls again, pierced only by the wistful cry of the curlew. Where the cows once lingered, strange white oval forms can be seen scattered here and there over the meadows, or lined up on their trackside perimeters. People call them 'dinosaur eggs'. Really, they are gigantic rolls of machine-cut hay. The machine rolls the hay as it cuts, and as each roll is completed it is automatically wrapped in white plastic sheeting and laid – like a great egg – on the ground. Later, the 'eggs' will be collected and taken far away, to the place where all the cows are now.

Amidst fields bordered by woods and lake stands an old timber-built cottage. As a family, we have often spent our summers here. The cottage has a living room, two small bedrooms, a porch and a little veranda.

Outside, a set of wooden steps leads up to the front door. I can tell you exactly how many steps there are. Every morning I sit on the steps and think. I think about all the life that has passed there, from when our children were taking their first steps to now when they have families of their own. I listen to the birds, watch the bees as they pollinate the flowers, follow the sun as it passes between the trees and drink a mug of tea. And I think about what I am going to write that day. If the weather is fine I write outside at a small wooden table, seated on a bench hewn from a log, and look across the yard to the trees on the other side. The table is covered by a plastic-coated cloth, which is bare apart from a tin on which I mount a spiral of insect repellent. I light one end and it burns very slowly, giving off a sweetly aromatic smoke that is alleged to drive away the mosquitoes that might otherwise invade my writing space. With fewer mosquitoes these days – an effect of climate change, perhaps – it is hardly needed, and I'm not even sure that the mosquitoes take much notice of the smoke. But I burn it anyway, as I quite like the smell. It is a sign that I am thinking. As the spiral of repellent is slowly consumed it seems to me that my thoughts curl up, like the smoke, and waft into air.

For the rest of the year, when I am not here, I dream about my bench and table and about the steps to the cottage. Nowhere is there a more tranquil place to be. Nowhere is more conducive to intense reflection, for my mind can withstand the stress of churning thought only when it is otherwise at peace. And nowhere are the multiple rhythms of the world, from the glacial to the atmospheric, so perfectly nested. The cracked boulder, the twisted tree, the empire of the ants, the sighing wind and the suns that reflect from ripples on the lake, the memory of a lost kite, the fading path and absent cows, the dinosaur eggs, the steps on which I sit and the table at which I write these lines: these are among the many stories woven into the fabric of my favourite place. I won't tell you exactly where it is, as this would give away my secret. But it is somewhere in northern Karelia.

CHILDHOOD GROUND
ABIDING PLACES

Richard Long

The cliff ledge den
The look-out tree
The bicycle racing track in the wood
The dumps
The long grass place for stalking
The cave in the cliff
The slide
The footpath where we dug a trap
The smoking cane place
The place of the secret grave on the scree
The tobogganing zig-zag
The place where we dug quartz with hammers
The place of some soot behind a wall
The swampy place

City of Bristol The Downs and the Avon Gorge 1983

A Wood Over One's Head

Richard Mabey

It was pinned to a beech tree in the lane like a poster announcing the circus was in town. 'WOOD FOR SALE'! Bold letters, no stated price. A path tumbled down into a dry valley, then up again, statuesque beeches to the right, frayed ashes trapezing to the left. Through their trunks the haze of bluebells looked liked dry ice. The prospect made me giddy. What was I doing, dreaming of buying a wood when I didn't even own a house? The reasons I gave my friends were sociable and sensible. I wanted to see if a modern community could go back to the woods, if all I'd read about woodland history and management could be put into practice in the twentieth century. But thirty years on I recognise that there were other kinds of neediness at work. I was almost forty years old and single. I think I wanted to make something, leave a legacy, maybe have a place where I could go feral among the trees again as I had when I was a kid. What I hadn't anticipated was that I was to become embroiled in implicit debates about the privileges and abuses of ownership, and about woods as autonomous ecosystem as against managed artefacts.

One problem was that to dis-own a wood, so to speak, to take it out of the province of the functional and commercial, you first had to own it, and play the property game. You had to be prepared to deal with fences and planning law and the insidious pressure to *do* something. I did not accept this frame of mind with much grace, even at the very beginning. In the months I was negotiating with the agent, I mooned about in Hardings Wood (as it was called), hiding in the undergrowth when yet another bidder with a Norfolk jacket and a clipboard hove into view and made me wretched with gloom and frustration. In the end I sealed the deal by contacting the vendor directly, and being emotional about my romantic plans for the place. I would have to pay the same rate as a forestry company, so it was no skin off his nose.

Even objectively it was a more promising site for me than a commercial operation. The wood was slung like a hammock over a dry valley half a mile from the village of Wigginton, and in the north corner there was a patch of some commercial value – a beech plantation established in the 1890s. But most of the tree cover was natural regrowth after the place had been gutted of timber during the Second World War. There was ash and cherry in the valley, oak and holly on the clay plateau, all worthless as timber. And some time during the 1960s the last owner, an absentee wood merchant over-excited by an ephemeral subsidy scheme, had over-planted the whole site with matchwood poplars. They became infected by honey fungus and were dying on their feet. The wood was dark from the dense regrowth, but full of ferns and flowers that relished the shade. I wandered about among its strange and unremarked tuftings – beeches shaped like candelabras, dynastic badger setts, orchids glimmering in the deepest shade – and wondered what I could make of it. I was full of hubris then, expert in suppressing the fact that in the long term the wood would survive and flourish even if I did absolutely nothing. But I was passionate to get engaged, to let in some light (in more than a literal sense), to make the place wilder, woodier, more beautiful in some ill-defined way, to feel I had enhanced the earth's growth a mite before I was added to the leaf litter myself.

The novelist E. M. Forster owned a wood in Sussex in the 1930s, and confessed that he too was troubled by this compulsion to intervene. Possessing Piney Copse, he wrote in an essay entitled 'My Wood',

makes me feel heavy. Property does have this effect ... [it also] makes its owner feel that he ought to do something to it. Yet he isn't sure what. Restlessness comes over him, a vague sense that he has a personality to express – the same sense that, without any vagueness, leads the artist to an act of creation.

I never felt that kind of grand creative impulse towards Hardings, but there was no vagueness about my idealistic fantasy of restoring one small plot of the Greenwood to the People. I declared my ambition to establish a 'parish wood' by cutting the fence across the entrance.

And then, with the help of local friends and allies, I canvassed the village, asked for memories of the place, invited the inhabitants to come and help with the 'work', whatever that might turn out to be. The response was mixed, revealing the different declensions of possessiveness people can feel about places. A taxidermist, bizarrely, was the one soul to express outright hostility, protesting that activity in the wood might disturb his illicit trapping vigils. The Master of the local foxhounds imagined that sharing a few whiskies might persuade me to open the wood to the hunt. A handful of villagers fretted that the phrase 'community wood' presaged coach parties from Islington. Not that they seemed engaged as a community themselves. When I talked about our scheme to the local primary school I was shocked to find that not a single child had ever slipped into the wood, despite its comparative closeness. No dens, no bike scrambles, no dirty games in the deep ditches. Things had been different half a century before. The oldest villagers could remember the 1930s, when the local woods were worked by cross-cut-saw teams, and kids gathered up the debris in shopping bags as fuel for home. One woman showed us a basket plaited from willow and hazel by the Italian POWs who had looked after Hardings Wood during the war.

It was no great surprise that on our first working day locals were outnumbered by friends and fellow woodland enthusiasts. A score of us assembled one autumn Sunday with the beech leaves turning golden and the bracken tipped by frost, and realised we hadn't a clue what to do. There was little evidence of any ancient management practices we might carry on, certainly no preening 'heritage' model to live up to. That morning all my nebulous visions about the place collapsed at the stark prospect of making the first cut. Why do *anything*?

So, a little nervously, we talked. Those present shared their feelings about the place, and how they felt it might be enhanced. Tree identities and the merits of space versus shade were debated. There were different points of view, but in the end we seemed to agree what might be done. We happened to have met by a woodland pond, a very dark and overshadowed body of water, and clearing a glade around it so the sun could get in seemed uncontentious. Pardons were granted to characterful oaks and hollies whose case was argued before this impromptu forest court. At the end of the day we found we had a created a curious but pleasant miniature landscape, like a patch of savanna around a waterhole.

And that was pretty much how work would proceed over the next few years. It would be fanciful to call it on-site democracy, yet it wasn't some rigid pre-established management plan either. What gave our actions a kind of coherence was that we were all responding to the prompts the place gave us as much as to our personal visions. The network of footpaths (there were none at the start) were trodden out by people following animal tracks and natural contours and the magnetic pulls of viewpoints and big trees. Everyone felt that letting in light was a priority, so thinning dense stands of ash and sycamore and poplar soon became routine.

For the first time in half a century villagers came to enjoy the wood. I once chanced upon a couple of watercolourists seated among the bluebells in straw hats and looking much more a part of the place than I was. There were new customs established too. On Ascension Day the children from the village school tramped over the fields, and in a clearing among the freshly leafed beeches sang hymns to new life and the mysteries of transubstantiation. In summer, after exams were over, there were secular rites and woodland sleepovers.

Some part of my own dream of ushering a parish woodland into existence had happened. But with hindsight I was driving the agenda much more than I admitted to myself at the time. On one occasion I acted as an outright commercial forester. The big beeches which had been planted on a field adjacent to the wood at the start of the twentieth century were, on a forester's time sheet, ready for thinning. But of course they didn't *need* thinning. They would have survived as a group of trees perfectly well for another two centuries. Nonetheless, they had been planted for timber, and thinning them would contribute to our philosophy of enlightenment and, I reasoned defensively, help pay for a pick-up truck to fetch our cut wood ... I salved my conscience with the high-minded phrase 'continuity of intention'. And one November day I found myself progressing through the wood with a professional surveyor, deciding trees' destiny and the future interior landscape of this part of the wood with the help of cans of different-coloured aerosol paint. My mentor would choose those trees that might eventually make fine timber. I could pick those that were picturesque or promising dead wood habitats, or just tickled my sentimental fancy. Between these, and marked with red dots, were the trees that could comprise an immediate money-making harvest, mostly close to the chosen ones, so that their removal would give these more space to flourish. I was pleased to learn that the whole process is known in forestry jargon as 'selection'. It sounded as if we were preparing a Tree Show for the Royal Academy.

It was in my private time in the wood that I came closest to understanding my complicated and sometimes contradictory relationship with it. From spring to autumn I spent time just mooching about the place. Walking the same tracks two or three times a week I could spot the tiniest changes: which ash seedlings had put on an inch in height; where windfall branches had dropped from; how our minimalist experiments with the light were affecting the rhythms of growth. When I return to the wood now, fifteen years after I moved away from the Chilterns, I find those two decades of intense memory are still there – 'like a peat core drawn from my mind', I jotted in my diary.

I paid obsessive attention to the flora of the place, which was shifting partly because of the work we were doing, partly from its own cryptic cycles. One May, working on my hands and knees, I counted eighteen colour variants in the bluebells, from pure white and white stripes on pastel blue to dark indigo. I had volunteered to survey the wood for the Hertfordshire County Flora, and a generalised ecstasy over the spring florilegium wouldn't do. So I learned to evaluate glumes and lemma in the woodland grasses (our single tuft of the rare wood barley was a conspicuous bearded oddity among the crisp anemones). I tracked the migrations of supposedly immobile ferns from their redoubts on the medieval woodbanks to nondescript addresses among the planted beeches. I realised that our exquisite wood-vetch – sweet-pea-scented, liquorice-striped and the only colony in the county – depended for its survival on the disturbance we created along the tracks. After ten years Hardings had the highest score in the county, relative to its size, of what ecologists call 'ancient woodland indicator species'.

In winter my relationship with the wood became more physical. The mid nineties were an exceptionally rainy time. Often I'd go there after a downpour and hear an unfamiliar sound: the lap and gurgle of water running over stone. The current of rainfall pouring down the lane had found an easy left turn at the wood's entrance and made off down the hill. It fingered its way into every track and rabbit run. It carved out runnels down to the bare flint, piling up dams of woodland flotsam – beechmast, dead leaves, a leavening of fine gravel – and laid out terraces with miniature pools and rapids. For a few hours most rainy days I had an upland stream on my patch.

The heaviest downpours sent flash floods rasping through the wood. Everywhere the water took short cuts, dashing down badger trails, bursting through hedges from the fields next door. In the valley one day it built up to a torrent that tore clumps of fern out by the root. It snapped off a branch from a fallen tree and drove it forward like a snow plough wiping a swathe of ground ten yards long clean of vegetation.

It occurred to me that this might be a prompt for a piece of beneficial landscaping. Why not facilitate moving water in the dry valley? It is what would have been there in post-glacial times, and would have helped form the topography of the place. Re-introducing it is what the earthmover Capability Brown would doubtless have done. And there had been a watery motion in the valley more recently. In the 1930s, when the Rothschild family owned the wood and many of the houses in the village, they'd lain sewage pipes from the cottages down the hill to evacuate their contents among the cherry trees. Fifty years on trees would still not grow in the eutrophic midden that resulted, and insisting that this unwholesome traffic was stopped was the first action I took after buying Hardings. Joining up the pipes with the village gutters in the hope of rather more splendid flows during storms might have been theoretically possible, but it would have been an absurd and unnatural artifice. The valley had been dry for thousands of years. It was part of the identity of the place, not something to be tinkered with as if it were a gardener's plaything.

Sometimes I would work in the wood by myself in winter, sawing up logs from thinnings we had generated on a working weekend. More often I would saunter round the place with a pair of heavy-duty loppers doing just the sort of tinkering I despised. I clipped the brambles round my favourite primrose patches, so they would make a better show. I lopped sycamores that were shading ashes, and ashes shading young beeches, as if I had certain knowledge of the proper hierarchy in trees. As for the pesky poplars, I was in the habit of looking for ones about to topple and nudging them into a position where they would take other poplar branches with them when they fell. And I remember the excuses I made to myself for this finicky primping in a place I liked to think of as halfway wild. I was doing something no less natural than the local badgers or a tribe of bark-beetles might do, making corners of the wood commodious for themselves. I reckoned I deserved a niche along with the rest of creation.

But William Wordsworth's admonitions to presumptuous land-owners nagged me. In 1811 he had visited Foxley in Herefordshire, seat of the philosophical high priest of the Picturesque movement, Uvedale Price. Wordsworth admired the estate, but not the owner's habit of lopping branches to open up a view, or levering a few rocks into the splash of a stream. '[A] man little by little,' he chided, 'becomes so delicate and fastidious with respect to forms in scenery: where he has a power to exercise control over them and if they do not exactly please him, in all mood, and every point of view, his power becomes his law.' Foxley 'lacked the relish of humanity' of a country left more to itself'.

The odd thing is that I experienced not a mite of the tinkering instinct outside my wood. Everywhere else I was delighted by muddles, by the glint of obscured flowers, by views from, not views of. Wordsworth was right. It was the licence given by ownership and power that encour-aged gratuitous intervention.

In 2002 I moved to Norfolk and, with no wish to become an absentee landlord, sold Hardings Wood to a village trust – a sadness for me, but a boon for the wood, which now had a written constitution and a guarantee of open access in perpetuity. When I go back I think I have been too hard on myself. The wood does have Wordsworth's 'relish of humanity', but an obstinate, self-willed temperament too. In response to what we did there during my tenancy, it's been generous. The footpaths we trod out have firmed up, but not dogmatically, and wander pleasantly wherever a fallen tree or a new badger digging intervenes. The gaps in the beech plantation have filled with spectacular natural regeneration, of more than ten species of tree. The whole wood has been a dramatic demonstration of the fact that trees can start their lives perfectly well without being stuck in the ground by humans. We did plant a few saplings, mostly gifts it would have been churlish to refuse, but their weedy growth was a caution by the side of the self-sprung wildings. New species arrived – wild daffodil, nesting buzzard, fallow deer. And I suppose one could add to that list a benign strain of *Homo*, not overbearing or presumptuously stewardly, just making a space for themselves alongside their fellow creatures.

Tekels Park

Helen Macdonald

I shouldn't do the thing I do, because motorway driving requires you to keep your eyes on the road. I shouldn't do it also because pulling at one's heart on purpose is a compulsion as particular and disconcerting as pressing on a healing bruise. But I do it anyway, and it's safer to do it these days, because this stretch is being transformed into a smart motorway, so the long slope of the M3 as it falls towards Camberley is packed with speed cameras and 50 mph signs, and when I'm driving there on my way somewhere else I can slide my car into the outside lane to bring me closer and slower to the section of fence I'm searching for, running west and high under skies white as old ice.

Perhaps a hundred thousand vehicles pass this place each day. Back in the mid 1970s I could lie awake in the small hours and hear a single motorbike speeding west or east: a long, yawning burr that Dopplered into memory and replayed itself in dreams. But like snow, traffic noise thickens with time. By the time I was ten I could stand by Europe's second largest waterfall, listen to it roar, and think, *it sounds like the motorway when it's raining.*

I shouldn't look. I always look. My eyes catch on the place where the zoetrope flicker of pines behind the fence gives way to a patch of sky with the black peak of a redwood tree against it and the cradled mathematical branches of a monkey puzzle, and my head blooms with an apprehension of lost space, because I know *exactly* all the land around those trees, or at least what it was like thirty years ago. And then the place has passed, and I drive on, letting out the breath I'd been holding for the last thousand feet or so, as if by not breathing I could still everything, movement, time, all of the dust and feet that rise and fall in a life.

Here's an early memory. A ridiculous one, but true. I learned to speed-read by trying to decipher military warning signs that bordered the roadside on my way to primary school. KEEP OUT was simple, but DANGER – UNEXPLODED ORDNANCE took me months. I needed to read the words *all at once*, because my mother's car was moving and the signs were very close. Each weekday morning I'd stare out of the window as the army land approached and wait for the words to appear so I'd have another chance at them. The feeling I had then, of wanting to apprehend something important that was passing by me very fast is the feeling I have now when I look for the place behind the motorway fence where I grew up.

I was five in my first summer in the Park. It was 1976. Cape daisies bloomed and died in the flowerbeds and pine cones in the trees behind the house crackled and split through endless indigo afternoons. Standpipes, orange squash, dry lawns, and a conversation in which the matter of *drought* was explained to me. That's when I realised for the first time that not every year was the same, or perhaps that there were such things as years at all. My parents had bought this little white house in Camberley, Surrey, on a fifty-acre walled estate owned by the Theosophical Society. Mum and Dad knew nothing about Theosophy but they liked the house, and they liked the estate too. There'd been a castle here once, or Squire Tekel's early nineteenth-century approximation of one, all faux-Gothic battlements and arrow slits, peacocks and carriages. After it burned down the Theosophists bought the grounds in 1929 for £2,600 and set about turning it into a place for them to live and work. Residing here was *a privilege*, the residents were told. *A privilege for service.* Members built their own houses, bought tents and a second-hand Nissen hut for a newly-created campsite. They grew food in the walled kitchen garden; opened a vegetarian guesthouse. In the 1960s, after leaseholders were granted the right to purchase the freeholds of their properties, outsiders like us began to populate the place.

Theosophy had been banned in Nazi Germany, so many of our neighbours were refugees from the war, and others were the black sheep of good families: elderly women, mostly, who had refused the roles society had reserved for them: the quiet Lolly Willowes of Surrey Heath. One wore ancient Egyptian jewellery she'd been given by Howard Carter; another kept a great auk egg in a drawer. Spies, scientists, concert pianists, members of the Esoteric Society, the Round Table, the Liberal Catholic Church, the Co-Masonic Order. One resident sent his beard clippings back from Nepal to be burned on the estate bonfire. On discovering that I had gone to Cambridge, another, years later, inquired of me where I had stabled my horse – for he'd had dreadful trouble finding livery for his hunter while a student there in the 1930s. Everyone had lives and pasts of such luminous eccentricity that my notion of what was, and wasn't, normal took a battering from which it's never recovered. I am thankful for that, and for the women in particular, for giving me models for living a life.

But most of all I'm thankful for the other freedoms I had there. After school I'd make a sandwich, grab my Zeiss Jena 8x30 Jenoptem binoculars and strike out for my favourite places. There were ivy-covered walls and specimen trees, redwoods planted to commemorate the death of Lord Wellington – they called them Wellingtonias back then, of course they did – and creosoted summer houses with fly-specked windows. 'Arthur Conan Doyle liked to sit here,' I was told, of the smallest summer house beneath the sparse shade of a balsam poplar, the one with original prints of the Cottingley Fairies hanging on its cream-washed walls. There was a round, shallow pond on the Italianate terraces that held an intermittently broken fountain, smooth newts and great diving beetles, and from which vespertilionid bats dipped to drink at night; there was a nine-acre meadow with decaying stables on one side, acres and acres of Scots pine, and damp paths obscured by bracken, rhododendrons, swamp laurels with piped-icing flowerbuds; and there were roads that went nowhere, for when the motorway was built on land compulsorily purchased from the Theosophists in the 1950s, it cut the estate in two. I loved those roads. Bare feet on the rotting tarmac down by the straight avenue of sessile oaks that ended in drifts of leaves and a new desire path that curved right to trace the perimeter of the motorway fence. One dead-end lane at the back of the Park had ten-foot sandy banks I'd scramble up to get to the vast grey beech carved with hearts and dates and initials above, and I was awed by the notion that anyone had found this tree, because I'd never seen anyone near it, *ever*, and one afternoon I dug up a rotted leather drawstring bag from the humus beneath it that spilled threepenny bits into my hands. There had been glow-worms here, and snipe, and ponds, before the motorway came, I was told. Everything on the other side was already houses.

I was permitted to roam unchallenged because everyone here knew me – though they'd have quiet words with my parents after they'd yet again spotted me knee-deep in the middle of the pond looking for newts, or walking past the guesthouse with a big grass snake, two feet of supple khaki and gold twined about my arms. Reg the gardener took me for rides on his tractor-trailer, and we'd putter down the road singing music-hall songs he'd taught me:

> It's the same the whole world over
> It's the poor what gets the blame
> It's the rich what gets the pleasure
> Ain't it all a bloomin' shame?

And while Reg rolled a cigarette I'd race off to explore the bracken and scrub in the back woods, where rhododendrons had grown to near-trees with branches shaped by ancient prunings. They were *superb* to climb when I was small: frames of right-angled kinks and acute wooden curves I could hoist myself into and up, and sit inside a canopy of dark leaves that clicked and pattered with tiny rhododendron leaf hoppers that on closer inspection resembled the brightest of bestiary dragons. In the back woods too was the wood ants' nest, that glittering, shifting particulate mound which moved from year to year and reeked of formic acid. You could turn blue flowers pink if you tossed them on the top before the ants carried them away, and for a while I'd prepare skeletons of the dead birds I found by folding them carefully in little cages of wire mesh and lodging them on top of the nest. When I pulled them free weeks later they'd been reduced to clean white bone that never quite stopped smelling of ants.

Almost by accident I'd been granted this childhood of freedom and privilege, partly through a quirk of location, partly through my parents' trust in the safety of this place, and I lived in the familiar setting of so many of my children's books, from *The Secret Garden* to *Mistress Masham's Repose*, though I wasn't half as posh as their protagonists. I was a state-school kid running free in crumbling formal parkland that might have been written on paper as a metaphor for the contracting empire, or a wilder life, or social transgression, or any number of dreams of escape forged in the imagination of writers years before I was born.

I didn't know how unusual my freedom was, but I knew what it had given me. It had turned me into a naturalist. And for a new naturalist like me, the nine-acre meadow was the best place of all. So much of what was there must have arrived in hay brought for long-dead horses, as seeds from lowland meadows: scabious, knapweed, trefoil, harebell, lady's bedstraw, quaking grass, vetches, diverse other grasses and herbage. And butterflies, too, marooned in this small patch of the nineteenth century: common blues, small skippers, grizzled skippers, marbled whites, small coppers, and grasshoppers that sang all summer and pinged away from my feet. The other side of the meadow was different, and more what you'd expect on acidic soil: a low sea of sheep's sorrel, stars of heath bedstraw, white moths, small heaths, anthills and wavy hair grass brushed with fog by the sun. I knew that meadow intimately. It was richer, more interesting, had more stories to tell than any other environment in my life. I'd press my face in the grass to watch insects the size of the dot over an 'i' moving in the earthy tangle where the difference between stems and roots grew obscure. Or turn over and prospect for birds in the thick cumulus rubble of the sky.

So many of our stories about nature are about testing ourselves against it, setting ourselves against it, defining our humanity against it. But this was nothing like that. It was a child's way of looking at nature: one seeking intimacy and companionship. When I learned the names of these creatures from field guides it was because I needed to know them the same way I had to know the names of my classmates at school. Their diverse lives expanded what I considered home far beyond the walls of my house. They made the natural world seem a place of complex and beautiful safety. They felt like family.

When you are small, the things you see around you promise you they'll continue as they are forever, and you measure life in days and weeks, not years. So when the mowers came one day in early August to cut the meadow as they had done every year since the meadow was made, and I saw what was happening, I burned with terrified outrage. There was no time to think about what I was doing. I ran. I stumbled. I sat in front of the mower to make it stop, then mutely, passively, held my ground in front of the bewildered driver, who came down to quite reasonably ask me what the hell I was doing, and I ran home crying. I didn't understand how hay meadows work. All I saw was destruction. How could I know that the mower's job was to hold history in suspension, keeping the meadow exactly where it was against the encroachment of heather and birch and time?

Every year the meadow grew back and thrived and was as rich as ever, right up until we left the Park in the 1990s. A decade later, I returned on a summer afternoon. Driving up Tekels Avenue the passing scenery possessed the disconcerting, diffuse, off-scale and uncanny closeness of things in dreams. I was frightened of what I might find when the car crested the curve down to the field. But there the meadow was: impossible, miraculous, still crowded with life.

Then I went back in my forties, less scared now, more certain of myself and what I would find there. But I was wrong. Someone who thought meadows should look like football pitches had treated it like a lawn and mowed it repeatedly for several years until the exuberant moving life I'd known and loved was gone. The meadow now looked how that man thought it should look: blank and neat and flat and easy to walk upon. I cried when I saw it: a woman weeping not for her childhood, not really, but for everything that had been erased from this place.

Losing the meadow is not like losing the other things that have gone from my childhood: MacFisheries, Vesta paella, Spacehoppers, school lunches, Magic Roundabout toys, boiled sugar lollipops when

I'd finished my meals in roadside café chains on holiday trunk roads. You can mourn the casualties of fast capitalism for your own generation, but you know they've merely been replaced with other programmes, other media, other things to see and buy. I can't do that with the meadow. I can't reduce it to nostalgia *simpliciter*. When habitats are destroyed what is lost are exquisite ecological complexities and all the lives that make them what they are. Their loss is not about us, even though when that meadow disappeared, part of me disappeared, too, or rather, passed from existence into a memory that even now batters inside my chest. Look, I can't say to anyone. Look at the beauty here. Look at everything that is. I can only write about what it was.

When Henry Green started writing his autobiography in the late 1930s it was because he expected to die in the oncoming war, and felt he did not have the luxury of time to write a novel. 'That is my excuse,' he wrote: 'that we who may not have time to write anything else must do what we now can.' He said more. He said, 'We should be taking stock.' I take stock. During this sixth extinction we who may not have time to do anything else must write what we now can, to take stock. When I sat on the verge that day and wept I told myself over and over again that he was a nice man, that perhaps he had simply not known what was there. Had not known what was there. And I thought of something that I was talking about with a friend just the other day: that the world is full of people busily making things into how they think the world ought to be, and burning huge parts of it to the ground without even knowing they are doing it, utterly, and in the process accidentally destroying things. And that any of us might be doing that without knowing it, any of us, all the time.

A few years ago the Park was sold to a property developer. Today when I drive past the fence the pull on my heart is partly a wrench of recognition when I see those trees, knowing they are the standing ghosts of my childhood. But it's also the knowledge that with care, attention, and a modicum of love and skill, the meadow could be incorporated into the site plan and turned into something very like it had been only a few years ago. The pull on my heart is also the pain of knowing that this is possible, but that it is very unlikely. Centuries of habitat loss and the slow attenuation of our lived, everyday knowledge of the natural world make it harder and harder to have faith that the way things are going can ever be reversed.

We so often think of the past as a something like a nature reserve: a discrete, bounded place we can visit in our imaginations to make us feel better. I wonder how we could learn to recognise that the past is always working on us and through us, and that diversity in all its forms, human and natural, is strength. That messy stretches of species-rich vegetation with all their attendant invertebrate life are better, just *better*, than the eerie, impoverished silence of modern planting schemes and fields. I wonder how we might learn to align our aesthetic and moral landscapes to fit that intuition. I wonder. I think of the meadow. Those clouds of butterflies have met with local extinction, but held in that soil is a bank of seeds that will hang on. They will hang on for a very long time. And when I drive past the fence these days, staring out at 50 mph, I know that what I am looking for, beyond the fence, is a place that draws me because it exists neither wholly in the past, nor in the present, but is caught in a space in between, and that space is a place which gestures towards the future and whose little hurts are hope.

CLIFTON SUSPENSION BRIDGE

Patrick McGuinness

Beside the school is a suspension bridge. To get to the playing fields across the gorge, the boys have to cross it. They do this three times a week, rain or shine. It has to be pretty wet for any match, even the crummiest remedial game, to be cancelled. 'It's *corpore* fucking *sano* time,' says Mr McT***, the heavy-smoking, whisky-perfumed form teacher who talks to the boys like mates from the pub, and discusses historical figures as if he'd known them personally. They like him, though he's tetchy and unpredictable, and when he's angry he's feral and looks like he'll bite. He's big and barrel-shaped, and wheezes like an old accordion when he bends over to tie his laces or pick up some chalk or a dropped cigarette. He remembers nothing, mixes up their names, turns up late and leaves early, but the boys think he tells good jokes. What they mean is that he tells dirty jokes. Some of the older boys go to his house at night to smoke and drink and watch films. When they come back they smell of adults.

They all have their reasons for going to the bridge: mostly it's to smoke or drink; later it will be to meet girls or just for the view. One boy, now a successful entrepreneur in Bristol, collects the pages of porn magazines from around the bridge, and from the caves and crags near the observatory, that have been thrown out by passing cars or hedgerow masturbators. Unless he's very lucky, they're usually damp and dew-soggy, so he takes them back and dries them on the school radiator. When they're dry he sells them. There is a price list: the whole pages are expensive, and there are discounts for the shredded or lopped-off partials. They are available to rent, too.

On windy days the bridge can sway, and lorries and buses have to make the detour down and along the gorge and then back up to the other side. In really bad weather it shuts. The temptation to look down into the brown sludge of estuary, the glistering oyster grit and the silt, the little drain-ditch of trickling water, thin as rain coursing down guttering, is hard to resist. In the sunshine the mud flexes and ripples. It doesn't need much light to look alive. And inviting – a cushion of shimmering brown silk. It's tempting to jump.

The schoolboy is struck first by the smell that rises and catches on the wind. It's the smell of estuaries: on the one hand, drains, and on the other, the open sea. They should clash, but here they seem to go well together, like sweet-and-sour cuisine: the one is blockage and rot and stasis, the other escape and freedom and drift.

And you can always jump. You can jump any time you want. Mostly it's curiosity rather than suffering that makes you look down and find yourself wanting it, sending your mind up ahead to imagine what it's like to fall; to fall and fall and fall. The boy often feels hypnotised by the view, by its completeness. Not many things feel so total as what he sees when he looks down here. It's not dying in itself that's attractive – he's nowhere near unhappy enough for that, though he likes to imagine precisely *how* unhappy he'd need to be: what sort of dosage, millilitre by millilitre of unhappiness climbing the notches of the desolation-syringe, degree by degree in the sorrow-thermometer … No, not dying so much as its hypothetical nature. It's the idea of seeing yourself afterwards that draws you in: lifting off, peeling away from your body like a pen nib rising from the letters it leaves on the page, then looking down at your shell as you leave it, then at the people in the distance. Though really it's you in the distance: you *are* the distance; dead, you've become it.

He imagines death as one of those aerial shots in a war movie they show in school, where they leave the soldiers behind and rise in their helicopter, and the soldiers run but can't catch up and they shout and cry out and stretch out their hands for their comrades, fingers meet and grip and hold on and then are prised part; and the helicopter rises, shakily at first, and then steadies and pulls away, sticky and reluctant, and the soldiers get smaller and the enemy catch up or mow them down, and everyone becomes a dot and then everyone is gone; then it's all jungle and then all just sky.

And, well, there's also the advantage of just not having to drag this beast of a body around with you, no longer being shackled to the burning animal you are.

There's a legend of a Victorian woman who jumped from Clifton Bridge and lived, as the saying goes, *to tell the tale*, thanks to her big dress ballooning out into a crinoline parachute. There's little possibility anyone would survive the fall today, the boy knows, since, one, the velocity at which you hit the water would kill you outright; two, your heart would explode from fear long before, the way dormice burst inside when you pick them up, or, three, you'd hurtle so deep into the mud that you'd suffocate. It's the lady's image the boy has in mind when he and his friends peer down, or drop balls of paper, sweet wrappers, handkerchiefs or penny pieces over the edge and try to time their descent.

A few feet up, water is hospitable. It opens up and lets you in. After about seventy it is like stone. It will break you as if you'd hit a quarry floor. They learned that in physics.

Another reason it's tempting to let the mind play with the idea of falling is that it's so banally possible: the parapet only a little over five feet high. For most of the boys that means barely shoulder-level. One modest high-jump, using the wood of the handrail for leverage, and you'd be up and over, over and down, down and dead. Maybe then the fall would feel endless, though it would take just a few seconds. You could live a whole lifetime backwards in those seconds: back to birth, as the myth goes, the dying watching their lives unwind before them in reverse. You're interested in whether the same story told backwards is the same story at all. It's the 1980s, so your reference points for backwards and forwards are different from what they are today: they're the fast-forward or the rewind button on a cassette player or a video recorder, or perhaps the lifted needle of a record player dropped approximately between songs. Much later, with the arrival of CDs, you'll hear the old tunes again, like your parents' Jacques Brel or Beatles songs, but on a CD. And for the rest of your life, with a small tug of disorientation, you'll listen out for, and fail to hear, the scratches in the songs that made them yours, and without which you had never until now heard them.

Back then, back in the then, back on the bridge, you think it'll take a few seconds and a whole lifetime to reach the estuary silt; the cool, shiny, hourglass-fine sand. Maybe you could change a few things too, second time around – who knows? Make corrections.

He sometimes takes his introspection, which, like the rest of him, needs exercise, for a walk there. It's probably the only part of him, even in that sporty school, that gets any genuine exercise. There's always someone else on the bridge and, though he thinks of it as a place of extreme loneliness, he realises, years later, that never once was he actually alone on it. There were always others, sometimes as many as half a dozen, all doing the same thing: looking out and over and down. Once he saw someone writing the number for the Samaritans, whose notice is posted at each end of the bridge, on the back of his hand with a biro. For now, he leans over, dangling his arms, the handrail wedged in his armpits. His grandmother is a dressmaker, and she made him his school suit. The way the wind nips and tucks at his clothes like a tailor reminds him of being measured for it. He's being measured for a suit of air, so he can be sleeved in the rush of falling.

Years later, he comes back to the bridge. The Samaritans number used to be local; now it's an 0845 number – like insurance companies, mobile phone companies, telesales. The parapet is the same height, but now it has been supplemented by a four-foot grille of steel that turns inwards at the top. To jump off now, you'd need a ladder.

He's an adult, and has his own children, but when he's back on Clifton bridge, he realises he has his child self on an inner thermostat: always on low, but never quite off. There is a photograph, long-lost materially-speaking, but still intact in his head: it's of his aunt and uncle from a small town in Belgium, who have come to visit him here in Bristol. It's the first and only time anyone from there came here. The three of them are on the Clifton side, at the mouth of the bridge, in autumn sunlight. They must have asked someone to take the picture, because everyone who should be in the picture is in it.

Going back in time is like climbing into an old photograph. He remembers it in sepia tone; remote as an old postcard. But it's a post-card of his life: the treacly air, the heavy school furniture, the gelatinous glaze of things seen through a syrup of time and tears. If he dived into the photograph now, or ran his fingers along its surface, it would be the texture of cream, not the hard floor of water below the bridge. He thinks of the school, a few hundred yards away, and remembers the smell of the place, the universal boys'-school aroma: floor polish, over-applied deodorant and badly wiped arse.

He remembers, too, the wooden desks with their – even then, even in his day – long-disused inkwells, rims impregnated with black and blue spillages. Cocks carved with compass-points and fuckwords etched into the grain, past the varnish and into the pulpy meat of the wood. All that stuff looks a little prehistoric today, as faraway and tribal as bison on cave walls. You can get the desks now on eBay – 'Complete with graffiti', the sellers announce, by way of authen-ticating them.

But the bridge is always there: tonnes of iron and steel but looking, in the distance, delicate as lace, the cables taut as the strings of a harp. Sometimes you can hear the wind pluck them and fancy you hear a song. It is the song of the air, which is the sound of falling. The boy thinks he'd like to hear that song through to the end, that he'd like a long, long fall so he can hear it over and over and never hit the ground.

We think of haunting as a people thing: something essentially sociable, however unnerving. Ghosts are domesticated creatures, because we have invented them to replicate our actions, which they repeat – repetition is important to the ghost-life: like pets and children they need routine – slowly but often with surprising exactness. They are spectral replays of our matches, won or lost, and we impute to them something of ourselves we do not like to see: an inability to move on, a hunger for return.

As a child I found ghosts disappointing for these reasons: how constructed they were, how made up they were of us. It was our lack of ambition for ghosts that disappointed me; as if, with all we knew about the unknown, we couldn't imagine something better for them than repositories of our unfinished business. I'd have liked them to pull away a little more, to peel off from us, but no: they were hemmed in by their patterns, which were our patterns. A lost opportunity, I thought; for us in our imaginations and for them in their imagined reality. There are rules and regulations for ghosts, and the primary one is that you can't haunt somewhere you've never been, not properly at least, and though there have been ghosts who erred into other stories, other hauntings not their own, the effect there is comical, of actors stumbling into the wrong play.

Three bridges haunt me, though really I'm the one haunting them because I keep returning, and keep remembering the overlaying selves I see and feel whenever I cross them, or look up at them, or stand on one or other of the shores they connect. I explain to my students, early on in the first year of their studies, that the difference between a simile and a metaphor is like the difference between a bridge and an estuary: the bridge links two bits of land, and reminds you that they aren't linked at all. Like a bridge, the simile connects two things at the cost of reminding you that they aren't really connected. The metaphor is the estuary, in which two elements, earth and water, infuse and overlap and merge without its being clear which is which. At the right time of day, you can cross it safely, and at the wrong time of day you can sink into the silt or be swept away by the mad tides and the intricate, unpredictable currents.

The bridges I haunt and am in turn haunted by have something in common: that they are thrown (that is the verb for a bridge: you *throw* it) across estuaries. I remember being offended to hear, back in school, about time's forward flow – the old Heracleitan river you never step into twice. This seemed a satisfactory way of thinking about world events, battles and victories and some (but not all) politics; but as an account of human beings and their relation to Time, it seemed pretty cursory and left a great deal out. From Clifton bridge, looking over the parapet, it also seemed wrong: up there you could imagine Time more as an estuary – with its constant land/water level-shifts, its intermingled elements, its rises and falls, its drain-and-glut, its cross-currents and backstitching, its mud and silt and overlapping in-betweenness – than Heracleitus's river. At some point early on in my life, I must have fixed on that – and back then, not even consciously – as my metaphor for time and memory.

My three bridges are these: the Humber Bridge, which we caught sight of coming from Belgium, where I was brought up, to England; Clifton Suspension Bridge, which loomed over my schooldays at Clifton College, where I was from the age of nine to the age of eighteen; and the Severn Bridge, which welcomed me to Wales, the country that became my first and (I hope) final home – though I had had many houses.

When I arrived in Bristol, my English was piecemeal and full of holes. It sounded faraway in my mouth, not quite mine. Far away, but also someone else's. I felt like a ghost who had broken the revenant rule: a ghost in the wrong haunting, an actor in the wrong play. Speaking English was like wearing a dead relative's clothes, which is not such a dramatic analogy, since my father's Irish-Geordie family were either all dead or nearly so. The ones who were alive seemed already to be turning in like leaves, crisping at the edges. They lived in Newcastle, Doncaster, Bradford, Cullercoats. I always had the sense of somehow trying the language on for size. It had the feel of folded things. When, as a teen-ager in Bristol, I started buying trendy second-hand clothes – this was in the period, the mid 1980s, when the charity shop was seguing into the vintage clothes shop – I felt I'd known that smell for years, that I finally recognised it: it was the smell of English, and of my English self. Someone had died in it and it had been washed and pressed and put on a hanger in the Salvation Army store on Whiteladies Road for me to come and buy and climb into. As my Belgian grandmother was a dressmaker, and I spent a lot of my childhood with her while she worked, I took and still take many of my metaphors for fitting and *fitting in* from the world of *couture*. So I knew right from the start when things fitted and when they didn't.

When I was doing my O levels, I found, in a shop on Park Street that specialised in dapper, dressy second-hand clothes, a grey single-breasted linen jacket with a blue-and-green threaded piping, and a lining that was the colour of shallow water over estuary mud: a silvery-brown silk-shimmer that tugged at the light and drew it in. It fitted me perfectly, but had been tailor-made for someone else. Whoever it was must have been exactly like me in every physical respect, and really it was I who fitted it. It was bespoke, just not for me, which is how I thought of English, and how I still think of it: made for someone exactly like me, but not me. I associated it too with a betrayal of my grandmother, who used to make me my clothes and took huge pride in them. That I should now be buying them from others, and tailor-made at that, albeit at one ghostly remove, was treachery. Finding that jacket coincided, for me, with getting my English right, with feeling that I finally *had* it, that I'd mastered it and made it mine. That was an illusion – in fact, it had mastered me, just as I fitted the jacket rather than vice versa. I started to find holes in my French where once there had been holes in my English. The *mot juste* still came to me, just not any longer in French. Now I could say more than I felt in English, but in French I felt more than I could express. In tailoring terms, French had become the lining, and English the jacket.

I wore that jacket for our post-O-level party, an amateurish rave on the rocks near the bridge, with ghetto blasters, newsagent-sourced booze and ineptly-rolled joints. Two years later I wore it for my university interview – to study English – and kept it until my early thirties.

Wherever I am, I still haunt the bus stops around the bridge, and the benches where the foxes scavenge by the bins, and when I leaf through the portfolio of regrets that is my adolescence, I always meet myself in the vicinity of Clifton bridge, a clumsy shade in a sharp jacket, taking his melancholy for a walk across a gorge. But the estuary has everything I want and everything my ghost wants, because it is the opposite of Heracleitus and his river: it is water that hasn't yet flowed and sand that hasn't yet passed through the hourglass. Together they make a clay that hasn't yet been fired.

There's still time to change everything.

Here and There: or, the Plot

Andrew McNeillie

The deadline for this piece threatens like a sudden warning of late frost, one that should take me hurrying across the way to do what I can, to unfurl gauzes, cloudy bundles and unravel them over the tender broad-bean plants, like ribbons of heavy mist in the half-light.

The blackbird on her nest there watches me sharply but holds her nerve. Home I go, leaving her to sleep under the hard night sky that will, or will not, for nothing is certain, form a stiff and blanching frost come morning, winter's Pyrrhic victory if I don't look out – if the blackbird's unlucky and misfortune befalls her new-hatched nestlings in the bitter night. I must nurse my crop as best I can, as the blackbird nurses her new brood.

I was surprised to find her nest, in the corner of an upended wooden pallet through which some fingers of ivy and thorn had taken hold in the past year. Once I knew the nest was there it seemed too obvious, too exposed, but I never noticed it building, and the blackbird was three eggs in before I realised she was there. Safe in plain sight for now. Somehow I feel she's in my care, or that we share something, the spirit of a place, perhaps.

But it is December now, not spring. Now I must dig here, dig in, with my pen and black ink towards my deadline. 'Here' is a far cry, though only a short step, from my physical or material plot out 'there', on the nearby allotment, my only common ground (to speak unmetaphorically) in my retirement, and only hope of any. How I would love a field's-worth or two, a whole Sabine farm, but too late. I will never have the means for it. A token tenancy, it has become a special place to me nonetheless, though it is not strictly 'common' ground, but rented by our Society from the local landlord, owner of a vast demesne north of the Chilterns.

Some of us come and go, unable to keep on top of things, or else throw in the trowel, disillusioned by the reality of keeping Nature at bay with spade or hoe or potato fork. But those of us who hold out cling with some passion to our allotted portions of God's earth, small though they be, our feudal strips that might at any time be sold off to make room for a housing development. Upon which the outcry would be great but unlikely to stay execution. We form a loose but supportive community, respectful of each other's need for solitude, ready enough to help each other out, all within bounds. The powers-that-be are face-less. We are pawns whose protestations, when push comes to shove, will be bulldozed aside by a cabal of other interests. New housing is creeping up, encroaching along a nearby arc of the ring-road, in fields beyond the town's pale. The houses are jammed together without anything you might call a garden between them. My plot is little more than fifty yards out from the ring-road. Rumour is rife that developers are working in our direction, with their eyes on the allotments. I am not sure how much substance there is to them. There may be none, at least for now.

Our tenancy is ever a brief affair, you say. But until this year we were protected by our immediate neighbour. Call him Alexander. It is not his real name. He had a ramshackle barn and a couple of small crooked fields on our westerly border under the terms of an old-fashioned agricultural lease. He kept chickens, a few sheep, a cow and a calf, two or three bullocks or heifers to fatten, and likewise lambs, a pig now and then. The lie of his land was such that it would hamper development. The nature of his lease would make it troublesome to obtain planning permission. The lease ran and could not be cancelled while there was an heir ready and willing to take it on.

Alexander had no heir. He died. He was a rare breed, all but extinct now across the land. He'd left school at fourteen, perhaps earlier, and gone to work for a local farmer until he came into his lease. He kept farmer's hours, late and early, driving up in his white van at dawn, day in, day out, from his nearby council house, a loaded .410 shotgun across his lap, the window down, the vehicle scarcely moving along the lane as he looked to take a magpie or wood pigeon by surprise. He didn't like killing things. But the magpies stole his new-laid eggs by the dozen, given half a chance, and the wood pigeons cropped away at anything they fancied from winter brassicas to summer lettuce.

That Nature is red in tooth and claw he knew by second nature, but he was a thoughtful man too, though some doubted it; and you could see his caring nature in the character of his stock. They were calm and steady, and they flourished, his poultry bold and inquisitive, not easily put to flight. He maintained upwards of a dozen semi-feral cats. Some complained that the cats fouled their plots, especially when newly dug and planted. But they overlooked the benefits the cats brought, at least to Alexander's immediate neighbours. There were no mice to steal our newly planted peas or beans, no rats to do what rats do, to anything they fancy, and no rabbits either.

My plot is just across from his old holding. I often spoke with him. We became friends in a way. There was nothing he didn't know about growing vegetables, and he would advise me often but always in a round-about manner, acknowledging the vagaries of the seasons, and that he too got things wrong. After all, we are all at the unpredictable mercy of the weather. He succeeded and subsisted, however, and loved his way of life and knew he loved it. It was based on a primitive belief system. If you nurture the soil, and plant and sow, then you will reap and harvest. Along the way your faith must survive many trials by plague and blight.

Alexander was a local, a native, a kind of English crofter. It meant everything to him, to belong in his native heath. Sometimes he philos-ophised about the nature of Nature and, like the country mouse contemplating the town mouse, mocked both DEFRA's civil servants and campaigning environmentalists alike, for what he saw as their red-tape interferences, their ill-informed alarmism, their want of hard-won, hands-on experience. The spirit of place, however degraded his holding, however far from being a rural idyll, the target of thieves and of fly-tippers, haunted him in a way that can only be called mystical.

Never a smoker, he developed what used to be called 'farmer's lung', caused, he thought, in his case, by exposure to chemical dips rather than the bloom and mould in old hay. Latterly he would struggle for breath, especially on warm days. Sometimes I would see him standing stock-still, head bent, one hand resting on a fence post or anything else sturdy enough to support him (he was a big barrel-chested man) while a crisis passed.

Eventually it brought him down. He was buried in a field a quarter of a mile away, a small field he did own, by the sewage works, where he once kept a horse, and where he was interred, as was his wish, in 'a green coffin'. Thereupon the lease on his holding reverted to the landlord. Some people said he was a rogue. When things went missing, some pointed a finger at him, in a kind of reflex way. He did not enjoy the respect of everyone. But to my mind we were diminished by his passing. He was a reminder of a harsher reality, of what it was to scrape a living, hand-to-mouth, the lot of the poor the world over. What's more, we were weakened on what until now was our surest flank against the developers.

I think at first Alexander had me down as a middle-class dreamer, with New Age or Green tendencies: an educated fool, perhaps, persuaded I was doing my bit for self-sufficiency towards saving the planet. But little by little, in the first two years of my tenancy, he seemed to understand I was a lesser kind of mortal, a more down-to-earth specimen, for all my so-called education, with a taste for labouring and fresh vegetables. And I suppose, like him, I have some little scorn for humanity, in the spirit of Henry David Thoreau. I am surprised when I discover among friends and acquaintances individuals who claim either not to know what to do with fresh vegetables, or to have no time to spare for their preparation. But I don't see what I am doing as virtuous.

I was somewhat put out the other day when an old friend, a metropolitan man, praised my virtue for 'growing my own'.

Virtue is its own reward, I said. I am merely a materialist, in love with the flavour of vegetables cooked within minutes of harvest, pleased to readjust the balance in my mind–body equation by labouring out of doors. I cannot save the planet, nor contribute significantly to doing so. It is too late for that, and the scale of the problem too vast. If the recording angel thinks otherwise, then that's her business. I just enjoy my contact with the soil, the processes of nourishing and nursing it, and the dance the seasons lead me, a wilder dance by the year, it seems, these days, thanks to climate change, as we all go rattling off to hell in the proverbial handcart. I love to labour. I am eternally grateful that Adam and Eve were evicted via the little wicket gate from Eden. Or how boring life would be, deprived of knowledge and work.

My approach to things is, I suppose, to a degree existential. Knowing that something is the case is never enough without know-how. Labour teaches me know-how. Husbandry teaches me know-how. I dig. I have a mantra. 'Expect nothing, hope for nothing. Dig. Toil …' I sometimes say it to myself as I dig. I often say it to myself as I write. I sometimes call myself a lapsed Zen-Protestant. I feel more like a tramp in the pages of Samuel Beckett than a so-called transcendentalist à la Thoreau. (Notwithstanding my granddaughter's delightful way, when just two years old, of referring to my plot as 'the aloftment'.)

I am strongly aware in all this that to the town mouse I am more than faintly risible. I suppose I have Romanticism in my bones. What else is our appreciation of place and local habitation? I disappear before my own eyes into the rhythms of work. I will work in the cold. I will work in the rain. I like it when it is inclement once I am under way. But I do not like the carcinogenic sun on my head, the scorching sun *de nos jours*.

There is always work of one kind or another to do. I am living my dream or the compromised version of an old one, with which I've made my peace. No matter the thunder of traffic nearby, the violent clatter of tailboards as vehicles shudder to a halt, the hiss of air brakes, the boom of rappers and others blasting by in low-slung cars with full-bore exhausts growling, thundering there at a halt, with only a scraggy hawthorn hedge between us. Forget the pollutants that, to one degree or another, settle on my soil and plants.

A man at seventy is lucky if he can afford to live any version of his dream. He is lucky if his body will allow him to labour, as I have done now for at least eight years. He is lucky if his name comes up on the Society's waiting list before it is too late, and he has already left for a very different plot.

Not only do I love to labour, it's almost as if I need to, and not simply to preserve my sanity, or my version of sanity, in the face of the world as it is, in its 24/7 news-feed madness, its technocratic plutocracy, its deafening opinion (instant opinion), its abuses of language (going forward), its terrible politics, its violent upheavals. Its ... its ... its ... morose old men.

Digging and husbandry clear my head and keep me going, not least by speaking back to other places and times, time in my youth above all, when I toiled and moiled for my father, in the days when we were more than self-sufficient, from bean-row to bee-loud glade, and honey, on our patch of rough land above the Irish Sea in north Wales. Where we also had apple trees and sometimes, though rarely, a serpent, a grass snake. This ground I have now, this little bit of God's earth at the heart of Middle England, may be all compromise (it is not even third-best), but nonetheless it grounds me and frees me into reverie. Every place is unique. Did Thoreau say that? I seem to think so, but I can't remember where and perhaps I am mistaken.

It isn't new or alien for me to travel between place and page. For almost as long as I can remember, from late youth at least, it's been essential to me, as reader as much as aspiring writer. But the proportions and exchanges have altered, between there and here, here and there, and they keep altering, as now I am entered on my older age. I have just had my biblical three-score-years-and-ten birthday. No use you telling me it's the new sixty. Ask my aching limbs after a damp winter's afternoon's labour wheelbarrowing a dozen and a half loads of manure 200 yards to my plot from the communal midden. Or after as much time digging, or a-lugging water fifty yards from the standing tap, in summer drought, on a warm evening.

What I go to and return with in my mind is of a markedly different kind from even a few years ago. My orbits are more curtailed, my circuits shorter, my pace slower (though I rarely realise it is), my concerns different. But if anything I'm haunted more intensely day by day. 'There' looms and lingers longer, unbidden. It's not perhaps so much that I bring it back with me as that it follows me home like a stalker, and stays with me and tumbles in my head as I fall asleep, more intensely than ever, planning and scheming and taking pleasure in work done and things seen and felt, ushering me into oblivion. I think it has something to do with wear and tear in synapses and circuitry. No doubt toiling and moiling keep me fitter in mind and body than I might otherwise be if I sat reading all day, but a fifteen-mile walk staggers me now far more than ever a twenty-mile one used to.

I still walk out round the local farmlands, a latter-day Loony Dick, mooching about. They are my plot's hinterlands, vast swathes of them owned by the same peer of the realm that owns the allotment land. The efficacy of walking is thoroughly known and long established by philosophers. Sublime scenery might infuse thought with drama but I think, as in labouring, it is the motion that matters above all. Motion and emotion are only separated by a single vowel, as has often been observed.

The landscape just north of the Chilterns is of weald and otherwise lacks uplifting contours. The arable agriculture is highly mechanical and chemical. Birdlife here is frugally distributed (I will not speak of red kites) and little varied, despite the token extra widths of headland, set aside for grant money. In winter I will see large flocks of fieldfares and, most years, redwings. Once in a way I hear a curlew to my west, strayed over from the edge of Otmoor. It will always make my heart beat faster when I do. Sometimes there are clouds of lapwings. They nest here in some number. In spring I might see wheatears passing through, heading north-west; or on a dreary day in March catch sight of a merlin harrying a lark. When I first saw such species in these parts I was taken aback, and taken back, too, to Welsh mountains and moorlands and boyhood. I travelled between here and there and back, with their unexpected help.

Momentary correspondences are present anywhere and everywhere in all kinds of forms and particulars. It depends on how and where you were made. They seem to suggest themselves, but we meet them at least halfway, ministering to them. They cry out to be brought to book, caught in words, like that balloon steered by Yeats's poem into a shed. I tell myself this regularly. I tell myself to keep my feet on the ground. As if it might help me to do so, I went up to my plot the other day and, with a six-foot cane, surveyed and measured it.

It is the first plot you come upon as you leave the short lane, a byway between an A-road and the rugby club beyond.

Spin the wheels in the padlock to the right code and step through the wicket gate. Re-run Adam and Eve. My plot is the one on the right-hand side of the path. It occupies a corner. It is a corner of land and runs in something of a crescent where the path begins. In its main body it is neither square nor rectangular. This year I have acquired the greater part of a neighbouring plot, one run to neglect by a friend. He is in full-time employment and in his passion took on too much.

The Society measures things in perches or rods. That means little to me. So to make account of my now expanded ground I measured it all out with my cane. Thoreau, a land surveyor by profession, would have laughed to see me or to read my figures. He knew a perch or rod = 5.5 yards or 0.25 of a surveyor's chain. Looked at one way, I have more than 3.5 perches or rods by about 3. It still makes no sense to me when I work that out and round it up to equal 1/20th of an acre. Don't trust me. I am innumerate. The exercise fails to bring me down to earth but hoists me back into speculation. How can I describe and define my plot? There is no equivalent to being 'there'. Being 'here' I think runs it close, as a form of cultivation. Or what can we say of the world? Though I am not sure Alexander would not have made much sense of such a question. Rather it would probably have confirmed him in his original suspicions as to the kind of man I am.

Coda: Hedge Fund

In the last three or four years my walks have not always been ends in themselves, at least not in the autumn and spring. These walks have had only my plot in mind, or I should say its new hedge. Along the lane, to the right or broadly the south of my plot, is a fence, a few strands of wire and a stretch of sheep netting, supported by posts and angle irons. Nettles grow through the wire, at the top of the bank that drops at an easy gradient to the edge of my plot. I grew a chestnut from a conker and planted it on the bank. It flourished quickly but had to be lopped at about four or five feet. I began to poke chestnuts, hazelnuts, acorns, berries into the bank at quite close intervals. Some took root but it was hit or miss.

Then in my wanderings one soggy day at the back end of winter, sheltering from heavy rain, I found in a coppice a leafy floor through which sprouted scores of saplings – chiefly ash, some hawthorn – and I found that with a firm grip and sharp tug they would come out, bringing their root systems with them. I would take them in their dozens and replant them along my bank. I found a similar stretch of sycamore wood and brought back dozens of sycamore saplings, and the same for blackthorn and hawthorn elsewhere.

On a recent trip to my native heath I gathered a bag of sessile acorns and planted them in giant flowerpots. I still have to see how many Welsh oaks I can add to my hedge. At times this hedge takes over. I think of it first and my plot second. I have found that you can't just put saplings in the earth and leave them. You must clear the weeds and grasses from their stems and from around their roots; you must water them in times of dry weather. They can be strangled by other growth and perish.

At this stage in its development the hedge has a long way to grow, but already I see something of it, in two or three hawthorns that have put on a spurt of growth; already I can see how I will begin to lop and to weave one whip or miniature trunk, one branch with another, to create a shapely tangle, something with a nod in the direction of David Nash to it; to create in the end a high barrier to the world, a thing of wonder, full of light in winter, and of tender green foliage in spring, with cover for the blackbird to build her nest and other species too. I call it my hedge fund. I am hedging my bets in the hope I'll see it fully grown there, as I see it here, in my mind's eye, a thing of great wonder, a windbreak to my plot, a thin line of mixed wood, a conservation area in little, beyond which my plot will continue to thicken long after the new housing stock round the corner has grown to look outdated and generations of blackbirds have gone forth and multiplied.

A couple of weeks after I sent this piece off, I went up to the plot to find Alexander's smallholding demolished and a giant JCB scooping the assorted rubble into a truck. By the end of the week everything had been cleared to resemble a ploughed field down as far as the orchard where Alexander used to keep his hen huts and sometimes graze a beast or a few sheep. Our tenancy is ever a brief affair. Where are the nows of yesteryear? – as Tim Robinson once asked.

You might think it the beginning of the end. But not so. The event led to a meeting between representatives of our Society and the landlord's agent, at which a startling reassurance was given: the Estate will *never* sell the allotment area for housing or anything else. The cleared ground will become a wildflower meadow. Dare I revise my mantra to: 'Expect the best, hope for the best' – keep digging and toiling, here and there, as if for all eternity?

Embarking

Philip Marsden

I turned off the ferry road into the woods. Sunlight flickered through the windscreen and over the dashboard. The trees were oak mainly, sessile oak, which long ago had been coppiced and now grew as thin and twisting figures, stunted by sea-salt. It was late September and the leaves still showed green; only in patches of open ground, where the light fell on rust-coloured ferns, was there any sign that summer was over.

Through the trees, just visible now as the road dipped and swung to the left, was a ship. I could make out its white superstructure and its radar antennae and the low stern deck. It was an ocean-going research ship laid up between commissions; the name painted on the bow made me chuckle: *Deep Investigator*.

There was something odd about the road itself. It had been constructed half a century past, in five-yard squares of concrete. Where they joined, along the seams, were green lines of moss and grass. The road also was much too wide for a cul-de-sac and the single waterside cottage where it led; in places two or three trucks could pass each other without slowing. In the last section a cutting some thirty feet deep had been blasted through the killas. It was a ghost road.

I left the car in the cutting and walked on through a gate into the sun. I was in a large apron of concrete, made from the same squares as the road. Here was the river, the Fal, deep-watered and steep-sided and no more than a couple of hundred yards across. The single cottage lay off to one side, cutely thatched and small-windowed. Visible upstream was a V of wooded slopes and a distant bend in the valley. The oaks all dropped their skirts to the same level – the level of the spring tide. There was the gap too where the Truro river joined the Fal and, high above the confluence, with its scooped-out parkland and antler-like chimneys, stood Tregothnan, Cornwall's largest private house.

Right in front of me, just twenty yards offshore, was my boat – a white-hulled 1960s sloop, thirty-one foot long, with a solid-looking mast and a canvas cover tenting over its cockpit.

I had bought it in June, for a book project. I was going to sail it up to Ireland and Scotland, and write about it. Because the boat's wooden, I needed to keep it on a mooring through the winter to prevent the boards drying out and opening up, and because boat ownership brings with it a certain anxiety – going to check it was still there, undamaged during the season's storms, and not half submerged because the automatic pump had failed – the road leading down to the moorings became intensely familiar to me.

Until a few years ago the thatched cottage had been a seasonal pub: the Smugglers at Tolverne (*Teas, lunches, bar meals*). In winter it was always a hidden-away place, but in summer a great many visitors drove down to it, following the too-wide road through the woods. Since the pub closed, the route has sunk back into sylvan obscurity, its pitted surface edged by a mulch of leaves, its dodder-hung oaks unseen by passing cars. Only the young couple who live in the cottage, and a few boat owners like me, use the road.

That winter, driving down it once or twice a week, as the trees dropped their leaves and revealed more of the *Deep Investigator*, I found the broad road filled with expectation. It built to a peak before the reveal of the last corner: *would the boat still be there?* Such a sharpening of the senses stirred a sediment of deep memory – not just my own half-forgotten visits to Smugglers as a child – but a host of historical connections that came tumbling out as soon as I started looking into its past. With each new story, I noticed the appearance of the land beginning to alter – as if meaning could somehow affect topography, rather than the other way round.

In his 1955 *The Making of the English Landscape*, W. G. Hoskins suggested that what we see of the country's land surface is now almost entirely man-made. Rather than viewing it as something spoilt, a vulgarised version of pure Nature, he presented it instead as endlessly revealing, a story-book, a storehouse of memory, an archive waiting to be dusted off and read. Hoskins's approach – which has enlivened faculties of geographers, archaeologists and historians ever since – encourages a localisation of study, a move away from the regional and the abstract to the immediate, to that scale of territory that is not just more visible but more closely related to human experience. Uncover the past of particular places and history can break free of the textbook, come alive in the open air.

'The view from this room where I write these last pages is small,' concludes Hoskins. As if pulling from his pocket a gate-fold map, he then reveals the centuries. He points to the traces of bankside buildings recorded in the Domesday Book, to the Saxon name for the river, a twelfth-century charter proposing the fishpond, eighteenth-century hedges, the distant chimneys of a Victorian 'big house'. 'Here in this room one is reaching back, in a view embracing a few hundred acres at the most, through ten centuries of English life, and discerning shadows beyond that again.'

Some years ago, I began researching the story of Falmouth. I never imagined it would yield enough for a book; personal interest only. But I soon found myself immersed. County archives, state papers and records offices turned up a glittering hoard of stories and individuals. I was amazed that a not-very-large town could produce so much material. But it wasn't just that: put together, those lives and their locale began to tell a much bigger narrative, of an entire nation, an entire era. It left me with the heady feeling that you could take any small town, any field or woodland, and discern the whole – in the way that each microscopic strip of DNA contains the genome for a complete organism.

The initial zeal calmed, as zeal does, and revealed something more interesting. Hoskins concedes that his own window is particularly rewarding: 'Not every small view in England is so full of details as this.'

Rather than significance being equally distributed, certain pockets of land become hotspots of history. Arbitrary features like river crossings, prominent hills or natural harbours concentrate human activity, or accrue significance: when you come to them, you cannot help but be aware of some strange quality, the sum perhaps of all those others who have passed through, and all they have felt and all that they have done and thought in that particular locale.

Such a place is Tolverne and its road. Several things combine to give it an advantage. The estuary is very deep. It turns a ninety-degree bend. It gives both shelter and a certain discretion for those like the free-traders of old who required it. There was always a ferry here. Before it was a pub, the cottage was the ferryman's cottage, and had been for 500 years; countless people stood on the shore waiting to cross, or disembarked here with the expectations of return or reunion. Such is the geography of the long tidal fingers pushing into Cornwall that ferries have always been needed; less than half a mile from Tolverne is another, King Harry Ferry, still in use today with a thirty-car chain-powered craft, running six times an hour.

On the hill above the cottage is the ancient barton of Tolverne. The Arundel family who lived there grew rich from the ferries, and by the sixteenth century had begun to expand their horizons. In the 1580s John Arundel left Tolverne to take part in Grenville's expedition to set up a colony in Virginia (or rather a nest of privateers to prey on the Spanish silver trade). Arundel was the commander of the first ship back and was knighted by the 'pirate queen' herself, Elizabeth I. Emboldened by the spirit of the age, Sir John then left Tolverne again, this time to search for the mythical island of Hy-Brasil. He lost all his money, the estate was sold and the family permanently impoverished. Even now, four centuries later, when you approach the house, with its ivy-clad walls and its missing windows, trying to work out whether it's inhabited or not, it's easy to imagine the reckless days of the early nation-state.

Below the house, not fifty yards from the road itself, is a thicket. One day I pulled up the car next to it and, pushing aside brambles and holly, came to a place of flattened ground and half-collapsed walls.

In the handwritten notes of the historian Charles Henderson, I had read of the chapel: dedicated to Henry VI, whose canonisation was thwarted only by England's estrangement from Rome during the Reformation. On down the road, the thatched cottage of Smugglers itself dates from the 1400s. All alone beneath wooded slopes, it too looks ageless.

Then there are the ships. This stretch of the Fal river makes a handy boat-park for spare cargo capacity. The number of ships is said to be an indicator of the global economy. After the banking crisis of 2008, more than half a dozen were laid up here. The oil crisis of the mid-1970s had brought thirty-six. Now it was just the research ship *Deep Investigator*; in February she left to do some deep investigating in the Baltic.

One winter, years earlier, an old Soviet factory ship ended up here. The *Kommunar* had spent two decades trawling and buying up fish stocks from the world's oceans. But what worked for the planned economy failed when it collapsed. By 1995, with a string of unpaid harbour dues behind her, the *Kommunar* had a writ from the Admiralty taped to her radio mast; she was legally under arrest. Having just returned from six months in Russia, I used to visit the men who remained on board, taking them supplies. The skipper was of Chechen origin and told stories from seafaring in West Africa and the Far East, and his crew of seventy-five who heaved fish in over the stern, processed and canned it. Now he presided over just two, and a ship that no longer had power. Off Tolverne, in the ship's chilly companionways, its empty hold and the rubbish-filled decks, the last stages of the Soviet Union were being acted out. In March the three men left, unpaid, for St Petersburg. The *Kommunar* was towed off to Turkey for scrap.

And then there's the road itself: why so wide?

For tanks, for troop trucks, for staff cars, for the men of the 29th Infantry, of the US 5th Corps who, in June 1944, embarked at Tolverne for Normandy and the horrors of Omaha Beach. The thatched cottage and the steep wooded slopes were the last piece of friendly territory many of those men ever saw.

As early as 1942, plans were being made for an Allied invasion of the continent; officials were hunted along the south coast of England for suitable sites. With its deep waters and narrow sides, the Fal at Tolverne fitted the bill. First came teams to widen the ancient ferry track. They cut into the rock to level the last section. They felled trees at the shoreline and built an artificial beach with blocks of granite and shingle. They suggested pulling down the thatched cottage to make room. But it had a phone line, so became a coordination centre.

US forces arrived in Cornwall early in 1944. At Tolverne they felled more trees, they dug latrines, built storage huts and cookhouses. They piped in fresh water from a source a mile away and held it in a tank above the shore. A checkpoint and barrier were placed on the road and its surface was widened further, to accommodate rows of Sherman tanks. Down on the water a pontoon of wood and steel pushed a third of the way across the river, to the edge of the channel. The shoreline was covered to create a hard, but the concrete dried white and had to be tarmacked to be less visible from the air. Secrecy surrounded everything.

Through May 1944, barges and landing craft began to assemble in the narrows above King Harry Ferry. The troops themselves were based in sausage camps around Cornwall, so called because of their shape, stretched out along the edge of the county's roads. At the end of the month, the camps were sealed, the roads closed to the public and hundreds of trucks transported the men to the coast. At Tolverne, General Eisenhower drove down the widened road, past the tanks and armoured cars. Thousands of troops gathered, along the shore and on the decks of numerous ships, to hear his eve-of-battle address.

The noise of the preparations was something local people commented on; they just weren't used to the clang and hiss of traffic. After the Americans had gone, in landing craft along the English Channel to meet up with other groups, then south to the bloody beaches of Normandy and the largest invasion in human history, it was said that at Tolverne 'you could hear a pin drop'.

Seventy years later, Tolverne is again a backwater. The old pontoon has gone, and a new one put in – shorter, designed for leisure craft. On still afternoons, on board my boat, I would go up and stand in the bows to check the mooring line. The tide brushed past the hull and made ripples against the buoy. The only sounds then were curlew, the squawk of a heron or the rasp of a black-headed gull.

At the time of D-Day, the cottage at Tolverne was the home of the Newman family, and remained so for years afterwards. Only in 2010 did they finally leave. I had come to know Peter and Elizabeth Newman a little while visiting the *Kommunar* in the mid 1990s; I still saw them once a year when they came back to the village show to judge the dog-racing. They had retired to Truro and a flat in a large Victorian house.

In April, shortly before I was due to sail to Ireland, I went to see them. The house had high ceilings and a wide communal staircase. A ship's figurehead stood outside their apartment door. On the walls of the sitting room hung early charts of the river around Tolverne, aerial photographs of Tolverne, a watercolour of Smugglers Cottage fronted by marigolds. There were photos of the ships that ended up at Tolverne – the SS *Uganda* which had served as a hospital ship in the Falklands War, and the *Windsor Castle*, which looked like a small freighter but was a gentleman's yacht.

'People always said to me – Peter, you'll never leave Tolverne. They'll carry you out of there in a box. But in the end, we were ready to retire.'

He looked to Elizabeth, who agreed: 'Forty years of cooking in the pub seemed about enough, really.'

It was Peter's father who first took the family to Tolverne. In the early 1930s, before Peter was born, Rodney Newman was living down-stream at Devoran working as an engineer. He used to go up the river in his boat. Seeing the cottage at Tolverne always made him daydream of living there. But it was the home of the ferryman and always had been.

Then one evening, in 1933, there was an accident. Returning late from Truro, the ferryman's punt struck a rock in the darkness and sank. He drowned. Rodney Newman went to the Tregothnan estate office soon afterwards and, to his surprise, was given the keys. He loaded his boat with furniture, a piano and with his young family motored up to the cottage. You're mad, his neighbours told him, going to live up there, all isolated and alone. But by the time war broke out, the place to them was the centre of the world. Rodney was running passengers up and down the river, and his wife was letting out rooms for B&B. He remained there throughout the war, joining the river patrol, towing dummy ships up to the deserted stretches of river to draw the bombs. When Eisenhower came, Mabel Newman served him tea and biscuits.

With the GIs gone and war over, the Newmans resumed their pleasure-boat business and the B&Bs. They opened the pub and tea room. They became a much-loved part of river life, with their blue-and-white Tolverne ferries running from Falmouth to Truro and back again. Large ships came and went, spending months in front of the cottage, dwarfing it with their bulk. Their skeleton crews used the US Navy hard to receive supplies. Over the years the bar filled with ships' memorabilia.

When Rodney Newman died in the late 1950s, his son George took over. He ran the ferries while his mother continued with the B&Bs. The waters of the Fal might look benign, but water's water; one evening, mooring the ferry, George fell overboard and drowned. Mabel carried on alone until her younger son Peter was ready to take over.

Peter and Elizabeth ran Smugglers for the next forty years. Each summer, US veterans came to visit; each summer they grew fewer, slower of limb and stockier. In the woods, Peter cleared the scrub around the traces of the 29th Infantry's brief passage through the site – the Nissen huts, the sheds and latrines. In 1994, half a century on from D-Day, a small group of vets visited Tolverne to unveil a bronze panel set into a lump of granite on the foreshore:

The plaque commemorates the fiftieth anniversary of the departure of thousands of American troops from this beach in landing craft bound for Omaha on the Normandy coast for the invasion of Europe.

Above it was engraved an entwining of the Union Jack and Stars and Stripes.

'I arranged for that plaque,' explained Peter, just as he had arranged for the handwritten signs showing the remains of the D-Day preparations. Most of the signs have now gone. His collection of memorabilia was offered to the Tregothnan estate. Without the pub, without the visitors, it had little appeal. In 2012, the whole lot was put up for auction in Penzance.

That afternoon, after visiting the Newmans, I returned home by the car ferry. I turned off to Tolverne, towards Smugglers. Spring sun flickered in the windscreen and over the dashboard. Last autumn's leaves were still pasted to the fringes of the road; the woods were stirring from the floor up, with bluebells and white ransomes scattered beneath a tangle of bare-branched oaks.

I was preparing to leave. In Truro I had bought some new lanyard for the boat's jack-lines and some chrome polish for the coach-roof windows. I had picked up the mainsail from the sailmakers, repaired and cleaned. I loaded them all onto the dinghy and rowed out. The wind was blowing hard from the west but the cloud was high and broken. I let my gaze rest on Smugglers Cottage, thinking of what it had witnessed. It looked, if not actually bigger, somehow more substantial.

During those final days, toing and froing to Tolverne, my mind was abuzz with boaty dilemmas – thinking how best to stow the Zodiac on board, and the outboard, what food to take, which charts to buy, which books to put in the saloon. I'd had the sea-cocks serviced, and the engine, and ironed out one or two problems with the rigging. I'd rolled on the self-furling headsail. I'd recruited a friend from Falmouth to help with the passage to County Kerry; after that, going on up to the Western Isles, I'd be on my own. It was not something I'd ever done before.

One afternoon in mid April, I took the last of the gear aboard and, with the lockers full of food, and the tanks full of fresh water and diesel, I was as ready as I'd ever be. I sat in the cockpit. For the umpteenth time I checked the weather on my phone. Another twelve hours of easterly meant a nasty swell going down to Land's End, but from then on, for the two days it would take to Dingle, it looked not too bad.

On board that afternoon, it was hard not to think of that other embarking, in 1944, and the part the weather played then, delaying the invasion by a day or two. It was hard not to think of the thousands of young Americans who boarded the landing craft here at Tolverne, and the apprehension they felt crouched on the boxed-in decks, and the much greater danger they faced, and the history they made when their boots splashed onto Omaha Beach. It was hard too not to think of John Arundel, setting off to Virginia and then for Hy-Brasil; and those who had drowned here – Peter's brother George, and the ferryman in 1933.

Then too, as Hoskins put it, you could gaze over the same site, the same view, through many centuries of activity, 'and discern shadows beyond that again'. Half a millennium of ferries crossing the river, and the numberless passengers and, before that, the traffic of small craft that passed along this slim stretch of water for hundreds, perhaps thousands, of years: medieval pilgrims boarding ships at Tregony – now several miles inland – bound for Compostela (the amount of silver and the dedication of the vanished church of St James's testament to their number and their destination); the early missionaries from Wales and Ireland, who sailed up these creeks to establish monastic cells, and whose names survive in the shoreside villages of Kea, Lamorna and Ruan Lanihorne; and those ships before that with their cargo of alluvial tin bound for the Mediterranean, where it was forged into the bronze weapons that shaped the ancient world. And beyond that, even less recorded, the seafaring groups who spread megaliths and early agriculture along the Atlantic seaboard, and for whom the Fal's long and safe navigable waters provided easy passage to higher ground.

I stood and looked ashore. In the cottage now lived a family who ran the moorings and had a charter boat of their own. I could see Colin crossing the hard to the pontoon. His three-year-old son was running before him, plump and tottering in his all-in-one waterproof suit. He reached the water and stopped, then he heaved a rock into the shallows. The splash made him yelp with joy. He stood there for some time, watching the ripples as they spread and disappeared, and the place where the rock had vanished.

SEAVIEW: THE ANTHROPOSCENIC

David Matless

Anthroposcenic: Landscape emblematic of processes
marking the Anthropocene

Breezy summer nights roar. Surf and undertow cradle sleep. Ten feet
to the cliff edge from salted glass, sound washes inside; over the two
steps, the slippery mat, the kitchen corner, the banquette and bedrooms.
Seaview caravans, the constant sea.

And on a winter's night, sleep in trepidation. Unseasonal clinging
as sea surges, banked up with northerlies, water lifting to low pressure.

Atmosphere's release, valves open, vans wobbling; metal gale-tested, rust salted. That which never ends proceeds regardless, to a possible fall.

Cliffs of till undercut, sodden soil slipping, trapped flints and bones seeing first light for an epoch. The caravan shudders, lists, slips a little, then some more. Fencing descends with the cliff-edge long grass, the trimmed grass follows, the van tilts to topple. A one-way rollercoaster to the beach. Cupboards fly, windows and waves break. Unrivalled sea views.

Things have fallen since things have been built on soft cliffs. Turn the lining of England's east coast to find ex-places offshore. Boats net odd human remnants, ears claim phantom chimes. Melancholy gathers on the shore, haunting hubris. Treasure hunters rummage the wake.

And so human misery, and beachcombing joy, proceeds as it has proceeded. Yet the shore gathers new freight, other stories colonising floods and falls. Coast signals climate, seas rising for reasons other than their own. Humble tumbling vans catch in larger nets. As new epochs are labelled, the world becoming Anthropocene, sea views turn Anthroposcenic, their landscapes emblematic.

Labels enable, yet stain. Beaches colour with abstraction, miniature gaieties tainted by epoch. In seaside amusement, the penny drops. So enjoy it while you can, and don't let it spoil the holiday. Keep choking on lolly-stick gags: the sand was wet, and the sea weed.

Holidays at East Runton; forty years ago, with predictions of a new ice age, and in newer hotting times. A beach mile from Cromer, rock pools and sand, the wave-cut platform and forest bed. A minute from door to paddle, cliff's topping to North Sea summer icing; always a chill.

Once upon a horizon, seascape showed day ships and night lights; at anchor, or giving warning. Now turbine blades turn from shallows, nocturnal red twinklings. Ships and birds evade, seascapes filled to mitigate rising seas. Atmospheres dance in the cool night air.

The sewage outflow, marine direct, is gone. The bobbing turds of memory pass. Paddle with assurance in improved waters. Descend the beach from soft to firm, tentative over shingle and flints, to revealed sand, and sea collapsing on the ebb. Firm enough for a bowl.

Inshore craft beach with the catch, hauled by tractor to the slip; bathers descend, sea creatures ascend. Boxed crustaceans pique young curiosity, marine still life. Tides fall to platform chalk, miniature canyons for sea streams. Weed and whelks wait twice daily, crabs strand, anemones wave. Young fingers, nipped and sucked, touch knowingly.

Along the shore, exposed by retreat, mammoths emerge, laid down 600 millennia. Cohabiters of the ancient human poke from till. On this 'Deep History Coast', mammoth back and coastal bulge merged in logo, past surprises project, in Anthropocene resonance. Strollers glean relics.

Before descent, check the sea timers. The public served via provision of tide clocks: plan your day for high and low fun. Kites flown, castles moated, waters damned. Beach burial helps sharpen sense; sandy and damp, up to the apple, the vivid scenery of the stuck.

So diurnal turns accumulate, epochs meet through a fall, odd storms renew. Horizons fill, structures fall, words mark. Views become Anthroposcenes, emblematic prospects, as soft cliffs toast: 'to the sea'.

WADERS

Andrew Motion

1

After the accident, when summer brings
slow afternoons with nothing left to do,
I take what used to be your garden chair
and park it underneath the wayward ash
that sidles forward where the garden swerves
and hides the house from view. In secret then
I conjure up the notebook I have found
among your bedside things and open it.
Blank pages. Thoughts you never had, or had
but could not bring yourself to say. Should I
imagine them or write my own instead?
I close my eyes and scrutinise the white
that also lies inside me while the ash
rattles its pale green keys above my head.

2

The milk float with its thin mosquito whine
straining through larch and elder from the lane,
the nervous bottles in their metal basket
intent on music but without a tune,
the milkman in his doctor's stubby coat
and sailor's rakish dark blue canvas cap

are all invisible, imagined/dreamed
beyond my curtains in the early light,
along with tissue footprints in the frost,
our rinsed-out empties, and the rolled-up note
exchanged for bottles with their silver tops
the blue tits have already broken through
to sip the stiffened plugs of cream before
we come downstairs and bring our order in.

3

To think the world is endless, prodigal,
to part the hedgerow-leaves and see the eggs
like planets in a crowded galaxy,
to hear my mother's voice advising me
the mother-bird herself will never mind
if I take only one and leave the rest,
means nothing more than showing interest.
As does the careful slow walk home, the ritual
of pin-pricks through both ends, the steady breath
that blows the yolk and albumen clean out
but keeps the pretty shell intact, the nest
of crumpled paper in the cedar drawer,
the darkness falling then, the hush, and me
bringing the weight of my warm mind to bear.

4

Beyond the grazing and the bramble bank
where on another day I might lie down
and press my ear against the trampled earth
to hear the rabbits scuffling underground,
a headland round the Ashgrove leads me on
past wheat fields which still show the buffeting
of last night's storm, towards the Blackwater.
The stream has long since burst inside my head,

the banks collapsed, the water-meadows drowned,
the mesh of overhanging branches bowed
with plastic voodoo junk and hanks of wool.
Then I arrive and see things as they are:
a settled surface with a clearing sky,
and shining gravel drifting inside clouds.

5

My father with no explanation stays
behind at home; my mother drives away
and takes me with her to the Suffolk coast
where I lie down all day on rounded stones
and will the sun to thaw my frozen brain
while she ... I've no idea what she does,
until the evening she manhandles me
to stand beside her in the cypress shade
which makes a double-darkness on the lawn
and watch the round moon roll into our sky
as Neil Armstrong takes his one small step
and pokes his flag into the silver dust
although we cannot see him, nor he us
except in ways I think my father might.

6

Before our time they used my room to store
apples collected from those crooked trees
now wading waist-deep at the garden end
in frilly white-capped waves of cow parsley,
and laid them out in rows not touching quite.
I know all this because the floorboards show
wherever they had missed one as it turned
to mush and left a round stain on the wood.
My bed stands over them and when at night
my eyes grow used to darkness they appear:

the Coxes, Bramleys, Blenheim Oranges
whose names alone can fill the empty air
with branches weighted down by next year's crop
and turn its scent half-sickly and half-sweet.

7

That lead tank like a coffin with no lid
lying between the cooler greenhouse-room
my mother uses for her cuttings-trays,
and one as steamy as the rainforest
with air so thickened by tomato plants
it lies like moist green velvet on my tongue –
that lead tank, that disgusting (almost)
store of syrupy black water is where Kit
my brother slipped, or threw himself to see
if that would make our father like him more,
and where, as I look down to see myself
alive and sensible, I envy him
his moment in a time outside our time,
free from the earth and all its appetites.

8

The low tent-tunnel of the laurel walk,
where no one but a child can stand today
encloses me but keeps the world in view
in sudden supple leaps and starts of light.
Here out of sight I wait to meet myself
with no idea of what myself might be.
I drink the musty air and bide my time.
I shake the sullen shadows from my head.
I feel the deep earth rising in my bones.
I make believe the shivering small flies
beside me on the leaves, the sparrow gang
that flusters in its shallow bowl of dust,

suppose that I want nothing more from them
except to stay here and not mean a thing.

9

I try my father's waders on for size
then take, with him encouraging, his rod
and wading-stick, his canvas bag, his cap
rigid beneath its crown of favourite flies,
and step into the river. From the bank
he says I look like him. As for myself
I only think of how to stand upright
with water hardening one second round
my ankles, and the next uprooting me
as though I have no purchase on the world.
My father shouts, Don't fight it. I obey.
I let the deluge settle round my heart
then lay me on my back and carry me
round the long sweep beyond my father's sight.

10

Those roofless kennels where the nettles shake
their fine-haired leaves and tiny bright green buds.
That almost-buried path of blood-red bricks
confined both sides by tiles shaped like rope.
The ruined square of cracked disrupted blocks
where once a summer house had turned and stared.
These are the former glories of the house
although I like their fall and brokenness
much more than grieving for a time I missed.
As also I like walking with the ghosts
that wander through the garden everywhere –
the mother and her son whose footsteps leave
no prints beside us in the grass as though
our selves are all the company we keep.

THESE ARE MY CHANGES

Adam Nicolson

When I look out of the window, almost everything I see – the stone wall on the edge of the garden, the already-craggy hawthorns beyond it, the track they shade between them, the chestnut fence and hedge the far side of that, the beeches and hornbeams just now gesturing in the wind from the west, lining the little valley below the farm that was first noticed in an Anglo-Saxon charter 1,100 years ago, plus the slightly gappy mixed thorn and hazel hedge of the field beyond it – all of these things, and their gates and fences, are there because I have put them there. Or, to be more honest, because I have asked and paid people to put them there.

These are my changes. In the twenty-five years since we came to live here on this ninety-acre grass farm in the Sussex Weald, Sarah and I have wanted it to look and be like this. When we arrived, no trees were growing on the ancient parish boundary: they had been taken out. A sort of stark, driven, impoverished wreckage of abused grazing and broken-down buildings filled the farm. There was no hedge dividing the Cottage Field from the orchard, nor Jim's Field from Great Flemings, or Beech Meadow from Way Field. No gates worked. The grazing was, in wide pools, so thick with thistles no dog would enter it. Stone walls had been buried in concrete. The whole place – a small dairy farm which had been unable to keep up with the demands of modern life – was crusted in poverty and failure. The big oaks around the farmhouse had been cut down to make way for new corrugated sheds. Ponds had been filled in. The farm had reached a crisis when inspectors found that the milk it was sending out had been diluted with water.

Perch Hill wasn't entirely lovely then, but we thought we could see loveliness in it: in its modesty and ancientness; precisely in its lack of *bien soigné*, silk-lined gravel; in its *echtness* – the word I loved at the time, its sense of being true to itself. The farm may have reached the end of a long road since it was first cut out of the Wealden oakwood in the sixteenth century, and it may have suffered all the abuse of the twentieth-century industrialisation of agriculture, but something supremely valuable seemed detectable beneath all that: the interfolding of human enterprise with the natural world, a beauty whose materials were oak and tile, brick and grass, cuckoos and finches, hay and hay barns, calves and lambs, with the promise of a summer ease whose memory would sustain us in the long soul-clamping, clayey winters.

That sense of implicit, concealed value – and the hope of redemption – was what was alluring here, and in service of that idea we quite deliberately, over two and a half decades, began to change this micro-slice of the world. We wanted to restore its virtues, looking to the old forms, the old hedge lines, the old arrangement of lanes and paths, the old materials, and in doing so have made something that does now seem beautiful: soft, divided, a Wealden farm in the shape Wealden farms are meant to be in, wooded, grassed, butterflied and dragonflied, the Sussex cattle grazing in the low meadows this summer, the sheep on the valley sides above them, the long grass shut up and soon to be made into hay, the cords of ash and hornbeam now lying, drying in the coppices where they were cut for firewood last winter. If a man from the mid-to late-sixteenth century came here now and was led blindfold past the house and yard where the cars are parked, and then walked these twelve fields and modest, slopy woods, the Wealden shaws filled in midsummer with their collapsed, drowned-out bluebells, he would see little difference from the moment he was last here. And he would, I hope, think it good.

But is that right? Quite often, I walk across these lovely fields and think we are faking it. Have we actually returned this farm to itself, or have we dumped ourselves all over it, requiring it to be what we wanted it to be, using those historical cues only in the way someone would do up a bathroom: scrape a beam or two, slap in some tongue-and-groove, get out the Farrow & Ball? The farm, like nearly every small farm in the Kent and Sussex Weald, is no longer providing a family's income. It is essentially a huge garden, mown and fertilised by beautiful conker-red cattle, with the simplest of aesthetics governing its look and pattern: nothing too showy, a kind of looseness in every part, so that nothing seems over-driven, but washed over with an Arcadian contentment that looks disconnected from any hint of getting or spending. This, it says, is a theatre of how things are. Or at least of how things would be if we lived in a good world.

Christopher Lloyd liked to say that a garden, to be its best, should seem as if the owner had died three weeks previously. That is the condition Perch Hill now mimics: not the thistledown chaos it was when we arrived, but in the relaxed form of order called by Renaissance theorists *sprezzatura*: a self-control so deeply absorbed and ingested that there need be no outward sign of it. Just as young men in Veronese frescoes loll in their satins against the pillars of their Palladian halls, so this little Sussex farm, which would never have known anything of the kind, is now being forced into the mould of expensive, laid-back contentment, a fantasy of Horatian beauty imposed by owners who earn their keep in other ways and elsewhere. What a fate: a real farm with real lives, real triumphs and real griefs, subjected to an entirely inauthentic mimicking of the *echt*, a piece of drama founded on the ending of the very life that gave rise to it – driven to the wall, in fact, by the metropolitan culture which is now presiding over the place where it died. Pastoral here erects a theatre over the murder it has just committed.

That isn't the sweetest of thoughts when chewing on the stub-end of a bit of summer grass, lying out in the Way Field watching the deer pause and graze above the sorrel and the buttercups. Sometimes I imagine the speech made by a hard-line landscape historicist to every-thing we have removed: the acres of concrete, the endless corrugated pole-barns, the over-large, over-nitrogenated, brutally productive rye-grass leys in the fields. How true all that was, he would say smilingly and generously, how exactly responsive to the situation those struggling dairy farmers found themselves in. They cut down the oak trees because they needed the sheds for the calves. They trashed the meadows because they needed the milk. They wanted to be as rich as you are. What you have done, Adam, is pure deceit. Landscapes reflect the money that creates them, and your pretensions are all for a kind of visual peasant-hood, a little Transylvanian flower-and-hedges idyll when the source of the cash used to create it is from some distant global capitalist system with its roots and tendrils in Shanghai and Frankfurt. For the last twenty-five years, you have been elaborating a lie.

Mmm. Chew on the grass a little longer. Watch the buzzard flick-cruising over the ash shaw, listen to the jays hawking in the oak wood, follow a jet down on its glide path into Gatwick, wait as the mist gathers in the river valley, look at your phone, take a picture of the pyramidal orchids for Instagram and remember something else, some earlier way of being.

> Almightie and moste merciful father, we have erred and straied from thy waies, lyke lost shepe. We have folowed to much the devyses and desyres of our owne harts. We have offended against thy holy lawes. We have left undone those thinges whiche we ought to have done, and we have done those thinges which we ought not to have done, and there is no health in us: but thou, O Lorde, have mercy upon us, miserable offendours.

That is from the first revision of Cranmer's *Book of the Common Prayer*, added in 1552, almost exactly contemporary with the young farmer who knew these fields when they were first cut from the Wealden forest. Its measured sentences and pointed, rhetorical repetitions, its near rhyming of *devyses* and *desyres*, the yin and yang of human weak-ness – all would have been heard and said every week by everyone who ever lived and worked on this farm. The deep clanging of the undone-done-done-ought-not-have-done bell would have rung through their lives, either in Burwash at St Bartholomew's (the saint, flayed alive, was the patron saint of the graziers, butchers and tanners of the Weald) or at Brightling in St Thomas à Becket, the favourite of the anti-establishment, independent woodcountrymen of the Weald. Over 400 years, after walking or riding back from matins or evensong on the day of rest, those sentences would have echoed in the minds of the Perch Hill people, self-repeating around their long hard days as they ditched and hedged, mowed and stacked, milked and threshed their way through their lives. Done, undone, ought to have done; done, undone, ought to have done: the calendar of a year, or a lifetime. No health in us.

That, maybe, is what this farm sounds like in its heart: a way of thinking a thousand miles from my own pastoral vanities. There is nothing in that of my lightweight ability to drift and pick, to engage and disengage as if nothing much depended on it. Here is the kind of seriousness and embeddedness I see in the mute enquiring eye of a cow as she comes up to me in a summer field, the flies all over her muzzle, the gloss of summer on her flanks, the most wonderful animal intimacy I know as she breathes milky gales all over me, a set of giant grass-fuelled bellows in a forge. Hello, her simple eye says. So you are still here too? We are doing what you have asked us to do, eating the grass, allowing our calves to suckle, being here, getting fat. Is that what it adds up to?

Again and again, in the order of service laid down by the great Tudor archbishop and martyr, the congregation were reminded of their own insignificance. Human beings were not as good as the universe God had made for them. Time and the things of this sublunary earth were their enemy. 'There was never any thing by the wit of man so well devised, or so surely established,' Cranmer told them, 'which (in continuance of time) hath not been corrupted.' This was a world in decline, whose only possible redemption was not in anything material but in the understanding that eternity was neither here nor now. The people were instructed to pray that everything around them should 'speake good of the Lord'. Showers and dew, the winds of God, fire and heat, winter and summer, dews and frosts, frost and cold, ice and snow, nights and days, light and darkness, lightnings and clouds, the earth itself, and all the green things upon it, the wells, the seas and floods, the whales and all that move in the waters, all the fowls of the air, all the beasts and cattle, the children of men, the spirits and souls of the righteous, the holy and humble men of heart: all these huge and potent presences were to join in one grand obeisance to a God for whom, let it not be forgotten, 'all hearts be open, and all desires known and from whom no secrets are hid'.

This landscape of comfort was nothing of the kind: it was a world of terrifying uncertainty overseen by a just-as-terrifying surveillance system. This farm, in other words, was not a landscape of power or sweetness but of humility, even of humiliation; not a place in which a vision of contentment could be casually imposed, but somewhere from which, while a living had to be wrought, nothing but a sense of vulnerability and transience could be absorbed. 'Lay not up for yourselves treasure upon the earth, where the rust and moth doth corrupt and where theves breake through and steale,' Cranmer told them, 'but lay up for yourselves treasure in heaven; where neither rust nor moth doth corrupt, and where theves do not breake through and steale.'

The archbishop, speaking through his parish priest, could not have made the binaries clearer: each half of his sentence was identical except for one simple negative applied to the earth, one simple positive to the world above. Here on this farm was not the place where value was to be found. To attempt to lay it up here was a futility. Cranmer's image of goods laid up, stuffed into the fuggy dark of the farmhouse attic, is as canny as it gets. Precious things pushed up there feel hidden and secure, invisible to man, but just as God is all-seeing and all-knowing, the three forces of destruction Cranmer mentions – the moth, the rust and the thief – are those that know all too well about objects festering in the attic, vulnerable there even as you hoard them, a dark place of cupidity and guilt.

Do you store up treasure in this world? Or do you remember your insignificance? Do you loll in silks? Or restrict the vanities of self-adornment? It is the great choice, the difference over which Englishmen fought a Civil War in the seventeenth century. When Charles I came to his execution in Whitehall in 1649, among the most shocking revelations for Milton and the other Puritans hinged on this difference. The book the King took with him to the scaffold for his last moments on earth was not the Bible but a copy of Philip Sidney's *Arcadia*, a book so relentlessly dedicated to the beauty and entrancement of this life, this world, the beautification of this landscape and the people in it, that heaven or the world to come didn't get a look-in. It was the defining fact for Milton of Charles Stuart's wickedness: he had traded the next world for this.

In that cavalier way, we have dressed up this farm as if it were a slice of perfection. But should we, like good Puritans, have looked beyond worldly décor and understood this life as something of passing and fragile beauty, one over which we as human beings have little or no control? That is the way the Puritan frames the choice: which will you have, hubris or humility? Make it beautiful or serve your time? Self-delusion or self-realisation? Arcadia or significance? Picnics or cosmic reality?

A few years ago, in one part of this farm, our hands were forced. I had always loved one of our smallest fields called Hollow Flemings, tucked down away in one of the small side valleys with which the land is pleated here. Dyers' greenweed grew in the summer grasses and Meadow Brown butterflies used to flitter across it in June and July, pairs of them dancing around themselves as they fled across the hillside in dark, double, guttering flames. It was where I would often go to read and write.

Then, one very wet winter, two things happened. The stream at the foot of the field, gorged with winter rain, started to cut deeply down into its bed. At the same time the springs in the field itself were running hard, lubricating the upper layer of clay in the field. A gap was created at the bottom, a readiness to slide over the whole field, and one morning I found about three acres of Hollow Flemings slipped, a little cliff at the top of it, a tumble of fallen and half-fallen trees at the bottom where the clay was now clogging the stream. Over the next weeks, still more of the land slumped downwards. It was clear that the use of that field was now over. We couldn't mow it or even fence it, and so we let it go. It was no longer any part of the farmed world.

What Wordsworth called 'the calm oblivious tendencies of nature … the silent overgrowings' started to take over Hollow Flemings. Brambles bubbled up into thickets which no deer could enter. Willows were the first to sprout beneath them, followed by the blackthorn and birches. Within a year or two young ash trees were raising their heads above the thorns. Now young oaks, some fifteen feet high, stand around the old landslip, the tips of their branches just beginning to touch. Deer graze in the narrow tongues of grass that persist between the clumps of new woodland. And then, this last spring, two nightingales made the brambly thickets their territories, one at each end of the landslip, sigh-shouting at the night sky for any wives that might be passing.

In one way, that field is ruined; in another it is reaching for a kind of wholeness. If the two earlier versions of this farm are presided over by Cranmer and Sidney, Wordsworth is the king of Hollow Flemings. In the late 1790s, in despair over the collapse of his hopes for the Revolution in France, and filled with guilt over his desertion of the young Frenchwoman who had borne his child, he wrote 'The Ruined Cottage'. It is his first great poem, and the first modern meditation on the relationship between our own ambitions, our failings and the ever-lasting facts of nature. He takes on the voice of a 'wanderer' who looks back to the time when, coming to the abandoned cottage, he had seen wild plants growing where the inhabitants had once cultivated a neat and human order. The wanderer remembered 'that those very plumes, / Those weeds, and the high spear-grass on that wall, / By mist and silent rain-drops silver'd o'er' had seemed not an image of 'what we feel of sorrow and despair / From ruin and from change, and all the grief / The passing shews of being leave behind', but something both far larger and slighter than that: 'an image of tranquillity, / So calm and still', which 'looked so beautiful / Amid the uneasy thoughts which filled my mind', that he turned away from them, from the ruin and from the resurgence of nature, 'And walked along my road in happiness.'

It is the most beautiful recognition that abandonment is not aban-donment, and that there is a third place between the Puritan world of submission and the Arcadian landscape of pleasure. A huge time-perspective floods into this farm in the wake of that understanding. A kind of tranquil everlastingness seems to be here now, a fusion of a worldly Arcadia with a Puritan heaven. We are irrelevant but we are not waiting for death. This place shifts and I shift. We co-evolve. Trees die, buzzards and kites arrive, the thistles, miraculously, retreat, the oak wood reclaims its own. Woods we planted now have to be thinned. New hedges are now old enough to be laid. Chestnut fence posts I remember smelling bitter with tannin when new-cut have now rotted and must be replaced. And I age as the farm cycles through its lives. Time is running through me when I look at these fields, as if I were a watergate in its stream, my bars fixed, the hum and quiver of my life nothing but the pouring of that liquid through me.

ESTUARINE

Sean O'Brien

The sea had gone away round a corner, leaving the huge door open, the hard blue sky taller and the vast khaki-coloured flats in a state of shimmering uncertainty. Pools big enough to swim in waited as noon approached. Surely it wasn't allowed? Streams ran urgently in near-silence on secret errands in the folds of the sand and mud. There seemed to be no directions.

We too were uncertain, left to amuse ourselves without orders, in a place, if that was what it was, that we had never seen before. We found we could hardly speak. The father slept among the dunes by the road, far off, in his white overall, the newspaper over his eyes. His work was done in bringing us here. The rest was up to us. The terrible liberty leaned like a god out of the stopped sun: *well then, well then?*

Somewhere at the back of us, behind the sand and stray wire and the old military road, on the far side of the landspit, the sea could still be found in a different dispensation, a bright breeze skating over the low waves as they marked time against the gravelled shore, carrying it away handful by handful. We had seen the sea for a few moments earlier on our way in. But that was not here, and it was hard to bring persuasively to mind as we knelt at the edge of a pool out on the flats of the estuary, settling without a word to make a dam, though whether to keep the water out or in I no longer know. The younger of the two brothers had a shit nearby, as though it was a point of honour to do so. The long turd was the colour of the mudbank.

All the time we were listening: there was a sound that was not happening – it would be like a warehouse full of ride cymbals being stroked to a tall silver roar, behind which everything else was gathered. It was an education in fear, in awe. The hard light was about to turn into noise. At a loss, we returned to the landspit.

The older brother smirked as we walked back on to the sandy margin. He was a thug and a bully, easily bored. At some point his father would hit him again.

We passed the sleeping father and pushed back inland until we found the airfield. In those days, when people said 'disused airfield', the phrase had something epic to it. These bomber fields had sprung up everywhere after 1939 and just as swiftly turned to phantoms of themselves. Here locked blockhouses sank among rotting sandbags whose contents had turned solid and then gradually blown away. The runway had cracked under the pressure of weeds. The control tower was a wreck, all the windows out. You could get in at the ground floor but no further. To be there was like being implicated in a crime we were too young to understand. No one would tell us the rules.

The older brother was bored. He threw a chunk of brick at the younger, hitting him on the head. We trailed separately back to where the father lay, so that the older brother could be punished. It was done, a formality of rage. Snot ran down the older boy's face on to his Aertex shirt. Time to go.

Somehow it had become a grey-purple evening as we drove back in the Jowett Javelin between the hedgerows on the white roads under mauve clouds. The car seemed to absorb the father's affection. He was a mechanic. To his sons, and to his wife, who looked like Diana Dors, he seemed to be just a formal black-haired Brylcreemed presence in a white overall.

The place we were leaving was part of the unconscious of the city, like the gravel ponds to the north, and the long, nearly immobile open drains that worked in parallel to the streets, weaving their slow brocade of cresses. The zone was bounded by the river, and by the curve of the chalk Wolds rising at the edge of the mud plain that had formed at the last Ice Age. What happened beyond that was someone else's business.

In the great silence on summer days, the air wavered in the heat. Long afterwards I discovered a reason for the peculiar empty quiet of the land (it may be what Larkin has in mind in 'wheat's restless silence'): it is a war grave for those who did not return from the Western Front. A lifetime later, on the way to Little Gidding, I found the same sense of elegiac disquiet in the empty fields on the Cambridge–Northants border, depopulated by plague. We had our own plague pits, in an ancient wood on the western edge of the city. We challenged each other to climb down to the parched forest floor among the twisted hawthorn trees. Risk it, go on.

After the trip to the landspit, that hinterland would be present to the imagination. Sometimes I would come to a blank halt in the back garden and sense what seemed like an alertness, an onlooking. It was present around the foul old drains we fished in by the bridges further down the street, and then further off in the deeper, more purposeful stretches that found their way to the sea or the estuary. When eventually the drains were filled in, the water simply rose to its original level whenever it rained. Water, said the water, this is what water is like. Watch it, smell it, think about it when you're somewhere else. Turn on the tap and hear its ceaseless conversation with itself.

We were always seeking permission to dig holes, to see the water arrive and gaze back at us. The boys' father had forbidden them to dig in the back garden behind their flat in the street of Dutch-fronted houses, but the older brother disobeyed him, and by the end of the day the pair of them had a neat circular pit in the clay, five feet wide and maybe three feet deep. The water had filled it to within inches of the top. The boys studied their handiwork, and the rest of us, who had heard the rumours, came to see what might follow.

For a time I stared into the ochre-yellow water, but what really drew my interest was a rotting tree stump nearby. It seemed to have been torn open. It was full of black insect eggs which no one could identify. The eggs were somehow terrifying, like stuff from outer space. The late-summer afternoon – it was one of those white, oppressive days that seemed peculiar to the city – wore its way onwards to teatime, and nothing happened. We lingered as long as we dared. Only as we trailed away down the street did we hear the shouting start. The father was home; the punishment could begin. That seemed part of the law: you never got to witness the whole thing, the whole story, the reasoning behind the anger and the hoarse cries the old brother made when being belted.

It was a summer that seemed unable to end. We might never get back to school. We sat on the high back wall of someone's garden, looking down into the tenfoot, one of the local concreted back lanes. It ran for half a mile between the rear gates of houses on adjacent avenues. In some sense the tenfoot belonged to us. Few people owned cars and those who did rarely used them. It was the era of the despised 'Sunday driver'. Adults were scarce on the tenfoots. If they appeared there they seemed to be off their proper ground.

Now we gazed down and along. A heavy silence had fallen. In the distance there was a disturbance in the air as if a mirage were forming. It seemed to be coming closer, bringing with it a hushing sound at first so faint as to seem beyond the limits of hearing – an idea of itself, a warning, a promise. Rain. The mirage was a wall of rain advancing steadily up the tenfoot. We watched it come, thrilled and delighted. Twenty yards away, ten feet, arm's length, and then it passed through us or over us, for a moment dividing the front of the skull from the back. I hoped that we and the rain might freeze in this position, evidence of a local, earthly miracle to which we were the only witnesses.

When the front of the rain passed by we dropped down into the garden. We knew without needing to discuss it that the deep trench we had been digging had become useful, as had the disused door we kept on hand for a purpose we had only then discovered. We climbed into the trench and pulled the door over us like the lid of a coffin. Much later I would read of how US soldiers in the Ardennes and Hürtgen Forest in winter 1944 wove nets of branches to protect their foxholes from the treebursts caused by German artillery. Down in our own foxhole under the coffin lid of the old blue door, we were on a permanent military footing. We were at war in the school playground with endlessly replenished armies of Germans and Japanese. Our mission underneath the door was to wait out the bombardment of rain. For some reason the water in that pit did not engulf us from beneath.

There was a breach. The reasons for it were not apparent but I spent much of the next summer in solitary amnsements.

I felt like a castaway on the island of the huge back garden that came with our ground-floor flat. It was a garden that someone had worked on a good deal before the house was divided up. There was a lawn edged by brittle Conference pear trees, with mossy concealed paths and a narrow jungle of elders next to a high wall. Beyond the lawn rose a parterre on which a dry fountain stood between two mature walnut trees, with a vast copper beech and an equally large mulberry tree in the offing. Beyond that lay the orchard. I had never seen anything like this place.

The fountain was obviously important. The fact that it no longer worked was taken as a given. This was the 1950s, when many things didn't work or were unavailable, and when, although rationing had finally been lifted, an austerity of possibility seemed to go unquestioned. Since I had the garden I had nothing to complain about. When I studied the fountain, with its wide drystone bowl like an ashtray full of black leaves, I saw that its pastness was what made it important. The unknown what-had-been underwrote its stillness. I found such places in books, too, in bits of de la Mare's poetry and, somehow, in the late-Victorian Lewisham where E. Nesbit's *The Treasure Seekers* was set. I think it was this place that tilted me in the direction of poetry.

When I first went with my mother to see the flat she was arranging to rent, I was sent out to explore the garden. Its sheer size, and the wooded obscurity of its remote far end, made me afraid. But gradually I acquired the ground and began to undertake some exploratory digging. Tiring of that I entered the large empty garage – this really did feel like trespass – to be dazed by the heat it stored like a battery, and beguiled by the narcotic smells there – turpentine, paraffin, boot polish, rust.

There was more fruit than we or our neighbours could find a use for: apples, pears, cherries, mulberries, gooseberries, redcurrants, black-currants, and the mysterious loganberry which I first encountered there. My father climbed into the Bramley tree and shook it for minutes on end while the fruit thundered down. A neighbour came with a ladder and a wheelbarrow and carted mounds of apples away. Still there was too much. Burrowed by wasps, fruit rotted on the ground, then froze in autumn.

We lived in the house of a suicide, though only much later did I discover this. The owner, a prominent businessman and local councillor who tried to break the General Strike, was disgraced when it turned out that he had been involved in extortion and improper dealings in the acquisition of land for housing estates. He gassed himself in 1932 while under investigation. What I knew as a child was the History Room, the large library in the ground-floor flat. It was panelled, and had stained-glass windows, and a tall wooden fireplace decorated by leering heads of Silenus gazing down as I sat reading by the fire, which was lit when autumn came.

Autumn required the acquisition of fireworks from compliant back-street shopkeepers, followed by an excursion to the Woolsheds. This vast wasteground of pitted asphalt and overgrown bramble bushes and bloodstained dock leaves had served some purpose, but none of us knew what. Though it was open land, this too felt like trespass. We might encounter groups of older boys who would want to fight, but it was worth it to empty all our bangers on the hardstanding by one of the old air-raid shelters and set the black powder alight. It was a military activity, into which the whole landscape was drawn, from the radiator factory to the railway goods line that bounded the Woolsheds on the southern side.

When the fireworks were finished we would squeeze behind a blank advertisement hoarding near the railway bridge, then scramble up the clinkered slope when a train approached. We lay there watching the great wheels grinding out sparks. If we followed this line we would eventually come to the docks, from where the landspit could be imagined, beyond the flares and glittering pipework of the refinery. When we slid out from behind the hoarding, filthy and exhilarated, we would wander the ground until we located the stream that slowly snaked its way southwards before it disappeared into a culvert and continued to some imagined confluence with a larger version of itself, and so on via glimpses at garden ends and from the steps of leaking, mould-white cellars, on to the river whose sudden tides swept over the silver mud. The pull of the water – river, sea, drainage – was irresistible. We knew that in some way we were its creatures, our task to keep wandering there until one day, suddenly, childhood was done with, and the smells of heat and rot and earth and waters, and even the names of our chance companions, were lost to us. We were leaving the flat because my parents could not raise the sum (£2,000 seems tiny nowadays) required to buy the whole huge house when the current owner decided put it on the market.

Nowhere else has ever seemed entirely real in comparison, or as amenable to being discovered and claimed. Many years later I stepped off a train at one of the little local stations. It was unmanned now, its buildings boarded, a new main road cutting it off from the river. But behind the traffic, in the huge sky, there was once more that absence of sound, with the sense of something about to happen, ever-ready. Water, mudflats, earth, grass, rain, an ancient hoarded heat and the long view down to the landspit – all this had waited with patient indifference and now once more required homage.

The Four Wents of
Craster

Dexter Petley

1

In a house called Kia-Ora, the last tenant had left a clothes peg, a
knitting needle and a blue mirror, like a mermaid's moonlight flit. Our
winter let, this fish-box of gutted rooms, flipped by tides upon a rocky
shore, the frost already at the gate. We ate off tea chests, made a bed
of straw, then slept in the window that first night, September 1994, to
watch the sea snarl at us like guard dogs on the end of a rusty chain.

Our first storm threw caution to its winds. We listened to breakers
threshing oil drums from Tyneside, boat sticks, lobster pots, ship's
furniture, a chandler's-worth of rope, telegraph poles, railway sleepers,
whole pine trees lathed of their skins by rolling salt. Next morning,
the horizon was a jagged edge as waves unfurled like ballroom carpets
over the stone pier.

2

October's sun rose on dropped wind, peeled its orange rim off the
world, the North Sea like a Sunday painting, dawn in salt on the
window glaze, frost rind slowly visible on thistle cupulae, the low tide
dubbed over skerry crusts blackened and slippery. The skyte of giant
kelps, sea belts, tangles and furbelows, edges and tips which lipped and
flicked like carp in summer ponds, or rudd at the evening's hatch. No
cold blue winter sky quite yet, only hushed reds stained the yellow of

piss on snow. Stilled white boats rode eight furlongs off Muckle Carr, two perfect swans low-flying south, nailed to the paper sky.

3

Harry next door came across for his coal shovel, overburdened by the news: *A woman's missing, aye,* he said. *Since Sunday.* They'd had to break into her house before, *once ago, aye, overdose or summ't. Her,* he said, *never went near pub.*

Harry, aged seventy-seven, born next door in this house his father had built in 1902 with stone he lugged from the quarry. A long-shore widower, Harry said you could spot the ones who wouldn't go in the pub. Looked like death, they did, when they followed the dog along the sea path. *No good that, keeping it in thyself.* The sea was no friend of Harry's. He'd learned the electrical trade instead of hauling net on his father's herring boat. The only sea in Harry's ears came from a D-Day shell on Omaha Beach, two shattered drums and a face like it saw bodies on every other tide. When I set off after driftwood, pushing Harry's barrow, he had to say it: *Aye, an' yer might find her what's miss'n, washed up wi' the wood if wind shifts t'Sooth.*

A yellow Sea King out of Boulmer hovered half a mile out, tail swinging like a weather vane as the wind shifted east and the sea gouged at rock like a cat biting between its paws. Luxury foam bulged on the tideline, heaped into creeks till a fox of wind set it into a brown flight of sheep, breaking from the fold. Above a rim of crushed horizon-yellow, a black sky screwed down like a fruit press. Gulls bent into crow bars against the brunt.

4

A blurred photograph of the missing woman appeared in the weekly *Gazette.* We'd stowed our lobster pots away for the winter that morning, in the outside bog with the jerry cans and driftwood. The lobsters had moved out into deeper water a week before the first storm. Till then, the inshore gullies had yielded them reluctantly. Half a dozen dogger crabs in a good week, a 14 oz lobster for the bonus. Even Harry had let his bait go to bad, shot with maggots, over-salted. The lorries were out gritting lanes by night. Coach trips filled the village pub some afternoons. Trees were bare, stripped of dead leaves already. The sea tight under bleached candescent suns. The overflow iced solid, drains clogged in frozen hair, puddles like toenails of ice.

She lived alone in one of the coastguard's cottages. Five feet seven inches, brown hair greying at the sides. Nobody knew what she'd been doing when she disappeared, sometime after 10 p.m. on Saturday night. Today the sea was table-flat, red tinged from a sleepless night. A lazy day. You could drop off the horizon, never be seen again on a day like this, one sharp edge of a cube. No shags on the long rock, no gulls on the pier. Glass pools and new shiny furrows caught the sunlight, made a mud sea, white glints like stacked plates, a thousand seagulls following the plough. From our distance, in the low slanting light, we saw a cotton field in the light's trick. In the same way, who dared see anything in the photograph? Perhaps her mother had taken it with a handbag camera, free with five coupons off the soap. She might be standing anywhere, dutiful and featureless. It could be yesterday, or 1950. She might've been her own remains, a face beyond a salted window.

5

The clocks went back. I missed the sunrise. The first day of winter fledged on a calm sea, a bed sheet under yellowing blue sky. The bereavement sea on a sensitivity card; sad, loss-white gulls in gentle soul-shaped flight. Rest in Peace rocks. Ezekiel 36:16 on a paper scroll in the grass, dropped there by a walker.

Night fell at six o' clock now, muffling out the sea, my watch cut short by double glaze, a riot shield, undertaker's glass. Behind drawn curtains, you couldn't guess the sea was there, just fifty yards off. It might have been a brass plaque, on a wall behind the curtain, in memory of the lost, the drowned; or coffin rollers, an incinerator pit, or simply nothing, the bottomless dream itself. Was this how Harry saw it, as the village waited for one of their own to come ashore? You couldn't help but feel a tension seething, tide-like, around the house. I ran from

room to room trying to find its beginning. The cats flew in two directions as I careered into Alice's study. One astonished face beside a
screen, but the cats decided to run with me, and Alice laughed and
joined us. We all ran outside, flattened against the darkness, and there
was Harry in his slippers, mossing out to the coal shed to feed his fire,
one shovel at a time. He saw us pale as moons. *Aye*, he said, *did yer see,
man? They took a body oot the sea this afternoon. The life-boot an' the helicopter.
Aye, tha's aboot reet. They coom up, them bodies, seven o' ten days after.*

6

Once through the swing gate, each passer-by paused below my window.
To wipe dog egg off a shoe, cup hands and light a smoke, drop a tissue,
point a camera. But always, at some point, looking up at the house for
sale behind them. Behind, because they always stood and faced the sea.
'For Sale', only it had been five years on the market. Our landlady and
her aunt had quarrelled over the asking price and the division of spoils.
A dream view in a postcard village, famous for its smoke-house kippers.
A drab and shabby house on private links protected by the National
Trust, behind a padlocked five-bar gate. Roof shot, no insulation,
unheatable, corroded metal windows, cracked pebbledash, a yellow front
door you never opened. Their Kia Ora, our Shangri-la: we had an open
fire in the parlour, straw mattress, no furniture, just boxes and a five-
quid peach-coloured sofa from *Loot* which we'd strapped to the Land
Rover roof and driven home from a thousand-acre housing estate in
Newcastle.

Glen passed my window, a dozen times a day. Duffel coat and
schoolboy hair, ex-hotelier, simplified by a stroke. Sometimes his sister
kept him company, but she preferred to walk the dog alone, a chapel
spinster, waxed jacket, tartan skirt, marching by like her life's task was
to ring the Inchcape Bell. Once, they stopped together out front. She
took Glen's comb from his duffel-coat pocket and ran it through his
hair as he made a suffering face for me to see. Glen waved up at me
each time he passed. Sometimes he'd wave at a blank window, or it was
so salty he didn't know if we were in, or which room he should wave

at. If it was cold outside, he made exaggerated semaphore just to let us know, rotating arms which hugged and strummed his flanks. He had a word for everyone he passed, usually about his stroke six years ago, how stopping work and taking the sea air had saved his life.

A widower collected driftwood in a handyman's cart with pram wheels. *Took it bad, him*, Harry said. *Dooz'n' mix, avoids pub, he.* I watched him push his bodge at dusk like it was his wife's hearse. Black cap tight and low, looked neither right nor left. As darkness took over, the sea sounded like a city at night, hum-visible through the deaf glass, when all these widowers must have wondered, more than once, if jumping in would make it stop.

7

On 5 November, a fog rolled in from Forties, Tyne and Dogger, screening sea from house. There was nothing in the paper about a body. The day was warm but from the east. They said, according to Harry, that the cold was there, in front. You could see them coming, the calm, cold days; slow bulks on the horizon, the seagulls all at sea. Harry said a Polish trawler ran aground once. The whole commie crew legged it across the fields in the dark, were never heard of again. The villagers looted the boat. It broke free and sank, but the captain's chair washed up below the house and Harry nabbed it, stuck it by his hearth. *Come through*, he said, *I'll show it yer if yer not busy. Kettle's on.*

It was in the *Gazette* the following Friday.

MISSING WOMAN'S BODY IS WASHED UP

... on a County Durham beach. Jennifer Pauline Jobling, aged 47, was last seen on Saturday 16 Oct in the village of Craster ...

She'd gone a long way, staying with the tide as far as Seaham. The tide ran south and today the wind pushed against it. The body Harry saw had been a practice dummy. I watched a sheet of white board skit along a wind-lane, following the course taken by the lobster boat. At one point it lifted clear and somersaulted corner-to-corner for 200 yards.

The low tide ruffed white over slippery rocks covered in truncheons of seaweed stem, its own push no match for the wind.

8

Scant timber washed up in a north-east wind, none at all in a westerly. The signboard from the castle came ashore below the house. Someone must have sawn it clean through, then dragged it 200 yards to the cliff edge and toppled it over into the sea fifty feet below. Some boat sticks came in, split middles discarded in the harbour after a hard launch just across the way. The puddle at our gate enlarged, dug out by nobbled treads on the farmer's pick-up. He dropped bales twice a day for the sheep, counting his raddled ewes. The grazing hardened. Dead crisp packets whipped against the fence and into the sea. The sheep went far and wide, beyond the headland, rarely near the house now the grass was yellow. Shags deserted the shoreline, keeping to the Carrs at low tide. Anglers' lanterns burned all night now the codling were inshore and taking peeler crab. Oystercatchers bradawled the inland mud for lobworms, running all the way in pairs. These were dark mornings and we rose before the sun now. I'd drop Alice at the station in the dark, an early train to Newcastle. Two calm hours of flat sea before a red sun became lost in the drizzle of grey sacking clouds. Mid-morning, a wind drove them back to harbour and the horizon was a dark, indigo bar.

9

The day of her funeral was *Dreadnought*-grey. Coasters on the horizon, some bright red and blue, the sea at rock-face like washing suds, Christmas emptiness about the grass and muds, the puddle a broken side window, single shatterings too thick to prize out, its ridge-backs frozen in. The village had been invited to 'open house' at Keeper's Cottage, the incumbent widow's sixtieth birthday. Two women in black were there, up for the funeral of Jenny Jobling, her last hours served with port and sloe gin. She'd gone to Lesbury to talk to the vicar, left him at seven-thirty, walked the seven miles home, in the dark through cold wind and rain, then jumped into the sea below her cottage. The

New Year, still weeks away, was already poised to grow over this bare patch of time.

10

A shower of frozen salt-grit pecking on the window woke us Christmas Day. It turned to snow, powdered the mud. A robin stabbed at the cat food. Harry said: *The postman delivered her cards, man.* Whose cards? *Her, her what come oot the sea.* The snow passed like a Christmas wedding. New Year's Day slammed gates, rained in your eye and made side flares of your trousers. On the Hough, a wind to slit the dead woman's cards open.

11

Eastern snow, yellow January skies mid-morning, till on a white foam sea waves looked like mountain ranges, foam and snow tumbling off walls, sleet driven horizontal, gulls frenzied along the spume line. The cat watched ice run down the window, his paw always tentatively drawn. He preferred to configure it thoughtfully before touching the glass and failing to connect with what he didn't recognise. Like it was his first invention, he'd never seen snow before. Likewise, the sea was just a noise in our eyes. The cat might see in the dark, but like me he couldn't see through a blizzard.

The full moon held steady in a gale, high over the puddle first, the puddle water running like roach fry fleeing a pike, darker when the wind lulled, silver-swiped when the gale dived across it. The sea stretched silver like the puddle. I could see the horizon at midnight. Ships passed through it. I could see a coaster's rivets a league offshore. You could follow gusts for a hundred yards. The sea became the moon. I could jump into the moon. I cut the picture of dead Jenny Jobling from the *Gazette* and stuck it to the wet window.

12

In February, the rough sea was like a great slice of veined fat. The 'For Sale' sign disappeared one night, the gate blown flat off its hinges, face down in the mud. The game that afternoon was to kick the football off the cliff edge, into the gale, then watch it snatched back and fly by, spinning uphill behind us for a hundred yards. Just putting a hat on knocked your teeth out. A wind to split the cat in half, the salt skinned your face, our knees trembled. It took two to shut the door or fetch the coal, and walking with the storm behind was like being under arrest, frog-marched into a whirlwind. And in the night, again, we heard fragments of the village join the corrugated roof of the woodshed to escape over the fields like Polish mariners as waves pounded across the village.

In the clean-up days, we joined the wader count, collecting bodies for the ranger, counting guillemots and razorbills, washed up in their emaciated thousands. We stacked them into the fish boxes which had come ashore with them, and as we did so we heard the bleet of lambs below the Hough on the westerly, a spring wind, and saw a fox passing in a quandary. The curlews walked from rock to rock again, the west wind blew the sea flat, sounding like the all-clear after an air raid. A school of dolphins jammed the wind lane off the Carrs, rolling in pairs, wearing the new sea on their backs. Driftwood burned blue from the drying salt.

13

The first day of spring, and Harry had one bad night in every two. He said the daffodils wouldn't appear till it was summer everywhere else. The wind blew off the land now, making desert waves, mackerel-backs of sea. It threw vapour like smoke in shots across the surface, and the sun cast milky rainbows, colours flashing as they moved. The plughole gurgled constantly.

Dunstanburgh Castle re-opened. *National Toast*, as Harry called it. It was a human world again. The visitors returned, as if from hibernation, still unsteady on their feet. The first weekend a woman with blood on her hands ran to our front door. Her son had slipped on the rocks. An hour later, another woman ran through the gate shouting for help, past our house, away along the sea path towards three people half a mile away.

Then one mild afternoon a third woman ran, this time from the castle. As she passed my window, her face was hard and white and grim. She returned in a car, with the castle keeper's wife, behind a four-wheel-drive ambulance, and you could tell by the lack of urgency. Two lads, laying their lobster pots off the rocks for the first time that year, stood and watched it all the way. In the yard, Harry and I stood side by side. Harry said the salmon were running close, up along the gullies. He wouldn't mind betting there'd be a net or two going out the night. Then the ambulance returned and he shut up. John the keeper was already dead, a man I waved to as he passed each morning, walking the mile and a half to the castle, swinging one of the sticks he carved himself, his jacket freshly waxed, his trout bag with its flask of tea and sandwiches.

14

Next day, canoeists were driven back into harbour by a shift in the wind. Lambs huddled in the lushest grass. A cold wind, still vicious enough to slash open weak shirt collars and race up ungloved cuffs. The foam remained unspent.

On Easter Saturday, the farmer sprayed nitrogen pellets over two women pushing babies. No driftwood on the spring tide, yachts instead of coasters, fox droppings of bunny fur, radishes pushing through. Harry buried his onion sets, pushed deep or have them blacken in the wind. This was no renewal. A stillborn, shrivelled month, the long struggle into a short cold summer. Harry faced his seventy-eighth year in the same window. I was forty and the novel was dust. Alice had finished her dissertation. Then a man with a cold knocked on the back door. He said he was a writer too, had watched me typing in the window several times in winter. I said I'd kept his seat warm, when he said he'd come to buy the house.

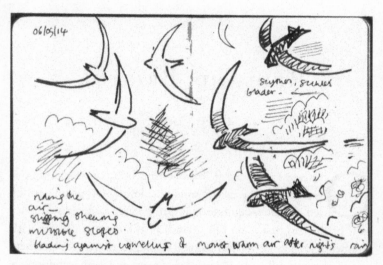

swifts arrival sketched from the allotment, early may

peacock butterfly, brambles & thistle, june

common-spotted orchid & yellow rattle, late may

Redland, Bristol

Greg Poole

Our house is on one of Bristol's many hills. Looking down our road, if it was a river it would be flowing fast north-east. Its left 'shore' rises quite steeply facing south-east, and so catches most of the sun that is on offer. Much of the slope is covered with allotments. Despite all the horticultural digging, between the plots there are still plenty of yellow meadow-ant nest mounds. Green woodpeckers furtively probe the anthills with dibber bills and long ant-licking tongues. They leave behind droppings that look like cigarette ash from a tightly packed roll-up. Walk to the top of the slope and you get a great view over the city.

I moved back to Bristol in 2004 to live with my partner, Susan. With much effort we destroyed the old Anderson bomb shelter at the end of the garden and erected my printmaking studio in its place. Around the same time we started to cultivate the allotment which is just the other side of the back gate. I was a novice gardener, and treated the project of clearing what was something of a wasteland more as groundwork than gardening. I made a series of stepped beds using boards hauled from skips, copying the approach that has been adopted all over the allotments.

One part of the allotment escaped my pickaxe-and-shovel approach. There was an area of lawn about the same footprint as my studio, about 4 x 4 metres, and we weren't really sure who it belonged to. Our allotment neighbour used to mow it; another neighbour would occasionally picnic on the lawn with his young children. Both moved away, and I carried on the mowing tradition. Then in 2012 I noticed the purple blotched basal leaves of two common spotted orchids. Although not rare plants they seemed 'wild' in this tamed terrain, and got me really excited. If there were orchids there, what else might grow? I asked the council allotment manager if it would be OK to cultivate this area as a wildflower meadow, and got the permission to go ahead.

In the autumn of that year I mowed 'the meadow' as close to the ground as I could, raked it vigorously, then sowed yellow rattle seed onto what was pretty well-scalped ground. The rattle is well known as a parasite on the roots of the coarser, more vigorous grasses, suppressing them and consequently allowing space for slower-growing, less thuggish species to move in. So in spring 2013 I watched anxiously to see if the rattle would come up. Because the spring was so cold it was very slow to appear, but by the end of March there were lots of seedlings. The rattle has a distinctive leaf even when first sprouting. It has tiny round teeth, and the segments between veins are cushioned like a more succulent plant. Lots of their seed lies on the surface right through the winter, and more recently I've been able to see their tawny, ravioli seed pods break open and the first white filament of a root come snaking out, coated with minuscule hairs. It took more strongly in some areas than in others. An area near the orchid leaves was reduced to a mat that already looked more like downland, a bed of clover hosted a jungle of rattle. It did what it was supposed to, leaving a lot more open areas and reducing the crowding effect of the coarser grasses.

The square of turf morphs through the growing season. Through the winter it could pass for poorly maintained lawn and is a lumpy 'flat' space. By the end of March the surge has begun, the green flowering tide is rising. 'High water' is reached somewhere around early June, and the level is up by over a metre. The raised 'surface' is a shifting cloud of delicate grass heads and flower forms. Up to the high-water mark there is a tendency for the flowers to be in the yellow spectrum (rattle, trefoil, daisies, dandelions), which then spills gradually into magentas and purples (orchids, thyme, knapweed, scabious, self-heal).

One of the effects (symptoms) of cultivating the mini-meadow has been hours of staring at 'lawn', gradually learning to identify the basal leaves of each species. Sketching has helped with this. In that first rattle spring I noticed more tiny orchid leaves (up to fifteen so far), minuscule and without spots, but clearly orchids. At first I wondered if they might be a different species of orchid. After hunting for ages in books and online the best description I found of the common spotted orchid's lifecycle was in the seed catalogue. It produces dust-like seeds which need to come into contact with a particular fungus soon after germination to help them get nutrition. The pair then live underground together in a symbiotic relationship for two or three years. So my little unspotted leaves were the first showing above ground of a process that is already two years minimum in the making. Despite my best efforts most of those little leaves got grazed off by slugs. Just one of these 'new' orchids has produced a flower spike (it has now flowered for three successive years). The new one is a much more delicate affair than the beefy mature specimens. So it seems you might be able to age orchid spikes? I'm hoping that despite the slug casualties the others are fortifying themselves under the soil, and that one year there will be a mass flowering.

At the same time as sowing the rattle I'd bought varieties of wild-flower seeds that corresponded to species I see locally on similar terrain. With more patience I could have just waited to see what emerged, but I greedily wanted an instant mini-meadow covered with ant mounds along with the plants that I associate with them. Thyme, ladies' bedstraw and above all bird's-foot trefoil.

Oddly, four years on, although I've learned more patience and realised that things take their time, I've also realised that some species are quite easy to proliferate. Cut off a 'branch' of bird's-foot trefoil with a promising bit of root, poke it into the ground a bit further along, and it will usually take pretty well. It is a hardy, deep-rooted plant. It is also easy to snip off a bit of thyme, a section that has little rootlets on the underside of its creeping stems, poke it into the top of an anthill, and four times out of five it will take. With these successes I started to feel more of a connection with the plants.

The bird's-foot trefoil was abundant by 2015. I took out all those boards that I'd used to hold up the banks and planted the sloping soil with trefoil, thyme, rock rose, etc., to stop the banks collapsing. I figured that anywhere a mower couldn't go I would try to make a wildflower bank. I was cultivating flora and insects instead of slugs and snails (which used to hide behind the boards).

One of the first gratifying effects of the burgeoning flora was seeing Common Blue butterflies egg-laying on the bird's-foot trefoil, their main food plant. Before the arrival of the trefoil, we would see the occasional blue, but they would be transient. This year (2016) I started to be able to identify them individually. I was hoping that there would be swarms of them, but in fact only around ten appeared. They vary quite a bit in colour, from a thin sky blue to something with more violet in the mix. After only a day or so they get nicks or rents in their wings and are pretty easy to get to know on first-name terms. Cookie-cut left hindwing, Rip-right forewing, etc. Knowing them in that way meant I could tell how short their lives as an adult were. None lasted over two weeks, and I only saw two females. I didn't witness any mating or egg-laying, but saw much feeding and basking on the bird's-foot trefoil. Small Coppers are still passers-by, and I haven't managed to get their food plant, common sorrel, to grow as yet.

Small Skippers have been around from the start. According to the great Jeremy Thomas and Richard Lewington guidebook they lay their eggs in the stems of Yorkshire fog grass, and the caterpillar spends the winter in a cocoon inside the stem. To reduce the fertility of the ground I mow the meadow in late summer and remove the grass. Unless those skipper caterpillars are very low down in the grass stems then I'll be removing them too. So far small skippers keep materialising in June, but I'm not quite sure how. Each butterfly species has its favourite food plant, and they vary a lot in their strategies for getting through the winter. One will exist as an egg, another as a caterpillar buried in the soil (I think Common Blue is one of those), some as a chrysalis and a few as hibernating adults. It's hard to get a handle on which needs what to make it through the bleaker months.

There is potential for conflict having a wildflower meadow on an allotment. Some of the veg growers might see the meadow as a weed breeding-ground. One plant that really gets people going is common ragwort, with its reputation of being poisonous to livestock and children. There aren't any livestock up there, and children are really unlikely to graze on ragwort (apparently it would take huge amounts to do any damage), but the plant still has a bad name. Lots of the insects that are mentioned here seem to love to feed or rest on ragwort flowers (sucking up nectar), and with a slight mind shift they are a really handsome spike of flowers. To strike some kind of political middle ground I now hoik them out as they start to seed.

One insect that does more than suck ragwort's nectar is the Cinnabar moth. A bold red-and-black fluttering in the meadow is likely to equal Cinnabar moth. Vivid red bars run along the leading edge of the satin black forewings, the almost completely red hindwings are tucked away on landing. Its caterpillars are banded yellow and black and decimate ragwort leaves, leaving behind just a bare stalk. Since leaving the ragwort to flower on the meadow I see more Cinnabar moths each year. Perhaps there is an optimal balance between Cinnabar moth and ragwort numbers, and in due course maybe there will be enough moths to keep the weed bashers happy.

Before studying this scrap of 'meadow' so intently I'd never learned to distinguish between species of bumblebee. There is a great app available for phone and tablet, and by using that it wasn't long before I could identify six common bee species on the allotment. Buff-tailed, Common Carder, Early, Garden, Red-tailed and Tree. Amazing how things that were once a generic 'bumblebee' can become distinct characters with a very particular identity. Garden and Buff-tailed for example: both black with yellow and white stripes. At first I would distinguish them with a kind of bar-code mentality, but then, with more watching, they start to seem very different creatures. The Garden bumblebee moves faster, and is smaller and blacker. Black bear to the Buff-tailed grizzly, I think its yellow is less warm too. The app tells you about head shape and tongue length, which I thought must be for identifying captured specimens. Then one day I realised that I could see the tongue of the Garden bumblebee hanging down as it flew from one rattle flower to another. The Buff-tailed visiting the same rattle flower is lumbering in comparison to the nimble Garden. It weighs down the whole flower and, because it hasn't got a long tongue, it has to go round the back of the flower and bite a hole to get access to the nectar. Common Carder (more of a ginger, striped affair) and Garden were by far the commonest feeders on the rattle.

When I'm up there digging, sketching or in turf-watch trance it is very handy to have the equivalent of guard dogs to alert me to any birds of prey that may pass overhead. The local herring gulls pursue any passing raptor, making a persistent mewing alarm call. They go particularly nuts for osprey or heron. So twice in early April I've been alerted to osprey heading north. Usually it is only the commoner species, buzzard or sparrowhawk, but several times they have chased red kites (who have almost always been drifting due east). Just once while watching newly arrived swifts moving ahead of a band of rain I saw a hobby following along.

The micro meadow isn't really big enough to give a home to larger creatures, but both foxes and badgers pass through. The foxes occasionally bask in a sunny spot, or on frosty winter nights I hear their mating calls from the studio. We rarely see the badgers, but they leave their mark. When the meadow flora is at high tide some large creature goes rolling around, flattening swathes of it. I'm pretty sure it must be baby badgers. I've just once seen the youngsters chasing each other around our vegetable beds at dusk.

A few years ago I bought a bat detector. This converts the high-pitched calls of bats to a much lower frequency, easier for us humans to hear. We had regularly seen tiny pipistrelles hawking for insects. I think having the detector forced me to pay more attention and it wasn't long before I noticed a larger species of bat. It looked a bit like a snipe doing its display flight. I traced its path through the binoculars held in one hand while pointing the detector with the other. The funky, lip-smacking sound coming from the detector was like a soundtrack to my demented pitching and rolling trying to keep up with the bat flight. When I checked on its identity, the frequency and lip-smacking quality were enough to identify it as Leisler's bat, the UK's second largest species.

The bat detector also came in handy for locating and identifying grasshoppers and crickets. Fairly annoying for anyone else in the vicinity, it sounds like cranked-up static on a CB radio. Each orthopteran species has its own distinctive calling pattern, and many are at quite different frequencies. The one that really dominated the airwaves on my first excursions was the long-winged conehead. It sounds like a helicopter coming into land, and drowns out the more gentle sounds of meadow and field grasshoppers. The coneheads prefer ranker grass and they are difficult to spot, but by moving the speaker around I could gradually home in on them. Long-winged conehead is rapidly extending its range, and has probably only been in these parts for ten years or so. Now there seem to be huge numbers of them.

Years ago I had a phase of painting up sheets of coloured paper for making collage. After painting lots of sheets in tints of red, to then go out and see a post box was like some kind of electric shock for the eyes. I was reminded of this with my recent studies of the individual Common Blues. After an afternoon squinting through close-focus binoculars (Pentax Papilios) at the Blues I then went out jogging in the local parkland that borders the Avon Gorge. I'd read on an interpretation board that there were both Small and Chalkhill blue colonies around the gorge. I couldn't quite believe it – these are scarce species, and this is only a mile or so from home. In hope I took a detour from my run, Papilios in hand, and went looking near the interpretation board, which seemed as likely a place as anywhere. There, resting on a woolly kidney vetch flower head, was a paler blue butterfly. The spotting on the underside was radically different from 'my' Common Blues. The creature is actually minuscule, but these spots looked huge, and then it opened its wings and the soft, celestial 'Chalkhill' blue nearly took my head off.

There is a sense of the Incredible Shrinking Man about all this study of the plot. Insects are the worst for bringing out the nerd in me. This year I've bought a guide to the 270 species of British bees, and another for a similar number of hoverflies. A whole range of previously unnoticed or unidentified species are now revealing themselves. Just for starters there have been Nomad and Mason bees, and a Leafcutter bee made its nest in the door lock of my studio.

Part of the value of cultivating the mini meadow has been getting to know individual species more intimately, their annual cycles and how they change their appearance with time. The sustained close observation of the inhabitants leads to a sensitisation that has made a trip into the wider countryside a heightened experience.

long-winged conehead, September

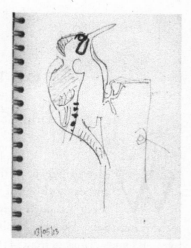

green woodpecker yaffling from
lookout post

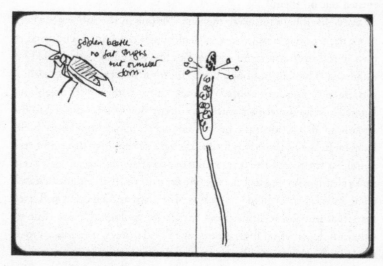

flower beetle and plantain, june

About Time

Fiona Sampson

We live halfway up a valley. The stream that made it is small and easily dammed – by a wooden fruit crate, a dead sheep – though after heavy rain it can fill the lane and make it impassable for cars. The banks are is lined with oak and ash trees, and immediately in front of our gate there's a tall perry pear. The valley is narrow enough to feel deeper than it is; its fields are steep, but such good grazing that it's mostly cattle rather than sheep that are turned out on them.

We've lived here for three months. No one in the valley goes back more than a couple of generations, although the family who used to own it still lives and farms locally. But the place has been settled for millennia. The faint fold of a bank rings our hill, trace of the earliest settlement. The stone-lined runnels into which our neighbour Russell's cattle sometimes stumble, coming down heavy-footed to the stream to drink, are said by the county's archaeology team to be Roman. In Saxon times this ford at the valley's shoulder also supported a mill. At the top of the lane, a mile or so further upstream, is a pond that's clearly man-made. Like the one set next to an abandoned church a few miles west of here – which is obviously, and creepily, still used for ritual purposes – this pond makes no geological sense. But its situation does: set on high ground with wide views, it marks a cross-roads leading to four villages.

Today, unusually, the wind's from the south. It blows up the valley, stirring the trees with a rushing roar that's echoed by tractors harvesting the maize just over the ridge. In the autumn brightness every leaf and blade of grass, and every sound, has a dazzling clarity.

It's hard to talk about living in such a new place. Nothing here yet casts what I picture as a sort of shadow, the perspective knowledge we rely on (without realising we do) to give our experience order, or depth. Things here are overwhelmingly themselves; they aren't backlit by having been repeated over and over. I had no idea how important this kind of repetition was until we moved here. Then I found that all the connectedness of my daily life had suddenly stopped: no more wind off the Severn. No glare across the fields at dusk. No more hearing the stream behind the elder hedge.

I'd lived in our old home for seventeen years. It was time to move. Still, seventeen years turns out to be a stretch: long enough, anyway, to have been paradoxically foreshortened by the repetition that came from living it. In the old house, what was happening in any given *now* had begun to collapse into a sequence of all the other times it happened, and often I could no longer separate individual events – or even days, weeks or months – from each other. This was true above all of annual occurrences, like raising the beanpoles or picking sloes, the first pipistrelle that jinks around the eaves on a spring evening (it turns out that we have them here, too) or the first cry of a returning lapwing, faint and electric in a March wind. Such moments felt both new and old, fresh and familiar. But it became true also of daily repetitions: walking the dog on the back track past the Dutch barns. Blackbirds' alarm calls at dusk.

Here, by contrast, both past and future have disappeared. In a way, moving to the valley is a return to childhood. I don't know what tomorrow will be like, or the winter. I don't know the order in which the orchard trees will turn yellow. I've no idea where the footpaths will become slippery in autumn. I don't know where smoke lingers and where it drifts, nor which fields drain where onto our lane.

Because we're living in a place whose routines and repetitions are new to us, we take notice of them in new ways. Last week the beef herd that browses the big front field at Kilforge got separated. One afternoon we noticed Alan at work, loading the weaners into his lorry.

After weeks of being fattened together on summer grazing, the young were being taken away from their mothers. I've seen this separation innumerable times before but only with sheep, never cattle. So I was taken completely by surprise when, at dusk, the valley echoed with groans, shouts and howls, the herd sounding as if it were about to break through the hedges, each beast gone as mad and dangerous as her size warranted. The bellowing went on all night, haunting and distorting our dreams. Maybe cattle don't understand that they're being farmed: perhaps it's true that they don't recognise the abattoir. But with the loss of their calves a contagion of grief – whether or not it was truly realisation, whether or not just some kind of mood – passed violently to and fro on the hills above us.

From the top of our own hill the calves had looked oddly immaculate. I used to imagine I could pick one up between my thumb and forefinger, like a piece from a toy farm. It's already become one of our daily pleasures to watch the herd of pale, pinkish-white Charolais on the slope opposite. They've worn three red paths, ringing the field above the valley trees at nearly regular intervals like contour lines on an OS map. Whenever I look up – as now – the cows are there, pacing vaguely along and all of them heading in the same direction as each other.

Why is this dreamy kind of repetition so comforting? It almost feels as though, if you knew a place well enough, it could shelter you from time. Living here, I'm learning that old buildings – houses, barns – old chairs and tables and even tools (a second-hand spade, the shears my parents bought when they set up home together) do this too, creating a kind of shortcut into repetition. As I move around this house it comforts me to know I'm repeating gestures that have been made here over and over by generations of unknown predecessors.

Sometimes the landing window stands open at evening, letting in the changing light and particular noises. If I forget whatever it is I was meaning to do and pause to watch dusk fill the orchard, I know I'm doing so in the very spot where those earlier inhabitants stood. When what I can see contracts, first to the near trees and at last to the stumpy damson nearest the house, I know it contracted for them too. Like them, I hear the birds run through their alarm calls – blackbirds on the wing with their clockwork *chakachakachaka*, pheasants cocking up one after the other all the way down the valley – then gradually quieten. Like them, I hear that pause as a last aftershock of the evening chorus.

Living in a place means letting it carry you forward. *Habitat* seems a good word for this. It suggests living going on, rather than our *doing* living. A few nights after they lost their calves, the cows were roaring again. This time another kind of estrangement – or perhaps it was simple astonishment – set them off. After its week of practice runs, the full harvest moon had risen at the end of the valley, on and up over Ballingham Hill. It was swollen and yellow with harvest dust, and it filled our roof light like a beacon.

I got out of bed and went to the window. The herd, crisply visible on the hill opposite, were grey-white silhouettes in a grey-white field. As I watched, first one cow and then another stretched her neck to groan, and really it seemed to sing. Calling to the moon, each became a long-necked, implausible beast. The singing cows, ardent and off-balance, were surely monsters out of somebody's dream. But not yet, I thought with a kind of surprise, out of mine.

Moonlight has a strangely affectless quality – I can't think of any better way to describe this than humourlessness – something it shares with fluorescent light. I was still watching the cattle from our attic window when I noticed that we were all facing downstream together, as if in some bizarre congregation. When the first cow on the ridge raised her muzzle and thrust forward her lower jaw in a trumpet of astonishment, I could even feel as if, for want of a more accurate way of putting it, I agreed with her. Of course, even in my own dazed, nocturnal state I didn't imagine the cattle were having thoughts like *congregation* or *downstream*. But I did feel as though I was thinking like them. It seems my old mammal self isn't so very evolved after all. For what could I do but feel a burst of moon-madness, the kind of longing that resembles nothing in the world so much as a roaring cow?

I let down the blind and got back into bed. *Finished?* asked P. sleepily. As if *I* were the trumpeter on the hilltop; as if I *had* been unable to keep my feelings to myself. *All done,* I said, and he rolled over and was asleep again.

But I didn't find it easy to fall sleep. Perhaps I was *not* all done. The moonlight deposited its large white squares on the ceiling. Just beyond the triple glass of the roof light, the night was still busy. The barn owl from Justin and Caroline's place was making desultory conversation in the wood. There was the occasional *whoop!* of a tawny owl. Closer at hand, the nightjar skirred away so loudly that I almost thought he was perched on the roof ridge itself.

He's probably halfway to Africa by now. But the thought of him makes me smile, reminding me as it does how panicked I was the time I first heard that uncanny call. We were sleeping out in the old garden, which lay among Oxfordshire water meadows. (At the time, I didn't think of this as eccentric.) I was woken by a strange flutter-tonguing, a sound unlike any bird song I knew. It kept moving round and around us, low to the ground, until at last it entered my dream-fugue – as alien landing craft.

So the other night, when P. began to snore, I slipped out of bed again, restless and eager for more, even if not quite to be scared. I opened a window, shifted a cushion onto the sill and swung my feet up beside me. As I looked out once more across the little valley, I wondered again who else had done this before me, and whether they too were sometimes unable to sleep and would get up to spy on the night valley and its inhabitants.

Now I saw that the herd on the Kilforge acreage had begun to move. Slowly, as befitted their size, Alan's giantesses were drifting once again towards Ballingham. Here and there one or two paused to lift a head and give a last, thoughtful bellow. Mostly they had fallen silent. They slowed, grazed, and moved on, according to their own mysterious logic: just as they're doing this morning, up there once again.

THE PLASH

Adam Thorpe

Everything could be seen down there, right to the bottomless depths. Even your face was visible until you withdrew it, distorted like an astronaut's pulled down by the G-force of the launch. It was a place of wonder, in full colour, tinted gold by autumn. It was generally in autumn that this far more perfect world came into view, and sometimes in spring. In winter it was hidden by solid ice that my stamps of Tuf heel (with built-in compass) could barely crack.

The ensuing Arctic thaw brought danger. Setting out over the creaking wastes, I had nothing to hold on to – just balance and pluck. There'd be the sound of a latch dropping, and the trapdoor would tip in a single solid piece, icy water lapping over one edge, the other lifting a few inches free from brown tufts of couch grass. 'Oh no,' I would shout to my invisible companion, the nameless essence of loyalty, 'I think I'm a goner!'

Smashing the frozen seas with my heel was like the punching-in of a window: it was associated with theft. I felt a certain regret. That the ice had survived the passage of tractors or the odd Land Rover was already a miracle. Few vehicles came this way. After all, the only reason to turn off White Hill onto the track was to go to the farm. Steeper than any road I knew, White Hill started in the market town of Chesham, with its pet shop and toy shop and the Embassy cinema and the family optician's where my mother worked as a receptionist. The town still felt rural fifty years ago, yet it was directly connected to London's heart, being the furthest stop on the Metropolitan Line. Puffing back up the hill took you to our row of houses at the top, just a minute or so further than the sign which said, TO DUNGROVE FARM.

The track was pot-holed. My adventuring seas were a mundane puddle. 'Puddle' sounds diminutive, too like 'piddle': the language lacks a word for something bigger, unless we revive 'plash'. My plash filled the chasm of an exaggerated rut. It lay several hundred yards along the track, just where the latter curved to the right: the farm was visible on the low crest. To the left was a stile half buried in the verge, leading through arable fields along a footpath that eventually, after two unpeopled miles of the rolling Chilterns, came to my Sunday school, little St George's church and, more importantly, the Five Bells pub. My parents would have their ritual Sunday pint there after the service. My sister and I, banned from the interior, would play in a beech copse across thick pasture until a shout from the far-off stile would drag us back to the stuffy little Simca, now smelling of beer and tobacco.

I never went into the farm. The courtyard made me nervous: it was eerily silent, although it was a working place with cows and arable, exhaling urinous suggestions of manure. I didn't know at the time that it was farmed centuries earlier by Thomas Harding, one of the last Lollards condemned to the stake. His chief crime was to insist that the Bible should be rendered into the native tongue. He was executed almost within sight of Dungrove, halfway up White Hill, in 1532. Spared the agony of the flames by an onlooker who knocked his brains out with a faggot, he is remembered these days with a carved stone marking the spot. In similar vein, perhaps, our path to Sunday school is now part of a Heritage Trail.

Water attracts boats. Haphazard dinghies of leaves; tree-bark galleons with salty crews. Sometimes I press-ganged ants, or ladybirds who would flee the deck by air. My brother, eight years older than me, would come along now and again and fashion me a sail from a leaf and a mast from a twig, adept with his penknife. It would generally keel over at the first breath of a breeze. Rafts were more successful – twigs lashed together with wiry stems – but they lacked romance unless my laser imagination etched a castaway waving his shirt. His vessel was not much bigger than a king-size postage stamp.

The flinty contours were the outlines found on a seafaring map: they included the odd island and various harbours. Amazingly, I never acted God and adjusted the coast. Heroic journeys were started. Reefs were washed by tropical seas. I was often alone because, perhaps mistakenly, I felt my intense fantasies would be diluted by sharing them with a friend, who'd drag me back to a world of beehive hairdos and the Beatles thrumming from the tranny in the kitchen. At times a blue sky threw a squall of glitter over the surface: puddle as Mediterranean glamour. At others I sensed the infinity of space the wrong way up, small clouds slipping between, birds become fish. I stared into a giant lens.

Its position on a bend meant that it was maintained over and over by the wheels that took the curve leaning in, exerting more force on one side, the increased weight gouging the seabed minutely deeper. Perhaps only some ten years earlier the wheels would still have been wooden and iron-rimmed, accompanied by punching hooves. No repairs were ever carried out: no gravel, no bitumen, no sludge of builder's sand or crushed bathroom tiles. It was understood that the defect was perma-nent. I was fascinated by this persistence because I feared that any day now the track would be spread with the ultimate tedium of tarmac, like a blank screen. But the track remained unmetalled. The gash in it was timeless, in a way. It might well have been there since the Tudor era of Thomas Harding – or even earlier. Stubborn and refractory, it would have been familiar to the farmworkers in the wagon or the kids in the cart as a bouncing of the boards a few minutes from the yard. Tiny flies came to sup on the brackish water, as did birds. There were no tadpoles, however: the water was too ephemeral.

When it began to recede, the inlets showed their banks, as ribbed as a giant ammonite fossil. Not tyre treads but cultivated terraces. Soon, the places where my torpedo foot had stirred explosive billows of underwater smoke were turned to desert rock. A gulley buttressed by flint outcrops. Real rock showed: the gulley was serious enough to be bedded here and there with what I imagined were the tectonic plates of the planet. At school we'd studied Pompeii and the marks of wheels in cobbled streets, the hard stone worn away to grooves as smooth as sculpture, natural rails for the traffic. Who was to say that the Romans hadn't travelled up here to an earlier version of Dungrove, or to some fancy country villa with statues?

Without water, or the waters of my imagination, the rut could turn embarrassing. A shallow depression. I didn't like to look at it. Sometimes I had to wait weeks for proper rain. Or else the rejuvenation occurred during school weekdays in the winter, when it grew dark too soon for me to reach that distance up the track after tea. By the weekend, the water would often be gone, leaving only a tantalising glint of mud.

The track itself was tantalising, right from its beginning at White Hill: it was bordered on either side by a broad and grassy verge foamed in the summer by cow parsley, spreading at the foot of brambled hedgerows several feet wide, whose clustered blackberries we would strip for jam every September. To the right were huge sloping fields, cowpat-spattered; to the left, at least for the first half-mile, the hedge concealed the long back gardens of Cheyne Walk, a 1950s lollipop close that had stretched its tentacle into the former fieldscape. We lived on the corner of the close. My London mother would insist that we were not actually part of Cheyne Walk: she had a very English dislike of cul-de-sacs, associating them with twitching net curtains and suburban boredom. My parents met in Paris, my Derbyshire father was bilingual. Our family car was the small Simca, but tucked behind our garage door was a 1938 Type 57 Bugatti, gleaming black, bought during our time in France: old cars – even Bugs – were cheaper than new ones in the 1950s. We were, in many ways, in the wrong place.

One of my mother's best friends, however, hailed from the close. Mrs Crisp was the plump and jolly Avon lady. She would give me sixpence for feeding her hairless sausage dog when she was away. Woofie was an unappealing creature who would yap and tremble as if mildly electrocuted the moment I appeared. Needless to say, we had a plethora of unused Avon scents in the house. When, in my gap year, I took a job for three months as a machine operator in a Chesham factory making neon bulbs, the women packers all wore Avon. For some chemical reason the perfume would go stale by the lunch break, and that distinctive powdery muskiness is inextricably bound up with my Buckinghamshire youth.

To be honest, there was very little difference between the houses of Cheyne Walk and our own road that led into it, except for the semi-detached element. We belonged to a row of about ten identical homes built at the end of the 1950s by an architect impressed by Moorish arches in Spain: every box-like house boasted a deep and curved front porch in white stucco. Large cracks would appear in them, for reasons no builder could ever quite fathom. Some fifty years on, this mildly pleasing and repeated motif, something which gave me an obscure sense of reassurance and belonging as I walked past our neighbours, has mostly disappeared behind an anarchy of fiercely individual extensions and improvements.

I'm looking at our house on Google Street View. The porch has gone, and the garage is now a downstairs room, but the all-over rendering (if less chalky white), the drainpipes, the roof tiles, the diamond-shaped leading in the windows, these are the same. I travel the length of the garden where our fence consistently teetered over in strong winds. The fence has changed, and where I'd swing like the child in Thomas Hood's 'I Remember, I Remember', and similarly think 'the air must rush as fresh / To swallows on the wing', is now the garage. The area's electricity generator, humming under yellow skull-warnings of death beyond what was the foot of our lawn, appears identical. At the front, we were separated from White Hill itself (finally arrived on the flat summit) by a raised swelling of grass, so we weren't really a street. Beyond was the road and then some rather stockbrokerish houses, one of which held a Colditz survivor who would reminisce with my parents about the war. Behind us, the close gave way to a welter of fields and woods spreading over the hills as far as the eye could see.

It was all very English. When I first arrived at the age of five, I had spent most of my brief life in Paris, Beirut and Calcutta. England felt chilly and grey and somehow less friendly or exuberant. 'Exuberant' was a word beyond the pale of my limited vocabulary, of course, belonging to all that I was yet to explore: a hinterland of glittering riches. I was learning to write properly, tracing repeated letters on lined paper; pegging the alphabet onto its washing-line. Even now I can feel the almost physical thrill of those apparently tedious lessons. As if even the individual letters themselves, clumsily pencilled into being, were plump with entire poems and stories: seed-grains of towering trees and intricate flowers.

On the 1877 OS map of the immediate area, all you can see on either side of the road's slow-travelling worm is the unblemished white of fields. They are bordered by tiny bobbles of cartographic trees, deemed solid enough to cast an etcher's flick of shadow. Oak? Elm? Beech? The creaking shuffle of horse and plough, the summer haywains, a kiss under the wagon. My bedroom faced those phantom fields when I first read, at the age of eleven, Laurie Lee's *Cider with Rosie*. That book, more than any other, inspired me into writing. It also deepened a sense of loss: that an entire rural existence, a way of being and of knowledge, had been erased in the name of progress – both social and scientific. When our own modest lawn insisted on sprouting the stems of wheat or oats, as well as wild plants like bird's-foot trefoil and 'eggs and bacon', my father – who knew the old ways as a boy on the moors – explained that it was the old field pushing through, its dormant seeds reviving. After all, our house was only a few years old, sheltered by a young silver birch I had always imagined to be ancient.

This revenance excited me for reasons that had nothing to do with botany. I would look out from my room over the shallow roofs and out towards the tops of the oaks that marked the farm track trailing away to the south, and imagine the suburban post-war houses vanished – including our own. It surprises me now, that this palimpsestic, historical impulse started so young. Wasn't this my home, cosy and familiar? The green double-decker London Country bus, having chugged gamely up steep Eskdale Avenue, would deposit me at Codmore Cross (a name that still conjures the warm-muffin feel of school's end), and I'd race back to slump in front of *Blue Peter* or *Crackerjack* or *The Adventures of Robinson Crusoe* in fuzzy black-and-white. Why did I wish it all gone, depopulated, the clock spun back to tussocks or crops or unbroken beech wood?

That past was exciting mainly because it was lost, in the way treasure gains a magic from being buried on a coral island. It was not as if the present-day fields thrilled me that much, except as playgrounds. The steep pastures that dropped down from Dungrove Farm to the thick hedgerow of White Hill offered wonderful views over Chesham to the sloped horizon beyond, but they were chiefly enticing as the site of my international sledging championships in the freezing winters of the 1960s. They were also the aerodrome where my brother's balsa-wood plane, weeks in the making on a table in our bedroom, its tissue stiffening under the vaporous dizziness of dope, stalled at a point higher than the crowns of the bordering oaks and crashed ignominiously into a cowpat.

1877 seems impossibly far back, yet neither the track nor the field boundaries had budged a lifetime later, according to a 1952 OS map shorn of those thoughtful trees. Now, apart from the cul-de-sac's ganglion and the zip-like grey of further buildings along the roads and lanes, they haven't budged in the six decades since. We arrived in 1962, just four or five years after the building works had ceased. I vividly recall imagining the science-fiction feel of the date 1965, when it would all be white spacesuits and pills for food. A relentless optimism reigned, a complete faith in scientific progress. The Cuban crisis and myxomatosis were hiccups. Yet I rebelled against this very early on, and I'm not sure why. A handful of tradesmen still used horses. We had our own Steptoe, clomping past with his blinkered pony and flatbed cart, yelling something unintelligible that we eventually deciphered as *Any old rags, any old lumber?* I was already nostalgic for ploughhorse and haycock, which in our area might still have been visible just a few years earlier. Hayricks were certainly around, and I was to help build them when home from university a decade later following my parents' move to the edge of the Berkshire downland – more securely rural yet within earshot of the M4 motorway.

At any rate, I felt I had just missed out. The puddled track to Dungrove carried me back. Tracks and paths are as stubborn as wood and field boundaries, stitched into history, into the older landscape. They share something of the vanilla-and-dust aroma of those maps I'd call up in later years from local libraries: evidence of bottled-up time. At thirteen, in anticipation of my parents' move to Africa, I was sent to board in Wiltshire amidst downland thick with prehistoric mysteries.

The house was swapped for a maisonette down in the valley on the Berkhamsted road, near a straggling beech hanger. The wood was sufficiently large for me to roam in it every day as a brooding adolescent, dreaming of girls and poetry, pencil-sketching the hills and vales into uncertain permanence.

These days, to enter the archives of the past, I just tap on my keyboard. I don't need to move at all; not even to explore my old childhood haunts. At time of writing, our row of houses and Cheyne Walk have been trapped in an amber of miserable grey. Low cloud, little shadow. It has probably rained over the last few days. 'Cluttery' weather, as the old farmhands would say. It makes my revived memories depressing, even dismal. I click my way back to the entrance to the track. The sign proclaiming DUNGROVE FARM has gone. The sun comes out, suddenly. It gleams brilliantly on tall and full-flowering cow parsley. I advance fifty yards in three taps: all that I'm permitted. The odd new house has been squeezed in between the track and the fields and even Cheyne Walk (somebody preferring money to a garden), but the great hedgerows are intact. The gift of sunshine stays.

I peer forward into the virtual distance, impossibly far from my adventuring seas, my reefs and dreams, my other-world fantasies of deep-down nymphs and bottomless heavens. It all seems both close enough to touch and simultaneously vanished for good, never to return. Granted another few hundred yards, perhaps we would see the flash of it: the unlidded lens, bright as a living eye, catching the light and casting it back, mirroring the world while it can.

AT THE EDGE OF THE TIDE

Michael Viney

The screensaver on my computer shows the strand on a sunny autumn morning, the sea calm for once and unfurling on the sand in slow, gleaming doorsteps of foam. Whatever the real weather on the shore below, it offers an encouraging start to the day. It reminds me of early walks on the strand with my eyes closed, the sun a warm vermilion in their lids and the rustle of the waves on my right to keep me straight. For all but a handful of days in the year, there's no one else to bump into.

'Strand' is Ireland's word for beach, which speaks to me more of the massed and clattering, sometimes lickable, pebbles at Brighton, where I was young. The only stones on this strand are scattered platters of green sandstone, carried in with the holdfasts of kelp wrenched up in winter storms. The stones are embossed with white hieroglyphs, calcareous tubes of seabed worms. Their bright rococo doodling made me gather enough to clad the chimneybreast above the woodstove, a typically laborious endeavour when we settled here some forty years ago.

That was the time for such middle-aged departures – 'deep ecology' from Arne Naess, 'self-sufficiency' from John Seymour. An acre on the wilder coast of County Mayo, on a final tendril of road, seemed the right setting for effortful experiment: hens, goats, potatoes, peat-cutting, fishing with a spillet, all that. The view – mountains, islands, an infinite ocean – was sustaining in itself.

So was the rawness of this corner of the coast: a great delta of sand curving back round the dunes, its fringe of fields framing a pair of lagoons, one shielded by a dark, ivied cliff. Between lakes and dunes, the astonishing, wind-levelled lawn of the *machair*, the geographers' 'plain' from the Gaelic, on north-west shores of Ireland and the Hebrides.

Even the strand was suitably untamed. To reach it, down the stony lane – the boreen – to the shore, meant fording, first, a little river from the mountain, at times just a rattling splash, at others a surging, impassable flood. A little way on, past drying furls of seaweed from the last spring tide, the main flow from Mweelrea carves a long, curving channel to the sea. The crossing-place from the boreen is marked by a row of rocks, once set hopefully as stepping stones. Now one has to follow, sometimes in thigh boots, the shifting consensus of tractors taking feed across the channel to sheep on the *duach*.

The farmers' homes are strung out towards the mountain on narrow acres striped up the hillside a century ago. Above our own small house the land is corduroyed with grassed-over ridges that grew potatoes and oats before the Famine: they need a prance from one ridge to the next. Also preserved, among marshy rushes and erratic glacial boulders, are foundations of the old crowded cabins. Three hundred people lived in this townland where a dozen or so dwell today. On one boulder I can picture, a set of little stones is clasped in a matrix of moss. They were gathered, I must suppose, by a petticoated toddler, helping to clean a field some two centuries ago.

The history of this hillside includes clearance of the land and its families for a Scottish rancher's blackface sheep. The dislocation can be read into what's left of a wreck on the strand, the points of its ribs sticking up, now and then, from the sand. Just once, in our memory, a big storm stripped enough sand away to expose it right down to the keel, scattered with lumps of limestone ballast and shards of black pottery. It was probably an old coaster and probably pre-Famine, but nobody can say when it was blown ashore. That's telling in itself: folk history or even common fancy should account for every quirk of local landscape. Less and less of the wreck survives. A number of the big oak ribs, pierced for dowelling, have been dragged away by tractor to serve as gateposts in the fields behind the shore.

The sea has erased another somewhat uncertain monument. When we came to live, the big delta of the strand had as its odd focal point a pyramidal mound as high as a house. Originally a tide-severed spur of the dune system, it supported the last few square metres of a small and ancient monastic chapel and its accumulated graves, some of drifting war-dead salvaged from the sea. As the spring tides undermined it, the mound began to sink, spilling out bones and headstones. Eventually, chewed to the sandy core by a January storm surge, it collapsed, leaving stones in a jumbled circle on the strand. We salvaged a headstone, a rough-edged slab of slate inscribed by a journeyman mason in the early 1800s. The surname still thrives in the parish, but no family cared to claim it. It survives in the garden path, face down.

The strand is so exposed to gales and breakers that fishing in the tarred canvas currach has dwindled to the use, on occasional calm Sundays, of a very few boats, lashed down to rocks in niches of the headlands. Our own hauls of rays and flounders, for the freezer, were made with a long line of mackerel-baited hooks, set parallel to the shore, anchored at the very bottom of one tide and recovered at the ebb of the next. Such efforts, in weather that could utterly change overnight, diminished with the years. They were mocked by a memorable event in which a storm left the strand littered with fish, gills snapped forward in the undersea maelstrom that drowned them. We gathered weighty bags of fish for the freezer – pollack, ling, cod, haddock, hake, whiting – and left the prickly rockfish to the gulls.

For the hillside community, the sea's offerings were led by Laminaria, the offshore forest of kelp. Uprooted by storms or in annual senescence, it is tossed ashore in toffee-brown drifts. The fronds are good as fertiliser on the land, but their real value lay in the stems, the 'sea rods', worth wading in for, waist-deep, in competition at dawn. Stacked to dry and burned in stone 'ovens' on the shore, their charred clinker was the raw material of iodine, the burnings rolling pungent smoke inland. The eclipse of iodine by antibiotics is already good for reappraisal in the running battle with sepsis. The kelp is now harvested for alginates, smoothers of ice cream and toothpaste.

The shore's more enduring gift has been the sand itself, rich in calciferous marine fragments – 'the dry shells, the toe- and fingernail parings of the sea' in Michael Longley's poem. Carried up by horse and cart, the sand made a soft bed for cattle in the byre and a liming of land as their manure was spread. That was before tractors grew as powerful as tanks and the scale of sand quarrying became insupportable. In the finite budget of a bay of sand, great withdrawals by winter storms are held offshore, to be repaid in summer's soft selvedges. Steal too much from the sand budget and the ocean claws even harder at the dunes.

There is another grand recycling between the strand and the machair, the broad, green sward behind the dunes. Dunes and machair abound in snails, from the big, brown kind known to gardeners, through smaller sorts ringed with bright bands of colour, to rare and miniature whorled species no bigger than a match-head, surviving from post-glacial times. What delighted me was to realise that the land snails build their shells from the calcium of their lost ocean cousins, carried on winds from the strand. In winter, I have found long lines of 'garden' snails wedged into the leeward cracks of driftwood fence posts, their shells sand-blasted to delicate shades of blue. On some mild, moist mornings in early summer, walking the dunes risks crunching on copulating molluscs.

I have beachcombed most hopefully in winter, often in the wake of gales, wind hissing around my boots and leaving worm-stones and otter shells balanced on pedestals of sand. In the early years of smallholder mechanics, I marched the tideline with an improvising eye. Spanish fish boxes, New England milk crates, swathes of fishing net and tangles of rope, stray buoys, colourful trawler-balls. I was rarely first along, following instead the close-stitched prints of fox or stoat at dawn (for dead seabirds and crabs) and tractor tracks of the farmer who lives beside the strand.

Now that ships' cargoes are carried in containers, there is rarely much cast up that's of use to the community. There was, once, a great arrival of clean, finished timber – stout planks for roofs or scaffolding. They vanished in a day. Then, even more mysteriously, came hundreds of little cedar tiles, like the lids of school pencil boxes. These, at least, were left to me, fragrant and challenging for some better purpose than wedging rocking furniture on a bumpy flagged floor.

So much for the material, Swiss Family Robinson side of things. More importantly, as one might hope, the strand has been my primer in marine life – or rather, death. Our windowsills are heaped with predictable bric-a-brac: sea urchins, dolphin vertebrae, bird skulls, crab carapaces. Some things are fragile and beautiful, as in the ocean-drifting, translucent violet snails, *Janthina*, that Rachel Carson pursued on her side of the Atlantic. I keep mine safe in a clear plastic box. In another is the little skull of a Ridley's turtle, winter vagrant from the Caribbean. And hanging on my study wall, like a ribbed African shield, is the carapace of a big loggerhead turtle, salvaged from the strand in a wheelbarrow and left buried for months at the bottom of the garden.

What's rare can be a matter of who's around to see. In the 1980s I came upon the seventh recorded stranding (then another, a few years later) of 'True's wonderful beaked whale', *Mesoplodon mirus*. The early common name for this slim animal, a rare deep diver after squid, reflected the delight of Frederick True, a Smithsonian curator who described the new species from a corpse washed up in North Carolina in 1913. A solitary pair of conical teeth at the very end of my whale's lower jaw warranted the call to a distant zoology professor, who came to confirm their distinctive shape (as if squeezed between finger and thumb).

This first whale was salvaged for its skeleton by the Ulster Museum. Great chunks were neatly butchered by a mammal technician, then wrapped in plastic bags and ferried up the fields to his rented van. His work, conducted on a rainy Sunday in a pit dug around the whale, was watched attentively by my farming neighbours, standing together carefully upwind. When the technician dropped his big knife, it was returned to him gingerly, at the tip of a spade.

The number of Ireland's whales, alive or stranded, has since become a national wonder, thanks to the leadership of the voluntary Irish Whale and Dolphin Group. Leaping humpbacks and blowing fin whales are now regularly spotted from southern headlands; cast-up corpses are promptly noted and available for autopsy. Two recent True's, which are still very rarely stranded, carried plastic fragments in their stomachs.

A singular, lentil-sized pellet of raw plastic is called, for some reason, a 'nurdle', of which more than 100 million tonnes are produced every year. Shipped around the world in this form, the pellets have been spilled into the ocean by the billion and gulped for zooplankton by seabirds, fish and other marine life. I noticed them first in 2000, among seaweed at the strand's furthest lap of the tide.

I was stirring the weed, as usual, in the hope of adding another sea bean to my dish of them: sea hearts, horse-eyes, nickars. They are fruits spilled into rivers from tropical pods in Cuban or Central American forests, reaching our islands on the North Atlantic Drift after perhaps 400 days at sea. The glossy brown skin of the sea heart invites fondling, like a worry bead, and its toughness once served the teething of babies of this coast.

It's ages since I added another, but how long since I really looked? Perhaps drift-seeds have grown fewer, the forests of the Caribbean cleared for golf courses and celebrity homes. I still host, however, from transatlantic drift, a couple of coconuts still in their husks and a box fruit, *Barringtonia asiatica*, a four-sided fistful with a husk like Shredded Wheat. It was the first ever recorded on a European shore and reached a children's programme on telly.

My passion for the natural world has long had the company of two close friends in this landscape. One is an ornithologist, David Cabot, who lives across the lake, his lifelong study the barnacle geese that winter on north Mayo's islands. The other is the poet Michael Longley, who comes from Belfast to borrow Cabot's cottage and immerse himself in the landscape.

David and I made a film about him, where I had him paddle in a chill November surf, framed against a fiery sunset, to recite his poem 'Sea Shanty'. As the shot ended, the camera still ready on its tripod, a young otter chose to dash along the shallows, straight past us: a magical conjunction. Again, filming with my wife, the dog seated beside us at the crest of the dunes, an otter gave us a whole digital minute of its life. It climbed the dune from the strand and paused within our long winter shadows, then dashed off through the marram to the distant lagoon.

Rinsing off the sea salt with a swim in fresh water restores the insulation of the otter's soft underfur. But retreat from the sea to the cover of the dunes can have another end. Once, slowly walking the tideline with the sun behind me, I watched an otter bound from the surf with a flounder in its jaws and lollop up into the dunes to eat. Crouched among the marram, it was swooped upon by a raven that tried to bully it off its meal. At last, giving up on the whirring assault, the otter skidded back down the sand, fish flapping from its jaws, the raven skimming it back to the sea.

Such explicit drama is rare. I look for footprints leaving the tideline (a neat arc to each paw, the pads rounded and separate, impressed like petals). At the bank of a stream running into the strand, a tall, green tuft of well-fertilised grass is topped by a new wisp of spraint, black and glistening with chitin. I sniff its musky scent, content the otters are still there.

In Ireland's conservation texts, this sprawling corner of the coast is named as 'Dooaghtry', for a little, reed-fringed lake behind the dunes – one the otters sometimes wash in. They are given passing mention in the ecological synopsis of the National Parks and Wildlife Service, along with choughs, the buoyant, carolling crows whose red bills prod the machair, and the whooper swans of winter that croon to the echoes from the cliff above their lake.

In the botanical priorities of habitat conservation, Dooaghtry's special claim is its exceptional wealth of a liverwort, *Petalophyllum ralfsii*, a European rarity, its lettuce-like beauty best judged under a hand lens. Reduced to a scatter across Europe, it thrives in carpeted thousands on the moist sands of Dooaghtry. Michael Longley suggested this 'snail snack, angel's nosegay' for my farewell wreath.

One change in the landscape we mourned together moved him to these lines:

> Now that the Owennadornaun has disappeared
> For you and me where our two townlands meet,
> The peaty water takes the long way round
> Through Morrison's fields and our imaginations.

The Owennadornaun was the little river whose ford near the bottom of the boreen was so rich in the spirit of place. A sill of rock made a shallow waterfall just above the crossing, with the sun above the mountain to catch each ripple and splash. It was here I saw my first dipper, walking under water, and where, in summer, sand martins came to nest in holes in the bank. There were pied and grey wagtails dancing at the edge and, once or twice, a sandpiper.

This has all gone. The ford's loose cobbles, rolling beneath the tyres of summer cars, were thought an affront to tourism. And it's true that many 4x4s did press on, through the channel to the strand, there to spin great circles for fun or get stuck in the soft bits with the tide coming in. These transgressions were erased by the big spring tides of September. But a car park behind the strand, with a summer loo, was clearly essential to setting up the Wild Atlantic Way. It meant diversion of the little river and a road bridge built above its bed, this now remaining dry and quite birdless.

We are three ageing men, Cabot, Longley and Viney (me the oldest by a hare's leap), but we have shared a life and a landscape out of time, an ecosystem lean but lovely and enduring. We have a pact for the sequential scatter of our ashes on the little promontory fort above David's lake – a sprinkle of more calcium for the snails.

BINSEY

Marina Warner

The sanctuary where the high altar stood was out of bounds for us girls at the convent; women could arrange the flowers, but only boys could be servers. The Second Vatican Council was to redraw the rules in the mid sixties and allow females to help the priest saying Mass and, later, give out communion and even speak. But in those days before 1965, priests were the only men we saw apart from one or two gardeners: once a week in the shadowy, hushed booth, another holy enclosure, the confessor would be hazily outlined behind the colander of the dividing screen, surrounding him with a constellation of little haloes around his head as we whispered our sins. Every morning, wearing a long, rough-spun, brown robe with a rope knotted thrice for the three vows of the Franciscans, a friar would come and, as I stuck out my tongue to receive the wafer, I would peep, from lowered eyes, at Father Alfred's big strong hairy toes and thick ridged nails in sandals. He was our favourite because he got through the service quickly; some of the older monks were more devout and lingered on every word, and we schoolgirls were hungry for our breakfast; not infrequently, one of us would faint into the aisles. When I asked my friend Lindsay what it was like, losing consciousness, she answered, 'It's like going to Africa.' After that, I wanted to go to Africa, too, but when I did pass out, I found nothing except plummeting seasickness and loud thrumming in my head. On special occasions a Jesuit would be invited from Farm Street in London to give a sermon or take us on a three-day retreat; these were men who wore black suits and shiny, covered shoes.

Our nuns had been known as 'Jesuitesses'; Mary Ward, the founder of their order, had led a turbulent life, caught up in religious struggles, first with the Reformers in England and then with successive popes, because she wanted to teach girls, just as boys were taught by Jesuits. Jesuits had also been persecuted for being clever – we knew the history.

When I first arrived in Oxford at Lady Margaret Hall, the most celebrated poet-priest and Jesuit since Gerald Manley Hopkins was living at Campion Hall, but, unlike Hopkins, Peter Levi was infinitely glamorous, his prodigious gifts and his family history and his celibacy making him an irresistible object of desire for many, many people of every gender and age. His father had a business in oriental carpets, inherited from his father, who had come to England from Constantinople; Peter's stature was much enhanced, in the eyes of his many admirers, by his origins and expertise in Greek-Mediterranean-Levantine culture in all its polyglot variety. But it was his mother, Edith Tigar, a fervent Catholic from Yorkshire, who was the dominant influence: Peter's older brother Anthony had also become a Jesuit and his sister Gillian a nun. The triple surrender of the siblings to divine love, the family's self-fashioning according to the religious ideal and its constraints, marvellously amplified the pulsing aura around Peter. I knew a woman who was genuinely, determinedly, in love with him, and several others who were eager to try to make him surrender. I was fascinated myself, but I was struggling to abandon the faith that had ruled my whole life so far, and I was wary: it didn't feel right to me that a priest should be so alluring and have a taste for good clarets and eating out in restaurants (including the most expensive in town, the Elizabeth). He enjoyed his own seductiveness to others, like a beautiful girl who toys with her conquests. I never heard then of any consummations – and this invulnerability added to the perturbation that I felt around him.

We met in a field near Heythrop College where he was making a retreat and couldn't wait to be interrupted, or so I'd been told. It was early summer with high blue skies and a silky gleam on the crops and he came through these fields up the hill towards us, with a slight limp from a childhood attack of polio. It was the year he was ordained, I've now learned from the biography by Brigid Allen, and he was struggling with his superiors, who weren't happy about his lack of obedience.

The clandestine rendezvous – the tryst – had been arranged by Alasdair Clayre, folk-singer-songwriter, the English Joan Baez and Bob Dylan in the making (this was 1964), who happened also to be a Prize Fellow at All Souls. Alasdair was about ten years younger than Peter, and had a car – a rare thing among students in those days; how he managed to make the assignation to meet at that spot, beyond the grounds where Peter was meant to be enclosed, has vanished from memory – but there we were on a ridge in the Cotswolds, joyfully meeting the poet-priest. I was a bit shocked; I was intrigued; I was awed.

Peter Levi wasn't Father Alfred, or anything like the Farm Street confessors who had come to my school. He was then thirty-three years old, nearly twice my age; he was smooth-skinned and lissom, and had what's called an olive complexion, though no olive, either in fruit or leaf, ripe or unripe, oil or soap, is ever that colour: he was appealingly sheeny brown like a sweet chestnut when you first open its spiky shell to see it lying in its cottony nest, and he spoke confidingly and self-effacingly and rapidly, the chevrons of his brows punctuating the flow of put-downs and thumbs-ups from a fabulous range of reading and looking – all the while quoting, poetry especially, in many languages.

Later that term, he took me to see the medieval shrine at Binsey by the Isis, as the Thames is called there, where it flanks Port Meadow and runs into the capillary streams and canals that web the fields: I remember him pointing out a small building drifting in the meadow below us (we must have been approaching from Godstow and had been visiting the ruined abbey there), and talking about hermits and sacred wells and sanctuaries and places that are holy over long stretches of time. Later, in what is his longest-lasting work, he translated Pausanias's *Guide to Greece* for World Classics; he also went travelling – on horseback – in Central Asia with Bruce Chatwin. But that day at Binsey, he was telling me about the allée of trees running from the village to the little church, which had been cut down in 1879 and inspired Hopkins to write his impassioned lament and praise-song, 'Binsey

Poplars', with its unexpected but precise image of the sun, caught in branches, and made all the more fiery by rubato syncopation:

> My aspens dear, whose airy cages quelled,
>> Quelled or quenched in leaves the leaping sun,
> All felled, felled, all are felled;
>>> ...
> Ten or twelve, only ten or twelve
>> Strokes of havoc unselve
>>> The sweet especial scene,
>> Rural scene, a rural scene,
>> Sweet especial rural scene.

For my generation, Hopkins was the voice – and the eyes – of a radiant English dreamworld in which Blake was the pre-eminent seer, but which included many other intense spirits with local connections to Oxford: Pre-Raphaelites and Ancients, whom I felt were my elective affines, for they had foreseen the hopes and dreamed the future my friends and I were thinking we could bring about. Hopkins's great requiem, 'The Wreck of the *Deutschland*', sounds all through the feverish world of Muriel Spark's *The Girls of Slender Means*, which is set in 1945 but came out in 1963. At least, this is how I remember the feeling of discovery and the longing for enchantments beyond the dull and risk-less mainstream, with Peter talking to me about Samuel Palmer, and directing me to see Palmer's paintings and drawings in the Ashmolean, his ripely glowing suns in small hallucinatory rural scenes, as sweet and especial as Hopkins could have wished for. I was urged by both Alasdair and Peter to read David Jones, the poet and the painter – *In Parenthesis* and *Anathemata* were up there with Dante and Keats, far more cherished than Shakespeare (condemned by another of my mentors in those days, the historian Richard Cobb, as 'coarse, ruffianly stuff'). Hopkins, Palmer and Jones – these were luminaries, points of reference intersecting quite often with Catholicism, but not invariably.

There was more, much more – Peter was an ebullient and generous mentor; later some of these thoughts flowed into the lectures he gave as Professor of Poetry at Oxford. He imparted thoughts, not inner feelings – at least to me – and I had no inkling of his troubles, that he was so much at odds with the vows he'd made; I thought he was just a worldly priest. But at a party Alasdair Clayre gave in All Souls, Peter had already met Deirdre, the wife of Cyril Connolly, and it seems to have been a *coup de foudre* for both of them; after Cyril's death, he left the priesthood and married her. He was by all accounts much, much happier, but his unsettling aura was dimmed, not only for me.

For many years I avoided churches, and even wayside shrines and religious music made me uneasy, but now, with the years of Catholic daily life long past, I can enjoy visiting such places again, and I'm attracted to many aspects of them; setting aside the interest I have in the buildings themselves and their interiors, there's quietness, a quietness that often hums with centuries of voices. So in some ways I still envy those who can pray, but am reconciled to the spectral echoes that old sanctuaries sound for me. Walking to Binsey across the meadows and the river has become my favourite walk in Oxford; the last time I went, the hedgerows on the lane to the church had been slashed by a machine – a chainsaw? – and the dense, deep tangle of elder, dog rose, hornbeam, hazel, snowberries and hawthorn was mangled, left in broken stems to die down on the earth floor as compost. This is the country way of doing it, no doubt, but it gave the early-autumnal rural scene, still fruiting, still flowering, a battered, neglected look. Hopkins's words, when he cried out, seem to have lost no point:

> O if we but knew what we do
>   When we delve or hew –
> Hack and rack the growing green!
>   Since country is so tender
> To touch, her being só slender,
> That, like this sleek and seeing ball
> But a prick will make no eye at all,
> Where we, even where we mean
>   To mend her we end her …

Still, that summer bryony was mantling it all, exuberantly covering up the clumsy human husbandry, and on the last stretch of the lane, as it leads to the chapel itself, an avenue of lime trees has recently been planted; the third generation since Hopkins's aspens dear, they're still so small their crowns are globular, somewhat like standard roses.

Very old, cobwebby yews grow close in to the chapel in the church-yard. There are a few Victorian tombs and some more recent arrivals, including an infant which is under a tiny wooden marker; over the drystone wall a small herd of goats graze in an enclosure, the billy often leaping up, like the rampant, golden, Babylonian goat eating a thorn bush in the British Museum, with two nanny goats and a few kids usually at his side. On the north side of the church, some wrecks of river craft are slowly rotting in what remains of a boatyard for vessels working the web of streams and cuts that run into the Thames and its 'wind-watering weed-winding banks'. A peahen puffed up her salt-and-pepper feather cloak and shrilled furiously to ward us off her patch.

Apart from the farmhouse and the ramshackle outbuildings, the stoved-in boats and straggling animal pens that run up to the church-yard walls as if rising against a breakwater, the little gabled church with its double bell tower stands alone, a destination and an end in itself. It's a hidden place, shaded and old, built to a human, not divine scale; a speaking place even in its silence.

The shrine began in Anglo-Saxon times as an oratory, dedicated to St Margaret of Antioch, but its popularity since the twelfth century as a site of pilgrimage arose because of the well in the churchyard – the treacle-well – which is sacred to St Frideswide, the patron saint of Oxford. Margaret was one of the most beloved saints of medieval Europe, the special protectress of women who are being harassed because she resisted a pagan king who wanted to marry her and was then attacked by the devil in the shape of a monstrous dragon, and swallowed alive; but her holiness was so strong that the devil couldn't digest her and so regurgitated her safe and sound.

Gory miracle stories such as Margaret's were the staple of my child-hood; mostly featuring indomitable heroines (abused children, maltreated virgins, wronged queens), they're often bizarre, sadistic and stark, very close to fairy tales in mood and matter. The legend of St Frideswide is no exception. Her name means 'strong hope' or, according to another source, 'bond of peace', and she was a high-born heiress – the daughter of a sub-king, Dida of Eynsham, and his wife Safrida; her dates are conjectured at 680 to 727 or 735. She had lost her mother when she was a child, and wanted to become a nun; but she was being pressed to marry another potentate, Algar. She didn't want to, in any case, and certainly not Algar (this is an unexpectedly common situation in fairy tales, too). In other versions of her legend, she is pursued by several suitors; sometimes they come accompanied by a throng of soldiers. As in many stories of early female saints, the rejected suitor seeks revenge and sets out to rape her (marriage by abduction), then putting her in a brothel to punish her. 'Since she has thus rejected me,' Algar declares,

'I will commit a wrong against her;
And when I have done all the lechery I desire with her,
I will give her to whoever wants her – [to] flagrant and bold
    lechers,
[So] that when she leaves me, she will be [a] common whore!'
He leaped upon his palfrey and took the way forward.

But Frideswide calls on the help of St Margaret, and escapes. She takes a boat down the Thames and lets it drift; it carries her safely and sets her down at Binsey; there she conceals her aristocratic birth and becomes a swineherd (again resembling Peau-d'ane – Donkeyskin – in the fairy tale, best known from Charles Perrault's spirited verse narrative, but a widely known medieval legend). Algar still comes after her, remorselessly, but when he reaches her refuge, he's struck by lightning and blinded. Soon after, he's thrown from his horse and breaks his neck.

The posse he's brought with him are all struck blind too, but Frideswide shows mercy on them, prays to St Margaret, and a spring instantly wells up. With its sweet and fragrant water she restores their sight.

The word 'treacle' now conjures up golden syrup; its old significance, as balm and salve, has been lost. The well at Binsey was 'for long collapsed and fouled', according to T. J. Prout, who served as vicar for thirty years and in 1874, five years before Hopkins wrote 'Binsey Poplars', purified it in the spirit of Anglo-Catholic enthusiasm for the old cult practices (holy water, bells, prayers to saints and belief in their miracles) previously abhorrent to Protestants.

The well itself is now again a murky sump, like a blind eye deep down in the ground, under a Gothic arch with steps leading down, green and slidey with mosses and draped with the delicate quatrefoils of rambling penny royal, but still catacomb-like, damp and eerie. A well of this kind isn't far from a privy in appearance, a meeting-point between foul and fair, wild nature and human organisation, yoked together by need, a disturbing memento of our creatureliness.

The miracle of this cure and many more that followed brought great fame to Frideswide, as a holy woman, healer and abbess. After her death, a cult grew up attended by many miracles; so many that the little church at Binsey proved too humble for the crowds and her bones were transferred to a far more beautiful and magnificent priory church in Oxford; the city of Oxford was given into her care, and her tomb became a great medieval healing shrine, specialising in eye problems and in psychological troubles.

Young women were especially attracted to seek the saint's help. Some were suffering from rejection by a man they wanted, yet others were bitterly disappointed in their hopes for a loving partnership. The symptoms reported are remarkably recognisable for us today, though we would term them 'hysterical'. Pilgrims reported illusions and mental troubles arising from sexual problems: Alveva had gone mad after sexual intercourse; Beatrix, from Wiltshire, had suffered from a headache for two years after sex with her husband; Helen, who had lived with a priest for three years and then been rejected by him, had fallen ill with sleeplessness and internal pains; Cecily had had a phantom pregnancy. A girl called Mathilda had become blind for six years and been 'spurned' by her family, but in the shrine she bled from her eyes and found her sight restored.

In 1524, as the Reformation under Henry VIII was beginning, Cardinal Wolsey dissolved St Frideswide's Priory and took the proceeds for a new foundation, Cardinal College, named after himself. After his fall from power, this would become Christ Church, the seat of the cathedral of Oxford (the famous bell in Tom Quad, a landmark of the city, was originally the bell of St Frideswide's priory, and was moved to the college in 1684). St Frideswide's tomb was smashed and her relics scattered.

Hopkins doesn't allude to any of this in his poem, but it's interesting to contrast the Anglo-Catholic effort to redress the history of past desecration with Hopkins's contemporary vision of iconoclasm as nature damaged, as transcendence forfeited by a heedless act of vandalising trees, trees which used to catch the god-like sun in their branches. The restoration of the cult and the fabric did not compel his attention; instead, like Monet in his garden, he set down with marvellous sensitivity the movement of light and water under the vanished trees

> That dandled a sandalled
> Shadow that swam or sank
> On meadow & river & wind-wandering weed-winding bank.

I walked there again recently because I thought the shrine would appeal to the friend who'd given us lunch that day, a friend who had been a nun at one time long ago at my school. But she didn't want to swap stories about miracles and holy places and treacle-wells. Instead she took one quick turn through the chapel and left, saying, 'It doesn't have the right smell.'

The fissure that opened up between Rome and Canterbury half a century ago was not narrowed by the Oxford Movement's revival of liturgy and cult; it was a case of *les extrêmes se touchent*, but the stand-off continued. It was only when my friend seemed so irritated by the trappings of the old religion at Binsey that I realised I had come back with her because there was a kind of logic across the years, after my first encounter with the chapel through a priest who would also give up his calling. I was disappointed she didn't feel the enchantment of the place, and it dulled it for me too, a little, seeing her distaste.

The streams that run through the town and its surrounding fields and meadows have carried stories with them over the centuries, and Binsey now is much more celebrated for its connections with *Alice in Wonderland* than with Frideswide. Yet the two young women are closely entwined, as Lewis Carroll, being himself a deacon in the Church of England during the period of intense medievalising religious renewal, drew on local legends for the odyssey he imagined and recounted to his audience of little friends.

In 1856, Alice Liddell's father Henry had taken up his post as Dean of Christ Church and its cathedral, so when his daughter Alice and her siblings were growing up, they would have often heard their father preach by the tomb of St Frideswide, which had been newly restored; Alice would have recognised that Lewis Carroll was only teasing, in that knowing and whimsical way of his, when he talked about the treacle-well that afternoon in 1864 as they took the same course downstream to Binsey that Frideswide had centuries before.

During the Mad Hatter's Tea Party, the Dormouse starts telling a story about three children who lived at the bottom of a well. Why? Because it was a treacle-well. 'Why?' asks Alice again. Because, says the Dormouse, they were drawing treacle.

It's baffling, another of those maddening impasses that Alice keeps encountering in Wonderland. The sensible girl replies that the children would be very ill if they lived on treacle.

Maybe some images from the trip when Alice Liddell gathered 'dream rushes' from the riverbank helped inspire a sculpture that she carved when she was grown up: a bas-relief on oak which decorated a door in the mission church in Poplar, London, that Dean Liddell established; it was bombed in World War II, and has since been demolished, but the panel was rescued and brought to Oxford, to the church on the Botley Road dedicated to St Edmund and St Frideswide. It's a huge edifice, far too huge for the community that lives around there now, and no longer in use, so I had to write a letter requesting permission to visit, and one afternoon the retired vicar came with the key to meet me and show me around. We found, leaning against a wall, the wooden bas-relief that Alice Liddell carved. It's an ogive panel, and unexpectedly skilful – did Alice Liddell miss her vocation? – and shows St Frideswide looking like a Virgin annunciate kneeling and praying, with a single oar untended in its rowlock as she drifts towards Binsey in a swan-necked skiff between the wind-wandering weed-winding banks of the Thames.

Note

I would like to acknowledge the help of Cressida Connolly; Brigid Allen, 'Levi, Peter Chad Tigar (1931–2000)', *Oxford Dictionary of National Biography*, Oxford University Press, 2007; online edition, 2011, http://www.oxforddnb.com.ezproxy2.londonlibrary.co.uk/view/article/73779, accessed 29 August 2016; Brigid Allen, *Peter Levi: Oxford Romantic*, Signal Books, 2014; Josh Spero, *Second-Hand Stories*, Unbound, 2015; Henry Mayr-Harting, 'Functions of a Twelfth-century Shrine: The Miracles of St Frideswide' in *Studies in Medieval History presented to R.H.C. Davis*, eds., Moore, R. I., Mayr-Harting, Henry (London: Bloomsbury, 1985, pp. 193–206); and Sherry L. Reames, ed., *The Legend of St Frideswide of Oxford, An Anglo-Saxon Royal Abbess* in *Middle English Legends of Women Saints*, University of Rochester, 2003. For Hopkins's 'Binsey Poplars', I accessed https://www.poetryfoundation.org/poems/44390/binsey-poplars.

The Echoing Green

Ken Worpole

> Such, such were the joys
> When we all, girls and boys,
> In our youth-time were seen
> On the echoing green.
> William Blake

1

'Without common land no social system can survive,' wrote the architectural historian Christopher Alexander in 1997, a prescient warning at a time when the privatisation of public assets was gaining increased traction as the new political common sense. More recently, in July 2016, a House of Commons Select Committee on 'The Future of Public Parks' began public consultation by asking 'what the advantages and disadvantages are of other management models, such as privatisation, outsourcing or mutualisation.'

What have voters done to deserve this resurgent ideological attack on the public realm? Parks are almost the last symbols of common land rights left in towns and cities, and perhaps this is why they attract so much ideological opprobrium from free-market economists, for whom the commons is now an antiquated and outdated ethical sphere.

Having lived close to Clissold Park in Hackney for nearly fifty years, I know only too well how much the park's majestic chestnut and plane trees, wide skies and open horizons, undulating grassland, ornamental lakes and gardens – along with the regular *passeggiata* of familiar and unfamiliar faces – have provided a source of pleasure and refuge to the many who use it, often daily. As with the woodland glade in *A Midsummer Night's Dream*, parks are places of enchantment from which visitors emerge refreshed, changed or renewed.

For the three million visitors it attracts each year, Clissold Park is one of the larger public open spaces in this part of London, and has been so for more than a hundred years, but its future is once again threatened. This is because the provision of public parks remains a 'non-statutory' service, which means municipal authorities are not required to provide them if they feel they can't afford to, and in an 'age of austerity' non-statutory provision is the first to suffer, as is now happening.

Cuts to parks budgets are biting deeply across the UK, according to the Heritage Lottery Fund's report, *State of UK Public Parks 2016*. While more popular than ever – with over 90 per cent of families with children under five and 57 per cent of all adults using them regularly – parks services across the country are being outsourced to community groups or their management, and maintenance handed over to private contractors in order to save money. In 2014 Liverpool City Council, for example, announced that over the following three years its annual £10 million parks budget would be cut by 50 per cent. Many other councils have announced similar levels of reduced funding. 'Parks take a long time to fall apart,' says Dave Morris, chair of the National Federation of Parks and Green Spaces, adding that 'it's not immediately noticeable, like a library closing'. But over time the effects are just as socially (and environmentally) disastrous. Sooner or later there is a danger that many city parks will take on the character of the bleak, deserted grasslands of those edgeland prairies, where only dog walkers, footballers and joy-riders venture.

The amount of public parkland in any town or city is an accident of history: some places have prodigious amounts of open green space, while others have just pockets. To complicate matters, there are distinct typologies of urban parkland, ranging from the ornamental garden to the prestigious civic park, and from the garden square to the public commons or recreation ground. Allotments, canal towpaths, closed burial grounds, memorial gardens, bowling greens and many other serendipitous green spaces add to the urban mix. Each has its own history and customary 'rules of engagement', which are often implicitly understood by their users, occasionally reinforced by local by-laws. These typological distinctions are fascinating, each bringing with it rich historic associations, not just with aesthetic issues, but also differences in their respective 'moral economies'. A park is never simply just a green space, but an ever-changing *mise-en-scène* of social theatre.

Clissold Park itself is a classic *hortus conclusus*, a former enclosed private house and grounds, that over time has mutated into a modern city park, a successful hybrid of the Renaissance 'public garden' and the historic recreational space of the English commons, where markets are held, sports played, and funfairs and travelling circuses encamp for a short while. It is intriguing how these historic typologies of cultivated and open land have been commandeered and re-purposed in recent times by the internet with its 'walled gardens' and 'creative commons'.

The park and its mansion, Clissold House (Grade II-listed), originated as a family estate in the 1790s, under the ownership of a Quaker banker, Jonathan Hoare. After several changes of ownership during the nineteenth century, in the 1880s the 53-acre estate ended up in the hands of the Church Commissioners, who proposed selling the site for development. A vociferous and successful public campaign led to its purchase by the Metropolitan Board of Works in 1886, and it was opened as a public park by the newly formed London County Council (LCC) on 24 July 1889. It remained with the elected London authority until 1986 when, with the abolition of the Greater London Council (GLC), house and park were transferred to Hackney Borough Council, in whose large and richly variegated portfolio of land holdings it now rests.

For some years after Hackney Council – like many other London boroughs to which the former GLC parks were transferred by government diktat – struggled to maintain Clissold Park adequately. This was for reasons of cost as well as a lack of management expertise necessary to maintain such large historic parks and their built heritage. In the 1980s anxieties about the decline of the park and mansion spurred the formation of a voluntary user group, Clissold Park User Group (CPUG). This grew in size and expertise over time, and, though starting from a fairly adversarial relationship with the local authority, now works closely with council officers. Initially this was for one reason only: the arrival of the Heritage Lottery Fund's urban parks spending programme in 1996. Whatever one's reservations about the morality of using lotteries to underwrite public amenities – and I certainly have them – there is no doubt that the HLF parks programme, which has now provided more than £800 million to UK parks over the past twenty years, has transformed many out of recognition, and provided the greatest renewal of parks seen in Britain for more than half a century.

A grant of £4.5 million to Clissold Park in 2008, matched by £4.1 million from council funds, restored the mansion to a pristine condition, and refurbished every aspect of the park and its hydrological features, together with new tennis courts and extensive play provision for young children and sports enthusiasts. The grant came with significant conditions, notably that the park and mansion required their own dedicated management team, together with on-site gardening staff, a business plan for the house, and an educational programme for working with local schools. The enhanced status that Hackney's parks service now enjoys as a result of the HLF programme has put its management team back on the top table in the council hierarchy – but for how much longer?

2

Many other city parks also have their origins in large private family estates acquired by municipal authorities in the late-Victorian era. In the history of modern cities it is the moment when the new civic gospel and the natural world came together, and in doing so created a new landscape form that has over the past hundred years been replicated across the world. The architect Terry Farrell has said that while Britain imported most of its ideas on city form and townscape from Europe and beyond, its true claim to fame is that it gave the world the public park.

The Victorian concern with formality in public life meant that the early parks were designed and managed as spaces of moral uplift and social regulation, though over time such regimes fell out of step with changing social mores. It was Sunday every day in the Victorian park: best clothes and best behaviour. Plants and trees were labelled for public edification in English and Latin; children's free play was strictly restricted to one small area, if allowed at all, and informal sports were prohibited.

Times changed, and parks had to change accordingly. Thus, when the veteran municipal socialist George Lansbury was given the minor Cabinet post of Commissioner of Works in the 1929 Labour government – he had been deliberately sidelined by Prime Minister Ramsey MacDonald, who loathed him – Lansbury took to the job with gusto. He ended up as the only minister of that short-lived government to acquit himself with an enhanced political reputation, notably through his commitment to widening access to public parks. 'Railings were pulled down, shelters for parents put up, paddling and swimming pools for children constructed, play and recreational equipment installed in the parks over which he had jurisdiction,' wrote his biographer, Bob Holman.'Mixed bathing was allowed in the Serpentine and Hyde Park was revamped as "Lansbury's Lido". His aim was to make the parks attractive to and open to families of all kinds – and he succeeded.'

Other cities followed Lansbury. During the 1930s across Britain the Victorian park underwent a process of greater democratisation in design and amenity. This was sufficiently impressive to attract the praise of admiring observers from abroad, such as the eminent Danish architect, Steen Eiler Rasmussen, who devoted five chapters of his seminal 1937 work on London architecture, London: The Unique City, to praising the lively conviviality of London's parks, as did the great Dutch historian and philosopher of play, Johan Huizinga, in his 1938 study Homo Ludens.

Those new public parks designed from scratch, rather than adapted from existing estates, were usually part of the development of the wealthier housing districts and suburbs, and were sometimes regarded de facto as a private amenity for those living in properties overlooking or adjoining them, as had been the case with the more prestigious London parks. Conflicts between residents immediately fringing the grander parks, and users from other parts of the city, soon emerged (and still rumble beneath the surface in many places even today).

Other changes resulted during both world wars, when large areas of urban parkland were transformed into allotments for food-growing, a trend re-emerging today as community groups request permission to convert under-used parkland into productive use. For some years now the organisation Growing Communities has had its own smallholding in Clissold Park, supplying local farmers' markets and cafés with salads and herbs, while training volunteers in horticultural skills. During the Second World War people were encouraged to take advantage of 'Holidays at Home' schemes, eschewing travel abroad or elsewhere in Britain in favour of using local parks, where programmes of events and activities were provided to help sustain civilian morale.

3

Parks have their fair-weather users, as well as hardened regulars. In the summer months Clissold Park provides a popular place for picnics, informal sports, funfairs, Turkish, Kurdish and Afro-Caribbean festivals, along with a deer park and animal enclosures to visit, and swans, ducks and geese to admire on the lakes. Meanwhile people queue to be photographed against the brilliant floral displays for wedding and family photographs. There are free summer music concerts in the formal gardens, play schemes for children and young people, the butterfly tunnel is opened and one of the last surviving municipal paddling pools comes into its own.

T'ai chi, yoga, martial arts, meditation, circus skills and tightrope walking can all be seen being practised daily, alongside impromptu football games and organised matches on marked-out pitches. It is estimated that more than 500 people use Clissold Park regularly for jogging. Local surgeries promote organised 'health walks' in the park, now popular among older people from all of Stoke Newington's diverse communities, and the 'One O'Clock Club', a legacy from the post-war London County Council that installed them in all of its major parks, has provided indoor and outdoor play facilities for the under-fives for many years, as well as a much-needed meeting place for isolated parents and carers. Thanks to Lottery funding there is now a popular 'wheels park' for skate-boarders and riders of BMX bikes. No other public amenity in this densely populated area offers such a rich variety of attractions and activities every day of the year, and for free. Hence the 3 million visits each year.

Among the hardened regulars out in all weathers are dog owners and professional dog-walkers. The growing number of dogs in the park is a divisive issue locally, though owners are always keen to remind other park users that they are out in all hours of daylight and often the first to spot or report anything untoward. Nevertheless, the fact that so many dogs run freely is a problem for the Orthodox Jewish and Muslim visitors who use the park and share a common aversion to dogs as human familiars. This is where parks draw on the legacy of the commons, as places where conflicting needs and interests – and there are many – have to be negotiated. Apart from conflicts about dogs in the park, there are cyclists competing with pedestrians on the footpaths, players of team sports in conflict with those looking for peace and quiet, and festival organisers whose (strictly rationed) events cause concern for residents living nearby. Regular public meetings of the park-user group provide a mediating forum for trying to resolve such conflicts, and may indeed be one of the voluntary forum's principal functions.

This was the theme of an article by the American journalist Michael Goldfarb in the *New York Times* some time ago, when he wrote admiringly about the park he found himself living close by. 'In a world splitting at the seams, Clissold Park is like a dream,' he wrote. 'Some of the most intractable conflicts in the world seem to have been resolved – or at least temporarily ignored. Kurds and Turks, Jews and Muslims, working-class and middle-class people (this is Britain) all co-exist, enjoying the lawns, the deer park, the ponds, the rose garden and the wading pool.'

Not all use is negotiable, especially after dark. Despite the fact that the park is locked at night, its after-hours use increases in the summer months: homeless people sleep there, and it provides a setting for sexual encounters and drinking schools. To my knowledge at least two people have hanged themselves from the trees, to be discovered by distressed park staff the next morning. Some years ago it was also the scene of a frenzied stabbing attack on a woman jogger after dark, which proved serious but not fatal. The morning after the police closed the park for a fortnight, and every gate was sealed and permanently guarded. An air of gloom settled upon the immediate neighbourhood. On the Sunday after re-opening the minister of the nearby Anglican church organised a carol-singing procession through the park, led by a professional jazz trumpet-player. It was a large, ecumenical gathering in which several hundred people processed along every park footpath and avenue, holding candles and lamps, singing. With this largely spontaneous ritual the park was reclaimed from its enforced sleep.

Despite such rare and shocking events the park remains overwhelmingly a sanctuary and safe haven. At its busiest it is used by thousands of people in the course of a day without any formal policing, in sharp contrast to many other public spaces in the city which now seem to swarm with private security guards. For me, this attests to the moral economy of traditional park culture, which acts to temper behaviour in the interests of the wider public comity, providing the strongest argument as to why they are safer in public rather than private hands. While conflicting uses are mostly resolved informally, the elected local authority retains the power to arbitrate on any major conflicts of use within the park, possessing as it does, in my opinion, a democratic legitimacy that a privatised or outsourced park would lack.

4

Parks also serve as proxy memorial gardens, and in some towns in recent years this has reached critical proportions, especially where sites of burial or cremation are located some distance away. A handful of local authorities have embargoed the installation of further park memorial benches, after complaints that their parks were acquiring the ambience of remembrance gardens. Some years ago the anthropologist Leonie Kellaher and I interviewed a number of park managers on the ways in which parks were increasingly being used for these purposes. Apart from dedicated benches and memorial trees, we were told of people surreptitiously interring ashes in areas previously favoured by the deceased. Furthermore, many of the trees planted without permission were of an inappropriate species, planted at the wrong time of year, dying soon after.

As a result, many local authorities now ask that those wishing to dedicate a tree to the memory of a loved one sponsor a species already designated as part of the park's long-term planting programme. They are also asked to forgo individual memorial plaques, which, it is felt, compromise the communal aesthetic of the public park or garden, and the unanchored, amorphous spirit of this *rus in urbs*. A park can be a place of memory without words.

What gives parks this privileged status as one of the few remaining 'sacred spaces' in the modern urban landscape? Primarily there is a perceived connection to a pre-existent and enduring natural world – tenuous though the municipal park version of 'nature' may be – and thus with more seasonal rhythms of life, increasingly distinct from the digital timetable of the 24-hour city. This may be especially important for people who have come from rural cultures and who retain a strong pull to being outdoors whenever possible. And while the seemingly immutable world of Clissold Park has nevertheless witnessed enormous changes at its borders – the Georgians, Victorians and Edwardians have come and gone, tower blocks have risen at its perimeter, been demolished, and today rise again – it remains for many a still centre in an otherwise fast-turning world.

Finally, of course, there is the crucial factor of the weather. 'Weather is the chief content of gardens,' wrote the idiosyncratic artist and landscape designer Ian Hamilton Finlay, 'yet it is the one thing in them over which the gardener has no control.' The same is patently true of the sensual *au plein air* world of the public park, which can possess a crowded festive air in the heat of a summer's afternoon, but at dusk on a winter's day can exude an other-worldly melancholy.

The year 2016 commemorated the 500th-anniversary year of the publication of Sir Thomas More's *Utopia*, and there has been much discussion as to where any residual utopian impulses or visions in the world might still be found today. Inequality is on the rise, and London's socially mixed communities are under continuing pressure from 'the invisible hand' of the housing market to segment even further into discrete enclaves of wealth and lifestyle. Yet parks remain among the last places in the city where all users are equal, and preferential terms of access or treatment cannot be purchased or parlayed. These outbreaks of arcadia hark back to ancient commons rights, and continue to embody the spirit of Blake's idyll of the echoing green: a rare place of enchantment open to all.

Further Reading

G. F. Chadwick, *The Park and the Town: Public Landscapes in the 19th and 20th Centuries*, Architectural Press, 1966.

Hazel Conway, *People's Parks: the Design and Development of Victorian Parks in Britain*, Cambridge University Press, 1991.

Travis Elborough, *A Walk in the Park: The Life and Times of a People's Institution*, Jonathan Cape, 2016.

Gareth Evans & Di Robson (editors), *Towards Re-Enchantment: Place and Its Meanings*, ArtEvents, 2010.

Liz Greenhalgh & Ken Worpole, *Park Life: Urban Parks & Social Renewal*, Comedia & Demos, 1995.

Heritage Lottery Fund, *State of UK Public Parks 2016*, HLF, 2016.

Leonie Kellaher & Ken Worpole, 'Bringing the Dead Back Home: Urban Public Spaces as Sites for New Patterns of Mourning & Memorialisation', in *Deathscapes*, edited by Avril Maddrell & James D. Sidaway, Ashgate, 2010.

Margaret Willes, *The Gardens of the British Working Class*, Yale University Press, 2014.

CONTRIBUTORS

Barbara Bender is Emeritus Professor of Anthropology at UCL. She spent twenty-five years researching and teaching landscape across disciplinary boundaries. Her books include *Stonehenge: Making Space* (Berg); *Stone Worlds*, co-author (Left Coast Press); *Contested Landscapes: Movement, Exile and Place*, editor (Berg). She has also spent twenty-five years working with the oral/archival Branscombe Project, a communal endeavour.

Julia Blackburn has written two novels and ten works of non-fiction. Her books are a mixture of memoir, biography and travel writing, alongside the process of thinking on the page. She has approached all sorts of subjects, but perhaps the unifying factor is her interest in people who are caught in a predicament of one sort or another. A Box of Shells' is an extract from *Time Song: Journeys in Search of Doggerland* which will be published by Jonathan Cape in 2019.

Sean Borodale works as an artist and writer. His first collection of poems, *Bee Journal*, was shortlisted for the T. S. Eliot Prize and the Costa Poetry Book Awards. He keeps bees in Somerset.

Hugh Brody's books include *The People's Land, Maps and Dreams* and *The Other Side of Eden*. His films include documentaries made with indigenous peoples of northern and western Canada: *Nineteen-Nineteen*, starring Paul Scofield and Maria Schell, and *Tracks Across Sand*, a set of sixteen films made with the Khomani San of the southern Kalahari. He holds the Canada Research Chair in Aboriginal Studies at the University of the Fraser Valley in British Columbia.

John Burnside's novels include *The Devil's Footprints* (2007), *Glister* (2008) and *A Summer of Drowning* (2011). He is also the author of two collections of short stories, three memoirs and several prizewinning poetry collections, including *Black Cat Bone*, winner of both the Forward and the T. S. Eliot prizes in 2012. His most recent novel, *Ashland & Vine*, was published alongside a new collection of poetry, *Still Life with Feeding Snake*, in February 2017.

Mark Cocker is an author, naturalist and environmental teacher who writes and broadcasts on nature and wildlife in a variety of national media. His eleven books include works of biography, history, literary criticism and memoir. The latest is *Our Place*, a personal journey into British environmental history.

Peter Davidson is Senior Research Fellow at Campion Hall, University of Oxford. His most recent book is a cultural history of twilight, *The Last of the Light*, published by Reaktion Books. He is working on a book about lighted windows in the dark, and on a further collection of poems for Carcanet. He lives in Oxford.

Nick Davies is Professor of Behavioural Ecology at the University of Cambridge and a Fellow of Pembroke College. He has studied cuckoos in the fens for the past thirty years and his book *Cuckoo – cheating by nature* is published by Bloomsbury.

Paul Farley is a poet and broadcaster. He has received many awards for his work, including the 2009 E. M. Forster Award from the American Academy of Arts & Letters, and is a Fellow of the Royal Society of Literature. His *Selected Poems* was published in 2014 by Picador.

Tessa Hadley has written six novels and three collections of short stories. Her novel *The Past*, published in the UK in 2015, won the Hawthornden Prize; a collection of stories, *Bad Dreams*, was published in 2017. She publishes short stories regularly in the *New Yorker*, reviews for the *Guardian* and the *London Review of Books*, and is a Professor of

Creative Writing at Bath Spa University. In 2016 she was awarded a Windham Campbell Prize for Fiction.

Alexandra Harris is the author of *Romantic Moderns, Virginia Woolf* and *Weatherland: Writers and Artists under English Skies*. She is Professorial Fellow at the University of Birmingham, and a Fellow of the Royal Society of Literature. Her radio programmes include a series on Woolf's walks in different landscapes and *A British History in Weather*.

Philip Hoare is the author of eight works of non-fiction, including biographies of Stephen Tennant and Nöel Coward; *Leviathan or, the Whale* (winner of the 2008 Samuel Johnson Prize for Non-Fiction) and *The Sea Inside*. His latest book is RISINGTIDEFALLINGSTAR. He is co-curator, with Angela Cockayne, of mobydickbigread.com, and is Professor of English at the University of Southampton. @philipwhale

Richard Holmes is a Fellow of the British Academy. He is the author of *Footsteps: Adventures of a Romantic Biographer*, and biographies of Shelley, Coleridge and young Dr Johnson. His study of scientists and poets, *The Age of Wonder*, won the Royal Society Prize for Science Books (UK) and the National Book Critics Circle Award for Nonfiction (USA). He has also written about ballooning in *Falling Upwards*. His most recent book is *This Long Pursuit*.

Tim Ingold is Professor of Social Anthropology at the University of Aberdeen. He has written on evolutionary theory, human–animal relations, environmental perception and skilled practice. He is currently exploring the interface between anthropology, archaeology, art and architecture, and is the author of *Lines* (2007), *Being Alive* (2011), *Making* (2013) and *The Life of Lines* (2015).

Richard Long is an artist of landscape and nature. His work takes many forms, but is essentially about making walks in both rural and wilderness landscapes which articulate ideas of time and distance. He often also makes sculptures of place along the way, marks of passage.

He has worked on all five continents. Since 1968 he has had over 250 one-person exhibitions worldwide. He was born in Bristol in 1945.

Richard Mabey is the author of some forty prizewinning books, the most recent being *The Cabaret of Plants: Botany and the Imagination*. In 2002 he moved from the Chilterns to Norfolk, swapping wood for water and a slim-line electric boat. He is a Fellow of the Royal Society for Literature, and Patron of the John Clare Society.

Helen Macdonald wrote the bestselling memoir *H is for Hawk*, which won the 2014 Samuel Johnson Prize and Costa Book of the Year, and was a 2015 Kirkus Award and NBCC Award finalist in the USA. She has also published collections of poetry and works of cultural history. She is a contributing writer for the *NYT Magazine*.

Patrick McGuinness is the author of two books of poems, *The Canals of Mars* and *Jilted City*, and the novel *The Last Hundred Days*, about the fall of the Ceauşescu regime. His memoir, *Other People's Countries: A Journey into Memory*, appeared in 2014. He teaches French and comparative literature at Oxford University.

Andrew McNeillie's seventh collections of poems, *Making Ends Meet*, was published in 2017. His memoir *An Aran Keening* was published by Lilliput Press in 2001. He is the founding editor of the literary magazine *Archipelago* and runs the Clutag Press.

Philip Marsden is the award-winning author of books that include *The Bronski House*, *The Spirit-Wrestlers*, *The Chains of Heaven*, *The Barefoot Emperor*, *The Levelling Sea* and, most recently, *Rising Ground*. He is a fellow of the Royal Society of Literature and his work has been translated into more than a dozen languages. He lives in Cornwall with his family and a number of boats.

David Matless is Professor of Cultural Geography at the University of Nottingham. He is the author of *Landscape and Englishness* (Reaktion 2016, first published 1998), *The Regional Book* (Uniformbooks 2015) and *In the Nature of Landscape: Cultural Geography on the Norfolk Broads* (Wiley-Blackwell 2014). His work explores the relationship of landscape and culture, with a particular interest in the landscapes of East Anglia, the landscapes of English identity, and the cultural geographies of the Anthropocene.

Andrew Motion was UK Poet Laureate from 1999 to 2009. He is now a Homewood Professor of the Arts at Johns Hopkins University and lives in Baltimore.

Adam Nicolson was born in 1957 and has written about the English landscape and its owners, the Hebrides, Homer, 17th-century England and the sea and its birds. Since 4 May 1994, he has lived at Perch Hill Farm in the Sussex Weald, where he keeps a small herd of Sussex cattle and a flock of sheep of mixed parentage. He is presently writing a book on the year Coleridge and Wordsworth spent together in the Quantocks and another on life between the tides.

Sean O'Brien is a poet, critic, novelist and short-fiction writer, Professor of Creative Writing at Newcastle University and a Fellow of the Royal Society of Literature. His poetry collection, *The Drowned Book* (2007), won the Forward and T. S. Eliot Prizes. Among his most recent publications are *The Beautiful Librarians* (2015), which won the Roehampton Poetry Prize, and his second novel, *Once Again Assembled Here* (2016).

Dexter Petley is the author of four critically acclaimed novels: *Little Nineveh, Joyride, White Lies* and *One True Void*. His latest book, *Love Madness Fishing*, is a memoir of boyhood among the rural poor in a 1960s Weald of Kent. Angling writer and mushroom-gatherer, he lives in a yurt in a Normandy forest, where he is working on a nature detective novel.

Greg Poole – artist – printmaker – illustrator – naturalist – was born in Bristol in 1960. A long-time council member of the Society of Wildlife Artists (SWLA), he is widely travelled, including several Artists for Nature Foundation (ANF) projects. His work features in numerous nature/art publications, and a one-man book was published in French: *La Riviera* (Gallimard). He writes a blog on his website: www.gregpoole.co.uk

Fiona Sampson has received numerous national and international awards and been widely translated as a poet. She also writes non-fiction including biography, writing about place, and criticism. Among her recent books are *Limestone Country*, *In Search of Mary Shelley* and *The Catch*.

Adam Thorpe is a poet, novelist, translator and critic. He was born in Paris and brought up in Beirut, Calcutta, Cameroon and England. His first novel, *Ulverton* (1992), is now a Vintage Classic. *Voluntary*, his sixth poetry collection, was a Poetry Book Society Recommendation in 2012. A work of non-fiction, *On Silbury Hill* (Little Toller), was a BBC Radio 4 Book of the Week in 2012. His latest novel, *Missing Fay*, was published by Cape in 2017.

Michael Viney, author of *Ireland* in the Smithsonian natural history series, moved from English to Irish journalism in 1962 and has written 'Another Life', a weekly column on ecology and rural life, in the *Irish Times* since 1977. His books include *Ireland's Ocean: a natural history* (Collins Press), written with his wife Ethna. He was elected to the Royal Irish Academy in 2017.

Marina Warner writes fiction and cultural history. Her most recent books are *Once Upon a Time: A Short History of Fairy Tale* (Oxford University Press) and *Fly Away Home: Short Stories* (Salt). She is Professor of English and Creative Writing at Birkbeck College, London, and is working on a book about Cairo in the fifties. In 2015 she was awarded the Holberg Prize, and in 2017 became President of the Royal Society of Literature.

Ken Worpole is the author of many books on architecture, landscape and social history, and works as a writer and researcher in the field of public policy. He lives with his wife, the photographer Larraine Worpole, in Hackney, where they have both been active in local social and environmental campaigns since the late 1960s. www.worpole.net